The British and the Vietnam War

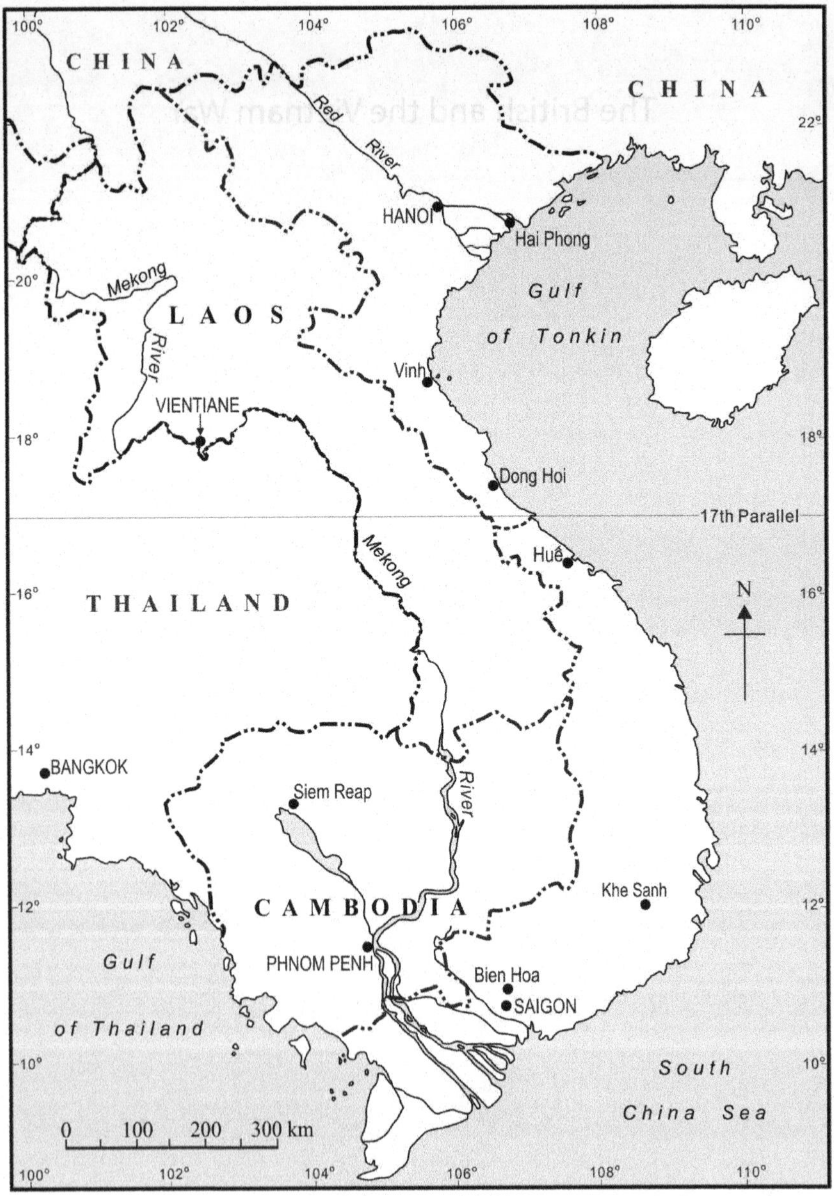

Map of Vietnam

The British and the Vietnam War

Their Way with LBJ

Nicholas Tarling

NUS PRESS
SINGAPORE

Published by:

NUS Press
National University of Singapore
AS3-01-02, 3 Arts Link
Singapore 117569

Fax: (65) 6774-0652
E-mail: nusbooks@nus.edu.sg
Website: http://nuspress.nus.edu.sg

ISBN 978-981-4722-23-0 (Paper)

National Library Board, Singapore Cataloguing-in-Publication Data

Name(s): Tarling, Nicholas. | NUS Press, publisher.
Title: The British and the Vietnam War : their way with LBJ / Nicholas Tarling.
Description: Singapore : NUS Press, [2017] | Includes bibliographical references and index.
Identifier(s): OCN 951206212 | ISBN 978-981-4722-23-0 (paperback)
Subject(s): LCSH: Vietnam War, 1961-1975--Great Britain. | Great Britain--Foreign relations--1964-1979. | Great Britain--Foreign relations--United States. | United States--Foreign relations--Great Britain. | United States--Politics and government--1963-1969.
Classification: DDC 959.70432--dc23

Typeset by: Ivan Foo/Gerakbudaya, Kuala Lumpur, Malaysia
Printed by: Markono Print Media Pte Ltd

For

my colleague Xin Chen

Contents

Acknowledgements

I wish to thank the staff at the National Archives in London and at the Auckland University Library for their unfailing assistance, and acknowledge the support of the New Zealand Asia Institute at the University. I also wish to thank Dr Brook Barrington for reading and commenting on the typescript, and to offer gratitude and affection to Fiona and Rupert Wheeler, without whom the research would have been impossible.

Introduction

Anxious to maintain the support the US afforded them in the Second World War through what they called a 'special relationship', the British differed with it over China and Southeast Asia. The Geneva agreement on Indochina of 1954 was a focus of difference: the US was determined not to 'lose' Vietnam as it had 'lost' China. The British nevertheless again took the lead in negotiations that led to the Laos neutralisation agreement of 1962. The result was, however, that the US became more determined to defend southern Vietnam.

One of a series of works on British policy towards Southeast Asia in the period of decolonisation, this book covers only a relatively short phase in the long-drawn-out struggle that occurred in Vietnam. It was a crucial one, and hitherto not much has been published on the role of the UK. Under President Lyndon Johnson the US committed itself so far to averting the success of Communism that it bombed the North and introduced half a million American troops into the South. The moves were criticised in Britain as well as at home and in other countries. What Britain could do was, however, limited, even though it claimed to have a 'special relationship' with the US. By this time, indeed, its financial weakness, coupled with a shift of economic and political interest, had reduced, if not eliminated, its capacity to influence the US in Southeast Asia. But the left wing, and a widening section of the population, wanted it to do so, particularly as the air-war, and then the land-war, expanded.

The short phase covered by this book—as indeed that covered by Peter Busch's *All the Way with JFK? Britain, the US, and the Vietnam War* (2003), which reaches only the opening phase of the Johnson presidency—has indeed to be understood in the context of changes over a much longer period, going back at least to the closing years of the Pacific War. 'The Europeanised "Far East" has gone', as H.C. Walsh, the British consul-general in Batavia, had put it in 1942, 'and the organization of European activities there in the future will have to be rebuilt on entirely different foundations from those prevailing before 1939'.[1] British post-war planning sought to recognise this, and so did the adjustments made to that planning when the war ended suddenly. European activities would have to be based on accepting the strengthening of nationalism and the emergence of independent nation-states. If they were accepted, the Europeans would be acceptable. If they were not, the Europeans would have no future there.

Pre-war Southeast Asia, though dominated by the British, had been divided among other Western powers, Siam alone retaining its political independence. Would the Dutch and the French share the views of the British? At the end of the Second World War, the former at first believed that regaining the lost Indies was essential to their recovery, and they accepted the inevitable only in 1949. No one could argue that Indochina was economically essential to French recovery. But it was argued that it was essential to the perception that France was, despite defeat and humiliation, still a great power, and none of its post-war governments, based on insecure coalitions, was strong enough to adopt the bolder policies the British adopted in Burma and India.

The Cold War complicated what was already complicated enough, for though its initial focus was European, it extended to Asia, with the activities of the Soviet Union (SU), and then, with the triumph of Mao's Chinese Communist Party, with those of the PRC, taken in the West as a bloc but behaving ever less like one from the later 1950s. International Communism had been seen as a threat to European empires in the inter-war period, and to some extent the latter had collaborated against it. In the post-war period it seemed more of a threat. But the British did not see it as only something that had to be fought. They saw nationalism as the best antidote. They thus validated and urged on a policy that they were in any case ready to adopt. But that, too, was complicated.

The Russians presented a direct threat to Britain itself, and, as Britain had in face of the Nazi menace, it had looked to the US, ultimately with success, though at a price. What the British saw as a special relationship, developed in the Second World War, was needed still in the Cold War. Indeed it became the commanding feature of Britain's foreign policy, reducing its flexibility and constraining its initiatives. No one perusing the archives of the British Foreign Office (FO) could fail to note the number of telegrams sent to Washington, designed to ascertain its objectives or to test its reactions to possible UK initiatives and suggestions.

Nor is it easy to avoid the feeling that the relationship was more special for the British than for the Americans. No doubt it became increasingly so as Britain, greatly weakened by the war, failed fully to recover. It was estimated that Britain had lost one quarter of its national wealth between

1939 and 1945.[2] Yet it was committed, during and after the war, to creating a welfare state, and also, in face of its imperial responsibilities and the challenge of the Communist bloc, to substantial defence expenditure. It needed a 'special relationship' with the US, but it also needed to play its part in the developing Cold War. In the absence of a full economic recovery, governments were to find it impossible to reconcile those objectives.

The US indeed often found it useful to have an ally whose cooperation demonstrated to domestic as well as international audiences that it had not abandoned an earlier isolationism in order now to act in the unilateral style of an imperialist, dispelling, in the words of Roger Makins of the FO, 'a haunting possibility that she may slip back to a new form of isolationism (it would really be a form of imperialism) and try to "go it alone"'.[3] But the US was conscious of a leadership role. And that carried with it assumptions that the British had not made even when in the 19th century they had the predominance among the powers that the Americans now had. The quality of their diplomacy differed not only because it was made in a different way, and in a very different institutional context, but also because the US was a 'superpower' of a kind that Britain had never been. Britain had always been a European power, a power among states, conscious of the values of a pragmatic approach, not expecting complete or lasting solutions. That approach had become only more important with the passage of time and the lapse of power. Beneath the more specific differences between the two allies lay fundamental differences of attitude to the world, to ideals, to the long term.

After his Asian tour of 1949, Sir William Strang, the permanent under-secretary at the FO, had looked for 'a combination of British experience and United States resources'.[4] But some of the specific differences were indeed larger than others. The frequent telegrams and occasional anger were all the more numerous in respect of East and Southeast Asia because of a fundamental difference between the two leading Western allies in respect of China. Their post-war policy towards that country deemed to have failed with its 'loss' to the Communists, the Americans did not recognise the new regime that Mao proclaimed in October 1949, and any chance that they would do so in the foreseeable future was eliminated by the Korean War in 1950. In keeping with their overall notions about the world of states, as well as their hopes of sustaining something of their old position in China, the British wanted to handle the new regime by engaging in normalising diplomacy rather than imposing isolation. The UK recognised the Central People's Government and secured diplomatic representation there, though at a much less effective level than they would have wished.

But US recognition was not offered till the 1970s, well after the British had finally abandoned a strategic role in Southeast Asia. 'The American policy of non-recognition, and the dragooning of her friends and allies to follow suit,' an FO official wrote in 1965, 'was misconceived and has probably been counter-productive—though how any United States Administration can abandon this line under present or foreseeable circumstances is quite a different matter.'[5]

The difference was not merely a formal one. The US military, vastly more influential as the Korean War prompted the US to build up its national defence, tended to plan in terms of a possible war with China, and certainly seemed more ready to contemplate it than the British, who feared it would precipitate a major war, if not a third world war, in which nuclear weapons might be deployed and Britain itself destroyed.

The policies in Southeast Asia thus also differed. Even before the Korean War, the French were at war with the Democratic Republic of Vietnam (DRV), proclaimed by Ho Chi Minh in Hanoi in September 1945 soon after the Japanese surrender, and had emphasised its Communist rather than its nationalist aspect in order to win US support as the PRC reached the frontiers of French Indochina. Already struggling from mid-1948 with a Communist-led 'Emergency' in Malaya, the British, too, were sufficiently concerned to want a demonstration of American support in Southeast Asia. But they wanted so to define that support that it would not provoke China. The object was to constrain China until it was clear that it would indeed behave like the 'normal' state the British wanted it to be. This was a difficult line to follow. Indeed the records show that British opinions, even within the FO and among its staff, were often divided.

Arguing for an influence over American policy, the British presented the Emergency as part of a common struggle against Communism. But other factors could be brought into play, so that Britain might advocate policies that could otherwise have undermined the special relationship. One was the foreign policy of India, independent as a dominion from 1947 and as a republic in the Commonwealth from 1949. A relatively weak though populous state, its policy, as defined by Prime Minister Jawaharlal Nehru, was one of 'non-alignment'. It meant that India would not take sides in the Cold War but that it would not necessarily be inactive, and that it would reserve the right to act as a major state among states. Though Nehru's anti-colonialism was often seen as too extreme by the British, they valued India's stance in part as a means of moderating American Cold War policies. They could allege the need to take account of 'Asian opinion', by which essentially they meant Indian opinion.

'One of the happiest portents in this part of the world is the interest being taken by the Americans in the defence of Indo-China,' Hubert Graves wrote in July 1951, soon after arriving in Saigon as British ambassador to the State of Vietnam, the French-sponsored counter to the DRV. True, it was based on the wish to 'block, as they put it, the southward surge of Chinese Communism, and not merely for the purpose of eliminating disruptive elements within Indo-China'. But so long as the French conducted the campaign with skill and vigour, the Americans would 'maintain a helpful interest in this key position'.[6]

The British were indeed looking for some kind of US commitment to Southeast Asia that would yet not involve a provocative approach to China. Aiding the French and boosting their morale had to be done without risking a wider war. If action against China were necessary, it must stop short of naval blockade and widespread bombing, the British chiefs of staff insisted early in 1952.[7] 'It would be silly to waste bombs in the vast inchoate mass of China, and wrong to kill thousands of people for no purpose,' as Prime Minister Winston Churchill put it.[8] US Secretary of State Dean Acheson reassured his counterpart, Anthony Eden. In any case, he did not think the Chinese would invade: they would proceed by aiding the Viet Minh [the DRV] in their struggle.[9] But if there were no 'southward surge', in what way would the Americans be involved in Vietnam and for what purpose?

Fatefully they were to become committed to the State of Vietnam, influenced, it seems clear, by their determination to limit a further 'loss' to Communism—the success of Ho following that of Mao—and perhaps to retain a foothold for redeeming it; influenced, too, by their experience in Korea: with a strong leader, and a well-trained army, the Communist threat could at least be held, if not pushed back. That line they pressed on the French in vain. When the French found in the Korean peace negotiations at Geneva in 1954 an opportunity to terminate their active military involvement in Vietnam, the US would proceed to carry out the policy it had urged. Its Syngman Rhee it found in Ngo Dinh Diem, who was quick to displace Bao Dai, the head of state, and it built up a Vietnamese army, more indeed on a Korean War basis rather than on the anti-guerrilla basis that would turn out to be more relevant. President Dwight Eisenhower described the rationale of the policy with misleading simplicity. 'You have a row of dominoes set up, you knock over the first one, and what will happen to the last one is a certainty that it will go over very rapidly': Vietnam, Taiwan, the Philippines. That would take away, 'in its economic aspects, the region that Japan must have as a trading area', leaving it with 'only one place to go, towards the Communist areas'.[10]

Geneva

Britain's policy had diverged. By the time of the Geneva conference, when it became clear that the French would be withdrawing, the British were prepared to accept a temporary partition of Vietnam, and prepared also to accept that it might well be followed by reunification under Viet Minh leadership. Anthony Eden, the foreign secretary, indeed modified Britain's policies. Laos and Cambodia would be independent states, neutral in all but name, and Premier Zhou Enlai agreed that China would respect their independence. The line would no longer be drawn along the Tonkin frontier but along the Mekong. James Cable, who was later to become head of the FO's South East Asia Department (SEAD), recalled that Eden 'held the view … that our job was to draw a line in South East Asia of the kind that had been drawn in Europe, but with the difference that Cambodia and Laos were to act as neutral buffers between Eastern and Western spheres of influence'.[11]

Dealing with the Chinese—admitted to the Geneva conference, though not a member of the United Nations, where the Republic of China based in Taiwan still held the China seat on the Security Council (SC)—was in itself a victory for the British approach. At that time they were responsive both to the general trend in international relations after the death of Joseph Stalin in 1953, and to the particular prospects opened up by the Berlin conference. They wanted to avoid US intervention, Korea-style. That ruled out their own military intervention: 'it is impossible for the Chinese army to take part in operations in the territory of Vietnam,' the Central Committee decided, 'because this counterpoises China to other peoples of Southeast Asia. The United States would use this participation for establishing a bloc extended from India to Indonesia.'[12] More positively, they sought recognition as one of the five major powers. A moderate stance at Geneva would boost the PRC's 'claim on peaceful co-existence' and create new channels of communication with Britain, France and other Western countries.[13] As Geneva got under way, China demonstrated its policy by concluding a treaty with India that endorsed what became known as the 'five principles of co-existence'.

In the midst of the Geneva conference—while Eden and Churchill were in Washington—Zhou had at rather short notice visited New Delhi. At the end of 13 hours of talks with Nehru, the two issued a joint statement on 28 June which enunciated the five principles in a form which clearly envisaged their general application when, as they put it, they would 'form a solid foundation for peace and security'. They also expressed the hope that they would be applied in Indochina, 'where the political settlement should aim at the creation of free, democratic, unified and independent States, which should not be used for aggressive purposes or be subjected to foreign intervention'.[14] Thus, while Eden was seeking to win American support for a settlement much on those lines, Zhou was rallying Asian support.

Eden's efforts were unsuccessful, and his attempts to pursue them used methods that may have damaged the special relationship in a way that undermined any chance of success for his ill-judged Suez adventure of 1956. In a speech of 29 March 1954, US Secretary of State John Foster Dulles had called for 'united action'. His intentions were unclear at the time, and historians have also found them difficult to interpret. It seems most likely, as he told Roger Makins, now British ambassador, that his aim was to stiffen French resistance. The *New York Times* had indeed suggested that the administration wanted the French to stay on for one to two years, at which time an American-trained Vietnamese army would be ready to take over. Eden and the FO decided that no announcement should be made until Geneva had begun, and that the aim should be 'a lasting alliance', not an ad hoc coalition, and preferably one towards which India might have at least a benevolent attitude.[15]

Discussions with Dulles in London produced a communiqué, but the two parties disagreed on what had been agreed. Dulles immediately began to set up a working group on collective security, while Eden insisted it was 'most inopportune'.[16] The differences between the two statesmen were remembered at the FO, though not always accurately. Like the Stimson/Simon controversy over the Manchuria crisis, they became rather a matter of legend.

There was a further difference, more widely remembered, though perhaps also somewhat in terms of a legend. That turned on the imminent fall of Dien Bien Phu, which the French forces had made a stronghold only to find themselves beleaguered. Would the Americans carry out an air strike to help them? Dulles was not ready to do that, but he still wanted to keep the French in the war. What he was ready to do was not clear, but his vagueness, and Admiral Arthur Radford's specificity, suggested that the US was prepared to take military action. In retrospect it is clear that its intention was still to 'shore up the French will', as Livingston Merchant put it.[17] The Americans' methods, however, alarmed the British and contributed to their desire for a settlement. Eden's diplomacy was credited with averting a war. What the US was aiming at stopped short of that, however. Its objective was to sustain a Franco-Vietnamese military effort until it became possible to make it a Vietnamese effort, backed not by American troops but by American training. The idea of training Vietnamese troops and inspiring them with independence was already entrenched in American thinking partly as a result of the Korean experience. President Eisenhower was to remain committed to it even after Geneva created quite a different situation.

Late in June, while the Geneva conference was still in being, Churchill and Eden visited Washington, one of the objects being to clear the air on Vietnam. Russia and China wanted a settlement, Eden told Cabinet on 22 June, but might have difficulty in restraining the Viet Minh, 'who are in a position to demand a high price. It may prove even more difficult to persuade the Americans to accept whatever settlement can eventually be reached.' One task in Washington was (a) to persuade them to give the French at least a chance of reaching one in the next few weeks. (b) 'We must continue to make it clear that we cannot consider intervening in Indo-China and we must do our best to restrain the Americans from doing so.' (c) 'We must again make it plain that we can accept no further commitments in regard to "united action" in South-East Asia until the outcome is known. (d) But we can express willingness to examine at once and in secret how best we can proceed to strengthen our common defences. (e) We should discuss how the principal Asian powers in that area can best be associated with this work. (f) But we should not agree, before Geneva is over, to any wider and more publicised meeting, at which Siam and the Philippines would be the only Asian countries present, to plan and proclaim an anti-Communist alliance.'[18]

The Americans were likely to press for a pact, Eden added. What form might it take? A NATO, like the pact of 1949? A Locarno, like the mutual guarantee of 1925? '[T]he two types of pact were not mutually exclusive,' he claimed. 'In Asia, as in Europe, there might still be need of a collective defence organisation, even if a Locarno agreement were reached.'[19] The idea reappeared in his Commons speech on 23 June. He envisaged a kind of Locarno, 'a reciprocal arrangement in which both sides take part', and a kind of NATO, the pact created by the US and the Western Europeans in 1949. '[B]y refraining from any precipitate move towards the formation of a N.A.T.O. system in South-East Asia, we have helped to create the necessary conditions in which both systems can possibly be brought into being.'[20]

Next morning the 'two tier' idea was discussed at a meeting of Eden and FO officials. The Locarno-type arrangement would consist of a guarantee of the agreements on Indochina—either part of the agreement or a separate undertaking—by powers participating or by others, like India, Australia and New Zealand, which might associate themselves with it. The powers would be free to act individually, so that the Communist powers would have no veto. The NATO-type arrangement would be confined to the non-Communist powers. 'Its essence would be to guarantee the countries, particularly Burma and Siam, lying on our side of the Indo-China area.' Securing the participation of Asian states might be 'difficult'. An attempt to secure a Locarno should be made first. If it failed, the NATO agreement would be more likely to secure acquiescence, if not participation. Even if Locarno were secured, NATO should still be proceeded with 'as a second line of defence'.[21]

Whether the two were compatible was indeed doubtful. How would the Chinese see a pact if they accepted a Locarno? And another 'flurry' in Washington followed the Commons speech, many Congressmen and Senators reacting violently against the proposal 'both as requiring some form of diplomatic recognition of Communist China and as sanctifying, by guarantee, a Communist conquest of Northern Indo-China'.[22] 'Change the name Locarno,' Eden said, 'if it stinks in the United States.'[23] It was, however, not so much the name as the thing itself. The US would be entering an agreement with China and guaranteeing a 'loss' to Communism. Later Eden was to tell the House that he could not get reciprocal guarantees because the Communists wanted a 'collective' guarantee, a veto.[24] The real difficulty was with the US.

Dulles objected to the Locarno-type scheme, inasmuch as 'an affirmative guarantee ... amounted to moral approval of a Communist success. This was unacceptable.' The US might, however, be able to associate itself with the agreement by declaring, in line with Article 2 (4) of the UN Charter, 'that it would not use force to upset it'. That did not 'apply [imply?] approval of the Communist regime in the North'. Eden liked the idea and suggested it be studied along with possible alternatives. The Americans pointed out that the British paper seemed to exclude Laos and Cambodia from the area covered by the pact. That was 'because, in practice, we would never achieve an agreement at Geneva which did not neutralise those countries'. Bedell Smith, the US delegate, suggested that there was 'no reason why the political guarantee should not include them even if the military stop-line were further south'.[25] According to the American record of this meeting, Dulles asked why, if a *de facto* settlement divided Vietnam, what remained should not be 'guaranteed by a collective defence system'. Eden 'did not exclude from the defense provisions those parts of Indo-China which might be salvaged', even though, Harold Caccia added, they could not be 'turned into a defensive position'. Would subversion, he asked, bring the pact into operation? What if the Communists won elections?[26]

The Americans suggested drawing up a communication to France, stating 'the type of Indo-China agreement which they would be willing to respect, even though one or both might not be parties to it'. A communication from the French made it, they said, more desirable.[27] Prime Minister Pierre Mendès-France, who had set himself a deadline for a settlement, was apprehensive of 'a violent and irrational reaction' against partition 'on the part of Vietnamese patriots'. He hoped the US would not encourage it, but would encourage them not to refuse an agreement intended 'to save everything that can be saved'.[28]

Dulles, Eden and their advisers drew up an agreed minute, indicating that their governments hoped that any agreement would be one that (1) preserved the integrity and independence of Laos and Cambodia and assured the withdrawal of Viet Minh forces; (2) preserved at least the southern half of Vietnam, and if possible an enclave in the delta, in which connection they would be 'most unwilling' to see 'the line of division of responsibility' drawn 'further south than a line running generally west from Dong Hoi'; (3) did not impose on Laos, Cambodia or 'retained Vietnam' any restrictions that would impair 'their capacity to maintain stable non-Communist regimes', including the right to import arms and employ foreign advisers; (4) did not contain 'political provisions which would risk loss of the retained area to Communist control'; (5) did not 'exclude the possibility of the ultimate unification of Vietnam by peaceful means'; (6) provided for peaceful transfer under international supervision of those wishing to move from one 'zone' to another; and (7) provided effective machinery for international supervision of the agreement. The two powers would be willing to respect an agreement along those lines.[29]

Points 5 and 6 were added at Dulles' instance. The latter related to Catholics in the northern delta: the president thought that 'some arrangement had to be made for their safety', particularly given Catholic opinion in the US. The former point—originally drafted to read 'does not oblige Vietnam to renounce any attempt to achieve unity by peaceful means'—was designed to 'render the situation in Indo-China similar to that existing in Korea' and was necessary to win Congress support for association with the settlement. Eden said that the Communists would like it, too, 'though for quite different reasons. He agreed with the thought, but feared that … it might prove a two-edged weapon.' What was in mind, though not specified, was elections. Dulles said that they 'must be put off and we could do it on the grounds that under present conditions they could not be fair'. Eden suggested redrafting to make it less easy for the Communists to call for immediate elections: hence the 'ultimate' phrase.[30]

These were the aims which Britain and the US set out for Mendès-France to achieve. '[W]hilst the U.S. Government could accept a settlement which passed the agreed tests, they would not wish to be associated as one of its promoters,' Dulles indicated.[31] '[W]e consider "respect" as strong a word as we can possibly employ in the circumstances,' he was to write to his ambassador in Paris.[32]

Denis Allen of the FO thought 'some fairly useful progress had been made towards getting things back on the rails between the Americans and ourselves'. There was also 'plenty of room for future argument ... about whether any given settlement ... that the French may manage to get at Geneva does or does not measure up to the conditions laid down ..., and it is quite likely that on the day the Americans will be looking for reasons to disapprove the agreement whereas our inclination will be to find good grounds for approving it'. He thought, however, the Americans were becoming 'a little bit more flexible'. The 'rather vague' word 'respect' might help. 'Perhaps the "respect" will become warmer or chillier according to the nature of the agreement reached but so long as it remains "respect" of one kind or another we may be able to avoid parting company with the Americans on this issue.' Eden would attach importance to this. 'Things might well be awkward for us in South East Asia if we find ourselves undertaking commitments, however shadowy, which were not shared by the Americans.'[33]

Allen did not seem to consider the possibility that the US would undertake commitments which the British might not share. Yet the agreed minute covered the possibility of sending advisers to 'retained Vietnam'. The French were apprehensive that the Vietnamese, led by Diem, might turn to the US in opposition to their deal with the Viet Minh. It was also possible that the link could become a more positive one, especially in the light of the longstanding American belief that they could foster an independent regime and army in Vietnam as they had in Korea. The words the president used at his press conference on 1 July did not exclude such possibilities. He would not, he said, be 'a party to any Treaty that makes anybody a slave'. Asked if that meant he would not cooperate in any way with an armistice agreement that would partition Vietnam, he replied: 'No, ... I don't say that I won't go along with some of it.'[34]

Zhou had met Ho Chi Minh at Liuzhou in southern China early in July. If Britain had to work on the Americans, the Chinese prime minister had to work on the DRV leaders. The result, too, became another matter of legend. 'It is possible to gain all Vietnam through peace,' Zhou said, uniting it through elections when the time was ripe. Peace had all the advantages. 'It can isolate the U.S.A.'[35] Subsequently he advocated the policy—including the 'temporary' division of Vietnam—at a meeting of the Laodong Party's

Central Committee.[36] The Chinese premier later reported to his own government that Ho had expressed the opinion that the five principles were entirely applicable to the consolidation and development of friendly relations among Vietnam, Laos and Cambodia.[37] To an enlarged meeting of the politburo, Zhou explained that the objective at Geneva was 'to limit and break the American plan for expanding its world hegemony. The key issue is to achieve peace in Indochina.' The conference had reduced tensions and 'blocked the U.S. plan to expand its world domination'.[38]

In a three-sided meeting on 16 July Soviet Foreign Minister Vyacheslav Molotov, jointly chairing the conference with Eden, argued for fixing the date of the elections, or at least specifying that they should be held in 1955. Mendès argued that if a date had to be fixed, it had to be a distant one. There was much to do before elections could be held. 'In any case, time must be allowed for wartime passions to cool.' Eden thought the best solution would be for 'the two parts of the country to meet to fix a date for elections after the regrouping of forces had been completed'. The three also discussed the line. Molotov argued for the 16th parallel: it was only, after all, 'a purely provisional measure for a short period pending the reunification of the country'. Conceivably, Mendès concluded, one party might yield on elections, the other on the line.[39]

Next morning Zhou called on Eden. Given goodwill, he said, he thought the issues could be settled. He had come, however, to ask whether the Paris meeting meant that the plans for a Southeast Asia alliance were going ahead, and whether the three Associated States would be part of it. 'If so, the outlook for a peaceful settlement would not be good.' There had been 'no new development' about the proposed alliance, Eden replied, which he had himself advocated for many years. He had explained in the House of Commons the difference between a Locarno-style arrangement and a Southeast Asia alliance which would be 'the counterpart of the Soviet Chinese alliance'. It was not the intention, so far as he knew, that the Associated States should be members. 'The Americans had made it clear that they had no desire to create bases in those States.'

'China's policy in regard to South-East Asia was quite simple,' Zhou replied. 'They approved of a Locarno-type arrangement which as many States as possible would join, so that a large area of peaceful co-existence in Asia should be created. But the proposed South-East Asia Alliance would split the area just as N.A.T.O. had split Europe, and would make peaceful co-existence very difficult.' Nu and Nehru shared his views, he said. 'As regards the three Associated States in particular they should be independent, sovereign and neutral.' Eden insisted that it would not be 'in any way incompatible' with an Indochina agreement, with which the US and, he hoped, Asian countries would associate themselves.[40]

At a meeting with Eden and Mendès, Bedell Smith agreed that the Associated States would not become members of any pact if agreement were reached.[41] On Eden's instructions Harold Caccia explained to Chang Wen-tien, the second Chinese delegate, that Smith had agreed that if a settlement were reached which the US could respect and if, as a result, the Associated States undertook not to join military alliances, then none could be a member of the proposed pact. Chang 'accepted that the Associated States would be similarly debarred from becoming a member of the military pact with China'. 'Although we have naturally said nothing to the Chinese,' Eden reported home, 'General Bedell Smith and I recognized that the territory of Laos, Cambodia and Southern Vietnam might be covered by the South-East Asia Pact, even if the Associated States could not themselves be members.'[42]

On the evening of 19 July, Smith told Mendès that the US, though it would issue a declaration undertaking not to disturb the agreement, would not sign it, 'nor could they even take note of a clause (let alone agree) which might provide for consultation between the members of the conference in the event of there being some disagreement later over the execution of the terms of any eventual agreement'. Eden thought that 'unreasonable'. If he could not get over the procedural difficulties, however, he would prefer 'an agreement for the cessation of hostilities with some procedural difference between the United States position and our own' to no agreement at all and the continuation of the war.[43] Churchill agreed.[44] So did the Cabinet.[45] Eden talked to Molotov. The decision was to make a formal declaration and list the participating countries.[46]

The parties had accepted Zhou's proposals—Eden thought they were in fact drafted by Krishna Menon of India—for membership of the international control commission: India, Canada, Poland.[47] Zhou seems to have proposed delaying the elections, and he also got the Viet Minh to accept a more northerly line.[48] Mendès and Pham Van Dong thus announced agreement on a 'demarcation line'—a river near the 17th parallel—and on a date for the elections, July 1956.[49] Eden chaired the final meeting on 21 July. Smith made his declaration.[50] 'The result,' the British co-chairman said in his closing speech, was 'not completely satisfactory, but we had stopped an eight year war and reduced international tension at a point of instant danger to world peace.'[51] It had to be assumed, Eden told the Cabinet in London, that when elections were held in Vietnam, Ho would win. The essence of the settlement was that Laos and Cambodia were 'an independent and neutral buffer between China and Siam'.[52] It was, as he had told his colleague Oliver Lyttelton, 'faute de pire'.[53]

The conference documents included an agreement on the cessation of hostilities signed on 26 July 1954 by the C-in-C of the French Union forces and the C-in-C of the People's Army of Vietnam (PAVN). That provided for a provisional military demarcation line and a demilitarised zone (DMZ) on either side of it to act as a buffer; for the regrouping of forces; and for a ceasefire. 'Pending the general elections which will bring about the unification of Vietnam,' ran article 14, 'the conduct of civil administration in each regrouping zone shall be in the hands of the party whose forces are to be regrouped there.' The agreement on the cessation of hostilities also prohibited the introduction into Vietnam of reinforcements and additional personnel, other than those rotated, and the introduction of arms and other war material, other than replacements. Article 18 prohibited the establishment of new military bases throughout Vietnam. Article 19 prohibited the establishment of foreign bases and required the two parties to ensure 'that the zones assigned to them do not adhere to any military alliance and are not used for the resumption of hostilities or to further an aggressive policy'. The two parties were responsible for the execution of the agreement. The international commission was to 'ensure the control and supervision of this execution', the three members presided over by the Indian representative.

The Final Declaration of the conference, dated 21 July, took note of the provisions in the agreement and the agreements over Laos and Cambodia. The essential purpose of the Vietnam agreement, Article 6 recognised, was to settle military questions and end hostilities: 'the military demarcation line is provisional and should not in any way be interpreted as constituting a political or territorial boundary.' General elections were to be held in Vietnam in July 1956 under the supervision of the International Control Commission (ICC) '[i]n order to ensure that sufficient progress in the restoration of peace has been made, and that all the necessary conditions obtain for the free expression of the national will'. Consultations were to be held between the two zones from 20 July 1955 onwards.

Bedell Smith's declaration took note of the military agreements and said that the US would 'refrain from the threat or the use of force to disturb them', and that it would 'view any renewal of the aggression in Vietnam in violation of the … Agreements with grave concern and as seriously threatening the international peace and security'. In reference to Vietnam he drew attention to the Washington Declaration of 29 June 1954 that in the case of nations divided against their will—Germany had been in mind—the US would seek to achieve unity through UN-supervised free elections. In reference to a statement by the representative of the State of Vietnam, the US reiterated 'its traditional position that peoples are entitled to determine their own future and that it will not join in an arrangement that might hinder this'.

Eden had rejected Dulles' call for 'united action', but he made use of it to secure the Southeast Asia Collective Defence Treaty, concluded at Manila in September 1954. In that, often referred to as SEATO, since a rudimentary organisation was set up, each party agreed to act 'in accordance with its constitutional processes' against aggression against any of the parties, or in respect of any states or territories designated in a protocol. The treaty is normally presented as an American initiative. But its origins are better understood by taking account of the British point of view, and more particularly in the context of the difficulty Britain had in reconciling its relationship with the US and its view of the policies that should be followed in East and Southeast Asia. The arrangement, Eden had insisted, should be framed, so far as possible, to secure Asian participation. Certainly, as he had told Dulles, India should not be alienated.[54] In that he was hardly successful: only three Asian states were to join, one of them Pakistan. Eden insisted that the extension of the protocol to non-member states and territories was not in breach of his understanding with Zhou: that was the reason they could not themselves be members. Those designated were Laos, Cambodia and 'the free territory under the jurisdiction of the State of Vietnam'.

The US chief of staff had no enthusiasm for the treaty and was opposed to the creation of any permanent machinery. It involved, as Dulles himself put it, 'committing the prestige of the United States in an area where we had little control and where the situation was by no means promising'.[55] In practice they were to make little use of it, though it has been argued that it acted as an effective deterrent even so.[56]

Ngo Dinh Diem

The reservations the US made in July 1954 were full of ambiguity: what would result was unclear. The Vietnam adventure into which it tumbled had its origins at this time, but also changed in the following years, so that it is difficult to decide who made the commitment, when it was made, and what was its nature and extent. 'The basic error of Viet-Nam started with not taking Roosevelt's advice, in permitting the French to return to Viet-Nam,' the veteran American diplomat Averell Harriman put it in 1968, 'but the most appalling mistake was Dulles taking on the French responsibility in the southern half of Viet-Nam, which everyone knew was politically unstable.

There was no real chance of maintaining it as an independent country without strong military assistance from the outside.'[57]

Initially it was intended to support the government in Saigon, the State of Vietnam. In October 1954 Eisenhower wrote to Ngo Dinh Diem, the prime minister, offering aid, the purpose being 'to assist the Government of Vietnam in developing a strong, viable state capable of resisting attempted subversion or aggression through military means'. The US expected the aid would be 'met by performance on the part of the Government of Vietnam in undertaking needed reforms' and trusted it would contribute to 'an independent Vietnam … so responsive to the nationalist aspirations of its people, so enlightened in purpose and effective in performance, that it will … discourage any who might wish to impose a foreign ideology on your free people.'[58] But, though the letter referred to 'nationalist aspirations', it was not coupled with any intention of helping to win the reunification elections: rather the reverse. What was in mind was avoiding further 'loss' to the Communists.

Would the Vietnamese have accepted an enduring division? Neither the attitude of the Saigon government nor that in Hanoi suggested that they would. Vietnam had indeed been divided before—more or less in the same place—but the Trinh and Nguyen regimes of the late 17th and 18th centuries had accepted, in the person of the Le ruler, the nominal unity of Vietnam. The French had divided Vietnam into three, but nationalism had reinforced the long-standing Vietnamese sense of unity. Maintaining a separate regime in the South would not attract patriotic support. If unification were not secured by the elections, it was, moreover, certain that the DRV would try to secure it by other means. Increasingly, however, what was perhaps more properly conceived as a civil war came to be perceived and presented by the Americans and others as a matter of protecting an entity called 'South Vietnam' from 'aggression' from the North, while the North supported a Liberation Front in the South.

The US had undertaken not to disturb the agreements by force. That did not mean that they were willing to implement them, nor to follow their implications. And there was no way in which the British could make them do so. Indeed, the special relationship rendered it impossible to do much more than persuade, and when their power further declined, they were unable even to attempt that. They did not, however, altogether abandon their efforts before the late 1960s. This book focuses on the last few years of that history. They were marked, not surprisingly, by utter frustration.

The history may, however, properly begin with the Geneva agreements, since the role of the co-chairmen became, somewhat by accident, an enduring one, and with the initial controversy over the holding of the elections that the agreements envisaged as the route to reunification. '[T]he United States let France fall but did not allow Ho to claim victory and move on,' as Robert Buzzanco puts it.[59] Dulles' view—as expressed in a meeting with Vice-President Richard Nixon and others on 24 July 1954, three days after Geneva concluded—was that 'we would have to take the position in 1956 that conditions were not favorable for the free expression of the will of the population'.[60] '[O]ur real objective,' he told the National Security Council (NSC) on 12 August, was 'to avoid having any such elections.'[61]

The idea gained ground in the American embassy in Saigon and among the Vietnamese. Tran Van Do, the State of Vietnam foreign minister, told Graves that it was 'mathematically certain' that the Viet Minh would win and therefore elections were 'out of the question'. That was 'a very unfortunate attitude to take at this moment', Graves replied.[62] But the American counselor, Kidder, saw no harm in letting it be known that elections would not take place: it 'would discourage the tendency which would otherwise inevitably develop among the South Vietnamese to reinsure themselves with the Vietminh in the expectation of a Vietminh victory'.[63]

Britain was morally, though not legally, obliged to facilitate elections, an essential feature of the Geneva settlement, Cable commented. 'If we were to connive at its evasion, the very worst impression would be produced, particularly on India and perhaps on Canada. It would also give the Vietminh a perfect excuse for renewed aggression or infiltration.'[64] There was a fundamental question, W.J.M. Paterson thought: 'whether we should pay lip service to our ideas of democracy and at the same time subvert them in Communist fashion or whether we should take our chance (and probably lose) by permitting free elections. The Americans favour the former which will only result in another Chiang Kai-shek or S. Korean type of regime in the East. This will be a source of discord and will destroy an Asian belief in our good intention. We should therefore speak to the Americans.'[65]

They tended to regard the elections as lost, as Cable put it, and their policy was to delay or prevent them. If there were no elections, they might consider it important to retain Diem as 'an impeccably nationalist figure'. Britain could accept neither approach: 'we should do all we can to impress on the Vietnamese politicians that the elections are a certainty and that the only hope of saving their necks is to set their House in order.' The chances were 'slender, but any other policy ... will only lead us straight back to the dilemma from which the Geneva Settlement was at least a temporary escape: the choice between acquiescing in communist domination of all Vietnam or intervening militarily, and thereby risking general war, to prevent this'.[66]

The FO briefed Eden for tripartite talks in Paris in December 1954. 'As long as the Americans are thinking in terms of frustrating the elections and maintaining the separate status of South Vietnam, if need be by force, in violation of the Geneva Agreement, Mr Diem's potentialities as an unimpeachably nationalist and anti-Communist figurehead outweigh his administrative incompetence. We, however, cannot accept a policy based on deliberate violation of the Geneva Agreement. It is doubtful whether the elections can be won outright, but we should at least strive to prevent a Communist majority in the South.'[67]

The essential point to be made was the need to coordinate the policies of the three governments. Britain's claim to be 'fully consulted' rested on its status as signatory (and chairman) of the Geneva settlement; on its position in the Commonwealth, and its influence with the Commonwealth members of the supervisory commissions; and on its responsibilities in Malaya 'and the fact that we have the only non-local forces in South East Asia outside Indo-China'.[68]

Dulles and Eden discussed Indochina on 16 December. Dulles admitted that Diem was 'lacking in many of the necessary qualities of leadership', but there was no agreement on 'feasible alternatives'. He discussed General J. Lawton Collins' plan for building smaller but more effective Vietnamese forces. 'In the main,' he confessed, 'we had to rely upon the Geneva agreements and reluctance to risk a major war to act as a deterrent to military action by the Communists.' The important thing was to gain time. 'It might in the end still not be possible to save Vietnam, but at least we could use the intervening period to strengthen Cambodia, Laos and Siam as much as possible. If we did this then we might be better able in a year's time to withstand the loss of Vietnam than we were now.'[69] A tripartite meeting went well, but the British did not raise the question of elections, content at this stage, perhaps, at least to have secured a say in the making of policy on Indochina, and perhaps reassured by Dulles' general tone.

Subsequently, moreover, the State Department sought to correct the impression that the US was now more ready to consider a prime minister other than Diem. It had never expected him to be 'a great administrator', Robert Hoey told Michael Joy, 'but, in the circumstances, they thought he was doing as well as could be expected'. The trouble was, Joy replied, that he was 'behaving as though he had all the time in the world. ... if it became apparent that Diem's government was incapable of organising the country to the extent necessary to win the elections, in the South at any rate, somebody else would have to be tried.' Surely, Hoey interjected, 'nobody imagined that we could win the 1956 elections?' What then was US policy? Joy asked. 'Hoey admitted in confidence that he had been unable to obtain any guidance whatever from his superiors about this. All that they would do was to point to the disastrous effect American withdrawal now would have on the other free countries of the area. Hoey could not say whether they thought this would be a greater disaster, than being voted out of the country after pouring in assistance of every kind.'[70]

'The lack of any sense of urgency on the part of the Americans in this matter is not easy to understand,' Lord Reading commented, 'especially after their frenzied activity in the spring of last year.' 'I should like to be clearer than I am what we hope to obtain in Vietnam,' Eden minuted. '... Could Mr Allen tell me what he thinks our objective is?'[71] Allen's answer drew on discussions within the FO about the elections. The object, Cable had suggested, should be 'to gain time without exposing ourselves to a charge of violating the agreement'. A properly thought-out scheme, put to the Indians and Canadians and pressed on the government in Saigon, might delay Communist dominance of all Vietnam: the elections might lead to a constituent assembly, and a transfer of power in the South might be 'postponed' till it had adopted a constitution by a two-third majority.[72]

The implication of the Geneva agreement, B.R. Pearn of the Research Department wrote, was indeed that the electorate would be choosing the members of a constituent assembly, though the references to the restoration of peace suggested it might have a governmental role as well. He went on to consider the voting age, the compiling of electoral rolls, the number of representatives and the size of constituencies, the supervision of polling, the counting of votes, and the announcement of results. Hard and fast rules were needed, embodied in identical laws by the two regimes. Pearn thought that the control commission should organise the consultations between the two zones due to commence after 20 July 1955, and help them to reach an agreement on a common electoral law. Could it impose a solution if they failed to agree? Its role and functions would in any case have to be embodied in a formal agreement accepted by both *de facto* governments. If the assembly were constituent, a new election should follow. Organising that would require an executive government, perhaps created by the constituent assembly, acting ad interim as a sovereign parliament. The actual transfer of power should then ensue, and that might require ICC supervision too.[73]

Assuming the Viet Minh would win, Cable added, the aim should be to 'delay and mitigate any subsequent transfer of power in South Vietnam to the Vietminh, but without thereby infringing or appearing to infringe the

Geneva Agreements'. Insisting that it was a constituent assembly was the best method.[74] Delay would hold out some prospect of political survival for southern politicians, suggested F.S. Tomlinson, the new head of SEAD, and so encourage them to greater efforts.[75]

The ideal solution was unification under a non-Communist government, but, given the strength of the Viet Minh in the North and the 'supine' government in the South, there seemed at present no chance that the 1956 elections could have that result. The choice, Allen told Eden, appeared to lie between unification under the Viet Minh—which might show 'some will to independence' but could not be 'relied upon'—and 'the semi-permanent division of the country'. The continuance of the existing division, 'with the tacit acquiescence of both sides', offered a chance of containing Communism in North Vietnam, preventing Laos and Cambodia from being outflanked and Malaya from being threatened, and it ensured China a friendly state on its southern frontier. The Vietnamese, however, had a 'natural desire' for unity, and it was 'strongly in our interests' that Geneva should be upheld: 'its breakdown would expose not only South Vietnam but possibly also Laos and Cambodia to seizure by the Vietminh and, in view of our commitments under the Manila Treaty, would involve grave risk of war.'

There was a danger that the Vietnam government, which never fully accepted Geneva, would seek to avoid the commitment to hold discussions with the Viet Minh about elections in the belief that the US would acquiesce in their indefinite postponement. Britain must seek an agreement with the US and France on 'the best means of securing a Government in South Vietnam capable of governing effectively, of negotiating toughly with the Vietminh about conditions for the 1956 elections and of making an all out effort to win them'.

The powers should also consider what advice, if any, they should give the Vietnam government about the conduct of the negotiations with the Viet Minh to begin in July 1955 and their 'possible outcome'. Two main issues would have to be considered. 'How is freedom of elections to be assured?' It was difficult to see how they could take place in the North; and if the government of Vietnam secured freedom for its parties to campaign there, it would have to allow the Communists to campaign in the South. 'It might therefore prove not only difficult but even dangerous to reach agreement upon a single electoral law for the whole country. The alternative would be separate elections in North and South. This would presumably result in the election of a solid block of Communists in the North who would dominate any common Assembly. A second question was the object of the elections. The Geneva agreement did not specify whether it was to elect a president, a government or a parliament which would then form the government for the whole country. One option might be to insist that the object was to elect a joint constituent assembly and that, pending adoption of the constitution, North and South would remain under existing governments. That would 'at least postpone unification for a little longer'.

The negotiations would be difficult, in themselves, 'also because what is agreed for Vietnam may be used by the Communists as a model for Germany. ... It would probably suit us that they should be protracted. It might be best of all if they were to drift into deadlock and if the deadlock were in turn to lead gradually to acceptance by both sides of the idea of a semi-permanent division of Vietnam.' It would have to be tackled discreetly, and it might be best, if possible, not to broach the questions with the French and the Americans yet.[76]

An 'able' paper, Eden commented.[77] It indeed advocated the kind of diplomacy that appealed to him. A partition had to be achieved, however, without openly defying the Geneva agreements, and it had to displace the very different strategies the Americans had adopted, though with a not dissimilar objective. 'Able', indeed, but hardly realistic. 'The idea that a diplomatic deadlock would deflect the Vietminh from their goal of unification was mistaken.'[78]

Early in April the FO sent instructions to the embassies in Washington and Paris. It was essential that the Vietnamese took part in the preparatory electoral talks in July. They might 'ultimately be faced with a choice between elections on demonstrably unacceptable terms and refusal to participate in such elections. If this happens, however, the Vietnamese must be in a position to demonstrate to the international community and to world opinion in general that not they, but the Vietminh, have made elections impossible.'[79] Any attempt to evade Geneva, Makins told the State Department, the Viet Minh might represent as destroying its validity. If they then renewed their aggression, 'public opinion in Great Britain would not wholeheartedly endorse counter-action under the Manila Treaty'.[80]

It was clear, as Cable wrote, that the US did not want Britain 'to have a voice in the shaping of their policy in South Vietnam. As we are not employing any resources of our own in that country, the only compelling argument we can employ is to warn the Americans that we will not share the responsibility for the consequences of a policy from whose devising we are excluded. If, that is to say, American policy results in civil war in Vietnam, or in the loss of the country to the communists, they must not look to us to clear up the mess.' It was worth risking 'a major row' with the Americans only if they violated the Geneva agreement.[81]

Early in June 1955 the DRV declared its willingness to hold the consultative conference on elections the following month.[82] But in Washington, as Makins reported, there was a feeling that Diem's arm should not be twisted, and if Britain pressed Diem, its policy would diverge from that of the US.[83] 'We must not be frightened of this,' declared Eden, now prime minister.[84] At the Geneva summit, however, the three Western governments agreed simply to advise Diem to reply to a letter from Pham Van Dong proposing consultations.[85] Harold Macmillan, now foreign secretary, thought that the British should not get out of step with the US and not press Diem unduly. They must still, however, urge him to undertake the consultations.[86]

Allen elaborated that line. 'Failure to honour our Geneva commitments will alienate Asian opinion and may provoke intensified efforts by the Communists to overthrow M. Diem by subversion.' Those in turn might lead the Americans to call on Britain to discuss 'measures ... for the common defence' under the Manila treaty. 'Our problem therefore is how to uphold Geneva without doing violence to our interests in the maintenance of a non-Communist Vietnam and of our solidarity with the Americans.' The best hope of resolving it lay 'in continuing, with the Americans, to urge M. Diem to enter into consultations about free elections, in the hope that the argument about the necessary conditions for freedom will result in deadlock, which in turn will lead both sides to acquiesce in continued division of the country after July 1956'. Allen doubted whether representations would succeed, but 'we should be able to show that we are continuing to keep the pressure upon him'.[87]

For Eden upholding Geneva was something of a personal cause. The urgency went out of British policy when Macmillan took over. The attitude to elections became more than ever one of lip service, but the co-chairman, Molotov, was ready to accept it. The FO sought a new modus vivendi with the Communist bloc that would 'shelve the original Geneva provisions for nationwide elections, while keeping the ceasefire in being and enabling the International Commission to continue working in Vietnam'.[88] In April 1956 a meeting between Lord Reading and Andrei Gromyko, Molotov's successor, accepted that there was no point in holding a new conference and that reunification had to be postponed indefinitely.[89] A joint Anglo-Soviet request to the Commission powers and relevant parties in Vietnam implicitly asked them to 'adapt the Geneva Agreements to the facts of the present situation in Vietnam'.[90] An anodyne message, Cable later termed it.[91] The co-chairmen did not propose a new date for elections nor a permanent division of Vietnam. The issue was left: 'a festering sore,' as SarDesai puts it. '... The Vietnamese question was thus in effect left up to the two *de facto* states, who would not admit their separate identities and yet would not be allowed to merge them through military measures.'[92]

South Vietnam

The Americans were pleased, but the Viet Minh were to take the course the FO had anticipated. The next three years were a period of apparent quiescence on the part of the Communist bloc, but it was, as Phillip Hughes has put it, 'not the dawn but rather the twilight of peace in Indochina'.[93] In 1954 the DRV had looked for unification through elections. Ho Chi Minh had told the Sixth Plenum: 'it was our aim to wipe out the puppet administration and army with a view to national unification; now we practice a policy of leniency and seek reunification of the country through nationwide elections.'[94] Failing to secure the unification of Vietnam through the elections Geneva envisaged, the DRV turned to other means. But initially leaders in the North, focused on state-building, resisted the wishes of comrades still in the South to resort to violence, in face of the repression to which Diem resorted.

Le Duan, who had remained in the South, presented his Northern comrades with a 14-point plan adopted by the Nam Bo regional committee that recommended military action, but it was seen in Hanoi as premature.[95] The bitter popular opposition state-building aroused in the North gave Le Duan another argument: a struggle for unification would rally the masses and bolster the Party's position.[96] At its 15th plenary session in December 1958–January 1959 the Central Committee came to the conclusion that 'the main direction of the development of the revolution in South Vietnam is one of violence'.[97] Training cadres were sent south on a substantial scale, and two groups were established to build the supply routes.[98] The Committee also authorised the establishment of a broad-based national front in the South.[99] The decision marked the ascendancy of Le Duan, and the proponents of armed struggle were entrenched in the Party bureaucracy,[100] but there was as yet no commitment to overthrow the Southern regime by force.[101]

In December 1960 the Party's Central Office for the Southern Region (COSVN) established the People's Liberation Front for South Vietnam (FLN, NLF). According to its manifesto, it undertook 'to unite all sections of the people [in the South] … in order to struggle and overthrow the rule of the U.S. imperialists and their stooges—the Ngo Dinh Diem clique—and realise independence, democracy, peace and neutrality and advance toward peaceful reunification of the Fatherland.' It was also designed, it is argued, to win international sympathy, to show the SU and the PRC that they had no reason to continue opposing armed struggle, and to counteract the American argument that the opposition in the South was all Hanoi's work.[102] Early in 1961 the Southern Region Liberation Army (PLAF) was organised, often called the Viet Cong (a combination of Viet and cong san [Communist]; VC).[103]

Told by Le Duan in 1960 of the change in policy, the Russians had expressed concern. The US would not allow reunification. The better course was to continue the guerrilla struggle that Diem's repression had prompted.[104] Nikita Khrushchev's SU adhered to the coexistence policies of the mid-1950s and sought some kind of accommodation with the US. The Chinese, who had exercised such an influence on the DRV in 1954, had by contrast abandoned the cautious coexistence policies of the mid-1950s and become deeply critical of the SU. Zhou supported the DRV's new position.[105] But those who saw the DRV merely as an instrument of either of the major Communist powers were quite mistaken.

In the US Vietnam was often seen through a Korean lens. The war there had been fought to avoid another 'loss', and Vietnam, too, was to be 'retained'. There, too, you might back up a Syngman Rhee in the form of Ngo Dinh Diem and build an alternative regime under him as president of a republic. But in Korea you had fought a major conflict, ended with an armistice and a line on a map, and the Seoul regime consolidated its hold in face of an opponent who continued to threaten. The war in Vietnam had been quite different, and the regime was not consolidated, unlike the South Korean. Eden and his FO colleagues of 1955–56 had 'time' in mind: the division might, especially in the light of history, become 'permanent'. The DRV was anxious to avoid that, and, election failing, did not long delay its challenge that Le Duan urged upon his colleagues.

Militarily Diem's American advisers thought in terms of a big war, Korean-style. The threat, as Chester (Chet) Cooper put it, was of guerrilla actions in the countryside, encouraged by southerners returning well trained, not of invasion across a border, but the Americans had a 'Korea complex'.[106] 'The thinking among American leaders … reflected previous U.S. combat experience in Korea,' as Robert Brigham writes.[107] 'We were waging a different kind of war,' as Nguyen Cao Ky, a later South Vietnamese leader, put it, 'a guerrilla war inside our own territory.'[108]

Increasingly, too, the Americans referred to 'South Vietnam' and to 'aggression' against it. There were legal doubts in the UK and in the US as well. In 1956, Cable wrote nine years later, the co-chairmen had tried to 'paper over the cracks'. But, he went on, 'it would be better to avoid any suggestion that South Viet-Nam is today legally a separate entity subject to external aggression'. That was incompatible with Geneva, and the South Vietnamese government had always rejected the idea of a permanent partition.[109] The then foreign secretary himself, Michael Stewart, took quite a different view. These were two countries, and it was strange to find a Communist country attacking its neighbour for not holding elections.[110] In the US Richard Falk, who edited the vast work *The Vietnam War and International Law* (1968), insisted that Vietnam was not two countries with sovereign governments, but 'one nation with two zones of temporary governance'.[111]

To whatever extent the US administration shared such legal doubts, it had its political doubts as well. It had no more wish to unleash South Vietnam against the North than it had to unleash South Korea. But the soldiers it helped to train had a diminished sense of the legitimacy of the regime they served. Many of the original Army of the Republic of Vietnam (ARVN) officers had collaborated with the French, and many rural Vietnamese saw the ARVN as the army of collaboration. 'The Communists were far more successful in convincing the citizens of Vietnam that they owned the nation's past sacrifices. The party was the self-proclaimed caretaker ... of Vietnam's patriots, forcing the RVN government to create a nation from dust. The RVN's inability to use the past had a significant impact on its army's alienation and lack of ideological commitment to the national struggle.'[112] Nor could the US allow the soldiers the 'all-Vietnamese' legitimacy the other side could claim. In Vietnam's case 'retention' was at odds with nationalism.

In 1964 one of Diem's successors, Nguyen Khanh, declared that the ultimate object of the Southern 'Vietnamese National Liberation Revolution' was the reunification of the Fatherland.[113] One of Secretary of Defense Robert McNamara's assistants argued that the US could offer 'moral support to this ultimate objective'. But the Vietnamese had to be clear 'that we do not intend to provide military support nor undertake the military objective of "rolling back" Communist control in North Viet Nam. Our purpose is to force the North Vietnamese to cease their ambitions to extend their control both in South Viet Nam and Laos.'[114] Nguyen Cao Ky claims that LBJ said 'No' to his 'simple bold plan' to send his troops across the border and set up a base in North Vietnam.[115]

The American objective—as defined by William Bundy, who played 'an enormous role' in defining US policy in 1961–68—was 'preventing the fall of South Vietnam to the Communists', which he believed would lead to 'a fairly rapid extension of Communist control, or complete accommodation to Communism, in the rest of mainland southeast Asia right down to

Indonesia'.[116] It was in a sense a 'negative' policy, relating to US 'credibility' in the region and beyond. Unable and unwilling to 'roll back' the Communist hold on North Vietnam, the US did commit itself to a positive but also again an intractable task, creating a southern state in face of a movement prepared to back its claims to national legitimacy by the use of violence and terror.

In Laos the Americans had openly intervened in opposition to the neutralist policies that the premier, Souvanna Phouma, thought were the only ones his country could possibly follow after 1954. They built up an army—Korea-style—and put their faith in its leader, Phoumi Nosavan. In their eyes Laos was not a buffer, as Eden had seen it, but a bastion. But Kong Le's neutralist coup of August 1960 had produced a new situation. The British sought to avoid a wider war. The accession of the new Kennedy administration made the conference they supported possible. It got under way in Geneva in May 1961 and finally produced the following year a scheme of neutralisation, though it was not to be honoured, nor could the UK and SU co-chairmen ensure that it was.

During the conference Caccia, now ambassador in Washington, suggested that some Americans had concluded that the decision over Laos was reached because Britain and France failed to support military action. They were similar to those who blamed Britain for restraining the UN Command from pursuing the ground forces across the Yalu River in 1950 or for preventing the bombing of Dien Bien Phu in 1954. 'They discounted both the dangers of Chinese Communist reaction and the wider implications of a major war involving China', and in the last analysis favoured a preventive war before China became a nuclear power. They saw Britain as a scapegoat in the absence of a decisive American lead in the direction they favoured. An increasing element in American opinion had, however, reached the conclusion 'that the anti-Communist Laotian is a will o' the wisp, hovering over a bog of indefinitely extending commitments', and that President Kennedy had chosen the right course.[117]

Co-Chairmanship

In June 1961 Tomlinson's successor, Fred Warner, had meanwhile prepared a memorandum for Lord Home, the foreign secretary, for use in a discussion with the minister of defence about allegations that Britain was 'dragging its feet' over Laos. 'Most Americans connected with South East Asian affairs have never forgiven Britain for preventing them from going to war over Indo-China in 1954 and for bringing about a settlement which handed over half of Vietnam to the communists.' The Americans were never really happy with the Geneva agreements, 'even during the first five years during which they worked pretty well and gave us an unexpected respite and opportunity for building up a stable system in Indo-China'. Policies prevailed that brought about 'the present dangerous state of affairs'. British criticism of those policies was 'most unwelcome', but they had some effect even on the Eisenhower administration and 'carried great weight' with Kennedy and his secretary of state, Dean Rusk. 'They have prevented the Americans from carrying out wholeheartedly their more aggressive policies.' Those in favour of those policies said 'that we have been dragging our feet in the interest of avoiding any unpleasant fighting'. 'The truth of the matter is that we want to handle South East Asian problems in quite a different way from the Americans. We feel we have right on our side because our policies in India, Pakistan, Burma and Malaya have worked very well, and we feel that if in those countries we had pursued the sort of policies which the Americans favour they would not now be fairly stable regimes but would probably be in the same position as Laos or Vietnam. Furthermore, not only do we think we are right but we think we have a right to speak, partly because we are Co-Chairmen of the Geneva Conference and partly because we may at any time be involved in a war as a result of what happens in Indo-China. But … so long as we continue to give what we think is the best advice, we shall be accused of dragging our feet.' There was no alternative to being exposed to the accusation 'so long as we feel that military intervention would be premature'.

The US had always wanted to pursue 'much more aggressive policies' in Southeast Asia than Britain, and the accusation of 'dragging our feet' was inevitable. 'In so far as the present American administration would be quite glad to extricate itself from its difficulties in Indo-China and has difficulty in doing this because of opinion at home, it is perhaps no great tragedy if they put a lot of the blame for unpopular decisions on to us. But the cumulative effect is bad, and leads to suspicion of our policies in other parts of the world as well.' The effect could be mitigated by expressing Britain's views only 'when really serious issues arise'. In the last resort, Warner thought, 'the Americans will not take military action unless they are sure that we will stand by them, so that we have in fact some sort of veto over the decision of life and death'.[118]

In November 1961 Warner dictated 'a few thoughts', prompted by Permanent Undersecretary Sir Frederick Hoyer Millar's saying 'how much he doubted the wisdom of our involvement in Indo-China'.[119] The connection, Warner's memorandum read, arose from co-chairmanship of the 1954 Geneva conference and membership of SEATO, two responsibilities often in conflict. 'As Co-Chairman the Secretary of State has to play a conciliatory role and try to restrain some of our allies, while as members of S.E.A.T.O. we are constantly being dragged by the hair into the more aggressive anti-Communist schemes of the Americans and the Thais. The result is that we are seriously handicapped in the first role and poor allies in the second.'

Nothing was said about the co-chairman's responsibilities in the 1954 agreements, which had grown up by custom without Britain's 'having an opportunity to accept or reject them in principle'. In the new Laos agreement that was being hammered out, it was proposed to formalise them. The disadvantages were 'a great deal of unwelcome responsibility and work. … We are also obliged to act as peacemakers in a part of the world where we have no direct interest. If we exercise our role effectively (as in Laos) we are brought into conflict with United States policy. … When we do not do our job properly (as in Vietnam) the role is *for the moment* useless and ridiculous.'

The advantages of the role were, however, 'considerable'. If a war started in the Far East, 'we are going to be involved or, at the very least, our interests are going to be seriously prejudiced, whatever we do. Therefore the greater our ability to stop such wars the better. The system of Co-Chairmanship undoubtedly provides a buffer between the rival blocs and a means of getting international negotiations going when the situation becomes really dangerous. It is very doubtful if it would work if the Americans were Co-Chairmen instead as they would not be flexible enough.'

SEATO risked drawing Britain into issues not perhaps of vital importance to it, like the loss of Laos. But there were 'compelling reasons' for remaining in the organisation. 'If we leave it, it will disappear (at least in its present form)', and though some other system of US guarantees would replace it, 'the shock to non-Communist countries in the area' would be 'considerable'. SEATO had also 'got very much tied up with imperial defence', since Australia saw it as 'their principal shield against the Communist landmass to the north'. But the main consideration was that if the British and French left it, SEATO 'would probably soon get itself involved in a war which would either seriously damage our interest in the area or into which we should eventually be dragged willy nilly'.

Had Britain not been acting as co-chairman and as member of SEATO, Warner believed, there would have been war in Laos. If it had been left to the parties principally concerned, there would have been no conference. 'Although we covered ourselves with opprobrium I have no doubt we were right.' In Vietnam the task was harder. 'The North Vietnamese are determined to overrun the South and I have the impression they have been given carte blanche by the Russians to do so as a reward for good behaviour in agreeing to a Laotian settlement. In these circumstances the

Co-Chairman are not able to put on the brakes.' Nor did the US want negotiations any more than it did in Laos. 'The difference is that there is nothing much to negotiate about because you cannot have a neutral South Vietnam. What we can do, however, is to try and prevent a war in South Vietnam through restraining S.E.A.T.O. But we cannot play this game indefinitely because President Diem's Regime is crumbling and in the last resort the Americans will go in to save him. Therefore, our main role at the moment is, neither as Co-Chairman nor as members of S.E.A.T.O., but simply to give advice as friends and allies of the Americans, but it is not much good opposing them and criticising everything they do as they are simply not going to be dissuaded from their present path, at least until things have got very much worse.'

The conclusion was, Warner thought, that Britain had been able to use the co-chairmanship and SEATO membership 'to advantage'. But its position in Indochina was 'highly artificial. We have no real interest in the area and, although it would undoubtedly be disastrous, I think that Britain could accept the whole of Indo-China going Communist.' It became involved in the two offices because of its 'general interest in the Far East ... inherited from our former Indian Empire'. Apart from Hong Kong, it had nothing that required military protection. 'Singapore is not an interest in itself but a means of defending our interest. This being so, our posture seems rather ridiculous. We have 14 major units in the area but all of this only permits us to put one British battalion into the field at present if we have to defend Laos, Vietnam and Malaya, and the machinery by which we deploy this tiny military force (S.E.A.T.O.) commits us to all sorts of adventures which we can ill afford.'

Warner was aware that Prime Minister Macmillan wanted Britain to play a role in alliances in the area acceptable to Australia and the US, but 'considerably less onerous in military terms than our present commitments'.[120] So long as Britain remained co-chairman and SEATO member, Warner wrote, 'we are bound to be involved in everything which happens in Indo China and we had better make the best use of our opportunities. If, however, we feel now that we cannot discharge in Indo China our obligations under S.E.A.T.O., because of shortages of manpower and money, then the sooner we tell the Americans the better.' If Hoyer Millar wanted that question to be examined, there should be an interdepartmental report on 'the effects on our defence effort of involvement in Vietnam, because that fighting may start quite soon'.[121]

Edward Peck, the supervising undersecretary, agreed generally with Warner but added some points. First, Britain still had 'very considerable commercial interests' in the area, and even if they did not require military protection, it was important for Britain 'to have a say politically'. Second, the influence of the British in Southeast Asia as 'disinterested decolonisers' was 'out of all proportion to our military strength', but 'some military strength is necessary to give us a say in American policy in the area'. Third, 'for good or for bad we are in SEATO and in South-East Asia jointly with the Australians and New Zealanders. The Commonwealth Brigade in Malaya is a unique "tripartite" military unit and it would be a retrograde step to disband it. Our SEATO obligations may be a nuisance but it pays better to honour them than to be in breach of them.' Lastly, while the mediatory role of co-chairman might earn 'more kicks than ha'pence, … if we did not seek to perform it a conflagration, certainly local and possibly world-wide, might have arisen in South-East Asia on at least three occasions in the past six years.'[122]

British 'Firmness'

In his book *All the Way with JFK?* Peter Busch seems at times to put a mistaken stress on British policy towards the escalating struggle in Vietnam. He suggests, for example, that Britain argued against a conference on Vietnam at this time.[123] Some delegates at the Geneva conference on Laos indeed hoped that it would be complemented by one on Vietnam, and the British ruled it out. Their prime argument, however, was that the Americans would not accept it. An agreement on the Laos model would not do for Vietnam, Rusk told ministers. If the Russians made the suggestion, it would have to be resisted, Lord Home told his colleagues.[124] The same doubt arose when Sihanouk sought support for the neutralisation of Cambodia.[125]

That the preferred destiny for Southeast Asia was neutralisation was a long-standing belief in the FO. A brief prepared for the Washington conference early in 1956 suggested that 'a genuine neutrality, provided that it is not based on a complacent disregard of the true aims of Sino-Soviet Communism, need not be inconsistent with the interests of the West. By its neutrality the neutral bloc enjoys a relatively high degree of security from overtly Chinese or Russian action.'[126] The idea was, however, at odds with the special relationship and could not be pressed on the Americans once the Korean War had enhanced the commitment to Southeast Asia into which the British had originally persuaded them. The neutralisation of Laos was thus in some ways an advance on a long-held policy, in other ways a retreat. For the US became more committed to South Vietnam. Britain sympathised with Sihanouk's notion of a 'neutral belt' but could not advocate it.

That did not mean that the FO, still pursuing the Allen/Eden policy, considered at that stage that South Vietnam should be abandoned to its fate. What it wanted was to avoid a larger war. It recognised, too, that Vietnam could not be neutralised, as the Indians advocated. Britain did not, however, want the Americans to introduce troops, and in 1961 it tried to persuade the Indians, who chaired the control commission, to make it more active. A welcome shift of view on the part of a former head of the Laos ICC was noted. He urged that the Laos conference should not extend to Vietnam. That would make it difficult to get a solution for Laos. Nor, he thought, should Britain 'buy any neutral belt proposals if a reunified Vietnam were the price to be paid, since he felt sure that a reunified Vietnam would go Communist'.[127] Was the change of view due to China's threat to India? The border dispute had been sharpening. China, an Indian note declared in September 1961, had shown 'aggressive designs and imperialist ambitions by unauthorisedly occupying large areas of Indian territory in violation of the solemnly agreed Panch Sheel principle of respect for each other's territory'.[128]

Advising the prime minister on a visit by Nehru in November 1961, the FO suggested that there was no chance of establishing a neutral and unified Vietnam along the lines being worked out for Laos. It was therefore 'in the interests of world peace that stability in South Vietnam should be restored on the existing basis of partition in Vietnam'. The ICC had recently decided that it could investigate complaints. Britain hoped it would become more forthright about armed North Vietnamese 'interference ... in South Vietnamese territory'; otherwise the US and its allies and the Communists might drift into 'a limited war in South Vietnam'. That would be 'a terrible tragedy after we have averted it with so much trouble in Laos'. The stationing of Western troops in South Vietnam, the prime minister was advised, 'would complicate the chances of a settlement over Laos and would be a violation of the Geneva settlement'. It would be 'a particularly difficult situation' for Britain as co-chairman. A more vigorous ICC might help restore stability.[129]

Lord Lansdowne was given similar advice for his visit to India. 'We do not agree with the Indian view that Vietnam can be neutralised. The North has no intention of behaving like a true neutral and only pays lip service to the notion as an excuse to swallow up the South.' The time was not ripe for international discussion of Vietnam. Any suggestion that the Laos conference should extend to Vietnam would worsen the situation and might frustrate a settlement in Laos. If South Vietnam fell into Communist hands, 'the shaky neutrality of Laos and Cambodia would quickly be overthrown'. The Indians thought that 'the present situation should not be allowed to drift especially with Diem trying to involve the United States directly in South Vietnam—a development which might not lead to a solution but on the contrary would perpetuate instability'. They favoured a Geneva-style discussion, the fundamental need being somehow to establish the neutralisation of Vietnam that 1954 failed to achieve. Britain thought that would be 'an ideal solution' if it covered all Vietnam, but 'the aggressive Northern Communist regime' would never submit to it. Any suggestion of neutralising the South was 'unrealistic'. Any negotiations involving the Sino-Soviet bloc would only consolidate the 'very great gains' of the Communists. 'The time for negotiations on Vietnam will be when President Diem has won the battle against the Communists in the South. We could then talk on equal terms and go for an agreement by both East and West to respect the *status quo*.' The FO did not think that Maxwell Taylor, whom Kennedy had sent to Saigon, would recommend the introduction of combat troops. It hoped that the US would make 'no dramatic moves' before the Laos settlement was achieved, and that it would 'go about the task discreetly'.[130] What Britain was seeking at this time was surely a return to the *de facto* partition of the 1950s.

The detailed presentation Busch offers of the Thompson (British Advisory Mission [to Vietnam]; BRIAM) mission is more fully convincing. Visiting Kuala Lumpur in 1960, at a time when 'insurgency' was increasing, Diem displayed an interest in the methods used in Malaya to fight the 'Emergency', quite different, indeed, from those for which the Korea-style ARVN was being trained. A visit by Robert Thompson, followed by a report in May 1960, Diem found persuasive, but he did not want a British advisory mission. The situation within South Vietnam continued to deteriorate. The US was failing to establish a viable regime able to defend itself at home, Ambassador Henry Hohler and the FO concluded. The ARVN's American training was 'wrongly directed in that too much stress was laid on preparation for outside aggression and not enough on internal security operations'.[131] The British had another interest. A mission would be a further means of reaffirming the special relationship damaged by the Suez crisis. The Pentagon was at best unenthusiastic, but BRIAM was finally agreed upon in mid-1961. 'Such a scheme,' Home had told the Treasury, 'would hearten the Vietnamese and please the Americans, fulfil our SEATO obligations and to that extent encourage the Thais and Filipinos, as well as commending itself to the Malayans, Australians and New Zealanders. Above all it might just tip the balance against a very expensive war in which we should all get involved.'[132] Fighting off the Treasury, Home later argued that the mission had an influence in excess of its size 'in giving us more of a voice on matters which might involve us in serious consequences if our interests were overlooked by the Americans, and in relieving us from American pressure to contribute in more expensive ways to the assistance of Vietnam'.[133]

The British were rightly concerned about the deterioration of the situation within South Vietnam. The main priority was to make a gesture to the Americans that would stop short of military participation, and avert the further extension of the conflict. It advanced Macmillan's wish to secure warmer relations with the US, as Peter Lowe puts it. But 'it could be dangerous if it led the Americans to deduce that growing British military involvement could follow. … The British were prepared to bend the rules in Vietnam and, in certain respects, to act in ways not compatible with the role of co-chairman. … But no British government could send British forces to fight in Vietnam.'[134]

Busch finds a 'firmness' in Britain's attitude that he assimilates to its firmness over Indonesia and Malaysia. There indeed it is easier to discern. The UK had taken up a proposal to create a 'Greater Malaysia' out of Malaya, independent since 1957; Singapore, a city-state since 1959; its colonies of Sarawak and North Borneo [Sabah]; and the protected sultanate of Brunei. But, having ensured its claim to West New Guinea, Indonesia 'confronted' the new scheme after the Brunei revolt of December 1962. What had begun as an attempt to reduce Britain's responsibilities, while yet retaining the use of its base at Singapore, in fact added to its defence burdens and the expenditure Macmillan was anxious to reduce. But it determined to stand firm and wanted Malaya to do so, too.

Standing firm is easily misinterpreted in respect of China, too. The kind of threats bandied about in Eden's day were not a thing of the past, but the US avoided deploying them and shaped its Vietnam policy accordingly. But the British valued its 'deterrent strength'. What it had wanted in Southeast Asia was presence but not provocation. That was still the case. 'Firmness' was needed, but a different approach might become possible in time.

The 'deterrent strength' of the US, as the FO was to put it in March 1965, affected China's policy. The only areas so far 'lost' were North Korea and North Vietnam, and 'we do not accept at this stage the inevitability of giving ground'. Local nationalism and traditional resistance to China might in the long run be 'potent factors in containing the spread of Chinese domination. But the question is whether these will develop better if American support is withdrawn now, or maintained as long as possible in the hope that meanwhile the stamina of south Asian states should increase, and that Chinese policies may soften.' In some cases the UK and the US might have no choice; 'but so long as the choice exists ... we think that hanging on involves the lesser risk. The Americans may or may not lose in Viet-Nam, but even if they lose, the higher the cost of success to the Chinese and their friends, the less likely they are to start the same process in another country.' The PRC was only 16 years old, and even in that period its policies had changed. 'What its final attitude will be is far from clear, and meanwhile there is much to be said for playing for time.' Changes in leadership and a greater sense of security might mean that China's policies would 'soften', and the neutralisation of Southeast Asia result, rather than its submergence. 'But such a deal is clearly not possible at present.'[135]

In other words, 'firmness' should continue. Ultimately, however, the 'neutralisation' of mainland Southeast Asia might follow. In the meantime, what the FO considered premature was taken up by President Charles de Gaulle. That was seen as striking a blow for French prestige, in which the Fifth Republic would redeem the humiliations of the Fourth, and presenting a criticism of the Indochina policy of the Americans who had helped Diem to hustle the French out after 1954. Critical of the Laos agreement—no one, he said, ever suggested a Communist satellite should be neutralised—Ngo Dinh Nhu, Diem's brother, warned against French policy: the French, he had told the British ambassador, Henry Hohler, in the summer of 1962, 'supported the concept of neutralism because they wanted the Americans to leave. They hoped that they would then be able to recover their former position.'[136] At the end of a meeting of the Council of Ministers on 29 August 1963, it was indeed to be announced that France was ready to help in the realisation of a Vietnam 'independent ... from the outside, in internal peace and unity and in harmony with [its] neighbours'.[137]

SEAD, Warner had told Hohler, had indeed worked out a proposal covering the neutralisation of North Vietnam, 'which could be examined if the need ever arose'. It should not be mentioned, however, 'because it is at variance with our present policy of avoiding any kind of international negotiation and of seeking to restore the situation in South Vietnam by military means'.[138] Talking points prepared for Macmillan's visit to Washington in April 1962 had suggested that, thanks to US advice and assistance, the military situation in South Vietnam had to some extent been stabilised. The next six months would be 'critical', but the FO thought the South Vietnamese could still defeat the insurgency. The Diem regime was 'unpopular and inefficient but any abrupt change now would be for the worse'. If there were a further attempt on Diem's life—in February 1962 two air force pilots had bombed the palace[139]—prompt recognition should be given to the military regime which would probably follow.[140] In Ottawa the prime minister might again suggest that the next few months were crucial: if there were no coup, the turning point might be reached by the end of 1962. The UK accepted the Americans' assurances 'that they desire no military advantages or bases in South Vietnam and that, if the Communist campaign ceases, American military assistance will be withdrawn'. If the situation improved significantly, it hoped that the Americans would consider 'a token withdrawal'. The British were 'not irrevocably opposed to a negotiation on Vietnam but think this should be considered only when the military situation has been restored'.[141] In the event Vietnam was not discussed in Ottawa, and it was only mentioned in Washington.[142]

As in 1961, so in 1962, the British government still hoped to avoid escalation but did not want a conference until the South Vietnamese position had improved. Those aims were consistent while you could still believe that the situation could be redeemed by limited measures. That was again evident from a discussion Warner had with Averell Harriman and William (Bill) Sullivan of the State Department after the conclusion of the Laos discussions in July 1962. Britain was 'still entirely in agreement with the Americans on seeking a military solution in South Vietnam, and would continue to hold off Communist attempts to start international discussions'. But the Americans had now put in 'a great deal of training, equipment and money to enable the Vietnamese army to turn the tide of battle. We should need to know fairly soon whether or not this policy was going to work.' If not, 'the sooner we all faced up to it, the better'.[143] The Americans might feel shy about speaking to the British, Warner told Sir David Ormsby Gore in Washington, and the FO did not want to give the impression that it was embarking on a different policy and looking for a pretext. The ambassador should sound out the governor (Harriman) from time to time.[144]

The year 1963 was marked by the crisis between Diem's government and the Buddhists. The US government had rejected coup overtures earlier, but in August, under the impact of the crisis, it shifted. The new ambassador in Saigon, Cabot Lodge, favoured a coup, as against his predecessor, Frederick Nolting, and so did Harriman. 'In the end,' as Nolting was to write, 'the American position came down to a disgraceful one: encouraging a coup while pretending we had nothing to do with it.' It 'created a political vacuum' in Vietnam.[145]

During the Buddhist crisis the British had adopted a cautious approach. 'I think we are right to lie fairly low,' Lord Home wrote. 'The Diem regime is not good but it is no use flushing it out if there is no alternative which there isn't.'[146] The struggle for Malaysia—in face of

Indonesian Confrontation—was also reaching its crisis. 'With so many other troubles in the world,' Macmillan concluded, 'we had better keep out of this one.'[147] The overthrow of Diem followed. Thompson's more favourable view of him had not been allowed to count.[148] Less than three weeks later, on 22 November, President Kennedy was assassinated. A new British prime minister, the former Lord Home, faced a new president, former Vice-President Lyndon Johnson.

A New President

The focus of this book is on British policy towards Vietnam during the Johnson presidency. Though Johnson recalled thinking that 'our failure to support Diem' had been 'mistaken',[149] he began, during a period of national crisis, with an assertion of continuity abroad as well as at home. But what did that mean for Vietnam? Though it has been much discussed, no one knows for certain what JFK would have done. His habit, Ilya Gaiduk suggests, was not to make clear-cut decisions: he 'chose to improvise, temporise, split the difference'.[150] Continuity was 'an ambiguous end'.[151]

LBJ began with a negative kind of declaration that recalled the mythical 'loss' of China. 'I am not going to lose Vietnam. I am not going to be the President who saw Southeast Asia go the way China went.'[152] A statement of 24 November declared that 'the central point of United States policy on South Vietnam remains: namely to assist the new government there in winning the war against the Communist Viet Cong insurgents'. It renewed Kennedy's indication that at the end of the year the programme for training Vietnamese troops should have progressed to the point that 1,000 US military personnel could be withdrawn, though it was also intended to continue the covert operations that Kennedy had approved.[153] Robert McNamara, retained as secretary of defense, wanted stronger action, and a programme drawn up on his instructions envisaged air strikes against the North in its Phase 2 and 3. But in January 1964 the new president was to authorise only a more modest Phase 1.[154]

In considering grand strategy, JFK and his advisers had rejected the resort to limited nuclear war contemplated by Ike's New Look, though they had not rejected the threat of annihilation and engaged in a build-up of nuclear as well as conventional forces. LBJ endorsed the approach: if there was to be a war, it must be a limited one. If the US invaded Vietnam, China would intervene, as it had in Korea. That would lead to pressure within the US for the use of tactical nuclear weapons, and the Soviet Union would be drawn in.[155] LBJ and his advisers seemed to have little choice but fight a limited war, if they fought a war at all. 'Why the administration could or would not make this iron logic apparent to the American people,' Randall Woods suggests, 'is another issue.'[156]

Perhaps the president thought it would undermine the larger threat. But it may also be that he had more in common with George F. Kennan than might be thought. In 1965 Kennan was to denounce the bombing of North Vietnam, to which the president resorted: LBJ had 'lost his head completely'.[157] Back in 1952 Kennan had told Arnold Toynbee that the best hope for humanity was 'an even and undramatic muddling along ..., avoiding great orgies of violence that acquire their own momentum and get out of hand'.[158] A popularised war could become an expanded war, and that would be risky. The restraints of limited war were imposed not only with China in mind but with the US itself.

Even after winning the November 1964 election Johnson pursued a gradualist approach. He wanted to keep the level of military action 'controlled, exact, and below the threshold that would provoke a direct Chinese entry'. That induced gradual escalation, which in turn gave Hanoi time to adjust to American bombing and 'develop strategies to frustrate U.S. moves'.[159]

The DRV concluded that, 'a global gendarme', the US could not use all its forces to fight in Vietnam, and it was thousands of miles away. 'This looks like the US can only use an arm to fight in Vietnam. Moreover, the arm is cut off from the body and is not supported by the whole body's force.' By contrast the Vietnamese revolutionaries were fighting with all their force and in their own country, and 'the rising trend of world revolution against imperialism' was with them.[160] The DRV had to find an effective strategy: protracted war, guerrilla tactics, international support. Its aim was not to defeat the US militarily, though many hoped to do so, but to 'defeat the will of aggression' of the US and prompt it to seek a negotiated settlement leading to withdrawal, a 'limited defeat', as Le Duan put it.[161]

Even such a war consolidated Le Duan's control over the policy of the DRV and, through a revived COSVN, over the FLN. In 1962, following the Laos conference, he had contemplated neutrality for South Vietnam at least on a temporary basis.[162] In reaction to Kennedy's moves he had sent 5,000 PAVN soldiers to join the PLAF and the guerrillas in the South late in 1961. The assassinations of Diem and Kennedy in November 1963 prompted him to decide on 'bigger war', despite the reservations of the guerrilla fighters, before the Americans could intervene further. The Central Committee resolved that the North must increase its aid to the South, 'to bring into fuller play its role as the revolutionary base of the whole nation'.[163]

The gamble would fail. What LBJ did even in 1964 showed that. The further steps Le Duan took prompted the post-election bombing of 1965.[164]

Those events were to bring the SU back on the scene. In Khrushchev's later years it had sunk into 'passivity, indecisiveness and vacillations about events in Indochina'.[165] A reconsideration had begun even before he was displaced by Leonid Brezhnev on 15 October 1964. The SU could not fail to offer the DRV assistance, lest it be open to sharp criticism from the rival PRC, though it was 'reluctant to sacrifice its relationship with the West, particularly Soviet-American collaboration'.[166] It began to ship air defence assistance, and at the end of January 1965 it was announced that the prime minister, Alexei Kosygin, would visit the DRV.[167]

Before the election LBJ was additionally cautious because he wanted to win it. Perhaps that provided the British, now that their policy of restoring the status quo as the basis of a deal had so clearly failed, with their best chance of urging restraint on their allies. But many of them now believed, with James Cable, that the war could not be won, and that did not make it easier to offer advice, though arguably it made it more necessary.

Chapter One
Election Year

When the Indonesian 'confrontation' of Malaysia developed, the UK sought American support for its policy and in return offered its support for US policy in Vietnam. That was limited, though a primary reason for maintaining a major base in Singapore was to indicate that Britain had a role in Southeast Asia and should be able to exert an influence on what the Americans did. It did not feel able openly to advocate neutralisation—as de Gaulle did—but welcomed the relative moderation of President Johnson's actions before the election of November 1964.

'Our primary purpose in Viet-Nam,' the State Department had told its embassy in Saigon on 12 December 1963, 'is to help the government and people of south Viet-Nam maintain their independence.' The goal was to return to the ceasefire established by the Geneva accord of 1954. 'If Hanoi will cease and desist in its subversive aggression against the Republic of Viet-Nam, and the Government in Saigon is thereby enabled to extend its authority without resistance throughout South Viet-Nam, a cease-fire will result.' As long as Hanoi continued to support the guerrilla war against the government of the Republic, the US would continue 'to furnish whatever assistance is required to help that government resist aggression'.[1]

Members of the British embassy in Washington tried rather vainly to find out how US policy was developing. Robert Thompson doubted that the new government of Duong Van Minh could summon up the determination to win the war.[2] In Washington Paul Kattenburg, head of a working group on Vietnam, offered gloomy comments, too.[3] There was nothing for the FO to do at present, Cable concluded. 'The war in Vietnam is an all American show and unsolicited advice from us would not be welcome. Nor does there seem to be any advice which we could usefully offer at this stage.' If, however, the gloomy forebodings were justified, the US government might soon be 'faced with a very unpleasant choice: either themselves to take over the direction of the war and to commit U.S. forces for this purpose; or else to contemplate a negotiated solution which would be bound to involve a considerable increase in communist influence'. In that case, the US might ask for Britain's assistance. It did so in 1954, Cable recalled, and Britain's refusal was 'primarily responsible' for the Geneva conference. It might do so again, for it was unlikely that in an election year the US would consider committing American troops 'unless they could do so with the full support of some of their principal allies. Unless Indonesian confrontation of Malaysia has ceased by then (which seems most unlikely) we should be unable to undertake fresh commitments of this kind and might well again prefer to press for an international conference instead.' That was a further argument for 'keeping the door open' for a conference on Cambodia. 'One of the main American objections to this policy—that it would encourage people to regard a conference as a solution for Vietnam as well—could turn into one of the strongest supporting arguments if it became clear that military victory in Vietnam was impossible.'[4]

Kattenburg gave Oliver Forster a copy of a letter Johnson had sent to Duong Van Minh, but would go no further. That pledged support. The aim would be to enable his government to protect its people from acts of terror perpetrated by Communist insurgents from the North. As the forces of Minh's government became increasingly capable of dealing with this aggression, American military personnel could be progressively withdrawn. The US shared the general's view that 'neutralisation' was unacceptable. 'As long as the Communist regime in North Viet-Nam persists in its aggressive policy, neutralisation of South Viet-Nam would only be another name for a Communist take-over.'[5] On the overthrow of Minh, Johnson urged his successor, Nguyen Khanh, to step up military operations. Neutralism was no answer, though if both North and South could be neutralised it would be considered sympathetically.[6]

Meanwhile Cable, now head of SEAD, brought Indonesia's Confrontation of Malaysia squarely into the British debate about Cambodia. Sihanouk sought a conference in order to guarantee its neutrality, but the US feared that it would demoralise the South Vietnamese. A Soviet note made it impossible to go on working for international affirmation of Cambodia's neutrality and no conference. It was necessary to choose between unsatisfactory alternatives, either accepting the call for a conference but trying to ensure, by advance discussion of drafts, that it would be limited and brief, or rejecting the proposal until governments had reached prior agreement on what the conference was to do. The first option might encourage neutralism in South Vietnam, and Cambodia and the Communist powers, promised a conference, would no longer cooperate in prior discussions. The second option might cause Cambodia and the Communist powers to 'abandon the idea of a negotiated solution and to treat the problem as a new East-West conflict in which Cambodia would align herself with the Communists'. If Cambodia then emerged as a Communist state, 'the effect on the struggle with the Viet Cong might well be worse than anything that holding a conference could produce'. SEAD favoured the first option.

The US might have different views. If so, the choice should be determined 'not by considering in isolation the immediate tactical problems posed by Cambodia or South Vietnam, but by Anglo-American agreement on future policy in South East Asia as a whole'. For example, if the US wanted to maintain the Western position as a whole, Malaysia must be safeguarded as well as South Vietnam. An 'Asian solution' that neutralised Malaysia would have such repercussions on the mainland that SEATO could not survive, and South Vietnam would become 'a precarious American bridgehead' in a Southeast Asia neutralist or Communist. And if the UK lost its bases, it was unlikely to be able to contribute to the future defence of the mainland. So, inviting American views on the Soviet proposal for a Cambodia conference, Britain should seek a clarification of US policy as a whole.[7]

Attorney-General Robert Kennedy's mission to Indonesia in 1962 had been followed by presenting the Dutch with a fait accompli on West New Guinea. In Indonesia the US thought that the best guarantee against Communism was to support Sukarno's nationalism, and the British feared that on a new mission Kennedy would press Malaysia into making concessions to Indonesia in return for a ceasefire.[8] He might, as *The Times* put it, be 'yet another victim of Dr Sukarno's well-known charm'.[9] Cable was advocating using discussions on Cambodia to head off a pre-emptive American move on Confrontation like the move on West New Guinea. The FO adopted the idea. The new foreign secretary, Rab Butler, sent a personal message to Rusk, designed, as Cable put it, to avoid a US commitment before the meeting of prime minister and president scheduled for February.[10] It expressed concern over Kennedy's proposal for an 'Asian solution'. A termination of Confrontation that led to the neutralisation of Malaysia under Indonesian influence would have profound effects on the mainland. Southeast Asia should be looked at as a whole.[11]

Nationalism, a draft brief for the Washington conference ran, had 'proved less resistant to Communist influence' in Southeast Asia than in India or the Middle East. The threat came largely from indigenous Communism, directly or covertly supported from outside. The Sino-Soviet dispute had not greatly affected it, nor could 'the sheer power and proximity of China' be regarded as the main cause of Communist success.

One of the main reasons, the brief asserted, was 'the continuing absence of any common Western policy. There has never been a steady, co-ordinated Western withdrawal that might, ideally, have left behind it a viable local nationalism.' Instead, individual Western governments had tried to defend 'a particular salient' which the others saw as indefensible: France in Indochina, the Netherlands in Indonesia and in West Irian, the US in Laos. 'In each case the lack of united effort and whole-hearted Western support doomed the attempt to failure, but each effort allowed the Communists to exploit for their own benefit the one force that could have resisted them—South East Asian nationalism.' Now it seemed that the process might be repeated 'by the British in isolated defence of Malaysia and the Americans in isolated defence of South Vietnam'.

The risk made it necessary to reconsider the theory behind previous attempts to hold untenable positions, 'namely that Western influence should not be withdrawn until this basis for viable and pro-Western independence has first been created'. That had worked with the Philippines and with Malaya. The opposite doctrine—'prompt withdrawal regardless of consequences'—which worked in India, worked also in Burma and Cambodia. 'Unfortunately it has long been too late to apply the lesson of Burma to South Vietnam. It was too late even in 1954, when the solution offered (but never applied) by the Geneva Agreement was (a) write off Vietnam (by allowing elections for its unification); (b) neutralise Laos and Cambodia; (c) defend Thailand (and with it Malaya).' Ten years later, if Vietnam were written off, probably Cambodia and Laos would 'rapidly fall under Communist influence', Thailand 'at best revert to neutralism', and Malaya would have to align itself with its Communist neighbours or with Indonesia, 'thus forsaking her British connexions and depriving us of the Singapore base'.

A negotiated settlement of confrontation that left Malaysia under Indonesian influence might have 'correspondingly widespread repercussions'. Malaysian neutralism would encourage similar tendencies in Thailand and in South Vietnam, far more than holding a conference on Cambodia; 'the loss of the Singapore base would largely eliminate the possibility of any Commonwealth contribution to the defence of mainland South East India'; and the US might then abandon a single-handed struggle.

Western withdrawal from either Vietnam or Malaysia would thus lead to the withdrawal of the present Western influence in mainland Southeast Asia. Arguably that was inevitable in the long run. 'The strongly pro-Western regimes now in power in Malaysia and Thailand cannot be expected to last indefinitely and, if there is any prospect of creating a stable

South East Asia able to maintain its independence of both East and West without the presence of western forces in South East Asia, this would be no less welcome to H.M.G. than to the U.S. Government.' Maphilindo, the proposed combination of Malaysia, Indonesia and the Philippines, thus had obvious attractions: such a confederation of 150 million people and rich resources 'would offer a real hope of creating a South East Asian power in its own right'. But if Maphilindo meant that Indonesia 'devoured' Malaysia, 'the new Confederation will start its life in an atmosphere of internecine and anti-Western hatred'. It would be a temptation for Chinese subversion, even a recruit to 'the Chinese half of the Communist bloc'. Malaysia's stability and development were 'the leaven which should permeate Maphilindo, not [the] ramshackle policies of an ill-ordered and expansionist Indonesia'.[12]

The brief was accompanied by a memorandum prepared by the FO's planning staff, drafted by Michael Palliser, that sought to situate British interest in Southeast Asia 'within the framework of our global interests and responsibilities'. The conclusion was that for Britain Southeast Asia was much less important than the Middle East or Europe, but that it was 'the one area of the world ... under direct communist attack', and the Americans saw the containment of that attack as vital to their security. 'Whatever they may think, it is doubtful whether they can contain it without our presence and support. They thus have a major interest in our continuing involvement. For our part, we have treaty and other essentially Commonwealth obligations in the area. Moreover, the Anglo-American relationship is so fundamental to our foreign policy that we could probably not risk the damage to it that any British withdrawal from South East Asia would entail.' The area was an example of 'inter-dependence'. But the US government had not yet realised 'how much they need us there and the consequent need to support us to the full'.

The memorandum summarised Britain's material interests in Southeast Asia. Private investment was mainly in Malaysia, but it yielded only about 7 per cent of total overseas earnings excluding oil, and new investment was small. Trade with Southeast Asia was only about 3 per cent of total trade, and half of it was with Malaysia. Britain earned almost as much from Latin America and traded with it more. Trade with the Soviet Union (SU) was about 50 million pounds more than with Southeast Asia. Set against such 'relatively modest material interests' was 'a very substantial ... military and non-military effort'. Defence costs in Southeast Asia were about 260 million pounds a year, 20 per cent of the operational part of defence expenditure. Military aid to Malaysia and counter-insurgency aid to Vietnam would cost 6 million, non-military aid 8.5 million, and representation and information about 3 million. 'So we are spending in this area over nine times what we earn from our investment in it and substantially more than the total of our trade with it.'

The justification was 'essentially political'. It derived from 'Britain's present position as the major partner of the United States in the world-wide effort to contain communist expansion'. Britain's contribution was concentrated in three areas. In Europe, though a direct Communist attack was unlikely, there was 'the need both to sustain the Atlantic alliance and ensure ourselves a continuing position of influence in it, and to demonstrate our solidarity with Western Europe will remain cardinal to British policy for the foreseeable future'. In the Middle East, Britain's objectives were 'the protection of the vital British (and western) oil supplies on advantageous terms' and the containment of Communist penetration. The main instrument was 'the military complex based on Aden', which cost 170 million pounds per annum, 13 per cent of the operational part of defence expenditure. In the Middle East Britain made the major Western contribution. In the Far East and Southeast Asia the US bore 'the lion's share'. But Britain's effort cost 1.5 times what it spent in the Middle East. It had obligations to Malaysia, to fellow members of SEATO, to the Commonwealth, to its Pacific possessions and to Hong Kong, 'all comprised within the common Western objective of preventing the spread of Chinese communism'.

Southeast Asia was 'under direct communist attack—an attack which is no less dangerous or costly to us because it is mainly in the para-military and subversive field [rather] than overt aggression'. If it were 'lost to Chinese communism', India, Australia and New Zealand would all be 'dangerously threatened. Indonesia's strident nationalism is, however unwittingly, abetting the communists. This is why British support for Malaysia has to be regarded as indivisible from U.S. support for Vietnam. If we withdrew or were evicted from the area (for example through the loss of Singapore) the United States alone could probably not contain the spread of communism; and no other Western power is willing or able to replace us. But we should recognise that this immense and relatively disproportionate effort is being deployed more in the general Western interest and in support of our American and Commonwealth partners than in defence of specifically British interests. Our continuing involvement—which means for example a settlement of the conflict between Indonesia and Malaysia on terms likely to enable us to remain for some time in Singapore—is thus arguably of more direct interest to America than to ourselves.'

That was not to suggest that Britain 'could or should shrug off' its obligations. 'Moreover, the Anglo/American partnership is such a vital element in British foreign policy and to our position as a world power, that we could probably not afford the damage to it which would result if we contracted out of S.E. Asia.' That the area was one of 'interdependence' had not been brought home to the US. 'The logic of it is that we should be entitled to more positive support from them than we have had hitherto.'[13]

'The theme of this brief,' Edward Peck commented, 'is to say to the Americans: "what South Vietnam is to you, Malaysia is to us" and "jointly we stand, divided we fall".'[14] Compared with American forces in Vietnam, the Philippines, and the 7th Fleet, M.R. Morland observed, Britain's military establishment in Singapore was 'quite small'. And the Americans seemed to fear Indonesia's going Communist more than Britain's loss of Singapore, 'which even we admit probably won't last for more than ?5 more years'.[15]

Washington Communiqué

In Washington talks between officials on 10–11 February preceded meetings at higher levels. The topics included Cambodia and the proposed conference. They also covered Vietnam. Given France's recent recognition of the PRC and its proposal for the neutralisation of Vietnam, 'the Americans would welcome a public gesture of support for their policy. They reiterated strongly their determination to persevere to a successful conclusion, and accepted that a collapse of either South Vietnam or Malaysia would seriously endanger the whole situation in South East Asia. Our support for the American attitude can be included in the communiqué balancing United States support for Malaysia.'[16] Harriman, Peck noted, was firm on keeping Sukarno's feet to the fire. What Britain wanted was a public declaration of US support for Malaysia and the British strategic position in Southeast Asia. Harriman indicated that it could be included in the communiqué 'if linked to a similar statement of British support for United States policy in South Vietnam, which we can readily give'.[17]

Secretary of State Rusk met Foreign Secretary Butler on 12 February. He was given a copy of the brief.[18] The British government, Butler said, wanted the communiqué to make its support of the US in Vietnam clear. 'This would, as it were, balance an expression of United States support for the independence of Malaysia. Britain did of course have to be careful about the wording in view of their co-Chairmanship of the Geneva Conference.'[19] At a subsequent meeting that included the president and the prime minister, Rusk said that he was satisfied that the US and the UK were 'in much closer agreement' on their policy in Southeast Asia. The quadripartite discussions on Malaysia had produced 'a satisfactory understanding' among the four powers. 'There was also agreement between the United Kingdom and the United States on policy towards Vietnam; and it would be valuable if both Malaysia and Vietnam were mentioned in the Communique to be issued at the end of the current discussions.' Sir Alec said it was 'welcome news that we were now much closer to the United States on policy in South-East Asia. As regards Vietnam, our position as co-chairman of the I.C.C. imposed a certain limitation on us; but we would certainly give all the support we can to the Thompson mission.'[20] In a private meeting with LBJ, Douglas-Home had offered similar assurances though saying Britain 'must help quietly because of its peacekeeping role under the agreements of 1954'.[21]

On 13 February the two issued a statement in which the prime minister re-emphasised Britain's support for US policy in Vietnam and the president reaffirmed US support 'for the peaceful national independence of Malaysia. Both expressed their sincere hope that the leaders of the independent countries in the region would by mutual friendship and cooperation establish an area of prosperity and stability.' In his press conference, Sir Alec declined to interpret de Gaulle's neutralisation policy but reaffirmed British support for American policy in South Vietnam. 'One could not generalise about that part of the world. Some countries must be defended, such as Malaysia; there were others for whom neutrality might be more appropriate.'[22]

Britain's idea of a 'balanced reference had in the end been accepted by Harriman with enthusiasm and eventually welcomed', A.A. Golds of the Commonwealth Relations Office wrote; 'and if there is any further back-sliding we now have both a public and a private text to quote to them'.[23] But the support—more like lack of opposition—won from the US in respect of Malaysia was won at some cost. It reduced the influence the British might exert on American policy in Vietnam, as well as, more immediately, exercising a further constraint on their own Cambodian policy.

In New York the Canadian foreign minister had told Butler of his concern over developments in American policy: officials at desk level in the State Department (SD) were, he said, considering an ultimatum to North Vietnam to stop aiding Communists in the South. It might work, but it might also lead the North Vietnamese to call in the Chinese and another Korean War could result.[24] The US government had always had 'a deep rooted belief that all Communist revolts are wholly dependent on outside organization and support', Cable commented.[25] No decision had been taken, Rusk said at lunch on 13 February, but if the US had to choose between defeat in South Vietnam or action in the North to stop support for the Viet Cong, the present mood of the administration was for the latter.[26] It seems that this was not true of the president. 'It's their war and it's their men,' he said on 20 February.[27]

Butler sent a message to Rusk at the end of February, when the British press was reporting that the US was contemplating an offensive policy, and he thought that might lead to questions in Parliament. The answer had to be that Britain's support on Vietnam was for a defensive policy, as America's was in respect of Malaysia. He would find it difficult publicly to support an overt military offensive policy in North Vietnam. The Joint Intelligence Committee (JIC) had concluded, too, that even a severance of supply links would have little effect, since the revolt was now self-sustaining. It was not worthwhile to run the risk of widening war in Southeast Asia with so little hope of achieving anything in South Vietnam. Further factors that would limit Britain's support were its Malaysia commitment and its co-chairman role. Could the British government have advance information of the plans of the US government, so that they could concert a line?[28]

Ambassador Harlech (Lord Harlech, formerly Sir David Ormsby Gore) queried his instructions. Contingency planning was proceeding, but action would depend on the situation in South Vietnam. It would be unfortunate if Britain displayed alarm before there was any need for it. Much would depend on China's reaction, and no doubt the Americans would keep punitive measures from affecting really vital Chinese interests. Sullivan seemed to think that the Chinese were in a cautious mood, their capabilities low, and that they were not over-welcome in North Vietnam.[29]

Cable was against altering the message. He had already argued that Britain could not support offensive action against North Vietnam. If US forward policy led to limited non-nuclear war, 'this would probably be protracted and indecisive and might encourage Indonesia to exploit Western preoccupation with Viet-Nam to intensify her confrontation with Malaysia'. Even diplomatic support would be incompatible with the co-chairmanship, already severely strained by support of a defensive policy but still possessing residual utility and of possible importance if a negotiated settlement had ultimately to be attempted. If Britain was not going to support an offensive policy, it should tell the US as soon as possible. 'This might influence their own decision, and, once we have told the U.S. Government, it would be easier to tell Parliament. I think this latter step is also desirable, as any evasiveness in our replies on such an important question might result in it becoming a political issue.' The major objection to 'frankness' was that it might prejudice American support for Malaysia, but the risks could be reduced by emphasising that Britain saw the support in both cases as for defensive—not offensive—policies.[30]

If the question of offensive action were evaded, Cable added when Harlech's telegrams arrived, it might become a political issue in Britain, and ultimately the damage to Anglo-American relations could be worse than any strain from 'initial frankness'.[31] But his superiors—Caccia and Butler—cut out the paragraph that said that Britain would find it difficult to support an overt offensive policy.[32] The indication that Britain's support was for a defensive policy remained, however, as Butler told the Cabinet on 3 March: the support was 'based on an assumption that that policy would remain primarily defensive in its emphasis'.[33] This small exchange implied problems that were to loom large in future discussions of the British role. What could be said to the US? And when?

Rusk agreed to keep in touch before any new courses were adopted.[34] The US could withdraw, escalate, or continue on its present course. The last was preferred. 'We shall do everything we can to make it succeed.' Unfortunately, the free world was not united. French recognition of the PRC was a signal to the Chinese Communists that their militancy paid dividends. 'The talk of neutralization is phoney, given the fact that there is not the slightest indication that North Viet-Nam is interested in breaking away from the communist camp. If neutralization simply means that the US abandons the support of South Viet-Nam, then neutralization is a formula for a communist takeover of Southeast Asia. We have repeatedly said to the other side that if they want to get American forces out of Southeast Asia the way to do it is to leave their neighbours alone.'[35]

The US did not seem to be contemplating an ultimatum, as the Canadians had suggested, but rather, as Cable wrote to Gordon Etherington-Smith—the British ambassador in Saigon—direct pressure on North Vietnam 'through more or less unavowed offensive operations'. He did not think it 'a particularly hopeful policy'. The insurgency, supplied and reinforced from the North, was basically self-sustained. 'If it cannot be suppressed in the South, I do not see how it can be suppressed at all or how the Americans could derive sufficient advantage from widening the fighting to outweigh the great risks this would entail. I cannot help feeling that there is a gambler's decision to try and recoup his losses by doubling the stakes.' SEAD was trying to think of 'more constructive alternatives', but without much success.

Meanwhile, the FO had been attempting to ensure that the prime minister's reaffirmation of support in Washington was understood as support for a defensive policy. One of the main considerations, Cable told Etherington-Smith, was recollection of what happened in 1954. Then the foreign secretary was 'reluctant to appear to be pouring cold water on

American schemes at the outset'. As a result Dulles 'got the impression that we were far more deeply committed to support the U.S. plans for rescuing the French in Indochina than was, in fact, the case. This misapprehension had eventually to be dissipated in a somewhat brutal and semi-public manner which did great harm to Anglo-American relations and had many unfortunate and lasting repercussions.' Hence, the FO was currently keen to be 'frank ... from the start'. Press publicity was another factor. A spate of Parliamentary questions had resulted, two by Harold Wilson, the leader of the opposition. 'I personally have been anxious to be reasonably frank in our replies in order to avert any risk that policy towards Viet-Nam might become a political issue in an election year.'[36]

The ambassador had reported Dennis Bloodworth's allegations that Ambassador Lodge and General Paul D. Harkins would advise McNamara, then on a mission to Saigon, to knock out targets in North Vietnam.[37] Should we urge our views on the US? Cable had asked. The timing was difficult to judge. If offered before a decision, there was a risk of irritating the Americans and perhaps causing needless alarm. After a decision, it might be too late to exert any influence. And what should we say?[38] As Fredrik Logevall puts it, 'British officials would have reason to ask themselves this question again and again in the months to come.'[39] The need to say gloomy things made it even more difficult to say anything. In fact, at this time, LBJ was continuing existing policy, more of the same, training: as he told the NSC on 17 March, he wanted 'a maximum effect with a minimum involvement'.[40] 'I've got to win an election,' he reminded McGeorge Bundy.[41]

Cable prepared a memorandum, based on JIC analysis. He listed possible Western objectives 'in descending order of attractiveness'. First was what he called 'the Korean solution', 'an independent anti-Communist South Viet-Nam whose territorial integrity would be guaranteed by the United States, but which would not require more than token Western forces to be stationed in the country'. That had been the US objective throughout, but it had been frustrated by the Communist insurrection, 'organised and assisted from the North, but now self-sustaining'. Some Americans thought that 'retaliation against North Viet-Nam might create sufficient fear of widespread and escalating hostilities to induce the Communist Powers to order the end of the insurrection and acquiesce in the imposition of this "Korean solution".' But the Communist powers were unlikely to issue such orders unless threatened with nuclear war, and the US might find it difficult, 'in view of the probable opposition of their allies', to obtain the support of their own public opinion for such a threat or 'make it sound convincing'.

It would be difficult to prove that continued insurrection was nevertheless taking place. South Vietnamese leaders might not support a policy that entailed prolonged hostilities or involved a threat of nuclear war. If they did, they might lose the support of their own people and armed forces.

Second, Cable considered 'the German solution', 'an independent, anti-Communist South Viet-Nam relying on the presence, during an indefinite period, of substantial Western forces to assist in external defence and internal security'. Instead of hoping to withdraw most of its soldiers by the end of 1965, the US would have to retain them indefinitely and 'commit them to direct participation in what would be essentially a "colonialist" war of the kind we fought in Malaya, but against far more formidable opponents'. Probably US opinion would not accept such an open-ended commitment unless some allies took part, but none were likely to agree. 'Moreover, any major increase in Western military participation could easily arouse Viet-Namese resentment and, by increasing disaffection and war-weariness, do more harm than good.' Increased Western participation would probably also provoke increased Communist counter-efforts.

Third on Cable's list was 'the Laotian solution', 'an independent, non-Communist Vietnam whose neutrality would be internationally recognised, but whose external defence and internal security would depend on indigenous forces with the background threat of renewed Western intervention to counter Communist interference'. That would be 'a bargain—probably reached in an international conference—of American withdrawal and the inclusion of Viet Cong representatives in a coalition government ... against an end of the insurrection and of North Viet-Namese interference', possibly with arrangements for international supervision and guarantees. But as soon as the idea was mentioned, 'South Viet-Namese readiness to continue the struggle would probably evaporate', and the Communists would have 'little incentive to make concessions unless the U.S. Government threatened to take over the war themselves'. If such a bargain were nevertheless reached, the Laos precedent suggested that it would be difficult to hold the Communists to the bargain or 'detect them in a sufficiently flagrant breach to make renewed Western intervention politically possible'. A Laotian solution would thus end in Communist domination and a reunification with the North or continued strife. Circumstances might nevertheless compel the US to consider such a solution 'if only to save face in a withdrawal enforced by, for instance, the collapse of the South Viet-Namese will to continue the struggle'.

Fourth, Cable considered 'the Geneva solution'. Reunification through internationally supervised free elections was agreed upon in 1954, but the

US supported the refusal of the South Vietnamese to put it into effect. Their objection then—that the Communists would win—still held good. It was thus improbable that the Communists would agree to any effective neutralisation of a reunited Vietnam. 'There was no evidence to support French wishful thinking that a reunified, Communist Viet-Nam would wish to follow a Titoist policy and would thus be partially neutral and non-expansionist.'

A fifth option was abandonment. 'The objections to this solution require no argument, but it is not certain that it could ultimately be avoided if South Viet-Namese morale continues to decline.' No satisfactory solution was in sight. The best course for the British might be to dissuade the US from embarking on a new course and suggest it should maintain its present defensive policy 'until further developments make some change appear feasible or inevitable. It is, after all, always possible that time might alter the present situation for the better.'[42] 'Micawber,' commented John Addis, previously ambassador in Laos, now in Manila.[43]

Palliser was also critical. Was it really true that the rebels could not be dealt with? The conclusion Cable reached was so disheartening to the Americans that it was not clear that it could be the basis of an approach. If the British counselled against escalation, the Americans would ask what they suggested. They could only say 'slog on'; and that might tempt them, in election year, to 'go it alone' in a tougher policy, while looking with 'a more jaundiced eye' than recently on British policies in Malaysia. It was better to await McNamara's report.[44] There was, it seemed, never a right time to say anything, let alone something bad.

Cable's paper was, however, sent to Harlech. The current regime was precarious, he was told, and the US might decide on a forward policy only to find a revulsion in Saigon, and another coup installing more cautious leaders.[45] Nigel Trench did not show the paper to his contacts, however. 'This was partly because we thought it might give the Americans a misleading impression of our attitude, and partly because it seemed, in the light of the extremely thorough study which the Americans had made of the subject, presumptuous of us to give them a potted version of our view of the problem.'[46]

In the meantime, Bundy's report on McNamara's trip, adopted by the NSC, committed the US to 'an independent, non-Communist South Vietnam ... free to accept outside assistance as required to maintain its security'.[47] Despite Palliser's doubt, the US was unlikely to adopt much tougher means for attaining its objective in election year, any more than it was likely to abandon Vietnam.

A Cable Proposal

Britain might have to consider the applicability of the 1954 agreements to the 1964 situation, Etherington-Smith wrote from the Saigon embassy, and its position as co-chairman 'now openly pledged to support United States policy in Viet-Nam'.[48] Cable referred to a telegram from Moscow that reported that the Russians had proposed a joint approach to the US. A British reply might offer 'the usual evasive and defensive counter' or, 'just conceivably, consider something more radical'. On the face of it, the Russian move was part of the 'ritual dance' the co-chairmen carried out: the SU pestered the UK to denounce breaches of the ceasefire agreement, usually producing a draft note leaked to the press; and the UK produced a rival draft, leaked in turn. 'This is all very futile and is possible because we maintain the fiction that the provisions of the Geneva Agreements still apply—which they manifestly do not.' They had been repeatedly violated, and neither the US nor the South Vietnamese were parties. 'Yet we have to go on pretending that the agreements exist and paying for an expensive International Commission to keep up a pretence of supervising what is actually a nullity.'

Might not relations with the Russians be placed on a more realistic basis? Britain might suggest, in reply to their latest proposal, that, given recent US statements, the North Vietnamese were 'displaying premature alarm'. It could go on to say that Vietnam was a difficult subject for joint messages, and there was not the measure of agreement there was in the case of Laos and Cambodia. Both North and South Vietnam, though abstaining from alliances directly incompatible with Geneva, had 'contracted close ties with other governments' and were clearly unwilling to renounce them in favour of neutrality.

In such circumstances, the British response might continue, the co-chairmen should recognise 'the facts of the situation as it has evolved and … devote their endeavours to bringing about a temporary *modus vivendi* which could reduce tension in South-East Asia. This could perhaps be achieved if the Co-Chairmen were each prevailed [upon] to persuade their respective friends, without abandoning any of their formal claims, to refrain in practice from any attempt to change the status quo in either of the two areas of Viet-Nam defined by the 1954 ceasefire agreement. If such undertakings were given and carried into effect, we could say to the Russians, the result would admittedly fall far short of the hopes enshrined in the original Agreements of 1954, but the situation would be far better than at present and a major threat to the peace and stability of the area would have been eliminated.'

The 'tentative' idea, Cable admitted, had 'a great many drawbacks'. Even most careful drafting might imply the recognition de facto of a State of North Vietnam. In addition, it would suggest 'equating' North Vietnamese interference in the South with such interference as the South had undertaken in the North. 'We would be implying that we would be prepared to take steps to persuade the Americans not to implement plans which the Russians must know that they have under preparation, for taking action North of the 17th parallel.' And in return, 'we would be asking the Russians to take action vis-à-vis North Viet-Nam which they are unlikely either to be able or to wish to do and to go on to use influence with the Chinese which they may no longer have'. Action of the kind in mind might also be held to imply a precedent for Germany and Korea, where 'reunification' remained 'the slogan of our side'.

The Russians might make no response and might indeed use the suggestions in their propaganda. Indeed there were many obstacles to overcome, and even if the idea were approved in London, the State Department would have to be consulted. But 'the whole Viet-Namese problem is in such an ugly and menacing impasse that I do not think we should be deterred from examining ourselves even the wildest ideas'.

The approach would have two objectives. The more important, but the less likely to succeed, was to suggest to the Russians 'the desirability of reducing the Viet-Namese conflict to the same kind of suspended animation as those now dividing Germany and Korea'. The second, less important but more feasible, was to extricate the British 'from their increasingly embarrassing position of responsibility, in their capacity as Co-Chairman, for the maintenance of a non-existent agreement on Viet-Nam at the same time as they have reaffirmed their support for U.S. policy in South Viet-Nam (a policy which even the Jesuitical casuists of South-East Asia Department find increasingly difficult in pretending to be compatible with the Geneva Agreements).'

Was such an idea worth pursuing? Would the US consider it worth pursuing? Would General Khanh agree that the 'slur' it cast on his fiction that he ruled all Vietnam outweighed 'the advantages to be derived from escaping the equally notional subjection of South Viet-Nam to the Geneva Agreements'? Would the Russians abandon their propaganda advantages? 'The whole idea ... rests on the assumption that the Russians are increasingly coming to regard the reduction of tension in South-East Asia as being in their interests.'[49] Cable was proposing a kind of recurrence of the status quo policies of the 1950s, in which indeed the Russians had partaken.

Ambassador Humphrey Trevelyan was in London. His second-in-command, Thomas Brimelow, commented unfavourably from Moscow. The Russians would probably interpret the suggested approach as 'an indication of weakness', possibly leading to an increase in Communist pressure. It would interest them only if South Vietnam were 'stabilized', and if North Vietnam were seriously threatened or escalation seemed imminent. Failure seemed certain if the ideas were put forward when the Communists thought that 'everything is going their way in South Vietnam'. If there were 'suspended animation' in regard to East Germany and South Korea, it was 'because they are held in a firm grip. This cannot be said of South Viet Nam.' The present role of the co-chairmen was indeed ritual, but 'the essential thing is to keep the machinery ready for use in case the crisis should deepen for one side or the other. This does not require us to take initiatives except when we think the time is right.'[50]

Trench thought the Americans were unlikely to accept Cable's idea 'unless the situation in South Vietnam had reached such a disastrous stage' that it was 'the only possible alternative to an admission of defeat'. It seemed dubious that the Russians would then be prepared to play, and if they were, whether it would have any effect on the North Vietnamese, who seemed to be 'leaning ever closer to the Chinese'. The Americans would be sceptical about any assurance from the North Vietnamese that they would not try to change the status quo in the South, and might argue that, if the Viet Cong were indeed self-supporting, as Britain maintained, such an assurance would make little difference. Unless the Viet Cong's fortunes were drastically reversed, Trench could not see why the North Vietnamese or the Chinese would accept the idea either.[51]

Etherington-Smith thought the Laos and Cambodia agreements worth preserving. The problem was 'how to get off the hook' in respect of Vietnam without upsetting the agreements as a whole. Cable's proposal was 'ingenious', but it could not succeed. 'In particular, … it would be most unwise for us to enter into any commitment, explicit or implicit, to oppose American action beyond the 17th Parallel.' Recently an attempt had been made to develop the legend that Douglas MacArthur would have won the Korean War but for Britain's sabotaging him. 'At all costs we must avoid giving the Americans any cause for asserting in the years to come that they would have been victorious in Viet Nam had it not been for our dragging our feet.'

What alternatives were there? The Geneva agreement might be anaesthetised, not destroyed. Britain might work behind the scenes to induce the Canadian and Indian governments 'to declare that violations by both sides of the Vietnamese agreement have now reached such a scale that they no longer feel it useful to maintain the pretence that the International Control Commission serves any useful purpose'. They would withdraw their teams, the Poles could do nothing, and the agreement would become 'dormant', though the legal framework would remain 'against a day when it might again prove useful'. The Indians, Etherington-Smith recognised, might be reluctant to follow a course that might not be to the liking of the Russians. But from such a beginning the Russians might behind the scenes be induced to accept 'a gentlemen's agreement to let Geneva sleep for a while'.

In public, meanwhile, Britain would maintain that 'such derogations from the Agreement as had our approval and support were justified by reason of North Vietnam's violation of the Agreement in conducting a war of subversion against the South'. If it were found necessary to provide SEATO assistance to Vietnam, that could be treated as an extension of the policy. The Geneva agreement had served well up to 1962. Now it had ceased to correspond with reality, 'the outstanding new development being the increasingly firm commitment of the United States'. Being co-chairman might soon become 'a source of intense embarrassment' unless a way out could be found.

The ambassador also commented on Khanh's attitude to reunification. Though impracticable, that had become 'an article of faith which could not lightly be abandoned by a country with a million refugees among its most dynamic elements', and he would not renounce it publicly. 'The situation in South Viet Nam, where the Communists have a near lethal grip, is of course basically different from that of West Germany and South Korea. The unsatisfactory position of those countries is a dream of desirability by comparison with the situation here.'[52]

Etherington-Smith's comment confirmed the view held by Trevelyan, with whom Cable discussed the matter: there was nothing that could be done 'to inject greater realism' into Britain's exchanges with Russia over Vietnam. Cable also doubted that Geneva could be 'anaesthetised' without killing it. The legal framework could not survive the departure of the ICC, and an admission that it had to be withdrawn because of extensive violations would be taken to imply that it was no longer relevant. The Communists, moreover, might counter by calling for a reconvening of the 1954 conference and blaming the West for the breakdown. 'After all why should the Communists let us scrap the Geneva Agreements in one country where these inconvenience us, but hang on to them where they suit our book?' They might, moreover, react by increasing their insurgency in Laos as well as Vietnam.

Britain must thus resign itself to the dichotomy between support for the US and co-chairmanship. The position could indeed become more difficult if the Americans took 'more drastic measures', but what they had been doing since 1961 was 'pretty clearly contrary to the Agreement', and Britain had 'managed to live with this without too much strain'. Maintaining the 'uneasy position' was 'unavoidable' if it wished 'to keep the framework of Geneva for possible use in the future'. Negotiating on Vietnam was 'not a subject that one can broach with the Americans at present, when their entire effort is devoted to the survival of South Viet-Nam'. But when the presidential elections were over, the next administration, presumably Democrat, would 'no doubt consider very carefully the long term implications of continuing the military struggle' and might 'give some thought to the possibilities of a diplomatic solution as an alternative'. That was not to say 'that we expect the Americans to look for a face-saving exit'. But they must be conscious of the 'uncomfortable possibility: that the growing war-weariness of the South Viet-Namese people will find expression in a third coup d'état and the emergence of a government in Saigon eager to attempt a negotiated solution'. If that happened, the Geneva agreement and the basis for contact with the Russians it provided 'might be very useful in enabling the West to salve something—above all United States prestige—from the wreck'.[53]

Geneva hampered the West, Thompson wrote from Saigon. Vietnam was 'one of the vital issues', he argued; the Americans were committed to the hilt and not going to withdraw. If Saigon called for SEATO intervention, the US could act under its umbrella, with token allied support, instead of acting alone, against Geneva, represented as imperialism.[54]

Cable did not agree with any of this. Vietnam was not a vital issue. 'South Viet Nam was never a viable part of the Western world and, if we had had our way in 1954, it would have been written off as politically untenable by being exposed to elections under international supervision. What is at stake is not South Viet Nam, but American prestige in South East Asia.'

Nor were the Americans 'committed to the hilt'. If there were a third coup in Saigon, and a government emerged that favoured negotiation or a neutralist solution, Cable did not think the US government 'could or would want to take over South Viet Nam as a colony and continue the struggle against the will of the South Vietnamese leaders themselves'. He suspected that 'the more far-sighted members' of the administration might, 'however reluctantly', have envisaged that possibility and were 'at present primarily concerned with holding the line' until the elections.

Nor did Cable agree with Thompson's belief that Britain should acquiesce in a decision to 'escalate'. The JIC had concluded that would solve nothing, and he suspected that 'the more sensible members' of the administration agreed. If it proved impossible to overcome the insurgency in South Vietnam, 'there is no solution to be found in widening the war, and ... we should resolutely oppose any idea of carrying Viet Nam to the nuclear brink. Saigon is emphatically not worth a world war.' Widening the war as a SEATO operation would not reduce the risks. 'SEATO is a red rag to every international bull.' The only difference it would make would be in the US, 'where it might render politically acceptable a degree of United States military involvement and nuclear brinkmanship that American public opinion might shrink from as an isolated operation'. But that was 'what we want to avoid'.

Thompson wanted to jettison the Geneva agreements 'because they constitute an obstacle to British participation in a wider war for the salvation of South Viet Nam'. Cable had wanted to get rid of the letter but reanimate the spirit of the agreements as a preparation for the negotiated solution that he thought would have to come. Trevelyan had persuaded him that his notion was not a starter. Thompson should be persuaded not to pursue his 'dangerous ideas'.[55]

The military situation was worsening, Cable had commented on 16 April. Khanh was insecure; the government's use of napalm and air strikes did not win allegiance. A crisis could emerge at any time: a desperate Vietnamese signal for more intervention, a coup of a defeatist/neutralist character, the disintegration of the administration.[56] The Viet Cong, Peck pointed out, had established no government base, and it would not welcome intervention, and thus occupation, by the Chinese. The FO should be thinking of 'stalemate' before the US election, and thereafter all sides might welcome a negotiated Geneva solution. 'But it would be unwise to breathe a word of this to any American at present.'[57]

Etherington-Smith had concluded that the initiative lay with the Viet Cong, and that even if Khanh lasted till after the US election, the deterioration of security in the rural areas would lead to a crisis soon after. The fall of Khanh, the ambassador said, would face the US with a choice between withdrawal and increased involvement. Cable thought there was another possibility: a new regime that favoured negotiation could help the US withdraw with less humiliation. But there was no point in saying that to the Americans. If the British played Cassandra, 'we may be blamed for causing a catastrophe which we had done no more than predict'. They should 'keep quiet, continue moral and non-military support for South Viet-Nam, but decline to be drawn into any additional commitments on the unexceptional [*sic* for: unexceptionable] ground that the defence of Malaysia must have first call on our resources'.[58]

Everything depended on what the Americans' policy really was in Indochina, Cable told Etherington-Smith early in June. He was not convinced that they had taken a final decision or would do so, if possible, before the election. Even if a diplomatic solution were possible, as Addis argued, this was not the moment. Meanwhile, the immediate crisis was in Laos. No doubt it could be argued—as by the French—that Cambodia, Laos and Vietnam were all part of a single problem, but 'this seems to be more of a mouthful than international diplomacy can at present stomach'.[59]

Etherington-Smith agreed that it was not the moment for a British diplomatic initiative. 'The Americans have not yet exhausted the options open to them, and … it would be disastrous if we were to take the lead in proposing negotiations before they were ready for them. … We simply must not give the Americans the excuse that they were getting along quite well with their problems in Indo-China until we, their Allies, cut the ground from under their feet. I do not believe that there should be any intervention in the form of a new initiative on our part short of the point at which we were convinced that this was necessary for reasons of the utmost national importance. We still seem to be a good distance from that and there is plenty of evidence that the Americans are themselves fully conscious of the risks inherent in the situation there.'[60]

De Gaulle

What should be the aim of British policy in Southeast Asia? asked Peter Murray, the ambassador in Phnom Penh. 'I suggest that our only viable and practical objective … is the establishment of a series of independent and stable countries, with sufficient unity, self-confidence and support for their own regimes to be capable of resisting outside pressure. This implies the ability to resist Western pressure as well as communist. In other words, such states must be expected to follow a neutral policy.'

China had the trump card of being Asian. 'The strongest card in our hand is local nationalism and the strong desire of the South East Asian countries to be left alone to develop along their own lines, to choose their own policies and to make their own friends.'

'No doubt,' Murray continued, 'in due course the Chinese revolution, as it succeeds and matures, gains self-confidence internally and externally and begins to raise the standard of life for the Chinese peasant, will slough off its more violent aspects and simmer down, like the Russian, into something more reasonable that we can hope to live with.' It might happen quite quickly once the old generation of leaders had died off, provided

China was 'treated with patience and consideration for her legitimate needs meanwhile'. The French were pursuing the right policy even if for the wrong reasons. American policy was heading for disaster. Britain's role should be 'to influence the Americans towards more flexible, more sensible and less emotional policies, based on their (and our) real interests, towards China in the first place, and towards the rest of South East Asia in consequence'. China's admission to the UN would facilitate Britain's task. And the UN could be made to assume a larger role in stopping local wars and policing trouble spots.[61]

For the UK indeed the neutralisation of Southeast Asia was ultimately desirable, but not yet. Recognising the PRC 14 years after the UK, de Gaulle had restated that objective. There was in Asia, he had said on 31 January 1964, 'no political reality ... which does not concern or affect China. ... Thus it would be absolutely impossible to envision, without China, a possible neutrality agreement relating to the Southeast Asian States, in which States for so many reasons, we French feel a very particular and cordial interest,—a neutrality which, by definition, must be accepted by all, guaranteed on the international level, and which would exclude both armed agitations supported by any one among them in one or another of the States, and the various forms of external intervention; a neutrality that, indeed, seems, at the present time, to be the only situation compatible with the peaceful co-existence and progress of the peoples concerned.'[62]

'We agree with General de Gaulle in regarding neutrality as the ultimate ideal for South-East Asia', a FO list of talking points for an interview of the French ambassador in February had begun. 'Neutrality, however, is only possible when the opposing forces within South-East Asia have achieved some sort of balance and there is at least a tacit agreement between East and West to leave South-East Asia alone.' The moment had not yet arrived. The government in South Vietnam was struggling with 'a dangerous revolution' and Malaysia faced with 'creeping Indonesian aggression'. They were allies of the West and 'touchstones of Western reliability. If the West abandons them, Western friendship and protection will no longer be wanted in Asia.' Neither, moreover, could be defended in isolation. 'If one falls, the other will follow before long. Although we and the Americans have each had reservations about each other's views in the past, we recognised at Washington that these two problems were indisputably linked, and undertook to give one another mutual support.' The French had even more reservations about US policy, 'but we hope that they will show the utmost restraint in expressing them during the critical months ahead. If the West is to withstand the twin threats from Djakarta and Hanoi and to restore the balance that must precede neutralism then Western unity will be indispensable.'[63]

Long-term the practicability of the proposals had to be doubted, the Australian Department of External Affairs considered. China had not 'overtly' broken the Geneva protocols. But 'no way has yet been found of guaranteeing to neutral states protection against covert subversion and interference (e.g. through minorities)'. Neutralisation would thus offer no guarantee against Communist takeover. 'Indeed the French accept that the D.R.V. would quickly gain control of the whole country as a means of developing independence vis-à-vis China and achieving a greater degree of contact with the West (read France) than the D.R.V. can afford while Vietnam is disunited.' But that assumed 'a tremendous ideological compromise for a communist regime, and a degree of independence of Chinese influence which does not seem possible for Hanoi. ... French hopes do not appear to be based on any inside knowledge of D.R.V. thinking.'[64]

In Paris the Australian ambassador sought comments on de Gaulle's concept at the Quai. De Gaulle's idea, or 'hypothèse', on desirable principles, de Villelume said, did not reflect 'a detailed *French plan* laid out in advance'. The Quai (the Foreign Office), Brèthes said, had 'no blueprint for neutrality for the Indo-China states', nor, he thought, had the Elysée (the Palace). South Vietnam had an army and 'the basic capability to stand on its own feet and live alongside a north Vietnam which itself seemed in no position to subjugate it quickly and easily—in rather the same way as South Korea lives alongside North Korea. The first step should be an arrangement worked out among Vietnamese themselves and first of all among South Vietnamese (a ceasefire). It was only by stages that such matters as the terms of international guarantees would come to be considered.'

Even the first phase involved 'thorny problems', he admitted. The political structure was 'woefully weak'; the government 'could scarcely be taken seriously'. Was that not a dilemma? the Australian ambassador asked. 'The sort of spirit he had mentioned as the basis of independence could not be built up either overnight or in the absence of pretty massive American aid. He replied that it would be better for American aid to take some other form than direct military participation.' It seemed clear, ran the report to the Department of External Affairs in Canberra, 'that French view with equanimity, to say the least, acceptance at pretty early stage of withdrawal of Americans as condition of settlement, and probably expect early replacement of present Government by a neutral-oriented one.'[65]

The most probable outcome, French Foreign Minister Couve de Murville told Ambassador Walker, was 'the communisation of South

Vietnam'. The only alternative was 'the indefinite prolongation of the American military presence. Had the Australians anything more hopeful to suggest?' There was no Vietnamese government, only 'a handful of Generals', the Americans, the Viet Cong: 'no political life. That was the essence of the problem.' Was Canberra aware of the rapid deterioration of South Vietnam? 'It seemed to the French that the objective of neutrality would be a lesser evil.' How would neutrality be guaranteed if the Americans returned to the US? Walker wondered. '[O]nly to the Philippines,' Couve interjected. Neutrality implied a balance of external forces, he replied. 'Both China and the United States would guarantee Vietnamese neutrality.' He went on to say that the US nuclear capacity was 'the only effective counter-balance to Chinese military strength'. China could not be contained by conventional forces: 'if it were not for the A bomb the communists would have taken Vietnam by now regardless of the United States military presence.'

J.B.S. Pedler of the British embassy in Paris told the Australians 'there was some evidence that the French were putting out the view quite deliberately that the North Vietnamese were Russian puppets and that Chinese influence was very weak in Hanoi, in order to advance the theory that a withdrawal of American military power from South Vietnam would not mean the domination of Vietnam by the Chinese, since the Russians could be counted on to act as a restraining influence on the North Vietnamese—i.e. that the Russians could be left to contain the Chinese in the Indo-China peninsula and that they would be better at doing this than the Americans.'

The Australians said that they had been fed with that thesis, but they agreed with the FO's view, 'that while it was extremely difficult to assess the exact balance of Russian and Chinese influence at Hanoi at any given moment, the Chinese were certainly in a very strong position, probably the dominant one'.[66]

The FO was, of course, interested in the views others took of the *hypothèse*. His ambassador, Charles Bohlen, counselled Johnson not to seek clarification of de Gaulle's views, but he wanted his French counterpart to say that he did not favour neutralisation at the present time. 'We are not asking him to drop his idea for all eternity.'[67] Bohlen gave Sir Pierson Dixon an account of his interview with the French president on 3 April. He had been instructed, he said, to try to extract an assurance from de Gaulle that the policy of neutralisation was 'merely a long-term idea', and he had tried on the general 'a formula to the effect that while neutralization of the area as a whole was the ultimate objective, the French Government recognized that this was not practicable in present circumstances until the pro-Western situation in South Viet Nam was firmly established.'

He failed to get any such commitment from the general. At one point he argued 'that he was in favour of Viet Nam being neutralized in order to prevent it being Communized'. Bohlen 'countered by saying that it was not realistic to expect that the Chinese would stop short at neutralization so long as the situation in South Viet Nam was relatively so favourable to them. The General had pooh-poohed this argument and had warned Mr Bohlen that the Americans would shortly find themselves in the situation of having to choose between recalling the Geneva Conference and working for a neutralization of Viet Nam, or using force against Viet Nam and possibly China itself.'

Basically, Bohlen thought, 'the General could not bring himself to face the prospect of the Americans being successful where the French had failed'. He also equated the Americans' difficulties in Vietnam with the difficulties the French had had in Algeria, and he was not going to help them out. He had no 'hard and fast approach towards the problem. It was not so much that he intended to do something, as that he was content to see the United States in difficulties.' Dixon commented that the French did not have to do anything in practical terms. 'Statements made here and there were in themselves a form of action.' Bohlen agreed: 'French statements about neutrality had had a most disturbing effect in a highly sensitive area.'[68]

Dixon himself called on Couve before he left for the Manila SEATO meeting in April and told him he found French policy 'rather obscure. We were all agreed that a neutral status for the whole of Viet Nam was the ultimate objective. The French seemed to be advocating neutrality as an immediate solution.' Nor was it clear whether they were thinking of the whole country or only South Vietnam. If the former, 'what guarantee could there be that the Chinese would in fact respect a neutral status for the Vietnamese'? If the latter, 'the counterpart surely should be neutrality for the North. Was there any reason to expect that the Chinese would agree to this?' The indications were the reverse. 'Would this inhibit the French from pressing for the neutralization of South Viet Nam?'

Couve evaded a reply. The French, he complained, were always reproached for their policy, but no constructive alternatives were offered. 'The fact was that there was no real Government in South Viet Nam …, and the American policy of trying to produce a solid South Viet Nam by running the country themselves was doomed to failure.' There was 'a coherent policy', Dixon replied, the object being 'to help the South Vietnamese Government to deal with and overcome the Communist insurgency and put South Viet

Nam in a position of security *vis-à-vis* the North. When this had been done would be the time to speak of lasting solutions. We had been successful in helping the Government of Malaysia to deal with similar problem of Communist infiltration.'[69]

After the SEATO meeting, Dixon reviewed French policy in Southeast Asia, which, he argued, de Gaulle saw in the context of 'the world game as a whole'. He was now concentrating on his new China and Third World policies, 'designed to combat the danger of what he calls a Russian-American "double hegemony"', and to increase the influence and prestige of France and incidentally China. Indochina was 'the perfect field for operations of the kind he has in mind'. He would 'no doubt think that it would be poetic justice if France could supplant the United States in 1964 or 1965, after an American defeat, as in his view the United States supplanted France in 1954'. But it was not resentment that moved him, nor French interests in 'the normally accepted sense of the term'. Much more, 'he believes he has a chance to improve his position in the world game'.

The 'element of vagueness in the formulation of French policy about South-East Asia' was 'no doubt to give room for manoeuvre'. Sometimes the general had spoken of a belt of neutral states south-east of China, sometimes of the need to extend it from India to the Pacific. He had spoken to the Australian ambassador of its including Thailand, while Couve had referred to states 'contiguous with China (though how Cambodia fits into this is not quite clear)'. Malaysia and Indonesia had not been included, though the general might include them in the future. For immediate purposes, his policy could be taken to refer exclusively to Indochina.

Even there 'ambiguities and obscurities abound'. The original statement about Vietnam of 29 August 1963 'referred to the need for internal unity as well as independence from the outside world'. Since then ministers, including French Prime Minister Georges Pompidou, had spoken of the principles as applying to North and South. At the SEATO meeting Couve was 'more cautious', speaking of 'neutrality for the whole of Vietnam starting with South Vietnam (though he did not explain how it would be possible to go on to North Vietnam after starting with the South)'. That was another way of putting what were said to be de Gaulle's instructions: 'that, for the moment, it was not possible to envisage neutralization being applied except to South Vietnam alone; it was not however expedient to say that this was the French Government's official view'.

Nor was it clear what the recommended neutrality would consist of. In the press conference of 31 January de Gaulle said it should be 'guaranteed internationally, and should exclude armed agitations, maintained by one of them in the country of another as well as the many forms of external intervention'. But provisions of that nature had brought 'neither peace nor freedom from Communist encroachment' to Laos. 'Moreover North Vietnam has itself a militant communist Government.' The French had not said what neutrality would mean there, but the Chinese ambassador in Vientiane had told the French ambassador there that it was inconceivable that North Vietnam should be neutralised. 'The French frequently say that they have no proposals to make, only a general prescription to recommend. This is literally true.' De Gaulle had 'established a position on the chess board. He is now waiting for an American castle to fall.'

The French believed that the war could not be won. Their policy was 'based on the assumption, and indeed one must suspect the hope, that the Americans will fail to improve the situation by the present means. In these circumstances they believe that sooner or later, and probably sooner, there will be a *coup d'état* in South Vietnam which will bring to power a neutralist Government or at least one which desires to seek an end to the war by negotiation rather than by military means.' Then the French hoped 'to play an influential role in promoting a Geneva-type conference and in bringing about a Laos-type solution for South Vietnam as a result of the conference, by which the Americans would be required to withdraw their military presence in Saigon in return for which the French would be entitled to install a small military mission as they have in Laos under the 1962 agreement and in Cambodia under the 1954 agreement. No French official … would dare to predict that this would keep South Vietnam out of the hands of the Communist North for very long.'

French advocacy of a neutral solution weakened the will to fight. 'By the mere reiteration of their ideas the French are therefore deliberately helping to make it more difficult for the Americans to improve the situation militarily.' Dixon doubted that they would 'give history a push' by fomenting a neutralist coup. 'They would however probably not hesitate to give any neutralist plotters who came to see them the impression that France could be counted upon to help them, if successful; and the French authorities certainly would not give anyone any warning if they heard that a *coup d'état* was about to take place.'[70] Peck agreed with the analysis.[71]

Addis, the ambassador in Manila, commented on the references to French policy on Vietnam at the SEATO meeting. De Gaulle's statement of 31 January was 'not so much a detailed plan of action as a general line of approach'. At the SEATO meeting Couve confined himself to questioning whether American policies would succeed and advocating an open mind about a negotiated settlement. Perhaps the debate would prove 'fruitful in the long run particularly in regard to the evolution of opinion in the United States'. Already French ideas had elicited a statement by Ho Chi Minh that they deserved 'serious attention'. British policy, Addis suggested, should be 'large and flexible enough to encourage the French to pick up any such clues and explore further the possibilities of a negotiated settlement'. But he differed from Couve when he argued that neutralisation should begin with South Vietnam. 'In my opinion the processes of neutralisation must from the beginning be applied with some sort of reciprocity to both halves of the country.'

Rusk rejected the French thesis, but there was 'very little substance in his case'. Previous agreements, he said, had not been honoured: why should the US try again? 'This was really too disingenuous: memories are not so short.' It was the Americans who tried to wreck the 1954 conference, who refused to sign the agreements, 'who immediately afterwards set about carrying out a policy in Vietnam which was directly contrary to the purposes of the agreement'. The 1962 agreement was often criticised for not producing a more satisfactory situation in Laos, but Rusk knew 'that it prevented a war that would necessarily have extended outside Laos. There is also the consideration that the settlement in Laos can scarcely be stable unless there is some resolution of the present conflict in Vietnam.'

Addis summed up his views in 'a few simple propositions'. The present American policy in Vietnam could not succeed and would lead to 'defeat and disaster'. Spreading the war to the North could not 'restore peace and security in the South, or in the area as a whole', and would lead to 'even greater disaster'. There was a 'very slight' possibility of a negotiated settlement. It would probably be 'very unsatisfactory', and the search for it would 'shake confidence and stability in South-East Asia. But all these grave consequences are preferable to the certainty of a much greater disaster.' In Addis' view 'the French are doing a better service to the Americans in questioning their policy than we are in supporting it'.[72]

From Phnom Penh Murray commented on Dixon's despatch. If the Americans failed in South Vietnam—'and it is difficult to find anyone who believes that they can succeed, though final defeat may be staved off for some years'—then France 'may have served Western interests by retaining some position and influence in a neutralized South East Asia.'[73]

Undersecretary George Ball was sent to talk to the French president in Europe, and he related the outcome to Foreign Secretary Butler. He had alluded to the alternatives the US faced: supporting South Vietnam; and if that were ineffective, acting against North Vietnam. De Gaulle showed sympathy but insisted that the answer had to be a political one. A conference was needed.[74] 'The more the United States becomes involved in the actual conduct of military operations,' de Gaulle said, 'the more the Vietnamese will turn against us, as will others, in Southeast Asia.' Even if the US did not make war and thought it could reinforce the existing situation, it would not be able to bring the affair to an end. If the US began negotiations, Ball responded, the existing resistance would collapse. 'Either we must increase the Vietnamese will to resist or we must reduce the subversive efforts of the North.' Negotiations could not start before that.[75] According to Bréjean, Ball told Couve that the Americans accepted that some form of consultation with China and North Vietnam would be necessary 'in the long run', and a negotiated solution was inevitable. Did Bréjean mean that the Americans would accept the neutralisation of the South without that of the North? Bréjean said he thought so, 'taking the long view'. Would the American public accept that? He offered no comment.[76]

Dixon talked to de Gaulle himself on 16 June. He said he had told Ball that the US had no chance of winning in their military intervention in Southeast Asia. 'This was because the local inhabitants would not be prepared to fight so long as it was an American-led war. It was a mistake to think that white men could lead the South-East Asians into battle.' Ball had said that the Americans were prepared to take the war into North Vietnam. De Gaulle said they could do that. 'They had the means to do so. They could bomb Hanoi or even Peking. But that would not produce the solution they were looking for in South-East Asia. On the contrary they would inevitably find themselves faced in the end with the need to withdraw, and the longer they stayed the more humiliating the withdrawal would be. The only real alternative they had was to make peace.'

Speaking as if acting on reports from Lucien Paye, his new ambassador in Peking, de Gaulle said he thought the Chinese 'might be prepared to come to an arrangement under which the neutral status of the Indo-Chinese states would be guaranteed in return for an American withdrawal and undertaking never to come back'. It might suit them, 'making their début on the international stage, for the situation to be quiet in South-East Asia for the next twenty years or so. Beyond that one could not look. The General clearly implied that in the long run Indo-China would fall under Chinese domination.'

The present division between North and South Vietnam would continue, as would the compromise between the three *tendances* in Laos, and 'poor Prince Sihanouk would get his guaranteed neutrality. The whole arrangement would be guaranteed by Britain, France, the United States, China, the Soviet Union, India, Poland, Canada, and perhaps Thailand.

It would in fact amount to a new Geneva agreement, ... negotiated by a meeting of the Geneva powers.'

Was the general not 'over-optimistic' in thinking China would join in guaranteeing the neutrality of the four states? 'He replied that there was no alternative but to try, or the Americans would land us all in a major disaster involving perhaps a major war.' What would the government of South Vietnam be? Would the FLN or the Viet Cong take part? Would that lead to the Communist North absorbing the South? De Gaulle 'did not see things developing in that way'. Elections would have to be held in South Vietnam, as envisaged in 1954: 'the result should be to produce a markedly neutralist and anti-Communist Government.'[77]

The last question had been put at the request of the US ambassador. The answer seemed to him an 'improvisation'. The elections foreseen in 1954 were designed to unify Vietnam, but the general had spoken of its continued division. 'I doubt if he had given any real thought to the question of how a non-Communist neutral regime in South Viet Nam could be created.' The conversation confirmed Dixon's view that de Gaulle saw his Southeast Asian policy 'simply as part of a world game in which France is playing against the United States. He evidently thinks that China is certain to dominate South-East Asia in the end.'[78]

Michael Butler of the Paris embassy told Étienne Manac'h at the Quai what de Gaulle had said about elections. He was 'clearly taken aback'. Indeed he said he agreed that constituting a government through elections was 'scarcely ... practicable'. The Quai 'had been thinking tentatively of the formation of a neutralist government composed of some of the political parties in Saigon, some neutralists among the exiles and some of the better elements in the National Liberation Front'. He argued that the Front was 'far from being an entirely Communist and fellow travelling body', and that it should not be 'dismissed as being entirely dominated by Hanoi. It had a life of its own and the "national" elements, though they might be anti-American, were strong enough to be worth betting on.' That Butler thought 'pretty good nonsense', and he found it hard to believe that it was 'anything but an instrument of North Vietnam'.

The conversation then turned to escalation. The French were arguing that if the US stepped up its military assistance to South Vietnam and Laos, the North Vietnamese would, with Chinese encouragement, step up their military activities. Three or four divisions of North Vietnamese troops might be infiltrated into South Vietnam, Manac'h suggested, or the Pathet Lao (PL) might seize Vientiane. 'What could the Americans do then?' Butler argued that the North Vietnamese, using the Viet Cong and the Pathet Lao as their instrument, had shown over the past five years their determination 'gradually to gobble up Laos and South Vietnam', and the 1962 agreement had hardly caused them to pause. 'What hope was there of bringing the North Vietnamese and Chinese to accept any real neutrality for Laos or any independence for south Vietnam unless they were frightened of the consequences of not doing so? It was necessary to negotiate from strength.'

Ball had argued along those lines, Manac'h responded, saying that the Americans were determined to demonstrate their will to defend South Vietnam, maintaining, too, that they were ready to leave if the North Vietnamese stopped their indirect aggression on the understanding that they would return if it were renewed. That would be reasonable, Manac'h thought, if the US agreed to negotiate at once and recognised that it could not bring its strength to bear. De Gaulle, Butler pointed out, had said that the Americans would have to undertake never to return. Manac'h evaded the point and went on to explain why the US could not bring its power to bear. Air strikes could do some damage to North Vietnam, 'but meanwhile the North Vietnamese could take over the whole of Laos and South Vietnam and the Americans would be unable to do anything about it. … While the Americans fought in the air, the North Vietnamese would move forward under cover on the ground.'

It was no good arguing with the French, Butler concluded. Manac'h now stuck to the official line: he knew that de Gaulle had 'adopted a firm policy of exercising as much pressure as he can in order to get the Americans out of South East Asia'. But it was 'necessary to have arguments to meet the French arguments if only because they are doing their best to spread their views as widely as possible'. What line should the embassy take?

At the weekend Robert Gillet told Dixon the French understood Britain's position: it was really in agreement with France, 'but, because we wanted American support on certain subjects, were unable to say so. There might be certain nuances of difference about how to proceed but our aims were exactly the same.' Dixon questioned that. 'Though genuine neutralisation in the long run no doubt seemed to us desirable it was difficult to separate procedure from substance and we thought that the French were doing damage by talking so much about neutralisation as an immediate solution and by acting as they did.'

Dixon added 'that he belonged to a generation of Englishmen who were particularly sensitive to the dangers of negotiating peaceful settlements under military pressure, that was to say appeasement. We did not agree … that the only thing for the Americans to do was to negotiate. If they were to negotiate they must be able to do so from strength.'

Probably French embassies abroad had guidance to speak on the lines Gillet had adopted. Perhaps, 'especially in view of the firmer noises emanating from Washington', the FO should send some guidance to its embassies 'to prevent the French from succeeding in associating us with their appeasing policies by what they say to the governments of other countries, and incidentally using our alleged attitude towards South East Asia to support their general contention that we are satellites of the Americans without the courage to say what we really think'.[79]

British Critique

Peck agreed that de Gaulle's policy was pursued 'largely to annoy', but thought it worth trying to analyse, 'for possible future use with the French', why the British disagreed with his ideas. His central proposition was that the Chinese might agree to an arrangement under which the neutral status of the Indochinese states would be guaranteed if the Americans withdrew and promised not to return. 'If we could be sure that the Chinese would accept such a bargain and honour it, there would be no problem. Of course neutrality is the ideal solution, not only for the Indo-China States but for the rest of South-East Asia as well. None of us want to involve ourselves needlessly in this uncomfortable, frustrating and unprofitable region.' But the general had misconceived the problem. 'He seems to be thinking of a kind of Locarno Treaty, as was abortively proposed by Lord Avon [Eden] in 1954. But Locarno treaties and international guarantees generally can only act as an effective deterrent against overt aggression. A threat to unleash nuclear war on China (which is about all the Americans could do after a total withdrawal from South-East Asia) might effectively deter Chinese armies from crossing the frontier.' But that was not the problem. The Chinese operated through 'cut-outs', 'bringing their influence to bear on the Pathet Lao and the Viet Cong through the agency of the North Vietnamese'. It was not Chinese aggression that had to be countered, but 'the steady attrition to which the Pathet Lao and Viet Cong are subjecting not only the Western, but also the neutralist, position in South-East Asia'.

In such circumstances it was hard to see how the US could make 'an enforceable bargain' with China to restrain the PL and the VC. If, for example, an agreement were reached, and the PL then staged a coup giving them effective control of the coalition government in Laos, the US would have only two options, acquiescence and major intervention, 'perhaps an ultimatum to China', and it was unlikely that acts of attrition would ever be so clear-cut as to justify re-intervention in an area that had been abandoned.

Hence the FO view that if the PL and VC were to be stopped, 'they must be stopped on the spot', and given the 'feebleness and incompetence' of the anti-Communist forces, 'very considerable local American assistance is needed to stop them'.

There was 'some force' in de Gaulle's argument that, 'given the inherent rottenness of the political situation in these two countries', no amount of American aid would suffice, and the Americans would eventually have to choose between major war and withdrawal. 'But he should not attempt to blur the harsh sharpness of this choice by pretending that there is an easy alternative in the form of neutralisation. There is a chance that, if the Americans keep up the struggle long enough, the other side will eventually weary and that, if the general international balance of power has meanwhile shifted in American favour (perhaps through the extension of the Sino-Soviet conflict), genuine neutralisation may emerge as a possibility.' At the moment, however, a new Geneva agreement could produce no more than 'a formula for saving American face in withdrawing from Indo-China and abandoning Laos and South Viet-Nam, to fairly rapid assimilation to the authority of Hanoi, while Cambodia would then come under Communist domination without more ado'. De Gaulle could argue that such an outcome was 'inevitable', and that the Americans ought to accept it 'rather than risk gradual escalation into a major and futile war'. He might possibly stand a chance of convincing the Americans if he put the argument 'privately and frankly' after the elections. But he had probably 'ruined his chances of being taken seriously by all his provocatively dishonest double talk in public about the Neutralist solution'.

'We, for our part, regard this as essentially a problem to be played by ear. American prestige and emotions are far too deeply involved for them to be susceptible, at present, to the dispassionate presentation of a case, however logically and forcefully argued, for writing off as an unprofitable investment their ten year old commitment to Indo-China. We think it much better to go along with them as far as we can and to employ the influence we thus acquire to dissuade them from over-risky courses. We think the Americans are more likely to listen to the doubts and heed the warnings of a loyal ally than the outspoken criticism, as audibly spiced by Schadenfreude, of General de Gaulle.'[80]

Palliser offered what he termed an incidental reflection. 'It is that, whatever we or the General may think about American involvement in Indo-China, the fact remains that the Americans have succeeded for the past ten years in preventing Indo-China from going communist—as I take it would have happened if the Americans had not propped up South

Vietnam. This represents ten years gained. Maybe the Americans are not going to succeed and maybe we cannot in any case expect them to hang on for another decade. But surely time gained in South-East Asia is on the whole to our advantage; which is a further reason why French rocking of the American boat is so very unhelpful.'[81] 'Quite so,' wrote Peck.[82]

There had been talks between Paye and Zhou Enlai, K.M. Wilford reported from Peking. The Chinese had responded to the French approach because they wanted to see the agenda of a Geneva conference broadened to include all Southeast Asia and believed they had French support for that, and also saw 'a splendid opportunity for wedge driving'. From what Paye and the counsellor, Claude Chayet, had told Wilford, it seemed that the two countries had similar positions on Laos and Cambodia. The crux was Vietnam. Paye told Wilford on 22 June that his government wanted the neutralisation of both halves of Vietnam. When Wilford said that he doubted whether the Chinese would accept 'anything less than a fully socialised subservient regime in North Viet Nam', Paye said free elections might produce 'different regimes in both halves of Vietnam'. Wilford said he did not see that free elections in North Vietnam were likely, but it seemed that the French had them in mind as part of a settlement. Chayet said on 29 June that when this was discussed with Zhou, he seemed to be thinking of trading US withdrawal from the mainland and free elections in South Vietnam against the ending of North Vietnamese interference in the South. Chayet said the Chinese asked for French assistance in Hanoi in putting across such a deal because their influence with Ho Chi Minh was 'limited'. If true, Wilford concluded, that suggested that the Chinese were genuinely interested in a neutralisation solution, 'perhaps because they have hoisted in the strength of American determination not to be beaten in Vietnam and do not want military confrontation with them'.[83]

That determination had been demonstrated by the appointment of Maxwell Taylor as ambassador in Saigon. At a press conference on 2 June, Johnson had read Ike's letter to Diem of October 1954. His commitment was the same as Ike's, 'a commitment to help these people help themselves'. 'The United States,' he added later in the month, 'intends no rashness, and seeks no wider war. But the United States is determined to use its strength to help those who are defending themselves against terror and aggression.'[84]

'The Chinese,' wrote P.W. Waterfield, 'are "genuinely" in favour of the neutralisation of South Viet-Nam as a temporary expedient to get the Americans out. Once they are out, neutralisation can be eroded gradually.'[85] The request of the Chinese for French assistance in Hanoi, the embassy in Washington was told, probably had other reasons: to flatter France, to avoid acting as mediators themselves, to exploit French influence among the South Vietnamese in favour of neutrality.[86]

What de Gaulle was trying to do, Dixon wrote, was 'to exploit, for the benefit of France, developments which he regards as inevitable anyway. These include the domination of South-East Asia by the Chinese.'[87] Bernard Burrows in Saigon suggested that FO posts should say that the French argument that Britain agreed about neutralisation but could not say so was not true: 'we do not see how neutralisation of South Vietnam could at this stage be anything except a victory for the communists who would be enabled to pursue a policy of infiltration and subversion initially unimpeded; and that it is quite unrealistic to talk of a neutralised North Vietnam or a neutralised unified Vietnam.'[88] But there was, of course, something in the French view. That was apparent to LBJ's friend Philip Geyelin: 'If the British Government did not quarrel openly with U.S. policy in Asia, its private thinking was closer to the French than to the Washington view.'[89] The British were, however, playing it by ear, waiting for the right moment; but it never came.

Peter Ramsbotham reported a conversation with Brèthes. It showed up the contradiction between de Gaulle's apparent assessment that the Americans were about to be kicked out and that Chinese hegemony was inevitable, and Paye's reporting from Peking that the Chinese might have been impressed by recent US moves designed to demonstrate its determination to hold South Vietnam and would use their influence in Hanoi in favour of 'prudence'. Brèthes was inclined to accept Paye's reports. Hanoi was not under Chinese or Russian domination. 'The North Vietnamese had one priority—the reunification of the country.' If the Russians seemed likely to help, they looked to the Russians; if the Chinese, to the Chinese. 'It followed from this that the North Vietnamese might well not be receptive to advice from Peking to scale down support for the insurgency in the south.' Brèthes also suggested, more tentatively, that the Americans had only the North Vietnamese and the NLF to face in South Vietnam, 'and not a determined push by the Chinese using these two as their instruments'. If that was the case, 'it was not impossible for the Americans to find some way of redressing the position in the South, though the situation was undoubtedly very bad'.

On de Gaulle's policy of neutralisation, no one at the Quai knew exactly what he meant, Brèthes said. 'The words neutrality and neutralisation covered at least fifteen different concepts and the General had been careful not to spell out what he meant. He would, Brèthes thought, continue to wait on events, taking the line that the details were for the Vietnamese themselves to work out.'[90]

Waterfield agreed with Brèthes' analysis: the North Vietnamese were the 'activists' in Vietnam and Laos.[91] But Cable thought Brèthes was oversimplifying. As he said, the North Vietnamese were nationalists: they wanted to reunify their country and extend their influence to other parts of Indochina 'quite irrespective of the wishes of Moscow and Peking. The fact that they are Communists merely gives them the added incentive of spreading the gospel among the heathens.' There were also 'good rational arguments (particularly in the economic field) for seeking the unity of Viet-Nam'. Vietnamese unity, Cable thought, was more important to the North Vietnamese than to the Chinese or the Russians, 'who might regard the existence of these unfulfilled ambitions and the continuation of the struggle as a surer means of retaining North Viet-Namese subservience'. As long as the North Vietnamese were focused on the struggle, 'their need will be so great that they must strive to please those who can supply them and there will be no incentive to heresy'. In a united Vietnam the North Vietnamese might concentrate on 'internal consolidation' and be 'tempted by the idea of compromise or "national communism"'. Moscow and Peking might therefore 'attach more importance to the continuation of the North Viet-Namese struggle than to its early success'. To that extent, Cable agreed with Brèthes that the North Vietnamese 'expansionist drive was not started by Moscow or Peking and could not, without great difficulty, be stopped by either of them'.

That did not, however, mean that the US was faced only by the North Vietnamese and the VC. 'The Chinese cannot possibly afford to let the North Viet-Namese down. To do so would be to betray a Chinese national interest (a buffer state on their frontier); to accept a major setback for world communism and to offer the Russians the chance of stepping into the breach.'

Cable concluded that North Vietnam's position was 'not so much that of the classical satellite' as that of Malaysia vis-à-vis the United Kingdom.[92] 'The parallel with Malaysia would be closer if the U.S.A. were competing for Malaysia's support!' Peck commented. It was 'a very difficult question which I have been asking for the last six years with no adequate reply'. Cable's analysis was 'a very fair one', and he was 'sure the Chinese will have the last word. Therefore it is mere flattery for them to ask the French to use their influence in Hanoi.'[93]

In a press conference on Indochina late in July, de Gaulle called for a conference on the region. The powers with responsibility—France, China, the SU, and the US—should resolve to engage no more, and massive aid should be offered.[94]

Tonkin

Early in August Cable considered the future of the co-chairmanship roles, in the light of the Soviet Union's wish to discontinue its role in respect of Laos.[95] Since 1954, British policy in Indochina had had two main objectives: 'to prevent Cambodia, Laos and South Viet-Nam falling under Communist domination'; and 'to prevent the struggle within any of these countries becoming a cause of general war'. Britain's contribution to the first had been 'political. Our support for American efforts has, at certain periods, encouraged them to persevere in this thankless task, but the military and economic burden has been borne almost entirely by the U.S. Government.' But in 1954 and 1961 Britain made a major contribution to the second task. It was able to restrain the US from courses that might have led to war with China, backed by the SU. 'Our ability to restrain the U.S. Government also enabled us to exert some influence on the Soviet Government, who were, in their turn, able to influence China.'

In between major crises, co-chairmanship had been 'a safety valve, a means of adjusting minor grievances and, above all, an institutional framework that enabled all concerned, as long as they desired, to gloss over the fact the Geneva Agreements were not really being applied by either side.'

It had not done much to preserve Indochina from Communism. Some Americans would argue that, insofar as it restrained the US, the reverse was true. 'We, however, do not believe that Communist successes in Laos or Viet-Nam have been primarily due to Chinese or Russian help, still less to lack of greater U.S. intervention (which has always exceeded that of the opposition).' The root cause was political: 'the indigenous Communist leaders in Laos and Viet-Nam have been more successful than their anti-Communist opponents in securing the allegiance of the people.' Norodom Sihanouk, on the other hand, had kept Cambodia independent and neutral without Western help.

It was 'equally unlikely' that a negotiated settlement could have preserved Laos and Vietnam from Communism. China, North Vietnam and the SU would never have agreed to withhold assistance from the Communists without a reciprocal undertaking, and, 'in the unlikely event of both sides keeping their bargain, the indigenous Communists could, on past form, have expected to achieve power unaided'. That was why Dulles encouraged Diem to reject elections. 'He, and everyone else, expected the Communists to win.' That was also why de Gaulle's 'neutralisation' offered no solution. It could only work if 'the indigenous Communist party had not already secured the allegiance of a substantial element of the population'.

The US had only three choices, Cable continued: '(a) to put such pressure on China and North Viet-Nam that they will withhold aid from the Communists in Laos and South Viet-Nam while tolerating continued American aid to anti-Communists in those two countries; (b) to continue their present policy in the hope of further delaying the Communist advance and of gaining time for the emergence of an effective anti-Communist leadership; (c) to disengage themselves from Indo-China as soon as they can do so without intolerable damage to their own prestige.'

The US had spread the rumour that it would adopt course (a), but Cable doubted 'whether they would actually do so' and thought it 'most unlikely that such a course could achieve the desired results'. Course (c) was 'inconceivable' before the presidential elections and 'unlikely even afterwards', unless the anti-Communist leadership collapsed in Vientiane or Saigon. The US was thus likely to continue its 'essentially defensive' policy. If that policy did not continue to command the support of Laotian and South Vietnamese leaders—and 'recent indications' suggested it might not do so much longer—'Cambodia might survive as an independent neutral subservient to her Communist neighbours', but the Communists in Laos and South Vietnam had 'already made too much headway' to be 'content with less than the reality of complete power, even if they could be persuaded to give this the initial mark of a neutralist coalition régime'.

The likely alternatives in both Laos and South Vietnam, Cable continued, were thus (a) 'continued civil war with gradually increasing American involvement' or (b) 'American disengagement and Communist ascendancy'. The dangers of (a) had been 'greatly reduced by the Sino-Soviet split and the obvious reluctance of the Soviet Government to support China against the United States. But some risk remains and the chances of success seem remote.' Long-run Western interests might be better served by 'writing off Laos and Viet-Nam as politically untenable and concentrating on the defence of Thailand and Malaysia, in neither of which has indigenous Communism struck firm roots'.

Arguably Britain should 'seek to promote such a policy and to minimise the blow to U.S. prestige by organising a negotiated settlement that would facilitate U.S. withdrawal'. That was de Gaulle's policy, though he reserved the mediatory role for himself. There were, however, strong arguments against British intervention. It was not 'absolutely certain' that US policies would fail. Attempting to persuade the Americans to cut their losses would make Britain 'extremely unpopular', the scapegoat for their own failure. It might forfeit US support for the defence of Malaysia and 'impair Anglo-American relations generally'. Cable also doubted 'whether our intervention at any stage before the U.S. Government have actually decided to withdraw could help to lessen U.S. humiliation or obtain concessions from the Communists'. The task of extricating the US or mediating between it and the PRC should be left to de Gaulle. 'If our efforts can no longer help to preserve Indo-China from Communism and are no longer essential to prevent Indo-China becoming the cause of general war, there is no obvious British interest to require our continued involvement in the affairs of those countries.'

In the past, it could be argued that co-chairmanship enhanced Britain's prestige and diplomatic standing. If so, it was 'largely due to the extent to which we were thought able to influence the Soviet Government'. Recently it had exposed Britain to criticism both for supporting its friends and for not supporting them unreservedly. If the SU withdrew in respect of Laos, what could Britain do on its own to promote a settlement? Was it worthwhile to remain co-chairman in Cambodia and Vietnam, where cooperation with the SU had never been achieved, and the function had been mainly a source of embarrassment?

If Britain continued as co-chairman in Laos, its position would be one of 'responsibility without power'. The only influence it could exert would be on the US, and it would have lost its main justification for exerting such influence, its 'marginal ability' to influence the SU, and through the SU, China, North Vietnam and the Pathet Lao. Britain could influence the US 'as effectively as H.M.G. as we could as Co-Chairman without a colleague'. Shedding the residual co-chairman functions would avoid embarrassing pressure to intervene 'when we did not wish to do so'. 'In Cambodia and Vietnam, the main argument for hanging on to the Co-Chairmanship has been that the day might come when the U.S. Government wanted a negotiated settlement to the problems of the two countries and that it would accordingly be convenient to keep in being the theoretical framework of the Geneva Agreements even if these had long ceased to be applied in practice.' But if the SU admitted its inability to influence China over Laos, it would be no better placed in Vietnam. And in Cambodia the dispute was between that country and the US and its friends, the co-chairmanship simply exposing Britain to the embarrassment of putting 'unwelcome pressure' on them. 'We should gain a good deal by abandoning Co-Chairmanship in both Cambodia and Viet-Nam and it is not obvious that the slender chances of a negotiated settlement would suffer thereby.'

In the last analysis, Cable concluded, 'the argument against abandoning our Co-Chairmanship once the Russians take the initiative seems to be more a matter of appearance than reality. Although we should not actually be doing so, we might seem to be relinquishing the use of some residual influence which could have been employed to promote a peaceful settlement in Indo-China.' But if the Russians took the initiative 'it should not be too difficult to overcome this objection by careful presentation of the reasons for our decision'.[96] The FO did not take up the idea. And shortly Cable was himself arguing for a Laos conference. Was this the result of the Tonkin Gulf crisis?

Rusk had promised to keep in touch. 'We cannot ... be 100% confident that we should ... be given a fortnight's warning that a particular act of policy was due for decision,' Harlech wrote at the end of April 1964. 'We should not do this ourselves if our roles were reversed.' But there was 'a categorical assurance about keeping in touch', and he was 'satisfied that for the time being the Americans do intend to concentrate on winning the war in the South, rather than trying action in the North'.[97] Butler told the Cabinet in June that Rusk had offered the assurance that if the US proposed to extend military action in relation to Laos and Vietnam, 'they would inform us before doing so'.[98]

In May, however, the Americans were considering two plans, one for 'major stiffening of our effort in South Vietnam, essentially by marrying Americans to Vietnamese at every level, both civilian and military', and the other '[a]n integrated political-military plan for graduated action against North Vietnam'.[99] After warning and preparation, the US should use 'selected and carefully graduated military force against North Vietnam', unless warning and preparation and other efforts had produced sufficient improvement in non-Communist prospects in South Vietnam and Laos.[100] The idea—emerging in part from experience of the Cuba crisis of 1962—was that North Vietnam might react to 'signals' of American determination. But, as a National Intelligence Estimate admitted, the DRV might decide to fight, 'believing that the US would still not be willing to undertake a major ground war, and if it was, it could ultimately be defeated by the methods which were successful against the French'.[101]

The question was 'what should trigger-off the launching of these deterrents', P.J. Honey told Peter Wakefield after a sojourn at Stanford. State and Defense seemed to agree that 'the campaign should get going soon, but they were up against the President's political caution'. He was reluctant 'to embark on such a dangerous policy before the Elections'. Wakefield suggested, as SEAD believed, that the VC could sustain the insurgency on their own for some time. Honey agreed, 'but thought that the cessation of direction and encouragement from the North would quite quickly lead to the dissolution of the effectiveness of the Viet-Cong'.[102]

'I don't think it's worth fighting for and I don't think that we can get out. It's just the biggest damned mess that I ever saw. … No, we've got a treaty but, hell, everybody else's got a treaty out there and they're not doing anything about it,' the president had exclaimed in a conversation with Senator Dick Russell at the end of May.[103] 'I don't see what we can ever hope to get out of there with once we're committed,' he told Mac Bundy at the end of May.[104] '[I]f I have to turn back,' he said in early June, 'I want to make sure I am not in too deep to do so.'[105]

Back in February, J.K. Blackwell, the consul-general Britain retained in Hanoi, had warned against air strikes. They would have little military effect, and psychologically they would destroy what little chance the moderates, who included Ho Chi Minh, had of seeking a compromise with the South.[106] Cable was concerned that—either at US prompting or their own initiative—Khanh and the Vietnamese had come to regard action against the North as a substitute for pacification of the South. It would fail. The US government was mistaken to think that there was a psychological advantage in taking action against the North: it could be 'a dangerous boomerang'. Nothing should be said, however. 'The quieter we keep on Viet-Nam before American elections, the better.'[107]

Thompson argued that the VC would win in 1965. Negotiations should be opened up while a measure of control remained in South Vietnam. Otherwise the US would have to send in combat troops in some strength.[108] Cable thought that defeat might not come so soon. In any case the British should keep quiet. The US government would not welcome advice, and Britain might be made a scapegoat. 'If the position can be held until after the U.S. elections, it will be less difficult to discuss these problems if President Johnson is re-elected.'[109]

In the meantime the Tonkin Gulf incident—or incidents—had occurred. Had the US itself provoked them? Blackwell thought so.[110] Certainly USS *Maddox* was eavesdropping under the DeSoto spy mission Kennedy had authorised, and US-directed South Vietnamese units were launching Oplan 34-A guerrilla raids on offshore groups, another Kennedy programme.[111] The civilian leadership in Washington, Lloyd Gardner argues, was 'still looking for a proper way to signal Hanoi—Paris'.[112] The outcome was the Tonkin resolution, in which Congress granted Johnson substantial authority to act when he deemed fit. The US, it declared, regarded the maintenance of peace and security in Southeast Asia as vital. It authorised the president, as commander-in-chief, 'to take all necessary measures to repel any further attack against the forces of the United States and to prevent further aggression'.[113] The resolution, said Johnson, was 'like Grandma's nightshirt—it covered everything'.[114]

The president, said the *Times* correspondent Louis Heren, had requested the resolution as 'a warning to hostile nations not to believe that the forthcoming election campaign would weaken American resolve'.[115] It was designed, John Dumbrell writes, to bolster the Khanh regime, to help the re-election campaign, and to open the way for air strikes. It also exemplified the Cuba-style crisis management approach, intended to resolve crises by sending a clear message of intent. It was a signal to Moscow that the time had come to bring Hanoi to heel.[116]

The Tonkin resolution has been seen also as a cunning seizure of presidential initiative. If so, was it to do more or less? 'Our principal concern,' George Ball wrote in 1971, 'was that there might be a kind of orgasm of outrage in the congress and that some of the right-wing hawk Republicans might take such action that would be in effect a declaration of war or would put the administration in a position where we had to do things which we thought would be very unwise, that might involve bringing the Chinese in or offending somebody else.'[117] Johnson himself recalled that he 'wanted the Congress and the country to know what was being, or might have to be, undertaken. ... I also hoped this strong congressional endorsement would help influence North Vietnam to refrain from accelerating aggression.'[118] It did not prompt the DRV to send troops to the South, as has been argued:[119] it was already doing so. The bombing reprisal that accompanied the resolution led it to expedite the despatch of PAVN regulars, in the hope that a quick victory would avert the deployment of US troops.[120] The president's actions achieved the reverse of his aims. And they provoked the SU to act.

The president advised Prime Minister Douglas-Home of the episode on 4 August.[121] In a response he drafted himself, Sir Alec thanked the president for keeping him in touch. He would have Britain's support in the Security Council (SC) for the right to defend American shipping in international waters. Sir Alec said he would follow with great sympathy Johnson's 'efforts to stop this aggression without embarking on a war, the consequences of which none can foresee ... Let us keep in close touch.'[122] This was clearly a gentle attempt to restrain LBJ, though in fact, still awaiting the election, he was keeping his weapons in reserve. Foreign Secretary Butler made a statement on 6 August. The UK, it said, had made its position clear in the SC when it supported the US action, in accordance with the right of self-defence under Article 15. Her Majesty's Government (HMG) 'share the desire of the President ... to avoid the risk of spreading the conflict'.[123]

Cable's insistence that now was not the time to offer advice to the US did not mean that he had changed his basic views. Britain, he thought, should not join the US in putting obstacles in the way of a meeting of the three Laotian parties in Paris, designed to discuss terms for a 14-power conference, for there might be a real need for another Geneva 'less on account of Laos than of Viet-Nam'. If Thompson were right, and the early collapse of South Vietnam resistance was possible, 'it might be of great value to have an international Conference in progress on Laos. Its corridors would afford opportunities for informal exchanges on the situation in Viet-Nam and, once the United States Elections were over, it might even provide a precedent for a further conference on Viet-Nam. Because negotiations on Viet-Nam are unmentionable but may nevertheless be urgently needed, I think it wrong for us to assist in creating fresh obstacles to a Conference on Laos.'[124]

The British continued trying to ascertain what US policy was and how it was shaping without themselves blatantly trying to shape it. Early in October, Alan Renouf, the Australian minister in Washington, related what Michael Forrestal had told him and his ambassador. The Americans had come to the conclusion that Khanh could no longer remain as head of state, but Forrestal could think of no civilian substitute. As for future policy, Renouf thought they had come to the further conclusion that the war could not be won, and that the problem was 'how to arrive at negotiations on the best possible terms'. They hoped the line could be held till the presidential election. After that 'their policy would be to increase the tension and to initiate further carefully graduated steps in the process of escalation in order to make it clear that the Americans still held some powerful cards'. That might be combined with secret approaches to Hanoi and perhaps Peking. There was no question of another Geneva: 'the Americans would hope to negotiate a settlement in stages.' The British embassy's own contacts with the SD and the CIA had no hint of all this, Oliver Forster reported. 'What seems ... to be happening is that another high-level review of American policy is going on probably directed to the questions can the line be held until the Elections and what is the best way of proceeding after them.' The Australians might be premature in assuming the Americans had decided on 'what seems a most difficult policy of dragging the Communists to the conference table by a mixture of force and persuasion'. But that might be 'the policy eventually arrived at'.[125]

Chapter Two
Wilson and Johnson

The Foreign Office discussed what advice it should give the new Labour government late in 1964. Once the presidential election was over, British ministers should discuss Indochina with the Americans. FO officials were not optimistic and tended to favour negotiations. But how could that concept be put to the Americans without alienating them and perhaps incurring blame for the failure to 'save' Vietnam? Hesitant to offer gloomy advice, British ministers in the event offered none at all, though they gained the impression that US actions would continue to be moderate, or, as the foreign secretary put it, 'proportionate'.

The date for a US presidential election, 3 November, was, of course, known well in advance, and it had, as usual, helped to shape or defer policymaking meantime. The fall of Khrushchev, announced on 15 October, was unexpected. A British general election had been called for that day, in which Sir Alec Douglas-Home's Conservative government would be challenged by Harold Wilson's Labour Party. Would the FO be ready with an assessment of the position in Southeast Asia for the new government? Cabinet Secretary Sir Burke Trend asked Sir Bernard Burrows. He wanted something more immediate than the long-term report just produced in Palliser's Planning Department.[1]

That itself was distinct from the report of the Long-Term Study Group set up in May 1964 as an interdepartmental subcommittee of the Cabinet's Defence and Overseas Policy Official Committee.[2] Macmillan had been concerned that Britain was, given its economic position, politically overcommitted. The task of the officials in the committee set up under his successor was to report on British interests and commitments overseas. Britain's principal interest in Southeast Asia, it concluded, was that it should not fall under Communist domination. The Singapore base, and the forces on it, enabled Britain to contribute to SEATO and to support a second line of defence against Chinese encroachment should there be a collapse in

Indochina, and that gave it some influence over US policy in the area. It also enabled Britain to defend Malaysia while it was threatened by Indonesia, and to contribute to the forward defence of Australia and New Zealand. Britain's depleted economic interests did not add to the case for keeping the base. If it left Singapore, Britain's interests in Southeast Asia could not be sustained by non-military means unless it were neutralised. If it had no alternative facilities, it could contribute less to SEATO and hardly at all to Australia and New Zealand, and would retain no significant influence on US policy. Replacing the facilities would be prohibitively expensive, but if Britain had facilities in Australia it could meet its commitments, though more slowly. 'If relations between Malaysia and Indonesia could be put on a satisfactory footing, we should work for the neutralisation of South East Asia. This would be, however, a very long-term objective, and the outcome would depend almost entirely on the policies of China and the United States.'[3]

The Foreign Office's memorandum on long-term British policy in Southeast Asia, a separate venture under way in Palliser's department since earlier in the year, had meanwhile emerged in September. The argument was based on 'likely developments over the next ten years' but made no attempt to set a time-scale for the evolution of the policy foreseen. The paper assumed, the FO also explained, that if the Americans had no other choice, they 'would accept less than victory in South Viet-Nam rather than embark on another continental Asian war on the Korean model'. In the present circumstances, it argued, that was a reasonable assumption, but it could turn out to be mistaken. 'United States opinion on Viet-Nam remains hard. Given the present military weakness of the Chinese and the strong doubt that the Russians would help them in a war with the United States, Senator Goldwater is not likely to be the only American to feel the temptation to settle matters with China once and for all. The Chinese Communists are, no doubt, haunted by just this possibility.'

The paper assumed that there would be no major war, that the presidential election would not result in 'substantial modification' of US policies, and that China would remain 'a Communist country and the dominant Asian power'. A Chinese military threat 'must be taken into account'. China might well have 'no present plans for attacking any part of Southeast Asia. But the lesson of the Korean and Himalayan wars has not been lost on the South-East Asians.'

Britain's material interests in Southeast Asia had been 'on the wane' for 25 years. The colonial empire had vanished save for Brunei, which had not joined Malaysia, and its need for the region's primary products become 'relatively marginal'. Malaysia no longer brought a net balance of foreign exchange to the sterling area and was in fact in deficit, and, as Palliser had earlier pointed out, Britain now did only 3 per cent of its world trade in Southeast Asia, and its investments there yielded under 6 per cent of its total overseas investment revenue. Why, then, did Britain even so sustain at Singapore its largest overseas military base, entailing some 300 million pounds of defence expenditure, some 15 per cent of the UK's defence budget? Trade and investment could not now be protected by military means in any case.

The reasons were political. The first was 'that the whole area should not slide progressively into a vassal relationship with China and subsequently into communism'. In whatever way the relations of the PRC and Soviet Union developed, 'it must remain a major British interest to prevent the decisive change in the balance of world power that would result from the absorption of 230 million people into the Communist system', whether of the Soviet, Titoist or Chinese variety. The impact would be 'particularly damaging' to Britain if American opinion were able to attribute Communist success in a substantial degree to its failing in its 'responsibilities'.

The second major political reason for playing a role in Southeast Asia was indeed 'to contribute effectively to the global Anglo-American partnership and to maintain that influence in the shaping of United States policies that is cardinal to the conduct of our whole foreign policy'. A war started in Southeast Asia could ultimately imperil the United Kingdom. It thus had 'a major interest in being able to influence United States policy in the region'. The extent of that influence would depend in the last resort on the value to the United States of Britain's political and military support for its policies in Southeast Asia. Its military support could never be decisive or even significant. But successive administrations had, mainly for domestic reasons, attached 'great political importance ... to British association with their military commitments in this area. As long, therefore, as our military presence in South-East Asia enables us to exercise a major influence on United States policies, it is worth retaining for this reason alone.' If the United Kingdom offered the Americans support in Southeast Asia, the latter would be more likely to support the former in other areas. 'They tend to regard this area as more vital than we do, but there are other parts of the world where the reverse is true and globally, we need their support more than they need ours.'

The denial of Southeast Asia to a powerful enemy was, third, vital to Australia and New Zealand, in which British investment had increased, with which trade would remain substantial, and to which the United Kingdom was 'strongly bound by ties of race and sentiment', expressed in

Commonwealth membership. Finally, it was essential, if it was to be denied to Communism, that Southeast Asia should 'develop economically and enjoy reasonable political stability'.

The paper then considered the Singapore base and the military effort deployed from it. It was not essential for the Hong Kong garrison to remain effective, nor for sustaining communication between the Indian and Pacific Oceans. Another purpose of the base and its forces was to protect Malaysia under the Anglo-Malaysia Defence Agreement. 'But in establishing Malaysia in order (among other things) to provide the right political environment for our strategic deployment in the area, we have in fact created a situation in which our strategy is largely nullified by the need to use most of our available forces to defend Malaysia. In the long run, our interests will be best served by a political settlement between Malaysia and Indonesia.' In some circumstances, that might be 'incompatible with our continued tenure of the Singapore base'.

The base was designed to back up the United States and SEATO in their efforts to contain Communism. Related to the United Kingdom's major political interest in the region, that objective would 'remain valid for some years to come'. At present British forces were too busy in Borneo to be readily available for SEATO, but the base itself would be available for SEATO forces, 'including British air and naval forces even if no British troops were available'. The existence of the base was 'reassuring' to Thailand as well as Malaysia.

'British standing in the Far East has long been associated with the existence of a large base in Singapore.' If it were given up, other powers, such as Japan, might 'revise their policy towards us'. But its long-term military value was declining, and politically it was 'becoming, however gradually, a liability'. Future Malaysian governments were likely to be 'more radical … and less tolerant of foreign military establishments'. Without friendly relations, the base would hardly be tenable. Alternative means of protecting Britain's abiding political interests in Southeast Asia should be sought, 'so that we shall be in a position to withdraw from it if possible before we are requested to do so'.

Currently Singapore loomed so large in British policymaking throughout Southeast Asia that 'to devise policies when we may decide to leave it requires a radical re-appraisal'. The paper indicated that it would not try 'to specify the point in time at which we can abandon all military interest in the area; nor to discuss how, meanwhile, we could deploy military force once we had left Singapore'. It did, however, add that, at a very high cost, improved logistics could enable the United Kingdom to keep an amphibious force in the region, operating from a base in the Indian Ocean or Australia.

The problem of a British military presence post-Singapore was, however, 'really irrelevant to the fundamental question': whether the long-term aim should be 'to keep the bulk of South-East Asia "in the Western camp"', and whether, whatever efforts the West made, it could be done. 'To pose the question in this way is, in 1964, to provide the answer.' Over half of the area in terms of population was already 'non-aligned', less than a third allied to the West. The United States and Britain were respectively expending vast efforts to keep South Vietnam from Communism and Malaysia from 'local imperialism'. To reverse the situation would be impossible. If the West were prepared to fight, the Communists would do, too. 'In short, the peace and prosperity of South-East Asia require some kind of *modus vivendi*, declared or tacit, between the West and the major Communist powers, but especially China.'

The long-term aim should be 'a *neutralised Southeast Asia* which by agreement, tacit or formal between the Communist powers and the West should be allowed to pursue its own destinies without outside interference or commitment', the aim set out in a speech Butler had made in Copenhagen on 5 February 1964. 'Such a South-East Asia could still include a wide range of political systems and attitudes.' Some might be 'inconvenient ... economically', but that 'need not disturb us politically provided that the forces of extreme socialism are content (as now in Burma) to operate within their own borders'.

SEATO would be disbanded. Western military bases only drove nationalism into partnership with Communism. Nationalism was 'still the dominant political emotion' in the region, and such a partnership was bound to damage the non-Communist cause. It was also 'unnatural, in that national particularism—and, in its negative form, anti-Chinese sentiment—is at present the one force that may be able to inhibit the spread of Communist beliefs in the area and to enable an agreed system of neutrality to be established.'

The policy was, however, long-term, and its goal would not be attained if the West did not play 'a skilful and determined political hand'. A 'defeat' for the West—in Indochina or Indonesia—would be fatal. If the Southeast Asian alliances should not be maintained too long, they should not be terminated too abruptly. Confrontation would have to be ended before the British defence treaty with Malaysia was terminated. SEATO would remain 'a necessary short-term symbol of Western resolution in South-East Asia. To seek to jettison it too soon would outrage the Americans and expose the area to demoralisation in the face of the threat of Communist advance from North Vietnam or China.' That threat had to be contained long enough to convince China that the West could not be beaten militarily or by subversion 'without unacceptable effort on the Communist part', and that neutralisation was preferable.

The continuance or otherwise of SEATO would depend on the Americans, but they would be more open to Britain's influence if it had kept up its military support. 'So, if we are to work for eventual disengagement, we must, paradoxically, set our face against ourselves disengaging for the time being.' The paradox could be illustrated by Britain's role in Indochina. 'As co-chairman of the Geneva Conference, we have consistently used our influence for disengagement and neutralisation. But our influence, at least with the Americans, has in fact largely depended on our readiness to be present militarily in Singapore and to be active in SEATO.'

In short, Britain's 'transitional policy' had to try 'to combine firmness with mediatory diplomacy aimed at eventual neutralisation'. The firmness must include 'a substantial measure of support for American policies in Indo-China and a readiness to provide training and technical aid to enable the countries of South-East Asia, if they so wish to prepare adequate security and counter-subversion techniques for the day when they will have to stand on their own neutral feet—though even neutralisation need not necessarily preclude the provision covertly of aid that can until then be given more or less overtly.'

The paper proceeded to deal with '[t]he implications for our policies towards the individual states', first in the continental region, and then in the archipelago. In the former all were afraid of China and were 'bound in the long run to be subservient'. It was difficult to envisage their achieving 'any genuinely neutral status'. 'But a successful policy of neutralisation for most of them could nevertheless create conditions under which it was not worth China's while to upset the local balance—and probably stimulate fresh American intervention—by attacking or subverting non-Communist governments in the area, because the combination of neutrality and subservience made them no more harmful to her than e.g. Finland or Afghanistan are to the Soviet Union.'

Burma was an example, though not a model. 'The situation in Burma today, however chaotic, is acceptable to China and to the West because Burma is genuinely non-aligned and does not threaten the security of its neighbours.' The West accepted that it might 'lapse into Communism', but a more active anti-Communist policy might make it 'a second Vietnam'. China would no doubt prefer a Communist government in Rangoon. 'But there is at least a reasonable hope that China will not think it worth taking the risks involved in bringing about such a change.'

In Indochina the situation was very different. It was still possible 'that a precarious but acceptable neutrality comparable to Burma's' might survive in Cambodia, but it might be too late to entertain hopes of neutrality for Laos, 'where it seems as if a neutralist regime can hardly survive without more American support than is compatible with neutrality'. It was 'virtually impossible' to conceive of it in South Vietnam, where there seemed at present no alternative to a 'stark choice' between increased US involvement, with the danger of escalation, and US withdrawal, with the certainty of a Viet Cong takeover. Neutralisation in current conditions would presuppose a bargain under which the Americans withdrew and the Chinese restrained Hanoi from taking over, but no such restraint could prevent Viet Cong domination. 'The only hope ... seems to be that the Americans will have the will to keep up the struggle and that their opponents will eventually weary.' That might not be 'so forlorn a prospect' as it sounded, especially if the Sino-Soviet conflict shifted the international balance of power in US favour. 'At that point genuine neutralisation might emerge as a possibility for both Laos and South Vietnam. At present, however, if an apparently neutralist solution were to be negotiated, it could not be more than a formula for saving the Americans' face in abandoning much if not all of Indo-China to Communism. The situation may come to this. But it could not be described as being in the British interest. Present British policy towards Indo-China must therefore be confined to supporting the Americans in general and to using the influence which this will give us towards restraining them from graver risks of escalation.'[4]

Following Trend's invitation, Cable supplemented this memorandum with something more up-to-the-minute. 'The Americans have not been as frank with us as they have with the Australians; so we have no such definite knowledge of how they would view a possible negotiation,' it read. Three weeks earlier Bundy had said they would wait for the dust to subside in Saigon before they would reconsider their plans for action against North Vietnam. That, he said, might mean two or three months, 'though in the light of recent developments it is doubtful whether they have that much time in hand'. The FO guessed they would hope to hold the situation until after 3 November, then perhaps increase the tension, combining that with secret offers of negotiation through the various channels open to them.

Such negotiations might have two different objectives. One would be to induce the Viet Cong to call off their guerrilla war in South Vietnam. The assumption would be that 'the Chinese and/or the North Viet-Namese exercised some degree of control over the Viet Cong and would, under a threat of selective bombing or similar action by the Americans, be prepared to instruct the Viet Cong to call the guerrilla war ... off'. It was open to question 'whether they would obey such a call given that things are going so well their way', though there were indications that Hanoi exercised 'a fairly strong control' over them. It would be 'a long shot', but 'given the fear which we believe to haunt the Chinese that the Americans might launch a nuclear—or even a large-scale conventional—attack ..., this piece of brinkmanship might conceivably succeed'.

The alternative objective was 'to arrange an American withdrawal under cover of some face-saving arrangement'. That might indeed be the only option, given that the situation in South Vietnam was 'crumbling so rapidly', less as a result of the activities of China, North Vietnam or the Viet Cong than of 'increasing war-weariness', 'irreconcilable dissensions' among the leaders, and the spread of the National Salvation movement. The Americans' principal card would still be a threat of action against China and North Vietnam, but the objective would be more limited. They would want to play it in bilateral talks, but to secure international acceptance of any private arrangement with the Chinese, another Geneva would be needed. Britain's role would be 'to help them extricate themselves in a reasonable manner'.

Timing, however, once more came to Cable's mind. The present was not the moment to argue with the Americans: they would not be open to reason till their elections were over. Any attempt to make them face unpleasant facts and cut their losses would be 'futile', and it would be resented. If Britain's predictions came true, moreover, some would blame it for helping to cause what it predicted. Until the elections were over, 'it seems essential to lie low, say nothing and continue to express ... public support for U.S. policy'. When they were over, Britain must consider whether it should 'embark on a serious discussion and discover what steps they intend to take'. There would be 'no scope for an independent British initiative, more particularly since the pledge for mutual support of our respective policies in Viet-Nam and Malaysia has undoubtedly worked to our advantage over the last eight months'.

Britain's interests in Vietnam were 'marginal'. They included 'playing a part in the Anglo-American partnership; seeing that as little as possible of South-East Asia comes under Communist domination; playing our role of Co-Chairman in the interest of the Western position; and, of most immediate value to us, retaining U.S. support over Malaysia in exchange for pledging a degree of support for their policy in Viet-Nam.' The objectives could include arranging the protection or withdrawal of British subjects; discussing the effectiveness of negotiations with or without threat or use of military force; seeking international agreement on the future of South Vietnam 'in the manner best calculated to minimise the damage to American prestige'; and discouraging Indonesia 'from profiting by this Western débâcle to intensify her offensive against Malaysia'. But it was too early to try to pursue such objectives.

Ministers after 15 October would have to be advised that 'the problem, though gloomy enough, is almost entirely an American one', though Malaysia and Anglo-American cooperation gave Britain an interest in giving the United States 'general support' over Vietnam. It would be premature to open a discussion before the elections, but afterwards a 'realistic' discussion was 'more likely to produce a useful result than frantic and ineffectual pleas for restraint'.[5]

'Though of vital importance to the Americans, Vietnam is not a problem of burning importance for a new British Govt.,' Peck wrote.[6] Cable's new memorandum was in fact deemed too long and inappropriate and was replaced by a letter to Trend, suggesting that Vietnam was 'primarily a problem in Anglo-American relations' and that the question ministers would have to decide was how far to attempt to influence the US government. The letter included a version of the memorandum's final suggestions. That excluded the reference to 'frantic and ineffectual pleas'. Instead, the letter recognised that once the possibility of action against China or North Vietnam was raised, 'there may well be pressure from public opinion for any British Government to exert a restraining influence in Washington. This is something which we will have to go into more deeply when the picture is clearer.'[7]

Cable did, however, draft a further memorandum, since it might be necessary to act promptly after the elections, and he asked British representatives for their views.[8] The memorandum dealt not with Vietnam alone but with Indochina, which he had previously suggested was beyond diplomacy. Perhaps the Eden experience was in his mind. Britain had failed to secure an international conference on Cambodia, and lack of Soviet cooperation made it impossible to secure one on Laos on terms acceptable to the United States. As long as there was a hope of winning in Vietnam, Britain had agreed with the United States in rejecting an international conference on that country, since a negotiated outcome could not satisfy the United States. Instead, Cable continued, the UK had supported the US because it needed American support over Malaysia and in any case had no constructive alternative to propose.

Now it looked as if the anti-Communist struggle might collapse, and it might be impossible for the US to secure a satisfactory settlement in Vietnam itself, 'no matter how far they were prepared to go in threatening or taking military action against China and North Viet-Nam'. In Cambodia and Laos, however, there might be more scope for pressure of that kind, both to improve the position of those countries, 'and also to afford the Americans a more effective and practical outlet for their natural desire to restore their own impaired prestige in South East Asia'. Neither country was 'as internally rotten with Communism as South Viet-Nam'. In theory the neutrality of each was 'internationally accepted', and 'it might be easier to coerce the Communist Powers into concessions intended to give practical effect to Cambodian and Laotian neutrality than to induce them to restrain the Viet Cong from exploiting to the full their victory in South Viet-Nam'. Forcible US action in support of their neutrality would 'encounter much less international criticism than similar action in support of a lost cause in South Viet-Nam'.

At first sight there might not seem to be much scope for a Western initiative in Cambodia. Sihanouk professed to be in harmony with China, at odds with Thailand and South Vietnam and their masters. But if South Vietnam collapsed, he might have a Communist Vietnam as his neighbour, and it would be to Western advantage that he should seek protection from an international conference that would reaffirm and perhaps guarantee Cambodia's neutrality and territorial integrity rather than turn completely to China. In Laos the position was 'rather more favourable'. Souvanna Phouma, though neutralist, was inclined to the West, and the Pathet Lao needed external assistance. Strong US pressure, coupled with a reconvened 14-nation conference, might produce a solution rather better than that of 1962, 'a reconstituted coalition Government enjoying effective control over the whole country'. The US might not be keen to apply pressure for that purpose, but if the Communists' success in Vietnam were not to lead them to attempt the 'total absorption' of Laos, something along those lines should be tried.

There were subsidiary problems: the future of the ICCs, their financing, the future of the co-chairmanship. 'To put it its lowest, H.M.G. ought not to go on paying over half a million pounds a year to maintain the existence of three international commissions of ever-diminishing utility.' There was 'a strong case' for considering a Geneva conference on Indochina. In the light of comments and developments, a more detailed paper might be prepared for discussions with the US 'at an appropriate moment'.[9]

Talks with Rusk

In the British elections, the Labour Party secured victory by a very small margin, making the new prime minister extra-sensitive to its left wing. SEAD outlined Britain's policy on Vietnam and its connection with Malaysia for the new foreign secretary, Patrick Gordon Walker.[10] Ideas were being considered, Peck added, to give policies a new slant if the situation deteriorated 'still further'. Discussion with the US was essential, however, though unlikely to take any useful form until after the presidential election.[11] Gordon Walker was, however, going to Washington before then, and Caccia suggested he should see the papers before he went.[12]

Briefs for his talks with Rusk described Western policy in all three Indochinese countries as 'in a state of deadlock', but added that 'it would be unwise to suggest any new initiatives to the United States Government at least till after the American elections are over'. The situation hinged on the outcome of the Vietnam struggle. Unless the South Vietnamese produced an effective government, organised resistance would collapse 'within a few months or even weeks'. If that happened, the US would face 'an agonising choice between two thoroughly unsatisfactory policies'. One would be to attempt by increasing air attacks on North Vietnam to compel China and North Vietnam 'to order the cessation of the Viet Cong insurrection', a policy that 'would not necessarily succeed and might entail some risk of hostilities between the United States and China'. The second would be to attempt to negotiate a settlement, perhaps in conjunction with bombing. That would probably involve American withdrawal and the imposition of Communist rule, 'whether or not this was permitted by the Agreement', but there might be 'a chance of securing compensating concessions that would improve the situation in Cambodia and Laos'. The 'unpalatable choice of evils' would largely depend on developments in South Vietnam: 'a complete collapse of Viet-Namese resistance' might make the first option impossible.

All this ought to be discussed with the US government, but not before the elections. 'The U.S. have invested so much prestige in Viet-Nam, which is now an important electoral issue in the U.S., that we do not believe they would welcome a frank exchange of views at present. Indeed, even to reveal our pessimism about the prospects in Viet-Nam would be unwise at this stage. This is such a sore subject for the Americans that, if events turn out as badly as we fear, the Americans might be tempted to accuse us of having undermined Viet-Namese morale and will to resist and thus of having contributed to a collapse which we had only predicted.' In any case, the situation was so confused that it was not certain that 'all is lost', and the FO was not ready to offer specific advice. Britain's position as co-chairman might later give it a role to play, which could be prejudiced by offering 'premature advice' when the idea of negotiations was 'anathema'. The secretary of state might prefer 'to avoid being drawn too deeply into discussions of Indo-China during the present visit'. It might be better simply to express gratitude for US support over Malaysia, and indicate that the UK intended, as undertaken by Douglas-Home, to continue its support in Vietnam, 'while making it clear that we foresee an early need for reconsideration' and would welcome 'an opportunity for a thorough exchange of views' as soon as the US was ready.[13]

In Washington Gordon Walker told Rusk that he would like to be warned of any steps that might cause criticism, for instance in Parliament. The American secretary of state said there might be more involvement in Vietnam. Gordon Walker said that Britain could not give 'any very active help because of heavy commitments in Malaysia'.[14] He also told Rusk and the president that Britain would like more detailed talks at the earliest convenient moment.[15] Etherington-Smith thought the US effort as constituted could not succeed. Increasing aid was not the answer: more should reach the countryside. Better relations with the Vietnamese were needed: action against the North was no substitute.[16] The ambassador did not go into the basic question, Cable commented: could anything the US did maintain resistance to the Viet Cong? Nor did he consider the choice confronting it: extend the war or end it. Cable did not think the Americans could reorganise or change their attitude.[17] Back from Washington, the foreign secretary declared himself 'depressed by the prospects'.[18]

Preparing for the Prime Minister's Visit

On 3 November Johnson enjoyed electoral triumph. Prime Minister Wilson's visit on 7–8 December would offer an opportunity for discussion, Cable noted, but the leaders would be busy, and a preliminary meeting of officials should take place from 3 December. It could be on the previous quadripartite lines—UK, US, Australia, New Zealand—which would make it easier for the US.[19] Peck agreed, though the emphasis was then on Malaysia, not Vietnam.[20] Harlech thought it would be more difficult to talk of Indochina in that way, not less.[21] The FO accepted the advice.[22] Bill Bundy told Harlech it would fit in with Taylor's return to Washington on 27 November and the major review that would follow.[23] The idea, Peck told M.N.F. Stewart, counsellor in the Washington embassy, was to give the State Department the FO's assessment in advance. American support on Malaysia would be taken for granted.[24]

Etherington-Smith thought that Cable's up-to-the-minute paper overdid the notion that 'collapse' was imminent. The position might be retrieved, and, accepting that possibility, Britain would be better able to suggest ways in which the US effort might be made more effective. He questioned whether Vietnam was 'marginal' to British interests. Britain had an indirect interest in its survival as part of the free world and its impact on Malaysia and Australia.[25]

Peck agreed that, 'as a matter of tactical presentation to the Americans', the British should continue to advance the possibility that the war could be won by existing methods. The tentative idea was indeed to set out a series of assumptions about the future 'in ascending order of pessimism'. The first would be that the Saigon leadership might prove 'sufficiently stable and determined to allow the struggle to be continued on substantially the present lines and, over a period of years, brought to a successful conclusion'. But it would have to be clear that Britain considered that 'most unlikely'. If the Australians were to be believed, so did the State Department. The situation had worsened 'much less rapidly' than the FO had expected when the memorandum was first drafted. But the lull in Viet Cong activity and in opposition to the Saigon government might in fact indicate a belief that that government had not closed off the possibility of negotiation. That was always the FO's concern, though the memorandum might have laid more emphasis on disintegration.

Peck also dealt with the ambassador's suggestion that Britain's interest was not 'marginal', as the FO had implied. 'Fundamentally, our view of South-East Asia has always been that, in the long run, our hopes must be based on those countries which possess some degree of inherent political viability: Malaysia, the Philippines and Thailand.' In the other countries 'the rot had gone too far for us to entertain realistic hopes for more than a precarious, pro-Communist neutralism or, at best, a Western holding operation intended to gain time'. A Western military alliance could keep out foreign invaders, but it could not deal with an enemy within, unless, as in Malaya, that constituted but 'a small fraction of a minority race'. In 1954 'the Western front-line was drawn further forward than was, even at that time, politically defensible'. Admittedly the FO was then 'over pessimistic'. It did not expect South Vietnam to survive 'more than five years at the outside' and 'the heroic American efforts' had kept it going for ten. That was 'an undoubted gain and, if the Americans and Viet-Namese could win a few more years, we should be well pleased'. But if that proved impossible, and the Western powers had to 'fall back to their main defence line along the Thai border', it need not necessarily have 'disastrous consequences to Western interests, provided that American prestige can be salved and that Laos and Cambodia can be preserved as a neutral glacis'.

It was the importance of securing those conditions that made early Anglo-American discussions essential. 'Our fear is that a natural American reluctance to contemplate the possibility of failure in South Viet-Nam might inhibit contingency planning for an adequate fall-back position. When disaster threatens there is always a temptation to issue a "no retreat" order which, however useful for sustaining morale as long as the battle can still be won, can greatly aggravate the consequences of defeat.'[26]

Etherington-Smith doubted Peck's conclusion. Laos and Cambodia would not last long as buffer states: they could hardly be a neutral glacis. A new US effort was needed, even, perhaps, the introduction of a limited number of troops with a clear role. It was necessary to preserve an open mind as to what was likely to happen.[27]

Writing on 17 November 1964, Lord Walston, undersecretary at the FO, thought it was necessary to 'clear our minds', as, though the problem was 'primarily an American one, we are clearly in a position to influence American thinking'. The only alternatives were 'a far greater military involvement ... by the United States', which 'would have to envisage the possibility of bombing China'; and US withdrawal from South Vietnam 'with the probability of a Communist government taking over'. The first option was 'presumably not on the cards'. Given that the second option was 'inevitable', US/UK policy had to be designed 'to prevent as far as possible loss of face in the area', 'to prevent further physical infiltration of Communist influence into Cambodia and Laos', and 'to prevent any deterioration in the morale of anti-Communist and neutral countries in this area, including India'.

Those objectives could best be achieved if the US withdrawal took place after negotiation, and, if possible, as a result of an international conference, 'and above all when the United States can be seen to be making a renewed military offensive'. The US should 'step up military activities to the maximum of her powers during the next two or three months', and at the same time the UK, as co-chairman, should press for the reconvening of the Geneva conference, at which Cambodia and Laos should be discussed as well as Vietnam. If the conference took place when the Americans were 'in military ascendancy', 'there would be little risk of loss of face and it might then be possible to persuade the Laotian and Cambodian Governments, and the rest of South-East Asia, that American withdrawal was due to a desire for peace rather than to inability to win'. It was 'even conceivable' that a really neutralist South Vietnamese government would come into power, 'though unless this government were strong enough to maintain order in the country little would have been gained'. At the same time, 'we could take whatever steps were necessary to assure Thailand, Burma, India and Malaysia of our unswerving support for them against Communist aggression', and also step up economic and technical assistance in the area, 'showing these countries that we were not planning to abandon them'.[28]

In referring to a conference, Walston had alluded to a telegram from Sir George Clutton, the British ambassador to Poland—one of the ICC powers—summarising the views expressed by Jerzy Michalowski, permanent head of the Foreign Office there. The Americans would eventually find themselves prey to a dilemma, he said: withdrawing militarily, 'politically impossible', or 'having to occupy the whole of the country'. But, he added, at present North Vietnam was prepared to discuss a political settlement. It would not include reunification since that would mean a Communist South Vietnam. 'What he regarded as practical was a South Vietnamese government which was neither Communist nor anti-Communist, but strictly neutral in all respects. He thought such a settlement need not entail the immediate but only the eventual and gradual withdrawal of the United States military support.' Michalowski evaded answering Clutton's question: was this a North Vietnamese initiative? He suggested that a Geneva-type Cambodia conference might 'provide a façade for preliminary unofficial sounding on South Vietnam'. If Poland could help 'at any later stage in finding ways and means of settling the Indo-China question', it would be 'glad to do so'.[29]

Walston's attempt to combine an intensification of US action—a surge?—with a conference was surely unrealistic. More than the permanent FO officials, he also exaggerated the role that Britain might play. Yet a week earlier Stewart had reported a talk with Bill Bundy, the implication of which was that war could be taken north of the 17th parallel as a prelude to possible negotiations. The US would consult the UK, he indicated, or at least seek its reaction. The move, Stewart said, might lead to increased Viet Cong activity, with an impact in turn on the new Huong government. Bundy seemed to think that if that new civilian government did not last, another could be found.[30]

The Viet Cong had attacked the Bien Hoa airfield on 31 October, just before the presidential election, as Huong and his colleagues were celebrating the anniversary of Diem's overthrow. Five Americans were killed; 13 bombers were damaged or destroyed.[31] No retaliation followed. But on 2 November the president asked Bill Bundy to chair a working party.[32] That envisaged, as the SD told Saigon, an immediate programme for four to six weeks of expanded action within the present policy. 'Concurrently, we would propose to decide very soon that, if such an immediate program does not produce a change in Hanoi behavior, we would initiate in January a program of slowly graduated military actions against the North in conjunction with negotiating moves in which we would seek throughout to keep alive a clear threat of additional action if the Communist side does not modify its position.'[33]

W.W. Rostow, Denis Warner wrote, was confronting the issue of 'how to use America's overwhelming military power with minimum casualties to bring about something in which something like even-terms negotiations may be possible', and suggesting 'a phased use of naval air power against selected North Vietnamese industrial installations'. If they were bombed out in phases, it was argued, Hanoi could be forced to come to the conference table. 'This would be brinkmanship of a high order,' the Australian journalist commented. 'Even if it "worked" it is difficult to believe that proper safeguards to prevent an ultimate Communist take-over could be evolved at the conference table.'[34] The head of policy planning staff was renewing his emphasis on the 'signal'. 'The first critical military action against North Vietnam should be designed merely to install the principle that they will, from the present forward, be vulnerable to retaliatory attack in the north for continued violations of the 1954 and 1962 accords. ... It is the installation of the principle that we are interested in, not tit for tat.'[35]

Maxwell Taylor, the ambassador in Saigon, discussed the minimum level of government needed in the South 'to justify mounting military pressures against the North': one capable of maintaining law and order in the urban areas, securing military bases against the Viet Cong, gearing its efforts with the US government. Perhaps such a government could not be expected for three to four months, if then. If, however, the government faltered, or gave 'good reason to believe that it will never attain the desired level of performance', Taylor favoured going ahead anyway. 'The purpose of such an attack would be to give pulmotor treatment for a government in extremis and to make sure the DRV does not get off unscathed in any final settlement.'[36]

The working group raised the question of introducing a ground deployment in northern South Vietnam in order to 'demonstrate resolve and also give us a major bargaining counter in negotiations'.[37] No consensus was reached on that at the National Security Council Executive Committee. A further draft, produced after Taylor joined the group, was discussed with the president on 1 December. The position paper prepared by the executive committee the following day envisaged a first phase of 30 days, involving intensified action. Beyond that, if the government of Vietnam improved its effectiveness and Hanoi did not yield 'on acceptable terms', the US would be prepared for a second phase, 'graduated military pressures directed systematically against the DRV', chiefly 'progressively more serious air strikes'. The president would seek 'full British support', as well as support from Australia and New Zealand.[38] Johnson gave his approval on 3 December, though full of doubt and concerned for his domestic programmes. 'If we get into this war, I know what's going to happen. Those damn conservatives are going to sit in Congress and they're going to use this war as a way of opposing my Great Society legislation. ... They'll say they're not against it, not against the poor, but we have this job to do, beating the Communists.'[39] The president's advisers feared that neutralism would spread if nothing were done. There was no point in knocking the North if the South were 'not together', Johnson believed. 'I am hesitant to sock my neighbour if my fever is 104 degrees.'[40]

On 18 November Harlech had cabled that Rusk, McNamara and John A. McCone were planning a post-election review of Vietnam policy. They would possibly be joined by Maxwell Taylor, and the result would be submitted to the president at the end of the month.[41] By 7 December, the day now scheduled for Peck's arrival in Washington to prepare for Wilson's visit, comprehensive proposals would have been put to LBJ, Cable pointed out. They might include, 'possibly with a marked degree of preference, the idea of offensive action against North Viet-Nam and China to save the situation in the South'. He tried to take account of this in a draft of a basic paper for Peck's use, taking 'strong American feelings' into account.[42]

Peck would need an indication of ministerial views on certain points. If the US decided on offensive military action against North Vietnam and China with the object of imposing a settlement on South Vietnam, would HMG give token military support, give diplomatic support, adopt a passive attitude, or feel bound to press for a Geneva conference to stop the fighting and negotiate a settlement? Would its attitude differ if the US, while taking action, secretly indicated it would agree to negotiations once the situation had improved? Would HMG have to make it a condition even of diplomatic support that they would advocate a Geneva conference, even if they cooperated in delaying its opening till military action had taken effect?[43]

Cable's long memorandum was rejected by Peck, who did not think the problem could be presented in quite the way it did. He wanted to do more orally, especially with respect to Laos and Cambodia.[44] In the last few years Britain and the US had 'worked in close and harmonious co-operation' in their Indochina policies, the shortened memorandum began. Events had developed, however, so that re-appraisal was needed. The US had 'borne the main burden of the Western effort', and so long as Confrontation continued, Britain's capacity to support US policy was limited. Circumstances gave the US the leading role in shaping the future course of Western policy towards Indochina. But in view of its importance, 'and of its potentially controversial repercussions on public opinion in Britain and other Western countries, a preliminary discussion of possible contingencies and the steps that might be taken to meet them, could lead to the widest possible measure of understanding of future U.S. policies in Indo-China. It would be easier to support those policies if there is advance knowledge of what is intended.'

'The Western objective is essentially negative: to deny as much as possible of Indo-China to Communist influence.' It was not merely 'the relatively simple problem of deterring Chinese or North Viet-Namese armies from invasion'. It was a matter of convincing the rulers of Cambodia, Laos and South Vietnam that the West could and would do so, so that it was worth their while to maintain their independence of the Communist powers and of Communist sympathisers among their own people. It was also a matter of convincing the SU, China and North Vietnam that the West would prevent their intervening, 'by methods short of military invasion', to support indigenous Communists, and of encouraging and assisting the rulers to maintain regimes capable of enlisting popular support against attempts to establish governments subservient to the Communist powers.

The primary origin of the threat was North Vietnam, and behind it China. No solution for the problems of Laos and Cambodia would be realistic that did not take into account developments in Vietnam. The memorandum thus focused on Vietnam, while the officials' talks themselves could cover the impact of developments in Vietnam on Laos and Cambodia.

The paper proceeded, as Peck had indicated it would, 'in ascending order of pessimism'. The most favourable contingency was that the present government in South Vietnam, or its immediate successor, might be 'sufficiently stable, popular and determined' to allow the continuance of the struggle against the Viet Cong over a period of years, so as to restore at least the level of security prevailing from 1956 to 1959. The latest reports suggest the growth in the Saigon government of a desire for negotiations, and it would be impossible to defend South Vietnam against the will of the local government, or with the cooperation of a government without support, no matter what resources were deployed or risks run. But, given a basic minimum of 'authority, co-operation and resolve', it might be possible to take additional steps to reduce the flow of North Vietnamese assistance to the Viet Cong, thus increasing the chances of defeating them and convincing Cambodian and Laotian leaders that Communism was not bound to win. The insurrection was 'now largely self-sustaining in men, money and materials'. 'Its military efficiency would be impaired by any serious reduction in the flow of *specialised* weapons and *cadre* personnel from the North.' Still more, it would suffer if there were clear evidence that it had been compelled to reduce overt support and thus defer victory. But it was doubtful whether even major reductions would cripple the Viet Cong unless North Vietnam actually ordered the end of the insurrection, 'perhaps on the pretext that the "strategy of world revolution" would be best served by a tactical retreat on this front'. Would any form of Western pressure induce North Vietnam to go so far 'without alienating international opinion, provoking Chinese intervention and possibly even creating a situation in which the Soviet Government might consider that their interests lay in supporting China and North Viet-Nam'?

The memorandum turned to 'a less favourable contingency'. The Saigon government, or more probably a military successor, might propose, or agree to, 'drastic military action against the North', on the understanding that if it did not lead to a major reduction in Viet Cong activity, South Vietnam would enter negotiations. That kind of proposal General Khanh had hinted at earlier in the year, but it now seemed doubtful that the Saigon government could maintain support throughout 'such a drastic and dangerous operation'. The military operations, moreover, would have to be so extensive that the repercussions on other Communist powers and on Western public opinion would be 'hard to predict'. There would be great pressure on the UK to call an immediate Geneva conference.

Third came 'an unfavourable contingency'. The present Saigon government, or less probably a successor, would inform Western governments of its intention to negotiate, but defer any announcement long enough for Western military pressure on North Vietnam to create more favourable conditions in which to negotiate. The objective of the pressure would not be, as in the earlier contingencies, to win the war, but to arouse sufficient apprehension in North Vietnam and China to induce them to accept more favourable terms in the negotiations. Once the decision was made, however, it would leak out, lower South Vietnamese morale, and encourage Communist intransigence. In such circumstances, it would be difficult for the US to contemplate extensive military action against North Vietnam. Resistance in the South might collapse while operations were in progress in the North, and the political gains from such operations would be limited. 'Given a Government in Saigon bent on negotiations, it would be entirely unrealistic, no matter how much military pressure were applied to the North, to expect negotiations to produce a South Viet-Nam liberated from the Viet Cong insurrection, but nevertheless still retaining American military advisers and receiving American military assistance on anything approaching the present scale.' It had after all been argued that a conference confined to Cambodia would fatally undermine morale in South Vietnam.

The 'least favourable contingency' was not, however, a deliberate Saigon decision to prepare for negotiations: it was 'a sudden and irretrievable collapse in Viet-Namese morale'. The government might call for immediate negotiations or initiate them secretly. Or it might include members of the NLF, producing the same result more quickly. Alternatively defeatism might take hold in the Vietnamese armed forces, leading units to adopt a passive policy and to mass desertions. There might, finally, be a disintegration of governmental authority, 'with provincial leaders either refusing to obey orders or fleeing to the capital'. None of this was currently probable, 'but every month that goes by without offering to the war-weary Viet-Namese people and their leaders any firm prospect of an early end to the struggle increases the likelihood of a *débâcle*'.[45]

This shorter memorandum was, Peck planned, to be given to the State Department.[46] A longer draft memorandum listed the points to be made orally. It considered the contingencies in the shorter paper and also covered Laos and Cambodia, as had Cable's longer draft. If, it asked, there were a real prospect that the Saigon government would retain its 'authority, cohesion and control', would a continuation of present policies be enough to restore South Vietnam at least to the level of stability and internal security that obtained in 1956–59? The answer was surely no. Before mid-1963 the Diem government was 'as stable, united and determined as any government one could ever expect to see in Saigon', but it was not winning the war. Anti-insurgency operations could well be improved, but that would not overcome 'the growing war-weariness of the Viet-Namese people or the increasing emergence among their leaders of a desire of a negotiated, neutralist solution'. Only new and drastic methods could do that, possibly 'a combination of American military pressure against North Viet-Nam with secret negotiations, so as to reduce North Viet-Namese assistance to a level that would permit gradual progress to be made against the Viet Cong'. There were limiting factors. If it aimed at quick results, it might risk Chinese and even Soviet intervention. If it were too gradual, the South Vietnamese might not stay the course. In addition the Viet Cong might step up its action so as to destroy the Saigon government before US military measures could do too much damage in North Vietnam.

It was tempting to consider supplementing action against North Vietnam by depriving the Viet Cong of 'the use of Cambodian territory as a safe haven and as a supply route'. Probably the Cambodians, even if willing, would be unable to do that, and Sihanouk might react to Western pressure by increased cooperation with the VC and an appeal for Chinese assistance. Even the extreme course of partitioning Cambodia between Thailand and South Vietnam would be ineffective: they could not control a resistance movement led by Sihanouk and backed by North Vietnam. Moreover, Cambodia enjoyed 'a degree of international sympathy as the success story of the 1954 Geneva Agreement and as the supposedly innocent victim of South Viet-Namese aggression'. Every raid into Cambodia increased Britain's embarrassment at having to evade Sihanouk's requests for another Geneva and impaired the chance of sustaining its neutrality. Yet a victory in South Vietnam would be 'partly barren' if it had allowed Communism 'to strike fresh roots' in Cambodia. And if the battle were lost, 'a neutral Cambodia will be even more essential as a glacis between Viet-Nam and Thailand'.

Laos was 'less difficult'. The area used was under Pathet Lao control, and the Royal Laotian government might even welcome action against VC lines of communication. It would be necessary to ensure that the PL could not launch a fresh offensive elsewhere. North Vietnam might increase its action in Laos and the prospect of a negotiated settlement decline. But it should be possible to 'sustain the morale and cohesion' of the Royal Lao government, provided there were no military setbacks in Laos itself and the Communists did not appear to be making headway in Vietnam.

In all this, the talking points continued, the US, the Royal Laotian government, the South Vietnamese government 'and possibly other Western Governments' would be acting in breach of the Geneva agreements in Laos and Vietnam, and they would be on the defensive in respect of Cambodia. Continued existence of the agreements 'would constitute a serious propaganda disadvantage to the West'. It might be desirable to consider their winding up. That might be based on the Soviet threat to withdraw from the Laos ICC and the obligation imposed on the co-chairmen by Article 19 of the protocol to make recommendations on the termination of the commission by July 1965.

The talking points turned to the 'less favourable contingency', a South Vietnamese threat to negotiate unless the US acted more drastically. That would face the US in an extreme form with the dilemma that more drastic action might bring about Chinese or Soviet intervention. 'Moreover, the reliability and staying power of any Viet-Namese government presenting such an ultimatum would automatically be suspect.' The US would thus be 'asked to take greatly increased risks to save a regime of greatly diminished viability', not 'a tempting proposition'.

The 'unfavourable contingency'—that South Vietnam decided on negotiations—would make them inevitable. Even if delayed, the news would leak out, and South Vietnamese forces would be increasingly reluctant to fight. The replacement of such a government by 'more militant leaders ... would probably offer no real solution'. It would ensure greater publicity for the news that the first government had wanted to negotiate and make it difficult for the successor to rally support. The most the US could hope for would be a brief respite to employ military pressure, not to avoid negotiations but to strengthen the Western bargaining position at the conference table. The concessions such pressure could extract would be reduced by the knowledge that South Vietnam wished to negotiate, and the US would not be able to coerce the North Vietnamese into agreeing that it could keep forces in the South or 'compel them to accept other terms that would genuinely and effectively guarantee the continued independence of South Viet-Nam'. Probably the North Vietnamese would conclude that they could run considerable risks in insisting on the withdrawal of all military advisers and cessation of all military aid 'as indispensable conditions for any agreement'. In return they might accept an independent neutral South Vietnam, perhaps with future elections for reunification and some kind of coalition government including NLF representatives.

Even if the North Vietnamese could be induced to concede more favourable terms, it would be 'difficult, if not impossible', to prevent subsequent Communist violations of any agreement once US forces had withdrawn. Even if a coup were found to be necessary, it was 'scarcely conceivable' that it 'would bring them back again or justify major offensive action against North Viet-Nam or China'. Any settlement would thus 'ultimately entail writing off Viet-Nam altogether'. The most that military pressure could achieve was 'a form of settlement enabling U.S. forces to withdraw from South Viet-Nam in good order and with the minimum damage to U.S. prestige', and make it as difficult as possible for the Communists to take over 'without having demonstrably violated a freely negotiated international Agreement'. Those were 'not attractive objectives', and their attainment would scarcely justify more than minimum military pressure against North Vietnam and China. Indeed, the Western powers would have to 'look elsewhere for the concessions that might help to preserve their prestige in South East Asia and prevent the loss of South Viet-Nam from having profoundly damaging repercussions in other countries as well'.

The memorandum turned again to Cambodia and Laos. If that kind of settlement had to be accepted in Vietnam, Cambodia would become more important to the West, 'whose handicaps in that country would simultaneously be reduced'. Confronted by a Vietnam enjoying increased Communist support, Sihanouk might throw himself on China's mercy, particularly if Western hostility continued. But if it did not, 'he might well conclude that international endorsement of Cambodia's independence, neutrality and territorial integrity was still preferable. And with South Viet-Nam gone or going, it would clearly be in the Western interest to keep Cambodia out of the Communist Bloc and to preserve her as a neutral buffer between South Viet-Nam and Thailand.' Cambodia would return to 'the position of a few years ago', accepting aid from East and West and maintaining 'internal stability and external neutrality'. It should be brought into the negotiations and the 1954 agreement on its neutrality reaffirmed.

The Western powers would, however, have to seek in Laos 'their main compensatory advantage' from the Vietnam setback. That could not be achieved without 'considerable military pressure' on North Vietnam. The aim would be the supervised withdrawal of its forces from Laos and an effective supervisory commission freed from the single member veto. In addition the PL, though included in a restored tripartite coalition, would have to surrender their exclusive control of eastern and north-eastern Laos and admit neutralist officials and forces to the area. If such gains were secured, 'we would in effect have returned to the position originally envisaged in 1954, with Viet-Nam written off, but Cambodia and Laos as neutralised buffer states'. The gains would, furthermore, reassure Thailand and encourage it 'to place continued reliance on Western support'. Existing pledges of support for Thailand could be reaffirmed, also for the Philippines and Malaysia, given that Indonesia might be encouraged in its own ambitions by setbacks in Vietnam.

The repercussions elsewhere in Southeast Asia would be influenced not only by the nature of the settlement and the 'ultimate fate' of South Vietnam, but also by the form of the settlement and the way it was reached. Most leaders had probably already concluded that 'a complete Western victory' was unlikely and to some extent have discounted it in advance. If American withdrawal took place at the wish of the South Vietnamese government, and not as a result of military defeat or the failure of American resolve, it would not necessarily be regarded as 'disastrous'. 'An openly negotiated settlement reached by an international conference would thus be less disadvantageous to Western prestige and influence in South East Asia than a hasty American withdrawal enforced by the collapse of South Viet-

Namese armed resistance or the disintegration of the Saigon Government.' American military operations would be more readily accepted if seen as directed towards improving a bargaining position in negotiations rather than trying to avoid them. An international conference would give a degree of endorsement to the agreements and make it easier to expose and denounce evasion or violation.

In the least favourable contingency negotiations were forced on 'us' by the collapse of South Vietnamese resistance. 'A Viet-Namese Government that called for immediate negotiations might still be replaced by one willing to proceed in slower time.' The threat or use of 'drastic military action' might prevent the VC from fully exploiting the situation. But such measures could only be 'temporary palliatives' and the Western powers would be left in a very disadvantageous position for attempting a settlement. 'We ought … to consider whether the interests in South East Asia of the Western Powers would not now be best served by embarking on a deliberate policy of preparing for a negotiated settlement of the Indo-China problem.'[47]

Peck's plan to give the shorter paper to the SD before the talks in Washington, reserving the measures that might be taken to meet the contingencies it outlined for discussion during the talks, came undone. Harold Caccia, the permanent undersecretary, had decided that it would be a mistake to give the paper to the Americans. 'It might only make them feel we were interfering in a problem that was primarily an American concern and forcing on them views of unwelcome gloom.' Its existence was therefore not to be mentioned to US officials, though it might be drawn on in the talks, when Peck hoped to be joined by Trench and Forster, if not M.A.F. Stewart, too.

The second paper, on the points to be made orally, argued that if negotiations were inevitable, as seemed probable, it would be better to accept that and prepare for them rather than to be 'forced into them at the last minute by a sudden Viet-Namese collapse'. That was also controverted in the FO, Peck told Stewart. The main argument was 'less concerned with the truth of these arguments than with the propriety of putting them to the Americans. We do not want the Americans to follow what seems to us a dangerous and mistaken course, but still less do we want to incur the odium of persuading them to cut their losses.' The present inclination was thus to regard the primary purpose of the official talks as asking questions. What did the US intend to do in Vietnam? What repercussions did they expect? How did they intend to justify what they did outside and inside the US? 'The crunch will come if Bill Bundy tells us that the U.S. Government have decided, or are likely to decide, on a policy of offensive action against

North Viet-Nam and China.' Then it would be not for Peck but for the prime minister and the foreign secretary to handle 'awkward hypothetical questions': would the UK give token military support, give diplomatic support, remain passive, or call for a Geneva conference at the outset or 'when things got too tough'?

The FO, Peck concluded, did not wish to rush in to restrain its allies, as Bobby Kennedy had done over Malaysia. 'But it is equally important not to repeat what Lord Avon did in 1954, when he allowed Mr. Dulles to expect British support for a forward policy in Indo-China only to let him down with a public bump a couple of weeks later. If, therefore, the Americans did decide on a really tough policy and H.M.G. are uncertain of their ability to support this to the bitter end, then ... we ought to voice our doubts at the very beginning.'[48]

The secretary of state agreed to hold an office meeting on 27 November to decide the line Peck should take in his talks with US officials on 3–4 December. The talks were designed, another memorandum suggested, to ascertain US intentions and isolate the issues particularly affecting Britain before Gordon Walker met Rusk. The main object would be to ascertain the Americans' intentions rather than urge 'a ready-made policy of our own'. They had 'such a dominant role in Indo-China that they would certainly resent any obvious attempt on our part to shape their policy for them'. That was why the main paper largely confined itself to analysis, but, in the course of discussion, Peck hoped to bring out the arguments in favour of 'a negotiated settlement', and he outlined the points he hoped to make orally.

Unless the situation took a further turn for the worse, the US would probably be reluctant to accept the FO's pessimistic analysis, Peck suggested, 'or to admit that it may now be too late to redress this by drastic American military action'. By the time the foreign secretary saw Rusk, 'it may well be apparent that the U.S. Government intend to pursue a tougher policy than we may consider prudent or realistic'. Rusk might then want to know how much support the UK would offer. 'Nor will he be the only one to ask.' A parliamentary question on the subject was already down for 15 December.[49]

The office meeting was in the event held on the 30th. In the meantime the Washington embassy had reported what Forrestal had told the Australians were the recommendations to the president as they stood before Taylor arrived. They were for limited military action against the North Vietnamese, including increased air strikes in the Laos corridor and possibly north of the parallel, followed by secret talks with the Chinese or Vietnamese. If such measures did not stop support for the VC, slow escalation would follow, including sabotage and bombing of North Vietnamese communications and industry. It was likely Taylor would agree. The president was widely thought to be cautious, and Rusk worried about international repercussions. But the Americans were committed to saving Vietnam, so that 'some very limited measures against the North and Laos' were likely.[50] The decision—probably for limited escalation—was expected on 1 December.[51]

Peck's main purpose, said Gordon Walker at the FO meeting, was 'to probe American intentions': he hoped that they would choose 'a course of creeping and relatively unobtrusive attacks rather than any sudden and dramatic assault. The more gradual approach also had the advantage that it could be combined with secret negotiations.' Second, Peck was 'to enquire how the Americans propose to justify the [to?] international public opinion what they proposed to do in the way of attacks on North Viet-Nam'. He was to express the hope that the US 'would choose a course of action that would not make it difficult for H.M. Government to give them the diplomatic support which H.M. Government were anxious to provide. This support should not be too difficult as long as U.S. activities followed the relatively inconspicuous Laotian pattern, but … large scale attacks or the development of major fighting would expose H.M. Government, in their capacity as Co-Chairman, to great pressure to join the Soviet Government in calling a Conference.' Gordon Walker also wanted the UK as far as possible 'to avoid presenting our support for U.S. policy in Viet-Nam as a quid pro quo after [for her?] support in Malaysia'. He wanted to justify support on Vietnam on its own merits. 'Now that the U.S. Government had come to realise the importance in their own interests of supporting Malaysia it was no longer necessary to drive a bargain of a kind difficult to justify to British public opinion.'[52]

After the office meeting, Cable prepared a draft for the prime minister to discuss with the foreign secretary and the minister of defence. What the Americans intended to do would be known only after Peck's talks. At present it seemed that they would indicate that they had decided on a limited offensive against North Vietnam and would want to know whether they could count on British support for the policy, 'which may not succeed, which may involve the risk of Chinese intervention and a wider war, and which is likely to be unpopular with significant sections of British public opinion'. The only alternative to an offensive, however limited, was negotiations. 'In present circumstances these could only lead to a settlement gravely adverse to Western interests and deeply humiliating to the United States. If we are to retain the American co-operation we so badly need in South East Asia, we have no option but to promise diplomatic support for their policy in Viet-Nam, but we should leave them in no doubt that, if offensive action fails to bring quick results or threatens dangerous repercussions, we might later be under international and domestic pressures to use our position as Co-Chairman to promote negotiations. We should also stress our view that there should be no dramatic action. We should need to be kept informed of any change of policy.'

There was a risk that Vietnamese willingness to continue the struggle might collapse unless something could be done to offer 'a convincing prospect of early victory'. The US was therefore considering offensive action against North Vietnam, which assisted and directed the Viet Cong insurrection in the South. It might begin with 'small air-raids against key points on the supply route to the South, simultaneously and secretly warning the North Viet-Namese that these attacks would become bigger and more widespread, unless the Viet Cong insurrection was halted'. The plan could have many variants, but the US would try to avoid two extremes: 'doing so little that continued insurrection in the South brought down the Saigon Government before Hanoi was seriously hurt by the U.S. offensive; or doing so much that China had to intervene and thereby widen the war.' It might be too late for a limited offensive to save South Vietnam, but the FO agreed that 'mere continuation of the offensive' offered no hope of victory. 'We also agree that a decision to write off south Viet-Nam, though possibly the lesser of two evils, would have profoundly damaging repercussions on U.S. prestige and the Western position in South East Asia. Such a decision, moreover, is probably excluded by considerations of American domestic politics.' Not least because of Malaysia, Britain would have to offer diplomatic support. But, 'so that we cannot later be accused of letting them down', it should be made clear to the Americans from the outset that the British would be under great pressure to call for a conference should things go badly.

Both China and the SU had promised to help North Vietnam if it were attacked, but neither had made any specific commitment. If the Chinese thought American attacks endangered the stability of the North Vietnamese government, they would probably encourage 'all-out attacks by the Viet Cong in South Viet-Nam, but might initially limit their own effort to strengthening North Viet-Namese defences with anti-aircraft and other specialist units'. They would not encourage North Vietnam to negotiate 'on any basis that did not contemplate an American withdrawal from Viet-Nam'. The SU would give diplomatic support, but probably seek to avoid military involvement. Prolonged fighting might, however, lead to the resumption of military supplies to North Vietnam and even China. 'The Russians would, however, probably try to keep out of the fighting themselves, even if the U.S. air attacks extended to Chinese territory.'[53]

SEAD was asked to set out the commitments Britain had made on Vietnam and the US on Malaysia. The US had allowed the British to understand that, if they had to take the offensive against Indonesia, they could count on its diplomatic support, especially in the SC. The British government had that 'very much in mind' when the British representative was instructed to give the US full support in the SC discussion of the attacks on Vietnamese naval bases following the Tonkin incident in August. Britain was not 'formally committed', but American public opinion would expect support. It would probably regard Britain's attitude to Vietnam as 'the touchstone of Anglo-American relations, not only in S.E. Asia, but in general'.[54]

The UK had not managed to influence the decisions reached in Washington: hesitant to offer gloomy advice, it had in the event offered none at all, despite, or because of, the perceptive discussions in the FO. Peck's talks with William Bundy thus offered a preview of what the president might say to the prime minister, telegraphed by Harlech on 3 December. There were two steps: air action in Laos against routes used by the North Vietnamese, and if there were another attack like Bien Hoa, targets directly related to infiltration between the 17th and 19th parallels would be attacked. More steps would follow if there were no result. The aim was to signal to Hanoi, which had authority to call off the VC, but the first phase might only give it pause. Talks were not being considered at this stage. The president would seek more UK assistance.[55] Harlech told Bundy that Britain wished to support the US, but that there might come a point at which international opinion pressed it to use its co-chairman role. The ambassador recommended that ministers should support the limited action, which resembled what Britain might have to do in Indonesia, and ask to be informed of further decisions after 30 days.[56]

Arguably the British were gaining an impression that US action would be rather limited. According to the State Department, Bundy told Peck and Stewart that the second phase was not yet decided upon but was preferred to 'any alternative of more sharp and dramatic military action'. The crucial determinants were whether the Saigon government settled down, and whether Hanoi's leaders showed any sign of responding to the immediate programme 'designed to impress them with our determination and to foreshadow possible future actions'. Peck and Stewart indicated their personal support for these decisions and expressed the belief that HM government 'would be relieved we were not contemplating early drastic action'; but they noted that if military action did increase, it would be under pressure to take some lead in seeking a new Geneva or 'other visible negotiating avenue'. Bundy said the US was opposed to any visible negotiations 'at least for some time to come and in absence of clear indications that they could produce our objective of independent and secure South Vietnam'.[57]

Talking to the Australian and New Zealand ambassadors, but not to the British, Bundy mentioned the possibility of 'introducing division ground forces'. Could there be small units from Australia and New Zealand? His brother, McGeorge Bundy, told the president that there was 'no political base whatever in England, in any party, for an increased British commitment in Vietnam now. For ten years we have accepted a situation in which the British give political support, but avoid any major commitment on the ground of their other interests and their position as Co-Chairman of the Geneva Agreements of 1954.' The most Wilson could do would be to enlarge the Thompson mission and police training. If the US opened a second phase and needed to land a mixed force of US and other troops, it might get a small British contingent, but that might mean the Soviet co-chairman would help Hanoi. The price would be stronger support for Malaysia. It would be very hard for Wilson to do as much in South Vietnam 'as we need him to. It is hard to treat a thing as our problem for 10 years and then try to get other people to take on a share of it, just because it is getting worse (though we choose not to say so).'[58]

The FO had guessed pretty accurately, Cable wrote to Peck, but was too optimistic about negotiations and had not considered further requests for aid.[59] He suggested a line to take if the president asked for it. So far, apart from technical assistance and a little capital aid, Britain's main contribution had been to train Vietnamese policemen in counter-insurgency techniques in Malaysia, and to keep the British Advisory Mission in Saigon. That would end in 1965, because Thompson and other members wished to retire, and because the disorganisation of the Vietnamese government had prevented proper use of the mission's advice. One member would remain on attachment in the embassy. Britain had also supplied four police officers to work with the US Operations Mission in Saigon.

What the president would like was a token military force, 'but we cannot provide this without violating the 1954 Geneva Agreement ban on the introduction of fresh troops, military personnel, arms and munitions'. The best compromise would be to train more Vietnamese in Malaysia, to provide more police officers in Saigon, and to announce that this was being done 'as a token of our support for South Viet-Nam'. The public announcement would count most with the US, but might expose the government to 'more criticism at home'.[60]

American public opinion, G.E. Hall commented, was increasingly focused on Britain's economic problems. Its requests for help, it was suggested, justified an expectation that it would do more in Vietnam. US support for Malaysia was seen more as an additional request than as a quid pro quo for support in Vietnam. 'Whatever we may think of the wisdom of U.S. policy in Vietnam, U.S. public opinion will find it hard to accept more support of Britain without some further gesture on our part to help them in Saigon.'[61]

The First Wilson Visit

As soon as the new Labour Government took office, the Treasury had presented it with a gloomy economic assessment. The balance of payments deficit for 1964 was expected to be 800 million pounds, and the pound was under heavy attack. Rejecting deflation and devaluation, the Treasury advocated a strategy designed to increase industrial efficiency and competitiveness and to reduce expenditure on non-productive purposes. Wilson followed the advice, and had told the president on 23 October. That was the situation, too, when ministers met at Chequers on 21–22 November 1964 to consider defence and foreign policy and to readdress the question put to the Long-Term Study Group: what world commitments could Britain maintain on a shrinking resource base?[62] It was also the context in which Trend suggested the need to start a defence review. Committed to maintaining sterling as a major reserve currency and to avoiding a repetition of the devaluation that had taken place under the previous Labour government, Wilson agreed, insisting on a ceiling of 2,000 million pounds at 1964 prices for three to four years.[63] But ultimately that was at odds with his expectation that Britain could continue to play a world role, as he hoped, and the future of its position 'East of Suez' came into ever-sharper question. 'I want to make it quite clear that whatever we may do in the field of cost effectiveness, value for money and a stringent review of expenditure, we cannot afford to relinquish our world role—our role which, for shorthand purposes, is sometimes called our "east of Suez" role.'[64] The left wing, for its part, preferred cuts in defence to cuts in welfare. Even apart from the political issues, there was no chance Britain would offer aid in Vietnam. But it could be argued that Wilson did attempt a different kind of world role. As in his dirigiste efforts to restore the economy, he was to be utterly frustrated.

In this endeavour, it might be said, he was following Macmillan, whose own efforts to reduce defence expenditure had fallen away: 'his attempt to act as an intermediary between Washington and Moscow ...

only underscored the continuing image of British importance in the world, while even a limited withdrawal from commitments east of Suez would have had the reverse effect.'[65] Wilson's endeavour depended in part on what he considered his good relationships with the Russians, which he hoped would give him leverage with the US. But the special relationship had to remain: indeed, US support for the pound was part of an implicit deal.[66]

Wilson and his colleagues arrived in Washington on 7 December. A percipient Rusk urged his government 'to give full weight to the role of the UK as a world power. ... It could do certain things which the US ... could not do itself so well. We would look with greatest concern at a diminution of the UK's role, which was of very great importance to us.' The American people were isolationists at heart. 'Because of this, what others are doing has a great effect on what we ourselves are able to do.'[67]

On the 8th Wilson met the president and others. He recognised, he said, the American role in Vietnam, as Britain faced the same role in Malaysia. It was providing BRIAM and could increase its police aid, 'but the United States Government must remember that our position as Co-Chairman of the Geneva Conference implied that we might find ourselves in a very embarrassing international situation if United States action in Vietnam compelled us to activate our Co-Chairman role'. Rusk and the foreign secretary should discuss the matter.[68]

The president and the prime minister were present next day when that discussion took place, on the afternoon of 8 December. The problem, said Rusk, was 'how to prevent the further thrust from North Vietnam into the South. It was essential to turn back the North Vietnamese.' The Viet Cong was stepping up its effort in the South. So was the US, which now had 21,000 personnel in the country. The US, Rusk went on, had been trying to send signals to Peking and Hanoi of two kinds. One was political: leave your neighbours alone, lest there be 'great trouble ahead'. The other was physical, including such measures as continued reconnaissance flights over Laos, prompt retaliation in the Gulf, and positioning of forces in South Vietnam. 'The important thing was to show solidarity with Vietnam and for this purpose a flag must be clearly flown.' Rusk hoped that the UK would make more effort in the South Vietnamese countryside. He recognised Thompson's contribution, 'but stressed that it was important to have a significant number of people in the country in order to create the necessary international effect, both in Saigon and Hanoi, and, he went on to say, on public opinion in the United States'.

Mentioning Malaysia after all, Gordon Walker urged that the area should be viewed as a whole: 'Malaysia must be taken into account as well as Vietnam.' Britain had 8,000 troops in Borneo and 20,000 in Malaysia, a commitment comparable to the United States' in Vietnam. 'But he was emphatic that the United Kingdom could not have troops on the ground in Vietnam.' It was, however, prepared to help in ways that could be made public and would amount to an increased commitment: training more men in jungle warfare; having more police advisers in Saigon; and cooperating more in the medical field.

He realised the value of the 'signals' but stressed that 'it was important to avoid any possible misunderstanding'. He was co-chairman of the Geneva conference. 'If at any time some sudden dramatic action was taken by the U.S.A. which was out of proportion to what had provoked it, this would put Her Majesty's Government in a difficult position internally and internationally.' He would be under great pressure to call the 14-power conference. 'Any retaliation which the United States Government undertook should therefore be related to the scale of the action against which retaliation was being taken.' It should be of the kind successfully undertaken in Laos. Within that framework, the UK supported the US, and would not wish to call a conference without consultation. Finally Gordon Walker said that the UK 'would like to be consulted on any further steps which the United States might be cogitating'. The foreign secretary, it might be noted, was advancing the idea of 'proportionality'. That goes back at least to Hugo Grotius and his view that inherently unlawful actions should be undertaken only in response to imminent danger and be proportionate, not excessive.[69]

The prime minister referred to the parliamentary questions already set down about the possible extension of the war. They could be answered, Gordon Walker thought, by the communiqué, 'but it was important to clarify the position in the long term'. Rusk urged that the Geneva signatories should take 'a sharp view' of violations and of North Vietnam's 'massive aggression'. A total of 10,000 Viet Cong had been infiltrated in 1964. The co-chairmen should urge compliance. Gordon Walker said he would be taking that line with Gromyko next day.[70]

The joint communiqué of 8/9 December was indeed to recognise 'the particular importance of the military effort which both their countries are making in support of legitimate governments in South-East Asia, particularly in Malaysia and South Vietnam, which seek to maintain their independence and resist subversion'.[71]

SEAD sent an account of the discussions to the Saigon embassy for its information alone: it was not to be discussed even with the Americans unless they took the initiative. The account summarised Rusk's remarks. It included, too, the details Bundy had previously given. The telegram also covered the statement Gordon Walker had made, indicating that 'dramatic action … out of proportion to what had provoked it' would put the UK in a difficult position and put pressure on it to call a conference. He had also told Rusk that Britain could not put armed forces into Vietnam, but was prepared to offer additional help and publicise it. 'The upshot,' the telegram concluded, was that the Americans did not 'at present intend a major new initiative, though they might again consider this if the projected intensification of their aerial activities in Laos fails to evoke an appropriate response in Viet-Nam.' Britain had accepted no new commitment, but would 'try to increase somewhat the non-military aid we are already giving'.[72]

In summary, Britain did not use the Washington talks to recommend negotiations long discussed in the FO, but, as Cable put it, promised qualified support for a policy of military pressure aimed at winning the war rather than negotiating. He did not think it would succeed, but Britain had to give it a chance before suggesting an alternative. Indeed, having decided not to take the opportunity in Washington, 'it is arguable that we ought not now to express any view to the U.S. Government before they themselves take the initiative and ask for our comments'.[73] The Washington talks offered no more than a chance of probing, Peck commented. There was never an opening to suggest negotiations, which, as Harlech had said, would give lasting offence.[74] Would the timing ever be right? Yet retaining Singapore—itself a major factor in supporting the creation of Malaysia—was supposedly justified by capacity to influence the US.

At the end of December Wilson sought the foreign secretary's view on a possible British initiative aimed at enabling the US to extricate itself from a worsening situation in Vietnam. A response from the FO suggested that Britain should offer diplomatic assistance, by calling a conference or otherwise, at the right moment. But it was too early to do that. Less than a month had passed since Britain promised qualified support for putting pressure on North Vietnam to call off the insurrection. The US had been reluctant to take that very far given the instability in Saigon. If that got worse, the Americans might consider extrication. But they might also gamble on a military regime, in which case pressure on the North might accelerate. A British offer to help negotiate would at present be resented, and Britain should avoid the possibility of being the scapegoat. The US should be allowed to take the initiative.[75]

Gordon Walker asked for Harlech's views. 'The greatest danger I foresee in the present American policy,' the foreign secretary wrote, 'is that they might defer the decision too long, thus eventually finding themselves in a situation where they wanted to leave Viet Nam, but could no longer do so without major damage to American prestige.' But he thought Britain could not suggest the idea at present.[76]

There was, Harlech replied, no disposition to pull out, or to contemplate a conference that might lead to the communisation of Vietnam. The Americans, the ambassador said, were prepared 'to continue for a very long time their participation in Vietnamese struggle'. They would do so even if the military situation got worse, though that might encourage the militants to urge stronger action against the North.[77]

Chapter Three
Phone Call

In February 1965, despite, it seems, the president's hesitation, bombing of the North got under way: it would sustain Southern morale and induce Hanoi to pursue a political solution. A concerned Wilson wanted to visit Washington, but had to content himself with a phone call. The president's response was angry, but his aim remained unclear. That made it difficult to comment. The FO took a positive view of his Baltimore speech early in April. It also sought to use a proposed Cambodia conference to discuss Vietnam. Neither course produced results. Wilson resorted to a fact-finding mission by a former foreign secretary. In the meantime the FO and its ambassadors discussed the policies Britain might pursue.

Early in the New Year Wilson indicated that he planned to visit Canada, attend the UN General Assembly (UNGA) from 9 February, and also make a brief visit to LBJ.[1] Harlech was fairly certain that the president could see him on 10 February.[2] On 28 January the Cabinet agreed that there was no step that Britain could usefully take at that juncture, but it might ask the Americans whether they saw any scope for its intervention as co-chairman.[3] Cable referred to Harlech's warning: there was a risk of damaging relations.[4]

A brief for the prime minister suggested he might talk to the president about McGeorge Bundy's conclusions after his current visit to Vietnam, and about the reasons for Alexei Kosygin's proposed visit to Hanoi. The malaise in Saigon, a background paper explained, meant that the US was reluctant to risk an offensive, but that might be the only way of overcoming the defeatism that was at the root of instability. The aim was an improved negotiating position, but the gap between what the US could accept and what North Vietnam was 'tremendous'. The Russian objective might be to avert confrontation with the US, or to resume the competition with China for ascendancy in North Vietnam abandoned by Nikita Khrushchev. The US might postpone its decision, neither attacking nor negotiating. A Vietnamese government might initiate negotiations. It was tempting to argue that the Americans should concentrate on saving what they could, but the UK should not rush in with unpalatable proposals and become a scapegoat. And it had itself rejected 'peace at any price' in Malaysia.[5]

In Saigon Nguyen Khanh got rid of Tran Van Huong and installed Phan Huy Quat as PM.[6] The Buddhists seemed influential: Thich Tri Quang, secretary-general of the Buddhist Institute for Religious Affairs, was reportedly not frightened by talk of neutralism. Indeed, it was part of the Buddhists' programme.[7] Western correspondents in Saigon predicted 'the emergence within six months of a government that will present an ultimatum to the United States to get out of Vietnam'.[8] Peck, then in Southeast Asia, and Ambassador Etherington-Smith talked to Alexis Johnson, deputy head of the US embassy. Possibly a situation might arise in which a Vietnamese government invited the Americans to leave. Johnson thought Vietnamese confidence had to be restored. The only solution was to adopt a more aggressive policy in the North as envisaged in stage two of the Bundy proposals. The UK's attitude would help. Peck told him Britain would assist, but reminded him of Gordon Walker's statement that it might come under international or domestic pressure to call for a conference. Johnson saw action as a prelude to negotiation.[9]

The report from McGeorge Bundy, dated 7 February 1965, declared that the stakes in Vietnam were 'extremely high. ... The international prestige of the United States, and a substantial part of our influence, are directly at risk.' It recommended 'a policy of sustained reprisal', air and naval action which would get the US into the second phase of its December planning, if not beyond. The object was to improve the situation in South Vietnam: affecting the will of the North was a longer-range purpose. Current developments had 'produced a practicable point of departure for this policy of reprisal'.[10] He did not think that the chances of success for this policy were particularly good, but, he told the president, even if it failed, it would be worthwhile. 'At a minimum it will damp down the charge that we did not do all that we could have, and this charge will be important in many countries, including our own.'[11]

He was referring to the FLN attacks on the Pleiku airbase on 6 February, which were to be followed by attacks on the army barracks at Qui Nhon on the 10th. No action had followed Bien Hoa before the election. Gareth Porter argues that the new attacks provided a chance for his advisers to overcome LBJ's continued hesitation.[12] Randall B. Woods suggests that Pleiku pushed him 'toward a decision he did not want to make'.[13] 'Flaming Dart' attacks on southern North Vietnam were launched in retaliation on the 7th and 11th.[14] Kosygin was in Hanoi at the time. At a mass rally on the 7th, he had pledged Russian support against the aggressors, and when the raids took place, he of course condemned them.[15] Without the equipment that the SU was to supply, including surface-to-air missiles (SAMs), the North Vietnamese would not have been able to counter the long sequence of bombing attacks, Rolling Thunder, that were to follow. Louis Heren suggests that Flaming Dart prompted the supply of SAMs. 'One could perhaps argue that Johnson lost in [the war] when he avenged Pleiku with too little regard for the consequences.'[16]

Rolling Thunder did not, however, start at once, though China was more in mind. On 8 February the NSC favoured adopting Phase 2. But, asked James C. Thomson Jr, one of its staff, had the risk of Chinese intervention been considered? Chinese MIGs might respond to air attacks north of the 19th parallel, and US planes might cross the border in hot pursuit and apply repressive fire. That could bring Chinese troops in. Were the president and people ready to face ground war?—in 'a conflict already fuzzed by national doubts far exceeding any that attached to the relatively clear-cut Korean conflict (invasion and "UN" response)?'[17] The president himself hesitated.

On 13 February Alan Crick saw Chester Cooper on his return from McGeorge Bundy's mission to South Vietnam and mentioned press reports that the chiefs of staff wanted to raise the level of action against North Vietnam. Cooper agreed that 'in terms of purely military logic they had a case for arguing that individual actions on a riposte basis and without fitting into any wider, more effective plan were not best calculated to achieve the desired result of getting the North Vietnamese to call off their efforts in support of the Viet Cong'. But General Earle G. Wheeler recognised that there were 'political considerations'. Cooper said he and McGeorge Bundy were 'on the side of caution', and that characterised the president's attitude, too. They had been urging that 'any increased U.S. strikes would have to be increased with very fine gradations so that … the military situation would not be heightened too much before the negotiation possibilities could be explored and exploited. … Chester used the analogy of two lines of a graph and said that it was important that the "military" line should not shoot ahead of the "negotiation" line in such a way as to make it impossible for the latter to intersect.' Crick suggested that the US might run out of targets in southern North Vietnam and might have to strike at areas such as Vinh. But Cooper did not agree.[18]

What was proposed, Ball told the president on the 13th, was attacks on a joint US/South Vietnamese basis against 'military targets directly related to North Vietnamese infiltration', and attacks on targets such as railway lines 'in response to Viet Cong attacks on corresponding targets in the South', slowly increasing in scale. The fundamental objective was to increase US bargaining power vis-à-vis North Vietnam and China, 'to the point where a satisfactory political solution becomes possible'. The attacks should also tend to improve morale in the South and to curb infiltration.[19]

McGeorge Bundy urged a firm decision: if the US limited itself to reprisals for spectaculars like Pleiku and Qui Nhon, it left the initiative to the Communists. But it should 'avoid excessive noise'.[20] The start of regular strikes, finally decided on, was not announced. In retrospect Defense Secretary McNamara argued that LBJ should have taken the American people into his confidence when polls were strongly backing his policies. It was not merely a matter of his 'innate secretiveness'. He was obsessed with getting Congress approval and financing for his 'Great Society' agenda. And he also 'feared hard-line pressure (from conservatives in both parties) for greater—and far riskier—military action that might trigger responses, especially nuclear, by China and/or the Soviet Union. The president coped with his dilemma by obscuring it.'[21]

'The decision to use military power against the North, in the end, seems to have resulted as much from a lack of alternative proposals as from any compelling logic advanced in its favour,' Herbert Schandler suggests.[22] A logic was, of course, advanced. 'We had seen the gradual application of force applied in the Cuban crisis,' as Cy Vance later put it, 'and had seen a very successful result. We believed that if this same gradual and restrained application of force were applied in … Vietnam, that one could expect the same kind of result; that rational people on the other side would respond to increasing military pressure and therefore would try and seek a political solution.'[23] But Vietnam was not the SU, nor Le Duan Nikita Khrushchev.

The historian of the international diplomacy of the war Ralph Smith concluded that 'coercive diplomacy' did not work, given this limited application of force. Only a quick demarche might have succeeded.[24] But what else might that have produced? It appears that the most powerful man in the world could not use much of his power. His concern to secure consensus among the agencies induced caution. So did his concern over China, and over his own citizens. He was, Woods argues, 'frightened' by polls that showed that the conflict in Vietnam was seen as a challenge on the part of the Chinese Communists.[25] There was a risk that opinion in the US would press for a wider war.

Flaming Dart and Combustible Conversation

Michael Stewart, M.P. (not Michael N.F. Stewart in the Washington embassy), had taken over as foreign secretary when Gordon Walker lost the Leyton by-election late in January. On 8 February 1965 he asked the

US chargé to call, so that he could give him an immediate account of his answers to parliamentary questions about US military action. Some members of the Labour Party were anxious for a peaceful settlement, Stewart went on. He sympathised but would have 'found it much easier to respond to requests that H.M.G. should take some initiative towards negotiations, if these requests had been made after the attacks on U.S. military personnel instead of after the American counter attacks'. He did not wish to say anything in public critical of the US government, 'but we were allies and we ought to discuss important problems frankly'. How did the US government envisage the future in Vietnam? 'Was there not a danger that the Western powers were at present trying to prop up in South Viet-Nam a regime that was already beyond being propped up? If so, where were we getting to in Viet-Nam?' The chargé said he could add little to public statements. But the action taken was similar to that Britain had planned in certain circumstances to take against Indonesia. The presence of Kosygin in Hanoi made it 'even more imperative' for the US to act as it did.

Stewart said he would find it easier to carry British public opinion with him if the US were implementing its existing policy rather than adopting a new one. Did the chargé think that a settlement would be possible if the Viet Cong halted its operations, allowing the Saigon government 'to become once more master in its own house' and opening the way for subsequent US withdrawal? The chargé could not answer, but was sure that the cessation of VC operations would be a prior condition for his government. Stewart asked if North Vietnam could turn VC operations on and off at will. 'Or was there an indigenous element in the Viet Cong that would permit this to survive even without control and assistance from the North?' The chargé did not know, but thought 'the life-blood of the revolt came from the North'.

The Soviet government, Stewart then said, might revise its ideas about the role of the co-chairmen in Vietnam and propose reconvening the Geneva conference. It would not be easy for the UK to return a blank 'No'. No doubt, said the chargé, it would want to examine the terms. Stewart agreed, and said that another important factor would be the readiness of other governments willing to attend. But supposing they were, and constructive negotiations seemed possible, would the US still insist that fighting should be stopped before a conference could be held? The chargé thought it would be difficult for the US to negotiate with 'people who were still breaking existing agreements'. Stewart replied that if it did receive a proposal from the SU, the UK would consult the US before taking any decision.

Finally Stewart remarked that the second US attack had been one of three originally intended to be simultaneous. Was it still intended to carry out the third? The chargé thought not. If it were, the foreign secretary hoped that the US government would again inform the UK if possible in advance. The chargé was sure his government would do its best. The foreign secretary hoped his remarks on the long-term aspects would be reported and that the US government would let him know its views.[26]

The Indian government, which issued a statement on 8 February 1965, was 'seriously concerned about the effect which the escalation of the conflict in Viet-Nam might have on the neighbouring countries', and hoped that the UK would use its influence to secure a declaration by all the parties that they would suspend hostilities immediately. 'Once that had been achieved,' Kewal Singh, the deputy high commissioner in London, told Minister of State George Thomson on 10 February, 'the aim should be to convene a Geneva-type conference to work out a long-term solution.' Thomson said that the UK was 'anxious to do anything which would produce peace in Viet-Nam', but the problem was 'to decide whether any initiative which might serve this purpose was … available to them'. Would the Viet Cong, who believed they were 'winning a civil war', join in a ceasefire? All those involved, the US, the SU, and North and South Vietnam, should join in a declaration, Kewal Singh responded, and the UK, as co-chairman and as a country with 'specially close relations' with the US, was in a position to press for it. The SU did not seem anxious to revive the active role of the co-chairmen, Thomson responded, and 'it would not be sensible to convene another Geneva-type conference unless it had a real chance of achieving something'. Did India want to see American forces withdrawn from South Vietnam? That was a point meaningful only in terms of a final solution, Kewal Singh replied. The Indians believed that ultimately all outside influence should be eliminated from Vietnam. They had no desire to see China 'imposing her domination on South-East Asian countries piecemeal'.[27]

In a statement of 9 February 1965 the Chinese government condemned the Flaming Dart attacks. It supported the protests the DRV had made. Like the Gulf incident of August 1964, this was 'another undisguised war provocation'. The 'south Vietnamese people' had only been giving 'tit for tat' to the aggressors. The US had acted in flagrant breach of the 1954 agreements. If it made further attacks, other countries had the right to assist the DRV. The 650 million people of China would 'definitely not stand idly by'.[28] The statement was somewhat stronger than that of 6 August, Murray MacLehose noted, but the Chinese government clearly retained the option 'to continue to avoid direct confrontation if they wish'.[29]

Wilson's visit had been put off. Harlech had suggested on 2 February that it was doubtful that the prime minister would be able to address UNGA the following week. With the primary reason for his visit no longer existing, he did not think the president would necessarily welcome a visit. A speech to the Pilgrims would not provide sufficient cover.[30] But at 11.30pm on the 10th the prime minister spoke to the foreign secretary, and it was agreed that he should fly to Washington. After consulting Caccia, Stewart suggested he should consult Harlech, and Wilson spoke to him by phone at 1am on the 11th. 'He explained the Parliamentary situation in this country and the fact that alone of the major powers Britain was appearing to keep silent over South Vietnam and appearing simply to tag along in the wake of the Americans in what they had to do in South Vietnam. But it would be easier for him to do this if he was seen to be in discussion with the President of the United States.' Harlech spoke to McGeorge Bundy, and rang back at 2am. The White House was against a visit. 'It would smack too much of desperation. US action would be moderate. It would look bad if the Prime Minister were giving advice while American soldiers were being murdered.' It would be best to phone first.[31]

A report had been received of a Viet Cong attack on a club in Saigon, Wilson recalled in his memoir, and he feared LBJ's patience might 'falter'. He rang Washington. 'To my surprise, he let fly in an outburst of Texan temper.' He was entirely negative. Whatever it would do for opinion in the UK, a visit would be misunderstood in the US. 'I won't tell you how to run Malaysia, and you don't tell us how to run Vietnam. ... if you want to help us some in Vietnam, send us some men and send us folks to deal with those guerrillas. And announce to the press that you are going to help us. Now if you don't feel like doing that go on with your Malaysia problem.'[32]

McGeorge Bundy recalled that he had told Harlech, first on his own and then on the president's insistence, that a visit would be 'untimely and unhelpful', but Wilson was insistent, as he had a Cabinet meeting on Thursday. The president agreed to receive the call, which came through at 10.15pm. Bundy was present but heard only what the president said. It would be 'a very serious mistake' for Wilson to come over: 'there was nothing to get upset about, any more than it would be right for him to get upset about Malaysia.' A visit would be 'misunderstood'. The US response had been 'very measured and very reasonable', and it would be 'a great mistake for us to jump up and down and fly the Atlantic every time there was an issue of this sort'. Wilson said 'something about his problems in the House of Commons. The President said he had plenty of problems with his own Congress, and he thought it would be a mistake for the Prime Minister to try to use the President as an instrument in the House of Commons, just as he would not wish to use the Prime Minister as an instrument with the

Congress.' Wilson apparently said something about the hazards of escalation. The president replied that he was afraid of it, too, 'but he did not see what was to be gained by flapping around the Atlantic with our coattails out'. 'If the Prime Minister had any men to spare, he would be glad to have them.'

Wilson apparently returned to the charge, 'and the President asked him bluntly, "Why don't you run Malaysia and let me run Vietnam"? Would the Prime Minister think it would be good for the President to announce to the American press tomorrow that he was going over to London to try to stop the British in Malaysia?' Wilson apparently assured the president of British support, and the president promised a detailed memorandum on US policy. Wilson 'apparently said something about the difficulty he would have in explaining what he was doing and not doing, and all that he would have to talk about was a call in the middle of the night. The President replied with some sharpness that it was the Prime Minister and not he who placed the call in the middle of the night. The President was just answering it.'[33]

A British record covers both sides of the conversation. 'Our problem,' Wilson said, 'is that every nation in the world is making a statement. ... It is very difficult for us to be saying nothing at all except that whatever the U.S. decides to do we shall go along with of course. ...' He wanted to come over as soon as possible. The UK had supported 'what was right and measured. ... We are under very strong pressure from both sides of Parliament about the long-term solution.' The government had faced 'some very strong criticism that we have not been taking the initiative in calling a Conference. So far as any talks are concerned we do like to know what you think.' LBJ offered to send a classified cable. Wilson then mentioned the word 'escalation'.

'I have met escalation in many places,' the president interrupted, 'and I take it in my stride and I do not think our personal visits would do anything but dramatise and heat it up. ... now that things look a little bit dark we do not want it to appear that we are desperate.' He would send Ambassador Bruce a memorandum, and the PM could say he had 'an extended conversation'. Wilson said the UK would stand by the US. 'Every time they murder our people we are going to react promptly and measuredly,' LBJ said.

'Whatever measured response you take tomorrow we shall be backing that too,' Wilson responded. 'We have been extremely loyal allies on this matter and that will be the position tomorrow.' All he wanted to do, the PM insisted, was to reassure the House of Commons. 'Do you think I can do this on the basis of a transatlantic call in the middle of the night?' 'You were the one who placed the call. At the end of the call, Wilson asked if the memorandum/telegram could include the president's view of 'the long term situation'.[34]

Perhaps it was not just a matter of 'Texan temper'. The president was agonising over his decision. He was also anxious not to make it too public. A visit by a prime minister who offered no help would only hinder, perhaps making consensus more difficult to reach, perhaps adding to the president's own doubts or pushing him into or adding to the discussion of 'escalation'.

Cutting Losses?

Two questions were to be faced, Cable wrote on 15 February 1965: How could the conflict be brought to an end? And could or should Britain 'do anything about it'? He suggested that the Americans had to choose 'between imposing a positive policy of their own and merely reacting to the initiatives of others', Communists or South Vietnamese. So far they had followed the latter course. The latest attacks were 'still part of a policy of drift, because the U.S. Government have not yet, as far as we know, set themselves a specific goal or defined the means of reaching it. The attacks are intended to demonstrate American determination, but nobody knows precisely what, in concrete terms, the U.S. Government are determined to achieve.' What policy might it decide upon? Defeating the Viet Cong on the ground was no longer a realistic objective. Even if present techniques were improved, their effects would not overtake war-weariness and defeatism. That limited the choice of policies to two: 'raising the stakes or cutting losses.'

The first meant using American air power to inflict such intolerable damage on North Vietnam that the Viet Cong would be ordered to lay down their arms. Theoretically that was a possible objective, and the bulk of the Viet Cong might accept a North Vietnamese order to abandon the struggle. 'But could China, could even the Soviet Union, tolerate the damage that such total surrender would do to militant Communism throughout the world?' Would the US have to threaten them, too? The Communist powers might themselves raise the stakes by 'mounting a combined war of nerves and propaganda campaign to deprive the U.S. of Western support as Britain was so deprived at Suez', and 'using regular troops to conquer the South before American aircraft could complete the destruction of the North'. And 'how long would the South Viet-Namese leaders and the South Viet-Namese armed forces continue to approve the bombing of their compatriots in the North without calling for negotiations?'

It was doubtful that any lesser objective would justify the risks that coercion of the North would entail. Suspension of the introduction of arms and personnel would be difficult to verify and too slow to forestall Southern collapse. Any arrangement likely to be acceptable to the Communists would probably be insufficient to save South Vietnam: it would be difficult to define an understanding so that breaches of it were 'sufficiently manifest' to justify renewed US attacks; and the Communists might well be in a position to renew their operations when circumstances allowed—when Russia had improved North Vietnam's air defences, or had patched up its quarrel with China, or the US were heavily involved elsewhere.

The French had often suggested that the Communist powers would accept the continued independence of South Vietnam provided that the country was neutralised, US forces withdrew, and US military aid was terminated. As an alternative to the destruction of North Vietnam, it was conceivable that the Communists might agree. But, once the US had withdrawn, it would be easy for the Communists to resume their campaign to dominate South Vietnam, and they would probably not need to resort to violence at a level that justified renewed US intervention, even if American public opinion allowed it. There was in fact no compromise that did not entail abandoning South Vietnam to Communist domination, however skilfully it might be disguised.

If the US government decided on a negotiated settlement, the paramount consideration ought to be the repercussions, not in South Vietnam, but on the Western position elsewhere in Southeast Asia and the world as a whole. 'They will have to try and show that their abandonment of South Viet-Nam (because that is how it will appear in Formosa and South Korea and Thailand and elsewhere as well) was due to a Viet-Namese, not an American, failure of will and that it constitutes no precedent for future American policy in other countries threatened by Communism.' The best hope of achieving that lay in 'a preliminary show of American strength and resolution (which they are now making)'; a subsequent initiative for negotiations from the Communists or the Vietnamese but not the Americans; 'Communist concessions outside Vietnam'; and 'an emphatic reaffirmation of American readiness to resist Communism elsewhere'. If North Vietnamese withdrawal from Laos and the admission of Prince Souvanna Phouma's officials and troops to all parts of Laos were made a prior condition for US withdrawal from Vietnam, that might be a 'negotiable concession' that would reassure Thailand and strengthen the Western position.

It might be, Cable continued, that the US would find that both policies—raising stakes, cutting losses—were too difficult to sell to public opinion at home and that they would go on as they were, 'reacting offensively when provoked, leaving their objectives unstated and allowing events to determine their policy, rather than vice versa'. A period of international tension and disunity in Saigon might then lead to a Saigon peace initiative.

'The President would then have a scapegoat for American public opinion and an excuse for his Asian allies', but it would be difficult for the US to save its face and bargain for concessions. 'Without careful preparation and planning, any peace initiative from Saigon could precipitate a rapid collapse of morale and organised authority in South Viet-Nam, which could make it difficult for American advisers and forces to remain and, above all, to retain their influence and bargaining power during negotiations. The end result of a policy of drift might, therefore, have much worse repercussions elsewhere in South East Asia and in the world at large than that of a deliberate policy of cutting American losses.'

A policy of drift could have yet worse consequences if the Communists failed to recognise it and realise time was on their side. 'If the Viet Cong, for instance, instead of avoiding provocations, were to intensify them, the U.S. government might find themselves driven, step by step, into a policy of raising the stakes, yet without ever having formulated—to themselves, to their allies or, most important of all, to the Communists—their objectives or the precise conditions on which they would cease attacking North Viet-Nam. This might prove the most dangerous policy of all.'

If his analysis were correct, Cable believed that Britain 'should favour a deliberate American policy of cutting their losses in Viet-Nam, because this offers the best chance of avoiding the dangers of escalation while mitigating the adverse repercussions on Western influence and prestige'. Should Britain let the US government reach the conclusion by itself or try to influence its choice? 'We know that the U.S. Government are acutely sensitive on this subject and that advice from us would be resented. Before we can decide whether we need or ought to expose ourselves to such resentment and before we can judge whether our advice would ever achieve its object, we need to know more of the present intentions of the U.S. Government.' The analysis provided a basis for sounding them out.[35]

The fact was that LBJ wanted an independent South Vietnam, but he also wanted a Great Society. He cautiously accepted the Bundy line: what Geyelin described as 'a war of semaphore': 'not an easy strategy to grasp, if one accepts that Johnson's main purpose from the start was to pursue settlement by improving his bargaining position. The aim, in short, then becomes quicker peace through fiercer war—an unappealing proposition to sell.'[36] Such a strategy offered little opportunity for Britain to get a word in, by phone or otherwise: it had failed in December; it failed in February.

Peck forwarded Cable's memorandum to Caccia, the permanent undersecretary, with the suggestion that the foreign secretary might read it before he saw the American ambassador and the president's memorandum on

16 February. How far it would be tactful to probe US intentions could only be judged in the light of what the Americans were now preparing to disclose.

Perhaps deliberately, Peck added, Cable's memorandum was 'on the gloomy side'. Peck himself 'would not exclude the possibility that the U.S. retaliatory air strikes, with conceivably a further degree of escalation, would bring Hanoi to the point of calling off the Viet Cong, without involving a regional conflict which both the Russians, because they are too far from the scene, and the Chinese, because of their relative military weakness by air and sea, wish to avoid. The risk of weakening the U.S. position lies less in the possible introduction of Chinese land forces (hinted at by Chinese statements) than in the use of the Communist propaganda weapon. The U.S. Administration can withstand this only so long as their own public opinion—and to a lesser extent that of their allies—can withstand it.' The Americans had 'a degree of supremacy' in the long run and in controlled warfare that the Chinese and Russians knew they lacked. Therefore, 'a settlement negotiated from a position of strength could stick'.

It would only do so, however, if the British government used its position as co-chairman to organise an effective control system. The 1962 Laos conference produced a better form of ICC than that of 1954. 'But something more effective still is required to control any new settlement: otherwise the Americans will be right in saying that they do not agree with conferences held to ratify terror.' Nor would a Communist withdrawal from Laos really strengthen the Western position: 'Laos is too fragile for this to work.' Britain had no option, Peck concluded, but to hear the Americans' views, 'in the hope they give us an opening to discuss, without rancour, an ultimate solution. Meanwhile we must support them in public, while getting down to a discussion of realities in private.'[37] Caccia agreed, as he did with the conclusion of Cable's memorandum. He noted that other conceivable settlements were possible, for example the Korean armistice line, in which Britain was not involved.[38]

Johnson sent no message, it seems, but he did send Bruce to see Wilson and Stewart on 16 February 1965. He was instructed, he said, to keep the PM 'very closely informed of what the United States Government had in mind'; but late the previous night he had received a telegram to say its plan was 'not yet formed'. He had, however, been in Washington: what he could say was based on what had then been decided. That he put under three headings. First, there was 'a plan to increase the dispositions in Vietnam itself which would assist in the task of pacification'. Second, there would be a programme of 'measured and effective action against targets in North Vietnam', to be stopped 'when the aggression against South Vietnam stopped'. The retaliatory strikes would be kept south of the 19th parallel; there would thus be 'no danger of direct contact between American and Chinese forces since the Chinese MIGs could not operate that far south'. Third, 'there was the question of a request for talks to discuss the future'. Adlai Stevenson, permanent representative at the UN, would discuss the prospect with Secretary-General U Thant. What the US had in mind was a preliminary conference including the US, the SU, China, France and the UK, together with North and South Vietnam. '[A] good deal of thought' was being given to the relationship of the conference to the Security Council: 'they wanted to avoid any question of a veto by the Nationalist Chinese'; also, at least three participants would not be UN members. 'The programme of retaliatory strikes would have to continue throughout the conference if necessary until a ceasefire had been agreed to.' What would be the conditions of a ceasefire? Stewart asked. 'One condition might be that the Viet Cong would agree to refrain from taking any further military action and to remain where they were', but the South Vietnam government 'might wish to be able to exercise their authority on their own territory'.[39]

The following morning Bruce said he had received further instructions from the State Department. It had recommended, and thought the president would concur in, 'continuing air and naval action against North Vietnam whenever and wherever necessary. Their thinking had been, and continued to be, that any such action should be limited and fitting and adequate as a response to the continuous aggression in South Vietnam directed in Hanoi.' A statement—probably by the secretary of state—would follow the next military action. That would reflect three elements in American thinking. One was to intensify pacification in South Vietnam, and taking every possible step to attack Viet Cong concentrations and headquarters. Second was the execution of 'a joint programme of measures and limited air action against selected military targets in North Vietnam', a programme to be put to the SC. Third, the SC would be given a detailed presentation of the case against North Vietnam as an aggressor. 'The United States Govt. did not expect to touch upon their readiness for talks or negotiations at this time.' In public statements, it 'expected to make it clear that military action would continue while aggression continued. ... There would be no comment of any sort on future actions except that all such actions would be adequate and measured and fitting to aggression.'

The US seemed to have changed its mind about negotiations, Wilson commented. 'The plan now appeared to be to step up military action without making proposals for a political solution; this was the pill without the jam. This would make it difficult for the outside world and in particular for the

United Kingdom who would, of course, have to support the United States without seeing any light at the end of the tunnel.' Bruce did not know why the plan had been changed: he would report Wilson's view. If Stevenson went to the SC and merely made charges of aggression without insisting on readiness to negotiate, 'he would be in for a very rough reception', Wilson responded. He would consider whether to send a message through Harlech.[40]

It was essential, Lord Walston commented on Cable's memorandum, to know which course the US intended to pursue, 'acutely sensitive' though it might be. 'I feel they should be pressed, with the utmost tact, to face the realities of the situation, to make up their minds, and to tell us what their choice is. The longer this choice is delayed, the harder it will be to make it objectively.' A telegram to Washington of 17 February had started the ball rolling. Could the Cable memorandum be sent to Lord Harlech, asking him, 'with all the very considerable tact at his disposal', to present the choices to the Americans? A 'speedy decision' was of intrinsic importance. But in addition 'our continued apparent inactivity is giving the Russians and Chinese the opportunity of spreading it about that H.M.G. is no more than a lackey of U.S. Government policy and can take no stand on its own without the approval of its dollar masters. There is already evidence that this line of propaganda is beginning to spread.'[41]

Fresh from his second meeting with Bruce, Stewart liked Walston's suggestion. 'In general, have we made sufficiently clear to the Americans our view that their abandonment of the conference idea will create great difficulties for us and them? If they present to the U.N. their first two points—pacification and further retaliatory measures—without the conference proposal, the reaction, even among those who genuinely want to be their friends, is bound to be adverse. I think they over-rate the value, to them, of presenting evidence of support from the North for the Viet-Cong; their enemies will refuse to believe this, while their friends believe it already. If, however, they change their mind again, and re-insert the conference proposal, then—although enormous difficulties remain—their position will be much strengthened.' Should he write to Rusk or should the point be urged on Bruce?[42] A telegram went to Washington, and Caccia spoke to Bruce.

Russian Initiative

In Moscow on 16 February 1965—after giving Trevelyan a Soviet proposal for a joint message on American bombing in Laos—Sergey Lapin discussed the situation in Vietnam. His main object was a new definition of the Soviet co-chairmanship in relation to that country. He started by referring to a message Xuan Thuy had sent to the co-chairmen on 9 February about the aggressive activities of the US, and asked whether Trevelyan had 'any reactions to proposals in connexion with this message'. He replied that he had none, and that he understood that the SU did not desire to reactivate the co-chairmanship on Vietnam, 'for which there was strictly no authority under the 1954 Agreement'. He would be glad to have clarification. 'Mr Lapin replied that when a fire broke out, the firemen should not argue over their responsibilities. We should use all available channels and possibilities to assist the victims of American aggression.' The 1954 agreements contained no reference to the continuing functions of the co-chairmen. But in practice they had acted, and the North Vietnamese had appealed to them.

Lapin conducted 'a highly emotional attack on bombardments by the Americans', demanding that they should cease at once and that all US military personnel should be withdrawn from Vietnam. The co-chairmen should declare that the bombing should stop and that there was no excuse for it. No negotiations could take place till it had stopped. Trevelyan said the co-chairmen should try to establish a cessation of all military activity in North and South and that the SU should use its influence in Hanoi to that end. Lapin denied that North Vietnam was influencing events in the South: the Communist partisan operations were 'a just struggle for liberation'.

The change in the Soviet attitude on the co-chairmanship, Trevelyan commented, was clearly the result of North Vietnamese pressure on Kosygin. The Soviet government had not yet prepared a joint message on the bombings, but one could be expected shortly. He needed material for an oral statement (a) on Britain's position on the co-chairmanship; (b) on its analysis of the Vietnam situation, including North Vietnamese interference and US bombing; and (c) '(if we can) Positive suggestions for action by the Co-Chairmen to lead to a peaceful settlement'. The sooner the better, so that Britain could answer Russian accusations that it had no positive proposal and only refused their draft messages.[43]

The FO instructed Harlech to inform Washington of the Soviet initiative. He was to say that Britain could explain its attitude on (a) and proposed to instruct Trevelyan to tell Lapin that Britain accepted that a tradition of joint co-chairmen mediation on Geneva disputes had grown up but that it conferred no special rights in respect of Vietnam nor imposed any specific obligations. In particular, the UK did not consider that either jointly or separately the co-chairmen had the right or duty to reconvene Geneva without the prior concurrence of all the other governments concerned.

Items (b) and (c) could not be answered 'without a more specific indication of United States policy and intentions than we have yet had', the telegram to Washington continued. 'Moreover, it would not be sufficient merely to provide evidence that the Viet Cong insurrection in the South was aided and directed by the North and to say that the United States attacks on the North were intended to counter this. The world is in no doubt of the strength of American determination, but neither we nor, what is more important, the Communist powers can be sure precisely what, in concrete terms, the United States are determined to achieve.' The US should 'define publicly what they envisage as an acceptable basis for a negotiated settlement in Viet Nam or, if they cannot go that far, at least specify the conditions on which they would be willing to cease attacks on North Vietnam and enter into negotiations'. Until the conditions were made known to the Communist powers, it was not clear 'how they can choose between taking steps which would satisfy the United States and a continuation of the armed conflict with all the risks this would entail'. And if they were not known to British public opinion, it would become 'increasingly difficult' to secure its approval. The problem had not been created by the latest Soviet approach, probably intended only to return Britain to the dilemma of the co-chairmanship that earlier Soviet statements had, 'perhaps inadvertently, tended to mitigate'. But the altered Soviet view made the problem more urgent.[44]

Harlech saw Rusk on the afternoon of the 17th. At first sight he thought the reply on the co-chairmanship looked 'excellent': keeping the Russians committed to it 'would tend to keep them on a peaceful track; they could also use it to contain pressures from their own side'. Harlech then went on to items (b) and (c). 'There was bound to be increasing pressure not only from British public opinion but from other countries for the working out of some formula for peaceful negotiations.' The Russians would exert pressure through the co-chairmanship, 'and there would be growing demands on us to take some initiative. It would be easier to handle this if American objectives and conditions for negotiations were made publicly known. It was no longer sufficient simply to highlight the iniquities of the other side; there now seemed to be a need for the Americans to state their intentions.'

On 'highlighting Hanoi's responsibility for the present situation', Rusk said, 'it was essential to try to get international acceptance of the elementary facts of North Vietnamese infiltration and control of the Viet Cong'. The Russians could not be expected to admit that publicly, but even in private, they 'showed no signs yet of starting from this basis of fact'. They continued to emphasise 'the indigenous nature of the Viet Cong revolt; the same line had been used by the Communists in the Korean war'.

On the question of US intentions, Rusk said he might hold a press conference later in the week. 'Meanwhile, he wished to point out that while there was no difficulty about stating American objectives publicly in clear and simple terms, to spell out in public the conditions under which the Americans would be prepared to negotiate would be to lose flexibility and the possibility of probing the other side's attitude: indeed, such publicly announced conditions might prove a major obstacle to talks. The same objections applied to a formal conference. If the Americans proposed an agenda or conditions for holding a conference, these might be rejected out of hand by the Communists and that avenue would then be closed; alternatively, a conference might break up in bitter disagreement and again the "court of last appeal" would have failed. We should then be in a worse position than before.'[45]

What Rusk said was 'disappointing on the core of the matter, that is American intentions', the Foreign Office told the ambassador. It had noted what the president said on 17 February. He declared that the American purpose was clear: 'to join in the defense and protection of freedom of a brave people who are under attack that is controlled and that is directed from outside their country.' Americans had 'no ambition there for ourselves. We seek no dominion. We seek no conquest. We seek no wider war. But we trust all understand that we will persist in the defence of freedom and our continuing actions will be those that are justified and those that are made necessary by the continuing aggression of others'. The actions would be measured, fitting and adequate.

'This was all right as far as it went,' the FO commented. 'But it did not go far enough, since no serious observer doubted that the United States did not seek domination or conquest or a wider war.' Britain also accepted that American actions would be 'measured and fitting and adequate to the continued aggression of others. But what was needed was some indication of American readiness to do something other than responsive military action. In brief, what were the circumstances in which they would be ready to talk? This need not at this stage commit them to any particular forum.' The FO did not consider 'that if the Americans were to spell this out in public, they would lose flexibility and the possibility of probing the other side's attitude. It could and would be argued that exactly the contrary was the case, since it would then be for the other side to show where they stood.' Harlech was asked to make use of these comments when he saw Rusk. The aim was not to make 'any unnecessary difficulties' for the US. 'But the point has come where they really must try to enable their friends to continue to back them wholeheartedly in public.'[46] Both parties seem to have a point: too much publicity could damage negotiations; but none at all made it difficult to offer support for US policy.

That evening Rusk had a short talk with Harlech before he went to see the president. 'In the light of our representations and after a careful review of the present situation … they were convinced that the time was not ripe for the United States to take an initiative pointing in the direction of negotiations.' But if the SU were encouraged to exercise some responsibility as co-chairman, it would appear more as a mediator than an advocate. There would be an advantage, too, 'in it being known that there was political activity on the part of the Co-Chairmen'. He confirmed American approval of the proposed reply to Lapin.

Rusk next suggested—following a draft by Bundy[47]—that Britain might propose that the first action of the co-chairmen should be 'to ascertain the views of the countries interested in the Viet Nam situation'. In their response 'the Americans would reply with a very full memorandum stating the limits of their aims and objectives in South-East Asia and outlining the conditions under which they felt a stable and peaceful South-East Asia might be established'. North Vietnam and China would no doubt offer 'very conflicting views', and the chairmen would have 'to try and find elements in the positions of the two sides which pointed in the direction of a peaceful solution'.

Harlech asked if those activities should be pursued behind the scenes or whether, as he greatly hoped, 'we could make public what was happening'. Rusk saw no objection. 'If we wished to announce that the Co-Chairmen were conferring and subsequently that they had agreed as a first step to ascertain the views of interested parties, he thought that this might be all to the good. Then when it came to the Americans replying to our request for their views he saw no reason why the American reply should not be published in full.' Later, Harlech heard that the president had approved the ideas.[48]

The FO said it was pleased with Rusk's response, but before acting on his suggestion, it wanted to be clear as to what the other members of the Geneva conference—presumably what Rusk meant by the 'interested' powers—were to be asked to provide. Merely to ask for their views would produce mere propaganda. 'What we want to ascertain from them is the basis on which they think a peaceful settlement could be reached.' In view of American 'susceptibilities', the word 'negotiations' should probably be avoided. An addition to the instructions to Trevelyan would propose, as a first step, a joint message to the members of the 1954 Conference (Cambodia, China, France, Laos, North Vietnam, South Vietnam, the SU, UK, US), in which the co-chairmen would note 'with grave concern the dangerous state of international tension now existing in connexion with Viet

Nam' and ask members for their views on the situation, 'and in particular, on the circumstances in which they consider that a peaceful settlement could be reached'. The composition of the membership was 'very close' to that proposed by the US, though it excluded the ICC powers, Burma and Thailand. No doubt the SU would try to amend the message to include some condemnation of the US, but the UK would reject that as unhelpful. In any case the full text of the recent ICC report had not yet reached the co-chairmen 'and will need prolonged deliberation when it does'.[49]

Rusk agreed to the proposed communication, subject to some amendments. He wanted the ICC countries—India, Poland and Canada—added to the list of recipients—since the original Geneva membership 'might leave the United States virtually isolated with the South Vietnamese, given our own special position as one of the Co-Chairmen'. The three countries had 'a clear interest in what goes on in Viet Nam'. He also wanted the word 'conclusion' substituted for 'settlement': his request arose from 'a somewhat inconclusive discussion about the significance of both words when translated into Russian'.[50]

The FO accepted these amendments and instructed Trevelyan to speak to Lapin accordingly. If the Russian response were sufficiently encouraging, Trevelyan should go on to suggest that neither Britain nor the SU should make a reply as members of the conference. 'It would be better for the two Co-Chairmen to regard their task as being to seek a consensus on the basis of replies received from other members of the Geneva Conference.' That might be even more difficult if they had themselves meanwhile adopted a statement. The FO would not make its proposal public until the SU's response was known, but might announce that Britain had proposed an initiative, without specifying its nature. If agreement were reached on a joint message, it would be advantageous for both governments to publish it simultaneously. The FO proposed to tell other governments in confidence when Trevelyan had made his proposal.[51]

Noting that Britain was not proposing a conference, Lapin told Trevelyan that he was glad that it was agreed on maintaining the tradition of cooperation between the chairmen. He did not, however, care for the proposal that Britain might make a prior announcement about the initiative. 'In the past we had frequently arranged by mutual agreement that the various proposals which had passed between us should not be published. We should discuss this question without publicity.' If Britain abstained from making a statement, it would soon receive the SU's reply. But if it announced the initiative, even without revealing its nature, the SU would look 'passive' and be 'obliged to make an immediate public statement of its own position.

Either we should both agree to publish nothing or we could exchange public statements.' On the substance of the proposal, Lapin merely commented that some governments, including France and North Vietnam, had already proposed a conference, and there seemed 'little point ... in collecting opinions which were already known'. Trevelyan urged him to give Britain's proposal serious attention. Lapin said the SU's proposal of 16 February—for a joint statement condemning American aggression—was also serious. 'The sense of his remarks was nevertheless that the Soviet Government would carefully study our proposal.'[52]

'Again and again,' Trevelyan reported, 'Mr Lapin came back to the point that if we make any statement about our initiative on Viet Nam, the Soviet Government will have to reply with a counter-statement.' Any British statement, the ambassador thought, would 'kill this approach stone dead, and most seriously minimise the chances of achieving anything with the Soviet Union on Viet Nam'. He recommended 'a complete blackout'. Foreign Office posts should be told 'to take no action and to ensure that no information gets out that we have taken an initiative'. No doubt the FO would ensure that 'special precautions' were taken to prevent leaks in Washington. 'I am saying nothing to colleagues here, except to ensure that the Americans say nothing.' Trevelyan thought that Lapin might have been expecting Britain to propose a conference and hoping that it would do so. 'The Soviet Government have been curiously silent on this and it may well have been their policy to try to get a proposal for a conference from us.'[53]

Any American indication of a further strike on North Vietnam, Trevelyan added, would make a Russian statement focus on condemnation.[54] Temporarily the strike was postponed, Harlech reported, but the US could not accept a ceasefire for any length of time.[55] Do not mention that consideration to Lapin, the FO told Trevelyan, on 22 February, but press him for a quick answer. Tell him that Britain had deferred any public reference to its approach. 'Nevertheless British opinion is keenly interested in this subject and it would be exceedingly difficult to remain silent beyond tomorrow evening. Unless we have by then reached agreement on the joint message ..., I would only say that we have been in touch with the Soviet Government with a view to seeing what might be done about Viet-Nam.' If necessary Trevelyan could accept a revised draft indicating a difference of view between the co-chairmen, provided it did not commit Britain to any criticism of US actions. But he should not agree to include a request for recipients to express their views on a conference. He should point out that the co-chairmen's message was 'primarily to discover whether there exists any basis for a settlement. Only if the replies indicate some possibility of narrowing the gap between the opposing positions would it be worthwhile for the Co-Chairmen to press for negotiations and a conference is only one of various possible forms of negotiation.' Even if not specifically asked, the recipients could express their views on a conference. 'There is no reason why the Co-Chairmen should attempt by the wording of their question to elicit a particular type of reply.'[56]

It was difficult, Harlech commented, to get the Americans to reveal their thoughts on long-term policy. The short-term difficulty was instability in Saigon. Silence on the long term might reflect genuine uncertainty about the course to follow. McNamara had told him on 22 February that three courses were open: (a) step up pressure without talks; (b) combine pressure and feelers; (c) stop attacks and agree to negotiations. Option (c), he said, was unacceptable, and he favoured (b). Apparently the president had still not made up his mind, but Harlech thought (b) most likely. At the same time, the Americans welcomed Britain's probe in Moscow as keeping open a channel of communication that had the advantage of engaging the Russians in a quasi-mediatory role. American determination could heighten the incentive to seek a peaceful way out and also urge restraint on Hanoi. 'There is little doubt that the Administration would like to extricate themselves from Viet Nam, but they are deterred not only by their attitude to China and their fear that a humiliating withdrawal from Indo-China would have disastrous effects on the whole area, including Thailand and Malaysia, but also by the repercussions which any such withdrawal would have throughout the world, and not least, in Europe, where the French would doubtless use this as evidence that, when it came to the pinch, the Americans could not be trusted to stick by their Allies.' The president seemed reluctant to make up his mind.[57] Indeed, bombing was held off till 2 March, though partly because of the weather.[58]

On 27 February Trevelyan summarised a speech Kosygin, back in Moscow, had given on TV. 'He told Soviet listeners for the first time that there was a real war on in Viet Nam, a war of foreign interventionists against the Vietnamese people; that American militarist circles (he was careful not to say the American Government) were entering on to the dangerous path of the extension of aggressive acts; that the armed acts of the United States against the sovereign State of the D.R.V. naturally caused serious anxiety to the Governments of many countries; that if the American imperialists continued their aggressive acts ..., the conflict ... would inevitably spread beyond its original limits'; and that the violation of international law and the UN Charter was 'a slippery path which might take one a very long way'. Kosygin addressed no threats to the US, but said that the SU could not 'remain indifferent' to the DRV's fate and would give it 'necessary help'. Aggression, he said, would not remain unpunished, though he did not say how. He forecast that the Americans would be unable to crush the national liberation movement. 'They would only increase the courage and stubbornness of the Vietnamese.' He demanded that they should withdraw—and from South Korea as well—and 'allow the people to decide their own fate'.

Kosygin attributed the bombings to the worst of motives: 'the United States were resorting to acts of military provocation in order to create a situation in which they could make one more attempt to break the will of the peoples of Indo-China.' But the policy would lead to 'total failure', as the realists recognised. He did not call for a conference on Vietnam (or Laos). 'He called for the strict observance of the Geneva Agreements to prevent the extension of the conflict and to find a path towards the solution of the problems of Indo-China at the negotiating table. The prime requisite for creating conditions for the search for paths leading to the normalization of the situation in Indo-China was the cessation of the aggressive acts of the United States against democratic Viet Nam.' The struggle in the South, he said, was one of the whole people, and the movement aimed at the end of foreign intervention 'and a national coalition Government, conducting a policy of independence, democracy and neutrality'. Three-quarters of the South and two-thirds of the population were 'already liberated'.[59]

What, Trevelyan asked, could be deduced from the speech? The Russians assumed that with South Vietnam substantially liberated, the problem was 'how to get the Americans out without major escalation'. The North Vietnamese did not seem to want a conference. Perhaps they feared it would give them less than the complete victory that seemed almost in reach. The demand for a coalition government in South Vietnam that the NLF had made might be intended 'both to reduce the pressures for a conference and to allay fears of a rapid and total Communist take-over'.

The Soviet government had apparently concluded that the US could not hold South Vietnam, but that its retaliatory raids on targets in North Vietnam were likely to increase. The North Vietnamese wanted more weapons, partly to defend themselves, and partly, though Kosygin did not say so, to enable operations in the South to be stepped up. The SU was willing to supply them, and that involved 'a risk of progressive escalation'. Kosygin might be worried that that would go too far, but he could not say so. The Russians 'may assume that the American forces will not carry retaliatory raids to a point which provokes Chinese intervention and a Korean-type war and that in the absence of retaliation on this scale the North Viet Namese and the Viet Cong will be able to continue and even expand their operations until they win'. Presumably they were also counting on the influence of 'realists' in the US and elsewhere.

The Soviet government accepted that its relations with the US would probably deteriorate at least temporarily. But that did not mean that it 'would regard with equanimity either a major extension of hostilities in Indo-China or a direct confrontation with the United States. They clearly want to avoid this, but are aware of the danger arising from the fact that they are not wholly in control of the situation.' Given the attitude of the North Vietnamese, the Russians were unwilling to call for a conference, but would not object if other governments arranged one. 'Kosygin's reference to talks "at the negotiating table" left every possibility open.' He did not refer to US 'prestige', though references to the issue occasionally appear in the press. It was 'an important element in the situation', but he thought that it was 'inevitable that at some stage the Americans will have to swallow their pride and get out'.

'What all this amounts to is an underlying Soviet assumption that the situation in Viet Nam will have to get worse before the United States Government can be brought to realize the inevitability of their withdrawal; that the risks involved are acceptable; that the expected deterioration in Soviet-American relations will be bearable, temporary and eventually reversible; that it will be possible to mobilize a good deal of support in the outside world against the adoption of a hard line by the United States Government; and that these problems and anxieties can at least be made to yield a few advantages to the C.P.S.U. in the Sino-Soviet dispute.'[60]

Oliver Wright in the PM's office thought Trevelyan's analysis 'bang on'. He himself had attended a CIA briefing on direct North Vietnamese involvement in South Vietnam, and it demonstrated that the Americans were in a 'hopeless' position there. 'The fact is that the Americans cannot win and cannot yet see any way of getting off the hook which will not damage their prestige internationally and the President's position domestically.' That explained his 'bear-with-a-sore-head attitude' in the phone conversation with the PM and 'the current absence of any Presidential "determination" on American policy in Washington'. Perhaps, 'with his passion for "consensus"', the president was 'waiting for domestic opinion ... to crystallise'. At the moment, it looked to be 'moving in favour of swallowing bitter pills, but is not yet ready to do so'. Wright thought that the best tactics for Britain were 'to keep away from the White House and concentrate on the State Department, where ways can be discussed which imply getting the United States off the hook without committing the White House either to admitting the existence of the hook or the desire to get off it. It is only when the President has got the politics of the situation sorted out that he will be ready to make a determination on the merits. It is not in our interest to badger the Administration: if the President, who is much more interested in domestic than in international affairs, suffers a domestic setback as a result of an international defeat, he will be less inclined to follow enlightened international policies for the rest of his term. And he still has nearly 8 years to go.'[61] 'Yes,' Wilson wrote. 'I very much agree.'[62] But he did badger.

Ten days later Trevelyan offered some further speculations. Lapin's approach of 16 February might have been designed to counter the impression that the SU was no longer interested in the co-chairmanship. Perhaps it was also intended to elicit a proposal for a conference from Britain, which it did not wish to make itself. Lapin's attitude on 20 February suggested that the SU then wanted to be seen as taking an active part as co-chairman. But no reply had ensued. The most plausible supposition was that the Chinese and Vietnamese were opposed to any action that might lead to a negotiation and were in no hurry to reply. Why then had the Soviet government approached the French on 23 February, specifically referring to a conference? Possibly it had gone ahead without consulting the Chinese or North Vietnamese, wanting to keep the idea of a conference alive. Alternatively, if, as the French thought, the Vietnamese and Chinese were consulted, 'the supposition is that though the latter do not want any Communist proposals for a conference, they would not object to the Russians eliciting such a proposal from the French, since this would have the effect of putting more pressure on the Americans and increasing the objections of world public opinion to their attacks on North Viet Nam.' The Russians' propaganda on Vietnam, Trevelyan added, had been less violent than expected. 'They give the impression of being unable to decide what to do next.' Visiting London, Andrei Gromyko was likely 'to be generally evasive but to close no doors'.[63]

Terence Garvey in Peking certainly thought China's line had hardened since the bombing and the Kosygin visit, 'at least in public. Chinese statements have not actually demanded American withdrawal as condition of a conference, but have stopped talking about having a conference at all. This may, of course, reflect only tactical desire to make life difficult for Russians, rather than real hardening of attitude.' Paye, the French ambassador, had, moreover, made 'rather rosy' assumptions, concluding, for example, that there could be something like the 'effective neutralisation' of South Vietnam.[64]

On 15 March, just as Gromyko was about to go to London, Roshchin offered an oral reply to the British approach and a draft message. Brimelow and he did not discuss it, as Gromyko was on his way. The text was a request that recipients should express their views on ending alleged American aggression, withdrawing US troops, and demanding that the US should observe the Geneva provisions.[65]

The foreign secretary met Gromyko on 16 March. Earlier in the day, Stewart told him, he had seen the disappointing Soviet reply. Gromyko said that all the governments involved had already expressed their views. Stewart said they had not dealt with the question of the basis on which a conference could be arranged or peace established. The main point, Gromyko insisted, was the attitude of the co-chairmen to events in Vietnam: in the Soviet view it was a matter of American aggression. In contrast, Stewart said, the UK considered the North Vietnamese had committed 'serious and continuing aggression against their Southern neighbour'. An aggressor could not lay down preliminary conditions for stopping his aggression, Gromyko declared: the aggression must stop first.[66] Gromyko also gave a press conference at the Russian embassy, 'a unique event'. The chief task, he said, was to end US aggression.[67] Gromyko discoursed on American wrong-headedness, the *Times* correspondent had written, but made no suggestions himself. 'The Soviet Government in fact appears still to be playing a waiting game. It is suggested that pressure from the Chinese leaves them little room for manoeuvre.'[68]

Gromyko 'stone-walled on every proposal to re-call any form of Geneva conference', Wilson later recollected, and also opposed Britain's suggestion of a limited conference comprising the two chairmen, the ICC powers, and parties to the fighting. He simply denounced the US and called for withdrawal.[69] His attitude was 'completely negative'. SEAD's conclusion was that the Russians had sounded their allies and found them 'intransigent'. But Stewart wanted to discuss a further British initiative with Rusk in Washington.[70] That, it seems, was for Britain alone to send the message, but Caccia and Stewart minuted that it should not be pressed if the Americans were doubtful.[71]

The time the Russians had taken to reply suggested that they might have entertained the proposal if not subject to pressure from China and North Vietnam to refuse to compromise, the Cabinet considered. Stewart proposed to explore on his visit to Washington whether the Americans would make some further public statement, including an indication that they were prepared to contemplate intergovernmental discussions about ending the conflict. 'In discussion it was agreed that there was no simple or obvious solution for a deadlock in which each party was seeking to insist that the other party must desist from aggression before there could be any question of negotiation. Nevertheless we should seek to persuade the United States Government to recognise the potential opportunities implicit in a situation in which the Soviet Government must be increasingly resentful of Chinese pressure; and we should therefore endeavour to ascertain how far they might be prepared, despite apparent Soviet intransigence, to acquiesce in our maintaining our initiative to promote a negotiated settlement of the conflict.'[72]

Rolling Thunder

Further air attacks had now taken place. At first, Etherington-Smith had commented, the basis on which the air strikes were started was 'far from clear'. It was thought they might be confined to occasions when American targets had been attacked 'in a spectacular manner'. The statement issued after the further raids on 2 March showed that this was not the case, since its references to Northern aggression included instances of Viet Cong terrorism against Vietnamese civilians. It thus seemed that the intention was 'to retaliate against Northern interference in the South as such and to go on doing so while that interference, whatever may be its form, continues. … In other words the attacks are to become a form of continuous military pressure on the North.' A conversation with Maxwell Taylor had confirmed that: attacks would continue until Hanoi showed that it was prepared to halt its aggression, and that meant 'not only that Viet Cong operations in the South should cease or at least be substantially diminished, but that Hanoi should stop sending men and supplies into the South'.

So much was clear, and, Etherington-Smith thought, understandable. Much else about American intentions was far from clear. If, as seemed likely, the Hanoi government did not respond, would the Americans increase their pressure, and if so how far were they prepared to go? So far only military installations close to the 17th parallel had been attacked. 'There are obviously a number of possible stages between this and the bombing of Hanoi. Do the Americans really expect to be able to force the Hanoi Government to cease their interference? If not, what exactly do they hope to achieve by their action?' Etherington-Smith's impression, drawn from conversations in Saigon, was that the Americans had 'not yet decided on their ultimate policy'. The air strikes against the North were 'intended to relieve a difficult situation in the South by introducing a new military factor which at least may bring limited advantages'. A officer of the Military Assistance Command (Vietnam) (MAC[V]) told Etherington-Smith 'that, since the West had been losing the battle in the political and counter-subversive field, they should concentrate on the military sector in order to gain time'. There were indications that the Americans were expanding their whole military effort and preparing to exercise more direct control.

How far they were prepared to increase pressure by extending their attacks to more sensitive targets remained to be seen. Etherington-Smith did not expect them to go very far 'for the present'. 'Their purpose seems rather to be to give the North every chance of reacting to this pressure without it appearing that they are being subjected to extreme intimidation. The conduct of such a strategy obviously calls for the utmost care and control both in planning and execution.' So far that seemed to be understood in Washington: 'action against the North has been studiously restrained and moderate', though that moderation 'must reduce to some extent the credibility of the air threat to the North'.

What would be the reaction of the North? Etherington-Smith did not expect any early reduction in support for the Viet Cong insurgency, nor much direct disruption of the flow of aid. Hanoi might calculate that the Americans would be 'restrained by fear of adverse international reactions'. But if they were not, the North could not be certain that China would risk war with the US in order to come to its aid, and in any case would not wish to be overrun by Chinese. 'Moreover, since the Hanoi communists are confident that the South will in any case be theirs in the long run, why risk such unpleasant consequences to get it a little sooner?' Such an argument might also appeal to the Russians. Etherington-Smith concluded that if the US seemed prepared to press its attacks to the limit, Hanoi might modify its policy, but the change would only be tactical. They would switch to the political field, encouraged, too, by signs of demoralisation in the South and the existence of neutralist sentiment. A temporary halt in Viet Cong operations might be accompanied by a move towards a negotiated settlement. Meanwhile, 'every manoeuvre and subterfuge' would be used to improve the Communists' position, so that the eventual settlement would be a step towards the ultimate goal.

The final outcome would depend on the establishment in the South of 'a political and social system which can resist communism', the ambassador believed. What the current American action might achieve was 'to make the communist task more difficult and to gain time for a further attempt to retrieve the situation in the South'. Meanwhile, the Americans were not yet looking for a negotiated settlement. Nor would they be wise to do so, 'unless they become finally convinced that the battle is lost in South Vietnam', since 'in present circumstances it appears inconceivable that any settlement would not be to the advantage of the communists'. Robert Thompson believed that the Americans should 'play things long, in the hope of a political improvement in the South or of some other development which could help to stem the communist tide'.

It was 'regrettable' that South Vietnam was suffering 'further upheavals', and the outlook was 'disquieting'. 'The air strikes ... have however given a temporary boost to Vietnamese morale and created a better atmosphere from which the beginnings of a recovery might develop. With General Khanh at last out of the way it is perhaps possible that things may pick up.'[73] Thompson's views had already been expressed in a letter to Peck; but there he seemed to see playing it long as 'helping general policy in S.E. Asia, especially over Indonesia, rather than suggesting that it can be expected to yield any real solution in Viet Nam in the long run'.[74]

Peck had also talked to Michael Forrestal, who had recently been in Saigon, 'emphasising that while of course we were solid in our support of the American action we did, as friends, want to know how they saw the situation progressing'. The Americans, he said, viewed the air strikes 'as a continuing process. Now that the first traumatic experience of U.S. strikes had occurred, international opinion would develop a callus over the sore spot and it was likely that they could be more easily continued over a period.' The Americans were conscious of the risks of provoking the North Vietnamese, and more particularly the Chinese, into 'more serious action. They envisaged a very careful co-ordination of the military and political effects of these strikes.' But Forrestal admitted that such was difficult to achieve and that 'the military once they had been authorised to bomb was very likely to overdo the dose'. The recent attack on Quang Khé by 160 aircraft he thought 'an excessive use of force'. He also recognised that 'bombing frequently strengthened the resolve of the people to resist'. But, over time, he thought, North Vietnam's capacity to supply the Viet Cong could be 'seriously damaged'. Peck stressed 'the need for the Americans to state their objectives, the circumstances under which they would be prepared to negotiate and the need for keeping channels open for possible discussion with the Russians and others'.[75]

In the House of Commons, left-wing Labourites proposed a motion under which the British government would declare that it did not support the extension of military operations to North Vietnam 'beyond retaliation in kind'.[76] The British government, Mac Bundy told the president, were 'nervous' because of 'a lot of yammering from their own [Thomas] Churches and [George] McGoverns'. They wanted to make explorations as to the possibility of talks and say they had been in consultation with the US.[77] Following a Rusk telegram, Wilson was able to tell the House on 9 March that if there were clear evidence of the end of North Vietnamese aggression, the US would be prepared to take its troops out.[78]

The day before, Marines sent to defend the base had landed at Danang, storming grimly ashore, as *The Times* put it, with a squad of press photographers barring the way, and Vietnamese girls and servicewomen 'intent on ensnaring them with flower garlands'. A 'signal', said *The Australian*.[79] General William Westmoreland had late in February asked for two Marine assault battalions to protect the airbase being built up at Danang. Taylor did not support the request: the troops were not trained for jungle warfare, and by taking direct part, the US would be giving a disincentive to the South Vietnamese to rowing their own boat. And once American troops were fighting and dying, it would be virtually impossible to reduce the US role and withdraw.[80] The step had nevertheless been taken.

An item in *The Times* of 12 March the prime minister found disturbing: the president, it said, would not contemplate negotiation until the North withdrew its guerrillas.[81] He called Ambassador Bruce in. Was the US altering its position? He had understood that the US would be able to remove its troops from South Vietnam if North Vietnamese aggression stopped. Now cessation seemed to be a prerequisite for negotiation. Even if the story were untrue, US policy had changed. The British government had agreed to support measured responses specifically related to provocation. That had changed without reference to a loyal ally. Britain could live with the original plan—stick and olive branch—and even with some toughening, if there were also some public recognition of readiness to negotiate. But if things went on as they were, the difficulty between the US and the UK would be as big as over Suez.[82] SEAD suggested that the US was still following the policy of December 1964.[83] Was concern over the Left the cause of this outburst? Perhaps especially so, given the item was so public. The PM had to be able to say he had protested.

In Washington M.N.F. Stewart was rather aghast. Before the PM went in to bat again, he should be warned of Louis Heren's unreliability. The Americans had not changed their policy: the British had, he maintained, been told they were moving into Stage II. What had been unsatisfactory was the failure to be frank about policies and intentions. 'They have made their ultimate objectives abundantly clear in public, but have never revealed the conditions on which they would be prepared to negotiate and the minimum objectives they would settle for.' Perhaps the foreign secretary would get something out of them.[84]

How far were the Americans 'consulting' the British over shifts in their policy, or at least keeping them informed, Peck wondered. They had been kept informed of the various strikes, and basic policy had not changed. The administration stood on the declaration Stevenson had made at the UN that if there were 'a prompt and assured cessation of aggression by Hanoi', US troops would be withdrawn. The emphasis, Peck assumed, was on 'assured', the implication being that US troops would be withdrawn only 'when an effective system of control has been set up to deter any further aggression, subversive or otherwise. In other words, it is the U.S. end-objective of negotiations for a settlement, not the basis on which negotiations might begin.' The position on that remained obscure, he told M.N.F. Stewart. Would the Americans agree to it when the DRV, increasingly pressed by air strikes, told the VC to 'lay off'? What if the DRV decided 'to grin and bear the raids'? Would the Americans agree to talks if an all-round ceasefire were agreed? But how could that be arranged without talks, or at least mediation, between the interested parties, including the Viet Cong, if the DRV continued to disclaim authority over them? US thinking on such questions was not clear, 'and at this stage it may be useless to raise them officially'.

On the military front, should the FO conclude that the Americans were moving into phase 2 without the clear-cut presidential decision that preceded phase 1, i.e., bombing of Laos routes and retaliatory strikes in North Vietnam? It looked as if a slide into phase 2 had begun when 'responsive attacks' were made 'in the context of general Viet Cong aggression and not specifically "tit-for-tat"'. The latest targets, moreover, were north of the 19th parallel. Perhaps the points could be cleared up at the SD, 'if this can be done without giving the appearance of nagging at them'. Or they could be left for the secretary of state's visit.[85] Policy had not changed, Stewart responded. Militarily the US had moved into phase 2. To the political questions Peck raised, he repeated, the embassy had never secured satisfactory answers. They should indeed be left for the secretary of state's visit.[86]

Stewart's Visit to Washington

No early Russian assistance could be expected in persuading the Chinese and North Vietnamese to negotiate, the brief for the visit began. Continued American military pressure would therefore be needed, Britain realised, 'both to hold the position in the South and also to induce the Communists to talk instead of fighting'. It was nevertheless 'important' that Britain should continue its efforts 'to find a basis for negotiations, even though these can scarcely be expected to bear much fruit at present'. Such initiatives would complement American military pressure by 'keeping channels open for future negotiations' and make it 'much easier' to justify support for US policies to British public opinion. The proposal was to develop the idea Rusk put tentatively to Gordon Walker, that Britain alone should send out a message along the lines originally suggested for the co-chairmen. The draft—on which the American view had been sought—was stronger, since a message from one co-chairman had 'less force' than one from both. Moreover, Gromyko had made 'one good criticism': 'there was no point in requesting views from Governments who had repeatedly expressed them already'. Britain thus proposed to ask members of the Geneva conference and the ICC powers for their views, not on the nature of the ultimate settlement, but on the basis for initiating negotiations directed towards achieving one.[87]

A background to the brief was headed by the question: Was US policy aimed at inducing North Vietnam to negotiate or to capitulate? Rusk's reaction to Britain's proposed message would probably provide an indication of US objectives. He might suggest that negotiations would never produce an acceptable settlement. If so, the secretary of state could ask 'whether military action alone—whether in the form of pressure on the North or as pacification in the South—could produce an acceptable solution leading to a trouble-free South Viet-Nam'. That seemed 'improbable': some compromise was 'likely to prove inevitable'. There was still 'sufficient determination in Saigon to justify the U.S. in running the risks inherent in their present policy and, if political stability can lead to a re-establishment of effective administration, a partial recovery is possible. Morale has sagged least within the Armed Forces, and if there were a sudden move by one or more factional groups towards an immediate compromise with the North, the Army would almost certainly act to prevent it. The danger is that, in the longer term, the present recovery of morale may be short-lived and that the military and administrative situation will continue to suffer erosion to the point where the Armed Forces can no longer count on the essential minimum of popular support they need to continue the struggle.'

Meanwhile, Rusk asked whether Britain was thinking of bringing the ICC governments into play now that the co-chairmen approach seemed to be dead: he would like to discuss that with the foreign secretary.[88] That fitted in with Britain's proposed approach, Cable wrote, but he doubted that the initiative should be confined to the three ICC powers. 'China and North Viet-Nam are even less likely to be influenced by an approach that excludes them. So perhaps is the Soviet Union. France (as last year over Laos) will certainly be annoyed and may adopt a still more unhelpful attitude out of pique.' Poland, moreover, might have to make 'a tougher reply' if it were the only Communist state approached. 'If all eleven countries are approached, the United States and South Viet-Nam will have a renewed chance to state their case, the Canadian reply will be helpful and those from Cambodia, France, India, Laos and perhaps Poland are at least likely to be sufficiently moderate to show up the intransigence of the Chinese, North Viet-Namese and perhaps Russians.' That would have 'a better propaganda effect' than the results of an approach to the ICC: 'one embarrassing Indian reply (mutual cease-fire and Conference); one tough Polish reply (American cease-fire); and one probably half-hearted endorsement of the U.S. position from Canada.'

Britain did not, 'in any case, expect practical results at present from either approach', Cable continued. Its objectives must therefore be 'to present U.S. policy in a more favourable light', 'to keep open for future use a potential channel for negotiation', and to make it easier to continue supporting US policy. Those objectives were better served by approaching the members of the Geneva conference as well as the ICC.[89]

The only serious question, McGeorge Bundy told the president, was the Wilson government's problem in holding to its support for the US on Vietnam. The prime minister was accused of uncritical support for the US, currying favour with the president, who let it be known in return that he would be an unwelcome visitor to Washington. The 'cooler men' in the Labour Party, 'as distinct from the Left Wing wild men', were 'said to be losing their patience'. This was, Bundy continued, 'a wild misstatement of the situation. None of it takes account of the very great damage which Wilson did to himself by his outrageous phone call to you—a phone call which has never been publicized.' But David Bruce said the situation in the Labour Party was 'real'. One course might be to let the Labour Party struggle with its own problems. 'The difficulty with this course is that since Wilson prefers his own survival to solidarity with us, he would be mortally tempted to begin to make critical noises about us, thus appealing to his own party and to the natural nationalism of many independent Englishmen.'

'The alternative is to see what is the least we can offer the British in return for continued solidarity in support of the essentials of our policy in Vietnam.' Bruce thought that the two governments should say that there was a 'full and continuous' exchange of views on the subject. 'Then we can put on some parsley about how glad we are to have Mr Stewart and how much we look forward to the Prime Minister's visit. In return, the British should undertake not to advocate negotiations and not to go back on their existing announced approval of our present course of action. They should limit themselves to expressions of hope that a path to a peaceful settlement will come, plus expressions of alertness, as Co-Chairman of the Geneva

Conference, to any opportunities for peaceful settlement which may develop in the future.'

Ambassador Bruce had left for Washington in advance of the foreign secretary's talks on 19 March. Before he went, Caccia gave him an account of the Gromyko talks, and then suggested he should bear in mind what the PM had said on the 12th. Two things were of particular concern to Britain. 'The first was to have an assurance that we knew exactly what it was the United States Government were trying to do, and how far they intended to escalate their military action in order to persuade the North Vietnamese to give up their aggression.' That was largely a confidential matter between governments. The second issue, one of 'public presentation', was 'the inadequacy of American public statements so far to explain to the world at large, in satisfactory terms, their conditions for talks leading to a settlement'. The British knew something on both points, 'but not enough either in private or in public'.

Bruce said he understood that. 'He could say so because he could not himself give me any full or clear statement on either head.' He did not know whether his government hoped that bombing up to the 19th parallel would bring sufficient pressure on the North Vietnamese 'to persuade them to desist from their present degree of aggression in South Vietnam', nor, if that failed, 'what the President's might be about responsive action … further north, such as military targets in the Hanoi area'. He would try to prepare the ground in Washington, but he thought the foreign secretary should speak to Rusk and the president 'extremely plainly on these points'. The president would be 'quick to see the difficulty for H.M.G. He was unlikely to take anything said amiss, and the only risk … was rather that the President might misinterpret the degree of H.M.G.'s concern if it were not expressed in terms which a Texan would consider sufficiently direct when matters at issue were of real importance.'[90] 'Yes, indeed,' wrote Foreign Secretary Stewart,[91] though it did not seem very good advice.

At press conferences the president had faced down questions about world pressure for negotiations. 'We have not had any indication …—any indication—from anyone,' he said on 13 March, 'that Hanoi is prepared or willing or ready to stop doing what it is doing against its neighbours.' He was carrying out the policies of Ike and JFK, he insisted on 20 March. The actions taken were made necessary by the aggressions of others. 'No one threatens their regime.' The people of Southeast Asia had 'the right to live side by side in peace and independence. And if this little country does not have that right then—the question is what will happen to the other hundred little countries that want to preserve that right.'[92]

Speaking to Etherington-Smith on 13 March, Maxwell Taylor confirmed that the attacks would continue until the North ceased its aggression. Hanoi, he thought, would eventually be brought to do that, though there was yet no sign of it. Asked what would happen if it did not yield, he said that 'would make things very simple, because Hanoi and the North would be destroyed'. Asked if that meant that, if necessary, the attacks would be carried to the limit, he confirmed that was so, 'though the scale of future attacks and the frequency with which they should be carried out would all require the most careful consideration and no far-reaching decisions had yet been taken'. Taylor added that this was his personal opinion, that of 'a bloodthirsty military man', and that final decisions would be taken in Washington. Nevertheless, Etherington-Smith thought, his views might not be at variance at least with those at the Pentagon.[93]

In a talk with Lord Walston on 22 March Robert Komer, Africa/Middle East specialist at the White House, 'implied that the U.S. have accepted that their eventual retreat from Viet-Nam is inevitable but this retreat can only be considered after demonstration of their overwhelming military power. This they are now doing and it should go a long way towards minimising the domino theory.' Coupled with that the US and the UK should concert economic assistance to neighbouring countries. Walston concluded that an approach to the president would be well received if it included wholehearted support for American policy, including the stepping up of air attacks, on condition that they had a definite term, say two months, not made public, and that at 'an appropriate moment' in that period the US would declare that attacks would stop forthwith if North Vietnam and China would come to talks 'at any place and with no further pre-conditions'. Komer had stressed that it would be 'easier for public opinion to take intensive bombing for a finite period than a gradual but indefinite increase in the number of attacks'.[94] The approach represented a shift from the relentless escalation envisaged in 1964. It also looked forward to Baltimore.

The record of the conversation did not, however, reach the foreign secretary before he began his talks with a private discussion with Rusk on the morning of 22 March 1965. 'He said that the aim of United States policy was to try to bring about some sign on the part of the North Vietnamese that they were prepared to cease their infiltrations and support for the Viet Cong in South Viet Nam.' Stewart pressed him to turn that into a positive statement, since it would then be 'much easier for public opinion and … enable the United States allies to continue to back them'. Washington could say that 'if the North Vietnamese were prepared to give such an assured sign the United States would be prepared to enter into discussions or negotiations'. The difficulty with that, Rusk responded, was that to mention 'negotiations' might encourage the North Vietnamese to think the US was 'weakening', and it might also have 'a bad effect on the South Vietnamese'. The policy was therefore to 'wait for a sign of change by the other side without talking about readiness to negotiate themselves. The North Vietnamese knew perfectly well what sort of sign would be needed.'

Stewart told Rusk of the UK's idea that it might ask the 14 powers 'to state their views on the basis on which negotiations might be initiated for discussion of a settlement on Viet Nam'. His first reaction was against it. 'His view, now that Russia had rejected our idea that the two Co-Chairmen should ask the countries concerned to state their views *on the situation generally* was that we should proceed by ourselves with this.' Rusk offered 'satisfactory assurances' that the US had no intention of sending ground troops into North Vietnam. He also said that the UK would be given 'fair warning in advance' before any 'switch' in US policy.[95]

Discussions on Vietnam resumed the following morning with officials present. Stewart began by referring to the reported use of poison gas. Rusk thought it was the kind of gas used for riot control. Stewart alluded to the 'extremely strong feelings ... aroused by the use of gas and napalm bombs which inflicted undue suffering and were of limited military value'. Rusk stressed the military value of napalm. 'This Viet-Namese war was not a Sunday-school party. It was a rough business.' If it was justified militarily, that should be explained in advance, Stewart said, 'not allowed to come out in the way it had'.

Stories about the use of 'gas' by the South Vietnam forces had appeared in the US press. A press release had described it as 'a type of tear gas'. That did nothing to stop the controversy aroused. 'Gas is a wretched means to achieve even the most valid ends,' the *New York Times* declared. MPs in Britain had been in uproar. The foreign secretary told the Press Club he had raised the matter with Rusk. 'I am, in fact, asking your Government—to quote your own Declaration of Independence—to display a decent respect for the opinions of mankind.' Johnson fumed, but officials persuaded him not to write to Wilson in protest.[96]

Stewart had also referred to the anxiety felt in the UK by a report that Maxwell Taylor had said that there was no limit to the extension of the war and that the US might enter the ground fighting. 'Whether or not the war escalated would depend upon what the other side did,' Rusk responded. Stewart said he understood that there was no plan to bomb the Hanoi area, but that the US was 'unwilling to say this specifically'. There was indeed no such plan, Rusk replied: it might subject the planes to MIG attack. The

Americans were, however, 'not prepared to impose limits on their own action without knowing what the other side might do. If they were to say that they were not prepared to bomb the Hanoi area this would also mean the removal of something which must be a worry to the North Viet-Namese.' The US had made it clear that it did not aim to destroy the regime but to stop the aggression. In answer to Stewart, Rusk said the UK would be informed in advance if the US thought of bombing the Hanoi area, and it would be informed of 'any major changes' in US policy. He referred to the president's statement that the US was not seeking to widen the war. Taylor's reported statement did not alter that.

Rusk thought the US might take up the suggestion that the UK had put to the Russians and the French that the co-chairmen should ask the interested powers for their views on the Vietnam question. The US might address the co-chairmen and the ICC members, giving them a reasoned account of South Vietnam, Laos and perhaps Cambodia, which would serve as 'a peg' on which the UK might 'hang an enquiry of the other interested parties for their views'. What would the statement contain? Stewart asked. It might refer to the need to respect the 1954 and 1962 agreements, deal with the activities of the North Vietnamese in 'crossing the frontier into South Viet-Nam', and 'express regret that there was no indication from the other side that they were yet ready to stop these incursions'. But the Americans would not 'spell out their pre-conditions for a conference because to do so would make everybody muscle-bound'. Many people were 'willing to be the midwife to a conference'. The US did not object, nor did it object to contacts designed 'to find out what the possibilities were'. Stewart thought it would be 'unfortunate' if the US made no reference to a conference. The US did not want one that would be 'fruitless', Rusk responded, 'and which might just end in a declaration of war'. Caccia suggested that the message might be 'so phrased that it could carry the clear implication that the United States would see no objection to a conference in certain circumstances'. Rusk said he was discussing the whole matter with the president: it was tentative till he had done so. He promised to show Stewart the message in draft. It was agreed that the British idea of asking the parties to express their views on the basis of which negotiations might be held should be 'held over for the time being'. Rusk was doubtful about it: in any case it would be best for the UK to await the suggested US message.[97]

Stewart was closeted with Johnson for 15 minutes, then others joined them, including Bruce. The president, the foreign secretary reported, said he faced three alternatives: full-scale attack on North Vietnam, quitting, doing nothing. None were acceptable: hence his present policy. Military measures would be 'appropriate, fitting and measured', but if necessary they might include an attack on Hanoi.[98]

LBJ, Bruce noted, was 'in talkative form. It was great theatre; he fed us oratorical sandwiches, with layers of gravity and levity.' He 'must have puzzled the British by the alternations of his manner. He told Stewart he had no objections whatever to negotiations if any one could offer a reasonable prospect of their succeeding.' After the foreign secretary had left, the president told Bundy and Bruce that he had not offered 'a single practical or helpful suggestion', nor had de Gaulle, nor any other foreigner. He repeated what he had told Stewart about 'fierce domestic pressures on him. Some favoured abandonment of all our commitments in the East, and retreat to Hawaii. Others wanted us to bomb the hell out of China. Others would kill all the civilians, as well as military, in the Hanoi district. He intended to continue to make measured responses to aggression from North Vietnam until it ceased. We had obligated ourselves under three presidents to assist the South Vietnamese to preserve their liberties, and that commitment would be carried out. He thought it insulting for politicians to come chasing over to see him, to expound for home consumption their condemnatory statements from the White House steps, unless they had practicable solutions to offer for American problems.'[99] So much for the advice Bruce had given to Stewart, not to mention the special relationship.

Subsequently, LBJ made a statement to his Cabinet, reported in *The Times*. He was ready to go anywhere, anytime, to meet anyone 'whenever there is promise of progress towards an honourable peace'. The US sought 'no more than a return to the essentials of the agreement of 1954'. Aggression must be stopped, and the US would support South Vietnam. The statement, said *The Times*, 'left much unexplained'.[100] A press release spoke of 'a reliable arrangement to guarantee the independence and security of all in Southeast Asia'.[101]

Conference on Cambodia?

From Hanoi, British Consul-General E.F. Woods commented on the effects of the bombing. The material result included the destruction of ammunition dumps and radar installations and the loss of man-hours to industry and agriculture. That could not be questioned. He was more doubtful about the psychological effects. The Canadian delegation, he thought, exaggerated it. 'In my opinion there is no indication that north [*sic*] Vietnam is any more prepared to agree to a negotiated settlement now than it was a month ago. It is anybody's guess how long it will be before the strain on the national economy and internal political "solidarity" will compel the government to adopt a less intransigent attitude.' But the Canadian theory was premature.[102] At SEAD Donald Murray agreed.[103]

Britain, Stewart had told the French ambassador, shared the US view that a precondition for a conference was 'that the North Vietnamese must abandon their aggression in South Vietnam. It might be possible to seal off the border between north and south. But there would inevitably be difficulties about controlling a cease-fire because there was not a clearly defined front between the two sides, as there had been in Korea. There was also the question of whether the Viet Cong would stop fighting even if Governments agreed on a cease-fire.' The danger the French saw, Geoffrey de Courcel replied, was that if the present situation continued, 'the South Viet Nam forces might simply stop fighting'. He thought Russia and China really wanted a conference 'despite their stiff official attitudes'. One way of making progress might be to start with a conference on Laos rather than Vietnam. That might be more acceptable to the US, Stewart thought.[104]

In Phnom Penh Sihanouk had convened a Conference of Indochinese Peoples, which resolved on 8 March that a conference guaranteeing Cambodia's neutrality, and another on Laos, could contribute to the return of peace to Indochina.[105] A conference would check US aggression against Cambodia, Chen Yi responded.[106] 'It would suit the Chinese to have a conference in being which was nominally confined to Cambodia and Laos,' the FO considered. 'If the going got too hot for the Chinese in Viet Nam, the conference could be switched to control the situation there without the loss of face to the Chinese and the D.R.V. which would be involved in reversing their present line and asking for a separate negotiation on Viet Nam.' But from the US standpoint 'it seems to us that all the previous arguments against a conference on Cambodia (in particular the effect on South Vietnamese morale) remain valid. From our point of view it is hard to see how any useful agreement would be reached on either Cambodia or Laos as long as the issue in Viet Nam remains undecided. If the United States Government ever do reach the point of finding a conference acceptable, then this would surely have to deal with the whole of Indo-China, as in 1954.'[107]

The bombing, Brèthes repeated, had hardened China's position. The DRV was unlikely to give in, even if the bombing extended to dykes and industrial areas. Then the US would have no cards to play 'unless they took the war into China or started using nuclear weapons. ... The confrontation was total—the only escape route seemed to be an oblique approach through some subject where the face of both sides was not totally engaged. This was why the French thought a conference on Cambodia could be useful as providing a lead-in to negotiations or at least a dialogue on Vietnam.'[108] In Warsaw Sir George Clutton pointed out that using a conference on Cambodia as a blind for initiating talks on Vietnam was 'an old Polish idea'.[109]

Manac'h restated the French position: given the Chinese demand for the withdrawal of US troops from Laos and Vietnam, there was 'no present prospect of a conference to deal with either of these countries'. The Russians also had their difficulties. The French were now in favour of a conference on Cambodia, 'whose problems were less intractable, and which could be extended to Laos and eventually to Vietnam without any of the parties having to withdraw from their publicly announced positions'.[110]

When in Washington, Wilson had mentioned to Rusk the idea of sending Gordon Walker on a fact-finding mission to Hanoi as a representative of the co-chairman. Rusk had no objection, but asked that the visit should be 'only one step of what might perhaps be described as a general fact-finding tour of the Far East'.[111] The US would neither approve nor disapprove, William Bundy indicated. Approving would suggest that Gordon Walker was going on behalf of the US and preparing for negotiations without any sign that the other side was interested in a peaceful settlement. But the US would not wish to disapprove 'an effort by an ally who carried the onerous burden of the co-chairmanship'.[112]

Wilson told the House of Commons that British policy was still 'to continue contacts and consultation with those most involved to discover whether there might be a possible basis for a negotiated settlement', and the government had decided to send the former foreign secretary on a fact-finding tour of the region, Malaysia as well as Vietnam in mind.[113] The most obvious advantage for the British government, *The Times* suggested, was to put off criticism from the left wing of the Labour Party.[114]

Since the US neither produced its own promised statement of policy on Vietnam, nor agreed to Britain's making the approach to the Geneva and ICC powers recently discussed in Washington, the only initiative left to Britain, Peck wrote on 1 April 1965, was to act unilaterally on the lines proposed to Gromyko. It would make the approach more palatable if it could be linked with Gordon Walker's visit.[115] The message went out that day. It invited the 1954 Geneva and the ICC powers to give their views on Vietnam, and in particular on the circumstances in which a peaceful settlement could be reached. It expressed the hope that the visit of the foreign secretary's special representative, Patrick Gordon Walker—it did not say the co-chairman's special representative—would give the governments of the countries he visited an opportunity for further discussion of their views.[116] The consul-general in Hanoi was instructed to send the message to the Foreign Affairs Bureau.[117]

In Moscow on 3 April Kuznetsov gave Trevelyan an oral communication proposing the convening of a conference on Cambodia.[118] This idea the FO followed up in Washington. Did the State Department see a move towards a Cambodia conference as fatal for South Vietnamese morale, as it had in 1964? There was advantage in 'keeping open a line of communication and discussion which might eventually help in Vietnam'. The FO would like to avoid sending 'our standard refusal'.[119]

The Quai was in favour. A Cambodia conference would be 'a useful start in tackling the Indo-China problem and ... open the way for discussions on Vietnam'. If Johnson's Baltimore speech of 7 April prompted hopeful reactions, a Cambodia conference would be less opportune, Brèthes thought, as it might not then seem 'the only way out of the impasse'.[120] The speech did not, however, produce reactions of that nature.

Baltimore

Lyndon Johnson had visited Southeast Asia as vice president in 1961. Before he left, Arthur Goldschmidt, his old New Deal friend, now at the UN, had showed him plans for Mekong dams: it showed how four countries could work together despite 'a lot of fussing'. 'It's a great thing when people of such different cultures can get together on power,' LBJ commented. On his tour he met U Nyun, the secretary-general of the Economic Commission for Asia and the Far East (ECAFE). He said the project envisaged not only dams and conservation but highway construction, linking 'old caravan routes and existing roads to provide an international highway that eventually will connect Asia and Europe'. The vice president, his Tennessee Valley Authority experience in mind, interrupted: 'I am a river man.'[121] Senator George McGovern, South Dakota, PhD in History, had advocated ending the war, neutralising North and South Vietnam, and cooperative planning to develop the Mekong to benefit all Vietnamese. McGovern saw the president in vain in late March. 'Goddam it, George, don't give me another history lesson.'[122] But the idea found its way into his speech at Johns Hopkins on 7 April, when he offered the DRV talks 'without posing any preconditions' and, making a reference to the Tennessee Valley Authority, also held out a 'billion-dollar carrot' in the form of an economic development programme for the Mekong in which North Vietnam might participate. An aide had found that the US contribution to the Mekong project so far had been USD5 million, less than four days' military aid. The State Department wanted the reference removed from the draft. After meeting Goldschmidt at Camp David—he had argued that the New Deal closed the gap between North and South in the US—the president put it back in. 'Uncle Ho can't turn me down,' he said.[123] He could. '[S]tinking dollars,' exclaimed Hanoi Radio.[124] It was a 'big swindle', said the *People's Daily*, the offer of unconditional discussions that Johnson made a 'hoax', accompanied as it was by 'three preposterous conditions'.[125] Those included an independent South Victnam.[126]

'This isn't going to work, Mac,' the famous columnist Walter Lippman told Bundy. 'It's just a disguised demand for capitulation.'[127] In fact, James Carter suggests, the administration never believed the approach would bring Hanoi to negotiate. The address offered nothing of substance. The objective, Johnson made clear, was to bring about 'the independence of South Vietnam', and the offer was to negotiate with 'governments', thus excluding the FLN. The speech briefly attracted some praise at home and abroad. 'In the end,' Carter judges, 'Lyndon Johnson's peace and economic development initiative was one of a number of political tools he hoped would allow for escalation and war, without provoking public debate that would detract from his Great Society domestic agenda.'[128] The president, Logevall concludes, had 'signalled no real change in administration policy, no slackening in the drive to defeat the Vietcong.'[129]

Wilson welcomed the speech, however.[130] The British embassy in Washington had had advance information of it. Given Johnson's declared readiness for unconditional negotiations—he had, in fact, said 'discussions'[131]—'the onus of pre-conditions now falls firmly on Communist side', the FO suggested. 'This puts the United States and ourselves in an advantageous position, but the advantage may progressively diminish unless we maintain momentum. The immediate prospects of a Communist response do not look very bright but there are a number of possibilities which we ought now to examine alongside the various alternatives or discussions which President Johnson outlined in his speech.' If the US thought the aim could be talks 'on the side', a Cambodia conference would offer a better chance than one on Laos, where the SU would probably object to extending the framework beyond Article 19. Alternatively, it might be possible to work towards a conference on all aspects of Indochina. If the overriding consideration was to maintain the military policy, 'we might also look at the idea of Panmunjom-type unconditional discussions with no commitment (and self-evidently no ceasefire) until an agreement of some kind had been reached'. The FLN could not be a party to any talks. If the Chinese insisted, 'the possibility of progress through "cease-fire" talks must probably be discounted'.

'We must not overlook that the Soviet Government are now in a dilemma.' Most world opinion would be behind the president's stand. A further possibility might therefore be to try to reactivate the co-chairmanship over Vietnam by proposing that a Geneva-type conference should be called immediately on the basis of the president's offer. The SU was probably in no position to accept one, and 'the end result might be a continued stalemate on present propaganda positions with no alternative but to continue the present military policy in the hope that the North Vietnamese will crack'. Nevertheless, the proposal would demonstrate 'that we are not simply waiting for a response' to the president's initiative. Discussions about a conference were 'most likely to produce the sort of signal from the North Vietnamese and Chinese for which we are now looking'. But the UK would also like to discuss with the SD a 'frontal approach' through the co-chairmanship.[132]

Trevelyan saw every advantage in agreeing to the Soviet proposal for a conference on Cambodia and in proposing joint invitations at an early date. Although there had been no indications in Moscow that the Russians would wish or be able to use it 'for a sideways approach to discussions on Viet Nam', the possibility could not be excluded. 'If the North Vietnamese agree to come, we may be able to approach the Viet Nam question indirectly. If they do not, because of the American bombing, a difference between the Russians and North Viet Nam will be exposed.' Communist propaganda would be deployed to present the continuation of the bombing as making the opening of talks impossible. A conference on Vietnam could not be directly set up while it continued. 'Our aim should surely be to leave it possible for the Americans to use the at least temporary cessation of bombing of North Viet Nam as a political weapon to bring about a cease-fire and conference on reasonable terms.' If the UK now proposed a conference on Indochina, including Vietnam, the Russians would respond that the bombing must cease. 'This would make a conference on Viet Nam more improbable than ever, as it will put the Americans under pressure to which they will not submit.'[133]

In Washington Sir Patrick Dean, Harlech's successor, thought that the purpose of the Baltimore speech was 'primarily to strengthen the position of the United States *vis-à-vis* their allies and the non-aligned nations and to put the onus for continuation of the fighting in South Viet Nam on the Communists'. Probably no results were expected in the immediate future. No doubt the president, Rusk and senior officials would wish to talk to Wilson and Thompson (minister of transport) 'about possible steps eventually to follow up the President's statement', but Dean doubted if it were advisable to put forward 'a large list of alternative steps so soon after the Baltimore speech'. Before the US government was 'ready to contemplate a further initiative', it would want time to test the response of the other side and assess the reaction worldwide. Dean thought the best course would be for the prime minister to initiate the discussion and try to get the president's approval to talk over the ideas in more depth with Rusk, or with Ball and Bundy. The embassy had already fed into the State Department the idea to which the FO gave most weight, a Cambodia conference, and that would provide a starting point for talks into which the other ideas could be brought.[134]

M.N.F. Stewart explained that 'rather muted' reply, partly by enclosing an article in the *Washington Post* by William S. White, who was very close to LBJ. It had to be borne in mind that the Baltimore speech was 'about equally balanced between conciliation of a kind and the expression of American determination not to abandon the struggle in circumstances which could lead to a virtual take-over of South Vietnam by forces which would either side openly with the North Vietnamese or would be too ineffective to resist continued, if peaceful, Communist subversion. In all of the background guidance … there has been a similar equal emphasis on the stick and on the carrot.' The president and 'a good many other Americans', Stewart thought, believed that they had 'gone a long way towards meeting the critics and the faint-hearted', and 'any attempt to push them further would for the time being be not only disregarded but resented'.[135]

The FO's guidance telegram welcomed the Baltimore speech as 'a framework within which it would be possible to resolve the present conflict'.[136] The foreign secretary declared that a great advance in Vietnam might follow the speech. The world had to look for a constructive answer to what the president said.[137]

The Four Points announced by the DRV on 13 April may have been an answer, though they had been included in a speech made by Pham Van Dong to the National Assembly on the 8th, and that had perhaps already been scheduled.[138] They called, first, for the recognition of the basic rights of the Vietnamese people, the withdrawal of all US troops, the dismantling of US bases, the ending of acts of war. Second, while Vietnam was temporarily divided into two zones, the Geneva provisions had to be respected. The internal affairs of South Vietnam, the third point declared, had to be settled by the South Vietnamese people in accordance with the FLN programme. Fourth, peaceful reunification was to be settled by the Vietnamese people without foreign interference.[139]

Ten days after the bombing started with Flaming Dart, a group of foreign affairs officials in Hanoi, led by Ho Chi Minh, Le Duan and Pham Van Dong, had begun to draft what was to emerge as the Four Points.

Unlike Geneva they did not provide for general elections with the aim of reunification. The third point, viewed in the US as a hard-line proposal, was, according to Luu Doan Huynh, 'something that could be reworded in the course of negotiations'.[140] George McT. Kahin and John W. Lewis thought there was an ambiguity in it, depending on where commas were placed: should 'in accordance with the FLN programme' properly come after 'settled'?[141] 'We will fight to the end!' *Nhan Dan* asserted on the 11th.[142]

The FLN's Five Points, announced in March after the introduction of US troops, denounced the Americans as warmongers; resolved that the South Vietnamese would drive them out and achieve an independent, democratic, peaceful and neutral South Vietnam, 'with a view to national reunification'; resolved to liberate the South and defend the North; acknowledged support from friends on the five continents; and resolved to fight and defeat the US and the Vietnamese traitors.[143] In August Nguyen Van Hieu was to indicate that negotiations would be useless unless the Five Points were accepted, including an acknowledgement that the NLF was the sole representative of the people.[144]

Wilson Back in Washington

The prospect of another Wilson visit was quite unwelcome to Johnson. The prime minister was, however, going to be in New York to address the Economics Club, and it was hard to avoid a meeting. 'Everybody just wants to come and lecture us … giving us hell.'[145] 'President Johnson is clearly impatient with foreigners these days,' the *Times* correspondent was to write. 'He has made up his mind about the war in Vietnam, and does not want to listen to any contrary opinion.'[146]

The prime minister did not go entirely empty-handed. The Baltimore speech had led the British Ministry of Overseas Development to prepare a brief for the visit. The World Bank had not been encouraging about the major Nam Ngum dam project, allegedly on technical grounds, 'but probably really because of the economic and security situation in Laos'. There were signs at the ECAFE meeting in Wellington, however, that it 'might be disposed to change its tune'. Investment could 'lead to or help to prepare the way for a political settlement, or it could be regarded as a probable consequential effect of a political settlement'. Britain had offered limited funds for the Mekong scheme, mainly for navigation improvement. 'If the Americans turn on the heat the obvious move would be to show interest in the Nam Ngum project. We know that they are themselves ready to look at this again in conjunction with the World Bank.' The project could make a contribution towards the absorption of labour from Laos and North Vietnam, 'either as a prelude to or as a consequence of stability in the area'. Britain considered that the project could only be 'safely and usefully' carried out after a settlement had been reached in Laos.[147] The Cabinet decided that it was desirable to offer a measure of support.[148]

The essential purpose of the Vietnam brief the FO prepared for the PM's visit was to advise him that accepting Russia's proposal for a conference on Cambodia was the best way of getting negotiations started on Vietnam. He had to persuade LBJ and Rusk. And it had to be done as soon as possible, lest the Russians withdrew under Chinese pressure.[149]

The meeting on 15 April went well after all. The president praised the Labour government's endeavours to support sterling. He explained his bomb-plus-olive-branch approach on Vietnam. He did not ask for British troops. Wilson explained his political difficulties and then spoke of peace negotiations, suggesting a joint approach with the SU as co-chairman. The president assented to a low-key approach.[150] Wilson felt 'reassured', as he later wrote, and pledged support in pressing the Soviet co-chairman to build on American willingness to secure a settlement at the conference table.[151]

It was agreed, the *Times* correspondent said, that Britain should continue the proposal for a conference on Cambodia: the terms for talks on Vietnam might 'emerge from it'.[152] But Sihanouk was to denounce the 'revolting cynicism' of the Anglo-Americans: they were merely using his country's objectives as a means of discussing Vietnam.[153] The Chinese, the FO experts concluded, had either torpedoed the conference or were happy to have it torpedoed. They 'did not want those concerned in a conference on Viet Nam to sit down together—even to discuss Cambodia—at this stage'.[154] The idea ran into the sand over the following weeks.

Bureaucratic Practice

Bombing Hanoi when Kosygin was there was extraordinary enough to attract more than one conspiracy theory.[155] Sir Paul Gore-Booth, looking back on it after his retirement from the FO, attributed it to error, and that to 'a failure, through a structural weakness in the United States Government, to co-ordinate political and military thinking and action'.[156] In Washington, indeed, policy seemed to be decided in a more irregular way than in London. The SD was but one of the agencies proffering advice to the president, whose decision-making, though culminatory, was both personal and consensual.

Unlike the SD, the FO in London did not have a rival in the NSC or the White House staff, nor was the PM also commander-in-chief. But there was some tension between it and the Labour government. The PM—whom critics such as Richard Crossman saw as having a presidential approach—was anxious both to meet the left-wing challenge and to play the role of an international statesman. Though FO staff members—Cable, for example—were far from unaware of the need to consider public opinion, they were concerned when ministerial initiatives cut across their recommendations. On Vietnam their views were well considered and, it may now seem to us, often showed remarkable foresight. But they were cautious, particularly when the relationship with the US was at issue.

Their views were shaped by the long-standing practice of 'private' correspondence between the FO staff and the representatives overseas and among the latter, a correspondence in which quite divergent views could be expressed. In the post-war phase—as Britain's power decreased—more central planning took place, first through the Permanent Undersecretary's Department, and then through the Planning Department, headed initially by Michael Palliser. How much planning there could be in so contingency-prone a field was, of course, questionable. It was more a matter of shaping opinion within broad parameters among the officials in London, the representatives overseas, and the ministers. Did that become so consolidated as to conflict with ministerial or prime ministerial initiatives? The answer seems to be no, with a touch of 'Yes Minister'.

The heads of mission in Southeast Asia, with some FO representatives, met in Bangkok on 31 March–2 April 1965, just before the Baltimore speech. The FO sent the conference a summary of comments on the long-term paper of December 1964, and also the draft of a paper by the Planning Staff on 'Vietnam and the Future'.[157]

That draft seems to have originated in February when Walston suggested that the FO should be thinking about steps to counter adverse repercussions in Southeast Asia should a new Geneva conference lead to American withdrawal from Vietnam.[158] As Cable had written on 24 February, that was a possible outcome of recent developments, but not the only one. The US, he said, had not finally decided to cut its losses, and would not necessarily do so through a negotiated settlement. Much would depend on the readiness of the Communist powers to make enough concessions to enable the US to 'save some face'. If they thought the US was already on the run, and no concessions were needed, 'this might well produce a reaction in the United States and a reversion to the idea of a show-down with China'. Much would also depend on developments in Saigon. 'The emergence of a stable and resolute Government there seems unlikely, but if it happened, it would be a further incentive to the U.S. Government to take a hard line. On the other hand, continued disintegration in Saigon might persuade the U.S. Government that both their domestic and their international prestige would be better served by letting the Viet-Namese opt out of the struggle on their own. This would enable them to argue that there had been no American failure of will, only a reluctant acquiescence in the spinelessness of their ally.'

If there were a negotiated settlement, its repercussions elsewhere would be influenced by its terms and the manner in which it was reached. 'In the worst case, if the United States were to appear to withdraw from Viet-Nam under pressure from American public opinion and their European allies but against the wishes of the Saigon regime, the effects on Western prestige in South-East Asia would probably be beyond repair. Such an outcome might also seriously affect the continued readiness of American public opinion to accept commitments in mainland South-East Asia and would certainly diminish the readiness of the United States Government to allow H.M.G. an equal voice in the shaping of Western policy in South-East Asia.' Prediction was premature, Cable concluded. The FO should think about it, but not finalise its ideas until the future was 'very much clearer. For one thing as long as confrontation continues—as it may for many years—we have no spare resources to devote to South-East Asia. Indeed we are already spending on that area much more than we can afford.' The Planning Staff should prepare a paper.[159] Peck agreed that it would be a valuable exercise, and on 1 March the secretary of state agreed that the study should go ahead.[160]

The draft started with the assumption that the Vietnam crisis would not lead to a general war. It was 'not impossible', but it was 'extremely unlikely'. The SU would contemplate war with the US only 'in defence of its most crucial national interest', and nothing in Southeast Asia was 'sufficiently crucial'. China would have 'fewer inhibitions' if it thought it could win, but it knew it could not do so without Russian support, which it knew would not be forthcoming. It would contemplate 'another localised war with America on the Korean model', but only if it believed Chinese security were directly threatened.

If the possibility of general war were excluded, there was a range of possible developments in Vietnam. Under option (a), US military pressure on North Vietnam, not countered by the other Communist powers or restrained by its allies, reached such intensity that the North Vietnamese abandoned further interference in the South and ordered the VC to do likewise, in which case South Vietnam would have 'a good chance of maintaining a non-Communist independence for a long time to come'. Under development (b), North Vietnam would secretly cease interference but not admit it. The Viet Cong insurrection could be resumed when Northern anti-aircraft defences had been built up. 'The South would have gained a respite, but perhaps not more.' Under (c), pressure from US allies, from the UN, and perhaps domestic opinion, prevented military attacks 'going far enough to produce even a tacit capitulation in Hanoi'. There were no negotiations. Fighting continued in the South on a reduced scale, and intensified efforts were made to produce a regime in Saigon in favour of negotiations.

Under scenario (d), the Planning Staff envisaged that the North Vietnamese, with or without Chinese armed support, would, as a counter to American military action, 'invade South Viet Nam openly and engage American ground troops'. The result would be a Korean-type war, likely to lead to the same sort of military stalemate, 'with the Americans unable to win for lack of the necessary land forces and the Communists unable to win for lack of the necessary air and sea power'. Alternative (e) envisaged negotiations, which might bring about a compromise 'reasonably satisfactory to the Americans and the South', a compromise that saved American face but little else, or 'a thoroughly unsatisfactory settlement in which the Americans acquiesce only because the South Vietnamese insist on signing'. Under option (f), negotiations were initiated contrary to American wishes on the insistence of the South Vietnamese and America's allies. Scenario (g) envisaged a collapse of resolution in Saigon 'so rapid that the Americans are unable to negotiate more than the terms of their own withdrawal', and (h) the agreement of the Americans, 'disillusioned by continued upheavals in Saigon or under pressure from their allies', to negotiations or a settlement unacceptable to South Vietnam.

The range of possibilities could be graded by the increasing amounts of American humiliation and by 'a decreasing readiness to accept military losses, doubts among the Western allies, charges of imperialism from the third world and threats and vituperation from the Communist powers'. The paper reduced the range to three categories—(a) negligible humiliation and maximum acceptance of the cost; (b) the reverse of that; and (c) some degree of each—in order to assess the likely consequences outside Vietnam.

So far as (a) was concerned, the paper emphasised that the US as a superpower had the resources and the 'international invulnerability' that Britain lacked at Suez and France in Algeria. The exception would be a commitment of Russian forces to a local conflict, unlikely to happen. In Southeast Asia, as the Americans were pointing out, the lesson of (a) would be that a country threatened by Communism could rely on US support sufficient to contain the threat. Those anti-Communists who wondered whether the price of being made a battleground might not prove as painful as giving in to Communism would be 'a small minority'. Two things were to be said against (a), however: 'First, it would involve Western actions of a ruthlessness unattractive to the consciences of many people in Western Europe and no doubt also in America. Second, it may well be a pipe-dream; the Communist will to resist in Viet Nam seems likely to prove too strong for any American military action to be able to bring about settlement on American terms, and there is also the danger of a complete political collapse in the South which would in effect leave the Americans with nothing to defend.'

In a category (b) situation, American prestige would suffer, but it would not be beyond repair any more than Russia's after Cuba. Chinese prestige would be enhanced, and the advance of Communism could hardly be confined to Vietnam, but the US could still find allies, such as Malaysia, Japan and the Philippines. The greatest damage would probably be domestic. 'Humiliation in Viet Nam could lead to a major American reaction against foreign involvements of all kinds', even in Europe. Isolationism could gain ground. 'The prospects for the security of the rest of the free world would then be very bleak.'

Category (c) would involve an agreement, explicit or tacit, under which both the Americans and the Communists would be content with less than their present objectives. The main difficulty would be to ensure that it did not break down. If the Communists renewed their endeavour to take over the South, the Americans would either have to tolerate that or recommit their forces. The cost of forcing a compromise would not be as great as forcing a defeat, but it would involve a degree of American humiliation, with greater consequences in Southeast Asia than elsewhere.

Those had been encapsulated in the Falling Domino theory. In 1954 the West accepted a compromise, explicitly in the case of France and Britain, implicitly in the case of the US. Since then the situation in Laos and South Vietnam had certainly deteriorated, but no other Communist government had emerged even in Indochina. A further compromise would set off a chain reaction, but the effects would be very different in the countries concerned. Most US allies would be unlikely to change their stance. The Asian neutrals would simply conclude that South Vietnam had been insufficiently non-aligned. The power struggle in Indonesia might result in a Communist takeover, but it would not be affected by events in South Vietnam. Even if the Pathet Lao took over the whole of Laos, 'the effect on the balance of power in Asia would not be very great, although the opportunities for Communist subversion in Thailand would undoubtedly be increased'.

Thailand was indeed the core of the Domino argument, the draft paper recognised. '[T]he Thais are notorious Vicars of Bray, and an American setback in Viet Nam would be bound to increase the number of them who think in terms of reinsuring with China. But the American-Thai alliance could probably weather the storm for, at any rate, some years to come.' Insurgency would increase, but 'the Thais' lack of appetite for fighting' would weaken that as well as resistance to it. If the Americans made Thailand 'a major bastion for the West, it would probably take the Communists almost as long to dislodge them as it has done in South Viet Nam'. Would the US be willing or well advised to make it a bastion? If American opinion hardened against further involvement on the mainland, that might lead to 'the happiest outcome of all', whereby Thailand was encouraged to follow in the footsteps not of South Vietnam but of Cambodia. 'This would enable the Thais to ease themselves out of SEATO (which could then be wound up without loss to its other members), to cultivate the Chinese in the manner of Prince Sihanouk or President Ayub [of Pakistan] and to give full rein to their ancestral talent for fence-sitting.' Western investments might suffer as in Burma, but they were 'not enormous', and trade need not be much affected.

In Malaysia morale would suffer if the Americans accepted a compromise in South Vietnam, and disenchantment with the Western connections increase if the Thais turned to neutralism. But the course of events would depend more on what happened in Indonesia. If Sukarno was followed by a Communist takeover, it would feel obliged to retain the British alliance, and the Americans would be eager to take part, even if they had decided not to make Thailand a bastion. If Indonesia did not go Communist, the Malaysians might be more tempted to make peace with Indonesia, 'perhaps by offering to phase out the British bases as a propitiatory sacrifice. If a comparatively stable military regime had emerged in Indonesia, this might not be such an unsatisfactory outcome from the Western point of view. It would get us off the Confrontation hook; it would open the way for a restoration of Western influence in Indonesia and perhaps for the eventual establishment of some kind of Maphilindo [Malaysia-Philippines-Indonesia confederation]; and it would deprive us only of a base of declining military value which we are in any case increasingly doubtful whether we can afford.'

The paper considered the scope for 'Western initiatives'. In relation to both (a) and (b), their main purpose would be 'to save the face of the defeated party'. If the Communist Vietnamese abandoned the struggle, 'they might find it easier to do so under cover of e.g. acceding to some kind of international appeal for a ceasefire and perhaps some kind of international assessment of the wishes of the population of South Viet Nam'. If the US accepted defeat, its withdrawal could be covered by some face-saving device like the UN interregnum in West New Guinea, although a UN label would have to be avoided (neither PRC nor DRV being members). The Western allies of the US would need to dissuade it from falling into isolationism in general, though disillusioned with Asia.

In a category (c) situation America's allies could play a useful role before negotiations began 'in helping to make the Communists' flesh creep and so to convince them of the need for compromise' by stressing the 'limited aims but limitless resolve' of which Leonard (Len) Unger had spoken to the North Atlantic Council on 3 March. If negotiations followed, 'the Western allies would have scope both for suggesting the form and purpose of any conference and for using their good offices'. If a negotiated settlement were reached, 'it would have to be based on each of the main parties refraining thereafter from provocations beyond a certain point; observance of these ground rules would require policing and perhaps also interpretation, and here America's allies would have a valuable part to play, both by taking part themselves and by persuading their closest friends among the neutrals to do likewise'. Given past experience, such a task would be 'extremely difficult and disheartening; and the problem of indigenous disaffection within South Vietnam would of course remain'.

Britain would be well placed to take part in these initiatives. 'Our past achievement, e.g. at Geneva in 1954 and 1962, and our quasi-diplomatic presence in both Peking and Hanoi would in different ways give us a national advantage in trying to convince the Communist powers of the seriousness of America's military purpose; "we pulled them back from the brink at the Yalu River and again at Dien-Bien-Phu, but we cannot do it a third time".' The co-chairmanship, however, would probably not offer much leverage. 'Russian passive if not active resistance would make the role ... an increasingly difficult one', and any new Geneva-type conference was likely to be 'under different and more neutral chairmanship. British sponsorship and stage-management of such a conference would not be desirable in any case, since it would make us an obvious target for any American tendency to attribute the absence of victory to the faint-heartedness of America's principal allies.'

Nor, the draft planning paper suggested, should Britain try to bring pressure on the Americans in favour of compromise even though the situation in Vietnam was 'still fluid'. British advice was 'not likely to be regarded by the Americans as a decisive or even a major factor, and we have our own reasons for knowing how tiresome backseat driving can be [an allusion to Robert Kennedy and confrontation]. In a context like Vietnam, where the American effort has been enormous and our own negligible, we may hope to help implement American policy but not to play a part in formulating it.'

If the lines of a Vietnam settlement emerged, however, and assuming they involved 'some measure of American retreat', Britain would have 'a real chance' to influence US policy towards Thailand and Malaysia. It might be able to persuade the US that Thailand should be 'allowed to evolve her own form of neutralism' instead of becoming a last Western bastion on the mainland. If Indonesia had gone Communist, 'we should aim to implicate the Americans as closely as possible in the defence of non-Communist Malaysia; this might well involve some sharing of our facilities (and expenses) at Singapore'. If 'a suitable military regime emerged in Indonesia', Britain would want US help in promoting a rapprochement between KL and Jakarta 'on terms permitting us to phase out the Singapore base in a manner which does the least damage either to our prestige or to our strategic requirements; a major factor in such circumstances would no doubt be American participation in a larger-scale Western rescue-operation to restore the Indonesian economy'.[161]

Reporting on 5 April 1965 on the conference in Bangkok that considered the two papers, Sir Anthony Rumbold found to his surprise that it was easier to reach agreement on policy in five years' time than on Vietnam. The divergences of view reflected 'differences of experience', but they were also the result of 'differences of temperament and vision'. Some were by nature sanguine, others more reflective. Some saw events as a struggle between 'great conflicting forces, good and evil, "free" and "Communist". Others view the world with a less confident and more critical eye.'[162]

The meeting did not accept the FO's view that an expression of future British policy should be deferred till the outcome in Vietnam was determined. Without it, it would be impossible to engage in talks with the Americans. The issue in Vietnam might not be known for a long time, and some issue might meanwhile emerge that would further defer it. 'Our aim should be to reach the widest measure of agreement with them on how we can best jointly defend our interests.' The meeting agreed that the long-term paper broadly defined those interests, and then discussed the principles of British policy. It agreed that a 'white' military presence on the mainland was currently necessary to defend Vietnam and Malaysia, but that the longer it remained, the more it might be resented. 'A British military presence should be maintained within reach of the area in conjunction with the Americans, Australians and New Zealanders. This would involve major problems of preparation and a decision as to how this should be done should therefore be taken without delay.'

Thailand should be provided with continuing guarantees as long as it wanted them, either through SEATO or, if that collapsed as a result of

French and Pakistani attitudes, by direct guarantees. Britain should be ready to join with the US, China and other powers in an agreement to respect the neutrality and territorial integrity of Cambodia, and it should also seek to preserve the 1962 agreement on Laos. If the threat from Indonesia had ended, Britain should bring about 'a gradual withdrawal from Malaysia and the Singapore base' and renegotiate the defence treaty. Britain should 'welcome nationalism, even at the expense of some of our short term commercial interests, in the belief that it will be an obstacle to the spread of Chinese Communism'.[163]

Turning to the Vietnam issue, the meeting agreed that the US administration had decided to regard it as 'a contest of wills' between themselves and Peking and Hanoi, 'but that they were still acting empirically in carrying out this decision'. Unfortunately, that had prevented the administration making its plans clear to the British. Attacking North Vietnam could be justified by 'the need to gain time' in face of the decline in South Vietnam's morale as a result of war-weariness and of fears that the US might abandon it, and by VC's military successes due to 'their ability continually to introduce fresh reinforcements and supplies'. The attacks on North Vietnam and the landing of Marines had raised morale. But that was not enough to gain time unless three conditions were met: 'political stability permitting the establishment of a reasonably effective Government', more effective pacification methods, and sealing off reinforcements and supplies from North Vietnam.

Etherington-Smith thought that if those conditions were met there was 'a small chance' that the Americans and South Vietnamese could restore 'at least the level of security and Governmental authority' obtaining in South Vietnam 1955–58. The rest of those present in Bangkok took 'a more pessimistic view'. The present scale of bombardments would be ineffective and would be followed by heavier ones. Those might cause the North Vietnamese temporarily to diminish their activities but not to abandon the struggle. The adoption of more brutal methods of war by the Americans would 'cause a strong revulsion of feeling against them in most parts of the world'. Sooner or later the Americans would have to choose between withdrawing from South Vietnam, 'leaving that country open to an eventual Communist takeover', and 'deliberately escalating to a wider war'. The most that could be hoped for was a continuation of fighting on the present scale for a period of years until the Communists were convinced 'that the best way of attaining their objectives would be negotiations followed by subversion', or a sudden intensification of US bombardments designed to 'demonstrate their overwhelming military superiority in the area, thus creating conditions in which they might feel that they could negotiate honourably'. In any case, the pessimists thought there was a risk of uncontrolled escalation, bringing in the North Vietnamese army or the Chinese or the Russians.

All at Bangkok agreed that it was an important British interest that the Americans should not be 'humiliated' in Vietnam. Most thought that it was also an important British interest that South Vietnam should not come under North Vietnam's control, 'but that in attempting to achieve this too high a price could be paid'. There was a difference of opinion as to the extent that it was a British interest that the Americans should not use methods that would outrage public opinion. Some thought that would lead to rifts in the alliance, and all agreed that open difference of opinion should be avoided. The idea of trying to promote a negotiation was considered, but though there were signs that the US wanted to keep open channels of communication, 'doubts were expressed as to the likelihood of any successful negotiation at the present time'.

The conference also considered the attitudes of neighbouring countries, as seen by the British representatives. A continued US presence in South Vietnam would be acceptable in Malaysia and Thailand for a long time, but negotiations likely to lead to withdrawal would 'cause a loss of confidence in the West and would facilitate subversion and internal unrest'. Burma would secretly welcome a continued US struggle as long as it had a chance of succeeding. 'American withdrawal would oblige Burma to trim her sails more closely to the Chinese wind.' Indonesian policy was currently 'so self-centred' that it might not be affected by the outcome in Vietnam. In Cambodia a continued struggle would be helpful only if American successes were 'immediate and impressive'. Otherwise, an end of the fighting in Vietnam, whatever its terms, 'would offer the best chance for a renewed effort to stabilise the neutrality and independence of Cambodia'. The same was true of Laos.

British action, it was agreed, should be directed towards 'helping to persuade public opinion that the obstacles to negotiations came from Communist Powers and not from the United States'. Opinion was divided over advising the US, if at all. Some thought Britain should declare its support and increase material assistance, then urge better methods of pacification. Others thought the US should be told that the cause was 'hopeless' and it should concentrate on extricating itself 'as soon as possible and with the maximum dignity'. In between those extremes some thought a conference on Cambodia might be pressed on the US 'as a step which might lead indirectly towards a Vietnamese settlement'. All those who thought any advice should be given wanted it done in the course of normal diplomatic contacts.[164] Were the diplomats restive over Wilsonian initiatives?

Gordon Walker

On 6 April the North Vietnamese rejected a visit from Gordon Walker: it was a 'unilateral approach', ignoring the Russian co-chairman's views.[165] The deputy director of the External Affairs Bureau pointed to the aggressive acts of the US but added that it was hoped that the time would come when talks would be of use.[166] The Chinese also rejected a visit. British peacemaking activities, said Zhou, were instigated by the US.[167] The Chinese claimed, MacLehose pointed out, that Britain's support for US policies 'invalidated the special position we once held as Co-Chairman' and made it 'unsuitable for a mediatory role'. It was unlikely that 'Chinese political irritation' would affect China's policy in Hong Kong or trade with the UK, but 'the prospect of any positive outcome is virtually nil'. In present circumstances, 'a low key is what suits our bilateral relations with China best'. Any political initiative Britain felt obliged to take might incur some cost in political relations.[168]

The FO's steering brief for Gordon Walker's tour—'described as fact-finding' but 'in fact an opportunity for the non-Communist governments to give their frank opinions to a single person on the possibilities of negotiations and on the form an eventual settlement might take'—pointed out that the North Vietnamese and Chinese reactions eliminated the American fear that Britain was 'embarking on some sort of mediation'. It would, however, be important 'to make it clear to all concerned that we have no illusions about a quick settlement and we realise that the problem is a long-term one, stretching back into the past and requiring much patience in the future'.

'From the Western viewpoint any settlement involving South Viet-Nam alone' would have to take account of 'the problem of removing the Viet Cong or neutralising the danger of renewed guerrilla warfare; disposing of the Liberation Front (either within a government or by complete exclusion) in such a way that it cannot impose a Communist *fait accompli* on South Viet-Nam; of the continuing threat from the Communist North; and of the requirement for effective international machinery for supervising the settlement and, if necessary, for sanctions against violations of it'.

Any settlement covering both halves should take account of most of those factors, 'but also of the problems of bringing North and South Viet-Nam together under a single authority (as a unitary or federal State); the risk of domination of the South by the North (a state of affairs which has existed for centuries before the present conflict), in which the North is infinitely better organised politically and socially to impose its will; the difficulties, both internal and international, of withdrawing North Viet-Nam, even nominally, from the Communist orbit; and the difficulties of international supervision of any settlement'. Any settlement would also have to consider the position of Laos and Cambodia and their attitude to a pacified Vietnam 'either in two halves or as a reunited State'.

The essential steps were 'to discover a means of first making contact with the Communist side, to establish the basis on which discussions should proceed, to reach agreement on the method of pursuing discussions of substance, and to arrive at a settlement involving a cessation of fighting and a provision for a political settlement either separately or as part of the general agreement'. A ceasefire might have to be negotiated prior to discussions of a definitive agreement, or postponed, as in 1954, to become part of the overall settlement. 'It seems unlikely, in circumstances where a dialogue had already been opened with the Communist side, that any of the parties would continue to insist that a cease-fire was a precondition of any discussions whatever.' The brief sketched a number of ideas for an ultimate solution, none currently realistic given the attitude of the governments concerned. Gordon Walker might accordingly prefer 'to refrain from expressing any view of his own on the final solution and to concentrate on the problem of initiating negotiations'.[169]

The first annex to the brief pointed out that a direct proposal for negotiations would meet with no response. The only possibility was to establish opportunities for contact on Vietnam in the course of other discussions, with the object of discovering whether there was any basis for beginning substantive talks, and also considering what form those talks might take. There were three conceivable opportunities for contacts—a conference on Cambodia, discussions on Laos, and contacts through the UN—and the annex placed them in descending order of priority. Substantive discussions could also take three forms: a new Geneva, a new conference on Indochina as a whole, and Panmunjom-style armistice talks. The prospects of the first were 'very slender'; progress through Cambodia was more likely than the second; an armistice would leave the Viet Cong 'poised in the South'.

A second annex discussed possible solutions. One was an Austrian solution for South Vietnam alone: '[a] self-imposed neutrality by South Viet-Nam declared to the world and recognised (but not guaranteed) by other powers.' Among the advantages would be that it could form with Cambodia 'a neutral belt'. A disadvantage was that North Vietnam would remain a threat of subversion. Second, the Austrian solution might apply to a Vietnam reunited 'by election or more probably negotiation'. That offered the prospect of a stronger state independent of China, it would promote the neutralisation of the rest of Indochina, and it would qualify for UN membership. But neutrality would, 'at best, be of the Yugoslav type';

and it could be dominated by well-organised Communist or Liberation Front elements. Third, the annex considered a Laotian solution for South Vietnam alone. North Vietnam would be a constant threat; the Liberation Front would probably dominate; and there would be, as in Laos, 'danger of factional fighting'. Then it considered a Laotian solution for Vietnam as a whole with a balanced or coalition government. That would remove North Vietnam from the Communist orbit, but Communist and Liberation Front elements would swamp the South. The annex also considered the Korean solution: a Western-oriented state of South Vietnam remaining under Western protection south of the present demarcation line. The solution would be 'totally unacceptable' to the Communist powers and probably to Laos and Cambodia, and South Vietnam would remain 'a permanent Western commitment'. It presupposed 'a position of military strength and recovery in South Viet-Nam' that was 'very unlikely indeed. It also presupposes "capitulation" by the Communist powers. This is therefore the least likely solution.'

The annex also referred to the French solution. Never precisely defined, it envisaged total withdrawal of Communists and Americans from all Indochina, 'which would then achieve unassisted self-determination and evolve in a neutral, Communist-inclined area, possibly on the lines of an Asian Yugoslavia'. The neutralisation of all Indochina was 'not an unexceptionable goal in itself', but the French also aspired to a renewal of their influence, 'possibly no more than cultural and economic at first but with more than a passing thought to political influence'.

A third annex dealt with supervision and insurance machinery. That set up at Geneva was expensive and 'largely ineffectual'. Some options might be mentioned in countries Gordon Walker intended to visit. One was improving the present machinery. That would require remodelling its structure and terms of reference, and the current Commission governments would have to be persuaded to continue. New machinery might be easier to set up and possibly involve other Asian powers, but doing so could involve the conference in considerable argument. A third option was the UN and its machinery. But the Chinese had recently snubbed the secretary-general's efforts: 'the problems of China and the United Nations would appear in an acute form.'[170]

Chapter Four
Mission Improbable

The US attempted, rather feebly, to test the effect of a pause in the bombing. Robert Thompson advised a holding action, rather than intensified bombing of the North, but that would have no appeal in the US. The British took up an appeal for discussions non-aligned countries had made in March. This the prime minister combined in June with the notion of a Commonwealth Peace Mission. He also sought to use the private contacts of a junior minister. The moves were vain. The US began to introduce ground troops on a substantial scale. The FO dropped the notion of a further Commonwealth initiative.

On 24 April 1965 Rusk gave Dean an account of the conclusions of a meeting in Honolulu in April, attended by McNamara, Bill Bundy and Maxwell Taylor. The North Vietnamese would not move towards peace unless convinced they could not win the war in the South. 'They still believe they can.' Though Hanoi would not be attacked, greater military pressure was needed. That would bring American planes within range of the missiles Russia was now supplying. A total of 100,000 would be added to the South Vietnam army, and additional US troops would be sent, though deployed so that the South Vietnam government did not get the idea that the Americans would bear the main burden. A Viet Cong attack was expected in May.[1]

Two thousand eight hundred sorties had been flown in the past ten weeks, George Ball had told LBJ on 21 April. The rainy season was an occasion for reconsideration. The stated positions of the two parties—an independent South Vietnam, the DRV's Four Points—seemed to call for surrender on the other side. The best approach would be to find some common ground that would enable Hanoi to pull back, even if it hoped to prevail at a later date, stopping fighting and infiltration if assured of the continued existence of a VC party in the South. Once a new government was installed, the US would withdraw, and reunification would take place if the people of South Vietnam wanted it.[2] But Ball was seen as a devil's advocate, and though there were other doubters—Clark Clifford arguably one—his proposal was not considered.

Independent South Vietnam had been attacked by North Vietnam, LBJ told a press conference on 27 April. 'The object of that attack is total conquest. Defeat in South Viet-Nam would deliver a friendly nation to terror and repression. It would encourage and spur on those who seek to conquer all free nations that are within their reach.' America's own welfare, its freedom, would be at stake. It had struck back, but its purpose was 'peaceful settlement', resisting aggression, avoiding a wider war. 'I say again that I will talk to any government, anywhere, any time, without any conditions.' The offer may be rejected, 'but it will remain open, waiting for the day when it becomes clear to all that armed attack will not yield domination over others'.[3]

Ball was in London in early May. There he stuck to the president's line, though hints of his own view came through. He met the foreign secretary along with Paul Hasluck, the Australian MEA, and D.J. Eyre, the New Zealand defence minister. Both Indonesia and Vietnam, seen to be connected problems, were discussed in an after-dinner conversation. On Vietnam Ball said the US did not rule out a political settlement, but it could not be 'just a face-saving formula. The United States were determined to see this thing through.' Only the Communists wanted the US to withdraw from Vietnam, Stewart said. But 'he had to admit privately that, though Her Majesty's Government had given whole hearted support to United States policy, there were a number of misgivings about the future: would military action on North Viet-Nam produce the necessary political result? Would it defect [affect] the organization of the Viet Cong in the South? When the time came for discussions what would the future be for South Viet-Nam?' Ball's answer was at best indirect. Only 24 per cent of the population were under the VC. The US was clear that it 'received its main control and thrust from the North'. Once Hanoi had decided 'that the game was not worth the candle and ceased to support the guerrillas in the South the military problem in South Viet-Nam would be quite manageable. ... Likewise once infiltration from the North stopped it would be possible to have a suitable Government in South Viet-Nam. The rebellion in Malaya had cleared itself up in time. This would also happen in Viet-Nam.'

The longer-term problem, Stewart suggested, was 'the pressure of China'. The aim should be the kind of relationship that existed between the SU and the world. 'China was not at present in the right mood. After it had been made clear in Viet-Nam and Indonesia that Communism should not be allowed to prevail, it would be necessary to consider bringing China into the community of Nations.' Ball refuted the Walter Lippmann thesis that China would one day come to control Southeast Asia, and that 'it would be better for the United States to recognise this sooner rather than later'. China would have to be shown—as the SU had been shown—that Communist aggression did not pay. 'The difficulty about bringing them into the community of Nations at the present time was that they were not prepared to come in.'[4]

Ball told Wilson on 5 May 1965 that the US was considering a bombing pause 'to break the rhythm of the bombardment in order to create the impression that the present attacks were not systematic. After a time the American forces might institute a longer pause and at the same time try and get through signals to Hanoi in order to see whether they were prepared to talk.' Had Britain any indication that there would be a response? The PM thought it an excellent idea, though he had no evidence about a Hanoi response. If there were none, the US would be in 'a sound moral position'. The president, Ball said, had given him 'the task of discovering whether there was an end to this situation. A ceasefire would raise very difficult problems.' The US believed it could negotiate only with North Vietnam, not with the Viet Cong. It had at least one regiment in the South, possibly two. Hence the American decision to send reinforcements. If nothing much occurred after the rainy season, it might mean interdiction was having an effect, and possibilities for talks might open up.[5]

On 10 May Ball asked the foreign secretary what replies the UK had received to its circular enquiry of 2 April. The Chinese, Stewart replied, had been 'extremely negative', the French did not consider it appropriate to reply to one co-chairman only, the Canadians had made a positive suggestion. He suggested that the US government might set out the way it thought a settlement might come about. Its intention was first to stop the infiltration, and then, according to Adlai Stevenson, to withdraw its troops, but that seemed to go 'rather further' than subsequent statements suggested. Ball confirmed that impression, 'but he did agree that if the North Viet-Namese were to assure the cessation of the despatch of men and equipment to the South and were to give up the command and control of the Viet Cong forces, the American attacks on North Viet-Nam would stop and they might possibly withdraw their forces. The problem was however how is such an assurance to be given in real terms? Owing to the need to examine the interrogation reports, intelligence summaries etc., the ability to detect the flow of men and equipment into South Viet-Nam carries a three months time lag.'

One way out of the deadlock, Stewart suggested, might be 'the sequence: assured cessation of infiltration; stopping of air strikes; then a conference. An alternative might be to have a conference first and supposing the other side were ready to talk without pre-conditions, the military action might well continue.' It was not unprecedented, Ball agreed, for a conference to take place while military action continued. If the other side were to come to a conference, the foreign secretary said, the three problems for discussion would be: '(i) the reduction or cessation of hostilities; (ii) how to guarantee the frontier of Viet-Nam; (iii) how to set up an independent or Allied Viet-Nam.' The US, he understood, was in favour of the third step as 'the ultimate solution'.

Ball wished to add a fourth element: 'the cessation of fighting in South Viet-Nam. The Viet Cong action must stop before the U.S. could pull out their troops.' Stewart 'interjected that the American case suggested that if the North did not support the Viet Cong, it would collapse'. That was not quite so, Ball responded. 'It was simply that the action against the Viet Cong would become a controllable action. If there was a real end to Northern command and control of the Viet Cong and a real closing of the frontier, demoralisation of the Viet Cong in the South would set in. If the flow of equipment were to stop, the Viet Cong are not now capturing enough weapons to compensate for their losses. There would then be time for the Saigon Government to take the necessary measures, i.e. amnesty, turning in of arms, offer of repatriation to those who did not wish to stay in the South.'

What mechanism could be created to achieve those objectives? the foreign secretary asked. There had been no discussion of such matters in Saigon, Ball said, 'as conditions there were not yet ripe'. Was Ball thinking of an elected government? The Americans were thinking, Ball replied, of local elections first, which 'would assimilate people back into the stream of orderly Government'. He did not exclude the idea of the NLF as a political party, 'but action of this kind would transfer the decision from the military to the political field'. Thinking on those lines was in hand in 'a very restricted group'. No details were available, and the South Vietnamese government had to be 'brought along'.

'The Foreign Secretary expressed anxiety that while the military situation was being determined by the Americans, it was the Government of Saigon which had it in its power to determine progress on conciliation.' The US government did not intend to become 'a satellite of Saigon' was Ball's jocular response. If a conference were to take place and hostilities to stop, 'the way would be open', Stewart said, 'for a representative government in Saigon and a neutral but not necessarily allied Viet-Nam'. A reply to the British questionnaire on those lines would be 'helpful, not so much on account of the irreconcilable elements in this country, but because both H.M.G. and the U.S. Government had been so intent on the military aspects of the situation that they had given the appearance at least of overlooking any move towards peace'. Ball agreed. But the reply must not get the Americans into trouble with Saigon, 'and the South Viet-Namese Prime Minister ... must not be given the impression that he was being sold out by the Americans'. Stewart concluded by saying 'that Saigon must learn to live with those of her citizens who were in arms against the Government'.[6]

At the restricted session of a NATO Council meeting dealing with Vietnam, the foreign secretary, Peck suggested, might wish to 'elaborate his previous thoughts' along a number of lines. First, the sequence ceasefire–conference–settlement was 'not sacrosanct': a conference could precede a ceasefire as in 1954. Second, the British aimed at a conference in being not necessarily on Cambodia but including representatives of Peking and Hanoi. In that way, third, 'Hanoi might be willing to make the "signal" so much desired by the U.S. in a way much less obtrusive than the rather indirect channels so far available'. In the FO view, however, there was, fourth, 'as yet no sign of any serious divergence of view between Peking and Hanoi, although the latter for tactical reasons may incline towards Moscow'. A fifth point Peck put in the form of questions. 'Will continued American bombing raids on North Viet-Nam induce the necessary "signal" or will they strengthen North Viet-Namese determination to resist? Would a deliberate cessation of bombing raids, with a threat of re-starting them, possibly bring about the same result more rapidly?' Stewart should steer clear of the 'delicate' subjects Ball had raised, 'namely how the war in the South is to be wound up after North Viet-Namese infiltration has stopped; what measures the Saigon Government must be induced to take to enable them to live in peace with all their citizens once they have laid down their arms'. Rusk was not likely to raise them.[7]

At the NATO meeting, Peck told Dean, the two points made by the foreign secretary were echoed by most of the other delegates. 'These were that, to facilitate the continued support their allies were anxious to give to American policy in Viet-Nam, it was most important that the U.S. Government should keep their allies fully informed in advance of their actions, of the reasons for them and of their judgment of the situation in Viet-Nam.' It was equally important that the Americans 'should take every opportunity to repeat in public statements the objectives of their policy in Viet-Nam, particularly their readiness for unconditional negotiations, their anxiety to avoid a wider war and to see a peaceful settlement in Viet-Nam and their efforts to encourage the emergence in Saigon of a Government that would meet the aspirations of the Viet-Namese people'. Rusk said he would do his best.

Dean was to remind Rusk and others of that. The foreign secretary felt that in recent weeks the UK had been consulting and informing the US, for example over Cambodia, far more than the US had been consulting the UK, and the president had 'got into the habit of talking and acting as if he had no allies'. That was 'particularly undesirable' when the British government's support for the US was exposing it to 'so much criticism from important sections of British public opinion'.[8]

Rusk met the PM on 14 May 1965. The PM warned him that any decision to bomb Hanoi would cause 'very real trouble' in the UK. No such decision had been made, the secretary of state repeated, nor would it be unless there was a major change in the situation. If, when the troubles were over, Rusk went on, South Vietnam wished to be non-aligned, that would be all right: it was North Vietnamese intrusion across the border that brought American pressure. 'Once this were to stop, the problem in South Vietnam would be reduced to manageable proportions, and South Vietnam ought to be able to deal with it itself.' The two also discussed the review of British defence expenditure. Rusk did not want the US to be alone acting for the free world.[9] The last topic and its implications for East of Suez were also included in a conversation Rusk and Stewart had on the plane from London to Vienna on 14 May. The foreign secretary told his counterpart that Britain was under constant strain: its effort was spread too thin. But—hardly comfortingly—he said that Britain would not abandon 'everything everywhere at once'.[10]

During the SEATO conference also held in May, 'various ideas' crystallised in Lord Walston's mind. There were only two satisfactory solutions to the Vietnamese situation: a complete Western military victory and a negotiated settlement. Few thought the first a possibility. The focus should be on the second. 'This being so, we should aim at negotiations taking place as quickly as possible. The longer the struggle, the greater the risk of general unrest in the whole of South East Asia: the more frightening does the image of American imperialism become in those parts: and the greater is the advantage that the Communists can gain in propaganda in Africa and other uncommitted countries. The longer the struggle, the greater the suffering of the people involved; the more China and Russia will be forced, however unwillingly, to work together; and the shadow of Chinese imperialism will be hidden by the physical presence of American imperialism.' Nationalism was one of the strongest forces in Southeast Asia. At present the Chinese were using it by presenting the US as the enemy of newly independent countries. The West should harness it and not be afraid if they adopted socialist or Communist policies.

Though negotiations were urgent, they must not weaken the Western alliance or the confidence of the Southeast Asia countries in the West's willingness and ability to defend them against Chinese or Communist aggression. The West must demonstrate strength and willingness to negotiate. The Chinese were 'surely highly satisfied with the present situation' and unlikely to take any action to bring it to an end. Intensified bombing would not alter their view. 'The only conceivable way of bringing Peking to the conference table is by pressure of world opinion—and this is not a very strong possibility.' Hanoi was in a different position. Again bombing was unlikely to bring the North Vietnamese quickly to the conference table. They were used to hardships.

'[T]he right course,' Walston proposed, '… would be a show of strength coupled with the mobilisation of world opinion on the side of the West—and with greater emphasis on the latter.' The events of the past month had been consistent with such action, though not necessarily the result of the same reasoning. Increased military activity had had a beneficial effect on South Vietnamese morale. In the course of it the president offered talks without preconditions and a billion dollars in aid. 'This had a good effect on world opinion, though it could have been played up more by the West. The main criticism by most of the uncommitted countries was that the bombing continued at the same time.'

Walston suggested that 'future tactics' should involve a significant two- to three-week intensification of the bombing, then an announcement by the Americans that they were still prepared to talk, that they would suspend the bombing for two weeks to give Hanoi and Peking the chance to answer, and that if no favourable answer had been received bombing would start again. 'This process could be repeated indefinitely, and each time Peking and Hanoi refused to come to the talks it would become increasingly obvious to the rest of the world that it was they who were forcing a continuation of the hostilities.' The initiative would thus 'pass to the West, who could vary the intensity of bombing and the length of time between attack and the offer of talks to suit their convenience and the reaction of world opinion. Such a policy would undoubtedly increase the strain between Peking and Moscow, and also between Peking and Hanoi: and at the same time it would leave no doubt in the minds of the other South East Asian countries that the West were worthwhile allies.'[11] Stewart agreed with much of this. His thoughts had been running on similar lines.[12]

In fact, under the 'Mayflower' initiative, bombing had been suspended, though no 'surge' had preceded it. The pause would not be announced, Mac Bundy had told Rusk, but the attention of Hanoi and Moscow would be called to it. It would not be a long one, but 'would indicate our own ability to move either way, depending upon the reactions of the enemy'. It would not be repeated or extended merely in return for a conference, but only for a major reduction in armed action in South Vietnam.[13] The US ambassador in Moscow could not deliver a note, the SD found. 'I am not a postman,' said Nikolay Firyubin.[14] Could the British consul-general in Hanoi do it?[15] The FO was concerned at the possible repercussions if he seemed to be involved in American military operations.[16] Go ahead, said Stewart.[17] The telegram was sent from Washington.[18] Then the US asked that it not be delivered.[19] Consul-General Myles Ponsonby had already left it at the Foreign Affairs bureau.[20] It was returned.[21] 'I was amazed that the authors of the communication could have expected any reaction other than that they received. ... there was not the slightest chance of a constructive response to it.'[22] The FO, Donald Murray told him, was anxious to leave no stone unturned and so agreed to the US request. There would be a parliamentary question on 21 June.[23]

The time limit had all but expired in any case. Other powers were not told that bombing would be resumed, the *Times* correspondent reported. He referred to Johnson's 'exclusiveness' and 'secrecy'. In the current version of superpower diplomacy, the job was done once the Allies had been pressed to take part in executing a decision already made. It was sufficient in this case to 'show that some attempt had been made to begin negotiations. What the objective is in Vietnam, what the United States is willing to settle for, does not appear to be known, certainly to the allies.'[24]

'My judgment,' the president had said on 16 May, 'is that the public has never wanted us to stop the bombing. We have stopped in deference to [Senators] Mansfield and Fulbright, but we don't want to do it too long else we lose our base of support.'[25] In June he remarked to the NSC: 'I didn't believe it would work, and it didn't. It did relieve the pressure of public opinion.'[26] The pause was 'not so much a pause as a hiccup', Ball later wrote. The Hanoi foreign minister had termed it a deceitful manoeuvre to pave the way for escalation: 'a perceptive appraisal,' Ball thought.[27]

Gordon Walker had completed what *The Australian* called his 'somewhat abortive tour'[28] on 4 May and his report on 7 May. The aims of the SU and the West, he concluded, were 'not very far apart—namely to secure some balance in the Indochinese peninsula which will enable the great powers to live together without danger of war'. The US could not aim at military victory, but only at leaving South Vietnam 'in such conditions that China does not come in and take her place'. China should exercise the influence of a land power, and the US of a sea power, both from outside the area. 'The best way to achieve this is a divided Viet-Nam with the independence of both parts guaranteed.'

Britain had to back the Americans in their present operations. 'Their military effort is their only possible policy. An American defeat would be disastrous, even if a victory in the normal sense is unattainable.' But 'we should search for a policy which, while backing America loyally, allows us a certain more apparent independence of view. We might perhaps let it be known that our analysis of the situation differs somewhat from the American. We see more division amongst the Communist forces, less of a solid chain from Peking to the Viet Cong.' Some in the SD would agree. 'We might also indicate what kind of ultimate settlement we envisage. We might, too, make more clear our opposition to the bombing of Hanoi.' Doing all this would be 'a delicate operation' and probably depended on America's 'getting into a position of greater strength'.[29]

The FO questioned whether the struggle was simply one between China and the US. The Vietnamese Communist movement was as old as the Chinese and began well before the CCP triumph. The Vietnamese constituted 'a dynamic and expansionist force in their own right and it is at least arguable that the North Viet-Namese are using China at least as much as China is using them'. That also made the idea of a divided Vietnam questionable. 'The viability of such a solution would, at the very least, depend on South Viet-Nam being able to achieve something approaching the national cohesiveness and unity of South Korea, a prospect which, however attractive, still seems very remote.' In any case British policy had to be governed by other factors, such as UK-US relations; developments in the tripartite relationship of China, the SU and the West; the risk of escalation; and the state of British public opinion. 'Moreover, although the situation is still too fluid to make it practicable to suggest what form it would take, … our objective should be a peaceful settlement', and negotiations should begin as soon as possible.[30]

The FO recommended that it might be better not to make a specific warning about bombing Hanoi, but to renew the request for 'more consultation and advance warning on their policy in Vietnam as a whole'. The British had consulted the Americans 'over and over again' about a Cambodia conference, as Cable put it, but they had 'latterly not been even bothered to tell us in advance when they put an extra brigade of troops into Vietnam'.[31]

M.N.F. Stewart considered Cable's comment on consultation a bit unfair. When they first started, the Americans told the British about each raid, but 'they not unnaturally stopped this when the raids became daily occurrences'. Leonard Unger was 'pretty frank' in a talk on 6 April, and so was Rusk when he spoke to the ambassador after Honolulu. Stewart thought that what he said then covered the move of the extra brigade. Stewart accepted Cable's general argument 'that the more we and other friends of the United States are consulted, the better. But given the limitations imposed from on high I do not think that Rusk and Company are doing badly by us.'[32] In other words, contacts at the SD level were limited while contacts at the highest level were inadvisable.

At the NATO session, Stewart had put to Rusk the two questions Peck had suggested. Was the bombing achieving the military objective of stopping the flow of supplies and reinforcements? And was it achieving its political objective of inducing the North Vietnamese to negotiate? Rusk's answers were 'rather vague'. Cable asked the JIC for an opinion. The answer to both questions was 'No', but the bombing did seem to have achieved 'two subsidiary successes'. It had 'greatly fortified morale in South Viet-Nam' and permitted the survival of a regime whose collapse had been predicted. And it might have prevented an increase in the flow of supplies that could have enabled the Viet Cong to go over to 'the third phase of revolutionary warfare: continuous large-scale military action'. Cable agreed with the JIC analysis, and also agreed that the war might go on for a long time, even if the scope of the bombing were 'gradually extended'.

Robert Thompson had come to much the same conclusion. His alternative proposal was that the US and South Vietnamese forces should withdraw to a limited number of secure bases, more or less abandoning the rest of the country to the Viet Cong. Over the next two years the bases would be consolidated, and then the Saigon government would renew the offensive, hoping that the interval of Viet Cong administration would have persuaded the peasant that it was a lesser evil. Cable did not find the proposal 'encouraging or convincing'. In his view 'no early or satisfactory ending to the conflict' was in sight, and 'any negotiated solution that preserves American face will be preferable to any of the foreseeable alternatives. Unfortunately American "face" is what the Chinese seem most concerned to destroy and it is hard to see how they are to be persuaded from this objective.'[33]

Robert Thompson

The Viet Cong, Thompson had argued, now controlled most of the countryside, and there was no stable government or effective administration in the South, nor real security in the towns. Three alternatives thus faced the Viet Cong. Now that they had encircled the towns, they could go into the third phase of Mao-style insurgency, the war of movement. That Thompson thought was unlikely, since they would be vulnerable to air power. 'In fact it would almost be to our advantage if we could entice them to enter this phase and to seek a Dien-Bien-Phu type victory. They could be clobbered which would give the government and the Americans a good chance to reverse the whole situation.'

The Viet Cong's second option was to maintain the pressure of guerrilla operations and continue eroding the government's position in the hope that a government would be formed containing elements that would do a deal with the NLF, negotiate a ceasefire, invite the Americans to leave, 'and establish an ostensibly neutralist coalition government'. The Americans might even be given six months to evacuate. But within a year or two a single Communist government of Vietnam would follow.

The third option was to continue the pressure but try to stage a 'mass uprising' within the towns. Refugees were pouring in, including Viet Cong infiltrators, and tension would increase. 'Some judicious terrorism will then get the pot nicely boiling', while the government could be relied on to deal ham-handedly with demonstrations. The Viet Cong could then promote a peace movement and 'a surge of anti-American feeling'. Thompson thought this was the option the Viet Cong were most likely to choose.

His answer was 'a holding operation of the key areas vital to the government, including the main air bases'. That might mean giving some ground, particularly some of the untenable district towns. It might also involve increasing the US combat strength to at least one or possibly two divisions of Marines. Beyond that, Thompson thought, the involvement would be 'unprofitable. It would mean that major American ground forces were committed in Asia and we would end up with a Korean type war with the fighting being done by the Americans and not the Vietnamese.'

What would be the attitude of the Vietnamese government and people? About 10–15 per cent were thoroughly committed in the war against Communism, and they had no Formosa to go to. 'The great majority of the peasantry do not want Communism but, in the present circumstances, are not prepared to stick their necks out. … As far as the war is concerned they have learned to duck and I do not think that there is all that degree of war-weariness which people talk about.' Normal life went on whether the area was under government or Viet Cong control. 'The war itself has become almost a way of life.' The South Vietnam government would still be able to recruit. Its forces now numbered 500,000, and at least in defensive actions they continued to fight 'reasonably well' despite heavy casualties. If some ground were given up, the government could concentrate more forces in the enclaves. The police were demoralised. Strong military forces would prevent crowd concentrations and avoid bloody clashes when demonstrations got out of control.

Quick results were impossible. 'There is no prospect of a pacification programme working at the present time from such an unstable base position. Nor should one lunge from a quicksand.' The position had to be held for one or possibly two years. That might give 'an opportunity for some individual Vietnamese to come through as a more dynamic leader and enable the government machine to be restored so that an advance from the base areas could be started in about two years' time'. The Viet Cong would have made mistakes. The government would be able to talk of liberation, not pacification. 'Perhaps the main difficulty in the whole of this holding action will be whether the American people are prepared to support a long-drawn-out struggle which will cost much blood and treasure and earn them little or no applause.'

The Communist bloc had worldwide aims. The Vietnamese themselves were not only concerned with South Vietnam or the 'domino fall' of the rest of Southeast Asia that could follow in 10–15 years. The Chinese wanted to prove that wars of liberation were more profitable than coexistence. More than that, the Communists wanted not only to inflict a humiliating defeat on the Americans: 'they want to drive them out of Asia stinking as brutal war-mongering imperialists.' That would contaminate them in other parts of the world. 'What is even worse from our point of view, such a defeat may give rise to such pressures within America that it will cause the American Administration in the future to fumble the ball during the difficult years that lie ahead.'

Such a holding action might not be a winner, but 'even if we still lose', it would mean that the Americans went down 'with their flag flying and it could reduce some of the politically strategic consequences of defeat'. If it succeeded, there was a chance of achieving Western aims, which, apart from thwarting the Communist objectives, 'should be to establish a definite stop-line to Communist expansion in Asia. To a certain extent Russia has been taught this lesson as a result of Berlin and Cuba and there is a generally agreed line which each side recognises that it cannot cross. With regard to China Korea was not enough and it may take ten years for this lesson to be taught.' Even if the holding action were 'only partially successful and delays a final defeat it will give us a few more years in which to consolidate the Western position in Thailand, Malaysia and even Laos'.

In the US Thompson had recommended that 'the tempo of the bombing in North Vietnam should be toned down', but that it should be continued as a 'measured response'. He accepted the American view that underground aggression should not go 'unpunished'. That was a lesson that had to be taught if there were to be a 'stop-line'. The bombing also reduced the infiltration flow and, by hitting communications north of the 17th parallel, might prevent the movement of large-scale DRV forces into the northern provinces of South Vietnam. 'To a limited extent it may improve morale in the South and allow a breathing-space for any holding action which is to follow.' It also demonstrated 'American determination and resolution'. But it would not force the Hanoi government 'to call the dogs off. As Vietnamese they are prepared to pay a certain price for South Vietnam and, as good, hard-core Communists, they are prepared to pay still more to inflict a disastrous defeat on American imperialism.' Other than the dykes, there were no targets that would force such a government to come to terms.

'The greatest danger from the present tempo is the effect which it is having not only on world opinion but on large groups within the United States.' Pressure for peace could force negotiations at the worst time. The prospect of negotiations would weaken 'any remaining will to continue the fight', and no settlement could remove the Viet Cong from the countryside or create a stable government in the South. 'Without these there is no possibility whatsoever (as laid down by President Johnson) of assuring the continued independence of South Vietnam.'

Thompson had 'never been happy', he wrote, 'about the prospect of maintaining two Vietnams', and reunification had only appeared credible 'from the North'. If the holding action were successful, there might be opportunities for seeking a different political solution, for example the creation of an independent sovereign state of Cochin China, and another in Annam. That would 'carry the political attack to the North'—Annam extended up to Vinh—and reduce the influence of Northern refugees in the South, 'a major step to stability'. Annam would be 'the buffer between a Communist Tonkin and a free Cochin-China'. There could be a common market and a customs union. Cochin China would be part of a Mekong Confederation, 'whereas neither Annam nor Tonkin are Mekong states'. But Thompson did not recommend advocating this solution at the moment.[34] Indeed it must surely have appeared too much like the old FIC.

The 'enclave' concept was not new, Etherington-Smith observed, and had something in common with familiar principles of pacification. It had been canvassed in respect of Central Vietnam, where floods had sent refugees into the towns, but not taken further, since it would have a depressing effect on South Vietnamese morale. Intensive air attacks on rural Central Vietnam had produced another argument for an enclave-like approach, which Tran Van Tuyen (deputy minister of planning) had tentatively advanced. Thompson argued that morale could hardly be worse. But in fact it had improved since he left Saigon, and it would be 'a grave mistake' to advocate an enclave policy, though on occasion enclaves might serve a practical purpose.[35]

At SEAD Donald Murray had found Thompson's analysis lucid. His proposal, however, would not be accepted by the US administration, since it required military concessions and patience, neither readily available, given domestic and internal pressures. Nor could the British government advocate a settlement with so little prospect of an end to the fighting.[36] Account should be taken of Etherington-Smith's letter, which put enclaves in the proper perspective, Peck commented.[37] In Washington M.N.F. Stewart wondered if he might talk to John McNaughton in Defense about Thompson's ideas.[38] Better not, Cable replied. Both SEAD and Etherington-Smith doubted their validity, and there was a considerable difference between Thompson's feeding in the ideas and Stewart's doing so. '[T]he rejection of a negotiated settlement ... is not an idea with which we can afford to be associated.'[39]

Etherington-Smith offered more criticism of Thompson's assessment, rather echoing Ball when in London, both, perhaps, relying on Americans in Saigon. The Viet Cong did not control the major portion of the countryside, though they could threaten it: it was 'one thing to create a state of insecurity ... and quite another to hold and administer'. Nor was the security in the towns as weak as Thompson suggested. Buddhist pressure had stopped, popular disorders virtually ceased, police morale improved. Thompson's suggestion that the Viet Cong were most likely to choose the third of the options he set out turned largely on the refugee problem, but that, too, had now levelled off. The 'mass uprising' theory would now be 'over-rated as a Viet Cong war-winning tactic'.

Withdrawal into 'small closely defended areas' would be 'interpreted as failure'. The abandoned population 'would feel that the government had not kept faith with them' and there would be 'a generally adverse effect on morale'. 'The Viet Cong would be jubilant and would hasten to establish "the people's government" wherever possible with ... extremely harmful international consequences.' Positions of real strength would be given up, 'particularly in the Hoa Hao, Cao Dai, and Catholic areas', and those who left would 'flood the "key areas"'. The regular forces would indeed have a firm base from which to operate. But the regional and especially the popular forces, removed from their environment, would be 'dismayed', since their main motivation was to protect family, friends and possessions, and they operated in their immediate vicinity.

Etherington-Smith also thought Thompson's remarks on the bombing were outdated. Since he left Vietnam, the US government had 'improved their position by their offer of unconditional discussions', and since he wrote his letter, by a 'pause'. The Americans had to 'strike a balance between, on the one hand, losing momentum and causing morale to falter by not pressing the attacks on the North hard enough, and, on the other hand, the risk of provoking a seriously adverse reaction of world opinion and/or escalating the war by stepping up the attacks too strongly'. The whole operation involved risks, as the president recognised, 'but my guess is that the Americans still have a considerable margin of safety in which to operate. Decisive intervention by the Chinese or the Russians seems unlikely.' World opinion had taken the bombings 'more or less in its stride', and there had been 'a surprising degree of actual support' in Southeast Asia itself.

Thompson's argument that if American forces went above two divisions 'we will be involved in a Korean-type war' was not 'explicit'. If he meant that that would produce 'a reaction from North Vietnamese or Communist Chinese ground forces', that was doubtful. 'There is already the best part of a division's worth of troops here and I suspect many more will come and I cannot visualize the D.R.V. or China attacking South Vietnam because another division plus worth of American troops land in South Vietnam. Without the aid of either the North Vietnamese Army or the Chinese how can the Viet Cong ever stage a Korean-type war? They have neither the weapons, the equipment, the aircraft nor the supplies to engage in such a war.'

Etherington-Smith was uneasy about the references to negotiations made both by Thompson and by Cable and in the FO despatch on the Gordon Walker report. His own view was 'that there is still a chance of saving South Vietnam from communist rule and that the effect on our interests if it is lost will be so serious that we should do everything we can to prevent this happening. … I emphatically do not subscribe to the view that we should do anything to promote or encourage a settlement which, while saving American face, means delivering South Vietnam to ultimate communist domination: in other words, a disguised form of capitulation.' The Americans did not contemplate that. 'For us to give any support to such a solution at this stage would … be dangerously short-sighted.'

British public opinion had to be considered 'as well as possible escalation risks and of course we should all like to see a settlement, on acceptable terms, of this bitter war'. But there was a point 'at which too much emphasis on negotiations ceases to be useful and becomes harmful. Constant reiteration of the need for negotiations when it is clear to everybody that the other side are not prepared to talk on any reasonable terms inevitably suggests that we are prepared to settle for terms which are not acceptable in an anti-communist sense, in other words to sell South Vietnam down the river. This impression, if it got abroad, could obviously be extremely harmful to our relations not only with the Vietnamese but also, I would guess with the Americans.' He agreed with Thompson that 'premature negotiations could be disastrous to the anti-communist struggle in South Vietnam'. The game should be 'played long and ... we should restrain our understandable anxiety to see an early settlement'.[40]

'What it really boils down to,' Cable commented, 'is that Mr Etherington-Smith and Mr Thompson are arguing about different methods of winning a war which, in my own view, cannot be won at all.' The ambassador's remarks about 'premature negotiations' were 'a little ironic'. Should his attention be drawn to Chen Yi's views?[41]

On 7 May Johnson promised that the US would do all it could to ensure the safety of South Vietnam from aggression. He was signing the supplementary appropriation bill which Congress had promptly approved. It told the brave people of South Vietnam: 'America keeps her promises, and we will back up these promises with all the resources that we need.' The weapons would be laid aside when peace came. 'But that was in the hands of others besides ourselves.' For months 'we have waited for a sign, a signal, even a whisper, but our offer of unconditional discussions has fallen on unreceptive ears'. The US would 'do whatever must be done to insure the safety of South Vietnam from aggression. We will use our power with restraint. ... But we will use it.'[42]

In Moscow Deputy Prime Minister Alexander Shelepin told Trevelyan that he regarded the speech as comparable to Churchill's Fulton 'iron curtain' speech. Some of what Soviet leaders said had to be discounted as propaganda, and the ambassador did not think they saw a direct threat to their country. They believed rather that the US had 'gone over to the offensive against the national liberation struggle'. If that succeeded in one country today, another would fall tomorrow, 'the Communist version of the domino theory'. It was, Trevelyan thought, in their interest 'to keep the question on this plane'. American bombing of military targets in North Vietnam had, however, transformed a national liberation struggle into 'a local war between States'. Soviet doctrine approved of the former but not the latter. 'Local wars, according to the doctrine, tend to grow, and the best course is to stop them as soon as possible.' The SU could not, however, urge a ceasefire: it was inhibited in part by the Sino-Soviet dispute, in part by its support for the North Vietnamese demand for a withdrawal of US troops, in part by the fear that any suggestion of compromise might be a mistake. Moreover, there was no assurance that their representations would be heeded.

What then would the Russians do if the American attacks continued? Unless the Chinese frustrated it, there would be 'a growing flow of Soviet weapons to the D.R.V. and increasing numbers of American aircraft shot down by such weapons', but it was unlikely that a Soviet-American confrontation would develop quickly and become a major threat to peace. Both sides probably calculated that the development of military operations could be 'carefully controlled', and that 'the pressure of world opinion for the opening of talks' would increase. Soviet leaders seemed to believe that the pressures that could be brought to bear on the US would prove greater than those that could be brought to bear on the Communist leaders involved.

If talks began, the Communists would first aim at stopping the attacks on North Vietnam, thus reconverting the situation to a national liberation struggle, and then creating conditions under which that struggle could be successfully resumed. Hence the demand for American withdrawal and the insistence that the Vietnamese should settle their own future. The president, however, had said the Americans would not withdraw. If each side stood on its current position, talks could not succeed, and hostilities might be resumed.

None of this had to cause the Soviet leaders 'any acute or immediate concern', Trevelyan thought. Indeed they might believe that the US could not bring about by military means a situation that would guarantee South Vietnam against a Communist takeover, and that the greater the effort it made, the more shameful the final withdrawal. Their present policies might, moreover, increase their influence in Hanoi and serve their purposes in the Sino-Soviet dispute. But they surely had anxieties. The world had learned that Soviet influence in Southeast Asia was not decisive. The SU had not been able to turn its co-chairmanship into positive action. Its leaders could not predict what their commitment to the DRV would ultimately involve. They could not control China's actions, nor could they be certain how far the US was prepared to go. If the scale of its attacks increased, there were likely to be strains within the Soviet leadership. It would be 'a testing time for them as well as the West'.[43]

'All that the Americans are asking is the cessation of North Vietnamese interference in the South,' Etherington-Smith commented from Saigon, and that was, he argued, in accordance with the Geneva agreements, which the Russians had hitherto supported. The North Vietnamese had never specifically admitted that they were responsible for such interference, and they too claimed that the Geneva agreements should be the basis of a solution. 'While it is true that each side interprets the Agreements differently, it seems to me that as long as there are some common terms of reference there is at least something which both sides could discuss.'

The ambassador in Saigon agreed with his Moscow colleague, however, that the prospect even of starting talks was 'not bright, and the tendency of both sides to take up ever more extreme positions does not seem likely to bring talks any nearer'. At present, too, the North Vietnamese probably looked on talks 'only as a means of finishing off by a process of negotiation what they could not do by direct military assault', and would not contemplate talks unless they felt 'pretty certain' that South Vietnam's will to resist 'had already been so undermined that peace could be made on communist terms'. Unfortunately China encouraged the North Vietnamese in those ideas. It would need 'a considerable improvement of the military position in South Vietnam during the next few weeks and months if the D.R.V. are to be shaken out of their present intransigence'.[44]

Non-aligned Countries

In a statement to the House of Commons on 3 June 1965 Stewart had repeated his sequence of conference–ceasefire–settlement, but also reiterated the lack of success of any of the initiatives to bring about a peaceful settlement. He suggested it might be possible to build on the declaration of the 17 non-aligned countries of 15 March delivered to the UK and other governments on 1 April.[45] Tito had organised a meeting of 'neutrals' in Belgrade in March.[46] Pursuant to the final declaration of the Non-Aligned Conference in Cairo in October 1964, that had appealed for negotiations without preconditions.[47]

Ambassador Bruce commented to the SD on the supportive nature of Stewart's speech, despite the restive left wing and 'growing uneasiness' among the British public. The Wilson government, he pointed out, depended heavily on the US undertaking to consult on major changes in policy or the conduct of the war.[48] Mac Bundy wrote to the president. He had shown 'skepticism' when it had been argued that the British government had been 'solid and helpful', no doubt recalling Wilson's attempt 'to telephone his way into a fancy trip to the White House' and Stewart's reference to gas. But Bruce had been astonished by Wilson's strength and skill in defending US policy and his mastery of his own left wing. 'The support of the UK has been of real value internationally and perhaps of even more value in limiting the howls of our own liberals.'[49]

An intensification of the fighting was predicted, Cable had written on 1 June, resulting, however, in no decisive advantage for either side. The Chinese would not intervene, but Soviet aircraft and missiles would be used, probably manned by Vietnamese. Higher US casualties could be expected, but there would be 'even less readiness than at present to negotiate'. Even if continued fighting convinced both sides that 'outright victory' was impossible, 'the emotions generated by such fighting may make it even more difficult than before to initiate negotiations without unacceptable loss of face on one side or the other'. That danger the Foreign Office had long had in mind, and one of its reasons for seeking a Cambodia conference was to create a forum for negotiations. Now that prospect seemed dim. 'Is there anything else we could attempt, whether to promote a settlement or to improve our propaganda position against the time when the fighting and the pressure of public opinion will have become fiercer?' Only the Russians could at present make an effective contribution to starting negotiations. Cable doubted whether Britain should merely wait till they were ready. Perhaps it could prod them. Or maybe publish a reply to the 17 nations 'on our own' just before the Commonwealth prime ministers meeting, so that the initiative could be pursued with the six uncommitted nations represented at it?[50]

Noting that Stewart referred to the idea in the House of Commons, Peck proposed to consult the Americans about it.[51] It would be suggested that the 17 nations should issue an invitation to meet to the governments interested in reaching a settlement in Vietnam. There was a risk that they might modify the proposal by including the Viet Cong or demanding an end to bombing, but the balance was in favour of the idea.[52] The draft response to them explained that the British government had so far remained silent since it was pursuing other initiatives with a similar objective, including the message of 2 April, the mission of Gordon Walker, and the attempts to promote a conference on the 'separate but related issue' of Cambodia. None had made sufficient progress to justify the hope that they would make an adequate contribution towards promoting a peaceful settlement in Vietnam. Britain now endorsed the appeal of the 17 countries and suggested that they agree to invite the governments interested in the conflict to meet under their auspices, at a specified time and place, 'in order to start discussions without preconditions so that a political solution to the problem of Viet Nam may be found'.[53] There was a risk that some of the 17 might try to modify their proposal 'to our disadvantage', but it would be emphasised that the suggestion referred to their original concept of 'discussions without preconditions'. The suggestion was sent to Washington.[54] The outcome was apparently positive. Perhaps the assessments Bruce and Mac Bundy had made were helpful with the president.

The plan was to discuss the proposal, but not the draft message, with the Commonwealth prime ministers when they met in London, then issue the message to the 17—seven of them were Commonwealth heads of government—before the Algiers conference of the Afro-Asian nations starting at the end of June. In the event the idea was shelved in view of the prime minister's consultation with members of the Commonwealth mission.[55]

On 8 June the State Department had formally announced that the American commander in Vietnam had been given authority to use his troops in offensive operations against the Viet Cong. The troops, said Robert J. McCloskey, could be used only if Vietnamese authorities asked, and alongside Vietnamese troops. Another step, remarked the *Times* correspondent, towards a Korea-style war.[56] A further statement the following day said that US troops would not be used in offensive action without the president's specific orders.[57] The president's tactics were as before, *The Australian* noted. He had been calling for peace for over a week: 'by speaking out for peace before stepping up the war he seeks to mollify world opinion and to impress the communists with a real desire to negotiate a settlement.'[58]

This would not make it easier for Wilson 'to run the Government on a shoe-string majority'.[59] Indeed he complained that the US decision to undertake a combat role made more difficulties for the UK. Was it consulted or given information? If not, it was 'a bit unreasonable to ask us to endorse everything they do and yet one sees the difficulties of any form of dissociation from it'. What could Britain do? Calling for a conference would be in vain. Raising the question at the SC Britain had always opposed, but it would put the Russians in a difficult position. Should the foreign secretary see the secretary-general?[60] Bundy had mentioned to the minister on 29 May the possibility of a combat role, Nicholas Henderson noted, though saying there was no intention of sending a lot more troops. The foreign secretary had approved press guidance to the effect that the Americans kept the British informed of their thinking and plans in general, but naturally not of each precise move. 'We had some foreknowledge of the announcement but not of its details or timing.' Britain was pursuing the 17-nation idea. But Lord Caradon could discuss the SC idea with Thant.[61] The PM agreed. Would a debate on Vietnam have any value? the delegation was asked. North Vietnam and China would not be there. Would there be a majority for a constructive resolution calling for a conference?[62] Thant saw no point in a SC meeting, New York replied.[63]

The foreign secretary, as Henderson put it, managed to assuage the PM's fears.[64] A FO minute had been left with him on 10 June. Britain's involvement in Vietnam was insignificant: Australia had sent fighting men there, and now New Zealand was following suit; Britain had none. 'Our major interest in the situation in Indo-China is to see that it does not escalate into a global or regional war in which we might be involved.' It was also true that Britain's interests as a non-Communist power would be 'impaired' if the US was 'defeated in the field, or defaulted on its commitments. As a major global ally we have an interest in *how* the United States wages its war.' Britain could meet those needs by keeping in touch with the Americans and showing them such assets as the co-chairmanship and a direct expertise on China. Its attitude also had a bearing on that of others, 'particularly the Commonwealth'.

Given the president's 'secretive nature', high-level approaches were difficult. Britain kept in touch with US thinking at lower levels. 'This is not always satisfactory or clear, but is the best we shall get. Moreover any closer consultation in the real sense of "would H.M.G. publicly approve United States action in such-and-such event?" would surely be extremely embarrassing to us.' Britain should expect to be informed on actions and policy, but not in detail, any more than the US would expect it over confrontation, and it could not exercise a veto. 'Consequently it is Britain's interest to give support to our major ally. Whenever we declare our determination to seek a peaceful settlement we should accompany this with an expression of general support for the Americans, while avoiding passing judgment on their specific actions. Behind this general public support, we should then have a better opportunity of conveying in private any criticisms we may feel justified.'[65]

Commonwealth Peace Mission

The PM had another idea. The Commonwealth prime ministers meeting was due to start on 17 June. 'Pacing the terrace at Chequers' early on the 14th, he tells us, he had the idea of 'a Commonwealth peace mission', which he discussed with his advisers, Oliver Wright and Derek Mitchell, and then with the foreign secretary.[66] He talked to Sir Robert Menzies that night, and in the morning Mitchell showed the draft telegram to Washington. The Australian prime minister said that instructing the Australian ambassador to support Dean had to be accompanied by emphasising that Australian support for US policy in Vietnam 'was in no way modified'.[67]

The telegram said that Wilson wanted to avoid an acrimonious debate at the CPM and a bad communiqué after it. He wished to avoid adding to the difficulties of the US, the UK, Australia and other like-minded nations, but also 'to see whether we cannot get some movement on the Communist side towards a Conference without preconditions'. On the first day of the CPM he planned to propose 'a mission to see in what circumstances [a] Conference on Viet Nam could be held and, possibly—to draw the terms of reference still more widely—to try to bring about a restoration of peace in South-East Asia'. A mission, say, of three prime ministers, might go to see the secretary-general, and then go to Washington, Moscow, Saigon, Hanoi, Peking, and back to Washington again, to discuss with the president the reactions in the other capitals. Led by Wilson, it might include, say, the presidents of Pakistan and Tanzania.

The idea had been discussed with Menzies but no other prime minister. They were 'not over-hopeful' that the initiative would lead to a conference and were 'resolved on no account to put forward proposals which would be unacceptable to the Americans'. Even if it failed—because Peking or Hanoi refused to receive it or took 'an utterly negative line'—it would advantage the West by identifying those governments that were making a conference impossible. Refusing to receive it would be 'a great snub to Afro-Asian opinion'. The PM and Menzies also considered that the whole approach would 'both strengthen the Russians versus the Chinese and increase Russian as opposed to Chinese influence on Hanoi'. Agreement was not sought in Washington, but acquiescence was. The object was to be helpful to the president, so that the CPM discussions took a constructive turn and 'the head of steam' at the subsequent Afro-Asian conference in Algiers was reduced. Should the PM contact the president by phone or teleprinter? Wright was flying over to provide background.[68]

Bruce was enthusiastic, Mitchell noted. He told the US ambassador on the way to his car that the idea had survived No. 10 and the FO because the PM said it was 'bound to be a winner, whether or not the Mission succeeded'. He had decided not to phone the president, the last call having been 'thoroughly unsatisfactory'.[69] It was, says Wilson's official biographer, 'a dazzlingly ingenious attempt to achieve his three main policy objectives in a single stroke: to maintain the Anglo-American alliance, to fortify the unity and standing of the Commonwealth, and to keep his left-wing quiet':[70] he says nothing about bringing peace to Vietnam. To the critical Richard Crossman, it was 'a stunt': 'the chances of success are very slim.'[71]

The US government was happy with it, Saigon was told, but no indication of that would be given to the prime ministers or to the public.[72]

Dean had talked to Mac Bundy about it at the White House. It was clear the initiative had been 'very well received in Washington and ... positively welcomed'. One problem worried Bundy, 'the problem of a possible cease-fire, whether as a request from the Marlborough House meeting or elsewhere. ... they had a problem with the Hawks there'. Shortly he expected an increased commitment of ground troops in South Vietnam as well as air activity against North Vietnam. An announcement of that while the Commonwealth mission was on its travels 'could well pull the rug from under its feet'. Perhaps in his opening speech the PM could explain the increasing VC activity and 'the inevitable American response'. In the rest of their conversation, Dean suggested a distinction between North and South. Attacked in the South, the US could not be expected to hold its fire. But 'it might be valuable psychologically if they were to volunteer, at some suitable stage of the initiative, to institute a second pause in the bombing of North Viet Nam'. Bundy said the idea had occurred to him, too.[73] The prospective increase in ground forces perhaps provided the context for the president's approval: it would accord with the tactics *The Australian* had described.

Faced with the unexpected suggestion, the heads of government meeting agreed to a mission, though President Julius Nyerere of Tanzania—which Zhou had just visited—was opposed,[74] suggesting that it would be putting China in the dock.[75] The mission would be led by Wilson and include the heads of government of Ghana, Nigeria, Trinidad and Tobago, and Ceylon. Its object would be 'to ascertain how far there may be common ground about the circumstances in which a conference might be held leading to the establishment of a just and lasting peace in Vietnam'.[76] It would meet the 'parties concerned', implying not merely 'governments', and thus the inclusion of the VC (FLN),[77] 'all the parties concerned', it insisted.[78]

Kwame Nkrumah's Ghana delegation produced a draft of the points on which guidelines for the mission should be based. Given the diversity of views within the Commonwealth, its first two points suggested, broad areas of agreement should be established so that the mission could approach its assignment 'meaningfully'. There was already agreement on some basic considerations, the third paragraph suggested: that the risk of escalation into general war was 'extremely great'; that the conflict could not be resolved by purely military means, since the Americans could not destroy the insurgency 'without much greater commitment of their power', nor could the Viet Cong force them out 'without greater and much more tried assistance from the outside'; and that a ceasefire and conference of those directly involved was 'the most reasonable solution'. During its consultations, the fourth paragraph suggested, the mission might be guided by the following 'ultimate objectives': immediate suspension of all US air attacks on North Vietnam; ceasefire on all sides to enable a conference to meet; the conference to aim to end the war, 'secure the withdrawal of all foreign military presence from South Vietnam and the neutralization of the area', establish for a period an international peace force under the auspices of the Geneva agreement along the 17th parallel 'to ensure the abolition of frontier violations', and 'establish principles for the eventual unification of the country through free and supervised elections'.[79]

SEAD suggested some amendments to the draft. Those it proposed for paragraph 3 were 'purely practical' in character, and not 'politically controversial'. The Ghana draft exaggerated the risks of escalation. It would be better to state that there was 'an inherent risk' of 'wider war'. The draft should mention the North Vietnamese as well as the Viet Cong and the South Vietnamese as well as the Americans. It should not imply, as the Ghana draft did, that reinforcements might enable the Viet Cong to expel the Americans. 'This does not seem to us realistic.' The draft should make it clear that neither side could expect a military victory 'without a major change in the situation'. It should allow that a ceasefire might precede or follow a conference. 'The fighting ... is a guerrilla war without any clearly defined front and it may well be impossible for the contestants to agree on a cease-fire without negotiating this in considerable detail.' In 1954 the ceasefire agreement provided for regrouping and withdrawal of forces and for arbitration and international supervision. The agreement occupied 13 pages and took months to negotiate. 'With the best will in the world, ... it might in practice prove impossible to arrange a cease-fire *before* a conference.'

The amendments SEAD proposed for paragraph 4 were 'politically important' and might prove controversial. First, it substituted for the immediate suspension of US air attacks on the North a clause providing for an American undertaking to suspend them and a North Vietnamese undertaking to suspend the movement of men or material to the South, leaving it open when those undertakings should come into effect. 'The U.S. Government have already told us that any cessation of American military action would have to be met by a corresponding cessation of military action on the other side.' It suggested that Hanoi should 'cease infiltration and aggressive activity in the South', and the UK draft sought to meet that condition. 'With Commonwealth delegates'—not supposed to know that the UK consulted the US—'the main argument might be that an appeal for cessation of military activities cannot be directed to one side alone and is more likely to be accepted by the U.S. Government if the other side have meanwhile given some indication of readiness for negotiations (i.e.

by agreeing to receive the Commonwealth mission).' The UK draft also amended the reference to conference and ceasefire, and it omitted the word 'South' to make that passage look less one-sided. 'In fact there is little foreign military presence in the North', and the North Vietnamese did not admit there was any. The phrase 'neutralisation of the area' was left: it was 'vague enough to be generally acceptable'. The international peace force, the revised draft suggested, should 'prevent interference from either part of Viet-Nam in the internal affairs of the other'. Neither side had, except by air, crossed the 17th parallel to any extent: the North Vietnamese had penetrated by sea or via Laos and Cambodia. Patrolling all the frontiers was 'not a practical proposition', while a force confined to the 17th parallel would be absurd. Finally SEAD's draft provided that the elections should be supervised 'internationally', as envisaged in 1954.[80]

The points were discussed at a meeting of the four heads of mission on 23 June 1965. The outcome was a document to be put to the full meeting of the Commonwealth PMs. If the mission was to approach its assignment 'meaningfully', paragraph 1 suggested, there should be 'broad areas of agreement'. There was already agreement on 'certain basic considerations', paragraph 2 continued. It included SEAD's clause on escalation; then the statement that the conflict could not be resolved by military means, shorn of any further references; and the Ghana version of the reference to ceasefire and conference without SEAD's qualifier. The word 'all' was, however, added to the phrase 'the parties directly involved' at the insistence, the FO told Washington and other posts, of 'certain members of the Mission', 'the logical sequence of the Mission's agreement to contact all the parties concerned', though it remained to be seen 'whether all the parties concerned would sit down at a table with each other, or whether the SVNLF are included in the Hanoi Delegation or not'. 'The Mission has in mind,' the FO added, 'that it might not be possible to arrange a cease-fire in advance of the conference and that a cease-fire might indeed be the first task of a conference when it assembles.' The point was appreciated, but deliberately not included since it implied the mission's failure to arrange a ceasefire.

The guidelines then suggested in paragraph 3 the 'ultimate objectives' that might guide the mission. First, (a), was the suspension of all US air attacks on North Vietnam; then, second, (b) 'A North Vietnamese undertaking to prevent the movement of any military forces or material to South Vietnam'. That was included, the FO observed, 'despite some difficulty from certain Missions'. It also noted that missions other than the UK wanted to call for the 'immediate' suspension of air attacks, but the word had been abandoned. Option (c), Ghana-style, called for a ceasefire on all sides to enable a conference to seek a peaceful solution. The objectives of the conference were to end the war; to secure 'the withdrawal of all foreign military presence from Viet Nam and the neutralisation of the area', a phrase covering the withdrawal of Russian and Chinese advisers from the North as well as American forces in the South, as the FO observed; to establish for a period an international peace force under the Geneva agreement 'to safeguard peace in Viet Nam'; and to establish principles for eventual unification through, as the SEAD had suggested, 'internationally' supervised elections.

If the reply from Hanoi were positive, the FO concluded, the mission would probably travel to Geneva, Saigon, Hanoi and Washington. If the reply were negative, the UK planned to resist any move by other members that the mission should travel to Washington and Saigon only. The agreement, the FO admitted, was less than complete: 'some points may not be acceptable to one or other of the Governments.'[81]

The Commonwealth prime ministers as a whole made some verbal changes. They modified the statement that the conflict could not be resolved by military means: 'there are grave doubts as to an early or final resolution by military means.' And they added 'assistance or' before 'material' to the North Vietnamese undertaking, and in the following clause put 'total' in front of 'cease-fire'.[82]

Etherington-Smith pointed out the 'particular difficulties' in face of arranging a ceasefire. Those included 'the difficulty of initiating negotiations and concluding any effective agreement owing to indeterminate status of the Viet Cong and Saigon Government's political objections to dealing with them', and 'the near impossibility of enforcing any agreement reached'. Viet Cong 'aggression' covered a range of actions from conventional military operations to sabotage and subversion. It would be 'practically impossible' to ensure they ceased, while the operations by government and American forces, 'mostly of an identifiable nature', could be easily controlled. 'The Vietnamese Governments have made it clear that they regard withdrawal of Communist troops and cadres as essential pre-condition of a cease-fire. The possibly impracticable stipulation is not unreasonable (the Malaysians made the same condition last year when there was talk of a cease-fire in Borneo).'

Etherington-Smith thought that 'the only practicable basis for a cease-fire would be agreement that both sides should rest on their present positions, i.e. that Viet Cong should remain in control of areas which they claim to hold. But it would be virtually impossible for political reasons for the Saigon Government to accept such an arrangement. It would mean abdicating their rights as the established government to maintain law and order throughout the country. The effect on their prestige would probably be disastrous. It would also leave the Viet Cong in a position to continue political subversion over a large part of the country to the great disadvantage of their opponents.' Thus continued pressure for a ceasefire would embarrass the Vietnamese as well as the Americans. The American ambassador said it was 'the one aspect of recent British initiatives which has caused him anxiety'. In his view it would be as difficult to conclude a ceasefire as to arrive at a final settlement.[83]

Aware of some of the difficulties from Thompson and Etherington-Smith, Peck said he had made the point in the official working party of the UK, Ghana, Nigeria and Trinidad. 'While it was evident that they had little conception of difficulties involved, it was also clear that in such company failure to agree that a comprehensive cease-fire was one of the objectives of the Mission would be to advocate original sin.' The question of whether a ceasefire preceded a conference, as in Laos in 1961, or vice versa, as in 1959 (1954?), was appreciated, though not mentioned in the guidelines. The final comment in Etherington-Smith's telegram was Peck's own view, 'but we cannot postulate failure of Mission's obvious first step'.[84]

The mission might turn into 'an empty window-dressing operation similar to the fruitless jaunt' of Gordon Walker, *The Australian* had sourly commented.[85] Would it even get going? In Peking the deputy director of the West European Department, Wilford had reported, thought that the proposal to engage in peace talks would not be accepted and the mission would not be received.[86] China had slammed the door on Gordon Walker, declared the *People's Daily*, and would slam it again. 'Truly this is the action of a nitwit making trouble for himself.' *Nhan Dan* rejected the mission as a 'vicious scheme', designed to please Washington and soothe indignation in the UK and Commonwealth countries.[87]

Kosygin told the ambassadors of the UK, Ghana and Nigeria that the SU was not prepared to receive the mission: the SU had no authority to discuss the question, which concerned only North Vietnam, the NLF and the US government.[88] Peking and Hanoi saw it as inspired by Washington, declared an article issued by the Cambodian press agency, and Washington had welcomed it with alacrity. The reaction was inevitable, given that Wilson was leading the mission. If Wilson wished to be conciliatory, he had to condemn US policy.[89] An article in the semi-official Phnom Penh journal *Réalités* said that Wilson was attempting this vain mission only to please the Left and to give LBJ an excuse to say he had tried a peaceful approach in vain.[90] In New Zealand, where he had been holding off the despatch of a battery, V Force, Prime Minister Keith Holyoake expressed his disappointment.[91]

In Paris Hohler called on the Directeur de l'Asie to bring the initiative officially to his notice. He and his colleagues, he replied, had discussed it, and the view had been expressed that the prime minister was not the ideal person to lead the mission 'since if the views of the Commonwealth on Viet Nam were regarded as a spectrum, Mr Wilson was well to the right of centre'. Hohler replied that he was chairman of the PMs conference and that it would be difficult to justify the choice of anyone else. The directeur apparently also thought it a mistake to publish the initiative 'without first preparing the ground by making enquiries through the diplomatic channel to ensure that it would be acceptable. By taking the Communist Governments by surprise, Mr Wilson had courted a rebuff.' Wilson, Hohler responded, had no doubt had in mind that the views of the Commonwealth governments differed widely. 'His only chance was to take everyone by surprise. If he had engaged in a careful process of diplomatic preparation, everyone would have started imposing incompatible conditions.'[92]

Bruce, the American ambassador, had told Wilson on 24 June that his government was concerned lest the mission went ahead with visits to Washington and Saigon and to Thant in Geneva even though the Communist capitals refused to receive it. The prime minister made it clear that the mission's intention was 'to make contact with the relevant Communist powers and that, if this was not possible in some form, the Mission would not proceed'. As a result of the initiative and other events, he said, 'the situation had been completely changed; for example, China and Russia were now at loggerheads. Useful pressures were being exerted on Hanoi and it was there that the Mission would have to see the Viet Cong—it was improbable that they would come down to Saigon and the Prime Minister would not be anxious to see them there if they did.' The most likely itinerary was now Saigon, Hanoi, possibly Peking and Washington.

Bruce welcomed the assurance that the mission intended to contact the Communists. He asked 'whether it was a fact that certain Commonwealth Governments were trying to jockey the Prime Minister out of the leadership of the Mission'. Wilson replied that 19 of the other representatives supported his leadership, only one—the Kenyan—reserved his position, and the issue had never become 'one for open debate'. Would the prime minister be able to control the other members when the mission was in Washington? Bruce asked. His aim, Wilson replied, would be to have at every place they visited only agreed press statements. If, however, members made separate statements, he would feel free to do the same. He expected to take all the press conferences, emphasising throughout that he was acting not as prime minister of the UK but as chairman of the Commonwealth mission.[93]

Wilson's leadership had indeed been in question. Nkrumah had told him there was no reason to step down. 'The important thing is to reassure the world that this Mission of Commonwealth Prime Ministers is independent and has an independent policy to the solution of the Vietnam problem. We should be sure never to give the impression that we are pro-U.K. or pro-U.S.A. If we can make ourselves clear on this point we will be in a better position to be received by all the parties concerned.'[94]

In Cairo, however, Zhou had described the mission as 'a manoeuvre in support of the American peace hoax'.[95] In Peking the mission, Wilford reported on 26 June, was 'sternly' rejected.[96] It was a new 'peace talks plot', rendering another service to the US aggressor.[97] 'This is "No", with knobs on,' Wright told his prime minister.[98]

In Hanoi Ponsonby tried to obtain some line on the North Vietnamese attitude by seeking an interview with the Soviet ambassador. Meanwhile, he had a conversation with a member of the embassy staff, who gave his 'private' views. He made three main points. First, he indicated that '[t]he Russians have consistently been telling the North Vietnamese that their country is [an] independent State and that they should make their own decisions free from outside influences.' Kosygin's reply to the Commonwealth proposal was a 'public affirmation of Soviet policy'. Second, he suggested that North Vietnam would find it easier to receive the mission if the NLF were initially approached unilaterally by the US in Moscow or any capital in which it was represented. The North Vietnamese, careful not to be seen to have direct control of the Front, would not act on its behalf. If such an approach were made, North Vietnam would be in a 'less isolated position', the Russian suggested, and he 'implied that Chinese pressure on North Viet Nam might be reduced if we could find the way to approach the N.F.L.S.V. without directly involving North Viet Nam'. Third, the Soviet embassy in Hanoi had detected signs that North Vietnam was adopting a 'more flexible attitude' to the Chinese in recent weeks.

Contacting the NLF obviously raised many problems, Ponsonby told the FO, but 'some unilateral initiative … might make North Vietnam begin to understand that the Commonwealth mission is genuine and sincere attempt to breach the impasse. At present I fear they are deceived by their own and Chinese propaganda.' The member of the Russian embassy to whom he spoke shared that view.[99]

H.F.T. Smith in the Northern Department at the Foreign Office had been wondering whether the SU was following a more helpful policy. It seemed to be pursuing disengagement from a situation it could not control, but not going back to Khrushchev's stance: 'the extent of their disengagement at present is that they are disclaiming a role in negotiations. At the same time this disengagement is expressed in words designed also to disentitle the Chinese from having a special role.' It might be that the Soviet leaders favoured the mission's going to Hanoi and indicating that they were 'not prepared to continue indefinitely an involvement in a situation in which the beneficiary of their support does not follow their advice'. Possibly the SU was moving away from putting its foreign policy 'in pawn in order to avoid a final split with the Chinese'.[100]

Peck saw Ponsonby's telegram as reflecting Russian pressure on Hanoi, designed to gain 'some form of recognition for S.V.N.L.F. in the expectation that this will give them a seat at a negotiating table. But as this implies a willingness to enter into negotiations that does not exist on the part of the Chinese, the outcome of the debate undoubtedly taking place in Hanoi, is, assuming Chinese pressure to be dominant there, likely to be a refusal to receive the Mission.' The Soviet suggestion was that the Americans should see the NLF. That raised the question whether the mission should offer to see them elsewhere than in Saigon or Hanoi, say in Moscow, Algiers, Prague or Havana, or invite them to Geneva. 'In our view the Mission should only do so if the Mission is able also to visit Hanoi. The UK's acquiescence in seeing the Front other than in Hanoi' and in a way likely to give it 'representative value' would be 'highly distasteful but perhaps not wholly unacceptable to the Americans'. Possibly the US could be informed that the mission as a whole might have to do this, but that the UK might issue a unilateral statement disclaiming recognition of the NLF. Further action would depend on Hanoi's official reply.[101]

That followed. The Hanoi government, Ponsonby reported on 28 June, refused to accept the documents on the ground that they were addressed to the 'North Vietnamese authorities', though it had not objected on previous occasions. Presumably it sought de facto recognition as the DRV, and might be suggesting that Ghana, which had diplomatic relations, would be acceptable.[102]

Trevelyan thought it looked as if the North Vietnamese might enter discussions with Commonwealth members less committed to the American viewpoint than the UK, on condition that they recognised the Viet Cong as a separate party. The Russians knew of the line, if indeed they did not concert it with the North Vietnamese. Trevelyan did not think they were trying to disengage, nor that their attitude was like Khrushchev's the year before. 'They are not willing to get out of step with Hanoi.' Maybe they were advising the North Vietnamese 'to leave open a way to negotiations; but in public they are not willing to take any initiative'. They could not usefully play a part until Hanoi was ready for negotiations. They were 'not willing to allow their position as co-chairman to drag them prematurely into the role of mediator', but thought the time might come when they would have a useful role to play. It would be going too far to say that the SU had put its foreign policy in pawn in order to avoid 'a final split with the Chinese'.[103] Rusk complained to Ambassador Anatoly Dobrynin that all Gromyko would say when asked what would happen if the bombing stopped was 'something like, "You stop first, then we'll see"'.[104]

Gromyko was affable when he attended a luncheon for George Kennan. The Soviet government was not authorised to negotiate for Vietnam, he repeated. The Americans must deal with the Vietnamese. Their Four Points were a reasonable basis for discussion. 'There would be no progress if the American approach was made in insulting terms as it had been on the last occasion when they stopped bombing temporarily.' The American ambassador, Foy D. Kohler, felt that there was 'a new flexibility in the Soviet approach', Trevelyan reported, 'that they wanted the heat taken out of the Vietnam situation by an American approach to Hanoi and by the cessation of American bombing, and that perhaps they wanted to imply that if such an approach were made, Hanoi would respond positively'.[105] It was also an indication that the Russians wanted to improve relations with the US. The latter followed up with a 'private' visit by Governor Harriman, which achieved more than expected, but 'less than my highest hopes'.[106]

Smith had suggested that the bombing would no doubt be an important issue during that visit. Perhaps some points could be made to the Americans. There was evidence, aside from Kohler's optimism, that the bombing was coming more and more to dominate Soviet thinking, and that if the Americans concentrated on South Vietnam, 'they might find a degree of acquiescence in Moscow', even though it continued to say that they must leave. The extent to which the Russians could disengage, Trevelyan thought, was 'strictly limited so long as the bombing continues'. Even if they were not struggling with China for influence in the Communist movement, they would find it difficult not to support a Communist state under direct attack, and they would be under pressure to involve themselves more closely, with 'the danger of a clash between American aircraft and the Russian surface to air missiles'. The bombing had 'brought the Soviet Union up against the contradictions in its own policy. It has shown Moscow the dangers of involving itself too deeply in an area where the Americans can bring strength to bear and where China's influence is greater than Russia's influence.' It had contributed to the Russo-Chinese split. Now the process could be better carried forward by stopping the bombing.

If that were to happen, the Russians might make renewed efforts 'to bring Hanoi to negotiation' and, if they failed, 'move further towards disengaging themselves'. That would be an advantage to the West. 'The split with the Chinese would go further. The Russians might even start to move in a small way to resume constructive relations with the United States and the West (e.g. discussions on non-proliferation and under-ground tests).' The Americans, however, 'might find this out-weighed by military considerations, by the argument that increasing attack on the North will bring them finally to the conference table, and by the political reactions in South Vietnam and in the United States itself'.[107]

At the moment, D.A. Greenhill thought, military considerations were dominant with the Americans. But it was worth putting the argument to Harriman, who was well placed, given his experience with them over 40 years, 'to find out what price the Russians might pay to be taken off the hook. If this price were to be a move to better relations with the West (test ban etc) it would be worth going for, but it is a lot to expect.'[108]

Peck agreed with Smith's reasoning but doubted if the point should be put to the Americans at that stage. 'We have done our best for them by including, as points (a) and (b) of the Guidelines ..., the suspension of air attacks and a North Viet-Namese undertaking to stop infiltration. Their own declared view is that they would only consider stopping the bombing if the North Viet-Namese gave some sign of stopping infiltration.' They claimed that the five-day pause (in May) was sufficient for North Vietnam to give a signal, but they also admitted that it took eight to nine weeks to determine whether a North Vietnamese unit was or was not operating in the South. The inconsistency might be 'probed further with the Americans'. Peck was not, however, in favour of briefing Harriman with the idea of a bombing pause. If they were to put it to the Russians, 'it must come as a decision of their own'. The minister in Washington might talk in general terms to Bill Bundy as he often did, without specifically suggesting that Harriman should discuss the issue in Moscow. 'The Governor is a pretty good Dove in his own right and I do not think that dovelike thoughts from our side will necessarily help his brief.'[109]

Sir Paul Gore-Booth, now permanent undersecretary, felt that, given Peck's doubts, 'we should not in fact try to nudge Mr Harriman's elbow'. In any case a message sent would have to go to No. 10 in draft. Some thoughts might be sent at a lower level 'for further excogitation'. But, 'given the state of affairs all round and notably our present attempt to reach the North Vietnamese', Gore-Booth was 'inclined to keeping our more radical thoughts for the moment to ourselves. But they are not wasted and may become topical very quickly.'[110]

Sir John Nicholls discussed the issue with Peck, Cable, Smith and Thomson, minister of state. They agreed that it was not desirable to try to brief Harriman. They also rejected the idea of giving the State Department 'a non-committal paper' asking how it viewed the indications of the Soviet attitude towards the bombing. '[W]e thought that this might be unwise in view of the possibility that H.M.G., either in the context of the Commonwealth Mission or otherwise, might decide to press the U.S. Administration strongly to stop or suspend bombing.' There might, however, be some advantage in getting some of the thoughts in Smith's minute into Harriman's mind before or during his talks. The embassy in Moscow, which had already been given an account of these minutes,[111] was so instructed.[112]

Harriman was given a list of the indications that the SU attached importance to the cessation of the bombing. In his talk Kosygin devoted 'little time' to the question. That was best explained, Brimelow thought, 'by the assumption that he did not wish to be pressed about a *quid pro quo*, a subject which the Soviet Government are unwilling to discuss'. Brimelow himself was suspicious about the statements from Russian journalists and others to which Smith had referred. They were not an indication that the SU would acquiesce in a rollback operation in the South, though it would accept one if it took place. 'The Russians probably believe that the Americans realise that they cannot stay in South-East Asia for ever, and conclude that sooner or later the communists of South-East Asia will have their own way.' If the bombing were to stop, and negotiations to start, 'we should find that the communist aim … would be to get the Americans out. … The Soviet leaders would love to see inflicted on the Americans a withdrawal from Viet-Nam no less humiliating than their own withdrawal of missiles and troops from Cuba in 1962.' If that were not attainable, they would settle for 'an arrangement which would prepare the way for an eventual National Liberation Front Victory in circumstances less immediately humiliating'.

The Russians were disappointed that the Viet Cong had not been successful and that Britain had supported US policies. But the 'slow and limited' escalation meant that the immediate threat to peace was small, and meanwhile they could score points off the Americans. 'The fly in the ointment is that the help given by the U.S.S.R. to North Viet-Nam has not been enough to prevent the American bombings.' At some point, 'possibly fairly soon', the 'galling' demonstration of 'ineffectiveness' might offset the satisfaction the Russians gained in the short run from criticising the Americans. There was no sign, Brimelow added, that they had tried or intended to try to bring Hanoi to negotiation. 'On the contrary, they are being demonstrably inactive. Nor is there any evidence that they are moving further to disengage themselves.'

Brimelow's own view was 'that the American effort in South Viet-Nam has not yet been great enough to ensure military success there; that the scale of the American attacks on North Viet-Nam has been nothing like big enough to bring about a negotiation on terms likely to satisfy the current American demands; and that political stability in South Viet-Nam is not yet in sight'. He saw no signs of 'a satisfactory negotiated settlement'. In those circumstances, the scale of American intervention in the South and of American bombing of the North might increase, 'with consequent devastation and war-weariness in both halves of the country'. In the hope of arresting such escalation, Harriman had been assessing the possibility of exploratory talks on a basis satisfactory to the Americans. 'The Russians were not forthcoming.' In those circumstances, Brimelow thought, a cessation of the bombing, though it would mean less devastation, 'would not alleviate the political problems caused by the militancy and intransigence' of North Vietnam and the FLN. 'On the contrary. A cessation of the bombing would be a relief to North Viet-Nam. It would reconvert the war into a national liberation struggle. It would be taken as evidence of American irresolution. The net effect would probably be to increase the pressures on the Americans to pull out.' If the bombing were to stop, Brimelow concluded, the Russians would still be supporting Pham Van Dong's Four Points of 8 April and still supporting the FLN.[113]

The Russians—and here Brimelow agreed with Smith—'would sooner see a settlement in Viet-Nam than the continuation of the fighting'. But the kind of settlement they were currently advocating was based on the Four Points. 'That, given the present state of mind of President Johnson, is not a basis for negotiation.'[114]

The Davies Mission

Harold Davies, MP, joint parliamentary secretary for the Ministry of Pensions—'a close friend of Wilson'[115]—had been in contact with North Vietnamese journalists in London, Nguyen Van Sao and Cu Dinh Ba, who had suggested that he would be welcome in Hanoi to see 'his old friend' Ho Chi Minh. He was one of five MPs who had visited Hanoi in 1957 as guests of the Fatherland Front.[116] Oliver Wright gave Peck a piece of paper that Davies might make over to his contacts, urging Hanoi to receive the Commonwealth Mission, which was seriously meant. If the reaction was negative, Hanoi should not close the door till he had flown out.[117] This was, as Peck put it, 'a private initiative', of which the prime minister wanted the foreign secretary informed.[118]

In principle, Peck wrote, the FO was 'against private emissaries of this kind', but 'the exceptional circumstances justify exceptional action'. Davies' brief should, however, be 'strictly confined to pressing the North Viet-Namese to receive the Commonwealth Mission as a whole and not individual members whose Governments may have recognised North Viet-Nam. He should have *no* brief to discuss conditions for peace or concessions by either side.' Anything the North Vietnamese said should be noted for reporting to the prime minister. 'It would lead to a fiasco,' Peck continued, 'if Mr Harold Davies were to leave the country and kick his heels in Bangkok and Hong Kong while the North Viet-Namese put forward unacceptable demands as conditions for receiving him in Hanoi.' Moreover, some announcement would have to be made, Peck argued. 'No cover story about social services in Hong Kong will hold water.' A junior member of the FO should accompany Davies. He could use the ICC plane, taking it from Phnom Penh or Vientiane, not Saigon.[119] The foreign secretary minuted for the prime minister accordingly.[120]

Whose initiative this was became the subject of speculation, once the initial secrecy about it had been breached. *The Australian* said on 9 July that it was reportedly initiated by Hanoi: Davies was approached by two North Vietnamese journalists. They said it was 'a personal visit and at his request'. The visit had 'no connection at all' with Wilson or the Commonwealth mission. Davies did not go at Hanoi's invitation.[121] Next day, allegedly quoting the FO, it suggested that Davies rang up the journalists and invited them to the House of Commons for a chat about the Commonwealth mission. He wanted to explain that it was no hoax. They left him for a day or two, and then invited him to repeat what he had said to Ho Chi Minh. Wilson 'quickly agreed' to send him. The journalists said that Davies suggested he should go to Vietnam, and that they agreed to arrange visas.[122] Perhaps it was another of the PM's own inspirations. Crossman was 'pretty sure this mission is only a gimmick'. Wilson would gain, but 'it is very un-serious'.[123]

The State Department was informed, and Unger and Bill Bundy welcomed the idea.[124] The North Vietnamese embassy in Vientiane was to confirm the invitation, Warner, the ambassador in Vientiane, was told. The FO did not want Davies kicking his heels there. Donald Murray of SEAD was to accompany him.[125] No visa was issued for Murray, his FO colleague, Warner reported. Davies went on alone.[126] But, though he saw members of the Fatherland Front, he was not received by Pham Van Dong, let alone Ho Chi Minh. Wilson suggested he might visit bombed sites, but he was not keen to bargain for an interview by making such an offer, and proposed to leave on 13 July.[127] Once they realised he was coming to press for the reception of the Commonwealth mission, he reported, the Vietnamese decided he should not see Ho Chi Minh or Pham Van Dong.[128] The visit, as *The Australian* reported, was seen in London as 'a cross between a diplomatic miracle and a diplomatic disaster'. A junior minister in a pro-LBJ government had set foot in Hanoi but had been snubbed by his old friend Ho.[129]

The North Vietnamese, Davies reported, were 'intoxicated with their successes on the battlefield and with their visions of victory'. They were winning the guerrilla war and expected to get negotiations on terms the US would not accept. They might be brought nearer to negotiation if given de facto recognition.[130] At a luncheon for the Foreign Press Association on 12 July, the PM defended the 'unconventional' discussions. 'The key to the situation is Hanoi', which was not recognised by the US or the UK.[131] He defended the venture in the House on 20 July. Hanoi was the key. That could not be turned in Moscow. 'There is no direct line from the West through Moscow to Hanoi.' Britain had to try all means to get through.[132]

In his memoir Wilson blamed the failure to receive Davies on the 'leak'. But John Young thought that 'ridiculous'.[133] Simon Kear thought it more likely that Hanoi never intended to let a FO employee—Murray, mistakenly described by Young as an interpreter[134]—into Hanoi.[135] The prime minister told U Thant that 'whatever happened, we should not give up trying. He did not mind rebuffs. What he wanted was results.'[136] But whether his 'stunts' were well judged could well be questioned, whatever they did for him domestically. And there was a risk that trying too hard and failing too often only made future endeavours—however much the PM was prepared to sacrifice his dignity—more problematic. Perhaps, too, the approaches made Hanoi think the US was desperate, since it saw Wilson as speaking for the Americans. Indeed that was Cable's assessment.

On 14 July Wilson suggested that the Nigerians might be asked to revive the idea they had of sending an official to Hanoi. Given Davies' failure, Cable thought not. The North Vietnamese could not be persuaded by anyone to start negotiations, because they thought they were winning. Only military reverses would persuade them, and further appeals to negotiate would do more harm than good, because they would believe that they were prompted by the Americans and indicated 'panic and despair in Washington'.[137]

In Moscow, meanwhile, the North Vietnamese had indicated to the Nigerian ambassador that they might receive a mission consisting of Kwame

Nkrumah (Ghana) and Sir Abubakar Tafewa Balewa (Nigeria), though they would refuse to receive Wilson. It was possible, Peck suggested, to assess the North Vietnamese gambit—the alleged readiness to receive those countries that recognised North Vietnam—in two ways. It could represent 'a genuine indecision on the part of North Viet-Nam, whether to accede to Chinese pressure and continue their intransigence in the face of American bombing attacks, or, despite Chinese pressure, to look towards Moscow to help them out of the dangerous position in which they find themselves by accepting a modified form of peace mission, leading perhaps to a settlement in their favour'. Alternatively, it could be 'simply a tactical move to enable the Viet-Namese to dodge an outright refusal to Ghana and Nigeria; they may hope thus to put the onus on the U.K. for refusing to allow certain members of the Mission to travel to Hanoi'. The first assessment suggested 'a chink in the North Viet-Namese façade', but the second seemed more likely to be correct.

There was a risk, Peck suggested, that Nkrumah, and perhaps Eric Williams (Trinidad) rather than Sir Abubakar, might be tempted to accept the Hanoi offer and go without Wilson. In that event the prime minister might wish to 'appeal to the unity of the Mission', in particular to the backing Nkrumah gave his leadership, and not allow Hanoi to 'dictate its composition'. That was the line taken when it was feared that a similar situation might arise with respect to visiting Peking, 'but it might be more difficult to sustain it in relation to Hanoi'. On the other hand a mission of two African leaders, or one African and West Indian, could not act with the authority of a four-man mission from the assembled Commonwealth ministers. If they wished to go on their own peace mission, 'we ought perhaps to insist that they are acting on their own and advise them to go also to Washington on their own'.[138] And face LBJ on their own?

The high commissioner for Ghana (Kwesi Armah) called on the prime minister on 8 July to indicate that Nkrumah was sending personal envoys to Hanoi, Peking and Moscow.[139] The focus, the FO suggested, should be on getting the North Vietnamese to receive the mission.[140] A Ghanaian delegation, including the high commissioner, left for Hanoi on 20 July. Ponsonby was instructed to offer assistance and to find out what was happening.[141] Wilford reported from Peking that, according to the Ghana embassy there, Nkrumah himself had accepted in principle an invitation to visit Hanoi.[142] Ho Chi Minh had, however, said he was worried about Nkrumah's safety because of the bombing, perhaps a polite rejection of the visit, as Qiang Zhai suggests.[143] But nothing was to come of the idea. Nkrumah concluded that North Vietnam was not yet ready to consider negotiations seriously.[144] The British PM wrote afterwards: 'what President Nkrumah wanted was not so much peace in Vietnam as glory for Kwame.'[145]

When the Commonwealth prime ministers had dispersed, Cable assessed 'where we now stand in Viet-Nam and how our policy is likely to evolve'. In the course of drafting compromises and retaining the support of the prime ministers, the UK had accepted that negotiations must include the VC; US air attacks should be suspended if the North Vietnamese undertook to prevent the movement of military forces and material to South Vietnam; US forces should ultimately be withdrawn from South Vietnam and the country neutralised; Vietnam should eventually be reunified through free elections. The US privately welcomed the PM's initiative, perhaps prompted by considerations similar to the UK's: the local battle was running in favour of the VC; further escalation might be needed; hence a case for trying to initiate negotiations before escalation went any further; the best way (other than escalation) to persuade 'the Communists' to negotiate lay in mobilising Anglo-American opinion, and the CPM was 'an obvious instrument'; even if it failed, it would demonstrate Communist intransigence, 'making it easier for Western public opinion to withstand the stress of the further escalation than [then?] to be expected'. The US was not committed to the concessions, but in practice it could not ignore the views of so many countries, and in that sense its bargaining position had been weakened. But as long as the Communists believed that they could secure military victory without risking a wider conflict with the US, they had no incentive for negotiations anyway. 'The Commonwealth Mission offered them a carrot, but the credibility of the American stick may prove a more decisive argument.'

The FO's prognosis was, however, 'pessimistic'. The US would probably undertake further escalation and the Communist powers make trouble elsewhere. And 'interested parties' were 'exploiting the natural uneasiness of British public opinion': there was 'every sign of an organised campaign' to stimulate and coordinate anti-American protests. That had not yet affected 'our basic support for American policy in Viet-Nam, but it has generated a certain discretion in the outward manifestations of this support'. If there were intensified fighting in the next few weeks/months, Cable thought that 'the relative emphasis in our dual policy—supporting the Americans and seeking negotiations—is likely to shift still further towards seeking negotiations'.[146]

Wilson's initiative was made at a critical time, Ralph Smith wrote, just as the Americans were deciding whether to enlarge their commitment. 'What Wilson was doing was to define Britain's position as one of peace-maker rather than ally in any larger war.' In that Britain would not take part: 'there would be no British role in the larger war, and no opportunity for British influence on American decision-making.'[147] Is that right? Britain was not taking part even now; and Wilson did not give up, even if there was no real opportunity.

Ground Troops

Then, too, the CPM mission was conceived mainly in terms of the bombing programme. LBJ had welcomed it, so it was said. But that was rather in the context of the escalation under discussion in Washington in terms of the introduction of large numbers of ground troops: on 7 June Westmoreland sought 44 battalions.[148] The 'graduated pressure' of bombing had not produced the results the Americans had looked for.[149] Talk of negotiations again preceded escalation, but escalation in a new form, quantitatively as well as qualitatively. It was still to be a limited war, but that now required sending in ground troops on a major scale. How many? The US, said the president at the NSC meeting on 11 June, had to contain the enemy 'as much as we can, and as simply as we can, without going all out'. By approving Westmoreland's request, 'we get in deeper and it is harder to get out. … We must determine which course gives us the maximum protection at the least cost.'[150]

As before, Ball played devil's advocate. 'We are drifting towards a major war,' he told the president on 18 June. The increase could go to 100,000, but no more, and the US should plan for a military-political solution that required no more, 'cutting losses and eventually disengaging from an untenable position'. Committing large forces would mean that 'the failure to turn the tide will generate pressures to escalate'.[151] The troops, he added on 1 July, would take heavy casualties in a war they were ill-equipped to fight in a non-cooperative or hostile countryside. 'Our involvement will become so great that we cannot—without national humiliation—stop short of achieving our complete objectives.' If the administration acted before committing substantial forces, it could 'avoid a long-term catastrophe'. Continuing and deepening the war would undermine the US world leadership more than 'a carefully plotted course towards a compromise solution'.[152]

McNamara recommended 34 battalions, plus the Koreans being sent, and possibly another 100,000 early in 1966.[153] At a long meeting on 21 July, LBJ allowed Ball his say. He doubted that 'an army of westerners can fight orientals in Asian jungle and succeed'. A prolonged war would display US weakness, not strength. 'The least harmful way to cut losses in South Vietnam is to let government decide it doesn't want us to stay there.' Let it move into a neutralist position. If the US wanted to make a stand, it should be in Thailand. Wouldn't all these countries then say the US was a paper tiger? LBJ asked: 'wouldn't we lose credibility breaking the word of three presidents? ... It would seem an irreparable blow.' 'The worse blow,' Ball responded, 'would be that the mightiest power in the world is unable to defeat guerrillas.'[154]

At further meetings there were more reservations. 'A commitment of large forces by us,' said Rusk on the 22nd, 'will lead to pressures on us to destroy Hanoi.'[155] 'We can't win,' said Clark Clifford at Camp David. 'Search out ways—by moderating our position—to allow us to get out.'[156] The NSC of 27 July formalised the president's decision for an increase to 125,000, additional troops to be sent as requested.[157] He was determined, as Chet Cooper later wrote, 'to fight the war with the minimum disruption at home, and the troop increase was not based on the estimated number required, but rather on the maximum number that could be employed without having to call up the reserves. Doling out additional forces with a view to balancing off military requirements in Vietnam and political consequences at home typified the President's approach. He wished to avoid giving the impression that the United States was, in fact, "at war".'[158]

A large request to Congress for supplementary funds would kill the domestic programme. 'I can get the Great Society thro right now—this is a golden time. We've got a good Congress and I'm the right President and I can do it. But if I talk about the cost of the war, the Great Society won't go thro.'[159] Yet LBJ did not think he could survive politically if he turned his back on what almost everyone in 1964–65 thought the moral obligation on the US to maintain South Vietnam's independence. Ball could never persuade the president 'that he could escape the opprobrium of the right if he pulled out and ran', as Jack Valenti put it.[160] And the British—whose views were so like Ball's—knew they could not try.

The war was a limited war, 'its goal not total victory but a return to the status quo as it had existed in 1954'.[161] You could not speak of neutralisation, lest you destroyed South Vietnam's 'will to war' and alienated the hawks forever.[162] But going to the public might prompt a burst of opinion in favour of a wider war, leading to a war with China, and to an end to the Great Society. As Bill Bundy recalled in the late 1980s, China 'did loom very powerful at that period, in the eyes of people in the area'. Ground forces had to be introduced, lest the US proved to be the paper tiger China said it was.[163]

The increment in the limited war was again accompanied by offers 'to begin unconditional discussions with any government, at any place, at any time', as LBJ put it at a press conference on 28 July 1965, though again they were combined with an insistence on the independence of South Vietnam. The US was ready to discuss Hanoi's proposals, 'our proposals and any proposals of any government whose people may be affected', and he was sending Arthur Goldberg, the US permanent representative, with a letter to the UN. The US did not covet a foot of territory. 'But we insist and we will always insist that the people of South Vietnam shall have the right of choice, the right to shape their own destiny in free elections in the South or throughout all Vietnam under international supervision, and they shall not have any government imposed upon them by force or terror so long as we can prevent it.'[164]

The FO had meanwhile contemplated and then abandoned another initiative: a different kind of desperation? Cable had suggested on 26 July 1965 what was called a 'chain letter' scheme, and Peck had responded that Commonwealth Secretary of State A.G. Bottomley was looking for an initiative.[165] The prospect of a mission visit to Hanoi having 'practically disappeared', perhaps alternative means should be adopted of profiting by the initiative to promote negotiations on Vietnam 'and to maintain some momentum in this unprecedented impulse of Commonwealth cooperation in international affairs'. With the possible exception of Kenya and Tanzania, all Commonwealth governments were committed to the principles in the statement of guidance, published as an annex to the final communiqué, and they might not object to persuading other governments to support them. A list of governments who might support the statement could be drawn up, and each Commonwealth government given four or five to approach. Britain could seek the endorsement of certain European governments, Canada some Latin Americans, Ghana and Nigeria some Africans, Australia and New Zealand 'the less neutralist Asian countries'.

Once that had been achieved, 'various possibilities would be open for further progress'. A public statement might be made simultaneously in all the capitals saying that '67 (or whatever the number was)' endorsed the statement of guidance and called on all parties to initiate negotiations accordingly. Alternatively a resolution could be sponsored in the UNGA. 'But the choice of such further measures would naturally depend on the degree of success achieved in securing the adherence of other Governments. Even if a respectable number of signatures were collected, there would be no guarantee that a resolution in the General Assembly would avoid amendment in an unwelcome sense and there would certainly be a heated debate which could prove embarrassing to the U.S. Government and their friends.' Perhaps the idea should not be mentioned at the initial stage. 'Unless a respectable number could be collected, it would certainly not be worth introducing a Resolution in the General Assembly and even a

Manifesto might fall a little flat.' The process should remain confidential as long as possible.

The UNGA was due to meet at the end of September, and the operation should be completed in good time to avoid procedural difficulties. Though China and Vietnam were not members, many had suggested that the UN should somehow be brought into the Vietnam problem, but it was not yet on the agenda. It would be convenient to meet the deadline for adding items without a preliminary vote, 20 August. If the plan were to be adopted, it had to be done promptly.[166]

Stewart sent the memorandum to Bottomley. Davies' report suggested that the North Vietnamese were too confident of victory to give serious consideration to proposals for negotiation, and it might be that no progress could be made before the Americans had 'succeeded in stabilising the military situation in South Viet-Nam—perhaps towards the end of the year—and the North Viet-Namese are forced to realise that their hopes of early victory are illusory'. It was also arguable that further British initiatives, 'particularly if these were of a dramatic nature', would do more harm than good, since the North Vietnamese, believing they were made at American instigation, would consider they indicated 'despair and defeatism' in Washington. They underestimated American determination 'and anything that encouraged these illusions in Hanoi could have very dangerous consequences'.

Public opinion at home and abroad might, however, 'misunderstand complete inactivity' on Britain's part, and it could be argued 'that, although the passage of time should provide the North Viet-Namese with stronger inducements to negotiate, the intensification of the fighting may also make these [negotiations?] more difficult to arrange'. There was 'also every advantage in exposing the North Viet-Namese to the continued pressure of international opinion in favour of negotiations'. Hence the suggestion of using the Commonwealth initiative, which would be better than a merely British one or any attempt to revive the appeal of the uncommitted nations (of 17 March). A Commonwealth initiative, the proposal would be less likely to convey 'a misleading impression of despondency in Washington as well as having a more international flavour'. It would 'gradually mobilise an increasing pressure from international opinion over a period of months and would reach its culmination at a time when there might be some hope (as there is not at present) of this exercising influence in Hanoi'. If successful, the move would provide an opportunity to use the UN, which would be 'welcome to many sections of public opinion'.[167]

Bottomley agreed with the 'general thought', but questioned the proposed procedure. The important consideration, he thought, was that while there was some doubt, particularly on the part of Tanzania and Kenya, about the mission, there was unanimous support for the statement of guidance. 'I believe that our immediate objective should be to build on this unanimity. From this point of view it would be a mistake and likely to prove disruptive of this unanimity to try to devise a procedure for separate approaches to foreign governments by individual Commonwealth countries, or to limit any approaches to non-bloc countries. What I suggest is that we try to get all the Commonwealth Governments to agree that the "Statement of Guidance" be brought formally to the attention of *all* foreign governments. In addition to these considerations, I think that, while it might be possible to allocate responsibility for approaching certain countries to particular Commonwealth members, it might cause resentment if in London we attempted to do this.' If a general approach of this kind could be launched, 'it might be followed by deployment of particular diplomatic effort where needed later'. The draft, Bottomley thought, might also include a reference to the UN: 'we might get ourselves into a false position if we were to make no mention at all of such a possibility.'[168]

Though it seemed rather to misunderstand the proposal, Stewart accepted the advice. But meanwhile a new development—related to the escalation—affected the timing of the approach. On 29 July Goldberg handed the UN secretary-general a letter from LBJ reiterating his willingness to negotiate and hoping he might help,[169] and next day Goldberg addressed the letter of which LBJ had spoken to the president of the Security Council, currently the British representative, 'suggesting some kind of action by the Council on Viet-Nam'. What did the US intend? the FO asked its Washington embassy. It noted that the message said that the US accepted the 1954 agreements.[170] Rusk said in response that the agreements were accepted on the understanding that the use of force was precluded as a means of unification.[171] The secretary-general was against a SC debate: it would be acrimonious.[172]

One of the FO's notions was that the Statement of Guidance might form the basis of a resolution to be introduced into the SC. 'Mr Rusk did not much like the idea. We are now looking for another formula.' Of course the preference was for a resolution calling for another Geneva conference, but there was not much chance of getting that past the Soviet veto. It was not clear what would emerge from the discussions in New York, but in the meantime it would be 'inappropriate', even 'embarrassing', to launch the initiative earlier envisaged. 'For us to recommit ourselves to the terms of the Commonwealth Statement of Guidance just at this moment might seriously restrict our freedom of manoeuvre at New York between the Russians and the Americans.' Further action should be deferred till mid-August.[173] The CRO agreed.[174]

When in London, Lord Caradon had said he would consult Thant on his return to New York about raising the Vietnam issue in the UNGA. Greenhill wondered if he had reached any conclusion. The question remained whether anyone else was likely to raise it and whether the UK should proceed with trying to get support for the 'Statement of Guidance'. 'We felt that it would be very difficult for men of good will in positions of responsibility in their country to refuse to accede to the principles', and the result could be 'a strong mobilisation of world opinion in favour of looking at the conflict in Viet-Nam in the same way as we do'. Just then Goldberg's proposal turned up, and now Thant's initiative—aware that a UN role might not be accepted by non-members, he was trying an 'exploratory procedure'[175]—offered a further reason for postponement. SEAD recommended it should be indefinite. Others were more doubtful. Greenhill was strengthened in his doubts when he was told that the Russians intended to introduce a resolution and attempt to isolate the Americans. 'The possibility of isolation would of course increase if the Americans had stepped up their bombing.' If it were the Russian intention, the proposal that the Commonwealth should now seek support for the Statement of Guidance 'would be a useful insurance in advance of the Assembly against the success of the Russian manoeuvre'. What did Caradon think?[176]

In September it became clear that the Western powers had no cause to raise the subject of Vietnam either in the UNGA or the SC, and the Communist powers were unlikely to do so, since the North Vietnam government had declared on 23 September that any UN resolution would be 'null and void'. Action on mobilising international opinion on the principles of the CPM's statement of guidance had been suspended. The secretary-general's personal initiative—designed 'to try to establish confidentially what common ground on a settlement might exist between the participants in the Viet-Nam conflict'—was continuing. That, and the wish to take Vietnam through the GA 'in a minor key' were strong reasons for definitely dropping the guidelines idea. 'Above all, the Americans would be strongly averse to it.' The SD, it now appeared, was 'even less warmhearted' about the guidelines than it was in the summer, in particular about the implication that the FLN should be regarded as an independent party in any eventual negotiations. The Americans saw that 'rightly' as 'playing the Communists' game'. Pushing the guidelines now would meet American resistance, 'and the advantages to ourselves would inevitably be outweighed by the disadvantages of stiffening American opinion on a matter where time and the course of events may well cause a reconsideration of policy'. Cable suggested 'that we quietly forget about the whole proposal'.[177] Peck thoroughly agreed—'if we can'.[178]

Chapter Five
Pause

The British reaffirmed that they would not send troops to Vietnam. The FO and its ambassadors discussed at length 'escalation' and the prospects for the rest of 1965, as well as the possibilities of a negotiated solution. Wilson raised the question in Washington. There the president decided on an extended Christmas truce. Not till the last minute was there a hint of a Hanoi response. Wilson's visit to Moscow, Cable suggested, might include a meeting with a Hanoi representative. But all that resulted was a meeting of the chargé and Lord Chalfont, and the Soviet leaders took a hard line with the prime minister.

In June 1965 Gordon Walker had been in the US to give a lecture. He noted that Rusk was more optimistic than McNamara. The ratio of government troops to guerrillas, the latter pointed out, was only 4:1. 'The campaign to raise 100 000 South Vietnamese troops was counterbalanced by heavy losses and desertions. … The only answer was more United States troops. More still would be sent and they would become actively involved in the fighting.' Gordon Walker asked whether the US 'could militarily hold on. He said—"Yes for the time being".' He seemed 'somewhat less than optimistic about longer-term prospects. He is rather baffled about the prospects of fighting a limited war. He said: - "None of us at the centre of things talk about winning a victory". He said it was not possible to tell the American people that victory could not be won.' Gordon Walker pressed on him 'the vital importance of not bombing Hanoi'. 'He said the United States had no intention of doing so.' He wanted Russia to make its influence felt. 'There was no other way out of this war. Several times he asked—"How can we get Russia to move?"' He said 'that all the United States wanted was an independent South Viet-Nam. The problem was to get Russia to use its influence for this.'

McGeorge Bundy was 'angry' with Gordon Walker for having said at White Sulphur Springs that it might be necessary to negotiate with the VC. 'This would adversely affect morale in South Viet-Nam.' Gordon Walker pointed out that Rusk had said that he was ready to sit down with the VC as part of another delegation—'a distinction that would deceive no-one'. Members of the Senate Foreign Relations Committee, Democrats, Gordon Walker found were becoming 'increasingly critical of official policy. They don't want to pull out, but don't see a way out.' Senator J. William Fulbright said that 'the only solution was one in which the Soviet Union helped to guarantee the independence of South Viet-Nam'.[1]

Gordon Walker's report and other conversations in Washington, M.N.F Stewart wrote, confirmed that the Americans were 'still determined to hang on' and insisted on 'the promise of some *quid pro quo* from the North Vietnamese and Vietcong' before they were prepared to make any concessions by way of a bombing pause. They had, however, produced no fresh ideas. Nor did they seem fully aware that military victories were but a temporary gain if not 'consolidated on the civil side'. It was difficult to get more than 'a sketchy answer' about pacification.

The Americans admitted that they were not going to win the war in the near future. How far would they go in responding to proposals for talks? 'The overt official stance had relaxed a good deal from say a year ago', but had set fairly precise limits. They agreed with Britain's proposal to revive the 17-nation initiative, they welcomed the Commonwealth Mission '(perhaps a bit too quickly, though this was the President's lack of finesse)', and said they would negotiate with a North Vietnamese delegation including NLF representatives. But they ruled out a bombing pause without 'some tangible *quid pro quo*' and were unwilling to accept the VC as an independent negotiating party. Nevertheless, 'there might be more flexibility if it came to the pinch'. David Klein, who worked in the White House on Western Europe and the Soviet Union, thought it might be worthwhile recognising the DRV, even though the embassy representatives pointed out that it would damage South Vietnamese morale. Perhaps some 'high calibre individuals in the White House' shared McNamara's pessimism and were prepared to consider ways of bringing the war to an end. The possibility of negotiations in mind, Rusk could not 'play with ideas so freely', and at the working level, Bill Bundy downwards, 'no-one would venture to say anything so heretical to an outsider'. Just possibly there might be 'more give in the American position' in the coming weeks. 'Reverses will make the Americans more inflexible; a moderate degree of success, even if it only amounts to holding the position, will probably make them more flexible.'[2]

Etherington-Smith wondered if Klein meant that recognition of the DRV might be part of a final settlement. Then the effect on morale in the South would not be so serious. And it would be in line with what the

Americans seemed long to have had in mind as their ultimate objective, 'to secure the establishment of South Vietnam as a separate state'. Recognition of the DRV would be 'a logical corollary'.

The ambassador also commented on the 'trace of pessimism' Stewart found in Washington. He had not noticed such a trend in Saigon. MACV had indeed become a little more hopeful than it had been. That was the result of a belief that more effective tactics could be developed, and also of the intention of bringing in large numbers of additional American troops.[3]

In Washington Sir Patrick Dean was expecting to see the president, Gore-Booth wrote on 22 July, and to be asked for a British military contribution. He and Peck discussed that with the foreign secretary and agreed that the main points were those Gordon Walker had made in December 1964: Britain had 50,000 troops in Malaysia and as co-chairman could 'scarcely get involved in military action in Vietnam'. Dean should say no more than that at the current juncture.[4] In fact, the president did not raise the question, Dean reported, but a request was likely. Renouf said that the US believed the UK could spare something from Malaysia, and that a mediatory role was unlikely to have much value in present circumstances.[5] Wilson and Stewart thought Britain could help with such things as mobile hospitals, but 'could not furnish anything which would kill anybody'. Gore-Booth suggested that Dean should make some move that would forestall a request Britain would have to refuse.[6]

That idea was superseded when the PM received a letter from the president. He was, he said, sending more troops to Vietnam. The aim was ending external interference in South Vietnam so that the people of that country could determine their own future. Could Britain offer increased assistance so as to indicate the solidarity of international support for resistance to aggression in Vietnam?[7] Cable noted that the president did not say in terms that he wanted a military contribution. The PM's reply should avoid all reference to the military issue, and the ambassador should cover it with the president's staff. That might avoid jeopardising personal relations between the president and the prime minister and discourage the president from sending a more explicit message.[8] Confine your reply to reaffirming support, the PM was advised.[9]

Calling on the prime minister, the American ambassador did not, however, substantively discuss the matter, and so the telegrams Cable had drafted were made warmer.[10] One indicated support for US policies.[11] The other instructed Dean to tell McGeorge Bundy, or make it clear in other ways, that there was no question of a military contribution. Any attempt to convert Parliament to that course might impair the level of political and diplomatic support. Britain was committed to Malaysia, while the US was still providing equipment for Indonesia. It was, however, trying to increase the police training it offered, and to get together a civilian surgical team for Vietnam. Britain's attitude, the telegram concluded, benefited the US by helping to restrain other European and Commonwealth governments from giving 'more vocal and forcible expression to their own apprehensions'.[12] The surgical team, Peck had stressed, should be civilian: Britain should not fall back on the Royal Army Medical Corps. Though the SU was supplying SAMs, any military contribution of a humanitarian kind might commit the UK 'more deeply than we might wish' and 'reduce our "mediatory status" in the eyes of some countries'.[13]

The 'virtual impossibility' of a British military contribution, Palliser told Sir John Nicholls after meeting Professor Richard Neustadt of Harvard, was 'understood at all levels in Washington except by the President himself'. He thought that he had made it clear back in December that 'the only really effective contribution Britain make would be some soldiers, however small the size of the force', and he scarcely appreciated what Britain had done since. As Neustadt put it, he wanted 'a few British soldiers to get killed in Viet Nam alongside the Americans so that their photographs can appear in the American press and demonstrate to American public opinion that the principal ally of the United States is contributing to a joint effort'. The president was not really looking for military assistance 'but for a symbolic political gesture'.

Palliser did not suggest that in present political circumstances Britain could conceivably send troops, though he doubted that a civilian surgical team would make 'any impression at all' on the president. But the question was relevant to any visit the PM or the foreign and defence secretaries might make to Washington in the near future. If he went, the PM would be 'exposed to extreme pressure from President Johnson to make some kind of military commitment to Vietnam'. If he maintained the refusal to do that, the meeting could damage the personal relationship. It might even induce the president to 'lend readier intention to the view … now being expressed in certain influential quarters', and hinted at by Bruce, 'that the U.S. should not go on propping up the British economy but be prepared to accept the collapse of the pound sterling as the only means of inducing the British people to face up to economic realities'.[14]

Dean himself, along with Cabinet Secretary Sir Burke Trend, suggested adding to his instructions a reference to the role of the ICC, which the Commonwealth initiative had attempted to develop afresh.[15] The PM himself wanted to add that the British position had been consistent throughout and the advantages still valid, if not more so.[16] Dean made all the points to Bundy, save one about the effect on other powers of the British stance.[17]

Rusk had brought up the question of a military contribution with Dean on 28 July. The president, he said, took the view that if worse came to worst over Confrontation, the US would be in it with Britain. Rusk hoped it could put one or two battalions into Vietnam.[18] But that was, of course, out of the question.

Evacuation?

Back in late June Etherington-Smith had, as before, advocated an effective pacification programme, with Britain offering advice, lest the US should escalate the military conflict,[19] as indeed it soon did. It was too late, Peck had replied. Britain should not exaggerate its expertise, and it would be difficult to restrict the military so as to allow the programme to be effective. Recruiting a team would be difficult. Most important, it would not be politically acceptable in the UK. The government was fighting a rearguard action to preserve British diplomatic support for American policy in Vietnam. 'They can only get away with this by constantly emphasising that our objective, and that of the Americans, is a negotiated settlement.' Since the CPM, the government could not afford to assume responsibility for a pacification plan, let alone spend British money on it.[20]

After Davies' mission, along with previous initiatives by Britain and others, had failed to produce any significant progress towards negotiations, it might be useful, Cable had suggested on 12 July, to take 'a fresh look at the obstacles and at possible methods of overcoming them'. Britain had relied on the argument that 'a compromise settlement would be preferable to the risks of escalation entailed by the pursuit of outright victory by either side'. The argument had sympathy at home and abroad but was not yet accepted by the contestants.

'The Communist powers, in particular, have substantial reasons for regarding continued fighting as preferable to negotiation.' In 1954 the North Vietnamese were persuaded by the Russians to forgo their chance of a military victory in the South, and then the elections that they were promised were repudiated. '[T]heir present insistence on American withdrawal as a condition of negotiations is thus an indispensable precaution against being caught twice in the same trap.' As Davies reported, 'they are euphoric in their conviction of imminent victory', and, believing that British peace initiatives were undertaken on US instigation, they thought the Americans were desperate. The Chinese shared that view, 'and also consider it essential to humiliate the U.S., thus demonstrating to the world that the Americans are truly "a paper tiger", and enhancing Chinese influence and prestige at the expense both of the U.S. and also of the Soviet Union'. Knowing more about the US, the Russians feared its diplomacy less and its military power more. 'They are also less involved and in much less of a hurry to see South Viet-Nam in Communist hands. Negotiations would suit them well, if only we and the Americans were not asking them to play the Anglo-French role in a new Munich. Even if ideological considerations permitted, how are the Russians to persuade the North Viet-Namese, who not only lack the pusillanimous pliancy of the Czechs, but possess an alternative major ally in the shape of the militant Chinese?'

The Americans, 'curiously enough', also thought they were 'tricked' at Geneva, 'where they had not expected the British and French to go so far in concessions to the Communists'. At a new conference they might be in a minority of one—'perhaps two if the South Viet-Namese remain staunch'—and could see 'little prospect of any negotiated settlement emerging that would not constitute an obvious and humiliating defeat of all the efforts they have made over the last eleven years to maintain the independence of South Viet-Nam'. Rather than accept that, the Americans would continue to intensify the fighting and were 'probably ready to accept a considerable degree of escalation, both because they see no acceptable alternative and also in the hope of forcing the North Viet-Namese to negotiate on reasonable terms'.

The South Vietnamese were 'deeply disappointed' that the bombing of the North had not brought victory, nor even respite. 'The morale of the Armed Forces is declining and the politicians are as disunited as ever. But they can expect the Americans henceforth to take an ever-increasing share of the actual fighting and there can be few Viet-Namese leaders who could expect themselves to survive a North Viet-Namese victory.' Political groups might emerge in favour of negotiations, but the Americans should have little difficulty in finding South Vietnamese to support them so long as they were willing to continue the fight.

In these circumstances, Cable concluded, further attempts to induce the Communists to change their minds were unlikely to succeed, and they could be counterproductive. The Communists indeed believed that the Americans would capitulate if pressed hard enough, a conviction 'unlikely to be shaken except by intensified American military activity, particularly if this succeeds in stabilising the position in South Viet-Nam or (though this might be less effective) in inflicting intolerable damage on North Viet-Nam and in posing a convincing threat to her allies'.

Two courses were open to the British government. The first, (a), was to remain passive, hoping that US military activity would induce the Communists to negotiate on acceptable terms 'without producing a degree of escalation dangerous to British interests or to the peace of the world'. The second, (b), was to persuade the US to negotiate on terms acceptable to the Communists. The choice depended partly on an assessment of the prospects of (a), already being studied, partly on an assessment of the dangers it presented to Anglo-American relations and to British interests. A humiliating American defeat, particularly one that took the form of the abandonment of Vietnamese allies, 'would only postpone, and not eliminate the threat to world peace'. Friends and foes throughout the world would draw the same conclusion: 'if the Americans could abandon one ally under pressure, then similar pressure could in the future induce them to abandon others. The next time there was a confrontation between the U.S. and the Communist world, the Communists would be that much more inclined to take risks and the Americans, conscious of their past capitulation, would be that much more intransigent and inflexible. A possibly fatal distortion and uncertainty would have been introduced into the balance of terror on which the survival of the world so largely depends.' Apart from the dangers to Anglo-American relations and to British interests, 'we should decide against pressing the U.S. to negotiate on terms that would involve abandoning their South Viet-Namese allies'. If so, and if course (a) were shown to involve 'unacceptable risks', one other alternative, Cable thought, might be worth studying.

One major obstacle to writing off South Vietnam was that the South Vietnamese would object and the US would thus be seen as abandoning an ally. 'Might it be possible, however, for the Americans to carry out this operation with the consent of the majority of the South Viet-Namese leadership by offering them a fresh start outside South Viet-Nam?' If there were a million irreconcilable anti-Communists in South Vietnam, the US government might undertake to evacuate them all and establish them on some Pacific island, perhaps an underpopulated island in the Philippines or the New Hebrides or other Pacific island colonies. If the migration were underwritten by a massive programme of US investment, to which Britain, France and other countries could contribute, 'it might be made acceptable both to the migrants and to their new hosts and even a thousand million dollars would be cheaper than continued fighting'. The idea, as Cable admitted, required much further study. It was indeed an extraordinary notion, though the later departure of the boat people and the US acceptance of the Hmong may put it in a rather different light.

In the meantime, Cable thought, Britain should abstain from further public initiatives, though he was later to suggest the chain letter. 'We have done enough to demonstrate our good will and to do more would be detrimental to our own prestige and future influence as well as, in all probability, actually to impair the chances of negotiations. Instead, we might devote the next couple of months to fresh emphasis on Communist opposition to negotiations, simultaneously trying, through all the confidential channels open to us, to convince the Communists of American determination.'[21]

Peck agreed with Cable's analysis, but not with his 'logical, but ... almost impractical' solution. He doubted if the US could, in Khrushchev's phrase, make the Vietnamese problem 'go away' 'by simply towing the non-Communist Viet-Namese out into the Pacific'. Transfer of populations was 'a very tricky matter'. Formosa sprang to mind, but there was no convenient Vietnamese island on which the non-Communist Vietnamese could take refuge, even though there was a tradition of Tonkinese labour being settled in New Caledonia and the New Hebrides under the French. 'The root of the trouble,' Peck continued, 'is that the Americans have pinned their flag to Viet-Nam as a vital interest of the United States and indeed of the Free World as a whole.' A similar flag had been pinned on Berlin, and it was as unthinkable that the Allies should leave Berlin as for the Americans 'to abandon what may seem to us a rather expendable corner of [the] South-East Asian peninsula'. Much as the Americans might feel a loyalty to the non-Communist population of South Vietnam, Peck added, 'they could not arrange for its removal without offering similar facilities to the non-Communists in North Viet-Nam'.

A solution had to be sought along more traditional lines, he concluded. 'The removal of the non-Communist population from South Viet-Nam would be in the eyes of the world a much more clear-cut abandonment of their promises than some fudged up settlement designed to save American face, even though this resulted in South Viet-Nam going under to the Communists in due course. Such a settlement might take the form of a Laotian settlement with the Viet Cong forming part of a government in Saigon, together with the Buddhists, the Catholics, the Militarists and other groups.' It might not last long, given that the Vietnamese lacked the Laotian genius for compromise. But with the ICC in effective control of the frontiers, 'it might last long enough for the Americans to withdraw without too great a loss of face'. An alternative would be to offer a limited exchange of population, which had a parallel in the Korean exchange of prisoners. The FO should look again at its earlier paper—presumably Peck meant the one prepared for Gordon Walker—in which it discussed the Korean solution, the

Yugoslav solution, the Laotian solution and the Austrian solution, to which might be added a Formosan solution and a New Caledonian solution.[22]

Sir John Nicholls agreed. Much depended, he thought, on what the Americans would consider 'an obvious and humiliating defeat'. His guess—not a very good one—was 'that they are not at the moment setting their standards very high, that they would accept negotiations if they were offered without asking too many questions, and that ... a fudged up settlement to save their face would probably be acceptable'.[23] Peck suggested adopting Cable's recommendation to avoid further initiatives but undertake further study.[24] The PUS agreed.[25]

The Prospects

The study of escalation to which Cable had alluded he had himself initiated, suggesting it be worthwhile to analyse 'that hard-worked phrase "the dangers of escalation"'. He adopted the approach of 'the American theorists': escalation was not 'a process of spontaneous combustion *resulting* from acute international tension; but a deliberate step-by-step *raising* of tension in order to frighten one's opponents into making concessions'; 'a more refined, more carefully graduated form of "brinkmanship".' Both sides had resorted to it, Cable argued, but the Americans had more reason to continue doing so. Without it, the Communists could expect to win the struggle in Vietnam. 'Americans are traditionally reluctant to commit themselves in ground war in Asia or to any war limited in scope but unlimited in duration.' They were also reluctant 'to credit the independence of Communist satellites' and believed they were best disciplined 'by pressure against their major allies': Cable referred back to the abortive proposals to avert French defeat in Indochina in 1954 by blockading and bombing China. The SU, it might be argued in Washington, could be deterred 'provided the threat of escalation to nuclear war is credibly posed at the appropriate moment'. Cable went on to list the steps the US might take to indicate its degrees of determination: readiness to persevere in a limited war; readiness to risk conflict with China and the SU; readiness to widen the war; readiness to contemplate the use of nuclear weapons. He also listed the steps with which China might respond if it alone supported a continued North Vietnamese refusal to negotiate and the steps the SU might take if it supported such intransigence.

Cable thought that escalation might create a crisis as intense as that over Cuba in 1962. Was it likely? Would the Communists employ escalating measures against British interests 'to induce us to put pressure on the Americans'? Could there be 'any stage at which British intervention might be desirable, whether to make escalation more credible (e.g. withdrawing a British "peace initiative" on the grounds that the Americans had passed beyond the reach of our restraining influence) or to restrain further American escalation (e.g. by appealing to American public opinion against their Government)?' Would the Communists provoke 'ostensibly local crises' as part of their escalation? What were 'the likely side effects on the British economy, British defence dispositions and our problems over Malaysia?' Should all this be discussed with the US, with NATO allies, with Commonwealth governments? Cable admitted he was 'committing the cardinal sin of asking hypothetical questions', but escalation accelerated, and he thought the problems should be studied.[26] A meeting of the FO's Planning Committee ensued in July.

Part of the FO's further study included a paper, sent out for comment on 18 August, on likely developments in the war during the rest of 1965. Reinforced by at least nine battalions of North Vietnamese regulars, the Viet Cong had been doing well. 'But for logistical reasons the North Vietnamese would find it difficult (and for other reasons, i.e. fear of American reprisals) might find it dangerous, to throw in their forces to the extent necessary to enable the Viet Cong to go over to positional warfare on a scale large enough to constitute escalation from the present situation.' Increasing US forces from the present 70,000 to nearly 200,000 ought to make it possible to stabilise the position in the South. A sudden collapse of South Vietnamese army morale, 'a successful Viet Cong-inspired outbreak of terrorism and rioting in the towns', or 'a political reversal in Saigon which would bring to power a government which wished to get rid of the American presence' all seemed unlikely in the next few months and were 'becoming less likely as the American forces became more important and American control of operations increases'. Those forces were, however, likely to suffer heavy casualties when engaged against 'some of the most skilled guerrilla fighters in the world on terrain of the latter's choice'. Military advice suggested that the Americans could get on top but not for another six months or a year.

American bombing might make it difficult for the Viet Cong to start positional warfare, but it would not prevent the North Vietnamese continuing the guerrilla war. 'An end to United States bombing is a major target of Communist propaganda, but there is no reason to think that the North Vietnamese would be ready to negotiate if it ceased. There is little or no likelihood of the Americans agreeing to end it without equivalent concessions from the other side, although they do not exclude the possibility of a further pause in certain circumstances.'

'The North Vietnamese have a considerable degree of independence of both China and the Soviet Union.' Their army was heavily dependent on China for war materials, and it would be 'a very serious step' for them to quarrel with China. It was doubtful, however, whether China would be in a position to veto a decision by the North Vietnamese to move towards negotiations, if they considered it essential. Their aim was to take over South Vietnam. Geneva, they thought, cheated them of military victory, and Diem and the US cheated them of political victory. 'They will be extremely reluctant to let the prize slip again.' At present they were 'showing signs of euphoria' and the bombing level was bearable. If, however, they came to think that early progress in the South was unlikely, they might calculate that a ceasefire and negotiations would give them a respite from the air attacks, a chance to regroup and secretly resupply the Viet Cong, 'and an opportunity to separate the United States from its allies and possibly gain some of their important objectives (e.g. recognition of the Liberation Front and the principle of a coalition government)'.

'The Americans are determined not to lose the war and will do anything necessary to ensure this.' Their aim was to bring the Vietnamese to the negotiating table on acceptable conditions. What they regarded as acceptable was unclear, though clearly they could not accept the Four Points of April 1965. Such points as whether the NLF should be regarded as a separate entity for negotiations, whether the South Vietnamese government was to be regarded as the legitimate government of South Vietnam, and whether a ceasefire would entail accepting that certain areas were permanently in Viet Cong possession would probably have to be settled before a conference involving all interested governments; and the way they were settled would greatly influence the outcome. 'The Americans would be averse to making unilateral concessions in a pre-Conference negotiation.' Some in the US would see advantage in terms of world opinion in ending the bombing, but while the North Vietnamese showed no sign of readiness to negotiate, the military would press the president to extend it. They considered that cutting the railways and roads leading to China, blockading the coast, and attacking the irrigation system in the Red River Delta would make it difficult for the North Vietnamese to continue their war for long. It was doubtful, however, that the United States government could 'abandon a policy of restraint even if it wished to'. Domestic opinion might become 'readier to contemplate drastic measures, but account would still have to be taken of hostile international opinion both within the Western alliance and in the uncommitted world'.

The Chinese considered that the Viet Cong were winning, the memorandum continued. They opposed negotiations, and they also opposed foreign intervention. But they did not, the FO thought, intend to commit their own troops in force unless China itself were attacked, or there was 'a danger of the imminent overthrow of the North Vietnamese regime', or American troops invaded North Vietnam. Hanoi would not want to accept Chinese troops, and China would be reluctant to expose its air force to the superior Americans. 'Chinese military help in Vietnam is, therefore, at present limited to logistical support and possible training and advice.' Politically the situation was welcome to the Chinese as 'justifying their doctrine of the present revolutionary nature of the international situation' and offering the possibility of a humiliating defeat for the Americans. It also strengthened them in their dispute with the Russians 'by confronting the latter with the serious dilemma of either sustaining the Chinese theories that they are colluding with the Americans (if they do not continue fully to support the North Vietnamese) or accepting a serious deterioration in their relations with the Americans (if they do)'. They were obstructing Russian help to the North Vietnamese.

It seemed clear that the Russians would like the North Vietnamese to agree to a conference. 'Their primary objective must be to get the bombing of North Vietnam stopped because it limits their possibility of manoeuvre in their dealings with both the North Vietnamese and the Americans and burdens them with an involvement which can bring no positive gain to the Soviet Union.' Since Kosygin's visit to Hanoi they had given North Vietnam a limited amount of military aid, including equipment for five or six SAM sites, but no modern fighters. They had no wish for a major military confrontation with the US. But their control over events was 'limited, owing to their relative lack of influence in Hanoi and they cannot appear to condone American air attacks on a fellow socialist country'.

At the end of the monsoon, if the South were reasonably stabilised and the bombing continued, the North Vietnamese might accede to negotiation, the memorandum continued. But they might decide to slog on. The Americans thought they were more likely to change tactics if the damage inflicted by air attacks on the North outweighed gains in the South, and so might start bombing the lines of communication between Hanoi and China, and even extend the attacks on industrial targets and start demolishing the dykes. That was unlikely to evoke escalated responses from China or the SU. If the Americans bombed SAM sites, the Russians would not admit they manned them.

If the Chinese decided on escalation, they might focus on Laos. The North Vietnamese were unlikely to ask for 'volunteers' in large numbers. Probably Chinese action would be limited to increased military aid, increased participation in maritime infiltration into South Vietnam, and 'more ostentatious military preparations in China'. The Russians were not likely to do more than increase their aid in air defence equipment. That did not exclude the possibility that they would make 'token moves … designed, by suggesting that there is a danger of escalation, to make Western flesh creep and to boost North Vietnamese and Viet Cong morale'.

By early 1966, the memorandum concluded, it was possible that the North Vietnamese would conclude that they were no longer winning on the ground. Would they hang on 'on the principle that they could outlast the Americans in South Vietnam and are prepared to take increased bombardment of the North'? Would they try to widen the conflict? Would they agree to negotiate?[27]

Philip Mansfield of the Paris embassy thought the paper should have a paragraph on the French attitude. De Gaulle now maintained that the opportunity to neutralise Vietnam, which he advocated in 1963, had been missed. But the French were looking for any signs that rigid Communist positions were evolving, 'even though they remain officially pessimistic that the American raids on North Vietnam and the recent successes on the ground achieved by the American Marines will bring this about'. The Americans had not asked for any help they could provide on exploring the ground for possible negotiations, and the British should not imply they had reservations about French efforts. Mansfield also wondered whether the paper dismissed the Four Points 'rather too finally'. The Americans might eventually accept a modified version as a basis for discussion, 'provided the North Vietnamese recognised certain counter-principles on their side. At any rate it seems likely that the North Vietnamese will continue to refer to them and will represent any modifications of them as concessions.' The French thesis, based on past experience of Indochina, was that North Vietnamese nationalism was 'potentially vigorous'. So long as the war lasted, it was risky for them to quarrel with China, but 'after a settlement they would be in a better position to assert their independence of China'. They would like to increase 'the considerable degree of independence of both China and the Soviet Union … they currently enjoy'. What the French had told the embassy about André Malraux's talks with the Chinese leaders suggested that they would agree with the memorandum's assessment, 'with the addition that the war successfully prevents a Russo-American *rapprochement*'.[28]

Etherington-Smith thought that 'the danger of the Viet Cong being able to break Vietnamese morale before the American build-up had developed sufficiently to sustain the Vietnamese is beginning to recede'. Intensified fighting could be expected in the coming weeks and heavy losses, but the Viet Cong attempt to destroy the Vietnamese army would be 'held', and towards the end of the year the Viet Cong might no longer be gaining. The ambassador did not expect the introduction of North Vietnamese forces on a greatly increased scale: 'there are distinct limits to the extent to which the Viet Cong guerrilla effort can be stepped up by anything the North can do.' Some kind of negotiations—a 'virtually negligible' prospect at present—might then appear, and the effect of the bombing might also become a factor in the Communists' calculations. Whether they would then decide to negotiate was hard to say. Their intransigence even when they thought they were winning would make a change seem like weakness and involve a loss of face. In any case, it would mean 'a decision taken in Hanoi that their aims could now be better pursued by this means than by continuing the war; it could never signify acceptance by Hanoi of the continued existence of a non-communist South Vietnam or the abandonment of their plans for its conquest. They would not ... ever reconcile themselves to this; nor, even assuming that they were to do so, would it be necessary for them to negotiate.' Encouraged by Peking, they might still continue to refuse all negotiations. 'Their calculation would be that, even though American intervention had defeated their hopes of an early victory, time was on their side and the national liberation struggle would eventually be victorious.' If negotiations took place, they would be protracted. If they did not, fighting would continue. But military action could not provide the whole answer: as Etherington-Smith had said before, 'hope of lasting progress will rest on the development of an effective pacification effort'.

Also as before, the ambassador hoped that Britain would do everything it could to 'sustain and support' the Americans. He was 'profoundly concerned about the degree of pessimism and defeatism about Vietnam ... discernible in British opinion and even in certain official quarters'. The public was poorly informed, and a campaign to assist a Communist victory had been allowed to influence more people than it should. Those opposing American policy were still, however, only 'a vociferous minority'. What people did not take into account was 'the extent of the dislike of Communism which exists among ordinary Vietnamese and their determination to oppose it'. Equally unfounded was the view that the Viet Cong was 'a powerful indigenous movement in South Vietnam'. Though there were many Southerners among them, 'the movement has to all intents and purposes been created by the Northern Communists who have given it its cohesion, its purposefulness and dynamism and, more particularly, provided it with the armed power which has enabled it to terrorise the population and on which its strength mainly rest[s]'. In any case, the US decision to intervene with its own forces had 'radically changed the position. It was quite wrong to take it for granted that South Vietnam is irrevocably lost.' The psychological factor was 'of the utmost importance; if people once got the idea that the Communists were after all not going to win, the situation could change quite radically'. The prospects were indeed 'very uncertain', but the situation was 'not yet hopeless'.

In any case, Etherington-Smith could not see what Britain stood to gain in anticipating a Western defeat in Vietnam. It would have serious consequences for Malaysia and 'for the whole balance of power in Asia and indeed in the world'. One way Britain could assist would be 'by promoting a sober belief that the West can succeed'. The course it chose to follow could 'help to tip the scales one way or another'. That was particularly likely if negotiations developed. Etherington-Smith was sceptical of their value to the West. The Communists would accept them only if they could achieve their objective through them: 'there would be no need for them whatsoever to negotiate if they thought they were beaten.' The idea of a compromise was 'fallacious'. The Communists wanted South Vietnam: 'how can there be a compromise between their getting it and being denied it?' There could be some 'sham compromises'. One would be a settlement affording South Vietnam effective protection against Communist domination, while compensating the North Vietnamese with 'economic benefits. Another would be an arrangement which, while making ultimate Communist control of South Vietnam inevitable, would be so worded as to conceal this effect and postpone its realisation for a certain length of time.' Etherington-Smith hoped that Britain would not support or press for that kind of solution. It should do what it could to avoid escalation into a major war. The risk of that was, however, 'not great', but if need be it should be accepted. 'For otherwise the West will be in danger of suffering a disastrous defeat and of being faced, in a few years' time, with a similar choice in far less promising circumstances.' Britain should continue to support US policy in Vietnam and do all it could 'to assist the Americans in their courageous and by no means hopeless attempt to stem the Communist tide'.[29]

Sent to Peck, though surely a comment on Cable's approach, Etherington-Smith's letter was answered by Cable. He accepted much of the analysis, but not the argument over negotiations. He agreed that it would be 'wrong to take it for granted that South Viet-Nam is irretrievably lost': he had after all 'never believed that Diem could keep going nearly as long as he actually did'. But given the circumstances of his downfall, 'the miserable succession of governments that have been shuffled in and out of power since his departure', the Viet Cong's degree of success, and above all 'the

American inability to confine the fighting within the framework of a South Viet-Namese domestic problem', the evidence for optimism was inadequate to allow FO officials to advise ministers to take the 'strong line' Etherington-Smith advocated, 'or, having regard to the political position' in Britain, 'for Ministers to accept such advice if we were to give it'.

For as long as Cable could remember, 'the basic British attitude' had been that only a negotiated solution was possible. Britain had not insisted on it when its allies, France and the US, took a contrary view and 'seemed capable of pursuing military victory without widening the war. But when, in 1965 as in 1954, the Viet-Namese conflict clearly threatened to escape from its local context and our allies began at least to display doubts about their chances of victory, we have felt bound to come out into the open and urge a compromise.' In 1965 at least the advocacy was combined with emphatic support for US policy going well beyond that of any other European nation, 'a major effort and a heavy political sacrifice for which a British Labour Government who are constantly taunted', Cable thought—correctly enough—'with having gone further in support of the Americans than their Conservative predecessors'. That was appreciated by the Americans, though they would have liked to see British troops in Vietnam.

The price of that support was British advocacy of negotiations and initiatives to promote them, and that had 'regrettably involved a certain amount of erosion of the Western negotiating position'. SEAD had as a result been preaching that 'enough is enough and that further initiatives could only be counterproductive by convincing the Communists that the Americans (who are naturally supposed to inspire all our initiatives and who have in fact concurred in them all) are on the run'. That line might be held, though the Americans had 'thrown a sizeable hammer into the works' with Goldberg's letter. Returning to the old line of rejecting negotiations until confident of a favourable outcome would have to await obvious evidence that the military situation had stabilised and South Vietnam had a government 'that at least looks united, resolute, respectable and possessing some popular support'.[30]

The paper on escalation was discussed with Etherington-Smith when he was on leave, and finalised at the end of September 1965. It concluded that, now that the Americans were on the way towards stabilising the position in the South, the North Vietnamese might 'review their policy in the light of their inability to secure early victory'. The Americans were 'likely to continue and perhaps gradually to step up their air attacks against the North, which might raise international tension somewhat further and result in a greater deterioration in Russian/American relations'; but that seemed 'unlikely to provoke any Chinese or Russian responses that could lead to further escalation by the Americans'. The North Vietnamese seemed unlikely to expand the fighting into Laos, or to reinforce the Viet Cong, which would be 'a long and difficult operation and … create serious logistic problems, given the level of American air attacks on lines of communication'. Their other options were 'slogging on with the guerrilla war' or seeking a pause for negotiation. The balance of advantage was in favour of the latter, but 'their stubbornness, their belief that the Americans can be defeated by guerrilla warfare in the end and the weight of Chinese influence' would all be in favour of the former.[31]

From the British point of view, Cable added, the major risk the paper foresaw was an extension of the fighting into Laos. Thailand might feel threatened and ask its SEATO allies to strengthen its defences. In 1962, 'we were able to get away with a token contribution of fighter aircraft,[32] but we might not get off so lightly next time'. The paper did not consider another possibility: the Americans might extend the fighting into Laos in order to cut the supply line between North and South Vietnam. Though military circles had considered it, Cable doubted that the Americans would adopt that policy unless they suffered heavy casualties, 'or saw no other prospect of making headway against the Viet Cong inside South Vietnam'. Comments were being assembled on a paper on the possibility of a negotiated settlement. The two papers might be considered together so as to try to decide 'whether the British Government could or should take any further steps, either to promote negotiations or to prepare for possible repercussions of the fighting in Vietnam (i.e. an extension of the conflict into Laos)'.[33]

Peck hoped the secretary of state could read the paper before he visited Washington. There was room for 'cautious optimism', he thought, but the distinction between the two options, 'slogging on' and 'seeking a pause for negotiations', was 'not quite so clear-cut'. The North Vietnamese might find that, with the increasing forces in South Vietnam and a corresponding weakening of the Viet Cong's ability to carry on the guerrilla war, the best policy might be a combination of the two, 'i.e. the guerrillas fade away, South Viet-Nam becomes ostensibly peaceful pending a U.S. withdrawal and a renewal of guerrilla warfare. This could happen without a negotiation. It is at this point that the Americans will have to deploy statesmanship to see that the Viet-Namese pacification sticks and that a stable Viet-Namese regime emerges.' The British could help by 'providing the right kind of advice and possibly administrators. The Americans might press the Secretary of State on the point: 5/6 policemen and a surgical team are probably not enough.'[34] 'Yes; I think we should be prepared to do this,' Stewart commented.[35]

A Negotiated Solution?

The draft paper 'The Possibility of a Negotiated Solution of the Conflict in Viet-Nam', also prepared by Cable, was dated 26 August 1965. The objectives of the two main parties were 'sharply conflicting', it pointed out. Ever since the US first took an interest in Vietnam, 'their basic objective has never been less (though it has sometimes been more) than to prevent South Viet-Nam falling under Communist domination'. The Vietnamese Communists, on the other hand, had always aimed as a minimum at the extension of Communist rule throughout Vietnam. No lasting compromise was possible. Either one side had to impose its will by force, or one side needed to concede the other the substance of its desires in return for some face-saving concession.

That was the device adopted in 1954. The US, however, found the formula unacceptable, as it was likely to lead to Communist domination of the South. 'It encouraged the efforts of the South Viet-Namese Government to ignore the provisions of the Geneva agreements and to consolidate an anti-Communist régime in the South.' But it did not denounce the agreements, nor allow the South Vietnamese government formally to do so. 'Instead the pretence was maintained that the military provisions ... remained in force and that, although the political provisions could not be applied at the time foreseen in the Agreements, these might conceivably be revived if more favourable conditions permitted at some time in the distant future. This was, in effect, a tacit offer by the United States to North Viet-Nam of a face saving formula,' Cable wrote, 'whereby North Viet-Nam was invited to acquiesce in the practical frustration of the Geneva Agreements in return for the willingness of the Western Powers to acquiesce in the theory that these Agreements remained in force and would one day be applied.' North Vietnam, rejecting 'this way out', sought to bring pressure to bear on the US and South Vietnam through the co-chairmen, and then turned to fomenting insurrection. At the same time, with its allies, it pressed for a conference or negotiations, overtures always rejected by the US and South Vietnam, 'with the slightly embarrassed assistance of H.M.G.', because the US realised that North Vietnam would not accept an independent South Vietnam as long as the insurrection might forcibly prevent it. A face-saving formula was again set aside.

Now, however, the insurrection, 'with ever increased support from North Viet-Nam', had made such headway that the US government was clearly wondering if its objective were 'still capable of achievement in the foreseeable future'. Given the costs 'in money, in lives and in the risks of dangerously far reaching repercussions', it was 'reluctant to continue indefinitely escalating … efforts in pursuit of an ever receding objective', and for some months had sought negotiations and relaxed the conditions on which it would enter them. It was not clear, however, how far that implied an abandonment of the basic objective and how far it was 'purely tactical'. Three interpretations were possible: (a) that the Americans hoped negotiations would produce a face-saving formula enabling them to 'extract themselves … without major damage to their prestige', even if that meant 'a disguised or deferred abandonment of their basic objective'; (b) that the Americans wanted negotiations but had 'not admitted even to themselves' that such was likely to be the result; or (c) that they were advocating negotiations as a propaganda device, designed to represent the Communists as 'intransigent warmongers'. Option (b) seemed the most likely interpretation, but American thinking might also contain elements of (a) and (c).

The North Vietnamese, however, probably took an even more cynical view, seeing the Americans as so hard-pressed and so conscious of the instability of the South Vietnamese regime that they wanted to obtain a breathing space. If there were a settlement that held out the prospect of achieving the Communist objective, it would probably be repudiated by the US and they would be tricked as they had in their view been tricked in 1954. No face-saving formula could be offered unless there were a guarantee that it would be implemented, and the only guarantee they envisaged so far was the Americans' agreement, prior to negotiations, to withdraw their forces. Their attitude was supported by the Chinese, anxious to humiliate the Americans and to show that they were 'a paper tiger'.

The paper considered the nature of a negotiated settlement, given that the basic objectives of the two sides were incompatible and neither could a force a capitulation. Any negotiations could have one of three results: North Vietnam conceded at least temporarily the substance of the American objective in return for a face-saving formula intended to disguise the extent of the concession; the US conceded the substance of the North Vietnamese objective in return for a face-saving formula disguising the concession or delaying its practical implementation; or negotiations dragged on interminably without agreement. Which course negotiations took would probably depend on the course of military operations. 'Neither side will make major concessions to the other as long as there is any prospect of avoiding this by early military victory.'

A settlement based on American success might include a ceasefire, a withdrawal to the North of those Viet Cong willing to go, phased reduction of US forces leading either to complete withdrawal or retention of only a token force, prohibition of the reintroduction of foreign military personnel and equipment, a provision enabling American withdrawal to be suspended or reversed in the event of specified North Vietnamese violations of the agreement, and provisions for international supervision of the military part of the agreement. Further provisions would be needed to give North Vietnam an adequate face-saving formula. Those might include the recognition of the unity of Vietnam and provisions for promoting that at a future date, such as the 1954 formula or a supervised plebiscite in the South, undertaken after 'a substantial period … for the re-establishment of peace and order'. In the meantime the governments of both zones should respect each other's territorial integrity and refrain from interference. Pending reunification South Vietnam would be 'neutralised' once the Americans had withdrawn.

If North Vietnam were reluctantly brought to accept such a settlement, 'it would only be in the hope that, as American withdrawal proceeded, the Communists would gradually be able to gain the upper hand in South Viet-Nam by political or covert means insufficiently ostentatious to bring the Americans back again'. The general terms of the agreement would have been such a setback that the Communists' prospects in the South would be 'prejudiced for years to come', but they would not have abandoned their objective. The South Vietnamese leaders would be in no position to object to such an agreement. The Russians would probably accept it, even attempt to counteract the influence the Chinese would exert against North Vietnamese acceptance.

The paper turned to consider the form a settlement might take if the Americans made little or no military headway. There would be no provision for the withdrawal to the North of Viet Cong forces, though regular North Vietnamese units might be withdrawn and there would be no provision for a continued American military presence or an American return if the agreement were violated. The unity of Vietnam would be recognised and elections or a plebiscite might take place, though any kind of international supervision would be difficult to provide for. Pending reunification, a coalition government would be established in Saigon, including representatives of the NLF. In the meantime both governments would refrain from interference in the other's zone, and South Vietnam would be neutralised.

Such a settlement would give the Vietnamese Communists all they wanted, 'and the only concession to the Americans would be to allow them to withdraw in good order *after* instead of *before* the settlement and to make reunification of Viet-Nam subject to delay and to electoral processes which the Communists would have little difficulty in rigging'. The US could not be brought to accept it unless the fighting spirit of the Vietnamese army had collapsed along with the politicians' will to resist. 'Such a débâcle might convince the U.S. Government that, if they were not to run South Viet-Nam as a colony and defend it almost entirely with American soldiers, they would have to get out on almost any terms before they were pushed.' The Chinese would try to dissuade the North Vietnamese from 'allowing the Americans to preserve the last few scraps of dignity'. Insofar as a government in Saigon was ready to continue resistance, it would see such a settlement as 'entirely unacceptable', and, 'in order to obtain some show of South Viet-Namese acquiescence and to satisfy their own public opinion', the US government might have 'to take special measures to secure the future personal safety outside Viet-Nam of a substantial number of South Viet-Namese leaders'.

Something in between these two types of settlement was also conceivable. 'A further possibility,' Cable added, recalling an earlier suggestion, 'is that the scope of negotiations might be widened to include Cambodia and Laos as well, in the hope that the Americans might obtain concessions over these two countries for what they would have to yield in Viet-Nam itself. For instance, something approaching the worst type of settlement in Viet-Nam might be made less unpalatable to the Americans if accompanied by sufficiently attractive proposals for North Viet-Namese withdrawal from Laos (which Hanoi would no longer need as a channel of communication between North and South Viet-Nam) and the effective neutralisation of both Cambodia and Laos.'

If negotiations began, both sides would open the bidding 'fairly high', and, on the analogy of the two Geneva conferences as well as Korea, they would be protracted. The Communists might hope that the longer they continued, the more the morale of their opponents would decline, and the better the terms they would secure. They might promote the process of demoralisation by 'allowing the general level of military activity in the South to fall', telling the Viet Cong not to initiate any offensive 'except when this was required to support diplomatic pressure at the conference table'. Such a policy might be especially advantageous 'because there would obviously be strong international pressure on the United States Government to refrain from attacking North Viet-Nam as long as negotiations were in progress (even if a cessation of bombing were not actually a pre-condition of negotiations). A defensive policy by the Viet Cong would thus simultaneously deprive the Americans of generally acceptable excuses for taking the offensive themselves (against North Viet-Nam or in the South) while allowing the Viet Cong to consolidate their power in the very extensive areas of the South already dominated by them.' A reduction in fighting might reduce international tension and promote a thaw in US-SU relations. But it would benefit the Communists more than the West. The longer the negotiations continued, 'the more the position of the Americans and South Viet-Namese will be weakened and the worse will be the terms of the ultimate settlement'.[36]

Gore-Booth had alluded to a marked passage on a telegram from Washington: 'How far will the South Vietnamese get a fair deal?' The answer would depend on a decision by the Americans, 'obviously not yet taken, about the best terms on which they can get themselves out of the present heavy and growing commitment'. It was 'primarily an American decision', but the British should have their minds clear on two points. One was the implications of the Geneva agreement: 'if they are in any way repugnant in the light of 11 years of history ought we to be careful how we go on basing ourselves on them?' The other was the basis of 'a "fair" choice, on the assumption that the Americans can fight the present situation to a conclusion which could be called a drawn match'. Bundy had been doing some fundamental thinking. 'In order to take an equality with the Americans on this we should do some fundamental thinking of our own. I should assume that what we would like to see, and consider it possible to see, is a South Vietnam which is a kind of "Austria minus" which will inevitably be minus because South Vietnam clings perilously on the edge of a continent instead of having what might be called continental backing. But one does need a system of determining the future which gives the non-Communists of South Vietnam a real chance. Is this to be gained by proper supervision (including North Vietnam, which will not be granted) or is there some other way of ensuring it?' It would be helpful to have thoughts on the two points before the meetings on Singapore and Confrontation,[37] meetings relating to Singapore's extrusion from Malaysia that month and the possibility that that could reduce Confrontation.

There had been 'a lot of confused thought flying about on "Back to Geneva 1954" lines', Peck commented, and the FO should clarify its ideas on that: perhaps only 5 per cent of the agreements would be relevant or valuable. The second point involved an acceptable settlement, 'which cannot, I fear, include towing the "loyal" Vietnamese out into the Pacific'.[38] The conclusions of Cable's new memorandum were, he admitted, 'rather pessimistic'. Possibly the Americans would have much more military success than expected, and the Vietnamese leaders display unity, common sense and efficiency to an extent not seen since the fall of Diem. Even so, he thought he had described the maximum attainable. Perhaps the Americans should be given 'a suitably bowdlerised version' of the memorandum. 'Hitherto we have rather tended to regard Viet-Nam as too delicate and embarrassing a subject for frank or far-reaching Anglo-American discussion', but it might be in the interest of both governments 'to break this tradition and exchange views with no holds barred. There might be some hurt feelings, but, once these had subsided, we should have a much better idea of American intentions and future Anglo-American cooperation might be facilitated.' When the Office had agreed on its views, the ambassador could be consulted on putting them to the Americans.[39]

The same idea had occurred to Addis in Manila. He had been reading statements Ball had made at the SEATO meeting in May about the Geneva agreements, implying that Vietnam was then partitioned, and indicating that the US would accept nothing less than the independence of South Vietnam, 'a small state on the periphery of Communist power'. But South Vietnam was not a state, and by insisting on its independence the Americans were imposing a prior condition outside the Geneva accords, which looked forward to the unity of Vietnam, and at odds with Johnson's Baltimore offer of unconditional discussion. Ball also defended the air strikes. Yet, Addis insisted, there was 'no reasonable prospect of the policy attaining its declared objectives of impeding the movement of arms and trained men into South Vietnam and bringing home to the regime in Hanoi the risks and costs of continued aggression. There is surely no worse policy than a policy that cannot succeed, and this has been the objection to American policy in Vietnam and Laos since the beginning.'

Ball had, however, admitted that there must be a political solution at some point. Addis thought that it was now only possible if the US accepted that the 1954 accords looked towards the unity of Vietnam and that a return to them meant the return to a process of unification. 'It must be accepted as very probable that Vietnam can now only be unified under Communist domination.' The negotiated settlement would have, in fact, to be 'a disguised form of pull-out', but it was an option still worth exercising. The idea now seemed 'horrible', but 'American prestige and American greatness are such that it could be lived down successfully in a relatively short time'. The Americans had pulled out from North Korea 'as the result of a military defeat and from Laos, as a result of a political defeat', and had lived it down. US policy had over-reached itself.

Addis recalled that he himself had many times argued against the 'stifling' of Britain's reservations and advocated telling the Americans of its 'misgivings' about their policies. 'After all, if your best friend and beloved elder brother is driving a car in which you are the passenger and you can see from your position in the back seat that he is getting dangerously near the edge of a precipice, do you keep silent?'[40]

Peck agreed that the US government was 'putting a considerable strain on history in their public references to the Geneva Agreements'. Originally the Americans were opposed to the Vietnam agreement, and their policy was 'still incompatible with its basic provisions'. But, as the Geneva agreements had become 'increasingly popular', the Americans were 'trying to adapt the agreements to their policy, rather than vice versa'. Peck sent Addis a copy of Cable's memorandum. '[W]e are again giving some thought to the possibility of a frank exchange of views with the Americans on the subject. As usual, however, it does not seem to be quite the right moment.' There were other things to talk about with them, and it would be some time before the North Vietnamese were ready for negotiations.[41]

Peck also discussed the Cable paper with Etherington-Smith, then in England. He was 'now more optimistic about the chances of a U.S. military success in some form or other', and of a negotiation from strength. The Washington embassy should be consulted, as Cable suggested.[42] Cable sent his paper to Trench in Washington,[43] and it was also sent to other posts.

Thomas Brimelow sent comments from the embassy in Moscow. Publicly the Russians maintained that the Americans could not win and that Pham Van Dong's Four Points were the only possible basis of a settlement. 'They may not believe in what they publicly maintain.' Johnson had said that the US did not intend to be defeated nor to withdraw. 'The Americans have the power to maintain a substantial military force in South Viet-Nam as long as they think necessary and to cause increasing damage to North Viet-Nam if time goes on without any prospect of a negotiated settlement.' The Russians would think the paper overestimated the readiness of the US to accept a negotiated settlement conceding a Communist victory 'under cover of face-saving phrases'. They might have 'a higher opinion of American determination than the paper assumes' and believe that the Americans would find it 'cheaper and easier' to stop the Communist advance in South Vietnam than to try to prevent insurgency in Laos and Thailand. If the Americans could not create an independent anti-Communist South Vietnam, the Russians might think they would go for 'a dependent and militarily occupied South Viet-Nam, with American forces there waging an undeclared but increasingly bitter war against North Viet-Nam'. They might also believe, as they say publicly, that the American offer of negotiations was not genuine, but 'only designed to create a better public posture for the United States while they pursue their policy of dealing heavier and heavier blows against the North'. They would not share the view that Cable's paper attributed to the North Vietnamese, however: they would consider 'that American determination is as yet far from broken'.

Brimelow turned to consider the terms for a settlement the paper set out and the possible Russian attitude to them. The settlement based on American success included the more or less total withdrawal of American forces and a prohibition on their re-entry. 'The Americans are hardly likely to allow themselves, if they win the fight, to be negotiated out of a position which they have won by armed force and which can only be maintained by armed force or the possibility of reverting quickly and powerfully to the use of armed force.' In the Russian view the Americans would probably be reluctant to reduce their forces to 'a purely token level'. The concessions designed to save North Vietnam's face that the paper suggested would please the Russians: they would facilitate the maintenance of covert Communist activities in the South. But such activities had to be prevented or hampered if South Vietnam were to be stabilised, and the Russians would not expect the US to agree to provisions of that kind.

If the course of events were to be determined by the military success or failure of the Americans, 'it is possible that there will be no negotiations at any time'. On the assumption that they won, 'there may simply be a gradual running down of the military operations in South Vietnam as American strength there becomes decisive. There may be no further operations thereafter as long as American strength remains decisive, but the communists will be at it again the moment the Americans lower their guard.' If the Americans lost, the only negotiations to which the North Vietnamese and NLF would agree would be 'designed to get the Americans out as quickly as possible and for good'.

Brimelow doubted whether the Russians had given much thought to an intermediate solution or to negotiations without agreement. 'They probably think that the Americans will try for some months more to force North Viet-Namese realisation of their strength and determination', and that until that phase was over, it would be premature to consider intermediate solutions. '[T]hey probably regard the opening of negotiations for any settlement as premature until either the burden of the present undeclared war has made the North Viet-Namese willing to negotiate, or the Americans admit that their present policy is mistaken. The Russians probably doubt at the moment whether the Americans are ready to accept any settlement as disadvantageous as those considered in the draft paper.'[44]

From Bangkok Sir A. Rumbold offered the reasonable criticism that the Cable paper took too little account of the American domestic scene. Decision about the conditions under which the US might negotiate would depend 'enormously' on what the president judged acceptable in the US. The Republican Richard Nixon had given a speech in Bangkok indicating his support for the administration, but also criticised those who showed excessive zeal in seeking negotiations. 'He took his stand on the position that the U.S. Government would be wrong to contemplate making any settlement about Viet-Nam which did not guarantee that South Viet-Nam would remain permanently free of communism and within the American sphere of influence.' After the lecture Rumbold told him that that 'presupposed an ability and willingness on the part of the American people to keep large numbers of troops in Viet-Nam almost indefinitely. It was the kind of burden which the British had become accustomed to carrying during the nineteenth century but I did not know whether the character of the American people had developed to the point at which they would be willing to shoulder such an ungrateful task as that of the semi-permanent occupation and policing of a distant part of the world.' Nixon said that was indeed the question, and he was not confident of the answer.

Rumbold mentioned Nixon, he told Cable, only to make a general point. Would the Americans be willing in the long run to spend the blood and treasure necessary to prevent an ultimate North Vietnamese success? 'They will not have the ruthlessness in the face of world opinion to reduce North Viet-Nam to a graveyard in order to achieve "victory", and there has been no evidence yet to show that the North Viet-Namese will not be able to continue the struggle in one form or another indefinitely.' The most likely outcome was a withdrawal, perhaps leaving South Vietnam with a slight hope for survival, unless there was a mutation in the American character that permitted large forces to remain in distant parts 'without the promise of "winning" and yet always half at war'. But meanwhile the administration, earlier 'unduly depressed', was now 'rather over-confident' and would see such an outcome as 'unnecessarily defeatist'.[45]

The paper, J.E. Ford of the embassy in Saigon noted late in September, took the view that the Americans sought negotiations because their resolve had been 'to some extent shaken'. That did not seem to be borne out by contacts with US representatives in Saigon and 'the relentless build-up of American troops and equipment. To us the Americans simply say that the consequences of defeat would be totally unacceptable and that therefore they *must* win. We see no sign of weakening resolve. The days when their policy was against bringing in U.S. combat forces seem very remote now. They are quite explicit that they can stand the cost in treasure and casualties, and they appear to have calculated the risk of dangerous repercussions and to have accepted them.' Lodge, again ambassador, had produced the slogan: 'Make the Viet Cong fall silent.' 'However long it takes' was another often-repeated phrase. The attitude seemed to stem from the basic thesis 'that communist revolutionary war as a method of imposing alien rule by force is incompatible both politically and morally with the rule of law. To abandon the struggle against it would be to abandon the whole ideological foundation by which the Americans like to believe that their world leadership is justified.'

Why then was there so much talk of negotiations? To a large extent the offers to negotiate had a propaganda purpose: 'the American leaders are conscious that a Great Power using its tremendous military resources to crush an enemy whose resources are relatively primitive would incur criticism from many quarters, unless the chance of an honourable peace were left open to the adversary.' But it was not merely a matter of tactics: it represented 'a simple and entirely genuine approach to the question. If the North Vietnamese and Chinese want to end the war, they say, let them come to the conference table. Any time. … But they will in so doing have tacitly to admit that their new kind of war cannot make headway against United States resolution.' When the Americans invited the North Vietnamese to start negotiations they did so 'without any idea of abandoning the basic American objective', and they saw 'nothing inconsistent' with that.

The FO paper might thus require some modification. The possibility that the Americans would accept a face-saving formula would seem less likely. The outline of what they would accept in the event of success probably overestimated what they would concede to North Vietnam and the Viet Cong: 'it seems highly doubtful that the Americans would contemplate complete withdrawal of their armed forces from South Vietnam, or the retention of only a token force; or agree to refrain from entering into a military alliance with South Vietnam; or accept provisions for elections on the 1954 formula. It seems more likely that they would take their stand on an independent and sovereign South Vietnam with no qualifications.' The paper might add a paragraph to the effect that proposals for negotiations 'would serve little purpose until a stage had been reached where the communists were (a) persuaded that the Americans would not give way and (b) ready to accept a settlement which would guarantee the indefinite continued existence of an independent and non-communist South Vietnam'.

There was much to be said, Ford concluded, for a 'no holds barred' exchange of views with the Americans. That could clear up discrepancies between some of the press reports from Washington and what appeared to be the real attitude of the Americans on the evidence available in Saigon. 'This in turn could reduce the risk of our getting too far ahead of the Americans and laying ourselves open to the charge of making things more difficult for them.'[46]

Trench had written from Washington about the speculation over third-party contacts between Hanoi and the Americans, mostly, he thought, emerging from 'the fertile minds of unemployed journalists', though in fact there were a number of contacts. Philip Geyelin told M.N.F. Stewart that Mac Bundy was 'pretty tight lipped about the question of communications with Hanoi', but that he had said that the US and South Vietnamese military position in South Vietnam 'was still too weak to allow negotiations in any real sense of the term'. Everyone agreed, Geyelin said, that the bombing of the North had 'virtually reached the end of its usefulness'. Johnson was 'in a state of indecision', 'anxious to get out' but recognising that he would probably have to let the military go over to the offensive before there could be meaningful negotiations. He wanted to have 'the best possible position both at home and abroad' before he did so. He wanted 'to be thought to have done, rather than to have done, everything possible to bring about talks before taking the next step'. The Americans, as Stewart put it, found it 'very difficult to forecast the shape of any negotiations which will not eventually lead to the Communists taking over South Vietnam'. There was also 'some substance in the Communist line' that US statements about negotiations from Baltimore on had not 'given the other side much to bite on, but then nobody expects or should … expect the Americans to make any major new concessions in advance'.[47]

Trench commented on Cable's paper. In general, the Washington embassy agreed with Ford's view, though not at that point with the idea of a 'no holds barred' exchange of views. That might play a part at a later stage, but at present the Americans' thinking had not 'reached a point where either we or they would get the best out of frank talks'. At the working level there was 'remarkably little indication that their thinking is anywhere near a coherent policy'. That might be seen as 'a sign either of short-sightedness or of a basic reluctance to consider negotiations at all, now that the situation on the ground in South Vietnam has reached a slightly more hopeful stage'. But Trench did not think that was the case. The State Department and the political side of the Pentagon were under no illusions about the determination of the North Vietnamese and the time and effort needed to bring them to a negotiating point. At lower levels, therefore, they were still thinking of terms of preventing a takeover, 'without anything more constructive in view'. The Bundys and others might not be so limited in their outlook, though Trench suspected that other preoccupations had prevented them from getting very far.

Basically far more interested in domestic than international politics, the president regarded Vietnam 'as a tiresome but at present necessary diversion of time, money and effort from his aim of creating "the Great Society"'. He would like to get out of Vietnam 'if he could do so with reasonable hope of not handing over the South to the Communists and without allowing Asian countries to believe that the Communists are the side to back in the area'. Possibly, as the situation seemed to be improving, he might go for a win rather than a draw, but there was no sign of that at present.

'Apart from the question of timing, … H.M.G.'s chances of influencing negotiations in the direction we think desirable would be prejudiced if we tried to push the Americans into discussions on the basis of a British paper. In view of our position as Co-Chairman they will naturally want in due course to take us into their confidence, if only to ensure that we play the game in the way that they think most effective, but since they are bearing the brunt of the fighting and expense, they would probably wonder why we thought we had the right to tell them how to play the hand, and this could lessen our chances of influencing them in the right direction.' The position of both the US and the UK had changed since 1954, though that did not mean that the US underestimated the value of UK support for its Vietnam policy. Trench proposed to watch the situation and report regularly whether the moment had come to broach the topic of negotiations.[48]

Trench sent a separate letter to Cable, not, as the preceding one was, circulated to other posts, explaining why he thought this was 'not the moment to tackle the Americans'. He had at last managed to get hold of Chet Cooper, Harriman's aide, for a talk on the subject, and he said there was a group of six to eight people working on the problem of negotiations. 'The existence of the team is not known to anyone else and must not on any account be divulged outside a very limited circle in London.' Trench did not know the names of all the members, but, besides Cooper, they included Bill Bundy, Len Unger, and John McNaughton of Defense. 'McGeorge Bundy of course knows that this work is going on, but so far no paper has been submitted to him.'

Without revealing the existence of the SEAD paper, Trench drew Cooper's attention to the role which the foreign secretary was likely to play as co-chairman when the time came for talks, and 'said that it would clearly be advantageous for us to have discussions with the Americans in due course in case the North Vietnamese suddenly made a proposal for negotiations'. Cooper agreed, but 'did not see much chance for this before the end of the year'.

Even now, he said, the Americans were 'better placed to respond to a call for negotiations than they had been in similar situations in the past'. If the North Vietnamese were unexpectedly to say tomorrow that they wanted to talk, 'the Americans would be able to respond with proposals for discussions to start in quite a short time, though naturally matters such as the stopping of infiltration in the intervening period would have to be settled before a firm undertaking for a conference on a specific date could be agreed to'. There would also be the problem of getting the South Vietnamese to agree.

Trench deduced 'that we should probably start off on the wrong foot if we put forward a paper of our own as the basis for discussion and that it would be better for us to enquire in due course what ideas the Americans had on the subject'. Since, 'for perfectly valid reasons', Britain did not have forces fighting in Vietnam and was 'not making any significant economic contribution', Trench thought 'the Americans would take it amiss if we appeared to be trying to tell them what they ought to do'.[49]

Palliser thought the paper too pessimistic. The Americans would stay long enough for negotiations along the lines of what Cable had suggested in the event of American success to become 'reasonably possible', and if the US ascendancy were great enough for North Vietnam to consider them, the Americans would settle for them.[50] Cable feared that American interest in negotiations would decline as the military position improved, and if North Vietnam remained intransigent, the US offer of unconditional discussions would not remain open indefinitely.[51]

Certain recent developments, wrote R.L. Wade-Gery, the secretary of the FO's Planning Committee, increased the 'need for us to make up our minds about the possibilities of a negotiated settlement': American successes might induce the North Vietnamese to accept the offered unconditional discussions or put forward new conditions for negotiations less unacceptable than the Four Points; they might encourage the Americans to look with less favour on negotiation; a committee of officials was considering what might be the US negotiating position and the FO might be asked, 'even if only informally', to express some views. Discrepancies in attitudes to negotiations resulted from American public statements, 'what we believe to be American intentions', what seemed possible or likely in practice, and what the prime minister and foreign secretary had said in public. The discrepancies had not mattered much while the debate focused, 'much to Western advantage', on the contrast between the American offer of unconditional discussions and the North Vietnamese insistence on 'the extravagant prior conditions' of the Four Points. Once the debate turned to the nature of the negotiated settlement, 'our position will be less advantageous and much more complicated'. The foreign secretary should be advised on two points: what should be said to the US government if it asked for British views? What should British ministers say in public?[52]

R.A. Longmire, writing late in November, thought the paper 'a brave attempt to tackle a thoroughly intractable problem'. Indeed it prompted 'the gloomy thought' that negotiations, 'at least in the near future, would achieve precisely nothing. The Communists would almost certainly make some gains to offset their present lack of success in the military field.' That being so, 'the best way to obtain a firm settlement in Vietnam is for the Americans to abandon the pretence that Vietnam ought to be reunified in the foreseeable future, to grit their teeth, send in more troops and continue the fighting until the South is clear of the Viet Cong and the position stabilised along the 17th Parallel. The tender plants of economic growth and democracy can then be carefully cultivated under American supervision. The process may take years (c.f. the 12-year emergency in Malaya) and the usual cries will deluge in—"too late", "neo-colonialism", "Americans do not know how to contain Communism", "the Americans don't understand Asians" etc etc. It is in the final analysis a test of American will-power—she certainly has the resources for the job. Anything less than this long haul carries the risk of buying a respite at cost of ultimate defeat.'[53]

Longmire really begged the question, Cable responded, by suggesting that the Americans should not negotiate but should seek to impose their own terms through military victory. That was what they had been trying to do since 1950. 'So far they have not succeeded and I personally doubt that they ever will.' But that argument was outside the scope of the paper inasmuch as it was concerned with what might happen if negotiations took place, not whether there should be negotiations, 'a point on which Ministers have committed H.M.G. publicly, repeatedly and categorically'.

Longmire had suggested that widening the negotiations to include Laos and Cambodia 'on the swings and roundabouts analogy as in 1954' would be 'a doubtful proposition'. The Communists would be quite unlikely to withdraw from Laos, 'and would Sihanouk cooperate on this basis?' The main attraction of Laos to the Communists was that it provided a corridor to South Vietnam, Cable responded. 'Once they no longer needed this corridor, it seems to me conceivable—though I agree it is unlikely—that they might bargain withdrawal from Laos against greater advantages in Viet-Nam.' Sihanouk's attitude would depend mainly on that of China. The paper, Longmire had added, did not make it clear 'whether negotiation would come after a ceasefire or while fighting was still proceeding'. If fighting were continuing, 'there would presumably be more pressure on the West (from left-wing opinion etc.) to make concessions'. The UK, Cable commented, had always argued that it would be impracticable to have a ceasefire before negotiations. The South Vietnamese had argued, 'with considerable justification', that they could not accept a ceasefire that left the VC 'free to stay where they were'. Cable thought that 'we should have to envisage the old pattern of agreeing provisions for the separation and regrouping of the forces before the cease-fire came into effect'.[54]

Exchanges with the Americans

The paper had been finalised on 19 November 1965. It now took account of the altered US attitude to negotiations. Since the Americans decided to commit large American forces, which had begun to stabilise the military situation in the South, 'some of the steam has gone out of the American quest for negotiations', and there had been signs that earlier offers, such as that of total withdrawal, were regretted.

The declared objective of the Americans was a negotiated settlement. It was not clear whether they regarded 'their quest for negotiations as entirely consistent with their objective of preventing South Viet-Nam falling under Communist domination'. In earlier years they had seen them as 'incompatible'. Three different interpretations were possible. One was that LBJ's resentment of the conflict as a diversion from his domestic programme might have persuaded him early in 1965 to ignore or postpone the obstacles to securing a negotiated settlement compatible with US objectives. A second was that, now that the military situation was going better, the Americans might believe that North Vietnam could eventually be forced into a settlement compatible with their objectives. A third interpretation was that while the US government recognised that its objectives and its declared attitude to negotiations were inconsistent, it considered 'advocacy of negotiations essential to improve their posture in the eyes of western and uncommitted public opinion at the expense of the Communists and count on Communist intransigence delaying negotiations long enough for American military success to transform the bargaining position'. The three explanations were variations on a theme: the Americans wanted both a non-Communist South Vietnam and a negotiated settlement; and they hoped that 'somehow or some day, these two objectives can be made less incompatible than they now appear'.

The revised paper did not alter the earlier analysis of the policy of North Vietnam: it believed that the imperialists would collapse and that the US could not be trusted if a settlement were negotiated. The paper also repeated Cable's analysis of the possible nature of a negotiated settlement. It concluded that American enthusiasm for negotiations was 'likely to diminish as the military situation improves': even an eventual North Vietnamese readiness to take part in unconditional negotiations would not necessarily lead to agreement.[55]

In December Trench talked to Cooper about the progress of the team working on negotiations. Its work was clearly far from finished, but it was difficult to make out exactly what stage had been reached, since they were talking in the White House Mess, and Cooper did not want his colleagues to get wind of the subject. Apparently the president had seen one or two scenarios and sent them back for revision. Cooper told Trench the need for discretion was as great as ever, and made no reference to the offer Murray had made when he happened to be in London to meet his wife 'to have ideas tried out on him'.[56]

Trench also asked about the likelihood, increasingly discussed in Washington, that the Chinese would intervene. The belief, Cooper said, was still that they would not do so unless North Vietnam were invaded, or there were attacks on Chinese territory itself, 'both of which eventualities could be excluded'. Various types of American action had been assessed. Neither more frequent attacks on railway lines between Hanoi and China, nor attacks on petrol oil lubricant installations in Haiphong, would 'push the Chinese over the brink, but attacks on Hanoi itself might be another matter'. Congress pressure for such attacks was, Trench thought, not unlikely when the mid-term election campaign began in the spring. The official SD line, elicited from Jacobson of the Office of Asian Communist Affairs, was still that the Chinese, whatever their warlike talk, would take no initiative that would involve them directly with the US. Cooper was, however, clearly 'not very happy' and suggested that Trench and Stewart might join him over drinks one evening to talk about China.[57] The Americans, Murray concluded, were not prepared to talk about negotiating positions. He guessed that the Chinese would not regard an aerial attack on Hanoi as justification for intervening.[58] In the meantime another pause was in place.

These interchanges overlapped others at higher levels. Back in September Ball had told the foreign secretary that the build-up of American forces had 'gratifying' results. 'Serious damage had been inflicted on the Viet Cong and there was evidence of reduced morale and increased defection.' The Americans had been 'careful to make it clear to the world that they were ready to have unconditional discussions at any time. They could not accept any solution which would not ensure independence for South Viet-Nam but were prepared for elections in South Viet-Nam and reunification through self-determination. They were ready to see all forces withdrawn as part of a final settlement.' Hints through 'circuitous channels' suggested that 'progress might be possible', but recent statements from Peking and Hanoi 'had if anything been tougher than before'. Those in Hanoi who favoured a hard line were for the moment in the ascendancy, and there was little prospect of negotiations. 'More pressure was needed. ... What the United States was trying to do was to persuade Hanoi that it need not abandon the ultimate objective of a reunified and even a Communist Viet-Nam, but must pursue this end by peaceful means. The problem was how to construct a mechanism for transferring the conflict from the military to the political level.'[59]

McNamara had assured the prime minister on 26 November that the US was prepared to go to the conference table without conditions. Wilson told him that Vietnam was no longer really a political problem in the UK: he had demolished opposition at the Party conference in Blackpool. But he was glad to know that the US position had not changed. 'He had one long shot at the back of his mind, but he thought it best to wait until he saw the President before talking about it.'[60]

The PM was going to address UNGA on 15 December 1965 and then go on to Washington. Vietnam was 'high on the agenda', the PM recalled in his memoirs. He received a telegram on arrival from 68 MPs—perhaps his own initiative—demanding that the US should stop the bombing, touched off by a report that one power station 14 miles from Haiphong had been bombed, and reports that McNamara had spoken at NATO of the 'near certainty' of war with China. Wilson 'pressed the President hard ... at least to suspend the bombing to test the sincerity of North Vietnamese hints that there might be a response on their side, possibly leading to negotiations. It was clear that his mind was not closed to this, and we discussed the modalities.' The prime minister repeated that if US aircraft bombed Hanoi or Haiphong, 'we should be forced publicly to dissociate from that action'. He recalled telling the president that when Confrontation ended, Britain would have to 'cut back sharply on the military establishment in Asia. I was not even asked on this occasion for British troops in Vietnam'.[61]

Ambassador Dean described Wilson's visit as very successful: he had 2.5 hours with the president, reassuring him, in the light of the Defence Review, about the continuance of Britain's worldwide role.[62] He explained Davies' impressions. The North Vietnamese drew a distinction between pre-negotiations and negotiations themselves. They might perhaps be induced to negotiate about negotiations before the main negotiations began, but they would not agree to move into major negotiations without insisting on their four conditions. The foreign secretary, who had been in Moscow, was not clear what the Russians envisaged. They insisted that bombing must stop before they took action, but were disturbed about the possibilities of escalation. Rusk said the conference might begin by 'escalation'. Representatives of the co-chairmen might meet in Geneva, then call in representatives of other countries for talks about Laos and Cambodia, and that might be extended in time to cover Vietnam. The PM sought the president's view on the Viet Cong proposal for a 12-hour Christmas truce. It was being considered, he responded, also a possible extension. Wilson said Britain's best role was to pursue every possibility of negotiations. Johnson and Rusk agreed.[63]

'After moving around in NATO,' Rusk said on 17 December, 'I find Wilson is a paragon of courage. The rest are doing nothing.' He really could not see, however, why he could not put in men to support the Australians. 'He wants a DSC for fending off his enemies in Parliament,' said the president. He told his opposition to bring the VC to the conference table 'and he'll produce the President'.[64] The remarks hardly suggest so positive a response to the PM as the FO records indicate. Perhaps he had more effect before he came. Mac Bundy had argued for a bombing pause—under discussion for some weeks—not only because of the alarming budget estimates. Wilson had 'some new Vietnam gambit up his sleeve. … We will spike his guns … if we have a pause in effect at the time of his visit.'[65] But whether his pressure had an effect or not, the president moved towards a pause, starting at Christmas.

Christmas Pause

Would it signal weakness? Would it encourage the Communists? 'The offsetting factor, and the one that became decisive, was that a pause would help to establish the *bona fide* interest of the U.S. in a settlement, thus making escalation more acceptable at home and abroad.' It was, as a SD paper put it on the 18th, 'the necessary peace punch to go with the military punch which is coming in January'.[66] 'If we are to have public support for our policies—if we are to blunt mounting frustration, it is absolutely essential that the public be constantly assured that we are doing all we can to get an honourable negotiated settlement,' as a White House staffer put it. 'A majority does not believe it.'[67] Others, however, looked another way. The National Council of the American Legion told LBJ: 'Loyal Americans do not want another "peace without victory" as in the case of the Korean War.'[68] Rusk thought a pause just might lead to a settlement on a Geneva basis, and the American people had to be convinced there was no alternative to war action.[69] 'We'll take the pause,' the president said. It was done by allowing the Christmas truce to remain in effect.[70]

'George, you wanted a pause and I'm giving you one,' the president told Ball on the phone. 'Now I need you to get it going.' He wanted, as

Ball recalled, 'a diplomatic extravaganza'. He enjoyed 'this frenetic to-ing and fro-ing (he delighted in his ability to send well-known people flying all over the world)', but in retrospect Ball 'thought the spectacle futile and unbecoming', though better than Nixon's Christmas bombing.[71] LBJ wanted to say, as he told Harriman, 'We have walked the last mile.'[72] Was it more about improving the American image than finding the key to negotiations? Cooper asks rhetorically in his memoir.[73] The ambassador in Rangoon, Henry Byroade, was to try to convey an aide-mémoire to the DRV through his counterpart Vu Huu Binh.[74] But, accompanied by the razzmatazz—113 countries were contacted and special emissaries sent to 34[75]—the approach was hardly subtle.

The resumption of bombing was deferred, Dean reported after Christmas, partly because, in order to justify the increase in the defence budget necessary for large reinforcements, it was necessary to show that the administration had tried every alternative.[76] The suspension, the president told the prime minister, was to continue into 1966.[77] Perhaps, Dean suggested, Wilson could suggest extending the pause till 20 or 23 January, the date on which the VC had reputedly offered a Tet truce. The Vietnamese had to be given time to sort themselves out.[78] That had not been the case back in May.

The foreign secretary saw no scope for any British initiative, nor for reviving the Commonwealth Mission, but suggested that the consul-general in Hanoi might bring the extended suspension to the attention of the North Vietnamese, and, as representing a co-chairman, express the hope that they might take advantage of it to start negotiations. The ambassador in Moscow might ask if the SU saw any scope for a move by the co-chairmen. Alexander Shelepin, a member of the Presidium, would be in Hanoi during the extension and Johnson might send Kosygin a message, hoping the SU would use its influence. No doubt the Americans would bear in mind that any direct approach to the Chinese via their Warsaw contact would diminish the impact of anything said to the Russians.[79] Wilson wrote to the president.[80]

On 29 December at a press conference Rusk listed what were called, no doubt with a not inadvertent historical overtone, the 14 Points, summarising all the statements the US had made about peace negotiations. 'We put everything in the basket except the surrender of south Vietnam.'[81] The US saw 1954 and 1962 as the basis of negotiation. It would welcome a conference. It was ready for unconditional negotiations, or unconditional discussions. A ceasefire could be the first business or preliminary. The US was willing to discuss North Vietnam's four-point programme. It wanted no military bases in Southeast Asia. It did not want a continuing military presence in South Vietnam. Free elections would be supported. Unification could be decided by 'free decision of their peoples'. Southeast Asian countries could be non-aligned or neutral; the US wanted no new allies. It was prepared to contribute one billion dollars to regional development in which North Vietnam could take part. The VC would have no difficulty in having its views represented at a conference after hostilities had ceased. Bombing would be stopped after it was stated what would happen next.[82]

Arthur Goldberg addressed the UN secretary-general on 4 January 1966, drawing attention to some of the points. The US was prepared to withdraw its forces from South Vietnam as soon as it was 'in a position to determine its own future without external interference'; its political structure should be determined by the South Vietnamese themselves 'through democratic processes'; and reunification of the two Vietnams should be 'decided by the free decisions of their two peoples'.[83]

Wilson had flown back from his Isles of Scilly holiday to meet Goldberg on New Year's Day.[84] The American ambassador to the UN had been sent as part of the 'extravaganza' to explain the pause and seek help in pressing Hanoi to respond. The prime minister suggested a message to Moscow, sent as co-chairman, in which he would say that he thought the US initiative was genuine and that it would be flexible over recognising the FLN.[85] The president agreed. The message finally sent was more cautious: it urged Moscow to use its influence for peace. The bombing was still suspended. The PM urged his counterpart and colleagues to do all in their power 'to ensure that the Parties leave the battlefield for the Conference table'. Kosygin had repeatedly said it was a matter for Hanoi rather than Moscow. But an opportunity for a peaceful settlement presented itself and once lost might be 'most difficult to capture'. A reference to the 14 Points was added.[86] Wilson, said *The Times*, had in fact made it clear that Shelepin should try to persuade Hanoi to take part in a new Geneva.[88] The consul-general in Hanoi was instructed to deliver a message from Britain as co-chairman, urging North Vietnam to take advantage of the pause. The aim was to make sure that it could not say that it did not know.[89] Ponsonby said the deputy director had accepted the message.[90]

Talking to the British ambassador at a New Year party de Gaulle said that no negotiation was possible until the Americans said that they would withdraw at the end of them. Sir Patrick Reilly said it would be difficult for the US to say that before negotiations started. The French president insisted that the other side could not accept a negotiation unless sure that at the end the US would withdraw.[91] He said the same thing to Goldberg. The US initiative would not lead to negotiations: withdrawal would have to be agreed upon in principle before they started. De Gaulle added that the Chinese had no interest in negotiations: he thought the Bloc would support Hanoi's uncompromising line.[92] If, however, the Bloc or the Chinese did not agree with Hanoi's line, they had no understanding of its 'determination to unite the country along its lines and to eliminate American influence in the area'.[93] Talking to the US chargé, however, Wilson was positive. He recognised that the SU thought it was a matter for Hanoi, and that China did not want peace. But it was a unique opportunity to get the parties together at the conference table. The cessation in May 1965 had not perhaps been long enough to enable Hanoi to assess the situation.[94]

Trench did not doubt that Johnson and Rusk wanted a conference to come about. The president wanted to spend money not on the war but on the 'Great Society', and Rusk saw the harm it was doing to the US in international politics. Even the military would on the whole like to get out, 'if only because they are fighting a type of war which does not come easily to westerners and in which their technical sophistication can be brought to bear over only a very small range of activities'. No one, however, wanted to negotiate from weakness, 'and anyway, as we are finding out, it takes two to make a conference'. Many of the military and some civilians thought that the 'relative restraint in air attacks' should be abandoned, the Hanoi/Haiphong industrial complex flattened, the dykes broken, but even their aim was to 'extricate' the US 'decently'. Only the 'peaceniks' thought that US troops should simply be withdrawn and the South Vietnamese left to fend for themselves. 'The Administration are quite determined that they cannot leave South Vietnam on terms by which they and the South Vietnamese would patently be the losers and the Communists—and in particular the Chinese—the masters of the future in Asia. Any withdrawal on terms which could not be plausibly represented as at least an attempt to allow the people of Vietnam to settle their differences on level terms would in American eyes—and rightly, in my opinion—have grave effects not only in South-East Asia, but elsewhere in the world, too.' De Gaulle, for example, would be able to point to evidence 'that, when it came to the pinch, one could not rely on the United States to stick by their allies'.

Some in Washington, Trench admitted, were not convinced that the president wanted to extricate the US from its difficulties in South Vietnam. 'They believe that he is very conscious of being the most powerful man in the world today, that he is determined to teach the "Commies" a lesson and that if the two hundred thousand American servicemen are not enough to teach the lesson, then he will just have to go on increasing the numbers until they achieve the desired result.' Trench found that theory hard to accept;

Johnson was 'a highly sophisticated political operator', and the war created 'endless difficulties' at home and abroad. Those who took a less favourable view of him saw the current peace drive as 'a lot of eye-wash'. Some was, such as Goldberg's visit to the Pope; but Harriman's visit to Warsaw and other capitals had more substance to it. Trench did not, however, rate the prospect of a conference within the next few months as 'very rosy'.

He expected, therefore, to see a further escalation in Vietnam. It was 'not likely to improve the situation significantly'. The influx of American forces in 1965 did, as McNamara put it, 'stop the Americans losing', but an increase in forces or air raids was 'going to take a very long time to bring the North Vietnamese to the conference table'. The only thing that would 'make them decide that the game is not worth the candle' would be 'progress in pacification'. By sending 'a relatively small force of regulars into the South', the North Vietnamese currently drew tens of thousands of American troops to the scene of action, 'with all the complications which this entails,—friction with the South Vietnamese, inflation, supply bottle-necks, etc.', while the Viet Cong on the whole retained the initiative and controlled the same area as before. 'If, on the contrary, the Viet Cong were to find the area under their control diminishing steadily, at the same time as they were suffering heavy casualties in the fighting, this might convince them that they would do well to stop while they were still in a good position.' But it was much easier to send another division to South Vietnam than to produce a workable plan for pacifying the countryside and induce the South Vietnam government to put it into operation.[95]

New Assessments

The FO's Steering Committee was due to consider the paper on the possibility of a negotiated solution after Christmas, Cable had noted on 17 December after it had been to the Planning Committee. It was originally intended to complement the paper on escalation, he noted, but the situation in Vietnam had changed since that was written, and it was now 'somewhat out-of-date'. He submitted an up-to-date analysis by Donald Murray. It took a pessimistic view. But given his basic assumption 'that the war must be won or lost on the ground and in the South', Cable thought Murray's 'depressing analysis … correct and his pessimistic prognosis probable'.[96]

The military situation in South Vietnam, 'to which the air offensive against North Viet-Nam is no more than ancillary', had reverted, Murray believed, to 'a dangerous immobility', in which the balance might be tipping against the US and South Vietnam forces. They numbered about 650,000

Vietnamese and 195,000 Americans. Most of the former were 'tied down on static or defensive duties with correspondingly little ability for mobile defensive operations'. The US force involved 'an immense air effort (both offensive and for transportation), advisory elements, fighting units, and a small naval effort'. The Communist forces in the South had been built up to match the American build-up. Viet Cong regulars were now put at more than 50,000, with 80,000–100,000 guerrillas in addition, and a new element had been introduced with comparatively large-scale intervention by over 100,000 North Vietnamese regulars. 'The Communist forces are masters of the art of concealment and deployment and have used both to off-set the American advantages of air mobility and striking power and to maintain their pressure and initiative.' They were learning how to withstand U.S. close infantry air support. They were able to maintain their supply lines, 'notably through Laos'. The increased size of the US presence offered them more targets for assassination and terrorist attack: those did not materially weaken the Americans or the South Vietnamese but secured 'disproportionate morale and propaganda advantages'. The previous American plans—'under which it was estimated that U.S. forces could start to deal effectively with the military effort by about the middle of 1966'—had been upset, Murray believed: 'the situation is again no more than being held', and there was 'no indication that any progress has been possible in evolving a coherent plan of civil pacification to reinforce any military success'. The Americans played 'no active role to consolidate the situation in areas once they have been swept'. The Communists could fill the vacuum more easily than the South Vietnamese government.

North Vietnam's 'mood of resolution combined with cautious optimism' was 'at least understandable and its premises may not be entirely false'. First, the North Vietnamese had sustained the present scale of bombing and believed, 'probably with justification', that an intensification, 'which they expect', would 'not materially affect their ability to prosecute the war'. The objectives of the US air attacks had been described as deterring Chinese intervention; punishing North Vietnam for supporting the Viet Cong and discouraging any further support; and degrading North Vietnamese military capacity. The first objective was at present 'irrelevant', and it had not prevented the introduction of 'some thousands of Chinese technical troops engaged in logistic support and reconstruction work between the Chinese border and Hanoi'. The other objectives were not being achieved. Second, the bulk of North Vietnam's regular forces, about 300,000, had not been committed, and there were reports of Soviet military assistance. The North Vietnamese might thus have 'good ground for assuming that they can continue the fighting indefinitely with Communist material help, with the single objective of persuading the U.S. to withdraw completely from Viet-Nam'. A parallel with the French might be in mind: the size of the U.S. forces was just about that of the French Expeditionary at its zenith, and they might consider the South Vietnamese forces were 'approaching the same stage of incapacity' as the pro-French indigenous forces in 1953–54. A combination of military frustration in the field, political frustration in the US, and the pressure of international opinion, they might think, would ultimately compel the US to abandon the struggle. North Vietnam might attempt the same 'stick and carrot' policy the US had adopted, 'dropping hints that the door might be open for negotiations, provided that this policy did not imply any deviation from the single objective of forcing a total U.S. withdrawal from Viet-Nam by whatever combination of military and political activity seemed most likely to succeed'.[97]

The situation was 'so uncertain' that the FO decided before Christmas that the Steering Committee would not discuss the long-considered paper on the negotiation. Cable agreed that the chances of negotiations were 'at present, remote and that, in any case, at the present rate of American concessions', the paper would soon be out of date. The Murray memorandum, however, remained 'uncomfortably valid'.[98]

As Cable was aware, Etherington-Smith had revised his earlier views. He had not expected the North Vietnamese to meet the military challenge the Americans now presented, but they had decided to do so. Hanoi's attitude remained inflexible: talking to Felix Greene, Ho Chi Minh had insisted that the Four Points had to be adopted before any approach to a settlement could be considered. No doubt the North Vietnamese hoped that increased pressure would create strains among their opponents. 'They may also expect that the increased bitterness of the fighting and the diminishing role of the Viet-Namese Government Forces in their country's defences will lead to mounting despair and disillusionment among the population and the collapse of Viet-Namese national will to resist.' The Americans would no longer be able to handle the war 'without having to make any major adjustment in their national life or economy'. Etherington-Smith concluded by repeating his view that Britain should offer what support it could. He also repeated his view—now clearly shared by Trench—'that real progress in the field of pacification would do more than anything to defeat the Communist threat and to reduce the risks of escalation'. He hoped a way could be found to improve the British contribution in that field.[99]

In the Soviet section of the Joint Relations Department at the FO, E.E. Orchard offered an idea for getting talks going with the Russians on a slightly different track, which might help to move things forward when the PM visited Moscow in February.[100] Put crudely, he wrote, it would involve substituting the concept of 'de-escalation' for that of trying to reach a conference in the next few months, and moving the Russians 'in the direction of thinking about spheres of influence and a possible return to the *status quo* in Viet-Nam'. Such talk would have to be 'completely confidential' and probably conducted with Prime Minister Kosygin in the first place. It could involve frankly appealing to political realism and 'playing, very cautiously, on geo-political considerations and Soviet susceptibilities about China'.

If recent initiatives met no response, then the possibility of a conference would 'almost certainly be killed for some months to come'. There would therefore be little point in discussing it in Moscow. Emphasis could instead be put on the dangers of escalation. As co-chairmen Britain and Russia should 'use our imagination to create a precedent for what might be called "de-escalation"'. It would be premature to urge a settlement 'while tempers are so high', and de-escalation would have to be a gradual process and was unlikely to be an easy one. The Americans had shown that they were willing in certain circumstances to refrain from bombing the North and might be persuaded 'to reduce the scale of hostilities in other ways'. The North Vietnamese could reduce their infiltration, and the Viet Cong 'begin to behave in a way which would justify eventual participation in a settlement'. Possibly the Control Commission could be activated in some way.

If the Russians showed any interest, the British might go on to discuss political concerns along the following lines. Given Chinese statements, it was not surprising that the Americans felt a need to contain Chinese Communism. The British were, of course, aware of the Sino-Soviet alliance and had no interest in trying to inflame relations between the two governments, which would be counterproductive. They were also aware of Soviet statements on revolution and national liberation, but noted that they had affirmed that revolution was the affair of individual peoples, not to be imposed from outside. Britain also stood for 'social progress and evolution', and like the SU placed peace and stability high among its priorities. It had noted the Soviet government's contacts with the North Vietnam government, and hoped they would lead to an improvement in the prospects for peace and stability in Southeast Asia. No one would like to see more Chinese participation in the Vietnamese conflict.[101]

Cable read Orchard's paper. He did not, however, think the Americans occupied a position of such military advantage that the Russians would accept Orchard's plan or commend it to the North Vietnamese.[102] But the PM, as he was to show, put a great deal of value on contacts with Russia.

There was still no reaction to the initiatives so far undertaken, Arthur de la Mare wrote on 14 January. The Americans suggested two further initiatives. One was a Security Council meeting. The aim would be to 'highlight the worldwide feeling that unconditional negotiations are desirable'. The FO had pointed out 'that a resolution might emerge unacceptable to them but which we should find it difficult to oppose', but the Americans tended to discount that. The other initiative, raised by Rusk and Vice-President Hubert Humphrey with George Brown in Delhi on 12 January, was a meeting of the co-chairmen, and perhaps ICC representatives, at Geneva 'or some other neutral ground'. That would be more effective, SEAD thought, but only if it were a meeting in London or Moscow of the co-chairmen only and in strict secrecy. If it were in Moscow, 'we might be able to ask the Russians to arrange for us to have secret talks with the North Viet-Namese there'. So modified, the initiative might, however, not meet Rusk's 'probable desire for some visible evidence of negotiations'. The question might also be discussed when Wilson visited Kosygin in Moscow in late February, but that would probably be too late. The Americans were showing 'some signs of restlessness', and it was unlikely that the British could persuade them to maintain the bombing pause unless other initiatives had shown results.[103]

There was no sign of any Russian steps after his talk with Kosygin in Delhi, Rusk told Dean on 22 January. He hoped the pause would last till Wilson visited Moscow.[104] The Russians, Demajo, the Yugoslav chargé, told Cable, were in 'an extremely delicate position. They were trying to acquire influence in Hanoi and they were preparing for a Congress of Communist Parties which would, they hoped, rally international Communist support for themselves against China. They did not dare give the Chinese any opportunity to say that the Russians were engaged in betraying North Vietnam to the Americans.' The Americans had to allow Hanoi and Moscow more time. 'If the bombing pause could be continued, there might be some hope of developing the initial indications of increased North Vietnamese flexibility.' A resumption would 'destroy the little progress made so far'. The great difficulty, Cable responded, was the absence of any signal from either capital. Neither the British nor the American approaches to the North Vietnamese had been rejected out of hand, but there had been no reply. The Russians said the matter was no concern of theirs. As a result it was difficult for Britain to recommend a bombing pause.[105]

Howard Smith thought Shelepin's visit to Hanoi had been concerned not just with aid but also with negotiations, but that would have been useless without extending Soviet influence at the expense of that of the Chinese. 'To this end Shelepin will presumably have sought to convince the Vietnamese that they can rely upon Soviet support in what he described as the defence potential of the North, and to demonstrate that this support is crucial to their survival.' Even if he made some progress, further developments would probably be slow. Smith thought it likely 'that we shall see a campaign to persuade the West that the Russians see some light ahead, that the situation is very delicate, and that everything would be ruined by a resumption of bombing in the North', a line that 'could of course correspond to the truth'. Sir George Clutton might 'seek the impressions of the Poles'.[106]

Bryan (H.B.) Shepherd, now the consul-general in Hanoi, commented on the lack of response. It was 'never really on the cards that the enunciation of the 14-Points like an unarranged bridge hand, with no priorities, suits, or trumps, would appeal to a Government that has such a very precise idea of what it would dearly like to achieve and of the priorities this imposes'. Aside from their effect on world opinion, their most useful result might be 'to oblige the North Viet-Namese to pay more serious attention to American war aims and to provide them with a sort of flexible basis from which ... the North Viet-Namese could later make counter-proposals'. In its simplest form the immediate failure to show any interest in peace moves derived from 'the conviction that reunification was promised in 1954 and was promptly frustrated by American action and that, if there were new negotiations, the Americans would only promise reunification if they were sure that it would not happen'. That was buttressed by the belief that the NLF would outlast the Americans and the Saigon 'puppet army'.

Negotiations, Shepherd continued, could be brought about only by a combination of military pressure and political flexibility. Could pressure be on the Chinese or the Russians to end the war? He thought not. Were there internal divisions in Vietnam that could be exploited? Not all the North Vietnamese were of one mind, and it might be that the NLF would be 'more ready for a compromise without promising unification in the near future, if it would give them the status of an acknowledged political party in the South'. If it were represented in the negotiations, 'the influence of Hanoi (and Peking) would be reduced: and is it not possible to envisage, sometime in 1966–67, that a widely supported Saigon Government, together with the Buddhists and other groups in South Viet-Nam would be sufficiently united to accept the N.L.F. as just another political group and to contain the Front by political methods as the French and Italians contained their Communists in the post-war period?'

Shepherd did not think that the Hanoi leaders would be reduced to submission by all-out bombardment, even of Hanoi itself. The town comprised only 4 per cent of the population. Government and people would disperse. The current air attacks were 'both frightening and effective in virtually forcing the Viet-Namese to move everything by night'. The economy had been slowed down, and military movements affected. But Shepherd's preferred policy would be to limit the bombing to military targets, to take the strongest possible action against the VC in the South, and to look for contacts with the NLF 'as an eventually recognisable political party, which could participate ... in negotiations for a political settlement'.[107]

Not surprisingly, Etherington-Smith agreed with much of this. But he repeated his criticism of the view that the North Vietnamese felt cheated of what they were promised under the Geneva agreement. Neither the Americans nor the South Vietnamese had subscribed to it. How then could the North Vietnamese have felt it would be implemented in precisely the way they wanted? '[I]n fact it suited their book to accept an Agreement whose value was debatable for the sake of the immediate advantages it offered them.'

The ambassador in Saigon also questioned the idea that the NLF might participate in the negotiations as a political party. The Americans had recently indicated that they would accept it as a political party in South Vietnam. Accepting it as an independent participant in negotiations was another matter. It would damage the prestige of the Vietnamese government and be difficult for it to accept. The Americans were ready to see it represented in a North Vietnamese delegation, but the Communists wanted it to gain 'official recognition'. Etherington-Smith added that though it might be possible to conciliate and even detach some of the 'nationalistic elements' in the front, it would also be 'a fairly tricky proposition'. Lodge thought the chances of success 'very uncertain'.[108]

The End of the Pause

On 24 January the president told the prime minister that bombing might resume at very short notice.[109] De la Mare did not recommend that the PM should 'seek further to deflect the President from this decision. Our own efforts in Moscow and Hanoi to bring about peace negotiations have met with no response. We have already exposed to the U.S. Administration our impotence as honest brokers.' It increasingly criticised the British because their ships continued to trade with North Vietnam. The enemy had been building up its military position while the pause was on. 'For Britain now to recommend further self-denial to the United States is merely to invite the retort that it is Americans, not Britons, who are paying for this war and dying in it; that our solicitude for peace is belied by our continued trading with the enemy; and in any event as peace promoters we have proved broken reeds. This rebuke may not be just, but it will be made, it will be believed, and it will stick.' The president invited suggestions. The only advice the PM could give was that he should ensure that 'unbiased world opinion—there will always be those who refuse to listen—rallies behind him to the fullest extent possible. To this end he should give as clear a warning to the North Vietnamese as is consistent with security that their refusal to entertain his proposal for unconditional negotiations must lead to escalation of the war.' Gore-Booth agreed.[110] The FO drafted a reply, which the principal private secretary (PPS) modified as 'too outspoken'.[111] It suggested providing the world with information about Hanoi's use of the pause to build up its forces.[112] The message was read at the president's meeting on 26 January.[113]

The foreign secretary and the minister of defence were in Washington to discuss the Defence Review, which had brought 'East of Suez' into question. Stewart met Rusk on 27 January. If Britain left Singapore while the US was still heavily involved in Vietnam, it would create 'a very difficult situation', Rusk said. In answer to a question, Stewart said 'that even if confrontation ended, it would be extremely difficult for the United Kingdom to consider sending troops to Viet-Nam'. Rusk made a plea for civilian medical care. 'In the United States there was a tendency to call the roll and see which of America's allies were in Viet-Nam. The Administration had used our Indonesian preoccupations in our defence, but in view of recent developments in Indonesia which most Americans considered favourable to us'—he was alluding to the Gestapu coup and the erosion of Sukarno's position—'this was wearing thin.' Rusk also commented on the Russians. In Delhi Kosygin had been reluctant to discuss Vietnam. Shelepin, it seemed, had a discouraging experience in Hanoi. Rusk thought the Russians had been obliged to give North Vietnam 'a great deal more support'.[114]

Denis Healey talked to McNamara and McNaughton. The latter said that the US would like to see Vietnam as a non-aligned neutral state. '[I]t would not make sense to hang on by holding half the country. He frankly admitted that the US Government did not know what kind of settlement they could hope to achieve. Broadly their object was to press their policy in such a way that northern Vietnam would accept the concept of a neutral State because they found the continuation of the present war intolerable.' If a non-aligned state could be achieved, it would, as Healey had suggested, need to be 'guaranteed by Western strength'. The US was anxious lest the Chinese might believe that after the war had been settled, the US would never again enter into a comparable commitment in Southeast Asia. Healey talked of a multilateral force, organised on an allied basis, though saying that he did not think British power would be 'significantly less' after the Defence Review.[115]

Both Stewart and Healey saw the president on 28 January, along with Rusk, McNamara and the two ambassadors. If bombing were resumed, the foreign secretary repeated, the president should make the military reasons as clear as possible. He said that if it were possible, the British would hope that the bombing pause could continue till Wilson had seen Kosygin in Moscow, though that was still a month off. Perhaps there were no solid grounds to think that the Russians would then be more responsive, but the visit would give direct access to Kosygin 'and might enable the door to be kept open'. 'The President replied that if he had any hope at all that there would be some positive response he would not hesitate to keep the door open.' But all the signs from the Russians were negative. He had never expected the pause to go on as long as it had. The Russians had suggested 12–20 days 'for the forces of peace to get to work'. The pause had lasted 30, 'and the American forces were suffering the military consequences'. If a serious reverse followed the pause, the military results would be bad enough, but he was even more concerned about the effect on internal US politics. Eighteen of the 20 senators at a recent meeting[116] wanted the administration to go much further than it had, and the other two offered only pious hopes. Each day the extreme senators, such as Stennis and Russell, became more vocal, the advocates of resumption more hysterical. 'Nothing could be worse than that the "War Committee" in the Senate should take control of the situation.' He expected a decision to resume 'fairly soon. If so, the bombing would be carried out in a restrained and sensible manner … designed so far as possible to help to relieve the situation in the South.' The president hoped there would be no publicity about the discussion. 'It would be very dangerous if it were thought that British Ministers had used their visit to urge a continuation of the pause in the bombing.' It was indeed 'paramount', Stewart told Wilson, that there should be 'no leak whatever'.[117]

Meanwhile Sir G. Harrison, Trevelyan's successor, had been tackling Foreign Minister Gromyko in Moscow. The co-chairmen perhaps had particular responsibilities, he suggested, and referred to Wilson's message of 3 January. What could he report? Kosygin, Gromyko replied, had only just returned to Moscow, and he had not been able to discuss the matter with his prime minister. Would Wilson prefer a reply now or during his visit? He would like to know, Harrison said, whether the Soviet government or Gromyko personally thought that 'there was anything that we could do together or separately'. The oft-stated Soviet position, Gromyko responded, was that the aggressors should leave Vietnam and go home. 'They were carrying out an aggressive war. The Soviet Government were not in the position of a mediator. They did not like to take such a position. ... They thought that the British Government had the possibility of exercising a good influence on the American Government. ... We had been too one-sided. They thought that if the British Government really wished to facilitate a solution we could exercise a positive influence, but they did not see that we were doing this.'

Harrison pointed out that the bombing had in fact stopped. The Americans, Gromyko said, made statements that they had stopped it, but that it might be resumed if their requirements were not met. 'What influence did this have on the other side? Very definitely negative. Even if it could be assumed that the Americans had good intentions, they spoiled them with such statements. If they had them. ... Considerations of national dignity meant that the possibility of a favourable effect was excluded.'[118]

Ho Chi Minh sent a message to Queen Elizabeth II on 29 January through the DRV representative in Moscow. It included an attack on the US position and called for the end of American bombing and warlike activities. Harrison saw the message as propaganda and returned it.[119] In Warsaw Foreign Minister Adam Rapacki told Clutton that Hanoi had drawn attention to Ho's message, especially the concluding passage which declared in French that the US must 'recognise' the Four Points.[120] The FO told Harrison to accept the message, and to invite the Vietnamese chargé's comment on the word 'recognition'. The 14 Points had already indicated that the US was ready to discuss them.[121] Harrison saw the chargé. The English version was official. The Vietnamese should translate into 'accept'.[122]

The FO did not see how it could go further, Clutton was told, especially as Ho's letter added the further stipulation that the US must recognise the FLN as the sole representative of the South Vietnamese people and negotiate with it.[123] Discussing 'this Gilbertian situation', Michalowski, the permanent head of the Foreign Ministry, said he would instruct the Polish ambassador in Hanoi to draw attention to the discrepancy between the English and French versions. He hoped to be able to say that the French version was correct: French was in continued use in Hanoi as the business language.[124]

In Warsaw on 2 February Michalowski told Clutton that Britain should have sought clarification not from a junior official in Moscow but from the Polish government, which could have asked the North Vietnamese government. He suggested the course that had been followed was at the request of the US government. Clutton denied that and recalled that he had pointed out the discrepancy to Michalowski. Had he had an answer from

Hanoi? It had replied, Michalowski said, 'that no useful purpose would now be served by pursuing the matter'.

'After further lamenting the delay in my asking for a clarification of the discrepancy he said that surely it would have been possible to have deferred the resumption of bombing for at least a couple of days while the Vietnamese message had been thoroughly studied.' Though dated 24 January, Clutton pointed out, the message had been handed to the Polish ambassador in Hanoi only on 28 January, and published that day even before it had been handed to the British ambassador in Moscow. 'Michalowski answered that he presumed this haste had been because the North Vietnamese believed that a resumption of bombing was imminent, a remark which can be interpreted two ways.' Michalowski was disappointed because of the part Poland had played as middleman between Harriman and Hanoi.[125]

'I am not happy about Vietnam,' the president had told a long meeting on 28 January, 'but we cannot run out—we have to resume bombing.'[126] On the 31st the president announced that bombing would be resumed after the 37-day pause,[127] though in fact it did not happen immediately.

The Americans asked the British to investigate 'weak signals' from Hanoi that they purported to have picked up.[128] On 3 February the FO passed on to the Washington embassy hints that Hanoi might be interested in discussions. Goldberg took the matter up with Caradon, and the Security Council, of which Goldberg had sought a meeting, was adjourned while consultations were undertaken.[129] Any concession was more likely to occur in confidential exchanges than at the Security Council. Caradon was authorised to speak to Nikolai Federenko, but the FO also issued instructions for direct representations in Moscow, Warsaw and Hanoi.[130] Federenko had told the SC that the SU believed that the issue should be settled within the Geneva framework. Britain was ready to join its co-chairman in proposing a reconvening of the conference or other initiatives. If the Russians replied on familiar lines—that it was Hanoi's business—the Moscow embassy could point out that the FO had instructed the consul-general to make an approach in Hanoi and was contemplating an approach to the North Vietnamese chargé in Moscow.[131]

These last-minute initiatives got nowhere. Firyubin replied that the only way to make progress was for the Americans to cease aggression and approach Hanoi directly.[132] Rapacki remarked, as Clutton reported, that starting, stopping and restarting bombing created 'a dangerous and deplorable precedent in international morality, since it implied that a great Power had the right at will [to decide] whether or not it should take military action against the territory of another and small Power'. There was a great deal in that, Clutton commented, from the point of view of world public opinion.[133] And perhaps it was not surprising that a Pole felt like that.

Wright at No. 10 tried to account for Hanoi's actions. It had perhaps interpreted the bombing pause as 'a sign of weakness' and believed that world opinion would prevent the US restarting it. Hence Ho Chi Minh's latest letter adding a fifth condition for peace talks, 'namely that the VC should be present as the sole lawful representatives of South Vietnam', was 'a total mis-reading of the situation'. The 'signals' might be 'no more than a surprised reaction to their own mis-judgments'. If that were so, 'there might be some grounds for cautious optimism. If the North Vietnamese come to realise they will have to give something in order to escape further bombing they may be more ready to talk.'[134]

At the same time, the president was despatching a letter to the prime minister saying that bombing would recommence on Monday, 7 February.[135] That would, of course, affect what Wilson might do on his visit to Moscow, not to mention its effect on the DRV.

Wilson in Moscow

The FO had meanwhile been considering what advice it might offer the PM. Even if the pause had continued—which would have given the PM more *champ de manoeuvre*—Harrison had doubted whether the Russians' leverage with the North Vietnamese, 'to say nothing of the Viet Cong', was 'such that they could ... deliver the goods in the form of agreement to enter into serious and genuine negotiations'.[136]

The long pause, Dumbrell suggests, 'cast long shadows over subsequent efforts to secure peace via Soviet diplomacy'.[137] It had, as Cooper recognised, been largely a matter of image so far as Johnson was concerned, but negotiations had been on the verge of possibility. If Wright's analysis was correct, the DRV had not realised that till too late. And the SU—which might have influenced it—did not want to be exposed by the PRC.

Harrison set out his analysis of Soviet policy more fully in the context of possible action at the UN, where Thant told Caradon he had suggested to the Americans a conference of the five great powers and representatives of North and South Vietnam.[138] The SU, Harrison pointed out, held that the UN had no standing in the matter, the PRC and DRV not being members. The right body was the Geneva conference, but the US should at first recognise or accept the Four and Five Points of the Communists of North and South Vietnam. The US did not accept those points, and so reconvening Geneva was impossible until either the Vietnamese or the

Americans or both modified their position. Until they thought the holding of talks had become possible, the Russians would take no initiative to bring them about, and would resist pressure to do so. They assumed that before any talks—and in the course of them—they would be 'the objects of Chinese suspicion, slander, hostile manoeuvre and open attacks', and that the best protection against that was 'the maintenance of solidarity with the Vietnamese Communists'. They were worried by the aggravation of the conflict, but feared that their intervention would be ineffectual and detrimental to their interests in their dispute with China. They would continue to try to bring pressure on the US, but felt that since Shelepin's return from Hanoi and the resumption of bombing, they could not press the Vietnamese.[139]

Harrison counselled against putting the Soviet co-chairman on the spot. Pressure on him would not induce him to take any initiative. The intervention of the co-chairmen might be useful when the American or Vietnamese attitudes had changed. 'But we are at present a long way off from that point.' The UK had 'a long term interest in preserving the position of the Co-Chairmen and in maintaining … the kind of relationship which will make a return to cooperation easy when the time becomes ripe for it'. The long-term relationship should not be prejudiced by short-term diplomatic moves that would not bring a peaceful settlement nearer.[140]

Meanwhile, Cable suggested that Britain might act on the repeated Soviet advice to deal direct with Hanoi. The prime minister could explain that the US would never accept the Four Points as set out, and question the ambiguities in North Vietnamese statements. If North Vietnam rejected a meeting, the prime minister could tell the Russians that that demonstrated the need for action by the co-chairmen.[141] Reproaching the Russians would get nowhere. Their attitude was, after all, 'the mirror image of our own attitude in previous years', when they called for conferences on Vietnam, Laos or Cambodia, and Britain, knowing that the US would not agree, refused to embarrass its American ally by joining in such proposals. Britain had also said that the co-chairmen had neither the right nor the duty to call a conference without ascertaining that other powers were ready to attend. Advising the PM to repeat the proposal might only urge him into a blind alley. Instead he should meet a North Vietnamese representative while in Moscow, explain the futility of expecting the US to accept the Four Points in their present form, question ambiguities in the North Vietnamese position, and renew Britain's offers to transmit any message or proposal. Calling on the chargé would be of no use unless he was told in advance. Preferably Hanoi should send someone to Moscow to talk to the PM.

Cable listed the advantages of his proposal. If the North Vietnamese agreed to talk to the PM, it might at least 'dent the surface of some of their more extravagant illusions' and possibly start a dialogue. It would be 'a bold and imaginative initiative'. That it would still be if the North Vietnamese did not agree to talk. Then it would also again demonstrate North Vietnamese intransigence to the world, and the PM would have a new argument with the Russians. Cable also listed the disadvantages. Particularly if they did not agree to see the PM, the North Vietnamese would 'once again be encouraged in their belief that the Americans are weakening and that Hanoi need only hold out long enough to be able to negotiate on its own terms'. HMG might lose some prestige, 'not only for having begun yet another unsuccessful initiative, but also for having exposed the Prime Minister to another rebuff from a Government whom we do not even recognise'. Cable thought the advantages outweighed the disadvantages, provided the proceedings were secret.

If his idea found favour, it would be necessary to decide whether the Americans should be consulted in advance. Because of the time factor, so he said, Cable himself favoured informing the US government, perhaps in a personal message to the president, at the same time as the North Vietnamese were approached, but consulting it only on what the PM should say when the conversation took place. The Soviet government could hardly object and might even cooperate in keeping the proposed meeting secret.[142]

The PM should concentrate on getting negotiations going, not on the nature of the settlement, Cable suggested. The FO did not know what the US would concede, but Washington telegrams about Ambassador Byroade's contacts in Rangoon suggested that its opening position would strike the North Vietnamese as unrealistic. 'So long as we stick to the immediate choice between negotiations or continued fighting, our position and that of the United States is easily defensible. But, if we have to start arguing about the Geneva Agreements or the attitude of the United States towards negotiations in earlier years, then our position is shaky and [the] North Vietnamese have some strong arguments on their side.' Britain was not supposed to reveal its knowledge of North Vietnam/US exchanges in Rangoon. It would be safer to say that it had no authority to speak on behalf of the Americans and was 'only trying to feel out the ground for negotiations'.[143]

Gore-Booth approved the idea,[144] and the foreign secretary sent a minute Cable drafted to No. 10.[145] It was, Wilson responded, a 'very interesting idea'. The North Vietnamese might refuse. 'I wouldn't mind the rebuff.' Should he meet a Viet Cong representative there? He thought yes.[146]

The FO agreed, but suggested that the possibility should not be mentioned in the message to the president. It might frighten him off.[147]

That message was sent on 14 February. Wilson told the president he would try to meet a North Vietnamese representative in Moscow, preferably 'some fairly senior man' from Hanoi, explain that the US could not be expected to accept the Four Points as they stood, try to probe the North Vietnamese 'about possible ambiguities or loopholes' in their proposals, and offer to transmit any messages. The meeting was unlikely to produce tangible results, but might 'help to get some of the realities of the situation through the barrier Hanoi has erected against the outside world' and demonstrate 'our will to peace'. If, as might well happen, the North Vietnamese representative refused to meet him, he would at least be able to tell the Russians that their cooperation in joint action by the co-chairmen was indispensable. Did the president see strong objection to the proposal? Wilson needed to know in 24 hours since he had to put it in advance of his visit.[148]

Johnson's response was very positive. He was glad that Wilson agreed that 'another hard attempt'—after Harriman's—'should be made to persuade the Russians to join as Co-Chairmen in convening the Geneva Conference'. His own attitude had been made clear since last February, but if Wilson planned to make his efforts public, he was prepared publicly to state his support before the visit. The president agreed that it was 'a good idea' to try to talk to the North Vietnamese representative in Moscow. He knew of nothing that would suggest that there would be 'a useful response', but it was 'wise to take every opportunity to impress the realities of the situation on the Government of North Viet Nam'.[149]

Harrison spoke to the Vietnamese chargé in Moscow on 17 February. He was ready to transmit Wilson's proposal for a meeting to Hanoi, but asked a number of questions: what were Britain's aims as one of the co-chairmen? What did it want the meeting to cover? Had its attitude on the Vietnam question changed? The aim of the PM, Harrison replied, was to seek further elucidation of North Vietnam's position. He would explain the British government's attitude. His government's attitude, the chargé said, had been set out in Ho Chi Minh's message to the Queen and many other heads of government and state. The prime minister, Harrison replied, hoped in confidential discussion to elucidate the views of the North Vietnamese authorities a little further, and would be willing to offer any further elucidation of British views that might be sought. The Vietnamese, the chargé responded, had noted that Britain was not fulfilling its duty as co-chairman but was supporting the US in its violations of the agreements and in its plans for aggressive war. It supported the renewal of the bombing and the attempt to discuss Vietnam in the SC, which meant the UN was interfering in Vietnam's internal affairs. It also allowed the US to use Hong Kong as a military base. Harrison thought those were all questions that could be discussed with the PM. At the conclusion of the interview the chargé repeated that he would transmit the message. He hoped the interview would remain confidential.[150]

The talking points for Wilson that the FO prepared set out his side of a conversation. He would start by stating that the British government wanted, and was convinced that the US wanted, 'a negotiated ending to the conflict in Vietnam'. The public positions adopted by North Vietnam and the US were 'not easy to reconcile', but the PM hoped that the private and confidential discussion might permit finding some basis on which negotiations could begin. He would seek clarification of points in Ho Chi Minh's message.

One was the participation of the NLF in any negotiations. If North Vietnam were willing for it to be represented on a footing equal to that of the governments of North and South Vietnam, he would put that to the US; but if the intention was to exclude the South Vietnamese government from the conference table, he did not think the US would ever agree, and he would not even be willing to propose it. The second question related to the first of Pham Van Dong's Four Points. If it meant that US forces had to leave before negotiations began, or that the US must promise withdrawal by a certain date whether or not an agreement was reached, the US could not be expected to agree, and Wilson could not recommend such terms. If it meant that the US should undertake to withdraw 'within a reasonable period of an agreement resulting from negotiations and subject to any safeguards contained in that agreement', Wilson would be glad of further clarification. The third question related to Dong's third point. Did it mean that the US had to agree in advance of negotiations and irrespective of their outcome that NLF should 'exercise supreme power in South Vietnam'? If so, there was no prospect of an agreement. If it meant that the future role of the NLF would be determined in the negotiations, he would be glad of further clarification. The fourth question related to Ho Chi Minh's call for a cessation of bombing and warlike acts against North Vietnam. If that were a call for 'a purely unilateral concession' by the US, it would be 'a serious obstacle to negotiations'. But if North Vietnam were also 'prepared to facilitate negotiations by making some corresponding concession of a military character', Wilson would again be glad of further clarification.

In the conversation the FO was adumbrating, the PM would then emphasise that he was speaking on behalf of the British government, and that he had no reason to suppose that his suggestions would necessarily be accepted by the US. He would also express his conviction that the Americans, though 'genuinely anxious to negotiate', would do so 'only on reasonable and honourable terms'. Rather than accept the Four Points in their current form, he believed that they would 'reinforce their present military effort out of all recognition' and would be 'prepared, at any cost, to go on fighting for as many years as may be necessary'. He did not think that the US could 'ever be forced to accept military defeat or a humiliating capitulation'. Negotiations were thus 'urgent and essential'. He hoped that the North Vietnamese government would offer their comments and let him know if it wanted him to make any communication to the US government. If so, Wilson would see that no publicity was given to the communication.[151]

Hanoi replied, Harrison reported on 21 February, that it could not send a representative to Moscow and that its ambassador was not in Moscow. If the PM wished to meet its representative, he could be received there by the chargé (Le Trang).[152] Wilson decided that the chargé should be asked to receive Minister of State Lord Chalfont, who was accompanying him. He would speak to the brief and 'try to take the temperature'.[153] The meeting was unproductive. The US should stop the bombing without prior talks, the chargé insisted. The UK was not fulfilling its obligations as co-chairman. Chalfont expressed his disappointment. It was never intended, he added, that the co-chairmen should be impartial, but rather 'balanced'.[154] Strangely, Wilson recalled that Chalfont had a six-hour talk with 'a high-powered delegation then in Moscow'.[155]

The PM's own talks with Kosygin were also unproductive so far as Vietnam was concerned. The Soviet premier said that the US had to withdraw from Vietnam,[156] and Leonid Brezhnev, the Party secretary, took an even harder line.[157] Wilson said he had not been 'unduly hopeful that the door could be opened to a solution of the Viet-Nam problem. In the long term the United Kingdom would like to see the whole area neutralised and its frontiers guaranteed by the Great Powers.' He accepted that there was no immediate possibility of an initiative on this problem.[158] What became clear, he later recalled, was 'the inability of the Soviet Government to exert any real pressure on Hanoi in the face of continuing militant Chinese pressure'.[159] So what could be done?

Chapter Six
Dissociation

The FO and its ambassadors continued their debate over Vietnam and over British as well as American policies. Cable insisted that the Americans had embarked on a lost cause and the British object should be to help them extricate themselves. Not all agreed. Though the prime minister dissociated himself from the decision to bomb Hanoi, his policy continued to be to offer support for US policy, in order to provide himself with some leverage for promoting peace through the SU. The Russians remained impassive, but in October 1966 they seemed to shift.

In October 1965 Cable forwarded to the Ministry of Defence the paper on Vietnam and Escalation. The major risk it foresaw for the British was the extension of the fighting into Laos. The ministry should perhaps consider the possibility that Britain might be asked to send forces under SEATO or otherwise. In 1962 the US bore the main burden. Would that still be the case? How much could Britain afford to provide Thailand with, Cable asked, if the Indonesian threat had died away? How much if it had not? What would be expected of it in order to complement US plans?[1]

While Indonesian Confrontation continued, Willy Wright responded, Britain could make at most only a token contribution to Thailand. If it had definitely quietened down, it could contribute more, perhaps at the level of Plan 8: a battalion group from the Commonwealth Brigade, a light transport squadron, and a fighter/ground attack squadron. He could not answer Cable's third question. 'No U.S. or other allied plans are known to us.' What might be provided in response to hypothetical expectations could 'only be a matter of seeing what we can afford in the circumstances and setting it against a political estimate of what is considered the minimum respectable contribution'. He did not think more could be found out about the Americans' military plans 'unless we are already discussing with them the political aspects of a crisis which may concern us both'. The defence staff could follow up an approach to the State Department. But he doubted 'whether it is sensible to think of such an approach until ministerial discussions, both on the defence review and on the follow up of the quadripartite talks, have taken place'. Those might provide 'an indication of the shape which Anglo-US defence cooperation in the Far East may take in the future'. Overriding all the considerations, Wright concluded, was 'the fact that now and in the future it would be contrary to our general policy to do anything that might result in our getting seriously bogged down and this militates strongly against any provision of U.K. land forces to Thailand'.[2]

Would the Thais ask for a contingent if fighting flared up in Laos? Cable asked Ambassador Rumbold. Could Britain get away with a token?[3] Rumbold found it difficult to answer. Warner thought that when the pressure on Laos mounted, the Americans' assistance would escalate *pari passu*, 'and they would find themselves committed to intervention without any formal decision'. A SEATO intervention as such would be avoided. 'What would happen would be that the war in Vietnam would in effect become generalised and there would be one campaign waged by the Americans against the North Vietnamese both in Vietnam and Laos.' Britain would have to decide what response to make to a Thai request for reinforcements, Rumbold concluded. If the US had decided not to regard the attacks as coming under the SEATO treaty, the kind of stiffening Britain offered in 1962 would be sufficient. The short answer to the question as to what Britain could 'get away with' was thus a token force of Hunters. If that seemed to be 'lowering us in the estimation of the Thais', that would not be 'a particularly important consideration'. If they thought 'that we have let them down this would not reduce the volume of our exports to Thailand nor would it make fewer Thais come to England to be educated. What the Americans would feel would be more important. But if it came to really serious fighting in Laos the Americans would surely be content that we should give the seal of our approval to what they did by making a token contribution.' That was on the assumption that Britain was not 'falling down on what they consider to be our proper jobs in other parts of the world, e.g. in Germany, in the Middle East and in Central Africa, not to mention in Indonesia'.

Had the FO considered the possibility that the US would decide to use ground troops to cut the Ho Chi Minh trail? That was recently mentioned by the *Times* correspondent as a possible outcome of McNamara's latest visit to Vietnam. Presumably it would take place only after the Americans had got Souvanna Phouma to invite them to defend Laos against fresh Vietnamese attacks, 'real or imaginary'. It would be represented 'however unconvincingly as a defensive riposte' to a Vietnamese onslaught. 'Such a development might … mark a turning point in our own attitude towards the Vietnamese war and result in a kind of crisis of confidence between ourselves and the Americans.' Rumbold could 'scarcely imagine that we would then find it either morally right or politically expedient to send any sort of reinforcements to Thailand'.

Rumbold did not care for the phrase 'getting away with it'. 'We are not shifty and recalcitrant schoolboys on the look-out to see whether the headmaster can be cajoled or deceived into overlooking our shortcomings. If we think that our national interest or the poverty of our resources make it necessary for us to withhold some support which our allies have solicited I would hope that we would tell them so without being too much inhibited by a speculation as to what their opinion of us might be.'[4]

In Vientiane Warner thought the Americans had no present intention of carrying the war to Laos, and had been assured by Bill Sullivan, as Cabot Lodge had assured Etherington-Smith, that they were trying to limit their activities in Laos so as to limit the danger that the other side would do the opposite. In any case there were good general grounds for believing that they would be reluctant to send troops into Laos: they had already taken on as much as they could handle in Vietnam. 'Surely the proper course for them is to get all their logistic, air and military bases set up in South Vietnam, to move cautiously out of them and establish safe surrounding areas and then to impose on the enemy their own wishes as to where and how they wish the war to be fought.' They were a long way from this, and meanwhile 'they cannot try new adventures and will have their work cut out to keep themselves from being clobbered'. Nor did Warner think the North Vietnamese wanted to open a new front in Laos.

The possibility that the war would spread to Laos was, however, 'drawing daily nearer. When a pair of dogs are fighting in the street they do not take much pains to stay on the pavement.' Either side might use Cambodian or Laotian territory to take a swipe at the other. McNamara was trying to prevent infiltration by heavy raids on North Vietnamese communications into Laos, but that had no chance of success. What would he do next? Perhaps he would extend the raids into Laos. That would not stop infiltration either. Commando raids into southern Laos might follow. There were all sorts of ways in which Laos could slide into war. The army might go to pieces and have to be strengthened by 'advisers'. 'We all know where that leads.'[5]

Etherington-Smith was 'puzzled' by Rumbold's suggestion that 'moral considerations' would operate against sending British reinforcements to Thailand. He could not see what they could be. 'If moral right is involved, surely it would be unmistakably on the side of the Americans and of

SEATO?' The Viet Minh started intervening militarily in Laos before the Americans and North Vietnamese forces were never withdrawn from Laos, as required by the 1962 Agreement. 'Similarly, in Vietnam, the North Vietnamese had been infiltrating armed men and political agents into the South in flagrant violation of the Geneva Agreement ... long before the Americans decided to intervene.' That being so, Etherington-Smith thought that the Americans could justifiably claim they were entitled to intervene in Laos 'if such intervention appeared necessary to counter Communist violations of Treaty obligations which were having a serious affect [*sic*] on the war in Vietnam. And from a wider point of view the American effort to stem the tide of Communist expansion in Asia is surely one about which we do not need to have any moral reservations?' Whatever Britain might be able to contribute in the event of escalation in Laos, he hoped that it would at least give the US its 'general support'.[6]

Rumbold did not let this go. He did not agree with the idea Etherington-Smith advanced that Britain had to choose between supporting, opposing or standing aloof from America's effort. 'At different times we do each of these things depending on the circumstances. And quite right too. Most of the time we support the Americans over Vietnam because they are our allies and because on the whole we approve of what we believe to be their objectives. Sometimes we oppose them but mainly in private, when we think that they are doing something stupid or wrong as for example when they recently threatened to pursue the Viet Cong into Cambodia. Circumstances can be imagined in which we would have to make it plain in public that we did not agree with what they were doing. The fact that our opposition is or might be ineffective is beside the point. And we sometimes stand aloof. We are not belligerents in Vietnam. I wonder whether you think we should be.'

Rumbold questioned Etherington-Smith's view that a 'moral justification' could always be found for actions that the Americans took to stem the Communist tide. 'Let us take an extreme example and suppose that if after the Americans had poured hundreds of thousands of men into Vietnam they still could not get the better of the Communists and so decided to use nuclear weapons. Would you then be in favour of our supporting them without reservation? I would hope not.'

Morals aside, 'it would be very difficult for our Government to continue to give whole-hearted support to the Americans if they were seen to be deliberately enlarging the war either geographically or in any other way. The British public would surely not accept the American claim that they were entitled to do anything they liked in order to make sure of stemming the Communist tide.'[7]

The bases the Americans were building—in Vietnam and in Thailand—were, Rumbold had suggested in November 1965, on such a scale that it might mean that they meant to stay in Southeast Asia.[8] '[W]e are always grateful for any light shed on an enigma which seems to be ever more tightly secluded within President Johnson's own bosom,' was Cable's comment on US foreign policy. 'My own impression … is that the Americans have never fully thought out thc implications and logical consequences of their policy in Vietnam on any long-term basis, but are proceeding, as British governments have so often done, from one short-term expedient to another.'[9]

'[N]o more than most governments and rather less than some,' Rumbold admitted, the US did not have 'a carefully worked out long-term policy for South East Asia'. But the bases being built had 'such a permanent air about them' that, if the US had no long-term policy, it clearly at least planned to keep American forces in both countries for a long time to come. The Americans would justify that by arguing that if they did not the two countries would 'quickly be subverted by the Chinese', and then 'the "free world" would suffer a terrible defeat[,] other countries would cease to have any confidence in the United States and so on and so forth'. The argument, however, was based on a purely American assessment of the correct way to prevent China's conquest of Southeast Asia. Many other governments did not share that assessment, including the British, or at least the FO. Its papers indeed questioned whether China had a strong desire to conquer Southeast Asia, and suggested that keeping white troops in the area would only encourage them to do so. The French government disagreed with the American assessment, and not merely out of a spirit of contradiction. The Soviet government disagreed, too, and it was at least as much in its interest to keep Chinese influence in Southeast Asia within bounds.[10]

Rumbold's thesis was in part founded on the 'durability' of American bases, but, Warner commented, appearances might be deceptive. The high standard of military installations did not necessarily mean that they were intended for long-term use. Warner agreed with Cable's view that over the last ten years the Americans in Southeast Asia had chiefly been reacting to day-to-day events. Now they were also reacting to contingencies, that is, 'looking a bit further ahead'. The bases in Vietnam were being constructed to deal with a situation that had already arisen. Those in Thailand were intended to deal with situations that might arise. Perhaps that was not very different from Rumbold's assessment, but Warner thought that the Americans were 'still acting in terms of particular considerations rather than of general ones'.[11]

Etherington-Smith had not abandoned his argument with his Bangkok colleague over Britain's support for the Americans in Vietnam. His views, he said, were not quite as Rumbold represented them: he had not suggested that moral justification could always be found for any step the Americans took 'in the name of stemming the Communist tide', nor that the British should support the Americans in anything they chose to do 'whatever our misgivings'. Rumbold suggested that the British should 'support, oppose and stand aloof from the American effort at different times, depending on the circumstances'. That was to confuse basic policy and day-to-day approach. Fundamentally the British had to decide whether to support, oppose or stand aloof. If they wished to support, that did not prevent saying that they disagreed in specific cases. But in general it should be done in private, and Etherington-Smith favoured the 'fullest and frankest private consultations'.

His view was 'that American objectives are so close to our own and that it is so greatly in our interest that they should succeed that we should do everything we can to help them'. He had no quarrel with the official position, though he thought the British could do more to help in practical ways, 'notably in the field of pacification'. He had never advocated that British assistance should take a military form, though not because of any objection of principle (two members of the old Commonwealth were doing so): 'for quite practical reasons it does not seem to me to be in our interest to intervene militarily in Vietnam at present.' It was possible to envisage circumstances in which it would become 'desirable—if not unavoidable'. He did not suggest that the British should always support the Americans. If they resorted to nuclear weapons, much would depend on circumstances, but the British should certainly not say in advance that they would not support any action of that kind: 'our enemies are prepared to use them, or the threat of using them.'

While he thought that 'most of us' agreed that 'stemming the tide of Communism in Asia' was an objective Britain should support, 'it is the means the Americans employ that present the real dilemma'. Thanks in part to Communist propaganda, the objective seemed to 'large and vocal sections of opinion … vague and slightly suspect', and the means aroused 'an instant and instinctive revulsion from the realities of US material power'. In public opinion the issue was 'not the tide of communism, but the tide of napalm'. That made it difficult for the British government to limit its criticism of certain actions to private diplomacy. 'We are liable from time to time to be forced out into the open with condemnation of the means and this will be taken by the Americans as tantamount to a condemnation of their ends. Why? Because the means which they are applying are the ones which their national character and environment dictate to them and denial of their right to use their unique powers and capabilities in the ways they judge appropriate in pursuit of an end which all regard as valid will continue to meet ... with stony silence in Washington.'

Was there any way out of the dilemma? 'Theoretically yes, by making such a substantial commitment to the effort in Vietnam that the Americans are forced to pay attention to our criticisms of their methods.' In practice, it seemed that Britain could not make that commitment. It would also help if the facts about Vietnam were better known to the British public. 'It has never ceased to amaze me that people should feel more indignant about American bombing than about the countless atrocities perpetrated by the VC.' Meanwhile there seemed to be no alternative to 'our continuing our present uncomfortable tight-rope walk between US ends, US means and an antagonistic public attitude at home'.[12]

Rumbold took up Etherington-Smith's reference to ends and means, but not in the sense he used it: he talked more of methods, policies and objectives. The relationship of ends and means, he wrote, had long been the subject of argument. 'What is certain is that means often modify or distort ends and the American record in Vietnam is a case in point. Alongside their original objective of helping the South to resist interference from the North there has grown up, because of the means they have employed and for no other reason, the quite separate objective of demonstrating that any enterprise to which they wholly commit themselves must always be successful. The need to demonstrate this point would not have arisen if they had been more cautious in supporting the South Vietnamese. If they had foreseen in the years 1955–1958 that their support for the South was going to have the effect of sucking hundreds of thousands of American combatants into the battle they would probably have been more circumspect in their choice of methods.' They might even have done their best to oblige Diem to hold elections. 'The result might admittedly have been a Communist Vietnam of a sort but it would probably have been nationalist as well as less tied to China than the North is now and we would all of us, including the Americans and the Vietnamese, have been better off.'

The Americans' policy had become schizophrenic. 'They obviously want to escape from their adventure if they possibly can, consolidate their relations with Russia and build their Great Society. But they also want to show that they cannot be beaten and considerations of honour together with an uncritical acceptance of the domino theory are driving them to plunge still deeper.' The world no longer knew what their war aims were. Their 14 Points were put out in 'a hole and corner way' as if they were 'slightly ashamed of them', and indeed they would not have been conceivable a year ago. Statements made seemed incompatible. 'Thus have the means employed distorted the ends sought to the point at which the ends have become unrecognisable.'

The 'general interest' required that hostilities be ended at a minimum price 'in terms of American face and Communist encroachment'. The Americans should be making a judgement about the price. Perhaps they were. Or was all the recent diplomatic activity—Rumbold was writing on 25 January—'just an Adman's exercise designed to put them in the best possible light before they prosecute the war afresh with increased forces and renewed vigour'? Rumbold hoped that it was more than eyewash and that the Americans were now reconciling themselves to paying a higher price to end hostilities. 'To the extent that we may have any influence over them at all it is in our interest to encourage them in this direction. For the continuation of hostilities is pretty fearful to contemplate. In the first place it is unquestionably a dirty war and *both* sides use revolting methods. Secondly if it goes on it is likely to spread geographically, to Laos to begin with, then to Cambodia and later on possibly to Thailand and even to China. If it spreads to China there will be a risk of nuclear weapons being used. And thirdly if it goes on, the honeymoon between Washington and Moscow which is the most hopeful development of recent times will be ended.'

Rumbold was 'not sure that the fact that we are not taking an active part in the war necessarily deprives us of all influence'. The Americans were anxious that the British should continue to play a part East of Suez. 'Moreover they like to be well thought of and to the extent that it is plain to them that most European countries including ours are uneasy about their policy in Vietnam that surely has an effect.' He was not, however, in favour of 'initiatives'. 'The Gordon Walker initiative alarmed the Americans without being effective and they were contemptuous of the Harold Davies initiative.' More important was the attitude the UK took, and it should look the same as that of other European countries.[13]

Rumbold's criticism of American policies, Etherington-Smith responded in February 1966, was a little too severe. He differed more with his suggestion that the US should extricate itself, 'even at some sacrifice in terms of face and interest'. The problem was not so simple. It was not a conflict in which a compromise was 'really possible'. The Communists wanted to take Vietnam; the Americans, South Vietnamese and their allies wanted to prevent their doing so. There was no halfway house. True, the Americans had suggested that 'a middle solution might be found by indicating that they were prepared to let the South Vietnamese people decide their own future in free elections'. But that was 'not really feasible'.

Some time would have to elapse before they could be held, and they would not be 'free', inasmuch as 'someone would inevitably be in control of the country—or different parts of it—and therefore in a position to influence them'. In any case, if the Americans were prepared to take a chance on a 'free expression of the national will', the Communists were not: Pham Van Dong insisted that a political settlement in South Vietnam had to conform to the NLF's programme, and Hanoi's latest demand insisted that it should be regarded as the sole representative of the South Vietnamese people. All the talk of negotiations was 'rather pointless': of what use would they be if there were no chance of agreement? Etherington-Smith was surprised that Hanoi had not long ago agreed 'to have talks which could have been made to drag on with devastating effect. To have got Hanoi into the position of refusing negotiations seems to me a distinct achievement of the West.'

Originally the Western powers could have taken the view that a Communist takeover of all Vietnam was no concern of theirs. 'The whole country would then have rapidly fallen under Communist rule, with possibly less serious consequences than would be likely to ensue if this happened now.' Three things, however, had given the problem particular significance. One was the 1954 Geneva conference, under which the powers concerned 'assumed a certain responsibility for the settlement of the problem, including … that of protecting South Vietnam against unjust encroachment'. Second was the American decision to support South Vietnam against Northern aggression, 'serving notice to the world that the United States intended to draw a line against Communist expansion in Vietnam'. Third was 'the increasing identification of the struggle in Vietnam with the threat from Communist China'.

As a result of those three developments, the Americans and their Western allies became committed to stopping the Communists in Vietnam 'and the price of failure was greatly increased'. A Vietnam united under Communist rule would be a direct threat to non-Communist countries in the area. The US would suffer 'an enormous loss of prestige', and other countries would doubt if its protection could be relied upon. Perhaps most serious, Mao's theory of revolutionary war would have been proved correct. Britain's interests would suffer as well as those of the US, and conceding victory would not be to its advantage. 'A capitulation dressed up as a compromise might have been acceptable from a Western point of view at one time, but … things have gone too far for that and no one would now be deceived by such a pretence.'

The right course for the Americans was the one they had chosen, and Britain should continue to support them. 'The massive deployment of

American military power … likely … in the coming months' would 'change the military picture considerably' and might produce 'a gradual improvement both in security and political stability'. That could 'in the course of time produce conditions in which a more lasting solution (not necessarily the result of open negotiation) could be envisaged'. Etherington-Smith still had some hope that a Communist takeover could be averted.[14]

Arthur de la Mare tried to focus on the question with which the correspondence began: was the Vietnam conflict going to spread to Laos, and if so, what should Britain do about it? He started with some assumptions: the fighting in Vietnam would continue for many months 'without bringing the Americans appreciably nearer to military success'; the Communists would concentrate on South Vietnam and were unlikely to take an initiative in Laos, though possibly increased US pressure there, or just conceivably a political upheaval, might change their minds; the president did not want to spread the war to Laos, but American military commanders pressed for cutting the HCM trail on the ground; and, as Warner said, whatever either side might intend, 'the trend of events seems to be setting towards an expansion of the conflict in this direction'. There was a risk that the conflict would spread to Laos in 1966.

Such an extension of the fighting would do nobody any good. 'If the Americans cannot defeat the Viet Cong on the ground in South Viet-Nam, there seems little reason to suppose that they will be any more successful by widening the area of conflict. The larger the front, the more important becomes the role of manpower as opposed to fire-power, and this must surely be to the advantage of the Communists. Moreover, the wider the spread of conflict, the greater the risk of Communism securing a foothold in territories at present denied to it, whether in whole or in part, such as Cambodia, Western Laos and even Thailand.'

Britain's interests thus suggested it should try to prevent the war from spreading. But what could it do? In practice, not very much. Laos could not be treated in isolation from Vietnam, and 'tentative efforts' to interest the Russians in discussing it had 'not got us very far'. Ho Chi Minh's message of 28 January and the resumption of American bombing appeared to have 'slammed the door for the time being on negotiations over Viet-Nam. For the moment we can only wait, with more hope than confidence, for the progress of the fighting to convince Hanoi that military success is unobtainable against the United States and that they must consent to negotiate a face-saving compromise.' The most the British could contribute towards preventing the spread of the war was to continue to advise the Americans against it. But, as Etherington-Smith said, 'the fact that we are not ourselves fighting in Viet-Nam makes it difficult for us to press advice on the Americans on military strategy', though ambassadors could present the case to US officials whenever they had the opportunity. But British arguments could not have a decisive influence 'if the twin forces of American military commanders and the indignation of American public opinion at their mounting casualties in Viet-Nam come to combine against us'.

'Supposing ... that we are unlucky and that the fighting does spread, probably at American initiative, what do we do then?' De la Mare could not predict that. 'Our policy on Indo-China is not now determined—and is unlikely in the future to be determined—by an objective consideration of British interests in South-East Asia alone. It tends to represent a balance between the conflicting pressures of our need for American support in other parts of the world and of the exigencies of the British political and parliamentary situation with objective South-East Asian considerations acting as little more than a make-weight. Naturally the two major influences fluctuate (at the moment, for instance, Rhodesia and Viet-Nam are counter-acting in a surprising way).' He could not foresee what the balance would be if trouble really started in Laos. But he guessed that, 'as over Vietnam, we will neither condemn the Americans nor support them militarily, but seek a middle way'.[15]

Alec Adams, the political adviser to the commander-in-chief (CinC) Far East, Sir John Grandy, commented from Singapore. The CinC agreed with Etherington-Smith on supporting the Americans. 'From the purely military point of view we are suffering from a certain coolness and lack of frankness in our relations with the Americans which we suspect is caused by their conviction that we are not wholeheartedly with them in their policy of containing Communism in South-East Asia. This has led to shyness on the American part in discussing national contingency plans for this part of the world.' There were, for instance, no properly integrated SEATO plans for air and naval action. To re-establish relations the CinC and others had visited Honolulu, but there was still a long way to go.

The Chinese, Adams continued, might not intend direct military conquest of Southeast Asia, but they certainly wanted to 'promote subservient regimes there'. Vietnam was a test case. If Mao's theories of revolutionary warfare were successful because the Americans were forced to withdraw, the same tactics would be applied in Laos, Cambodia and Thailand. In Thailand, indeed, 'we are already seeing an increase of subversion, if not the beginning of insurgency'. A Western withdrawal from the mainland would surely be followed by a Chinese triumph, 'with the most ominous repercussions in the terms of immediate re-insurance'.

Adams also commented on the construction of American bases in Thailand. Their relatively lavish nature did not necessarily mean that they were permanent: 'if they found that they did not want them after a few years they would probably simply hand them over to the local authorities.'[16]

More Arguments

Cable tried to answer the CinC's point about American suspicions 'that we are not wholeheartedly with them in their policy of containing Communism in South-East Asia'. It was necessary to distinguish the objective and the means: the UK agreed with the US on the former, but 'considerable differences' existed on the latter.

Britain's basic ideas were incorporated in the proposals arising from the Defence Review, recently discussed with the US, Australia and New Zealand. 'Though complicated by the need for economies in our own expenditure, these proposals stem from the view that British bases on the mainland of South-East Asia are unlikely to be politically viable for much longer. This means, if we are not to leave the area altogether, that we need to start preparing alternative bases, whether in Australia or elsewhere, as soon as possible, so that we shall still be able to play our part in the Indo-Pacific region even after our withdrawal from Malaysia and Singapore.' The UK would also like closer coordination and cooperation with its allies.

The Americans and Australians welcomed the evidence that the UK intended to contribute to the defence of Southeast Asia, but they did not accept the forecast of the probable erosion of its position. Cable doubted whether the Americans, 'in their heart of hearts', would confidently predict the future viability of the bases. Rather they feared that Britain's departure would 'increase the political isolation of their own position, particularly in Vietnam'. The Australians feared that Britain's ideas would get it out of Singapore before it was 'absolutely necessary'. But the reluctance to see Britain leaving the mainland would 'ultimately' give way, Cable thought, to 'a realisation that the British military presence in South-East Asia must be exercised from more distant bases or not at all'.

Vietnam was 'another matter'. It filled the foreground of the Americans' thinking to the extent that they found it difficult 'to focus on the wider picture or the more distant future', and as casualties increased and the prospects of military success continued to recede, their approach tended to become 'more emotional'. They fastened on the fact that British troops were not fighting in Vietnam, forgetting the political risks being run at home by the British government in 'constantly reiterating, in almost total isolation among the significant nations of the world, their public support for U.S. policy in Vietnam'.

The limitations on British support, however, did not arise merely from political considerations. 'We have also never been satisfied that American policy in Vietnam is a sensible one. Viewed in military terms, the record of the last ten years is essentially one of the piecemeal reinforcement of failure.' It seemed to Cable 'that we should all be a great deal better off—and so would the prospects of containing Chinese Communism in South-East Asia—if the Geneva Agreements had been applied after 1954 and Vietnam left to sink or swim. Even if a Communist Vietnam had resulted, this would probably not have been tied to China to the extent that North Vietnam now is.'

It was 'no good crying over spilt milk—notably the numerous opportunities the Americans had during the decade following the Geneva Agreements to negotiate on the terms they are now putting forward in vain—but these considerations inevitably modify our enthusiasm for the present American policy and our confidence in its ability ever to achieve useful results. We are sticking by the Americans to-day, therefore, because they are our allies and because it would clearly have disastrous consequences if they were forced to accept a humiliating defeat in Vietnam. But we do not see altogether eye to eye with them in their analysis of the situation, the methods they are employing or their prognosis of the ultimate outcome.' Until the Vietnam problem was finally settled, there would be some 'impairment ... of mutual frankness and confidence' in the military planning relationship, whatever the CinC tried to do.[17]

Not surprisingly, Etherington-Smith had 'some misgivings' about Cable's conclusion. '[W]hat he seems to be suggesting,' he wrote to de la Mare, 'is that we should sit back, watch the Americans make a thorough mess of things in Vietnam, and hope to do real business with them after this unfortunate affair is over. The underlying implication would seem to be that what happens in Vietnam is not of sufficient importance for us to have to do much about it ourselves and that, whichever way the Vietnam affair goes, we shall be able to carry on our policies for the rest of South-East Asia without having to modify them appreciably.' Could Britain really afford to take so detached a view? That depended on the consequences of a Communist victory in Vietnam. Etherington-Smith could not recall a recent official expression of opinion on that, but the question was important. 'And, if the conclusion is that a Communist victory in Vietnam would cause irreparable harm to our interests throughout the area, should we not be constantly asking ourselves whether there is anything more we can do, either directly or through the Americans, to avoid such a catastrophic development?'[18]

Hanoi would opt for talks only to facilitate a takeover, Etherington-Smith repeated. 'However skilfully any agreement is drawn up it is bound to load the dice either for or against an eventual communist takeover.' He again urged more British support for the American endeavour.[19] His views would not be 'generally accepted' in London, Cable commented. They seemed to be based on three premises: that Communist military strength in the South had two distinct elements, the 'main forces' and the guerrillas, which could be separately and consecutively defeated; that North Vietnam would be unable to match the continuing American build-up; and that 'popular attitudes and the influence of Vietnamese national characteristics' would help the Americans more than the Communists. All three premises Cable found somewhat suspect. It was hard to 'draw a distinction between regular and guerrilla operations': regular units were trained and had experience in guerrilla warfare. If they were defeated in pitched battles, the Communist forces might disperse into guerrilla bands, and that might make pacification more difficult rather than less. The anti-Communist forces, including 'auxiliary forces of dubious quality', numbered 836,000, giving them a numerical superiority of 3.5 to 1. In the Malayan Emergency—one of the few examples of the successful repression of guerrilla revolt—the margin of superiority was never less than 10 to 1. The Americans might have to bring in 'more reinforcements—perhaps considerably more', and so far the North Vietnamese had matched their every increase, 'not in absolute numbers, but in terms of the effect on the military balance in the South'.

Etherington-Smith argued that the Viet Cong enjoyed little popularity and that in the areas they controlled, 'their authority rests on fear'. The popular attitude to the Saigon government might not be different, Cable suggested. The Viet Cong had the advantage of 'a monolithic leadership'; the South Vietnamese government was 'perpetually exposed to dissension and opposition'. The Americans could match the Viet Cong's efficiency only by taking a greater part at all levels in the direction of the fighting and the administration. 'But the more effective American control becomes, the more obvious it will be, and the more repugnant it will become to the intensely nationalistic and jealous people of South Vietnam. Anti-Americanism is already a factor among important and influential anti-Communist leaders in South Vietnam.' It was 'highly doubtful', Cable concluded, that the US could defeat the insurrection, pacify Vietnam, and create a viable future for an independent non-Communist government. Nor could he see how a British contribution could help: if 235,000 Americans could not do the job—'or, as some have suggested will be the ultimate figure, half a million'—two or three British battalions would have no significant influence. Etherington-Smith's real argument was that greater Western—especially British—sympathy, support and participation might encourage the Americans to persevere if things continued to go badly rather than 'cut their losses and withdraw'. But that Cable considered 'would be entirely opposed to British and western interests'. The Americans had 'embarked on a lost cause'. Britain's object 'should be to help them to extricate themselves, not to push them further into the quagmire'.[20]

The government, Cable believed, should continue its policy of 'providing only diplomatic support and technical assistance, so as to preserve sufficient freedom of action to allow Britain, when the moment comes, to play a useful part in promoting the kind of negotiated settlement that would enable the United States to extricate themselves from Vietnam'.[21] Increased aid would mean sacrificing what Britain did elsewhere, de la Mare commented, and the position in Vietnam would make economic aid 'nugatory'.[22] Lord Walston would be happy to help in pacification, the main objective being to improve Britain's position with the US, but there was little that could be done in Vietnam. 'We must not forget that our ultimate objective must be to make it easier for the Americans to leave Vietnam without loss of prestige. It would be worth spending money to help achieve this—but not to bolster either the present V.N. Govt. or the Americans.'[23]

Lord Head

In early March 1966 M.N.F. Stewart reported on the attitude to negotiations in Washington. The president 'would clearly like to be freed from the expenditure of time, money and effort which the war in Vietnam entails and he wants to carry the country with him'. Often he expressed his willingness for negotiations. Chet Cooper was responsible for a study, being kept secret, on what might be secured or at least what should be aimed for. It was difficult to find out how that was going, but its basic assumption, Stewart thought, had to be that the war would continue until military pressure caused the North Vietnamese, still convinced that they could attain a military solution, to change their minds: the Americans were 'not likely to give up first'. That would not involve a capitulation, but 'at least a temporary political victory and a definite military victory for the Americans', in which it was made clear 'that the resort to force is not the way to settle international disputes and that the "wars of national liberation" advocated by Peking can be defeated, even on China's very door-step'. That had to be brought about by 'a continuation of the controlled use of force now employed by the Americans in South Vietnam', and if there were to be any escalation of the attacks on the North, they had to take place 'only after careful calculation of the political consequences'. As the war dragged on, there would be pressure to finish it with 'massive air attacks or something similar'. But the president, Stewart believed, was 'a supremely cautious man', unlikely to be rushed by anyone into 'dangerous military or political action'. Negotiations were unlikely until the North Vietnamese position changed for the worse. Then there would be an opportunity to say what should or should not be given away in order to try for a settlement, and British views might differ from American. At present, for example, Rusk considered the argument about VC representation was hypothetical. The Americans might make real concessions in due course, but at the present the North Vietnamese would simply pocket them and fight on.[24]

Stewart had just hosted a lunch for Lord Head, former high commissioner in Kuala Lumpur, who was on a private visit for some speaking engagements for the English-Speaking Union. The conversation developed into a virtual dialogue between him and Alexis Johnson. Head developed 'in a breezy style' the thesis expressed in a despatch about Malaysia and Singapore, but now applied to Asia in general. The Americans and the old Commonwealth could not hope to have precisely the kind of governments they wished in East and Southeast Asian countries, he argued, and it was above all a mistake to believe that keeping soldiers in them would ensure that their governments were friendly. They should remove their troops from the mainland as soon as Vietnam and Confrontation were over, 'otherwise "we shall find the poor bloody British soldiers or the poor bloody American soldiers shooting one lot of Asians for the benefit of another lot of Asians"'. He particularly referred to the Malaysian government 'as the kind of set-up that we could not afford to support and mentioned the Tunku's Edwardian outlook on life'.

Having thus extricated themselves, the four countries—the US, the UK, Australia, New Zealand—possibly with Japan, 'should be prepared to defend the independence of the countries on the borders of China by making it clear to Peking that if they started any monkey-business we were determined to resist them'. As a corollary, 'we should make a serious study to see whether it was militarily possible to guarantee a future settlement in Vietnam without having to station American or other white troops on the mainland of Asia', and 'get to terms with China, including arranging for her admission to the United Nations, though probably not at the cost of handing over Formosa to Peking'. In response Alexis Johnson put up 'a pretty good case on familiar lines'. Stewart thought he took Head's theories in good part and 'was unlikely to regard them as representing the policy of H.M.G.—we shall make sure of this'.

In reference to the correspondence about American intentions, Stewart reported that when Head implied that the US wanted to keep troops on the mainland ad infinitum, Johnson 'formally and categorically' denied it. The important words were 'ad infinitum', Stewart commented. A number of people in the administration and in Congress thought that some American troops, possibly part of an international force, would have to stay in South Vietnam 'for some years, to help guarantee whatever settlement may eventually emerge'.[25]

Lord Head seemed, Michael Palliser commented, to have expounded a 'tolerably faithful' account of Britain's long-term policy, approved by ministers. It was thus startling to read of the intention to make sure that Alexis Johnson did not see his views as HMG's. The FO should not allow Washington to see Head's views as 'heresy'. No doubt the British could have a long-term plan and conceal it, but in fact they had opened their mouths already during ministerial visits to Washington and Canberra. Should Stewart be put back on the rails? It would be better for the meantime to rest on the January talks and a Command Paper on the Defence Review, it was decided.[26]

John Addis

Unable to attend another 'sanhedrin' of British representatives in Hong Kong, Addis put his views into a despatch. He discussed post-war East and Southeast Asia 'from the old-fashioned point-of-view of the balance of power'—a stance he had previously favoured—rather than other aspects of the situation, such as the ideological conflict, 'Chinese expansionism', and the 'duty and determination' of the US to defend the rights of small nations.

China's power, he argued, had now been restored to the extent that the advanced positions taken up by American expansion could no longer be sustained. 'Like any other power which has over-reached itself, the United States wants to hold on. But the first test of any foreign policy should be whether it is feasible, and a policy based on congealing the present American position in Asia does not pass the test.' The inclusion of South Vietnam 'within the boundary of American power' did not correspond with the balance of power between China and the US. The right strategic objective was withdrawal. Once that was recognised, the tactical day-to-day questions acquired a new perspective, and apparently insoluble issues become 'practicable'.

'In so far as there has been a British policy in the Far East since 1950 independent of the Americans, it has ... been based on the recognition of the power situation in Asia and on the belief that, because Chinese leaders give the task of carrying through the revolution inside China priority over all other considerations and that task requires conditions of peace in China and on the borders of China, accommodations with China, particularly on the principle of a neutral belt, are possible, not as an overall settlement, but as a growing system of limited agreements and working arrangements.' The Korean armistice, the 1954 agreements and the Laos agreement of 1962 were 'instances of limited agreements within the context of that policy'. But, not realising 'the realities of the power situation', the Americans rejected, with too little British protest, 'the chances of political settlements in Korea in 1953–4, in Vietnam in 1955–56 and in Laos in 1960'. Nothing so good was now available. 'But that does not invalidate the policy of patiently continuing to seek for areas of possible agreement and of educating the Americans to make use of them.'[27]

In the FO Addis's views were regarded as provocative but not convincing. True, wrote John Denson (China and Korea Department), people talked too loosely about China's expansionism. If it was indeed not a military threat, it was a political one. 'The Chinese are a menace to our interests in that they encourage the development of national and social tensions and dissatisfactions which exist in many countries, and particularly the under-developed countries.' Given time and steady development, 'the kind of tensions on which the Chinese threat feeds will tend to disappear'.[28] E. Bolland thought Addis overplayed an 'old-fashioned' view. A Communist revolution had taken place in China, and its policies derived 'from an amalgam of Communist convictions as well as national interests'. The Chinese were not indeed expansionist in the Hitlerian sense, but they did wish to extend their influence throughout Asia and would like, 'sooner or later', to help other countries establish Communist regimes. They refrained from military attack partly because they considered that successful revolutions should be carried out primarily by indigenous forces, but also because the presence of the Americans caused them to avoid undue risks. Though they gave priority to the development of China, they did what they could to disrupt other regimes. It was the Chinese who needed to be educated, not the Americans.[29]

Addis had held such a view of the balance of power since 1956, noted J.E. Fretwell in the Northern Department: his experience in Laos had given it a 'more pronounced anti-American emphasis'. His concept of regional power balances and spheres of influence was 'largely out of date:

it does not take account of the effect of modern power, of the enormous pace of technological advance in the United States, or of the implications of distinctive ideologies which purport to be global in application'. The US position in Asia might require 'considerable adjustments', notably in due course in Formosa, 'but the idea of leaving it all to China because that is where the power balance now lies, seems to me to be founded on a whole series of erroneous assumptions'.[30] Murray thought Addis's despatch was 'wrongly slanted' in trying to reduce the Southeast Asian situation to a matter of balance of power. He had 'wrongly analysed American motives and the present American dilemma'.[31] Surely, however, Addis was arguing—like SEAD but on a different basis—that the US needed to be more realistic.

From Saigon Etherington-Smith, not unexpectedly, offered another critique of Addis. 'No one, including the Americans, would question ... that the long-term strategic objective should be withdrawal from the mainland of Asia. But, particularly in view of the strong anti-Communist feelings of many South-East Asians, this should not happen before the countries concerned have been able to develop their powers of resistance. A precipitate withdrawal would surely be the height of folly.' American withdrawal from Vietnam could hardly be justified in the present circumstances, 'given the certainty that the Communists would then take over ... and the far-reaching consequences for the whole of Asia which would be likely to follow. ... A retreat from Vietnam seems to me all the less incumbent on the Americans since it appears by no means certain that the battle there is yet lost; but even if ultimate defeat appeared inevitable, that would be no reason for hastening it. The fact that China may at the moment be prepared to be accommodating beyond her borders because she is preoccupied with domestic problems is in itself no reason for making concessions to her if it is likely that she will presently become more aggressive and seek to extend her power still further. It is rather an argument for yielding as little ground as possible.'

Etherington-Smith also questioned whether, as Addis asserted, the US violated the 1954 agreements, and argued that in any case it was Diem who ultimately took the decision not to hold the elections. The agreements seemed to many 'an understanding by all concerned that the division of the country into spheres of Communist and Western influence should be maintained indefinitely'. In that context it was Hanoi, and by extension Peking, that began breaching the understandings reached at Geneva by starting guerrilla war in the South in 1959.[32]

That line SEAD's Campbell could not accept. Etherington-Smith's was an 'utterly sincere' despatch, but its arguments were 'selected to form a pre-decided case'. The elections, which the Viet Minh had every reason to suppose it would win, were 'an integral part' of the Geneva bargain: 'the West Irian ascertainment procedures' offered a parallel. 'Ducking out of these elections can of course be justified in terms of anti-communist *realpolitik*; but we delude only ourselves if we do not recognise the price that has to be paid for such action: specifically, in this case, a conviction, which is not limited only to communist countries in the Far East, that the West and particularly the Americans, cannot be trusted to keep their side of a bargain if it does not suit them.'

Campbell claimed that Etherington-Smith did not touch on the debate Addis proposed—'what it is that suits our interests best in the long term in Asia'—though surely it was clear that he thought that those interests would be best served by staying as long as possible. The larger issue, Campbell continued, was 'whether it is, or ever was, in the West's interest to remain in South Viet-Nam'. If the American presence would 'continue to cause resistance, fighting and "imbalance"—as we must surely suppose that it almost certainly would—then Mr Addis has gained this point too'.[33]

R.A. Longmire of the Joint Research Department contested Addis and Campbell as well. Addis's argument was arranged to give the impression of the US as 'an expansionist, aggressive power' and of China 'as merely seeking her legitimate interests'. He 'deliberately' overlooked the existence of an 'expansionist Communism which has used a variety of means ... to weaken and erode the position of the liberal democracies of the West'. China did not need troops or bases outside its territory. More than once Addis said that the US had over-reached itself, but he did not give reasons for his statements. 'I would have thought that the available evidence pointed to the exact reverse—that American manpower and economic and military strength had only begun to be scratched. American will-power may be another matter.'

Over the elections Longmire agreed with Etherington-Smith rather than Campbell. The latter rejected the former's argument as based on anti-Communist realpolitik. 'But the objection would be valid only if the Communist record on elections was above reproach and if it was proved beyond reasonable doubt that the North Vietnamese had chosen Communism of their own free will. Since those conditions were not present, to force elections on an unwilling South would have been tantamount to throwing it to the Communists as an act of appeasement.' The refusal to hold an election was not 'a mistake'.[34] Seeming to ignore the Geneva agreement, Longmire reached conclusions at odds with the views of his FO colleagues.

In October Campbell sought to round off the debate. He did not agree with the idea that 'balance of power' arguments were out of date because of China's subversive methods or because of technological advances or the bomb. 'These are all elements in deciding *where* the balance will fall.' And Addis did not suggest handing Asia over to China: he thought the division of Korea was right in terms of the balance of power and believed a balance could be struck in Southeast Asia, too. Nor did Campbell accept Longmire's comment on the elections: it was known that the Communists were likely to win the elections when they were agreed upon, 'and no matter what our reasons for going back on our word the fact remains that we did so and that this constitutes a breach of faith'.[35]

Would it not have been more of a 'breach of faith' if an election had been forced on the unwilling South Vietnamese? Longmire asked. Would it not have been realpolitik to have sacrificed these people? 'But in any case, from the practical viewpoint, (and, I allow, with some—though very little—hindsight) the project of holding all-Vietnam elections was quite unattainable.' To overcome the valid objections of Diem and the South Vietnamese anti-Communists would have required pressure that no US government could contemplate. In Article 7 of the Final Declaration—providing for general elections in July 1956—the West was promising goods it could not deliver. 'All that this clause did in fact was to provide the Communists with a heaven-sent opportunity to cry perfidy against the West and subsequently to confuse a sizeable segment of Western opinion as regards the Vietnamese question as a whole.' The matter was not merely of historical interest. In any future negotiations, specifying deadlines should be avoided. Items 9 and 10 in the US government's 14 Points of January 1966 were rightly couched in general terms. 'We might, in fact, apply Communist tactics over the question of all-German elections in the Vietnamese context.'[36] Campbell still believed that Communist arguments on the Vietnam elections were more convincing than their opponents'. That was 'one of the reasons why we have such a difficult public opinion problem'.[37]

Addis explained that he did not subscribe to the 'domino' theory, 'at least in its crudest form'. Two US withdrawals—Korea and Laos—had not resulted in a catastrophic loss of confidence in other countries. 'This is after all of the essence of the balance-of-power theory. You withdraw from a position of imbalance to a position of strength and a more stable balance is created.' By advocating withdrawal from positions in which the Americans overreached themselves, Addis was not advocating a total abdication of power so as to leave a vacuum for the Chinese to occupy. 'It is of course essential not only to the balance-of-power theory but also to the neutral-belt approach that American power should be firmly maintained in equilibrium against Chinese power.' If the Vietnamese domino went, Laos might go, too, 'but that does not necessarily mean that other dominos in the area would also fall down'.[38]

Exchanges by personal or semi-official letter between British representatives in the field and FO officials in London were a common practice, exchanges among representatives in the field not uncommon. More novel in this phase, however, was the attempt to broaden non-official input into the making of policy. In the UK there was much less interchange with the academic world than in the US, but now the FO, perhaps influenced by the spread of teach-ins, sought to draw on and perhaps to influence academic opinion.

In 1966 the FO promoted a seminar at the University of Hull, which then had a Centre for Southeast Asian Studies. At first, Cable reported, the government's policy was criticised, but as the day wore on there was 'a tacit comprehension that H.M.G. could not, in practice, have acted very differently'. There was, however, a concern that the current British government had expressed its support for the US more categorically than the previous government, and a distinct preference for the more 'ambivalent' and 'equivocal' utterances of Home and Butler as foreign secretary.[39]

Wilson and 'Dissociation'

Wilson's policy was to offer support for the US, in order to give himself some leverage for promoting peace via the SU. But it did not win any enthusiasm at home. At the beginning of February the prime minister expressed his concern that some 90 MPs were apparently unaware of Britain's attempts to secure peace. An FO statement—of which the Vietnamese chargé in Moscow became aware—referred to 'support' for US policy, apparently prompted by a BBC statement that referred to 'full support'.[40] The FO did not brief the BBC, Stewart told Wilson. Its statement had been sent to the PM's office. If the statement had been less clear, there would have been more controversy.[41] Wilson told the president that Labour critics had been routed.[42] But clearly 'support' had its critics, 'full' or not.

At the end of March Labour won the general election with a decisive 94-seat majority. Wilson had done too well. His slender majority had been in some ways an advantage: 'for although the left-wingers may bite they cannot risk attacking action that might mean the defeat of the government', as the *New Zealand Herald* had put it.[43] With a clear majority, the dangers from the dissenters eased, but 'the scale of intra-party revolt increased', while the party at large was concerned about US policy.[44] Ayub Khan found the prime minister practising his putting on the carpet at Chequers. 'How's your handicap?' he asked. Wilson groaned: 'Gone up from three to ninety-seven!'[45]

The British government had indicated that it would have to dissociate itself from the bombing of Hanoi. The bombing of Dong Anh late in April was explained by the launch of SAMs against a raid targeted on Phu Ly bridge.[46] Bill Bundy said it did not indicate a change of policy.[47] But a month later Ambassador Bruce told the prime minister that the president had virtually decided to bomb oil installations at Hanoi and Haiphong. Wilson responded that he had told Johnson that if populated areas were bombed, the British government would publicly dissociate itself. 'Our general approach would be to continue support for the broad lines of American policy but to make it clear that we disagreed with this particular application of it.'[48] The PM sent a message to the president.[49]

Early in June Colonel Rogers of General Wheeler's staff—a 'humane colonel', Wilson says ironically[50]—gave the PM a briefing on the military background to the possible bombing of petrol oil lubricant installations in Hanoi and Haiphong. There was, he said, a consensus that a Chinese military reaction was unlikely. After he had left, the PM and the foreign secretary talked to Bruce. Stewart suggested that the military arguments did not carry the day against the political disadvantages. Wilson expressed his concern over the likely effect on the Russians, since he was convinced that they really desired an early end to the conflict. Bruce thought a further message to the president would be useful.[51] The proposed bombing, it ran, would make it more difficult to bring the Russians to a sense of their responsibilities and thus more difficult to reach an eventual settlement. Britain would have to dissociate itself. Wilson hoped to meet the president again, but it could not be immediately before the bombing, nor immediately after.[52]

Wilson met Rusk in London on 10 June. The American secretary of state asked whether, after Confrontation, Britain might send helicopters to Thailand. The prime minister ruled it out. 'Last year he got away with a tough line on Vietnam but the situation was now changing. The Vietnamese lobby was no longer standing alone and a big fight was brewing not only with the pacifists but with the sophisticated Europeanists. The East of Suez policy was coming under heavy attack.' Even limited aid would feed suspicion. The US could not give up, Rusk said. 'What is at stake is the value of our word and this is more important than 14m South Vietnamese or even all of Southeast Asia in the present context.'[53]

He told Wilson that bombing the oil installations in Hanoi and Haiphong was likely to be decided on in a week or ten days 'because the North Vietnamese were working hard to re-distribute their supplies'. The president hoped Britain would say it had been informed, hoped, too, that it would reaffirm that it held Hanoi responsible for failure to negotiate. He was keen, Rusk said, that Wilson should visit Washington 'at a reasonable interval after the bombing'. The plan to do so, the PM said, was 'relevant in part' to the possibility he would talk to Kosygin again and to Brezhnev. Perhaps, Rusk commented, he could take up the idea of trying to reconvene the conference on Cambodia. If the US thought the Russians would be responsive to such ideas, Stewart said, the decision to bomb Hanoi and Haiphong became 'even more incomprehensible'.

The PM thought that the bombing decision was now necessary for domestic purposes. It might make the prospects of his talks with the Russians less favourable. But they might consider Britain slightly less of an American satellite than before, and worth talking to in the context of their own preoccupations about Germany. Stewart also discussed Rusk's idea that Britain should call a conference in Geneva and see who came. 'If we found only ourselves there, we should surely be in a ridiculous situation.' The PM agreed that, since the bombing now seemed inevitable, 'the prospects of getting such a conference and hitching it to the Cambodia problem now seemed remote'.[54]

If he decided on bombing, Wilson wrote to Johnson, it would affect the prospects for reconvening a Cambodian conference, or suggesting a meeting at Geneva for those who wished to come, ideas that Rusk had put forward. But the president had the prime minister's sympathy in facing the choice he faced.[55] The PM also told the president that he and Rusk favoured a further visit to Kosygin and Brezhnev. Maybe he could go for the Moscow Trade Fair.[56]

The president hoped that the British government would not use the word 'dissociation'. He suggested that Wilson's statement might refer to SEATO and appreciate the action of its fellow members. His visit to Washington might be scheduled for late July.[57] The reply was disappointing: the president ignored the possibility of exploring peace negotiations with the Russians. A specific link with SEATO was not in the interests of SEATO, nor was it feasible for HMG.[58]

At a press conference on 18 June 1966 the president made a statement on Vietnam. The national interest required persistence in the present policy, designed to ensure that infiltration, subversion and terror, backed by North Vietnam, did not 'swallow or conquer South Vietnam', and to permit the people there 'to select their own government and to build a way of life which conforms to their own traditions and desires'. Meeting that objective, 'we must also reassure the world that America's agreements, once they are made, are not broken'. Attacks on military targets in North Vietnam had 'imposed a growing burden on those who support the insurgency in the South'.[59]

The statement, *The Times* commented, appeared to confirm that the US had decided to bomb oil dumps in Hanoi and Haiphong.[60] As Dean later said, the decision was 'necessary if only to satisfy growing American dissent from the right'.[61] Chester Ronning, the Canadian diplomat, had visited Hanoi 14–17 June and found, as Bill Bundy put it, 'no give in their position'.[62] The bombing would now go ahead, the president told the PM on 23 June.[63] Wilson replied that he would have to make Britain's dissociation clear, but he would also say that the US was right to continue to assist the South Vietnamese, and that the onus for continuing the fighting lay with the North Vietnamese.[64] The president, Rostow told Dean, could not understand why Wilson—now with a big majority—felt it necessary to dissociate himself even more.[65] Obviously he reckoned without the PM's increased 'handicap'. Delayed by the weather and an American leak, the strikes finally went ahead on 29 June.[66] US Navy ships and five fighter bombers struck the petroleum facilities in the vicinity of Hanoi and Haiphong.[67]

Wilson told the embassy in Washington that he had asked Stewart to discuss with Rusk—both at a meeting in Canberra—whether Britain, as co-chairman, could not take an initiative about Laos or Cambodia so as to emphasise that it wished to use the co-chairmanship as a means of helping the Americans to get a settlement in Vietnam, and not merely as an excuse for not providing military aid. He hoped to pursue that when he visited the president.[68]

The PM's statement of 29 June reaffirmed Britain's dissociation from bombing touching on the populated areas of Hanoi and Haiphong, but reaffirmed general support of US policy.[69] It was put out an hour before the Commons met, and then repeated in the House. Britain was convinced that the US was right to continue to assist South Vietnam until North Vietnam abandoned the use of force.[70] The statement was sent to the president on 1 July. The telegram also suggested that Wilson might go to Moscow before his Washington visit, ostensibly to the Trade Fair, but in fact to discuss Vietnam and Sihanouk's notion of enlarging the operations of the ICC.[71] The president hoped he would 'canvas all useful [negotiating] possibilities'.[72] More than 90 Labour backbenchers and eight Liberals tabled a motion calling on the government to dissociate themselves completely from American military policy. That, said *The Times*, 'was much more than a familiar left-wing mutiny'.[73] After a long debate the government's motion was approved by a majority of only 69.[74]

The tone of the PRC statement on the bombing, made on 3 July, was, as Bolland put it, 'violent and threatening', but, as Hopson said, it did not presage imminent intervention by the Chinese. Beset by the Cultural

Revolution, they were approaching recent developments with caution, and trying to increase the political fruits harvested from the American bombing 'rather than putting their own security at risk by directly intervening on the ground'. But they would probably increase material aid, and they would exploit the bombing in their dispute with the SU 'by making fantastic charges of Soviet collusion with the United States'.[75]

In Warsaw Foreign Minister Adam Rapacki spoke of the dangers of escalation after the latest phase of American bombing and of the risks of a degree of Chinese participation that might have an effect without provoking the US to justified retaliation. The cessation of bombing was a necessary precondition of any move to negotiations. In the winter pause, North Vietnam had sent hints that Washington ignored. Near the end the Americans said the signal was interesting, but too late. Clutton responded by rehearsing Britain's position: the cessation of hostilities was desirable, not only of bombing.[76]

Wilson in Moscow Again

In Paris the director of Asian affairs at the Quai told Reilly that Wilson would find any discussion of Vietnam in Moscow 'very tough going'. If the Americans stopped the bombing, the Russians might be able to change tactics, as an established Communist regime would no longer be under fire, and they could then possibly urge Hanoi to start negotiations whatever China's attitude was.[77]

In London the Russian ambassador told the chancellor of the Duchy of Lancaster that there was no prospect of a discussion on Vietnam 'unless its point of departure was an unconditional acceptance by the United States Government of the North Vietnamese conditions'.[78] The prime minister told the president that he intended to make it clear to the Russians that the US would continue hard pressure on North Vietnam, but he was not hopeful because their rivalry with the Chinese placed them in a 'diplomatic straightjacket'. They were, however, worried about such limitations, and 'the more convinced they are of your determination, the more we can hope to exploit their apprehensions'.[79] Was such optimism genuine? It was belied by actuality. Or was it just designed to appeal to LBJ?

The FO provided the PM with talking points. The Vietnam conflict cast 'an ugly shadow over the whole world', and the co-chairmen had 'an inescapable duty to consider together how they could try to bridge the gap between the two sides'. They were not expected to be neutral, but were regarded as being 'capable both of representing and influencing their own friends'. The US would not be deterred from maintaining its military presence in South Vietnam while North Vietnam and the FLN continued their military action there, but would be ready to consider a peaceful solution in unconditional negotiations. 'But the prospect of any useful action must depend on some change of view, or some susceptibility to influence, on the part of the North Vietnamese.' Could Kosygin see any way in which that might be brought about? If North Vietnam required a cessation of bombing before any other matters were considered, Wilson would be prepared to recommend that to the US, provided he could also convey an assurance 'that North Vietnam and the Liberation Front would stop the flow of reinforcements from North to South and all warlike acts in South Vietnam'.

It was not necessary for a ceasefire to be in operation before discussions began. Britain was ready to convene Geneva, but ready also to join in alternatives still within the Geneva framework but easier for North Vietnam to accept. The co-chairmen, for example, could meet in Geneva and quietly consider what could be recommended to reduce the scale of the conflict and create conditions for a wider meeting. Or they could suggest a meeting with the US, South Vietnam, North Vietnam, and 'representatives of the South Vietnam Liberation Front, all attending on the basis of equality'. Or given Indira Gandhi's recent appeal for a conference, a meeting of the co-chairmen and the three ICC powers, North and South maintaining contact with the proceedings through their liaison bureaux with the ICC? Or perhaps a third party that had the confidence of the co-chairmen could take the initiative? The SU, a background note added, was probably not ready to join in calling for a conference. In what circumstances, if any, would it help to promote peace?[80]

Wilson told Kosygin that Britain's ability to influence US policy depended on the general support it offered. Kosygin once more insisted that talks were a matter for the Vietnamese government.[81] At lunch Kosygin said that the Chinese were pressing to send volunteers—requested by Pham Van Dong as a demonstration of solidarity, the Warsaw Pact countries had issued a declaration in Bucharest on 6 July expressing readiness to allow volunteers to go to Vietnam 'in order to help the Vietnamese people in their struggle against the American aggressors'[82]—but the Vietnamese would not allow it. They might, however, have to give way.[83] There was, the PM telegraphed the president, 'no give whatever' in the Soviet position. The root cause lay in China.[84] Wilson's visit, like Mrs Gandhi's, only produced a public hardening of the Soviet position, it was thought in Washington.[85]

Before Wilson went to Washington, the FO provided a memorandum on the Chinese. Their statement of 3 July, though threatening in tone, did not offer to send volunteers to help the Vietnamese. Such offers had been made in 1965, 'always subject to the proviso that the Vietnamese should "require" or "need" them', but not recently. There were three reasons, the memorandum suggested, why the Vietnamese would not seek them. One was their traditional dislike of the Chinese 'imperialists who occupied Vietnam for a thousand years and held it in tributary status for nearly another thousand years'. Another was the possibility that the presence of Chinese infantry would attract US ground action north of the 17th parallel. Third, the North Vietnamese seemed to be 'still convinced that they can force a conclusion of the war on their own terms, by military and political attrition of the United States, as they won against the French'.

The North Vietnamese had not been brought 'anywhere near the point of such total collapse that only the introduction of large scale Chinese forces would preserve the structure of the State and Hanoi's capacity to continue the war. Even a further weight of bombardment would not necessarily bring matters to this point. North Vietnam is a primitive and undeveloped state with consequently greater resilience to the weight of conventional warfare than a more developed country.' Hanoi leaders had said they would continue the struggle from the hills, and, with material support from the Bloc, they could indeed make the pacification of the South impossible. Currently the British believed there were 20,000–25,000 Chinese troops in the North, though the Americans thought there were more. Most were construction and LOC (Lines of Communication) troops, others light anti-aircraft units. Expanding that presence so that Chinese took on more of the rear tasks was not inconceivable, but it seemed unlikely that the Vietnamese would request it in the near future. The Chinese, the memorandum concluded, were cautious and did not want to invite an American response against their territory. But almost certainly they would accept the risk if the US invaded North Vietnam or the continued survival of the North Vietnamese regime were in question. And it would be then that the Vietnamese asked for Chinese troops, 'a necessary precondition to China sending them'.[86]

De la Mare had toured Southeast Asia and the Far East. Many expressed concern at the UK's continued emphasis on 'Geneva', especially in South Vietnam, where some felt that American withdrawal and a paper agreement would amount to a death warrant. They preferred a Korea-type settlement, and pointed to South Korea's economic take-off. De la Mare thought that Britain should play down Geneva: that kind of settlement was neither desirable nor in Western interests. It would be better to work for a ceasefire, and, if successful, for negotiations. In Korea there was no 'political' settlement, but North and South 'tacitly accept that they must live side by side in peace'.[87] Lord Walston thought that 'Geneva' should be allowed to fade into the background, in case a better solution turned up. But the geography and politics of Vietnam did not lend themselves to a Korea-style outcome. Britain should concentrate on stopping the hostilities, and attempt to bring the Americans to accept that the sooner disengagement took place, 'the better for our joint policies and standing in South East Asia'. Britain's policies should be directed to achieving that 'without loss of face or discouragement to our friends there, even though we suspect that following upon withdrawal, Viet-Nam will go Communist'.[88]

That, Gore-Booth commented, was trying to do too much. If Vietnam went Communist, the West's friends in Laos, Cambodia and Thailand would have plenty to be discouraged about. When it came to American disengagement, 'we must play this very sensitively and with careful attention to opinion in the United States, Australia and South East Asia as well as to opinion here. There may come a moment when American disengagement is the price of peace and the price of avoiding escalation getting out of hand; but we must be very careful about pre-judging the moment at which we believe this to be the case.'[89] Perhaps, Walston wrote, he should have used the word 'Socialist' rather than 'Communist'. A 'Socialist' government in Vietnam would not discourage Cambodia, Laos or Thailand. What would discourage them would be Chinese domination of Saigon. It must be made clear that the fight in Vietnam was against Chinese imperialism and not against the form of government people could choose or go through the motions of choosing.[90]

The FO counselled against the PM's notion of sending another mission to Hanoi. It would fail, de la Mare insisted: Britain could not succeed where Ronning came back 'so utterly empty handed'. British peace missions were not merely unproductive: they were harmful. Britain's prestige was not a factor when matters of peace and war were involved. But de la Mare had to record that his recent visit to the Far East and Southeast Asia led him to believe 'that our peace efforts are widely looked upon in Asia (and perhaps elsewhere too, including the United States) as an ineffective attempt to hide our own political and military nakedness with a very flimsy and transparent garment indeed. Nobody in Asia really believes us when we talk of our special position as co-chairmen [*sic*]. We have lost our credibility as an effective peace-maker, and the longer we hide this fact from ourselves the lower our prestige will sink.'

Discounting prestige, de la Mare thought the peace missions had reached the stage when they jeopardised the chances of a settlement, rather than enhanced them. Going back to the North Vietnamese again and again when it was clear they would have nothing to do with such peace initiatives only confirmed their view 'that all we are trying to do is to bail out the Americans before they collapse under internal and external pressure. We therefore confirm the North Vietnamese in their fantastic assumption that all they have to do is to hold out until events destroy the United States. Because this belief of theirs is so fantastic we tend to think that we can persuade them into reason. We cannot. The more we run after them the more we confirm their conviction of unassailable right.'[91]

It was a matter of 'reconciling diplomatic credibility abroad with political credibility at home', wrote Gore-Booth. From the diplomatic point of view, he agreed with de la Mare. A visit would come too soon after the Bucharest communiqué and the 'unpromising' Russian response during the PM's visit. No proposal should be made at the moment, and no action taken till after his visit to Washington.[92] Walston agreed. The American build-up would have an effect in Hanoi: 'we must now remain both patient and cool.' There was no threat from the Left at the moment.[93] The foreign secretary agreed.[94] And so, after returning from Washington, did the PM.[95] There Rusk, however, had made other suggestions.

Wilson in Washington Again

Several times J.A. Thomson, visiting Washington for talks with SD planners, had been told that the president wondered why the PM was coming. One implication was that if the main reason lay in domestic considerations, the president would not be sympathetic. He was concerned about the impact on American public opinion, Victor Bator said. He hoped for a clear statement of support for US policy, affirmation that the conflict and its continuance were Hanoi's fault, and a refusal to say anything about the bombing of oil installations. Bator showed little interest in Wilson's visit to Moscow. He hoped that the PM would indicate in advance that he wanted to continue the exposition of Britain's role in the world he had made back in December 1964. A serious sterling crisis would be a major topic. If one occurred, the Americans would give further support, 'although they might try to exact a price for it'. The president's main concern was 'the long term malaise in British affairs'. Could Britain maintain its chosen role? Some of the president's advisers 'believed that the British economic position was trickling away and that this would continue'. LBJ himself was worried that 'such an important country and major ally as Britain might lose control of events and cease to play an important role in the world'. The PM should expose the links between the Defence Review and the National Plan, and give the president 'a clear and authoritative idea of how Britain intended to deal with both her internal and external problems, of the relationship between them and of what Britain could and could not do'. It seemed to Thomson that Bator was suggesting that the PM should restore the president's 'shaken confidence in the reliability of Britain as an ally'.[96]

The FO gave the PM talking points in its brief of 21 July. There was 'no give whatever' in the Soviet position, and no prospect of getting co-chairmanship activity going. 'Fearing that pressure in Hanoi may drive the North Vietnamese further towards the Chinese, and fearing also that the Chinese may themselves force the pace, the Russians seem to see their best course in terms of total, rigid impassivity.' The Vietnamese were convinced they could win, and the struggle seemed likely to continue for a long time. What did the president foresee? If the North Vietnamese became convinced that the present level of military assault was pointless, did the president consider that 'fighting might to some extent melt away and allow a *de facto* détente to come into being in the South'? Would he see any value in such a solution? It might enable the South Vietnamese government to establish itself 'internally and internationally … without necessarily proceeding to a formal "political settlement"'. But it might not work, since the situation was more complex than Korea's.

Britain would continue its support for US policies, though it could not promise in its present economic circumstances to extend its non-military aid. It was important that the September elections in Vietnam should go off well, given the criticism vocal minorities offered of US policy. Horror stories in the press were exploited by the Communists and their sympathisers, and 'general distress' might spread in Britain. 'There is a deep feeling about this. We can assuage it, and … hope to turn it in the direction of understanding for what the United States is doing, but it would be dangerous and indeed futile, to suppress it. Our support must be seen against this background.'

In a supporting note, the FO explained that there might come a point when the North Vietnamese wished to break off fighting, but not to lose face by entering negotiations, and so disengaging. Some Americans, perhaps including Rusk, might prefer such a détente to negotiations on the basis of Geneva, which, if successful, might jeopardise the future of South Vietnam.[97]

At the end of July 1966 Wilson related his Moscow conversations to the president at the White House. After dissociation, he says in his memoir, he expected to be greeted with 'the frozen mitt', and the financial crisis in Britain he feared might mean that he was greeted as 'a down-at-heel mendicant'.[98] In the event LBJ greeted him warmly and lauded him in extravagant terms. Was there, as Jonathan Colman suggests, 'a hint of sarcasm' in the president's calling him 'a man of mettle'?[99]

The president and the PM had met privately, then joined Rusk, McNamara, Ball, Trend and others in the cabinet room at 12.15pm on the 29th. The president said they had discussed their common problems, especially East of Suez, the German situation, and the British economic measures, together with some of the comparable measures the US might have to take. He now had 'a very good understanding' of the problems facing the UK and he hoped the PM felt the same as regards the US. The PM referred to his long discussions with Kosygin. No Soviet initiative could be expected in Southeast Asia, but in private he had revealed the 'great misgivings' the SU had about the Chinese attitude on Vietnam. The PM had been left with the impression that the Russians would welcome a reconvening of Geneva but dared not make any move themselves, lest the Chinese reacted by sending in 'volunteers' and so stepping up the war, a move from which they had hitherto been restrained by the North Vietnamese themselves.

Wilson then turned to the economic situation in the UK, alluding in particular to the seamen's strike and French selling of sterling. The government had decided 'severe disinflationary measures' were required. This showed that it was determined to defend sterling and avoid devaluation. It was also prompted to tackle with renewed urgency the structural reform of British industry. Some in the UK, and perhaps even a majority of the press, would prefer Britain to give up its worldwide role and concentrate on securing entry into the EEC, even on the terms de Gaulle stipulated, but those would 'imply both the end of our present relationship with the United States and the surrender of our world-wide role'. It was 'better to wait until the operation of the ordinary laws of mortality removed the French obstacle to our entering the European Community on acceptable terms'. It was in that spirit that the reductions in military expenditure he had announced had been conceived.

The meeting adjourned for lunch, when the president made his toast to the Queen. Colman may be mistaken, though the Churchillian references seem extreme and read rather as if the toast had not been the first drink of the day. 'For Americans,' the president said, 'Britain is a permanent friend, and the unbreakable link between our nations is our permanent interest.'[100] Rejecting Palmerston's notion, he surely had an interest in supporting what Wilson said he was trying to do.

Wilson had a discussion with the secretary of state. Rusk said he had been reflecting on the means by which North Vietnam had been induced to moderate its attitude to captured American airmen. That suggested it might be susceptible to pressure, 'judiciously applied'. One notion was a joint parliamentary and congressional démarche to try to persuade Hanoi to respond to Washington's frequently declared willingness to start discussions. Would it also be possible for the UK to approach non-aligned countries and urge them to represent to Hanoi the risk of escalation and the need to get some discussions going? Japan and the Commonwealth might have a part to play, and 'we might enlist the Pope, all living holders of the Nobel Peace Prize, etc.'

Rusk also wondered whether the PM might send a message to Kosygin, confirming, as a result of his visit to Washington, that the US was interested 'not in escalating but in de-escalating', that it had tried to convince Hanoi of that but had failed, and that 'an alternative possibility might be an arrangement whereby both sides would "pull back" on a *de facto* basis'. Wilson suggested that any such proposal might be combined with, or an alternative to, 'the suggestion that the United States should now stabilize the level of their troops in Vietnam and abstain from any further build-up in return for an undertaking that the Ho Chi Minh trail would be effectively blocked'. Rusk said he would have to consult Johnson and McNamara about 'the feasibility of a closure of the trail, which might have to be guaranteed by some form of international supervision', but he did not reject the idea out of hand.

Wilson said he would consider Rusk's suggestions. The first step might be to send two or three MPs to Washington to discuss the matter with such congressional spokesmen as the US government suggested. Then 'the Commonwealth might be mobilised to support the initiative. And the process might culminate in a new international mission to Hanoi.' He would give Rusk a considered view after he had returned to the UK and consulted his colleagues.[101]

If it were decided to follow up Rusk's suggestions, particularly the idea that the UK should approach non-aligned countries, it was necessary, de la Mare now wrote, to 'make quite sure what it is the Americans would like us to say'. Did they want the UK to advocate a settlement by means of an international conference, or did they want it 'to plump for a cease-fire, leaving the question of the political settlement to be dealt with after the fighting has stopped?' Within the administration, de la Mare believed, opinions about that strongly diverged. 'The difficulty about proposing a conference is that the whole world knows that the North Vietnamese are not prepared to have one': they said that everything would be settled when the Americans left. 'If we go on suggesting a conference many non-aligned countries will be confirmed in the belief they already hold that, in the light of the known North Vietnamese position, proposals for a conference by the United States, or by us who are widely thought to be their mouth-piece, are simply a propaganda manoeuvre intended to put the North Vietnamese in the wrong.' The UK, de la Mare believed, had 'already forfeited a good deal of our own credibility with third countries by having given the impression of insisting on a conference, and particularly on a "Geneva" solution'. The UK had also to be careful lest it be said that, in its wish to promote a conference, it was losing sight of the main issue: bringing peace to Vietnam. 'Many people hold that to propose an international conference which has no chance of success is tantamount to prolonging the war.' Britain might get a better response from non-aligned countries and in general if it took the line that the first step was to get a ceasefire, 'and then to think about a political settlement when the dust has settled'.[102]

A telegram to Washington, prepared in consultation with No. 10, asked for more information on all the suggestions Rusk had raised. On the substance of the matter, it took up de la Mare's point. '[U]nconditional negotiations on the basis of Geneva' provided 'a useful and logical framework for proposals', but the refusal of North Vietnam to negotiate on that basis without prior US withdrawal might make it more difficult for non-aligned countries to participate, 'both because they would think such a proposal useless and because they might fear they would appear to be taking sides'. It was difficult to verify a ceasefire, but it might be useful to include it as an alternative, 'or perhaps better as a proposal that a ceasefire should take place to coincide with the opening of discussions'.

On procedure, the telegram suggested that the PM might send a message to the heads of some non-aligned and Commonwealth governments, suggesting that the US was determined to see the war through, but alert to the dangers of escalation, and that it might be a good moment to propose ending the conflict by negotiations or ceasefire or a combination of the two, at the same time appealing to 'all concerned not to escalate further'. Kosygin might be told what Wilson was doing and asked 'at least not to take any action to make it more difficult for the non-aligned countries to act in this sense'. That might be followed by a UK/US parliamentary initiative addressed to other parliaments or by a public declaration with which other parliaments might associate themselves. 'We would have to be careful to avoid giving the impression that parliamentary action was simply being used as a smokescreen by the U.S. and U.K. Governments.' Any action with non-aligned governments could lose credibility or be wrecked if the Americans undertook any new military operation of a type on which non-aligned opinion was sensitive. Pointing that out was not intended to limit the US freedom of action, but it was a relevant factor.[103] What the FO had in mind was a possible American move into Laos or the DMZ.[104]

Rusk was on holiday, and Dean discussed the British telegram with Ball and Unger. They were discouraging. Rusk had, they said, 'not really envisaged a parliamentary/congressional *démarche*, partly because it would be very difficult to make it work and partly because any Anglo-American Parliamentary initiative seemed doomed to failure in advance'. Expressions of opinion by individual MPs could perhaps be helpful. The British government could put in some useful work at the CPM and with uncommitted countries willing to act. A message to Kosygin was a good idea.

Ball stressed the difficulty in accepting a ceasefire as a prelude to negotiations. 'This was not the classical form of warfare with fairly well defined fronts, when one could see whether the other side was complying or not, and the effect of a cease fire would in fact be to allow the Viet Cong to consolidate their hold on sizeable areas of country.' Dean argued the point the FO telegram had made, 'but without making much impression'. Eventually Ball said 'that the best way round this particular difficulty would be for us to induce people to ask Hanoi what corresponding steps they were prepared to take if the bombing were stopped'.[105]

The Americans, as R. Fyjis-Walker of SEAD put it, ruled out most initiatives. Messages to the non-aligned would make no headway, given that Mrs Gandhi's initiative had shown that the temperature in Moscow was 'glacial'.[106] Bundy had told Greenhill and Murray on 29 July that the US had invited the Indians to have another go. They could say that the US would reduce the bombing, if not stop it altogether, if North Vietnam gave some indication of a matching response: 'a nod of the head from Ho Chi Minh.' The Indian chargé in Washington was briefed.[107] In Hanoi the Indian consul-general was told, H.K. Matthews reported from Moscow, that North Vietnam might consider negotiations if the Americans stopped the bombing and publicly stated that they intended to withdraw within a time limit set by themselves.[108] In Hanoi Shepherd, however, thought the Moscow report doubtful.[109]

What were the State Department's views? The FO referred to de Gaulle's speech in Phnom Penh. Was there a 'nod'?[110] The French president saw Cambodia as a potential bridgehead from which the French might one day sally out and re-establish themselves in Indochina when other Western influences had been rejected or diminished, Chargé Leslie Fielding had explained in May. 'Above all, neutral Cambodia may one day underpin a regional "settlement" (or "sell-out"), with de Gaulle as architect and France as prime beneficiary.'[111] Departing for a world tour in August, the French president was expected to reiterate his country's opposition to America's military intervention in Vietnam and call for a political solution based on its neutralisation.[112] He received an enthusiastic welcome in Phnom Penh, and Sihanouk described him as Cambodia's 'most loyal friend', the 'best of models'.[113] In a speech before 100,000 people the French president urged a political agreement designed to establish and guarantee the neutrality of the peoples of Indochina and their right to dispose of themselves: the possibility of that would depend on a US decision to repatriate its forces.[114]

'We are willing to lay on the table at any moment our schedule for withdrawal from Vietnam,' the president told a press conference, 'if some-one can also lay on the table their schedule of withdrawal—and if we can give the freedom-loving, liberty-loving people of Vietnam any assurances that they will not be murdered, assassinated, or killed either by infiltrators or assassins.'[115]

In Washington Trench and Stewart asked Chet Cooper 'whether there had been any sign at all from the other side of willingness to discuss ways and means of calming things down'. None at all, he replied, and 'he was having quite a struggle to obtain agreement on his own side on the best way of setting about this'. He felt that 'well publicised exercises' such as the trips of Harriman and Goldberg were now more likely to do harm than good 'by having the appearance of publicity stunts with no genuine willingness to negotiate behind them'. Given the opening of the September UNGA session and the November elections, however, the administration would have to make 'some form of fairly resounding statement' if only to avoid the accusation 'that they were the war-mongers'. The best hope of results, if any, was in 'unobtrusive, unreported but persevering efforts wherever likely channels could be found'. Cooper also hoped to avoid too many public statements by administration spokesmen, 'which only served to confuse Hanoi'. He referred to various statements on the withdrawal of US forces: 'he himself had not been able to make out from them exactly what American policy was, so he was quite sure that the other side had no clear picture.'

Cooper agreed that no progress was likely until the November elections were over, since Hanoi and Moscow thought they would show a loss of support for LBJ. But he thought that Gromyko's visit for the opening UNGA meeting offered an opportunity, and by the end of the year the Russians might feel 'sufficiently sure of their position in the Communist world to be able to take some initiative over Vietnam without worrying about Chinese attacks on them'.

The State Department, M.N.F. Stewart thought, was 'putting a great deal of effort into their attempt to establish a dialogue with the other side', and its public expressions of willingness to talk were not 'mere publicity gestures'. There was 'so much talk about American escalation' that it was 'worthwhile emphasising once again their desire to end the war, provided that this can be done honourably'. True, that represented 'only one side of the coin, the other being the "meat-grinder" tactics aimed at inducing war weariness amongst the North Vietnamese and Viet Cong by showing that crime doesn't pay. But the object of both is the same.'[116]

The PM talked to Harold Holt, the Australian PM, who asked if he intended to revive the Commonwealth Peace Mission. It might be worth repeating the 1965 guidelines, Wilson thought, and perhaps keeping the mission in being, two new representatives replacing those no longer there, one of them possibly Lee Kuan Yew, prime minister of newly independent Singapore: 'basically a supporter of American policy but he also had a good radical reputation.' Holt said that Australia could not take the initiative—it had troops in South Vietnam—but wanted to be associated with any possible peace moves. To a lesser extent, Wilson responded, Britain was in the same position: 'despite our position as Co-Chairman, our own position of support for the United States made it difficult for us to be accepted as a valid peace interlocutor, at least in Hanoi and Peking.' Maybe two representatives could go to Hanoi, Wilson suggested. Holt reacted favourably. 'He said the important thing was to keep the door to a peace settlement continually open; one never knew when the Communists might suddenly change round and wish to start negotiations.'[117] The FO opposed the idea. A positive response, wrote Murray, was very unlikely and might discredit any efforts made when the time was ripe.[118] De la Mare, of course, agreed with Murray. The initiative would produce no result and 'bring the Commonwealth into disrepute by again laying bare its impotence on the Vietnamese issue'.[119]

That view seemed to prevail in Washington. Chet Cooper said that the present intention was not to talk about peace but to work for it. Reminded that the Commonwealth Peace Mission was still in existence, Bill Bundy confirmed Cooper's view. The president, he told M.N.F. (now Sir Michael) Stewart, was grateful for Wilson's attempts over the past year to bring North Vietnam to the conference table, but now the SD and the White House were agreed that open and publicised initiatives—American or otherwise—were 'counter productive' insofar as they damaged the credibility of the US determination to go on and also provoked the inevitable negative response from the North Vietnamese. Another Commonwealth initiative would be unwelcome, Stewart concluded.[120]

In New York, however, Gromyko said he wanted to talk about Vietnam to Goldberg.[121] De la Mare was in favour. And the British should not give the impression that they were so wedded to Geneva that they would look with disfavour on a solution on any other basis. Their objective was to end the war as soon as possible on terms that 'give the people of South Vietnam a reasonable chance of working out their destiny as they wish'.[122] 'Seems right at this stage,' wrote the new foreign secretary, George Brown,[123] who had been moved to that office when he opposed the deflationary package the Cabinet adopted.[124]

At UNGA on 22 September 1966, Goldberg, the US delegate, declared that the US sought a political, not a military, solution, one that assured the people of South Vietnam the right of self-determination. Reunification should be decided on by the peoples of the two Vietnams through a free choice without outside interference. 'We are prepared to order a cessation of all bombing of North Viet-Nam the moment we are assured, privately or otherwise, that this step will be answered promptly by a corresponding and appropriate deescalation on the other side.' President Johnson had said that the question of the VC's place in negotiation was not an insurmountable problem.[125] Hitherto the US had required an immediate and demonstrable reduction of infiltration in return for a bombing halt. The new proposal was to become a Phase A/Phase B negotiating position.[126]

Gromyko turned the proposal down, but he, Goldberg and Rusk had a long meeting on 25 September.[127] Gromyko told Rusk that bombing was the great obstacle, but when Rusk referred to the need for reciprocity, he had no response and could not say what might follow.[128] The foreign secretary also found Gromyko disappointing on Vietnam.[129] But he met LBJ on 10 October 1966 and told him the SU wished to improve relations.[130] He urged stopping the bombing. 'He could not say what North Vietnam or the NLF would do, but the reaction would be a different one.' The SU 'would like to see the end of the war'.[131] Was there an opportunity for the British? Had the moment come?

Chapter Seven
Kosygin Week

The idea of mutual de-escalation dominated the discussions late in 1966. If the US stopped bombing the North, what would North Vietnam do or pledge itself to do? Would the SU exert its influence on Hanoi? Foreign Secretary Brown's approach in Moscow was damaged by a parallel secret approach of which he knew nothing. The Wilson government nevertheless attached high hopes to Kosygin's visit to Britain in February 1967. Did the hawkish Rostow torpedo them?

Despite the doubt about new initiatives, George Brown had at the Labour Party conference in Brighton on 6 October 1966 put forward a six-point proposal for negotiations on Vietnam, designed to unite the party. North Vietnam and the US had stated at times that a Geneva-based settlement would be acceptable, he said, and he believed a settlement might be possible along the following lines: (a) a conference of parties to the war and other interested governments, held as soon as possible, which the FLN might attend; (b) when that was accepted in principle, the bombing should stop, and a pledge be given that it would not be renewed, unless the conference had met and failed; the introduction of US troops and supplies should also cease, as well as the despatch of North Vietnam troops and supplies to the South; (c) the high commands should as soon as possible simultaneously order that there should be no aggressive actions: a preliminary to a ceasefire; (d) while the conference was negotiating the ceasefire, it should agree on the main principles of a settlement, based on the Geneva essentials: (1) free elections in the North and the South within a specified time, say two years; (2) amnesty, full civil rights; (3) the governments chosen should freely decide if, and on what terms, North and South should be united as single state; (4) North and South Vietnam should be neutralised; (5) the US and North Vietnam governments should agree on a time for withdrawal, say within two years after the ratification of the political settlement; (6) the armed forces of the North and the South should be reduced and limited by the settlement; (e) all this would take place under international inspection and control, and there would also be an international campaign for economic and social rehabilitation; (f) the ICC, perhaps strengthened by representatives from other powers, should be responsible for implementation and have at its disposal a peace-keeping force like those on Sinai and in Cyprus. Brown proposed to repeat the offer to Gromyko at the weekend.[1]

There was no chance the DRV would accept it. The six-point British plan was a clumsy parroting of the Johnson hoax, it affirmed.[2] A Hanoi commentary described it as 'using a British band to play U.S. jazz'.[3] Moscow Radio had at once declared the proposals 'unacceptable: … almost an exact copy of those of the United States'.[4] Brown met Gromyko in New York on 9 October. 'The Russians are evidently sticking to their guns about not reconvening the Geneva conference unless asked to do so by North Vietnam.'[5] The foreign secretary repeated his proposals at UNGA on the 11th, and he also met Gromyko again.[6] The Russian foreign minister said it was not the right moment to convene a conference because the bombing must first stop, 'but he also said, for the first time, that Moscow is not without influence in Hanoi', the *Times* noted, and was no longer simply referring the British and others to Hanoi.[7] Izvestia criticised the proposal, for example its warning that bombing might be resumed. Perhaps, 'Monitor' commented, that 'belated blast' was designed to dispel the idea that the SU had given anything away in talks with Brown.[8]

The FO had briefed Brown for his talks in the US. Rusk's conversations with Gromyko should have shown whether there was any movement in Russia's position, given his remark in New York on 23 September that the US should not underestimate its influence in Hanoi. Brown might ask Rusk whether advantage could be taken of that to move to a settlement; whether Russia wanted to exact a price, e.g., guarantees about NATO nuclear testing; whether there was a role for Britain as co-chairman. His speech at Brighton, Brown might add, took the line that neither side could secure military victory, and that the only feasible solution was a ceasefire and negotiations 'in either order'. How did the Americans see the situation developing in Vietnam? Would American military success on the present scale force the Communists to think again or would a great increase in military effort be needed? Was there a chance that the conflict could 'end by a gradual dying away of the fighting'? There seemed no scope for Britain 'to offer help of any kind in this new situation at present', a background note told the foreign secretary, but it would be essential to remind the Americans of the importance it attached to a negotiated settlement and of the interest in Britain in action by the co-chairmen whenever that was possible. The Americans did not 'set much store by "Geneva" solutions', however, so Brown should not give the impression that Britain was 'committed to a "Geneva" settlement to the exclusion of other possibilities'. In the light of what the Americans said, Brown would be able to judge the line he should take with Gromyko.[9]

In Washington Rusk told Brown that he would be in favour of stopping the bombing while getting little back, but that made considerable political difficulties for the president. He agreed that the foreign secretary should go ahead with the peace plan outlined at Brighton and the UN.[10] The president clearly wanted to end the war, Brown told Wilson, 'provided he can do so with honour and dignity'. Its continuation stood in the way of all he was trying to do. 'He said that he was prepared to make a move to stop the bombing even if there was only a forty per cent chance that the other side would make some genuine, however small, move towards ending the fighting and beginning talks.'[11]

The president and his military partners met at Manila later in October 1966. The US got what it wanted, John McNaughton told McNamara: 'Display of not-US-aloneness, of resolve, of beginnings of an awakening responsible Asia, and of concern for the miseries of the Asian billions.'[12] Paragraph 29 of the communiqué declared that the Allied forces were in the Republic because it was the subject of aggression and had requested support. They would be withdrawn, after close consultation, 'as the other side withdraws its forces to the North, ceases infiltration, and the level of violence thus subsides'. Those forces would be withdrawn as soon as possible and not later than six months after the above conditions had been fulfilled.[13] That was put in because the president wanted something to hit the headlines.[14] It got them.[15] The White House called special attention to that item in the communiqué.[16]

The most dramatic part of the communiqué, Fyjis-Walker wrote at SEAD, appeared to be the expressed readiness of the participants to withdraw their forces from South Vietnam 'not longer than six months after certain conditions have been fulfilled'. Those seemed to be 'that the North Vietnamese have simultaneously withdrawn their forces, ceased infiltration and lowered the level of violence'. It also emphasised that the sole demand of the conference was that the North Vietnamese leaders would cease their aggression.

The public results of the conference, Fyjis-Walker thought, represented a success for the Americans' diplomacy. They had overcome those who wanted a hard line and wanted to discuss the formation of new defence groupings, the South Vietnamese, the South Koreans and the Thais. But there was a reference to holding regular meetings in Saigon in the future, 'a concession to the dissatisfaction of America's partners at the extent to which they are consulted about the conduct of the war'. Now there was 'machinery through which pressure can be brought to bear on the United States'.

The drawback of the conference was that it might not 'offer much hope of an advance towards a settlement'. It made no reference to the Geneva agreements. Russia should on the face of it take the Americans' acceptance of a six-month period for withdrawal as a welcome response to its suggestion that a specific time schedule would make their peace proposals more acceptable. But the acceptance was 'hedged around with conditions', and reportedly American officials were explaining that a North Vietnamese withdrawal would have to cover 'not only regular North Vietnamese troops but also Southern born hard core Viet Cong who have been trained in the North and reinfiltrated South'. It also appeared that the Americans and South Vietnamese were prepared to absorb the Viet Cong into political life only on terms that would seem to eliminate any chance that the FLN could continue as a political party. The North Vietnamese, Fyjis-Walker thought, would see that 'as the end of the Communist hopes and ambitions of the last twenty years and, in effect as a total capitulation to the Americans—a capitulation which in our estimate the North Vietnamese are not yet ready to make'.[17]

No doubt, de la Mare commented, the North Vietnamese public reaction would be 'violently critical', but it was possible 'that privately they may be assessing that a settlement which would leave them in control of their own territory (North of the 17th parallel) is as good as they are likely to get'.[18] '[I]n fact a Korean type solution,' Walston added.[19]

Rusk wanted the foreign secretary to follow up the contacts he had made with Gromyko. So far the Russians had refused to say what would follow a cessation of bombing, other than it would be 'different'. That would leave the United States open to criticism, and the result would be pressure for greater military effort. Some indication of de-escalation was needed, for example a reduction of infiltration. No piece of paper set out the road of de-escalation, but, if Brown wanted more after talking to Gromyko again, Rusk would see what more the Americans could say.[20] The FO sent a message to Moscow, and Gromyko said he would see Brown there on 22–23 November.[21]

Brown and Harriman

The FO prepared notes for a preliminary talk with Harriman in November. Soviet relations with China had been getting 'even worse', and official comment was now sharper than in Khrushchev's time. Had it led the

Russians to start a radical review of their policies towards major international questions? Perhaps they were now 'a little more willing to explore the possibility of progress with the West, or at least wish to give the impression that they are more willing'. In particular they might 'really want to do something towards ending the war in Vietnam', but the important question was whether they were prepared to make any concessions or take any risks to achieve that. There might, moreover, be 'a strong destructive side to Soviet policy'. A show of cooperation might extract some concessions or intensify divisions within the Western Alliance. The West should nevertheless not adopt a rigid position. The Russians might not exploit Kosygin's December visit to de Gaulle if a useful discussion had been set in train. 'It would certainly place some restraint on what they did in Paris, if we seemed to be making some progress, however small, on Vietnam.'

The talking points the FO prepared remarked on the promptness of Gromyko's response to a message suggesting another meeting, aware, as he was, that the foreign secretary 'wanted to probe for some indication of a response from the North Vietnamese to match an offer to end the bombing'. If there was movement within the Soviet Bloc towards negotiations on Vietnam, the West must move with it, and if possible give it 'added impetus'. Gromyko might show that the Russians were looking for a way forward. Then Brown would need to come back to Rusk to see what the US could say.

The US, Brown might say, needed 'a firm indication that there would be a matching response if the bombing stopped'. He was not, however, clear whether the US government could take such a significant action 'until they are satisfied that there has been a visible act of de-escalation from the other side'. He could try for that in Moscow, but he thought the Soviet government was 'not in a position to enforce positive action in Hanoi'. More likely it had concluded that its relations with the PRC had so deteriorated that it could and should 'take the risk of exerting influence on the North Vietnamese leaders'. But it might be groping for a position in Hanoi as much as Brown was trying for one with Gromyko.

Possibly Gromyko had prepared the ground in Hanoi since Brown talked to him in New York, and might be able to state that North Vietnam would de-escalate by reducing the infiltration, which would be 'visible ... on the ground' as soon as the bombing stopped. If Brown got as far as that, Britain would want to urge the acceptance of that as the 40 per cent of which Johnson spoke.

Gromyko might on the other hand say that if the bombing stopped, the SU would seek an appropriate response from North Vietnam. In itself that would be 'an enormous step forward' because Moscow would then be 'pledged to a positive effort to peace', a significant advance on Gromyko's current negativity. If Brown reached that stage, he would have to ask Rusk what the US could then do 'to help things forward'. He might suggest 'a visible reduction—though not a cessation—of the bombing', but he doubted if he should do that unless Gromyko hinted that would help him with Hanoi, and he realised it would be very difficult for 'your people'. Just possibly, the talking points concluded, Gromyko might offer to join in reconvening Geneva, and Brown wanted to be sure that he could accept immediately.[22]

At a dinner with Harriman on 6 November, Brown said he planned to take up with Gromyko where he left off in New York: what would Hanoi do if American bombing were stopped? He thought the US might have to stop the bombing without being certain. Harriman believed, however, that even if Hanoi agreed to an initial move on de-escalation, they would not proceed towards negotiations without further assurances. Tricked by the Russians in 1954, they were 'extremely suspicious'. Some contacts between the Americans and the North Vietnamese were needed at which the Americans could indicate 'where they are going to land' in the negotiations.[23]

Chet Cooper, who had been at the dinner, called on Denis Greenhill the following morning (7 November 1966). He had worked out a scenario, which he would not disclose to Harriman until they had returned to the US. It started from the point 'that the *only* time at which the U.S. Government might be ready to stop bombing without asking anything in return would be at Christmas'. The president might be persuaded to order a pause then, and he understood that the Pope would be asking him to do so. If all else failed, Brown might suggest to Gromyko 'that a Christmas pause was a possibility and might urge him to do some contingency planning for such an eventuality if the Soviet Government were really interested in making headway'. If during the Christmas pause, particularly in its early period, 'the North Vietnamese at Russian instigation could make some sign of de-escalation', the president might be able to extend it beyond the short period contemplated.

Cooper suggested as an example of the sign the North Vietnamese might make 'a marked reduction of terrorism in the south', 'a stop in truck traffic from North Vietnam to South Vietnam', 'a secret message from Hanoi to Washington that they were ready for some preliminary talks'. If it were possible to extend the pause, Cooper continued, he would suggest that the Americans should get into secret talks with the North Vietnamese. Through those they would 'reassure the North Vietnamese about the outcome of the negotiations'. If all went well, the way would be cleared for the co-chairmen to make a joint move when Kosygin visited London in February 1967, not necessarily to call a Geneva conference, but to take some forward step towards negotiations.

Greenhill encouraged Cooper to pursue his suggestion. 'He admitted that a difficulty might be the terms in which the President announced the Christmas pause. To meet the Russians it would have to be "unconditional" yet from the Congress there would be a demand for some indication of when it [bombing] might be resumed.' Cooper believed that could be 'got round'.[24]

Gore-Booth thought that it would indeed be 'the great difficulty', though he welcomed the positive outcome of the dinner party: the Americans would have 'to find a way of announcing a pause which would be unconditional *vis-à-vis* the Russians and their friends, acceptable to the American public and, in the end, revocable if everything went wrong'. The British should give Cooper time to feed the idea, if Harriman accepted it, 'into the machine'. Dean should tell Cooper that he was leaving him to pursue the ideas discussed here, though he would be glad to be briefed before he went to London on 17 November.[25]

Something was stirring in Hanoi, de la Mare believed, but the North Vietnamese were afraid of Geneva. He hoped the foreign secretary would be able to tell Gromyko that Britain and Russia had a special responsibility as co-chairmen, but should look at the problem both outside and inside the Geneva context.[26] The Canadian foreign external affairs minister (Martin) had a 'depressingly sterile' conversation with Gromyko. Perhaps, Donald Murray hoped, he would be more forthcoming with Brown.[27] 'I must still try,' Brown commented. 'But we had better play it soft.'[28]

At a meeting in Washington on 10 November, held after the return of Harriman and Cooper, Bill Bundy suggested that Brown's visit to Moscow offered better immediate possibilities than the new secret channel that was being opened up through Ambassador Lodge and Janucz Lewandowski, the Polish representative on the ICC. What if Hanoi agreed to some de-escalation? Pressure would build up for stopping troop movements, too. The US would not want to make substantial concessions before Hanoi was at the negotiating table, but Brown had to have something to contribute to the value of his talks.[29] A cable to London spelled out the two-phase formula, also sent to Lodge for his talks with Lewandowski, of which, however, the FO was not informed. The deal in its totality would represent what both Hanoi and the US agreed to as a reasonable measure of mutual de-escalation, but it would have two separate phases in its execution. 'Phase

A would be a bombing suspension, while Phase B, which would follow after some adequate period, would see the execution of all the other de-escalatory actions. Hanoi's actions in Phase B would appear to be in response to our actions in Phase B rather than to the bombing suspension.'[30] The immediate issue was to find out, precisely, if privately, what steps Hanoi would take if the US stopped bombing.[31]

This secret channel was not the first that had been used, nor, as James Hershberg has shown, was this the first used by Lodge and Lewandowski.[32] Cooper and Harriman thought Brown's trip had 'better immediate possibilities', but Rusk decided to give the Polish channel a try.[33] The US wanted to know what it would get if it stopped bombing, while Hanoi did not wish to appear to yield and wanted it to be stopped—or appear to be stopped—unconditionally. The device was a means of concealing the conditionality. All this, of course, could only be the start of negotiations. What would each hold out for then? And how would they get it?

Reilly reported Manac'h's analysis. The Quai, he said, thought the Russians would be less inhibited in the future about policies that might incur Chinese criticism, but had not reached the point at which they would be prepared to join the British in calling for a new conference on Vietnam. There were still two preconditions for that: the US would have unconditionally to stop bombing North Vietnam; and Hanoi would have to ask the SU to call a conference. Manac'h thought it 'just conceivable' that the Americans would be able to secure some kind of secret assurance that there would be an answering gesture, but the cessation of bombing would have to appear unconditional. 'He said that he also thought the Russians were encouraging the Hungarians, Bulgarians and Czechs to urge Hanoi to be more flexible, but Hanoi still had to bear the Chinese position in mind.'

The French ambassador to the PRC had called on Chen Yi on 16 November to ask for the reaction to de Gaulle's speech at Phnom Penh, which had only recently appeared in the Chinese press. He said his government welcomed the French president's call for the withdrawal of American troops, and agreed with the North Vietnamese government and the Viet Cong that the Americans must leave before a peace conference began. Such a conference should not be within the framework of the Geneva agreements, which were 'out of date'. A world conference was needed. The ambassador asked if China would continue to support Hanoi and the Viet Cong 'if they decided to accept negotiations after the Americans had declared their intention of withdrawing but before they had actually gone'. Chen Yi did not answer clearly, 'but said that the Americans could not be trusted'.[34]

Brown in Moscow

Brown and Gromyko had tentatively agreed to meet in January, but brought back the date to precede the Christmas truce,[35] though Vietnam was not the only item on the agenda. The foreign secretary was accompanied to Moscow by Lord Hood, deputy undersecretary, Sir Harold Beeley, representative to the disarmament conference at Geneva, Greenhill, Howard Smith and Donald Murray of SEAD.[36]

Brown took up the two-phase line, playing down his own emphasis on a Geneva. He put it to Gromyko before dinner on 23 November. It seemed that North Vietnam required the cessation of bombing to be unconditional, while the US required some assurance that if it stopped bombing, a measure of de-escalation would follow. 'The problem was to find some means of bridging the gap between the two sides.' Brown suggested the possibility that the two parties might agree secretly on mutual measures of de-escalation that would be put into effect once the bombing had stopped: 'the first step would be to stop the bombing and the second step would be further action of de-escalation by the American side to which the North Viet-Namese and Viet Cong would respond by similar acts of de-escalation; but with both phases forming part of a firm prior understanding.' There would thus be two phases: a cessation of bombing; then the execution of the other agreed measures of de-escalation by both sides. The idea, Brown said, would require careful study, and both Britain and Russia might have to help. Gromyko made no comment of substance. If the bombing stopped, he said, the situation would be 'different'; if something else happened as well, it would be 'very different'.

Next day Brown gave Gromyko a piece of paper, repeating what he had proposed the night before. At lunch Gromyko said he had not studied it, but assumed it was no more than a repetition of Brown's idea. That was so, said Brown. Presumably, Gromyko said, there was no obligation on him to transmit the proposal to anyone or to respond. There was no obligation, Brown replied, 'but he hoped he would do both things'. He would greatly value a response before he met Rusk in mid-December. He stressed it was a confidential communication and he intended to keep it that way.[37]

On 25 November Brown told Kosygin that if the SU supported his proposal, he thought he could get American support for it. 'He would like to know what were the Soviet feelings about a possible response from Hanoi.' Kosygin asked 'whether the proposal had been discussed and agreed with the Americans or was it Mr Brown's own plan'. Brown said it was 'his own personal effort. … He would not have put it forward if he had not had good reasons to believe that he could carry it through with the Americans.' Was that simply Brown's impression, Kosygin asked, 'or had he spoken to the Americans and received their approval'? Brown said he had long talks with Johnson and Rusk. 'He could pledge his word that if he could get a degree of help from the Soviet Government the plan could be acceptable. He was deliberately avoiding getting into a position where he was negotiating for the Americans.'

Kosygin explained that he had no authorisation from the Vietnamese to negotiate on any such matter. The SU was aiding North Vietnam against the US aggression. He did not understand why the UK had not said that the US was the aggressor. Brown said he could not accept Kosygin's analysis: it was oversimplifying. It was necessary 'to take advantage of this particular moment of time, which would not last, to do something positive'. Two dates were critical: mid-December, when he would meet Rusk; and Christmas, which might be a convenient moment when Johnson could take 'certain action'.

Denying he was oversimplifying, Kosygin repeated that he was not authorised to conduct any negotiations. Whatever opinion he might express would be 'an abstract consideration'. He had studied Brown's proposals with Gromyko. It seemed that there was a contradiction between the oral proposal made to Gromyko and the written one. In the first, as he understood it, it was stated that the Americans would consider both the Four Points of the North Vietnamese and the Five Points of the NLF. 'Before that there would be an end to the bombing and some measure of de-escalation in the military activities in South Viet-Nam. From the written document the impression was that conditions were now being imposed. … This was an ultimatum.' Following the written proposals would be going back to 'the old way of thinking which would certainly not bring any success. There was nothing new in these proposals. He had heard it hundreds of times: "you stop military activities in the South and we stop bombing". There was nothing new and therefore no new opinions to be expressed.'

The proposals put forward by his Vietnamese friends were 'correct and fair', Kosygin continued. If he were a Vietnamese, 'he would be determined to go on fighting the aggressor'. The only proposal that would be valid—and many countries were offering proposals—would be one that was acceptable to the Vietnamese. 'After all the fighting was going on in their territory, and the only way to put an end to this conflict was for the Americans to pack up and go in order to let the Viet-Namese choose their own way of life.'

Brown replied that he accepted that there must be a political solution, only to be found by negotiations. If the Four Points were taken as the basis for discussion, that would help, and if that meant they were flexible, that would help very much. The US would make no difficulty on the question 'as to who sat round the table'. As to the withdrawal of foreign forces, Goldberg had indicated in the UN that it would take place 'after a short space of time'. What he was trying to do, Brown continued, was 'to create favourable conditions for the start of negotiations. ... He was not offering a long-term solution. He was trying to create an atmosphere for negotiations. He was suggesting means by which both sides could save face.' Kosygin should forget the word 'conditions' and consider his proposal as a first move towards negotiations. He had asked Brown for the first of those steps. This was it.

'Supposing the bombing stopped and there was a conference,' Kosygin said, 'a Viet-Namese sitting down at the table would constantly look up at the sky to see whether the bombing was suddenly to be resumed.' It had happened before. There was 'a crisis of confidence of trust', Brown rejoined: the Americans feared that if the bombing stopped, 'there would be a build-up of forces and infiltration would continue. It was absolutely necessary to dissipate the atmosphere of distrust.' President Johnson had said that, if Kosygin would help, 'Mr. Brown could say that he knew he could deliver his friend. He could do that if Mr. Kosygin could give some indication of an assured reduction of military activity on the ground. Once this could be done the move to the conference table could be rapid.' The discussion had been exhausted, Kosygin said. Could he assume, Brown asked, that Gromyko would get in touch again? He could hardly say anything new, Kosygin replied, unless he pursued a different policy from his prime minister.[38]

At the airport later in the day, Brown assured Gromyko that the piece of paper in no way represented a retreat from what he had said the previous evening. 'His proposal should be received as a first of first steps, but his eventual object of course remained a substantive settlement through a conference or other means.'[39]

Brown found the Russians 'pretty cool', as he told the American ambassador on his return. But he would tackle Gromyko again about 10 December, so that he could speak to Rusk in Paris on the 16th.[40] Brown also discussed his Russian visit with Harriman. Had he told Kosygin that the Americans were willing to stop bombing in return for negotiations or only if there were responsive measures of de-escalation? Brown said he had told Kosygin 'that if there was a clear and firm assurance from a trusted source that the North Vietnamese would negotiate, this would help the situation. He had then said that if there was a similar firm assurance that the North Vietnamese would carry out a measure of de-escalation, this could likewise lead to positive results.'[41] The FO's guidance telegram described the Moscow talks not as negotiations but exchanges of thoughts.[42] We have to stonewall and say nothing, Bangkok was told.[43]

Brown, as promised, tackled Gromyko again. Were there any further thoughts, he asked on 6 December, before he met Rusk?[44] The reaction, as Murray put it in a note preparing Brown for his meeting with Rusk, was 'impassioned': he had nothing to add to what he and Kosygin had said to him in Moscow. It was difficult to decide, Murray suggested that the foreign secretary might tell Rusk, whether the Russians had put the package to Hanoi. Was there anything more that he or Rusk might do to help the Russians 'if they are groping for a position with Hanoi?' He was inclined not to nudge them again for the time being.[45]

Marigold

The fact was that US aircraft had attacked a military vehicle depot five miles from Hanoi on 2 December, and on 4 December a rail marshalling yard at the same distance. Substantial civilian casualties occurred on 2 December in Hanoi itself, perhaps, the consul-general thought, caused by an unexpended anti-aircraft missile or shell: anti-aircraft fire was intense, six US planes being shot down. Communist propaganda described the attacks as another serious step in escalation. In London there might, Murray thought, be parliamentary pressure on the government 'to show "consistency" with their dissociation in June, by freshly dissociating from, or at least condemning, the attacks'. There were two good reasons not to do so.

First, though they had led to casualties, the attacks were not specifically on targets 'touching on' Hanoi, like the oil installation attacks. Second, 'the most important objective in our Vietnam moves at present is to preserve the link of confidence with Mr. Gromyko, which in turn depends on being able to convince him that the Secretary of State maintains the complete confidence of the United States leaders'. An act of dissociation might reduce this confidence, and in any case would give the impression 'that we had lost it, or might be in the process of doing so'. Brown might, however, tell Rusk that attacks so close to Hanoi ran the risk of causing civilian casualties and handing the Communists a propaganda advantage, endangered the relationship he was trying to build with Gromyko, and caused difficulty in Britain, making it less easy to reject left-wing demands, still being made, for 'complete disavowals' of US policy.[46]

At the end of the month Brown considered a public move, but did not think the time had come for dissociating.[47] Governments that wanted to retain influence with the president, Dean had telegraphed after a talk with Harriman, should not go for dissociation. Those who did would not have much influence.[48]

Murray outlined possible courses. One was to telegraph U Thant, who, after criticising the bombing, had been asked by the US to try to bring about peace talks and had offered his three-point programme.[49] The disadvantage, as Murray pointed out, was that the UN was 'anathema' to China and North Vietnam, and such a move by Britain would not be 'sufficiently new to dispel heat'. A second course would be to telegraph Gromyko, but he was unlikely to budge on the co-chairmanship, and British public opinion was likely to know that. Telegraphing the president, a third course, would 'respond to feeling in the UK' but was 'likely to be regarded as a partisan move into which H.M.G. had been stampeded'. The form of language was 'unlikely to satisfy left wing', and it 'would put us in wrong with U.S. without positive gains'. A fourth option was to telegraph Johnson, Pham Van Dong and Air Marshal Nguyen Cao Ky, the prime ministers, with a 'positive proposal for armistice talks'. That would be 'a new initiative', diverting attention from 'simple condemnation of U.S.', and a refusal by the North Vietnamese would put them in the wrong. On the other hand China might make trouble over Hong Kong as a venue, and other venues were not under full British control or, like Mauritius, less accessible.[50]

After an office meeting, Brown approved a course that combined a number of these ideas and, he told Wilson, who was in the Scilly Isles, was cleared with Rusk, who consulted the president.[51] In support of Thant's efforts, as the foreign secretary put it, the UK sent messages to Rusk, and to the foreign ministers of the Republic of Vietnam and the government of North Vietnam appealing to them to nominate representatives who might meet to arrange a cessation of hostilities.[52] Brown also sent a message to Gromyko. He was sorry that his Russian colleague could not join in proposing the reconvening of Geneva, and regretted receiving nothing from him since returning from Moscow. Could he back up this new effort?[53]

LBJ responded positively to Brown's initiative at a press conference in Texas on 31 December: 'We have heard from the British. We are delighted to have their views and suggestions.'[54] The DRV rejected it, since it included no invitation to the FLN.[55] Hanoi Radio referred to the 'vile face' of US aggression, and the 'vile face of Mr Brown himself', in collusion with the US.[56] '[H]ypocritical words' could not cover up the 'foul contents' of the proposal. *Pravda* referred to pressure on the British government from public opinion, demanding dissociation from US aggression. Hence, 'in an effort to find a way out of an extremely delicate situation', it launched Brown's 'peace initiative'. Could its authors 'seriously think that any talks are possible while bombs are falling and shells continue to explode in Vietnam's peaceful towns and villages?'[57] The Labour left-wing criticised Brown for not endorsing Thant's Three Points.[58]

At this point the British were made aware of the Lewandowski venture, not by the State Department or by the US embassy, but through the journalist Harrison Salisbury, who got it from Pham Van Dong. That venture had also been damaged by the December bombing. According to McNamara, he and others had sought to delay the raids, but the president, still influenced by the after-effects of the Christmas 1965 pause, felt that postponement would be considered as weakness.[59] The Russian minister counsellor in Washington (Alexander Zinchuk) told Bill Bundy on 22 December that Brezhnev and Kosygin had discussed Marigold with Le Duc Tho early in December when he was on his way home from Hungary, but, because of the bombing, found it difficult to persuade or advise Tho to proceed with a meeting in Warsaw.[60] Rapacki insisted: 'The Warsaw meetings were bombed by U.S.'[61]

The fact was, it seems, that the president did not believe in Marigold. 'The simple truth … was that the North Vietnamese were not ready to talk to us. The Poles had not only put the cart before the horse, when the time of reckoning came, they had no horse.'[62] Brown himself was later to conclude that the Poles were in fact never in a position of being able to 'deliver' their friends.[63] In fact there was, as Hershberg argues, a narrow majority in the Hanoi Politburo for exploring the Warsaw contacts.[64] The breakdown of Marigold, Wallace Thies says, meant that the hawks in Hanoi renewed their ascendancy, and conduced to a consensus early in 1967 in favour of an all-out offensive in the South.[65]

The Americans let the foreign secretary go to Moscow in November without telling him what was going on, as Palliser told Wilson. Since the Polish representative in Saigon, Lewandowski, conveyed an inaccurate summary of the American position—'omitting in particular the two-phase agreement under which U.S. bombing would have stopped provided there was clear advance agreement about subsequent action by Hanoi'—at the same time as Brown was conveying an accurate version, it was not surprising that the Russians seemed 'puzzled' by his exposition and 'pressed him very closely on it'. Since it did not correspond with what Lewandowski was conveying to Hanoi, they must have concluded that the foreign secretary did not after all enjoy 'full American confidence', or that the two-phase agreement was 'his own bright idea and had no American backing'. If the Americans had taken the foreign secretary into their confidence, he could have told the Russians that he knew that the agreement was being discussed in Hanoi and suggested they check what the Polish representative was saying. Now the Americans were 'landed in a situation where their involuntary intermediary (Harrison Salisbury) is someone who because of his profession will be under the strongest temptation to publish … all that he is learning in Hanoi and thereby compromise such chances of success as this operation may enjoy'. It was, Palliser concluded, 'a rather gloomy story of muddle, lack of confidence and incompetence (either by the Poles or by Ambassador Lodge in explaining the American position to him [Lewandowski])'.[66] In fact Lewandowski had included as number 8 in his own Ten Points a rather obscure version of the two-phase proposal.[67]

Rusk's action, Dean was told, was improper. It also involved two risks, that the Russians would deduce that Brown was not, as he said, in the confidence of the Americans, and that the message would get to Hanoi in a garbled form. The Russians would thus be faced with two different proposals. 'In consequence each would discount the value of the other', and nothing would happen until they had decided which was authentic. Brown took no chances: he made over the formula Rusk had given him in writing. Kosygin asked him to postpone his departure for 24 hours so as to permit an adequate talk, and when they met pressed him hard on his credentials and on the meaning of the formula. In the event the Russians were 'needlessly puzzled' as to which message represented the US position, and the foreign secretary's ignorance of the Hanoi operation probably led them to doubt the extent to which he was in the Americans' confidence.

Probably they had got it all straight now, the letter to Dean continued. Perhaps Brown's stock in Moscow might even have risen as a result. 'But the risk which the Americans ran, both to their own interests and to the Secretary of State's reputation, by their lack of frankness, strikes us as amazing.' They certainly missed exploiting the first two dates mentioned to the Russians, the Rusk-Brown meeting in Paris, and the Christmas truce. The situation could have been quite different if the foreign secretary had been able to hint that he knew Lewandowski had been authorised to make similar proposals in Hanoi. 'We do not want an argument', Dean was told, but he should explain the matter to Bill Bundy.[68]

He raised various points in reply. '[W]e felt that we should honor Polish insistence that Lewandowski channel be kept totally secure.' The Brown message was the clear and solid one the US was sure would get through, and he was in a position to discuss the underlying principles in depth. Speaking privately, 'Bundy added that we recognized absolute obligation never to put British in false position and hence to provide them with all information they needed for any contacts they had. This applied to forthcoming Kosygin visit. At the same time, we were playing a multiple chess game and could not be expected to cut the British in on all boards at all times.'[69]

It was 'clumsy diplomacy' for the Americans not to tell the British that they were 'using a parallel track in a different way', Gore-Booth later wrote, but he did not think that it 'destroyed the usefulness of Mr Brown's intervention. … Simultaneous advocacy would have enhanced, not weakened, credibility. There was no point in the British claiming to be "mediators" as though they had invented or had some special copyright in the American plan.'[70] But surely that judgement misses the point that the two messages were not identical.

Certainly Wilson once more complained bitterly to Ambassador Bruce. Even now, he said, the UK might not know about the exchanges if Salisbury had not revealed them. A somewhat similar situation had occurred a year ago: but for Goldberg, Britain would not have been well informed. Kosygin was due to visit Britain, and the British government must be fully informed before the visit took place. Perhaps, Wilson suggested, Chet Cooper could come over to brief him. Bruce thought it best not to raise the matter with the president, but Wilson said that the broader question of confidence had to be raised at some point. Public criticism was growing, and that made the American failure to keep the British in the picture 'even more intolerable'.[71] The prime minister telegraphed the president, saying he was 'seriously concerned'.[72]

'I do not believe that we owe it to the British to keep them fully informed on every move in this game when 500,000 U.S. men are under arms and the British fighting contribution is zero,' Walt Rostow commented. 'Nevertheless, keeping the British tolerably happy is part of the job.'[73] But Chet Cooper was sent over. He discussed the Lewandowski affair. The prime minister expressed the hope that bombing would not be resumed during Kosygin's visit to Britain, given the hope of talks.[74] He had noticed, as he later wrote, that Kosygin had chosen for his visit dates that coincided with Tet, when there might be a ceasefire as in previous years. It would be easier to extend that, or a bombing pause, 'than to seek to create a cease-fire at any other time'.[75]

On 18 January the foreign secretary told the House of Commons that he was disappointed with Hanoi's refusal of his invitation.[76] Before he made the statement, however, he had been apprised that the Soviet ambassador in Hanoi had told Colvin that he thought the North Vietnamese might be prepared to enter discussions with the Americans '*provided they were in secret*'. They would have nothing to do with open and public negotiations. 'This fits in exactly with our view of the North Vietnamese position,' de la Mare wrote.[77]

Preparing for Talks with Kosygin

That view he repeated as the FO prepared its brief for the Wilson/Kosygin talks. On 27 January Walston met Harriman in Washington. The governor hoped that the British would emphasise that, in the American view, the SU had 'the ability and the responsibility to do something about North Vietnam. He went on to suggest that the Russians should make the North Vietnamese understand that, if they made peace, without Chinese acquiescence, the Russians would stand by them and help them.'[78] It would be wrong to advise the prime minister to be so forthright, Murray wrote, after consulting Howard Smith. The notion should not be put in the talking points, but in the 'background'.[79]

The draft of the 'background' suggested that there was room for progress in the 'public tier'. De la Mare was sure there was not. He was firmly of the opinion that peace had to come through direct negotiations between North Vietnam and/or the NLF and the Americans, and that contacts had to be secret. '[G]iven what we think is the attitude of the North Vietnamese, public initiatives serve only to make them more recalcitrant. But if political requirements at home make it necessary to be active in the public tier also we should at least try to avoid giving the impression of putting our money either on the Geneva Conference or initiatives by the United Nations.' The draft brief avoided mentioning them.[80]

The main point the British should make with Kosygin, the FO told Dean in Washington, was the need for 'some private sign out of Hanoi during the Tet truce'. Had Cooper any new information? The alleged conversation with Pham Van Dong of Wilfred Burchett, the Communist Australian journalist, might be an indication that Hanoi was trying to get some message across.[81] Dong had insisted that the DRV would fight on, but declared that when the US ended the war, 'we will respect each other and settle every question'.[82] Burchett had also seen the foreign minister, Nguyen Duy Trinh, who indicated that only after the unconditional cessation of bombing and acts of war could there be talks.[83] The US had also opened a contact between John Guthrie, deputy chief of mission at its Moscow embassy, and Le Trang, the DRV representative. After the 13th Plenum of the Lao Dong Central Committee 23–26 January 1967, he handed Guthrie an aide-memoire saying that the DRV would 'exchange views' if the US stopped bombing and all acts of war against it.[84] The Lao Dong leadership had called for a diplomatic struggle, though it had also called for a 'spontaneous rising in order to win a decisive victory in the shortest possible time'. Le Duan believed peace talks had to be preceded by a 'decisive victory'.[85]

At a press conference on 2 February, the president indicated that the US would be glad of unconditional discussions in any forum, and was prepared to talk about mutual de-escalation, but he was not aware of any serious effort by the other side to stop the war. The principles that the US believed should govern a peace meeting and a settlement had been made clear: the honouring of the 1954 and 1962 agreements and the right of self-determination for South Vietnam. Johnson was asked what would be a suitable step from the other side. 'Just about any step. … And we would be glad to explore any reciprocal action that they or any of their spokesmen would care to suggest.'[86]

Rusk thought the turmoil in China would make it easier for North Vietnam to talk peace.[87] Cooper went over to London again and, with Bruce, met the PM and the foreign secretary on 4 February. The line taken by the North Vietnamese, he said, was that if the US stopped the bombing, they would be prepared to listen to what the Americans had to say, but did not promise serious negotiation. Rusk hoped that Wilson could explore possible machinery if there were secret talks that reached a stage at which negotiation within a wider framework became desirable. Cooper himself, like de la Mare, thought that there would initially have to be a quiet deal 'under a palm tree'.[88]

The prime minister's brief was finalised by Murray in consultation with Cooper. In particular Cooper confirmed 'the continuing validity of the two-phase package' the foreign secretary had presented in Moscow, the concept resting on the secrecy of conditions for stopping bombing.[89] It was planned that he should leave just before Kosygin arrived on 6 February. In fact he stayed the whole week, 'hardly ever leaving the Ambassador's Office in the United States Embassy except to enter No. 10 Downing Street by the back door or to snatch a few hours of sleep at Brown's Hotel'. There, as a Foreign and Commonwealth Office (FCO) memorandum on the negotiations observed, 'he built up a reputation as the biggest American play-boy in London, returning always between 3 a.m. and 4 a.m. to his room, bleary-eyed and obviously exhausted', but not, of course, because he had been partying. In consultative sessions with Wilson and Brown, he was usually accompanied by Ambassador Bruce, 'who alone in his Embassy was privy to the close, and indeed almost constant, consultation across the Atlantic'.[90]

The Kosygin Talks

In a conversation before the main meeting on 6 February, Kosygin told Wilson that North Vietnam feared China and did not want more troops. As the situation got worse, and escalation continued, the Chinese would increase their pressure.[91] The main meeting followed at 4.30. Wilson started with the statement the North Vietnamese foreign minister had given Burchett on 28 January, authenticated by the statement of the North Vietnamese representative in Phnom Penh on 3 February, 'that there could be bilateral United States/North Vietnamese discussions if the bombing of North Vietnam were stopped'. The statements also referred to 'all other acts of war against North Vietnam', but Wilson thought they attached most importance to the bombing. He also stated the position in Washington as he saw it. The US government was faced with 'very strong public opinion'. Some wanted 'a rapid move to a *détente*. Other sections were talking—some in very dangerous terms—about moving towards a stronger prosecution of the conflict. The American Government wanted to take any opportunity of a move forward but they could not do so without some favourable gesture from the other side.'

The prime minister recalled the two-phase proposal the foreign secretary had outlined in November. 'There were ... two phases with three factors. Phase A would be the responsibility only of the United States, i.e. a cessation of bombing; Phase B would be a de-escalation by the United States and by North Vietnam and the Liberation Front. Both sides would however have been agreed in advance in a prior understanding.' The real issue was 'what assurance there could be that North Vietnam would take appropriate reciprocal action as part of Phase B' and what package the two sides would agree to in Phase B. The US needed some assurance, 'secretly if this could more easily be done'. In the short Christmas and New Year truces nothing happened to produce the necessary sign, but the Tet period of four days offered a better opportunity. If Kosygin could impress on the North Vietnamese the importance of an indication that they would be ready to make 'a positive and visible sign' that they would respond to a cessation of bombing, or, if direct and secret talks were too difficult, to discuss the possibilities through intermediaries, he would press the US to respond 'promptly and visibly' to a North Vietnamese approach.

If confidence could be established, it would be possible for both sides to proceed with talks or negotiations. It would, Wilson continued, be useful to know what ideas Kosygin had on the form of the discussions if they reached such a more formal state. The initial contacts would probably have to be secret, 'but a firmer framework would be required for real negotiations'. Something more restricted than Geneva might be possible, perhaps including the co-chairmen, the US, the governments of South and North Vietnam, and the FLN. There should be no artificial limit on the topics, which might cover the reduction or cessation of hostilities; the essential elements of the 1954 and 1962 agreements, including the withdrawal of any forces from outside Vietnam; 'arrangements for the free determination by North and South Vietnam of their future, including re-unification'; 'the recognition of the independence and territorial integrity of North and South Vietnam, or of the independence and territorial integrity of all Vietnam if the people chose reunification'; 'the international posture of South Vietnam including its relationship with other nations'; and provisions for the internal structure of South Vietnam, also covering freedom from reprisals and freedom for all political parties.

The SU, Kosygin responded, set out from the basic premise that North Vietnam was suffering from US aggression. He noted that, while Johnson and Rusk had at times called for a political settlement, and had said they had no wish to escalate the conflict, they had then done so. That aroused 'great wariness' in North Vietnam, and a lack of confidence in the basic intentions of the US in North and South Vietnam and in the SU, too. Matters were 'not at the stage which would give them the grounds for discussing any agenda for any possible Vietnam Conference. Instead he and the Prime Minister could and should attempt to find some common opportunity to assist in promoting direct contacts between North Vietnam and the United States.' If he and Wilson could take the North Vietnamese foreign minister's statement as a basis, 'and say to President Johnson, together or separately, privately or publicly, in the Communique or in a special message', that it was 'an acceptable basis for discussion', that was the best move they could take at present. 'It would enable bilateral talks between the Americans and the North Vietnamese to take place without any prior condition except a cessation of bombing.' Because of Tet, the present was the most suitable time. Kosygin added that he did not mean that he had reached an agreement with the North Vietnamese. 'He was relying on what they said publicly.'

Wilson agreed with Kosygin's use of the word 'assist'. 'An immediate way of assisting both sides would be to see that neither side took action during these few days that would undermine the confidence of the other side in their intentions.' If the North Vietnamese could give a sign of de-escalation, that of course would be of 'tremendous value'. Brown interjected that it would help if there could be a shutdown of movement through the DMZ during Tet.

Kosygin, Wilson continued, had said that if bombing stopped, he thought negotiations could take place. 'Would he be prepared to state this not only as an impression but as a firm view, and one which the United States would be able to take into account?' He said his understanding of the position was not based on what the North Vietnamese had said to him. 'Was there any possibility of getting the North Vietnamese to confirm within the next day or two that Mr Kosygin was correct in his understanding?'

Kosygin rejected both ideas. As for Brown's, he pointed out that the US was always bringing in new troops. As for Wilson's, the best way in which he and the prime minister could help, he said, was to support the statement of the foreign minister of North Vietnam. The SU could get in touch with Hanoi without delay, but there was no point in doing so. 'Indeed it would mean that they were getting into a negotiation, and that would not be helpful.'

Neither side, said Wilson, was convinced of the sincerity of statements by the other side. The SU had confidence in North Vietnamese statements, the British in American statements. 'Perhaps each would have to go bail for their friends. Her Majesty's Government could deliver their friends if the Soviet Government could deliver theirs.' Kosygin repeated his view that the two governments should say that they accepted the proposal made by the North Vietnamese foreign minister. There should be further discussion, Wilson thought. The press, Kosygin hoped, would be told only that the two leaders had an exchange of views on a number of international matters.[92]

The meeting, Murray commented, was not as discouraging as Brown's meeting with Gromyko had been. Tet—scheduled to last 8–12 February—could offer a chance; the Russians could assist towards American/Vietnamese contacts; North Vietnam was ready to consider negotiation. But the only proposal Kosygin made was for a message endorsing the Burchett interview.[93] At dinner that evening the prime minister referred to the misunderstanding in November/December. Could he tell President Johnson that Kosygin thought the Vietnamese foreign minister's statement was genuine? The important thing was that the North Vietnamese should give some sign. Kosygin said they had, and Wilson should tell the president he agreed with them: stop the bombing without conditions. He could not do what Wilson wanted, but would come up with a formula.[94] He had been in touch with North Vietnam since the afternoon.[95] He had called Hanoi and got a commitment to negotiate, Kosygin told Wilson.[96]

After the Russians had gone to bed, Wilson, Brown, Cooper and a small number of advisers met in the Cabinet Room late that Monday evening. 'There was considerable doubt on the precise implications in Mr Kosygin's attitude', though it was agreed 'that momentum must be maintained and that it would be essential to probe Mr Kosygin hard during the following day'. The group considered the relative merits of referring to possible future discussion in a wider framework, such as Geneva, or pursuing the question through a US/North Vietnam package. 'One possibility was that immediate advantage might be taken of Mr Kosygin's new attitude, possibly to the extent of telling him that the United States would not insist on mutual de-escalation if the North Vietnamese were genuinely ready to talk once the bombing had stopped.' To concede so much so early, however, 'would mean exposing the United States completely to Communist tactics, with nothing gained in terms of a reduction in fighting which could be used to justify in public the visible act of stopping the bombing'. Cooper argued strongly that the American twofold position was the basis from which to proceed at this point: 'if there was to be a cessation of bombing, there had to be some mutual de-escalation as well: alternatively the North Vietnamese could talk to the United States while the bombing, and indeed all the fighting in both halves of Vietnam, continued unabated. Talks, which might be indefinitely prolonged[,] were no adequate exchange for abandonment by the United States of the bombing weapon.' Wilson and Brown ultimately decided, with Cooper's concurrence, that he should report the position to Washington and request an urgent view on the line the prime minister could take, 'and the extent to which he could go in the certainty of United States concurrence' during the following day's talk.[97]

At breakfast on the morning of the 7th, Brown gave Cooper an outline of four points that might have to be pressed for in the communiqué, though he was not sanguine that Kosygin would agree. They were: that both sides agreed on the need for a negotiated settlement; that they agreed to assist in getting discussions started between the US and North Vietnam; that they recognised that useful discussions could not take place until the bombing was stopped and the level of military activity reduced on both sides; that they agreed they would keep in touch so as to continue their joint efforts. The State Department's comments referred only to the third point: the Americans would like it to indicate 'that the chances of successful negotiations would be enhanced if "mutual equivalent de-escalatory steps" took place'.[98]

De la Mare was unable to be present at the discussions, as he had to represent the Office at a dinner Healey was giving for Admiral Itaya. Murray told him what took place. 'My view is strongly that there is now an opportunity such as there has never yet been to make progress towards the settlement of the war.' The North Vietnamese, he believed, had 'for some time wanted to extract themselves from the war but have been afraid to do so lest the Chinese stop them by invading and occupying North Vietnam'. Now they felt that China's internal situation and its relations with the SU were such that the danger of Chinese intervention had diminished, and that it was a risk they could take, and the Russians had probably encouraged them to believe that. Burchett's statement referred to the DRV, but not to South Vietnam or the Viet Cong. 'This to my mind is the clearest indication that, if the United States will stop the war against North Vietnam the latter will leave it to the Americans and the South Vietnamese to settle South Vietnam in their own way.' The North Vietnamese statement was in fact a public offer to repudiate the VC and the FLN. That was, de la Mare thought, 'a very long step for the North Vietnamese to have taken', 'a hard decision'. To insist, as the US apparently wished to do, 'that they should publicly go beyond it and openly offer de-escalation in South Vietnam' was 'both to press them too far and to betray incomprehension, which they however will attribute to hostility and malice, of the import of the statement to Burchett. They will not believe that the Americans have really failed to see this import. They will conclude that the Americans do not want to stop the war, and neither the Russians nor we have any influence on Washington's intransigence. The result of all this can only be to bring about what the North Vietnamese themselves, the Russians, the Americans and we do not want—that is that the North Vietnamese be forced to conclude against their own will that their only hope lies in staking all on China.'[99] Was de la Mare exaggerating the China factor? Was he overemphasising the omission in the Burchett message? Was his inference too broad? The government had largely taken the line de la Mare advocated, Gore-Booth wrote on 13 February. 'Will it work?'[100]

It would be useful, so far as Parliament and the public were concerned, to say a good deal in the communiqué, de la Mare thought, but the North Vietnamese should not be frightened off. 'They are in an extremely difficult position in that they fear, to my mind justifiably, that the Chinese will take reprisals against them if they seem to eager to stop the war.' Hence they had not gone beyond the Burchett interview in public and were opposed, at least for the record, to avenues anathema to the Chinese, such as the UN and Geneva. The North Vietnamese might still rebuff blatant advances. 'We must remember that they have said only that they are prepared to talk to the Americans. They have not said that they are prepared to see us or the Russians take a hand in all this.'[101]

Along with Cooper's, the prime minister himself had also sent a message to the president: what would he regard as a sign from North Vietnam sufficient to stop the bombing?[102] The president replied that he was prepared to tell the Hanoi government that if they agreed to an 'assured stoppage of infiltration', the US would stop the bombing and the further augmentation of its forces in South Vietnam. It could not accept guarantees of safe haven from North Vietnam merely in return for discussions that so far had no form or content, during which it could continue to expand its military operations without limit.[103] 'Pure Rostow,' said Cooper.[104] Burke Trend and others questioned him as to the precise meaning of 'assured stoppage': did it mean 'a stoppage which had been verified' or 'a stoppage of whose existence the Americans had assured themselves'? Cooper was certain—as a marginal note—by Murray?—on the subsequent FO 'Study' said—that the phrase meant 'an assurance that infiltration would stop'. The British officials pointed out how important such nuances were and suggested he should get confirmation from Washington. 'He insisted that he already had chapter and verse for his interpretation', as a later FO note put it, 'and no check was made with the White House. This contributed to the serious misunderstandings which followed later.'[105] George Herring is quite unfair to Wilson when he declares him 'guilty at least of impropriety in passing to the Russians what was presumed to be an American offer without first securing clearance from Washington'.[106] Was Cooper trying to bypass Rostow?

A secret personal letter from the president to Ho Chi Minh was being discussed in Washington in 'the latter part of January'.[107] It was a response to the aide-memoire Le Trang had given Guthrie finalised as a result of the Wilson/Kosygin discussions on the 6th and 7th, drafted in haste, finished at 2.15 am.[108] Kosygin, Rusk told the Moscow embassy, insisted that Hanoi really meant to talk if the US stopped bombing. There were two difficulties with his offer to enter bilateral talks if the US ceased bombing and other military actions unconditionally and permanently, Ho Chi Minh was told: such actions would produce speculation that discussions were under way and would impair their privacy; and the US would be concerned lest Ho's government used the action to improve its military position. But the president was 'prepared to order a cessation of bombing against your country and the stopping of further augmentation of U.S. forces in South Viet-Nam as soon as I am assured that infiltration into South Viet-Nam by land and sea has stopped'. That would make it possible to consider 'serious and private discussions leading towards an early peace'.[109] The British were assured that the message was 'identical' in substance to the language used by the president in his letter to Wilson.[110] But that was not true.

On the basis of the message in that letter Murray had, however, prepared the brief for the PM for the talks with Kosygin on the afternoon of the 7th, seen by Cooper in its preliminary stages. Essentially it advised the PM to restate the A-B package in a form as close as possible to the president's message to him of 6 February, bearing in mind that the wording of the direct message the president had sent to Hanoi was not yet known.

The foreign secretary slightly amended the brief to state the A-B package in the clearest possible language, 'to make it plain that its two phases would be kept apart, with the first stage being carried out by the United States alone and the North Vietnamese action in the second stage seen as in response to United States action in the second stage, but as a result of a prior secret assurance'. Cooper was satisfied that that represented the US position, as it had in November, and he raised no objections to Brown's slight rewording.[111]

At the meeting with the Russians on the afternoon of 7 February (4.30pm) Wilson began with a reference to the Warsaw talks and the bombing of December 1966. Then he described the thinking in Washington. 'In realistic terms, those American leaders who deeply desired a settlement must be able to convince those who are urging that the military activities must be maintained, that by stopping the fighting the other side would not be placed in a position of military advantage.' But he was 'now satisfied' that the Americans would be 'prepared to move to further actions to strengthen mutual confidence if they were able to secure some assurance that this move would be reciprocated by the other side'. He believed they were now seeking to get word to Hanoi to the effect that they recognised the need for 'a first and visible step', and that that must mean the cessation of bombing. 'This, the Prime Minister believed, they would do, and they recognised that it must be presented as being done unconditionally. Therefore we had to use our ingenuity to divorce in presentation the stopping of the bombing from the consequential actions.' But the consequential actions were essential if the bombing were to be stopped.

Wilson went on to describe those actions. 'The United States were willing to stop the build-up of their forces in the South if they were assured that the movement of North Viet-Namese forces from the North to the South would stop at the same time.' The two stages would essentially be kept apart. But because the Americans would know that the second stage would follow, 'they would therefore be able first to stop the bombing, even if there was a short period between the first stage and the actions to be taken by both sides in the second stage'. In the second stage there would be 'balanced concessions'. What the North Vietnamese did in that stage would be seen in response to what the United States did in that stage, 'but it would be the result of a prior secret assurance'. The Americans, having stopped the bombing, would stop the augmentation of their forces, and the North Vietnamese their infiltration. The Tet truce—'a slight indication that the two sides had not lost complete confidence in each other'—was the best occasion for moving forward. What was needed was 'a further indication from Hanoi of a readiness to match the American reduction in hostilities'.

The fact that the US was contacting Hanoi was good news, Kosygin replied. It should be encouraged, and the UK and the SU should therefore support the proposal of the North Vietnamese foreign minister. If the US were handing over new proposals, the North Vietnamese would no doubt study them and reach their own conclusions. 'But he could not regard a cessation of bombing as, in itself, something for which the Americans should be praised.' As for the steps to be taken by the North Vietnamese, 'it was surely unrealistic to require them to stop the fighting everywhere: the people in the South were fighting, there were strong guerrilla forces among them, and there could be no question of stopping all this by a decision on the part of North Viet-Nam. The only realistic approach was a cessation of bombing to be followed by a move to the conference table.' No conditions must be attached.

Wilson agreed that it would be impossible for the North Vietnamese to give assurances that all the fighting in the South would stop. 'Nor would it be easy to prove in the early stages that an undertaking to stop the fighting was being honoured; there might well be incidents which could not have been controlled.' But what he said in speaking of the second phase was first that the US would stop bringing additional troops into Vietnam, and second 'that the assurance required from North Viet-Nam would not be that all fighting would stop throughout the whole of Viet-Nam but that the movement from North to South would stop, and this would be easy to observe and easy to carry out.' He thought it would be useful if he gave Kosygin the exact text of what he had been saying, and the Soviet prime minister agreed.

Once again, however, he repeated that 'the only realistic course was for the United States to declare openly that they were prepared to end the bombing and to come to the conference table'. All that the UK and the SU could do at that stage was to try to get them to say that, but if the US and the Vietnamese came together 'we could start giving one side or the other advice'. The SU and the UK wanted the US to make a declaration on stopping the bombing, Wilson rejoined. So did the US. 'What they required was one secret private assurance about what would happen afterwards in terms of de-escalation. This was the only problem that stood in the way of getting negotiations going.' He suggested they should think further overnight. Should they have a private discussion on Vietnam or return to the subject in a full meeting? Kosygin thought they might have a short private meeting before the next full meeting on 9 February.[112]

Wilson having promised Kosygin a text, Trend, Palliser and Murray met Bruce and Cooper after the meeting 'to check the record of the Prime

Minister's remarks and to edit them in a form which accorded with the United States position as described in the President's message to the Prime Minister and Mr Cooper's understanding of the background'. Murray delivered the text at Claridge's Hotel at 8pm, just before Kosygin left to dine at 10 Downing Street. Cooper took a copy to send to Washington. No doubt Kosygin would send the British version to Hanoi. If the US message had not been sent, the British text should be used. If it had been sent, any variation should be explained as a matter of style not substance, and the validity of the British text affirmed. Cooper found it had been sent, and so he followed the latter approach.[113]

'We have a problem,' Rostow told the president at 8pm EST on the 7th, 'real but soluble. The British took our proposal of last night and put it into A-B form; that is—first bombing halt;—then simultaneous stopping of infiltration and troop movements.' That was 'not how we stated it last night; or to Hanoi today'. The reason was that 'we gave Wilson and Brown the A-B formula and told them to peddle it in Moscow and, again, on this occasion'. Rusk was confident that if they bought the A-B formula, 'we can work it out to protect our interests'. Rostow agreed it could be done 'if we're short on the time-gap between A and B and mighty hard on verification'. If they bought anything, it would be the A-B formula 'rather than the tougher formula to Hanoi—where at lunch we virtually reversed the A and B. But that's a good initial bargaining position to be in—if bargaining it gets to be.'[114] In fact, the British had not received the proposal of 'last night' and were, as Rostow said, working from the A-B formula. And that had been changed, as he admitted, though they had been told the message to Ho was 'identical' in substance to LBJ's letter to Wilson.

On 8 February Kosygin spoke at the Guildhall. He referred to the possibility of joint action by the UK and the US in terms that might have implied that in certain circumstances the SU would join the UK in reconvening Geneva. As in 1954, he said, Great Britain 'together with the Soviet Union and other nations could make its contribution to the settlement of the Vietnamese issue on the basis of the Geneva agreement, which must be implemented by the United States'.[115] Late that evening the foreign secretary discussed that possible development with Gore-Booth and Murray, and it was decided he should probe Kosygin next morning. He should ask the Soviet prime minister if it were correct to interpret that passage in his speech as meaning that, if there were an understanding based on the two-phase proposal, the SU would join the UK in reconvening Geneva, 'even though both would know that the Chinese would almost certainly oppose and not attend'. In the early hours of Thursday morning (i.e., early on the 9th) a precise text was drafted by Gore-Booth, Murray and Cooper, and Cooper sent it to Washington.[116] The foreign secretary—always keen on Geneva—spoke to the PM. If Wilson did not raise the matter, he would.[117]

Under the proposal the co-chairmen would announce that they would invite the US to assure them that the bombing of North Vietnam would stop and invite North Vietnam and the US to assure the co-chairmen that they would take 'mutual and equivalent steps to halt the augmentation of their forces in South Vietnam'. If the assurances were promptly received, the co-chairmen would issue invitations for the reconvening of the Geneva conference on 15 February.[118]

For the meeting Murray primed Brown with a 'suggested line' for approaching Kosygin. The North Vietnamese proposal—cessation of bombing and agreement for bilateral talks—was not enough for the Americans, but they had already sent a proposal to Hanoi. If Hanoi wanted bilateral talks, they could secure them by agreeing to the two-phase proposal discussed on the 7th. If they would like to accept a Geneva conference, that would be possible. 'Your Guildhall remarks have aroused a certain expectancy. The world is looking to us. The protagonists are looking to us. We must get some sort of understanding before you go home and while the Tet truce still continues.'[119]

By the time Brown joined Wilson and Kosygin in a private talk at Claridge's at 10.45am on 9 February, the Americans were, however, still asking for 'more time to turn around the proposal'. Cooper therefore suggested that, if Kosygin's reaction were 'anything more than an outright rejection', Brown should postpone giving him any document until Washington's substantive comments had been received.[120] At the meeting the foreign secretary raised the Geneva question. Kosygin said there would be an outcry from the Chinese. He would put it to the North Vietnamese, but it would raise great difficulties for them in their relations with their northern neighbour. Could he have the suggestion in writing?[121]

In the evening Cooper received comments from Washington and gave Murray a copy of the telegram. Rusk had discussed the Geneva proposal with the president on the phone. The trouble with the second point was that 'augmentation is not good enough as a substitute for infiltration because that would mean that the other side would be free to go ahead with a rotation and sending arms and re-supply and all that kind of thing, you see. I think our original formulation—stopping infiltration—is the one we ought to stay with.' If they agreed not to augment, 'they can still send in arms and rotate their men and do the things we would have to do during that period'.[122] The

SD told the embassy in London it wanted 'infiltration' not 'augmentation', and that it would go along with either the two-phase proposal or the Geneva proposal, but would prefer the former.[123] A slightly amended version of the Geneva proposal was delivered to the foreign secretary at the Queen's banquet for Kosygin at Buckingham Palace, and Brown handed it to Deputy Foreign Minister Alexander Soldatov.[124] The text now provided for an immediate announcement by the co-chairmen that they invited the US to assure them that the bombing would stop; that they invited North Vietnam to assure them that infiltration into South Vietnam would stop and invited the US to assure them it would stop augmentation of its forces in South Vietnam; and that if all the assurances were received, they would invite members of the 1954 Conference to reconvene to work out a settlement of the conflict.[125]

Bruce and Cooper made further points when they called on Trend early on the 10th. They stressed that the US was not wedded to any solution involving a public declaration. They reported truce violations by the North Vietnamese, and said the US was concerned at the southward movement of road and waterborne transport in North Vietnam. And the US wanted Kosygin to know it was nevertheless considering extending the truce for a further three days, to the seven the FLN originally proposed. The PM put these points to Kosygin. When he emphasised that the US was ready to eschew proposals involving a public declaration, and restated the A-B package, Kosygin showed 'very great interest indeed' and asked to have the proposal in writing, though he already had the document of 7 February.[126] Murray drew it up. It was this document that Cooper declared did not need to go to Washington. He said, however, that he was sending the text to Washington for information. Wilson handed the text to Kosygin that evening when they were both at a reception at the Soviet embassy.[127]

A few hours later, about 10pm, Rostow phoned Trend and warned him that the US government had comments to make on the formulation that had been handed to Kosygin. At 10.45 he sent a formulation 'as cleared here at the highest level', to be handed to Kosygin.[128] The US, it stated, would order a cessation of bombing as soon as it was assured that infiltration had stopped, an assurance that could be conveyed in secret if North Vietnam wished. Within a few days—the period to be agreed with the two sides before the bombing stopped—the US would stop augmenting their forces in South Vietnam. The cessation of bombing would be apparent. The stopping of infiltration must become public soon after. If North Vietnam would not announce it, the US must do so at the time it stopped augmentation, and Hanoi must not deny it. Any assurances from Hanoi could reach the US direct, or via the SU, or the SU and the UK.

The message added comments for Wilson. Stopping augmentation would still allow for rotation; stoppage of infiltration meant cessation. The phrasing of the first sentence was designed to prevent the sudden movement of two or three divisions across the 17th parallel during the few days mentioned in the second sentence. The arrangement must not be translated into a Communist seizure of Laos. The ICC should provide observers to cover the DMZ and the Trail. Unless the US received immediate word from Hanoi that the arrangements were in effect, military action would be resumed against North Vietnamese forces in and north of the DMZ, but the bombing of the northern provinces of North Vietnam would not resume till Kosygin left Britain.[129]

The message seems to have resulted from a meeting including the president, Rusk and McNamara on 10 February, 3.19pm EST, for which Rostow wrote a memorandum.[130] Cooper had gone to *Fiddler on the Roof* on his first free night but was called out of the theatre for a call from Rostow that sent him to Grosvenor Square and then to No. 10. The message indicated, as he put it, that the US would stop bombing after it was assured that Hanoi had stopped infiltration. The US had reverted to a formula North Vietnam had rejected.[131]

Given the differences between this formulation and the earlier one, Wilson decided that he had no alternative but to catch Kosygin at Euston, where he was taking a train to Scotland. 'A messenger achieved this, by split seconds.'[132] Kosygin was given the message, but not the comments. Britain was ready to join the SU in making the approach, or in reconvening Geneva, Wilson's letter concluded.[133] After what Wilson called a 'jocular exchange', the PM and the foreign secretary agreed that they would be prepared to fly respectively to Hanoi with Kosygin, and to Washington with Gromyko.[134] Nothing so dramatic occurred, but there were telegrams and anger.

In a telegram to the president, drafted on the 10th, sent on the 11th, Wilson related his discussions with Kosygin, covering, too, the delivery of the revised version sent by Rostow. He asked that, before he met Kosygin again on Sunday, the president should inform him of any further developments, particularly as to the fate of the message he had sent to Hanoi. 'I shall be in a very difficult position if he knows more than I do.' The president, Wilson continued, could rely on his standing 'absolutely firm on the lines set out in your telegram to me and repeatedly stated since then by me to Kosygin'. That would remain Britain's position even if it meant 'recording a total disagreement on this issue with all that that will mean for me in terms of domestic politics'. Though the political position would be difficult, as indeed would the president's, Wilson was 'standing by the line in your last message to me, above all because I think it is right'. The next 48 hours would be crucial. But during that period, as during the previous week, 'we shall make no commitments or proposals as to the terms of settlement for Vietnam which do not square one hundred per cent with what we know to be your policy'.[135]

This telegram, it seems, was sent before the prime minister and his advisers had fully analysed the Rostow message, though they had got into a panic at the party. Early on the 11th Wilson reviewed the position with Trend, Gore-Booth, Murray and others, with the foreign secretary in touch by phone, but not summoned. 'They concluded that the text communicated by Mr Rostow ... represented a significant hardening of the American position in two important respects. It negated the concept that the cessation of bombing should be regarded as a prior, unconditional and unrelated step; it did not even allow that a package deal could be achieved if assurances were received from Hanoi that infiltration *would stop* at a given interval after the bombing; the bombing would not now stop unless and until the United States were assured that North Vietnamese infiltration *had actually stopped*. It also required that the stopping of infiltration should be made public a few days later, either by the North Vietnamese or by the United States, as justification for the stopping of the build-up of United States forces. Furthermore the United States intention to resume bombing of North Vietnam before Mr Kosygin left Britain was clearly a very serious matter.'[136] 'I was furious,' Wilson recalled. Had he been been taken for a ride? Had the hawks taken over? Was Washington confused?[137]

Gore-Booth, Murray and Murray MacLehose, PPS to the foreign secretary, then saw Bruce and Cooper and put these points 'very forcefully', with a warning that the prime minister would almost certainly send a message to the president 'expressing his serious concern'. They seemed 'somewhat bewildered'. The attractiveness of the A-B package, it was pointed out, had been destroyed, and requiring the North Vietnamese to take positive action before the bombing stopped ran counter to the US 14 Points. If bombing were resumed before Kosygin left Britain, Gore-Booth said, the prime minister would almost certainly have to dissociate Britain from the act, while it would have 'a tragic effect' on the closer understanding he was reaching with Kosygin. Bruce and Cooper were emphatic that a message to the president might be 'less productive' than strong messages from themselves, which they undertook to send immediately. The prime minister decided not to send one.[138] A draft had been prepared. Kosygin would conclude, it read, either that Wilson was not in the president's confidence, or that he had pulled a fast one. And if bombing were resumed while Kosygin was still a guest, no progress would be possible.[139]

At about 10.30pm Cooper notified No. 10 that he had received a reply to his messages, and at 10.40 he and Bruce discussed them with Wilson, Brown, Trend, Murray and others. Cooper brought an assurance there would be no bombing before Kosygin left.[140] He also handed over a telegram from Rusk. That sought to explain the US position. Three divisions were poised just north of the DMZ. 'We must be in a position to insist that these cannot be moved into SVN [South Vietnam] just before their undertaking takes effect.' The message sent to Hanoi had been in the terms of the formulation Rostow had sent: 'we must be assured that infiltration has stopped.' Rusk thought the Russians were aware of it, and the final draft would not come as a surprise nor impair British credibility.[141] Cooper added that the embassy had been advised of the extensive use North Vietnam had been making of the truce. Up to Friday night 2,050 trucks had been seen on the roads in the south of North Vietnam as against the normal 100 per day.

The foreign secretary was concerned that the US insistence on a harder line 'seriously impaired the British credibility'. Washington had had the piece of paper handed to Kosygin on the 7th, and he could not understand why, if there were an inconsistency, the British had not been notified. Wilson said that what concerned him was what he was to say to Kosygin on Sunday night at Chequers. Cooper said that the 'change of tense'—'has stopped' for 'will stop'—was a result of the violation of the truce and of the North Vietnamese build-up observed in the last few days. Why had he not been warned? Wilson asked.

The prime minister recalled that, in the light of the Lewandowski affair and the Warsaw exchanges, he had pointed out to the president, and more forcefully to the ambassador, that it was vital that he was fully briefed before Kosygin came. Cooper had been sent to brief him. But the information Cooper gave him on the 4th (Saturday) either did not reflect American policy or that policy had changed during the week. 'Why was he left in a state of incredibility for three days?' He had to consider what he should say to Kosygin. He could say that he was not, after all, in the confidence of the US; or that the US had changed its policy because of infiltration during Tet; or he could say that American policy was 'confused', and 'one member of the Administration was saying one thing and another was saying another thing'. That was in fact what he thought was the situation.

Bruce thought it would be 'quite credible' to explain to Kosygin that there had been a change in US policy because of infiltration during Tet, but to admit that the prime minister had not been kept informed. Brown intervened. If that was the right explanation, it was 'depressingly naïve'. He was anxious not to repeat the word 'dissociation', but 'felt that American action might well be pushing us in this direction'. Bruce wondered if the difference between the two proposals was very great. In that case, Wilson said, he was inclined to try to get Kosygin to accept the original text and then press the administration to accept it. Brown recalled that he had told Kosygin, on the president's authority, that if he could deliver Russia's friend, 'we could deliver ours'. Wilson added that he was at a complete loss over Phase B. That now required a public statement from the North Vietnamese. Yet six hours earlier Washington had asked him to make it clear that Washington was not pressing for any public commitment by the North Vietnamese.

Cooper thought that the Russians could be told that, given that the North Vietnamese had taken advantage of Tet, the Americans were 'concerned with an assurance that something had happened rather than that something would happen'. The PM could also say that Hanoi had had plenty of opportunity to respond had it wished to do so, but events showed that it did not. He could then turn to the substance of the change, explaining that 'what was really involved was a matter of timing, indeed of only a few days. When the Americans were told that infiltration had stopped, bombing would stop and a few days later re-inforcements would stop.' If Hanoi was really looking for a means to bring military activity to an end, Cooper thought that 'this question of timing should not be the crucial problem'.

Bruce suggested that Wilson did not need to begin his discussion with Kosygin at Chequers by alluding to the Friday text. He should probe Kosygin 'to see whether he was genuinely trying to influence Hanoi and bring about a settlement. If so, Britain and the United States were at the beginning of a negotiating position.' If, however, Kosygin was 'indignant at the outset', the prime minister would have to 'protect both his honour and his credibility'. Kosygin would question the latter only if he doubted that Wilson only knew of the change at the last moment. If Kosygin was 'not entirely rigid', Wilson might still 'point out that all concerned were now approaching the stage of negotiations and that each Government could in that process be persuaded to change its position'. Bruce thought the British government might be able to persuade the Americans to accept the formula he had first handed over.

The prime minister responded that he was 'worried over what might come out about this affair'. The Soviet government could 'make the British look like fools and not knaves and make the Americans look knaves and not fools'. Brown thought there might be accusations, private and public, 'that every time a move was possible towards negotiations the United States "mucked it up"'. The prime minister thought aloud about the public position he would have to take. The bombing would have resumed. 'It was therefore very important to get something constructive into the Communique, something which showed that the Soviet Union and Britain were trying to work together. What he had in mind was a Communique which reflected the joint recognition of a sense of urgency and a joint responsibility to act in a way manifestly to assist both sides in reaching a negotiated settlement.' It would go beyond a reference to the responsibilities of the co-chairmen. He showed Bruce and Cooper a draft.

Cooper suggested that the Friday message (Rostow's) 'might have improved the British position as an intermediary by showing that the Prime Minister was in an independent position vis-à-vis the United States'. He emphasised that the decision to suspend the resumption of the bombing till Kosygin left Britain had been an 'extremely difficult' one. It had indeed prevented a walkout, Wilson responded, but he 'could not understand the Americans even contemplating resuming the bombing while Mr Kosygin was here'. He would have liked the resumption to have been further postponed, so as to extend the opportunity of bringing the two sides together. Whenever it took place, it would shock world opinion. 'The fact that bombing was resumed would, he thought—thinking aloud—possibly allow him to take a more independent line in public. Our relationship with the United States did not mean that we must automatically back everything the Americans did.'

The meeting then considered whether the PM should send a message to the president, and if so, in what terms. It was agreed that he should state that he was in 'a hell of a position', but that he would try to nail Kosygin down to 'a continuing responsibility for Vietnam'. He would conclude by suggesting he visit Washington, since he felt 'an urgent need to re-establish a personal relationship with the President'. He hoped the president might welcome the communiqué in some way. British public opinion could be 'stabilized if the Government moved into a somewhat more independent position'. But 'things might not ever be the same again. Trust had been broken. ... neither side wanted another Suez. It was essential for the United States to put matters back on an even keel again.' But it would have to accept that he would stand by the earlier letter handed to Kosygin, not the later one.

The meeting considered the tactics to be followed with Kosygin. If there was no breakdown with Kosygin on Sunday, or if there was 'a glimmer of hope', Brown wondered if Bruce could secure a further suspension of the bombing. Bruce thought he might if there were 'a real break-through'. In that case, Wilson said, he would phone the president. Cooper added that if there were 'a situation of hope, not amounting to a break-through', it might be possible to restrict the resumed bombing to the southern areas of North Vietnam. Politically that would not help, Wilson said. 'World opinion, and indeed the Communists', would draw no distinction of the areas … being bombed or not bombed.'[142]

Wilson now sent two further messages to Johnson. The first pointed out that he would be in 'a hell of a situation' when he met Kosygin. The Soviet PM would doubt Wilson's credibility, and would himself have lost credibility in Hanoi. It was unlikely that any definitive progress could be made towards a settlement, but Wilson had to get Kosygin into 'as relaxed a posture as possible'. On the vital question—whether a cessation of bombing depended on a secret prior assurance from Hanoi that infiltration would stop or, as it now appeared, would occur only after infiltration had stopped—he faced 'very great difficulties'. On the Friday Kosygin had suddenly bitten hard on what Wilson had said, namely that all that was required was a private assurance that infiltration would stop, and that was because he knew, as Wilson did not, that the message to Hanoi was the tougher one. 'He thought I was telling him something new. I thought I was merely repeating what I had told him earlier with as I thought your authority.' He asked for a copy in writing, and told Wilson in the evening he had reported it to Brezhnev.

Wilson could get out of this position only by saying that he was not in the president's confidence, or that there was a sudden change in Washington that, 'as a loyal satellite', he had to follow. 'I cannot say either.' He would stand by the document he had given Kosygin before Rostow's message arrived, and tell him that if he would go along with it, 'I will similarly press it on you'. Kosygin no longer said he had nothing to do with the question: he now said Russia and Britain had to try to get a settlement. Wilson wanted to 'nail him to this position', though he must be disappointed that nothing happened during Tet, a time he had chosen for his visit. Both had to move to 'a slightly more central position', each, like lawyers representing clients, trying 'to get a settlement out of court ad referendum to the two clients'. If Kosygin accepted 'a continuing responsibility', it would be helpful if the president made some favourable reference after the communiqué. In view of the breakdown in communication during the past week, Wilson concluded, it was clear that he and the president should meet 'very soon'.[143]

In his second telegram Wilson expressed his surprise that if his first communication to Kosygin was going to be repudiated, he was not told earlier. Kosygin had been trying to put pressure on Hanoi, though others did not agree with him. 'He climbed out on a limb trusting in my confident assertion of where you stood. Now his enemies in Hanoi and perhaps in Moscow will be saying he was wrong to be misled by me.' Wilson hoped he could re-establish trust. 'I have known these Russians for 20 years and this week I have been trying to cash the cheque I have painfully built up over this time.'[144]

The president replied 'within a short space of time'.[145] He did not believe 'that the matter hangs on the tense of verbs'. Moscow had the two-phase formulation from Brown in November, and Hanoi had it from the Poles. It had shown no interest, and used three periods of no bombing—Christmas, New Year and Tet—for large-scale military movement and preparation. 'I wish someone would produce a real live North Vietnamese prepared to talk.' All Kosygin had done was to endorse the foreign minister's interview with Burchett. Operationally, the US could not stop bombing while three or four divisions dashed south from the DMZ before the promise took effect.

The president did not accept that the US statement of 7 February was inconsistent with the message to Hanoi or the formula of 10 February. On 7 February the US asked for an 'assured stoppage' of infiltration. In Wilson's version of the A-B formula, that became an assurance that infiltration 'will stop'. That was 'quite a different matter. We so recognized promptly … and telephoned Burke Trend that we were drafting and would transmit our response shortly.' No formula could be satisfactory to the US—or perhaps Hanoi—unless there were clarity on two matters: 'The timing of a cessation of bombing, cessation of infiltration, and no further augmentation of forces'; 'How assurance in the matter of infiltration will be established.' The cessation of bombing and stoppage of augmentation would, as Wilson recognised, be public.

Johnson ended by expressing appreciation for Wilson's effort. He would do so publicly. 'I'm always glad to know that you are in my corner but I would have some difficulty … in giving anyone a power of attorney. I hope for peace more than you can possibly know and will be much interested in what happens at Chequers.'[146]

Wilson took the point that in an interval between the cessation of bombing and the stoppage of infiltration, Hanoi might rush three or four divisions through the DMZ. He suggested that the prior two-way assurance might contain a timetable if possible underwritten by the Russians. 'What might be provided is that you would agree in advance to stop the bombing in return for their prior assurance that they would stop the infiltration, say six hours afterwards, or an even shorter timetable if that was considered necessary.' He might air the idea in talking to Kosygin that (Sunday) night. The PM added that he had not used the phrase 'power of attorney'. The key words were 'ad referendum'.[147]

The scene shifted to Chequers. Arrangements were made for a direct link between 'a responsible member of the United States Administration' in Washington and Cooper, who was installed in the 'Prison Room'—Lady Jane Grey's 'pathetic graffiti' could still be seen on the walls[148]—with a supply of food and drink and kept in touch with the conversations downstairs. The discussion with Kosygin dealt first with the communiqué. Kosygin rejected the draft passage on Vietnam prepared by Wilson and shown to Cooper and Bruce the night before. His own draft was unacceptable to the British side. Cooper and Murray prepared a redraft based on the Russian draft, which Brown negotiated with Ambassador Soldatov after dinner. The Russians accepted all but two of the points the British thought desirable.[149]

Last-Minute Proposal

Meanwhile, Wilson had persuaded Kosygin to agree to a short break. He held a quick meeting in the Prison Room, in which he outlined a last-minute proposal he would put to Kosygin if Johnson agreed. Trend, Palliser, MacLehose and Murray drafted it, and Wilson, who had rejoined Kosygin, had a quick look at it. Cooper telephoned the gist to the State Department, and Palliser sent immediate confirmation to Rostow through the private line to the White House.[150] The PM proposed to tell Kosygin that if he could get a North Vietnamese assurance before 10am that all movement of troops and supplies across the 17th parallel would stop, he would get an American assurance that the bombing would not be resumed. The timetable, Palliser added, was appallingly tight: Kosygin left Chequers in two hours' time.[151] The president, 'prepared to go the last mile', agreed that Wilson should go ahead. With the deal 'consummated, we would, of course, be prepared to move promptly to a neutral spot to engage in unconditional negotiations designed to bring peace to the area'.[152]

His reply had, however, not been received by the time Kosygin and his party left Chequers at 11pm. Shortly after, Rostow phoned Cooper and said that a favourable reply was on its way to Downing Street. It arrived shortly after midnight.[153] The PM put the proposal to Kosygin at Claridges about 1.30am. Kosygin said there was nothing new in it: it was repetition. That Wilson denied. At present there was a kind of unofficial extension of Tet: the bombing had not resumed. What the American message was saying was that if while the extended Tet continued there was an assurance that there would be no North Vietnamese movements to the South, then 'by the following night the same result would have been achieved as if the A and B formula had been in operation'. The proposal, Kosygin said, was in ultimatum form: the Americans were requiring an answer in seven hours. Wilson said he would try to get an extension. But he and Brown insisted that peace was available, and urged Kosygin to give the message his full backing in Hanoi. Kosygin agreed to pass the proposals straight to Moscow and ask for them to be passed to Hanoi. 'But he did not expect success. … the North Vietnamese could not be expected to abandon the South or to declare that all movement of supplies to the South would stop.' All that was asked, said Brown, was that divisions should stop moving through the DMZ.

Kosygin repeated that the North Vietnamese would not accept the proposals. They could only agree to what the foreign minister had said.[154]

Back at No. 10, Wilson telephoned Rostow to enquire about the possibility of an extension of up to 24 hours. The president was much concerned about the record.[155] Framing his answer in consultation with Rostow—drafting 'one would think', as Wilson later put it, 'for his local domestic gallery'[156]—he offered another six hours.[157] The message arrived in London at 6am. It would mean that bombing would recommence at 4pm GMT or at first light on the 14th in Vietnam. No word had meanwhile been received from Kosygin, and on the train to Gatwick Wilson and Brown told him of the new limit.

At 12.30pm Gore-Booth phoned the Soviet ambassador to make sure he could contact the Foreign Office if a reply from Moscow came through while Kosygin was in the air. At 3.15 he phoned again to ask if a message was on the way, and when Mikhail Smirnovsky said not, he asked him to phone Moscow to enquire. Smirnovsky was reluctant but said he would 'see what he could do'. A line was kept open between the FO and Cooper at the US embassy. Murray pointed out that the plane would not reach Moscow till 4.30pm, just after the deadline. Cooper subsequently told Gore-Booth that 'we could count on an hour beyond the deadline without specifically asking Washington', and a little later he told Murray that the timetable would be sufficiently flexible to enable Kosygin to land and phone someone. No reply was received from the Soviet embassy or from Moscow. At 5.40pm Downing Street received a message from Rostow to say US aircraft were on their way, though in fact Operation Junction City began only on 22 February.[158] Cooper had left London on the morning of the 14th.[159]

Kosygin had phoned Brezhnev—he was 'overheard (by telephone intercept)'—and told him there was 'a great possibility of achieving the aim. … All they need to do is to give a confidential declaration.'[160] Ilya Shcherbakov, the ambassador in Hanoi, told Pham Van Dong on the 13th, but the North Vietnamese were 'unmoved'.[161] What should be looked for, Kosygin told Llewellyn Thompson, were 'constructive steps', certainly not ultimata: the US should not send messages 'that something should be done by ten o'clock for it would receive reply that would make it necessary to start all over again'.[162] Ho Chi Minh replied to Johnson's message that talks could begin only after the cessation of bombing and all acts of war. 'The Vietnamese people will never give way to force; it will never accept conversation under the clear threat of bombs.'[163]

Aftermath

The communiqué of 13 February said that there had been a prolonged exchange of views. Both sides affirmed their adherence to the principles of 1954 and 1962 and set forth their views on ways to bring peace. They would maintain contact.[164] The most important aspect of the discussions, Gore-Booth told French Ambassador de Courcel on the 14th, was that the Russians had 'departed from their previous attitude of detachment': Kosygin had shown that the Soviet government felt involved. The French government, Courcel said, thought that the bombing should stop first. That would mean, Gore-Booth said, calling on the Americans to give up 'what they considered to be one of their most important arms in return for talks which (like the Korean talks at Panmunjom) might last for two years; the Americans would thus be giving something very substantial for, possibly, nothing'. He told Courcel that the SU, the US and the UK had made 'a really impressive effort to bring the war to an end, and a very small response indeed from Hanoi would have brought about success'. The work done was not, however, wasted: 'while it was a tragedy that more people would get killed and that the opportunity brought about by a truce had been missed, machinery for bringing about peace had been created and reinforced and, as the Prime Minister had insisted, would be available in future.'[165]

Wilson, however, was, of course, quite unhappy with the outcome. McNamara was apprehensive that he would 'try to make himself a hero' and maintain that 'if things didn't succeed it was really not his fault but ours'.[166] His statement in Parliament was, however, moderate.[167] But the State Department disliked his disclosure that agreement had been 'very near', as it put the US on the spot, since the proposal had been put only to Prime Minister Ky, and not mentioned to Australia or New Zealand.[168] And on 24 February he talked to Rostow, who allowed him to 'unload his feelings'.[169] The same day he also met Rapacki at No. 10, raised the question of Lewandowski, and alluded to the 'misunderstandings' during the Kosygin visit.[170]

In addition, the prime minister wanted to write to the president about the failure of the conversations. He felt that there was 'something of a breakdown in our communications during that week', and that it must have had some effect on Kosygin. The text of 7 February had been transmitted to Washington, and the British felt confident it was 'in full accord' with the president's views. On the 10th, when Brown and he went over the ground again without departing at all from what was said on the 7th, Kosygin seemed to see something 'new and encouraging in what we said', and it was put in writing. When it was reported to Washington, a message from the White House in effect withdrew it, 'and at the same time was equally a derogation from Tuesday's message'. The Sunday night message was gratefully received. Kosygin thought it was too much of an ultimatum, but Wilson believed he had commended it. He could not understand, he concluded, how the Tuesday message could have been in Washington for three days without his being told that it was on the wrong lines, and he hoped that the president could enquire what went wrong. He would also be glad to know whether the message of Sunday night still represented the position, 'however dark immediate prospects may look'.[171]

With the concurrence of Gore-Booth and de la Mare, Murray strongly opposed sending such a letter. The president did not think Hanoi was willing to talk at present, and probably believed that even if different but US-endorsed proposals had been put through Kosygin, the North Vietnamese would have responded with 'an uncompromising "no"'. The suggestion that he might hold an inquest into what went wrong might increase his frustration and not clear up the mystery, and, if he became irritated, 'the effect might be felt throughout Anglo-American relations, not only on the subject of Vietnam'. Currently Parliament and the public were reasonably satisfied that the UK, the US and the SU made a collaborative effort that was defeated by Hanoi's 'intransigence'. Reopening the question could lead to a leak about an Anglo-American argument. That 'would do us no good with the Americans and might make it more difficult, not less, to talk again to the Russians'. Accepting that there was a 'failure', the right time to remember it was when the FO was preparing for Brown's visit to Moscow in May, when it would be essential to reopen the Vietnam question. Then it would be necessary to have 'an absolutely firm understanding of American thinking'. When the PM visited Washington in early June, he could have a heart-to-heart talk with the president that would clear up 'any remaining issues of misunderstanding'. If the PM still felt he wanted to clear up the issue of the messages, Dean might be instructed to go over the whole ground with Rostow.[172]

Brown persuaded Wilson he should send just a short message. In the draft of that, he said he was worried about a deeper problem. He had discussed it with Rostow, and hoped the president could see Dean.

Meanwhile, he asked whether the message the president sent on 12 February to give to Kosygin still represented the position as he saw it.[173] FO officials were against any message. It would irritate the president, Murray argued, who had difficulties with Robert Kennedy on one side and the hawks on the other. The PM wanted to steer clear of mentioning the communication of 10 February and concentrate on the last-minute proposal. He was thus seeking to establish that the US proposal was that if the infiltration stopped, the bombing would also stop, and setting aside the separateness of the cessation of bombing. But the last-minute message was that if the North Vietnamese would immediately stop infiltration, the bombing would not resume. Now the position was slightly different.[174] No message should be sent, Gore-Booth insisted. If anything was to be done pending Wilson's visit, Dean should talk to Rostow.[175] Brown advised Wilson not to run the risk of irritating the president.[176]

The PM still thought the message should go. Rostow had probably not conveyed to Johnson a full and accurate picture of the 'very serious anxieties' he had expressed. 'I suspect that Rostow himself was largely responsible for the misunderstandings during the visit and I think he may well have reported to the President in the light of that responsibility.' Whether or not the president would be irritated, Wilson wanted him 'to be in no doubt of the fact that we are also worried at the way things went during that week. Moreover, while it could be argued that at a time when we need support from him over the German offset problem, we should not press him over Vietnam, I think on balance it is just as likely that he may feel some concern at the way things were handled in Washington while Kosygin was here and that a message reminding him of this could dispose himself sympathetically over offset.' He proposed to send the message.[177] Brown disagreed, but left the judgement to the PM, 'on the clear understanding that I would have made it the other way'.[178] The message went on 15 March.[179] The president replied. He would see Dean. His offers were still open.[180]

Palliser drew attention to the message the president had sent to Ho Chi Minh, which the FO had not seen, and Ho Chi Minh's reply, reiterating the Four Points, published in *The Times* on 22 March. Palliser pointed out the discrepancy between that message and the one Wilson had been authorised to give Kosygin on the 7th. The 'charitable explanation', Palliser wrote, was that the Americans themselves at first did not realise the discrepancy, and that it was 'loose drafting'; or that 'pressure was brought to bear on the President', and he toughened up the message sent to Ho, perhaps some 24 hours after the one sent to London. If so, 'why were we not told'? The 'uncharitable explanation' was that the 'hawks' got it toughened up, but were not prepared to tell the British about it before Wilson's first communication to Kosygin forced them to. 'Either way, the White House does not emerge with much credit.' Dean should be fully briefed.[181] The 'uncharitable explanation' seems to be the right one. And then the new 'Geneva' proposal, handed over at the banquet, gave Rostow the opportunity for a decisive rejection.

In the conversation Dean had, the president said he did not want to discuss the past, and so he had no opportunity to get across 'the damaging consequences of the long delay—between the Tuesday and the Friday night—in informing us of the change in the American position'. But Rostow's 'inability to hold his tongue', or perhaps his 'honesty', offered the information the British needed. Palliser's conclusion was that there was 'a fairly substantial change in American policy at the beginning of the Kosygin week', and that not only were the British not informed of it, 'whether deliberately or through inefficiency', but nor were Bruce and Cooper. 'I suspect that it is the realization by Rostow of their failure to keep their own special representative in the picture that impelled him to say … that in future there should be no question of the President having a special representative in London "even though no fault can possibly be laid at Chet Cooper's door".' The president realised that he and Rostow were at fault, but, as Dean said, he would never admit it. Palliser recommended that Wilson should not press the matter any further, at least until he saw the president himself.[182] 'I'm going to raise this very strongly in Washington,' the PM wrote, '—possibly at lunch.'[183]

Looking back on 'Kosygin week', Brown regretted that the PM's private secretary managed to get to Euston. 'Had I been consulted, I'd have said no, let them get it in the morning. They don't have a cipher machine on the night sleeper to Edinburgh and the Russians can't do anything with the message on the train. If we had waited until morning we should have had several hours to try to get hold of Washington, to urge them not to be so bloody silly. But I wasn't consulted.'[184] In his memoirs Gore-Booth refers to that criticism. 'With the gift of hindsight', he could see what the action should have been: a message to Kosygin to say they had received a worrying message and were checking it with Washington; and meanwhile he might wish to suspend current discussions and action. 'I was at home and was not consulted either.' At the end of a hard week, he might not have given the right answer anyway. Brown was 'technically right', but the error was not merely technical. There were 'strains within the British team at the top level. When such strains exist, there is almost certain sooner or later to be an error of top level decision and this was it.'[185] Differing over Geneva in this case,

Wilson and Brown were seldom in entire agreement, and the former had not consulted the latter.

'A historic opportunity had been missed.' Wilson blamed Rostow and the hawks. Two years later, he told a visiting US statesman 'that, in terms of influence on his master, the more I saw of certain of the White House advisers the more I thought that Rasputin was a much-maligned man.'[186] '[T]he whole thing petered out,' Brown thought, '… mainly because the American system is what it is, and the White House and the state department often seem not to know what the other is doing.' The hot line was 'not as reliable as it ought to have been. … part of the matter was that Mr Johnson did not like the Prime Minister very much, and the hot line from No. 10 that went allegedly direct to the President was inclined instead to go to Mr Rostow.'[187]

'The Russians wanted the world, especially the Communist world, to believe that they were the people the Vietnamese would listen to,' Brown thought. But Hanoi 'listened chiefly to China'. 'I'm pretty sure the Russians led us up the garden, and that Mr Kosygin never had any real authority to do what he claimed to be doing.'[188] Soviet officials, Ang Cheng Guan indeed concludes, were apparently greatly concerned that Kosygin's mediation efforts might 'diminish Soviet credibility and influence in Hanoi as well as its revolutionary leadership vis-à-vis the Chinese. This concern plus the U.S. bombing threat made it very difficult for Kosygin to play an effective mediating role.'[189]

Perhaps consoling himself, Wilson thought that something had been gained, a view Gore-Booth put to Courcel. 'In London,' *The Times* reported, 'it is reckoned a most hopeful sign that Mr Kosygin has now freely conceded, more than once, that peace in Vietnam is a Russian interest.' There was agreement 'that Moscow should use its influence on Hanoi—which Mr Wilson appears to think could be considerable—to bring the war to an end'.[190] In the House of Commons, he made the references that so annoyed the State Department, and in a later TV broadcast he referred 'mysteriously' to the 'intricate mechanism' that could be readily activated. David Wood, the political correspondent of *The Times*, wondered what it was.[191] Perhaps Wilson wanted to feel that he had established an arrangement with Kosygin that could at some point be effectively operated after all. But that assumed that the hawks could be overcome in Washington, and that Hanoi would take advice as well as armaments from Moscow.

At the Cabinet meeting on 14 February Richard Crossman had been pleased to puncture the prime minister's assertion that he and Kosygin had on two occasions during the week been on the edge of success, and that 'the mechanism for peace negotiations has now been established and in the coming months they would succeed'.[192] 'For all the excitement generated by Wilson during Kosygin's visit to London,' Louis Heren wrote, 'the British initiative was a bit of a joke. … There was no opportunity for so-called honest brokers, and after the Kosygin visit Johnson doubted Wilson's honesty.'[193] Kosygin's reaction may, however, lend some support to his British counterpart. 'What was really gained by restarting the bombing without waiting three or four more days?' he asked Ambassador Thompson. Only China profited from the US/SU failure to solve the Vietnam problem. It wanted the war to continue. It had triumphed, and the Chinese could say 'all those efforts were nothing but a masquerade'.[194]

Perhaps the British initiatives of 1966–67—Brown's as well as Wilson's—were always doomed: neither side was ready to stop yet. Or maybe there was just sufficient leeway to justify them, and to argue against the drawbacks of hopeless attempts. And the objective was after all worth pursuing, not merely as a way of appeasing the Left or responding to public opinion.

CHAPTER EIGHT
Committed Detachment

FO officials believed that ministers had tended to overrate Britain's ability to influence the Vietnam situation. A paper advocating 'committed detachment' was hammered out, but in the event not considered by Cabinet. Wilson continued to work on the Russians, though the co-chairmen had no direct role in the discussions that made a faltering start in Paris after the president announced his decision not to seek re-election.

The failure of the Kosygin talks to advance the prospect of peace in Vietnam was a deep disappointment to Wilson. It was not only a question of appeasing the left wing of his Labour Party, though after the 1966 election it was less restrained and its approach more widely shared. Nor was it a matter only of meeting a public opinion that, in Britain and elsewhere, deplored the bombing and, more generally, the way the war was being fought and was increasingly being mobilised and organised. It was a sign that Britain was no longer playing a world role, no longer, perhaps, capable of so doing. In trying to do so, Wilson was only showing that up.

The fundamental reason was, of course, Britain's failure to rehabilitate its economy. There lay another disappointment: the 'white-hot' technological revolution of which the PM had spoken failed to come about. From the earliest days of his ministry, the Treasury had argued that Britain could not afford to continue the world role of which the PM and others spoke. Cuts, especially in defence spending, became urgent. In Southeast Asia, they were deferred, despite Callaghan's protest, because of the commitment to Malaysia: what had begun as an attempt to retain the Singapore base a little longer, while unloading colonial Borneo, had led to a large-scale deployment of British forces against Indonesia's Confrontation. When the September 30 movement ended Sukarno's dominance, the British looked for an early reduction of their commitment. After Confrontation had ended in 1966 they were in July 1967 to announce what amounted to an end of their strategic role in Southeast Asia.

Neither his predecessors nor Wilson had been ready to commit troops to the Vietnam struggle. Their vision of the future of Southeast Asia was, it would seem, not far from the one articulated by officials in the FO as early as the mid-1950s and sometimes penetrating ministerial statements. The region should be one of independent states, living alongside one another, and not cat's paws of outside powers. It should be 'neutralised'. That had not been US policy, and, because of their overall dependence on the US, the British were not able to advocate it. Their view of the two Geneva conferences—in both of which they played a central role—differed from that of their allies, who had reluctantly taken part. Britain had wanted the US to be present in Southeast Asia after 1949, but not to make war.

The potential to influence US policy had been an argument for retaining Singapore. It accorded with the posture post-war governments had long pursued: Britain would offer wise advice, the Athenians to the New Romans across the Atlantic. Retaining forces in the East meant that they could argue that they were acting together and should share policymaking. That never worked very well. With Confrontation it worked still less well. By early 1964 Home's government was having to modify a Cambodian policy sympathetic to Sihanouk's neutralism in order to wean the Americans away from a pro-Indonesian approach during Confrontation.

A believer in personal diplomacy, his successor hoped to influence LBJ. But there were other issues on which Britain needed American support—the security of Europe and the stability of the pound among them—and it was impossible to win it with an offer of military help in Vietnam that, no matter how limited it might be, would symbolise a commitment. It became more a matter of offering—or, rather, not withdrawing—diplomatic support. That had some value for President Johnson, since Britain was still a significant European state, while France was critical of his policy. But it was not surprising that Wilson's personal diplomacy was not accepted with any warmth. Indeed, a vein of contempt can be found in many of the president's utterances in the White House. He was, of course, a man not easily persuaded, all the more perhaps because, beset by conflicting pressures and differing agencies and advisers, he was unsure that he had adopted the right strategy or was pursuing the right tactics. The chances that Britain could exert an influence from a depleted base were slim indeed.

Wilson looked to the Russians, co-chairman at Geneva, in the hope that they could exert an influence on Hanoi and so bring the North Vietnamese nearer to the terms for discussion or negotiation that Johnson laid out. Their attitude was seen to depend not only on intra-Politburo rivalries but on the attitude of the Chinese. From the later 1950s the PRC challenged the Russians for leadership of the world Communist movement on the basis that they were too ready to compromise, not revolutionary enough. In practice, the Chinese were bold in words but cautious in deeds. Their encouragement of revolution did not imply open intervention in support, but it did involve training and supplies as well as verbal endorsement and men behind the lines. The SU felt obliged not to take too firm a contrary line, and indeed to offer the Vietnamese weapons, including missiles, to resist the Americans, though much of what they supplied had to go through Chinese territory.

The idea that, but for the Chinese, the Russians could have influenced the North Vietnamese to the extent the British hoped may, however, have been mistaken, and the influence the Chinese had on them was almost certainly exaggerated. The North Vietnamese were very much their own men. Viewing this as a proxy war is misleading. And they were determined to reunify Vietnam. Though the FO aimed at a Southeast Asia of nation-states, officials too seldom recognised the nationalist element in the North Vietnamese cause. Creating an independent South Vietnam—generally said to be the US objective—was never conceivable in North Vietnam. What the Americans, or indeed Foreign Secretary Stewart, called 'aggression' the North Vietnamese could not see that way.

To some extent, perhaps, the British were captured by the rhetoric of the Americans. That shifted almost imperceptibly over time. In 1954 the talk, loose as it was, was about the partition of Vietnam, intended to be temporary. Supported by the US, the government in Saigon, heir to the State of Vietnam set up by the French under the former Emperor Bao Dai, rivalled the Democratic Republic, proclaimed by Ho Chi Minh in Hanoi in 1945. But as time went by the talk came to be of 'South Vietnam', against which the 'North Vietnamese' were the aggressors. The Saigon government indeed for the most part played down the notion that it might aim at ruling all Vietnam. But in fact this was a civil war in which outside powers, above all the US, were intervening. No doubt it seemed better to present that as the protection of a small state against 'Communist' aggression. But that did not make it easier to promote peace negotiations.

What the venue and format of negotiations might be was also at issue. Though, as secretary-general, Thant made various proposals, the UN was not a realistic option, given that neither China nor the Vietnams were members. The most obvious option was a third or a reconvened Geneva, though the US had never endorsed the agreements made at the first Geneva, and the North Vietnamese had been disappointed by it. Increasingly the emphasis was on bilateral US-North Vietnam negotiations, though that still raised the question of the participation of the FLN and indeed of the RVN.

Officials in the FO/FCO had sometimes argued that the UK could play no role, though they had loyally followed ministers who for whatever reason decided otherwise. After the initiative the British took during the Kosygin visit, de la Mare suggested that ministers might wish to review the situation in East Asia and its implications for British policy. Party and public opinion at home required that the government should be seen to be active in trying to bring about an end to the war. 'Our dilemma is that as long as Her Majesty's government are *seen* to be active their activities will not succeed. They may placate hostile or critical opinion at home but *they will not bring about or hasten the end of the war*.'

Overemphasising the role of China, de la Mare argued that the regime in North Vietnam was 'not waging this war as a completely sovereign power'. Either it was so much under China's domination that it was in reality China that was at war with the US and its allies, or it was 'so afraid of Chinese retaliation if it tries to end the war that it is no longer a free agent'. If the former were the case Britain had no role to play, since it had no influence in Peking. If the latter were the case, Britain had no *public* role to play, though it might secretly exert a little influence. The North Vietnamese took the risk of offending the Chinese with the Burchett interview, but had since been warned by the Chinese not to get involved in peace moves. They would ignore that warning only if sure that the negotiation would be secret. Every public initiative could only increase the difficulties of the North Vietnamese. Britain should therefore seek to discourage reconvening Geneva or UN intervention.

'Public silence is not synonymous with private inactivity. The greatest success of British diplomacy in East Asia in recent years, the ending of confrontation with Indonesia, was achieved by our maintaining strict operational silence. Success required that we content ourselves with a secret and self-effacing rôle and allow the appearance to be given that the negotiations were a bilateral matter between Indonesia and Malaysia.'[1] There were 'two presentational drawbacks'. First, opinion in Britain wanted to see it play 'a public and overt rôle'. Second, it enhanced 'the impression already widely held in the area and elsewhere that Britain wishes to dissociate herself from East Asian affairs'. They were drawbacks Britain had to live with. 'We are faced with the choice either of pleasing that element of public opinion which wants dramatic and much publicised initiatives, or of doing what we think right to try to bring the war to an end as soon as possible. We cannot do both at the same time, for they are incompatible.'

The second drawback, de la Mare continued, affected the area generally, and would become greater 'when the extent of our further military cuts becomes known. Irrespective of the rights and wrongs of these proposed cuts they will make a bad impression and have the wrong effect in the area.' The 'local people' did not want the British to go. 'In the past two years, and particularly since the end of Confrontation, there has been a great upsurge of feeling and resolve by the local people that they must play a bigger and more positive part in the shaping of their own destiny.' While the Vietnam War was going on, a 'radical and positive change in East Asian thinking has taken place'. But they recognised that they could not go it alone and that they still needed Western support. 'They are glad of massive American help, but find the American presence oppressive because it is so massive and they do not have full confidence in American judgment or in American methods. They want us there not as rivals of the Americans but as a reassuring if small counterweight.'

Here, however, was another dilemma. 'We know what we should *say* but what can we *do*? East Asia is becoming politically and economically an interesting proposition at the very moment when we have no more money to invest in it. We shall continue to maintain a limited military presence; but a military presence, even though locally welcome, is a negative role as long as it is maintained only for military purposes.' The forces retained in the area should be put to useful work, de la Mare argued. 'Our military presence should be, in the truest sense of the term, a Peace Corps.' He also recommended better coordination of the development and technical aid that Britain was still able to undertake in East Asia. Britain must show that it was still interested in the area. If it allowed the impression to grow that it was not, 'we shall not only lose our political influence but ... also make it much harder ... to get into the new and attractive markets which are certainly going to develop there'.[2]

The FO's Steering Committee suggested that the first argument should proceed from the PM's advocacy of secret diplomacy in the House of Commons on 14 February. The need to eschew public initiatives would have to be put to ministers with care. The second argument raised a question: how could the FO ensure that some of the defence savings were devoted to other purposes?[3] Further papers were prepared,[4] but the initiative was submerged in intra-departmental discussion, and curbed by the continuing financial crisis.

Meanwhile bombing continued, including in April 1967 attacks on Haiphong, despite Thompson's doubts that graduated bombing would induce negotiation.[5] A high-level DRV delegation visited Beijing and Moscow during Junction City. China argued that the North Vietnamese should persist in their struggle; the SU recommended a diplomatic solution.

But—although the DRV relied more heavily on Russian equipment than Chinese—Moscow could not induce it to negotiate, while refusing support would only enhance China's influence in Hanoi.[6]

Brown in Moscow Again

British ministers did not abandon their attempts to bring about negotiations. Vietnam was a topic during Brown's visit to Moscow late in May. He got nowhere, however. The failure of the efforts of both Britain and the SU during the Kosygin visit had been followed by an escalation of the conflict, he began, but he still thought the co-chairmen had a responsibility 'to try to find a way through'. His position was still the same. 'He could deliver the Americans on a wide range of possibilities which could lead to a de-escalation of the conflict, to bringing the parties concerned together in private, or to negotiations.' But there was still 'no indication of what Hanoi really wanted', nor of what Gromyko might do to '"deliver Hanoi" for any of the possibilities he had mentioned'.

The US, Gromyko responded, had extended its bombing. The first step was to stop it. Contacts in embryo were established at one time, but the Americans 'blew them up'. The action was surely 'part of some perfidious plan'. Americans 'talked of peace but continued to make war'. Sometimes they spoke of implementing the Geneva agreements, but it was they who were violating them in the first place. The Vietnamese were not going to give up. The SU would increase the assistance it was giving them.

Brown said he could contest many of Gromyko's remarks, but he did not wish to apportion blame. 'The most important point was whether Mr Gromyko felt strongly that the way must be found to bring the war to a halt. Simply to say that the United States must leave Viet-Nam got one nowhere. This was not going to happen. A way must be found for bringing the two parties together after, or conceivably before, a significant reduction of military activity.' No matter how many proposals he had made and urged on the US, he had never succeeded in obtaining a response from Hanoi or its friends 'as to what the response would be'. Could Gromyko make some suggestions? 'It was from the Soviet side that some suggestions must come, if Mr Brown were to succeed in persuading the Americans to stop.'

'When the delicate threads of contacts had been there, they had been roughly torn by the United States,' Gromyko replied, 'not by some political action but by increasing their military activities in the grossest possible way.' They should stop their bombing and withdraw. The Soviet government, he added, had noticed 'that Allies and friends of Britain, even members of the

Commonwealth, were becoming involved in the conflict and were sending forces to Viet-Nam'. Britain could work for peace by using its influence against that: Australia and New Zealand were involved, and now there was 'pressure on Malaysia'. They were, Brown commented, 'independent sovereign Powers', and Britain had 'no way of preventing them if they interpreted their obligations under some pact or alliance as involving them in the conflict'.

The foreign secretary asked four questions in order, he said, to see whether Gromyko thought they might find a way for getting the process of negotiation started. First, the North Vietnamese government required that the bombing should be seen to have stopped unconditionally, while the American needed to know what would happen thereafter. 'Could the Soviet Government say what Hanoi would do if the bombing stopped?' Second, it might be said that the US should not have engaged in ground operations in the DMZ, 'but then others should not already have been there. Could not the Co-Chairmen take action 'to pull the two sides apart? He was confident that he could persuade the Americans to move back if the Soviet Government could persuade others to move back. This too might be a way forward.' Third, 'had Mr Gromyko any ideas for getting the interested parties together in secret? Were there any steps that could be taken to bring this about?' Fourth, he mentioned a proposal Gromyko had not previously liked. 'Was it still out of the question that the Geneva Conference be reconvened as a starting point?'

Stopping the bombing would 'create a more favourable atmosphere', Gromyko responded, 'but he could not give a timetable of what the Viet-Namese would then do. No one could put a concrete plan on the table in advance. Indeed, the demands for a plan of action before the cessation of the bombing amounted to an ultimatum which the North Viet-Namese had already quite justifiably rejected.' As for actions in the DMZ, they should be 'put in the context of American aggression in Viet-Nam. Responsibility for the consequences rested with the United States Government. So far as contacts were concerned he could see no new conditions for the establishment of these. There had been certain unofficial contacts, but these had been destroyed by the United States.' As for using the Geneva conference for establishing contacts, 'the Soviet Government did not regard the existing situation as being propitious for such a step at present. In view of the continuing American aggression this was not a realistic proposal.' The remarks, Brown said, were 'very disappointing'.[7]

Gromyko showed, Brown told Wilson, that the Soviet government would not help on Vietnam. 'But his gramophone records were not strident. ... His attitude has been consistent with Soviet inability to move in Hanoi, and though he has dropped no hint of this, my guess is that this is the real position.' The Middle East—where Israel had launched the Six-Day War on 5 June 1967—occupied all the time Brown had with Kosygin.[8]

Wilson in Washington Again

Prime minister and president discussed Vietnam at the White House on 2 June. 'The Prime Minister was made familiar with the latest state of the polls on all subjects, particularly the pro-"hawk" polls on Vietnam and the increase in Presidential popularity whenever he acted or looked like a "hawk".' Wilson asked Johnson what his intentions were. Did he intend to invade the North? There was no question of that, Johnson replied: 'he was not going to do it.' As for the DMZ, the PM thought that the president's action was the most defensible of the actions he had taken that were criticised in the UK: it 'seemed to be designed to corral the issue rather than to extend it. If ... the President was attempting to stop infiltration through this area by cordoning off the entry routes', that seemed the right strategy. 'But he trusted that the President was not intending to cross the river.' The president denied 'any intention of doing so'. On escalation, Wilson quoted Kosygin on 'the danger of Chinese intervention'.

That brought him to the events of February, on which he had proposed to speak 'very strongly'.[9] 'The Prime Minister dealt lightly with the responsibility for the February shambles, but stressed the possible grave consequences and the need to ensure that it could not happen again.' He recalled the revision of the messages for Kosygin and said he had been left to choose among three theories: that the US had not kept Britain in its confidence; that there had been a change of policy under the pressure of the 'hawks'; or that 'there was a state of unutterable, anatomical confusion in the higher part of the administration'. Wilson said his view was the second, and Johnson 'did not try to deny this'.

The president felt that the Russians did not have—and had never had—the 'power to deliver' in Hanoi. In 1966, for example, after Gromyko had said that there was no hope of a settlement unless the US stated publicly its willingness to withdraw, he had said at Manila that it would withdraw six months after a settlement, but there had been no reaction whatever. Wilson drew Johnson's attention to two significant points. First, though he had no firm evidence, he thought Kosygin's visit had been timed for Tet. Second, 'there was the dramatic change in Kosygin's whole attitude towards involvement in the search for peace which first emerged during his visit'. Both the points 'suggested that, whether permanently or for one moment of time, Kosygin felt that he was in a position of influence'.

The president said he had been 'thinking hard' about his Vietnam policy. 'One fine morning in the near future he would probably drop a bombshell that would send everyone reeling.' The present policy was not achieving results, and was incurring increasing costs, particularly in terms of planes lost. 'He had given the generals their head, but of the 100 strategic targets on which they had insisted, they had already systematically bombed 85. He therefore intended at the right moment to change the policy, to confine the effort principally to the South, but also of course to continue to hit supply lines, desisting for a possibly considerable period ahead from any attack on the industrial infrastructure (the Prime Minister's phrase) of North Vietnam.' He would then see what the reaction was, 'having regard to all the North Vietnamese promises that, if he stopped the bombing, they would come to the conference table or produce a corresponding degree of de-escalation'. That would help him with 'part of his domestic pressure', and no doubt help the PM.

Wilson 'greatly welcomed' the intention but felt that the president should 'plan the diplomatic side more carefully'. He should be in close touch with Britain about the timing, and they could jointly consider whether, either through Dobrynin or through the British channel, they 'might try to get Russia interested'. The president did not attempt to argue—as Rusk had in Bonn, and he and Rusk had during the visit Brown had made to Washington in April—that Russia was taking 'a much stiffer line both on Vietnam and generally. The Prime Minister agreed that it was an open question whether Russia ever had any real influence in Vietnam, but added that it was equally arguable that, if they thought they had, that influence had been lost through a re-alignment of forces in Hanoi following the events of 10th February. The same question must be asked about Kosygin's position. Was he out on a limb in February and was he to some extent discredited by what then happened?'

Wilson had breakfast with Vice-President Hubert Humphrey on 3 June 1967. He said he was 'much reassured' by what the president said on escalation. Humphrey commented that this was 'what he had been fighting for and that the President had shown great courage and firmness in resisting the combined pressures of the four Chiefs of Staff'.[10]

Wilson visited Paris soon after his return from Washington. The FO provided him with talking points on Vietnam. In February, he might say, 'we got very near to breaking the deadlock on Vietnam'. He was not prepared to blame the Americans for failure, nor Kosygin, 'who showed quite clearly to me that he was prepared to engage in the search for a solution'. Hanoi was the enigma. The Russians might have had some influence there in January and February. 'But if they used it, the effort was self-evidently inadequate. What worries me, though, is that neither the Russians nor anyone else seems to have any scope for using moderative influence in Hanoi at present.' On Brown's recent visit, Gromyko made it clear that the SU was 'still not ready to act either in the general framework of the Geneva Conference machinery, or in any other way'.

It seemed, the talking points continued, that the North Vietnamese were determined 'to avoid reasonable negotiations now'. It looked as if they had decided to hold out at least till 1968, 'in the expectation that domestic and foreign pressures will cause the United States Administration to revise their Vietnam policy'. If so, it was 'very dangerous'. The visit to Washington had shown once again the 'great pressures' under which the president was working. 'But many of these pressures are in the direction of harder action in Vietnam.' The president should not, and could not, order a cessation of bombing on North Vietnamese terms. The 'balanced approach' was right: 'the North Vietnamese have got to give some indication of how, in practical terms, they would respond to a cessation.'

One problem was 'that if the President now stopped the bombing, apparently unconditionally, the world would assume that this was because meaningful negotiations with the North Vietnamese were going on, or were about to start. In other words essential secrecy would have been lost'. Was there any prospect, the French might be asked, of 'getting the North Vietnamese into secret talks in advance of any overt action?' If not, how did they see the deadlock being broken?

The background to the talking points noted that de Gaulle's extreme views—that the blame for the war lay with the Americans, that they must withdraw, and that Southeast Asia should be neutralised—had not brought him any success in his attempts to bring the war to an end. Envoys sent to Hanoi, Jean Chauvel and Jean Sainteny, had come back empty-handed. His own talks with North Vietnamese representatives during his visit to Phnom Penh failed to achieve anything. Perhaps as a result, he declared in October that he did not propose to make any attempt at mediation for the time being.

The North Vietnamese attitude to negotiations seemed 'completely rigid'. Recent pronouncements stressed the Four Points. The principle of reciprocity, the North Vietnamese insisted, had no relevance. They apparently believed they could stick it out until the presidential elections in 1968. 'There may well be a belief … that by next year political pressure in America, coupled with what they would hope to be a realisation that the effort in Vietnam was too expensive, would bring about negotiations, or an American withdrawal, on more or less Hanoi's terms.' The Russians would not use their influence to promote negotiations so long as the North Vietnamese were not ready for them, and they would go on supplying arms and equipment required to 'counter any intensification of the American military effort'. But they would continue to 'stop short of involvement which might lead to a direct Soviet/American confrontation, as might follow, for example, the provision of Soviet "volunteers"'.

In the US, the background concluded, there was 'considerable dissent' from administration policies, 'and even influential pressure for ending the present bombing policy because it is not paying off', though the latest polls put approval of the president's policies at 72 per cent. The numbers wanting total military victory had increased, and so had those wanting to escalate. Eighty per cent were said to believe that bombing was the best way to bring about negotiations. Eighty-one per cent believed that the war would go on for a long time. Sixteen senators, including Fulbright, had stated that, despite their criticism of Johnson's policies, they were against withdrawal. The president would regard such figures as a sufficient mandate to continue, if he wished, 'with an intensification of American military effort until the North Vietnamese sue for negotiations'.[11]

San Antonio

Kosygin had been in the US to attend UNGA after the Six-Day War, and a meeting with the president had taken place at Glassboro College (now Rowan University) on 23–25 June 1967. Johnson later recalled telling the Soviet premier: 'We do not want to conquer Vietnam. All we want to do is to prevent them from taking South Vietnam by force. If they take it by votes, that's a different matter ok. ...When infiltration and violence ceases we will get out.'[12] During lunch on the first day, Kosygin contacted Hanoi. Pham Van Dong said: stop the bombing, and we will immediately go to the conference table. On the 25th LBJ responded with an oral statement that the US was prepared to stop the bombing, but reserved the right to full freedom of action if talks did not lead to peace, or if the North Vietnamese used protracted talks to achieve a one-sided military advantage. A written message for Hanoi offered a cessation of bombing, accompanied by mutual restraint in military operations.[13]

This became the basis of LBJ's speech at San Antonio to the National Legislative Council on 29 September, given against a background of 'secret' discussions involving Henry Kissinger and others. 'The United States is ready to stop all aerial and naval bombardment of North Vietnam when this will lead promptly to productive discussions. We, of course, assume that while discussions proceed, North Vietnam would not take advantage of the bombing cessation or limitation.'[14] 'We'll talk when President Johnson stops sending his peace invitations by bomber,' said Vu Trong Kinh of the State Commission for Cultural Relations with Foreigners.[15] But, though Johnson insisted at a press conference that he was only explaining more fully what had been said before,[16] it was seemingly a less rigid line than Marigold's final bloom.

At UNGA on 21 September Goldberg had said the US was resolved to help South Vietnam defend its right to determine its own future. The US was prepared to order a prior cessation of bombing if assured that the Vietnam conflict would move promptly towards a peaceful solution based on Geneva.[17] Brown endorsed the Goldberg approach. 'He regretted that the leaders of North Vietnam had never said what they would either do or refrain from doing to help the process of peace if the bombing were stopped.'[18] Bernard Joseph Cabanes of Agence France Presse reported from Hanoi that North Vietnam would be prepared to begin talks three or four weeks after the US unconditionally stopped acts of war. *Nhan Dan* insisted, however, that Hanoi would make no bargains in order to stop the bombing. If Washington announced a period of cessation, no talks would be possible, for the halt would be conditional.[19]

Cabinet Paper

The foreign secretary reported to Cabinet on his discouraging talks in New York. In the UK, it was pointed out, there was a strong feeling that it was an unjust war, and, besides the moral issue, Britain was seen as supporting the US. It should publicly say that it was opposed to the bombing. On the other hand, it was also pointed out that North Vietnam had broken the Geneva agreement, and had rejected negotiations. If the US broke faith with South Vietnam, the confidence of other allies would be shaken. The government's attitude to the war had been stated at Brighton in October 1966. It did not support the war; it deplored escalation; it condemned bombing, but also condemned terrorist activities in South Vietnam. 'It was essential to keep this balance if we were to retain our power to influence events. Our attitude was understood by the United States and put us in a position to exercise our influence in favour of a settlement at an appropriate time.' Britain had taken initiatives, especially during the Kosygin visit, and the fact that the US had shown willingness to negotiate was largely due to Britain's influence. 'It was important to retain our influence to help in bringing the war to an end. A public declaration of policy might impair it. The Cabinet took note of the Foreign Secretary's statement, and invited him to prepare a paper for a later meeting.'[20]

So ran the characteristically depersonalised Cabinet minutes. Crossman records his intervention in Brown's account. The 'overwhelming majority' of the Labour Party, he said, wanted the government to stop supporting the Americans. Was the support offered on grounds of expediency or did Brown think it was a just war? Barbara Castle gave 'a great spiel about how we were losing the support of all Asia by supporting the Americans'. Moral postures were all very well, said the PM: 'what mattered was whether we had been able to do any genuine peace-making.' On 37 occasions, the UK had tried to intervene, 'never with success, but we still retained our mediatory position and that was the key to our policy and the reason why we were accepting all the unpopularity by not denouncing the Americans'. Mrs Castle insisted that 'we should at least be given a paper laying down the Government's position in Vietnam in some detail'.[21]

The Trades Union Congress had decided that Britain should dissociate itself from US policy. That meant that the Labour Party conference in October would vote for a similar resolution. Wilson and Brown would then find it hard, H.B. Boyne of the *Daily Telegraph* considered, to hold the Parliamentary Labour Party to the government's line of 'general, though occasionally critical', support for U.S. policy. Opposition in the Commons was 'no longer confined to left-wingers and habitual anti-Americans'. Many dissidents believed that the foreign secretary, as co-chairman, would be 'in a better position to seek opportunities to end the fighting if he represented a Government which was, as they put it, strictly neutral'.[22] At Scarborough the conference indeed passed the resolution. A few members of the Cabinet might be tempted to begin pressing for the motion to be acted on, David Wood of *The Times* speculated, and if it was Brown might then resign.[23]

In a minute of 1 November de la Mare recommended that, without publicly dissociating Britain from the US position, 'we quietly diminish our overt and public activity on the Vietnam issue, to the extent that this can be done without causing undue friction in Anglo-American relations or undue difficulty in Parliament'. He pointed out that LBJ was precluded from 'all-out escalation' by world opinion and by his re-election campaign, and that the North Vietnamese had the initiative. There was nothing Britain could do to alter or arrest those developments: all its initiatives had failed. He concluded that the co-chairmanship of 1954 'means nothing in the radically altered conditions of 1967 when we lack the physical power to make our views felt', and that that was recognised by North Vietnam, the

SU and also the Americans 'who, while paying lip-service to the value of our support, in practice set no store by our ability to achieve anything useful'. '[V]ocal world opinion, which is the only valid card of entry we could have into the argument,' de la Mare continued, 'is ranging itself uncritically and hysterically against both the United States and the legitimate and justified interest of the people of South Vietnam', and the only honourable part for Britain would be to campaign against the hysteria, but 'we lack both the power and the political conditions to do this'. Vietnam was 'not a vital British interest. In the light of the human suffering and misery there this is a brutal thing to say, but history will prove Vietnam to have been only a sideshow. The peaceful development of South East Asia, which is a British interest, will be gained not on the battlefields of Vietnam but in the factories and rice fields of Indonesia, Thailand and Burma. It is there that our role lies.' Given the need not to impair relations with the US, Britain could not openly dissociate itself from the US, 'even if we thought it expedient to do so, which we do not'. But it could tailor its support to 'a realistic appraisal of our capacity to influence the issue, which is nil, and to our interests, which lie elsewhere in East Asia where we can help consolidate and build on the foundations already laid for peaceful and democratic progress'. Britain should undertake no more peace initiatives unless one side or the other made a specific approach, and it should avoid drawing attention to the role of co-chairman, 'which bears no relation to present-day facts'.[24] De la Mare's minute was, he said on the 14th, approved by the secretary of state.[25]

Gore-Booth agreed with the general trend of de la Mare's minute, though suggesting that there was a morale value for the US in Britain's support. '[O]ur view in the Office for some two years has been that H.M. Government tended to overrate their ability to influence this situation and that some of the efforts that have been made to promote peace have been determined by domestic political exigency more than by a cool estimate of what we can really do', though he did not mean by this that the PM should not have made a major effort with Kosygin: 'I think that in all the circumstances this was right.' But Gore-Booth was less convinced by the 'defeatist' suggestion that the UK should not campaign against hysteria. That did not really do justice to the line consistently taken by the PM and the foreign secretary. Any doubts about that line arose from 'a reluctance to consider that the struggle in Vietnam has ideological as well as "nationalist" content'. A minister no longer in the Department used to argue that it was purely a nationalist struggle: 'the co-ordination a weekend ago through Communist-trained organization of the Anti-Vietnam demonstrations in several capitals shows what rubbish this is. … certain agencies which are pursuing a particular political end are seeking unceasingly to use for these political ends some of the best and most humane instincts in people, and particularly in young people. This is the difficulty.'[26]

De la Mare told Dean in Washington that the foreign secretary had accepted the views in these minutes, writing simply: 'I agree.' No change of policy was envisaged, 'only a change of emphasis'. Gore-Booth's query about his 'lip-service' remark was a side issue: 'the real point I wanted to get across was that with things as they are in Vietnam we have no role to play; and that being so the less we talk about it and the more we go about our own business the better.'[27]

The memorandum the foreign secretary had been asked to draft for Cabinet—what Murray called a 'carefully prepared and documented memorandum'[28]—had been received at No. 10 at the end of October. Burke Trend suggested on the 31st that the prime minister might wish to read it before it was circulated, consider if it were unsuitable, and what the timing should be. 'It is possible—admittedly by over-simplifying what the memorandum says—to read it as simply saying the Americans are right, that the North Vietnamese are wrong and that there is nothing we can do about it. This may, or may not, be true. But, read in this sense, the memorandum might touch off a rather unprofitable discussion in Cabinet; and it might be a pity to provide a gratuitous opportunity for the expression of anti-American sentiment at a time when we may be needing some practical American financial help. It might do no harm, therefore, if the circulation of this memorandum stood over for a time.' But the PM might think these were 'unnecessary forebodings'.[29]

Trend was saying in a delicate way that the paper was 'an astonishingly unsuitable paper' for the FO to put in, Palliser commented, and he agreed. 'I doubt if one can fault the facts. But it gives a rather crude impression of straight pro-Americanism. There is, for example, no attempt to explore the North Vietnamese motivations—their feeling that 1955 deprived them of victory, that they are not going to be had for mugs twice etc. It is not as black and white as this suggests.' How did the PM wish to handle it?[30]

On 10 November Gore-Booth spoke to Trend about the Cabinet discussion due on the 16th. Trend said Cabinet was 'now very divided about Vietnam', and the foreign secretary should put in a 'powerfully persuasive' paper. If he felt the policy right, he should say so, but he should take account of the drift of opinion in the Labour Party adverse to the Americans. The PM would probably be anxious to show that he was 'again active in promoting a settlement'. Gore-Booth told Trend the FO had just had approval of a submission drawing attention to HMG's inability to do anything effective. Trend thought the FO had to take account of the PM's 'inclination to feel that he had scored a near miss' with Kosygin in February. Gore-Booth said the FO did not agree: the PM's effort was 'worth making, but the evidence was that even if the Americans had not made things so difficult for us, the end result would not have been successful'.

Gore-Booth concluded that the paper would have to be 'more vivid', even 'more combative', than previous submissions. He made the following suggestions to the Department: (a) divide the argumentation between 'general sympathy with American policy' and questioning the necessity for the bombing; (b) stress the initiative of the new South Vietnamese government vis-à-vis Hanoi; (c) include an IRD (Information and Research Department) paragraph on the synchronisation of anti-Vietnam demonstrations through Communist front organizations; (d) draw attention to wider factors, such as Britain's distance from the scene compared with Australia's, and the American public's conducting 'a Great Debate in the classical American manner'. The vast majority deplored the situation, but the 'Antis' had yet to find a way to stop the bombing and the war and not hand over the South Vietnamese to the exercise of force. The paper would have to be 'a very serious piece of advocacy'.[31]

Murray spent the weekend writing a companion piece to the memorandum framed as a piece of advocacy for the present policy as approved by the foreign secretary, i.e., that articulated by de la Mare. But the foreign secretary's private office discovered on 13 November that the earlier memorandum had been suppressed by the Cabinet Office, to which it had been sent for distribution on 30 October. Murray did not know why, nor whether the foreign secretary had concurred. The effect was that the Cabinet would be 'taking "blind" a piece of advocacy without the carefully balanced information on which it has been based'. Perhaps the earlier paper should be attached as an annex to the new one.[32]

A meeting was held with the permanent undersecretary in the chair to consider Murray's weekend draft, and a redraft emerged. It included some of the argument in the 'suppressed' paper, while the factual part of it was made into an attachment. De la Mare agreed with it. The policy of 'committed detachment' was 'entirely in line' with the paper he had submitted. Brown approved it. 'It's a good paper.'[33]

The final paper, dated 15 November, the day before the Cabinet meeting, thus set out, as background, the basis of British policy. 'A lasting solution to the war', it declared, could not be military, but had to come by 'a negotiated settlement that will secure the legitimate interests of all concerned'. South Vietnam, it went on, was 'an international entity', and its people had 'the right to pursue their own affairs free from interference'. North Vietnam had 'not yet desisted from trying to overthrow the South Vietnamese Government by force with the aim of replacing it by Hanoi's own creation', the NLF. The government of South Vietnam had 'the right in international law to resist this and to request American help'. American policies were 'reasonable in their readiness to negotiate a political settlement'. The Geneva agreements were 'a reasonable and adequate basis for such a settlement'.

The South Vietnamese government, the paper continued, had stated that it had no territorial ambitions, nor any desire to change the regime in the North. But it resisted the claim that the NLF was representative, let alone sole representative, of the South Vietnamese. The recent presidential elections—in which 82 per cent of the registered electorate cast votes on 11 candidates—bore that out. Significant abstentions would have suggested support for Viet Cong or neutralists. It did not occur. Divided states raised many problems in international law. But Vietnam, as one of the successor states of the French Union, had been internationally recognised by more than 60 states, and it had the right, recognised by Article 51, of individual and collective self-defence. In resisting the North Vietnamese, and requesting US assistance, it was exercising those rights.

The US had given a number of specific assurances since 1954. It had also declared that its support for South Vietnam was, as a protocol state, in accord with its obligations under the SEATO treaty. Britain had made it plain, however, that it did not view its SEATO obligations in the same way. In any case South Vietnam had not formally invoked SEATO help. 'Even if she did, our view is that it is open to each party to put its own interpretation on the treaty requirement to "act to meet the common danger", and thus that each individual member would have to decide for itself how to respond.'

The Americans had said that they were ready for talks, negotiations, a conference. In Manila in 1966 they committed themselves to withdrawing their forces not later than six months after the end of violence and the withdrawal of Communist forces to the North. They had made low-level contacts, initiated bombing pauses, and encouraged third parties in their efforts to bring about a ceasefire and negotiations.

The North Vietnamese held to their Four Points and to the claim, reaffirmed by Pham Van Dong, that the FLN was 'the sole genuine representative of the people of South Vietnam'. The foreign minister had stated in January 1967 that talks could take place only after the unconditional cessation of US bombing and acts of war. There could, they said, be 'no equality of treatment for the aggressor … and the victim', and no reciprocity. All the proposals so far put forward had thus been rejected. 'Equally, all efforts to discover whether North Vietnam would, in fact, start talking after a cessation of bombing have failed.'

As a result of this North Vietnamese attitude and international criticism of the bombing, the president had moved from his position in February—that bombing would stop when infiltration had stopped—to 'a publicly stated willingness to order a cessation of bombing "when this will lead promptly to productive discussion", provided only that while discussions proceed the North Vietnamese would not take military advantage'. The North Vietnamese had made 'no responsive shift in their policy'.

Britain's responsibility was twofold, the background to the paper concluded, as a major power concerned with the security of Southeast Asia as a whole, and as co-chairman. 'For the first, it is accepted by our friends and allies that our military non-involvement in Vietnam does not mean that we have abandoned all concern with the security and stability of the whole region. Nor does it inhibit us from giving aid and support to South Vietnam and the U.S. presence there, because it is in our general interest that there should be a strong and viable South Vietnam so that the people of South Vietnam should be capable of deciding their future, and the question of reunification, free from foreign interference. We therefore believe that South Vietnam's resistance to encroachment from the North is right.'

As for Geneva, the co-chairmanship involved 'a responsibility without effective power'. The conference could reconvene only if its members would attend: not even the SU, let alone the PRC and North Vietnam, conceded that the time was right to do so. 'The essential value of the Geneva machinery is that it remains in existence, by tacit understanding between all concerned, against the day when it can be used; and that we test it periodically to see whether this day is near.'

The foreign secretary invited his colleagues to consider Britain's policy in the context he had set out. The North Vietnamese were determined to fight on to secure a South Vietnamese regime in all respects their creature, and the South Vietnamese, the Americans and their allies were pursuing a defensive war 'while constantly re-stating their readiness to negotiate a solution which would leave South Vietnam in peace'. The war was being fought 'with geographic and political limitations'. The North Vietnamese could not 'mount a military effort in the South which would swing the military balance in their favour', and the US was 'precluded by world opinion and the stresses of the presidential election campaign from all-out military escalation, such as the land invasion of the North or additional measures of air and sea warfare, aimed at bringing the war to a swift military conclusion'.

Each side was aware was that there were channels for direct communication with the other side. They had been used, but had only served to show that, until the situation changed, there was no alternative to continued fighting. Currently there was nothing the British or any other 'non-involved' government could do 'to mediate or to arrest or alter developments. But we have a duty and a capacity to maintain a continued readiness to act in the cause of peace when asked to do so by one of the combatants.'

In the US the components of the public debate included 'frustration, war weariness and a desire to end the whole involvement in Vietnam'. Probably a majority criticised the administration's handling of the war, but 'the desire to be "out" in a way which would hand over South Vietnam to the North, i.e. through an abdication of American responsibilities, is held by only a small—but vocal—majority. An equally vocal minority is demanding all-out escalation as a means of finishing the war quickly.' Meanwhile the Communist powers were 'mobilising a skilful world-wide propaganda campaign' that asserted that North Vietnam's intervention was 'blameless' and the military policies of the US 'totally immoral'. The majority of those involved in the current international wave of demonstrations were 'neither Communists nor fellow-travellers'. But the demonstrations were principally organised by the World Council of Peace, a Communist front organization dating from 1948.

There were, the foreign secretary continued, three alternative policies that Britain could adopt. One would be to align the country 'unswervingly' behind the US. That would be 'an act of folly. We would reduce our ability to play an independent role elsewhere, as well as in the Vietnam context; we would destroy our ability to offer advice and to criticise in private; above all this would be to act against the weight of British public opinion including that sector which believes that the Americans are in the wrong situation even if their motives are right.'

A second alternative was 'to express public criticism of the American position, ranging from complete dissociation to a demand for the bombing to stop, in the hope that this would advance the prospect of a negotiated settlement'. But that would not bring North Vietnam to negotiations. The Americans and the world in general would regard public criticism by the British government as 'synonymous with condemnation; and this would also place us in one sector of the domestic turmoil in America. By doing this we would lose the confidence and respect of the present and future Administrations there; and by estranging ourselves from the present Administration—on whom falls the burden of deciding on a Vietnam policy adjusted to domestic requirements and the military and political situation—

we would damage perhaps irreparably our understanding with the United States in other fields and areas of the world.'

The present administration and its successor would, in these circumstances, be unlikely to assert themselves in Britain's favour in such issues as protectionism against British goods, defence contracts, trade with Rhodesia, and votes on Gibraltar at the UN. Nor would the US be helpful over the balance of payments, and the application to join the EEC and the chances of solving the offset problem were both 'willy-nilly bound up with the international financial situation and our bargaining strength in it'. The world balance of power was also at stake. The Americans were unlikely to become 'consciously isolationist'. But if they felt they were defeated in Vietnam, and particularly if they felt that the result was brought about by their allies, they might follow 'a sporadic and unpredictable foreign policy', withdrawing here and over-asserting themselves there. That would be 'dangerous'. The Chinese and the Russians might not interpret American actions properly nor 'resist unwise temptations'.

At a time when Britain's power had declined, 'we should not lightly resign such influence as we have and can have with the most powerful nation in the world'. It would automatically entail a loss of influence with others, especially the Russians, who had a special interest in the relationship with the British 'because what we say is taken seriously by the Americans'. A loss of influence with the Americans would also lose influence with Australia, New Zealand, Malaysia and Singapore. 'It will be worse still if they believe we have contributed to American defeat in Asia.'

Brown favoured a third alternative, to 'recognise that there is nothing we can do for the present, but meanwhile to maintain our capacity to give private advice to the Americans and to maintain contact with other powers, against the day when both sides might want our services'. That policy 'would avoid ranging ourselves on the side of those who have hitherto offered no reasonable alternative to a cessation of military activities by the one power which can prevent South Vietnam being handed over to the rule of force'. It would also secure a position in which Britain could act 'when any of the parties engaged in the war believe that our services could help towards a settlement'. The time had not yet come. 'The North Vietnamese do not need us.' The SU considered that the co-chairmen had no role to play at that moment. The US knew that Britain was ready to help with peace moves when they were practicable. The South Vietnamese, 'though gaining in stature', were 'only gradually approaching the point where an initiative for direct North/South talks could add a new diplomatic dimension to the situation'.

The memorandum concluded with a section on the 'moral considerations'. The South Vietnamese had 'a right to freedom and a right to decide their own future for themselves'. A total American withdrawal would mean their subjugation to a totalitarian regime. If the South had a right to look for help, the degree of help they had secured could not be 'a matter of criticism or condemnation'. The North Vietnamese fought in the South 'with every means at their disposal, including the most repulsive atrocities', but had managed to mobilise a selective condemnation of bombing, with the implication that other forms of slaughter were 'in some way tolerable'. Not itself fighting, the UK, moreover, could not condemn bombing as a means of warfare, though it could argue for cessation if that might lead towards a settlement. Australia and New Zealand believed it was right to fight alongside the US, and in none of the non-Communist countries of Southeast Asia was there 'an outspoken demand for the United States to quit with the Vietnam issue unresolved'.

The foreign secretary recommended maintaining 'our present policy of committed detachment', viewing the Americans' 'present period of self-examination … with sympathy', and making 'our attachment to a peaceful settlement the foundation of our readiness to mediate if asked to do so'. Above all, he believed that the British government should 'eschew a position of moral condemnation of the United States because it would not be based on valid moral principles; it would not shorten the war; and it would not be practical politics'.[34]

In presenting the paper to his Cabinet colleagues, Murray suggested that the foreign secretary might care to say that it was right to make a very great effort during Kosygin's visit, but that the scope for a third party initiative was currently nil. 'This is not the fault of the Americans who … have tried hard to get some reasonable basis for negotiations, as San Antonio suggested, but the North Vietnamese were determined to reject all offers probably till after the [presidential] elections.' There was nothing Britain could do 'to arrest or alter the way things are going—because activity in any direction is likely to impair rather than enhance the ultimate prospects of negotiations'.[35] De la Mare unsurprisingly endorsed the advice.[36]

None of the three alternatives, Sir Burke Trend minuted for the prime minister just before the paper came to Cabinet, would be without its critics in Cabinet or the country. But the paper and its annex argued cogently that on grounds of morality and self-interest there was no real alternative to the middle course. 'To come out more strongly on the American side would be politically unacceptable and would destroy any prospect that we might one day have a valuable role to play as an intermediary in reaching a negotiated settlement; we would derive no worthwhile benefit from such action. To turn against the Americans publicly would be certain to have disastrous effects not merely on our own relations with them but on their policies generally; and the damage would be likely to be long as well as short-term. Any chance that there may be of influencing United States policy in Vietnam in such matters as bombing the North would disappear; and at the same time our relations with Australia and New Zealand would be seriously affected.' The arguments against the middle course would no doubt be mainly based on moral grounds. The annex showed, however, that aggression had come mainly from the North. Double standards were applied, and the Americans' failure to match Communist propaganda was as serious as their inability to win quick military victory in South Vietnam. But the success of Communist propaganda 'should not allow us to be misled on the policy that it is right for us to follow'. The problem in Cabinet would be to confine the discussion to the essentials of the problem 'with particular regard to the very severe limitations that there are on our freedom of action in our present economic circumstances'.[37]

The Commonwealth Office advised its secretary of state to support the foreign secretary's paper. A change towards either of the first two alternatives would be 'disastrous'. Malaysia and Singapore both believed that if the US failed in Vietnam their own independence would be short-lived. 'Australia and New Zealand are fighting alongside the Americans in the first overseas war in which they have not served with British forces, and a condemnation of that war would be most damaging to our relations with them. Coming on top of our decision to withdraw from the Far East, our apparent preference for Europe, and our seeming restrictions on Australian and New Zealand immigrants, we could not avoid giving the impression that we were no longer interested in preserving our links with them.' On the other hand, neither would expect Britain to follow the first alternative, 'nor would such a course be welcome in Malaysia and Singapore. Our existing policies have not been criticised by Commonwealth countries outside the Far East.'[38]

In the event the Cabinet did not take the paper on 16 November. Consideration was postponed, as the meeting was entirely taken up by devaluation. Precipitated by the worst trade figures since January 1964, as well as an indefinite dock strike announced in London and Liverpool,[39] devaluation was a catastrophe for Wilson, 'a profound defeat'.[40] The Americans were in no position to offer a loan: they were under pressure themselves, since the president wanted to run the war and the Great Society without tax increases—'if I talk about the cost of the war, the Great Society won't go through'[41]—and ran a deficit that conduced to inflation.[42] Chancellor of the Exchequer James Callaghan had to go, and Roy Jenkins replaced him. He was a strong critic of the East of Suez role. Devaluation raised defence costs, and Jenkins insisted that more cuts were needed: Britain's standing in the world had to depend on 'the strength of the economy and not upon a world-wide military role'.[43] The president was appalled.[44] 'For God's sake, act like Britain,' Rusk pleaded with Brown. '[B]y walk[ing] off the non-European world in terms of defence and commitment ... [we] have crossed a watershed in our ability to influence world affairs,' Dean wrote to Brown.[45]

Tet and Talks

Even so, British leaders continued an active search for a Vietnam solution. Attending the funeral of Harold Holt in Melbourne on 22 December, Johnson and Wilson again discussed Vietnam. The president told the prime minister that his problem at home was 'holding the ring between the two extremes': 17 per cent wanted to withdraw or limit the objective to stabilising the situation; 45–47 per cent wanted to step up the effort. Wilson said that he, too, was under pressure, now not only from the Left. But he could hold the position on the basis of the San Antonio formula.

Did the A and B formula still hold? Wilson hoped Johnson would let him know before his visit to Moscow in January 1968. It would be helpful if he could send someone to London shortly before he went in order to discuss and agree on what be said. The president agreed. There now seemed some doubt, Wilson suggested, about Kosygin's strength within the Soviet government. His position 'might have been weakened by being thought by his colleagues to have gone out too far on a limb of his own when he was in London'. There was also reason to doubt whether the Soviet government was confident about its relations with Hanoi. At Glassboro, the president said, Kosygin had seemed ready to use his influence with Hanoi, but nothing had come of it. 'He was beginning to wonder whether the Russians' real interest was ... to prolong the conflict and the American involvement in Vietnam as a means of diverting Chinese attention away from the Soviet Union.' If that analysis were correct, it underlined the need to make them aware of the pressures for escalation within the US.[46]

Unfortunately, Crossman wrote in his diary, LBJ's main concern was to talk to the Pope about mediation. 'This completely confirms my view that there will never be a role for Harold and George as mediators.' Apparently Brown had told the Foreign Affairs group of the parliamentary Labour Party that he had 'an understanding in Moscow that at any moment when we can get a breakthrough I can act as intermediary. The only basis on which I can stay in play is if the communists in Pekin and Hanoi believe that I can deliver the Americans. The U.S. trusts me not to deliver them unless they can get something sensible in return. I could deliver Johnson in two minutes flat from here if I could get something from Hanoi.' 'Tripe,' Crossman judged.[47]

A week later Nguyen Duy Trinh, the North Vietnamese foreign minister, made a statement to an Outer Mongolian delegation, subsequently broadcast on 1 January 1968. The US constantly claimed that it wanted to talk, but that it secured no reply. If it really wanted to talk, then, as stated on 28 January 1967, it must first of all unconditionally end all bombing and acts of war against the DRV. After that, 'the DRV will talk to the U.S. about the problems concerned'.[48] The use of the word 'will' rather than 'could' seemed, Rusk said, to be a new formulation, but left 'a great many questions still open'. He was 'cautious'.[49] But Mai Van Bo, North Vietnamese delegate-general in Paris, confirmed that talks would begin after an appropriate delay if the Americans unconditionally stopped the bombing.[50]

In Moscow Kosygin told Wilson that the US wanted to know the outcome before the talks were held. No, said the PM: they wanted to be satisfied that real talks would begin when the bombing stopped.[51] The UK, Brezhnev said, should dissociate itself from US policies.[52] Kosygin seemed to want Wilson to make contact with the North Vietnam embassy in Moscow. He was not doing so lest it prejudiced the president's communications, as he told him by teleprinter.[53] The SU might be playing a spoiling game, Johnson suggested in reply.[54]

'If the British Government dissociated themselves clearly and unambiguously from the American policy of aggression,' President Podgorny told Wilson, 'they could exert great influence on President Johnson. ... Britain alone of all the allies of the US really supported the US position.' Wilson disagreed. The San Antonio speech, in conjunction with Trinh's speech, could provide a road to peace. What was essential was to put the two together and get talks started. Dissociation 'would in any case make the achievement of peace more difficult. Someone who dissociated himself from what one of his friends was doing did not usually thereby gain greater influence over his friend.'[55]

'At the outset,' as the prime minister put it, 'the Russians took the predictable line that the San Antonio formula offered no scope for progress, because it constituted a pre-condition for the cessation of the bombing.' The US wanted to know the conclusion before the start. Wilson denied that was its position: 'it was clearly not only reasonable but essential that the Americans should know, if the bombing stopped, not what would be the outcome of the talks, but simply that talks would take place promptly and in a spirit of readiness to reach a political solution.' There was, in his view, 'a real opportunity for the combatants to arrange for productive talks promptly after the cessation of the bombing'.

As a result of what he said, Wilson continued, the Russians might take 'another look at their assessment of American intentions. They naturally tried to argue that we were too identified with the American position rather than with their own', but in the end they reluctantly agreed in the communiqué that they would continue to work for a settlement, singly or jointly. That went further than they went in 1967. 'Whether or not the differences between the two sides have been narrowed must now depend largely on the outcome of the current Viet Cong offensive in South Vietnam.' The prospects were 'obviously not too encouraging at present', and the PM hoped to hear from Thant whether Ho Chi Minh's representative offered any indication of prompt negotiations on reasonable terms.[56]

The communiqué indicated that on Vietnam the two sides had set out their respective positions. They reaffirmed their adherence to the principles of Geneva and emphasised the need for 'a political settlement of the conflict which fully respects the exclusive and inalienable right of the peoples of the region to manage their own internal affairs'. They pledged themselves to take actions singly or jointly 'to achieve this goal'.[57] Wilson told the House that there was a narrow bridge that could lead to peace.[58] Offensives in the South, LBJ said on 1 February, ruled out a bombing halt.[59]

Attacking Khe Sanh on 20–21 January was an attempt to draw US forces to that remote area,[60] and the Tet offensive had begun on 30 January. Trinh's shift of tenses, it seems, had been part of peace overtures, themselves part of the offensive.[61] The SU had advised the DRV to enter negotiations, while Mao had advised against a bigger war. But Le Duan wanted a big victory before negotiations in the president's last year: another gamble. He and his faction launched a pre-emptive strike against moderates in Hanoi. He believed he could achieve a decisive victory: mainforce units were to tie down US troops away from urban centres; and large-scale attacks in the cities would incite mass insurrection against the puppet regime.[62] The essential plan was for a morale-shattering attack on the Southern cities that would compel the US to pull back its firepower and de-escalate the war against the North.

The Central Committee determined 'to break the U.S. will of aggression, to compel it to accept defeat in South Vietnam, to stop all acts of war against North Vietnam, ... [and] to negotiate in order to end the war in accordance with our objectives'.[63] The ARVN did unexpectedly well. LBJ—after consulting Clark Clifford, McNamara's successor—rejected

Westmoreland's appeal for large numbers of US troops.[64] In retrospect, it is clear, the PAVN/VC suffered a devastating tactical defeat, but public opinion polls turned against supporting LBJ. The Second Republic saw Tet as a victory, but American reporters saw it as a defeat.[65] Le Duan toppled the president, not the puppet.

A few days before the offensive began, the North Koreans seized the intelligence ship *Pueblo* just outside territorial waters in the Sea of Japan; 'another attempt to divert us from our efforts in Vietnam,' the CIA concluded.[66] Visiting Washington yet again, Wilson found the president 'extremely troubled'.[67] The Russians featured in their talks on Vietnam. Johnson was convinced that their writ did not run in Hanoi: 'whatever they may want to do they have no power to deliver.' Given their supply of equipment, he felt they could influence the North Vietnamese to a settlement if they wished. 'It had been put to him … that the Russians had a powerful interest in keeping the Vietnam struggle going because it led to economic strain in the U.S., to divisions within the Alliance and within America, tied up a large U.S. army and enabled the Russians to exert some influence in Hanoi instead of being left to fight it out with the Chinese in that part of Asia.' The president went over the pre-San Antonio story, as he had in Melbourne. A full message had gone to Hanoi on 25 August, and he knew it got there. That specifically said that the Americans would be ready to discuss the Four Points, and while it mentioned that no military advantage should be taken of the cessation, it stressed much more that no action should be taken to make talks impossible, 'bombing the hut where they were taking place', as the president put it.[68]

At dinner Wilson recounted his visit to Moscow: he aimed to show that San Antonio and Trinh could be reconciled.[69] The following day the president said that the prime minister should inform the Russians of their discussions, emphasising—in face of Tet—that the US intended to see it through to the end. He should spell out San Antonio.[70] The president, Wilson duly told Kosygin, was determined, but he was also keen on a negotiated solution. Wilson had started out from San Antonio and Trinh's statement. Could he and Kosygin continue a dialogue?[71] Wilson also saw Smirnovsky and told him of the message.[72] 'There is a very narrow gap to be bridged—very narrow indeed,' the PM again told the House. 'Unfortunately the fighting of the last few weeks makes it more difficult to cross that bridge.'[73] 'I don't think Hanoi any more ready to negotiate today that it was a year ago, 2 years ago, or 3 years ago,' LBJ told his press conference on 16 February.[74] Indeed Kosygin answered that San Antonio would not do.[75] The exchanges were related to Washington in mid-March.[76]

At the end of the month the president made his famous speech: 13,500 more troops would be sent, but bombing would be cut back to south of the 20th parallel; and, he added at the end, he would not be standing for another term. President Nguyen Van Thieu had been consulted about the bulk of the speech, MacLehose reported from Saigon, but not about its final section. That drastically altered a package already distasteful. There was a disposition to believe that a turning point had been reached and that there was a serious danger that sooner or later the Americans would pull out.[77]

Details of the speech—though, again, not the concluding decision—had been relayed to Wilson in advance.[78] He proposed to go into action with Moscow. What was it the British should say?[79] The next move was Hanoi's, LBJ replied.[80] When it appeared on 3 April that Hanoi was willing to talk, Wilson wrote again: it was not clear how the British and the Russians could help at that point.[81]

Goronwy Roberts, a junior minister, had lunch with the Russian ambassador that day (the 4th). 'He said that he was very glad indeed that talks were in prospect but that the Americans had handled the matter badly. He would not commit himself to the reconvening of the Geneva Conference but said that whatever form the talks took they should be attended by all concerned. They should be preceded by a cessation of all bombing but he was silent when I added "and all fighting on both sides and movement of troops".' Why, Smirnovsky wondered, had the British and the Americans been so obstinate over Vietnam for so long? What he called 'obstinacy', Roberts replied, was 'well grounded apprehension of Communist aggression. ... It was comparable to the apprehensions of the democracies during the 1930s when Nazi totalitarianism was advancing from point to point. Many people wondered if Viet Nam was Communism's "last territorial claim"?' There was no analogy, the ambassador replied. 'The Viet Namese are creating their own revolution, not importing it. They are fighting to be free of the Americans as they fought to be free of the French. Once they are united they will be independent of all countries.'[82]

On 8 May Smirnovsky called on Stewart—foreign secretary again since 15 March, when Brown resigned—to deliver a message inviting him to Moscow for an exchange of views on 12–13 May. The meeting was finally arranged for 24–25 May.[83] Harriman and Xuan Thuy had just arrived in Paris, and the FO attempted a 'mind-clearing exercise', a reminder that progress might be slow. In agreeing to meet the Americans face to face, the North Vietnamese must have been influenced, it was thought, by the relative failure of the Tet offensive and of the siege of Khe Sanh, which would have shown that they would not get the Americans out by military means. Given the political confusion in the US, they therefore decided to see whether they could gain by negotiation what they could not gain by force. 'Bearing in mind that they would regard themselves as having been cheated in the negotiations in 1954, their most likely reason for deciding to talk now may be because they wanted a breathing space in order to redeploy their forces and adapt their strategy to long-term guerrilla tactics.' Alternatively the situation in North Vietnam was 'much worse than we think; but there was no evidence the North Vietnamese were negotiating from weakness'.

It seemed unlikely to the FO that they were influenced in their decision either by the SU or by China. The Russians would probably be 'genuinely pleased' that talks had been arranged, but would have no illusions about the difficulties ahead, or about their ability to influence North Vietnamese tactics. They would be 'careful to avoid any propaganda or action which could be interpreted as interfering in the way the Vietnamese are conducting their case'. As a result they would be unlikely to propose collective action, or seek the reconvening of Geneva, unless Hanoi wanted it, and that would probably not be in the near future. At the same time the Russians would maintain 'a strong propaganda campaign against the Americans' and would try to involve Britain, 'insofar as they can do this without involving themselves to the point of embarrassment to their relations with Hanoi. Their aim will be to exploit our relationship with the U.S. to the embarrassment of both ourselves and the Americans.'

The Russians would not be in any hurry for a settlement. 'We shall have to steer a careful course between pressures on H.M.G. to persuade the Americans to be active and concessionary (and the Americans may well have the weight of articulate world opinion against them if there are deadlocks and delays in Paris), and the need to recognise first where our own interests lie and secondly that only the Americans may be able to judge tactics at any given time.'[84]

British interests were discussed on 15 May 1968 at a FO meeting led by the PUS. P.A. Wilkinson, ambassador to Saigon, had drawn up some points for Gore-Booth to introduce into the discussion. The preliminary aims of the Americans were to get the fighting reduced as a prelude to a negotiated settlement, but they had not indicated 'what they will settle for in South East-Asia in the longer term except that the Communists must stop fighting in the South and leave. Can the Communists be induced to stop fighting and leave unless the Americans also leave, which in principle they have agreed to do six months after the end of hostilities?' Without the presence of Allied forces it would be impossible to establish a functioning democratic South Vietnamese government, and it would be impossible, 'politically, and perhaps practically', to reintroduce troops 'no matter how blatantly the Communists may organise their takeover'. Some Americans might wish to find excuses for stretching the six-month period for years, justifying their action on the ground, which might not be difficult to show, that hostilities had not ended. 'I fear this six months period was, like the "any time, any Place", an example of American "overspeak" and they will be almost universally condemned, once again, for a breach of faith. Where do we stand?'

It was arguable, Wilkinson continued, though he was less sure than he used to be, that if there had been no outside intervention the Communist takeover would have resulted in 'a sort of Titoist socialism, and the general situation could have been contained by American support for Thailand, the U.S. Seventh Fleet, and American dispositions in the offshore islands'. That might have been the case before 1963, or even before 1965, but it would not be a likely consequence of a US withdrawal, followed by a Communist takeover in 1968 or 1969. It was more likely that Laos, Cambodia and Thailand would come to terms with North Vietnam before being overcome by its army. Would the Russians and Chinese help the North Vietnamese? If the Americans looked like withdrawing, would British aid to regimes they were no longer prepared to support be justified? Even LBJ's Baltimore speech of April 1965 might be a case of 'overspeak'.[85]

A memorandum on British interests, intended as a background for the foreign secretary's visit to Moscow later in the month, reflected the officials' discussion. If, it argued, the Americans negotiated to a point where fighting could come to an end as a prelude to a political settlement, they would have to implement their Manila undertaking to withdraw their forces 'over an undetermined time scale but possibly in six months'. That would in present circumstances compromise their basic objective of securing 'a stable, viable and independent South Vietnam'. Without the protection of US forces, the American administrative apparatus—'which holds South Vietnam together'—would have to be withdrawn. The South would be exposed to 'a political take-over by the North within a time scale which might be foreseeable at the time of the settlement. The resulting situation [*sic*] in Vietnam, though it might well be Communist in spirit, is unlikely to be Russian or Chinese dominated; but it would certainly be nationalist with a very heavy list to the left and strongly opposed to the Anglo-Saxon West. Whether or not the political take-over itself would be military in nature, and whether any subsequent Vietnamese adventurism elsewhere (e.g. Laos and Cambodia) could be contained, will depend more on the military sanction which the United States will be able to retain in the region than on whatever political settlement emerges.'

A settlement resulting in American withdrawal would be seen by other countries in Southeast Asia as a reduction in the US capacity to protect the region as a whole and encourage them to come to terms with the Communists. The mainland countries would feel threatened 'by Chinese-inspired subversion or by an expansionist Vietnam, tempered by the extent of residual American assurances and protection'. The island and peninsular countries would suffer from 'a general malaise', and their internal problems would be accentuated. 'The whole region will become uneasy and could lapse into a form of xenophobic nationalism born of a sense of weakness.' The Russians would have an opportunity 'to increase their influence with weakish powers'. Britain's interests, commercial and political, would probably suffer 'in proportion to the degree to which the countries concerned become unstable, lean to the left and seek to reinsure there'.

If the Americans had recognised that negotiations would result in their withdrawal, 'their aim will be to find a way to retreat without too obvious humiliation, and if possible to find some half-way stage or guarantee that would give them some ability to continue to protect South Vietnam'. That would depend to some extent on North Vietnam's sense of strength or weakness and its timetable for absorbing South Vietnam. Effective international supervision would be 'virtually impossible'. Moreover, 'a "Korean-type" solution' had 'no analogy in Vietnam, where there is no front line behind which the non-Communist area can recover integrity in the absence of a final political settlement'. In these circumstances the Americans might consider protracting the negotiations, enabling them to build up South Vietnam in competition with the North's attempt to expand its political base. But 'any procrastination would be subject to dollar pressures and a large weight of political pressure, all requiring speed rather than delay towards a final solution'.

Britain's interests were likely to suffer 'in any situation except one where stable and well-disposed regimes are firmly in power': at risk would be 2.8 per cent of its total export trade and the sterling balances of the Commonwealth countries. At worst there could be 'a virtual suspension of economic activity', and if countries followed Burma's example Western trade would for a time be 'snuffed out'. Britain might lose its long-standing trading advantages—in Malaysia and Singapore and to a lesser degree in Thailand and Indonesia—and have to start afresh in competition with Europe and Japan. In such a perspective, Britain's interest was that US withdrawal should 'create as little disturbance as possible'. But a continued American effort had potential dangers for Britain's own position. Further pressure on the dollar could lead to a financial crisis in which sterling could be involved. A financial crisis could also encourage isolationist tendencies in the US, 'directed at accelerating the pace of withdrawal'.

Britain's interests, the memorandum concluded, would be best served by avoiding 'premature involvement' in the negotiations 'in any way which could hasten the process of American withdrawal with no improvement in the prospects for a stable political settlement favouring Western interests. When the point is reached at which our intervention is required or thought necessary, our objective will almost certainly be to help the United States find a way of retreating with the least possible stress in Asia or in the United States itself, accepting the risk that a Communist-dominated Vietnam will bring to the stability of South East Asia and hence to our interests there'. It would be important to try to hold the 'danger line' north of Malaysia, thus maintaining access to Malaysia and Indonesia, important for raw materials and as markets. 'The degree to which this line can be pushed further north will depend on the ultimate settlement, the extent to which the United States will try to maintain Thailand as a "bastion", and the countervailing sentiments for reinsurance within Thailand itself', 'which will be very strong', ran a note in the margin.

The foreign secretary's conversations in Moscow would be defensive and exploratory. They would be defensive in order 'to avoid Russian attempts to use us to pressurise the United States to accept inadequate terms in return for a quick end to the fighting, and to avoid involvement by the Russians in negotiations before we and the Americans are ready to broaden the scope'. The conversations would be exploratory in order to find out more about North Vietnamese strategy 'and the extent to which the Russians may be contemplating a "positive" policy in South East Asia in circumstances of stress following a settlement'.[86] P.F. Hancock offered a dissentient view: the US should disengage as soon as possible in order to avoid a unilateral demonetisation and its impact.[87]

Bill Sullivan and Daniel Davidson, members of Harriman's negotiating team in Paris, went to London to brief Stewart before he went to Moscow. They brought a message from Rusk. The foreign secretary should urge on Gromyko that Hanoi should respond to the cutback in bombing. The Russians should not expect political currents in the US to lead Johnson to take a softer line. They should be asked for their views on an ultimate settlement. It seemed, Stewart told Bruce, that the US wanted him to find out what immediate step Hanoi would take, but he doubted that it would give any such reply. He intended to 'take the line that it was right for the two co-Chairmen to be talking now about possible measures short of reconvening the Geneva Conference'.[88]

On his arrival in Moscow on 22 May Stewart said that his principal purpose was 'to lay the groundwork for an Anglo-Soviet role in the settlement if the Paris talks progressed'. There might come a time when the point arrived when they could help, 'and we are more likely to be prepared for doing that if we can exchange views first'. Gromyko did not give his view. The Russians had been insistent, *The Times* correspondent observed, that they could not initiate action in the absence of a request from Hanoi. The invitation to Stewart significantly coincided with the North Vietnamese delegates' departure for Paris. The SU wanted to use the UK to impress its views on Washington. And if the talks progressed 'it will want a voice for itself and a final peace settlement'.[89]

Stewart met Gromyko in Moscow on 23 May 1968. No real progress had so far been made in Paris, the Soviet foreign minister observed. While North Vietnam justly sought the complete end of bombing, the US seemed still to be elaborating the San Antonio formula. It was the duty of the co-chairmen, Stewart responded, to help overcome the current difficulties. The US had stopped bombing north of the 20th parallel. Johnson had indicated he would not run again for president, and said he was prepared to consider complete cessation. 'North Viet-Nam ought to consider what she could do without endangering herself to help towards a peaceful settlement. … If for example they could give the United States sound reason to be sure that the complete end of the bombing would not mean the exposure of United States forces in South Viet-Nam to greater danger, that would be a considerable step forward.' If they were so exposed, public opinion in the US might consider cessation 'a most unwise step', and that might lead to 'a marked increase in world tension'. The US had opened a new chapter. What happened next depended on North Vietnam's response. If, for example, the US could feel that it would observe the DMZ, 'the first obstacle in the Paris talks could be removed'.

The British government, Gromyko responded, were concerned that the US forces would be at a disadvantage, compared with their present position, if bombing were stopped. 'This was the weakest point in British policy on Viet-Nam.' The US was the aggressor and could not be put on the same footing as the country suffering aggression. In respect of the DMZ, it was 'applying a strange logic which the British Government seemed to support'. All the Geneva agreements had been broken: 'the Americans were isolating one small part of them in the hope that the situation in the zone could be made more favourable for them.' The SU and the UK 'were co-Chairmen of the Geneva Conference and not of the war'. The Soviet government would do all that was possible to see that the just cause triumphed.

They were not likely to agree, Stewart replied, 'on which of the two positions was the just one. They were more likely to reach agreement on finding some steps for either side to take which might bring a peaceful agreement nearer'. Both sides changed their position, the president at San Antonio and in his speech of 31 March, the North Vietnamese by their presence at the conference table, though the bombing had not stopped: they 'had narrowed the gap—not by insisting on rights and wrongs but by being more realistic on what could contribute to peace'. The DMZ was indeed only part of the Geneva agreements, but 'a measure of de-escalation' might lead to their full implementation. The US had made it clear that the future of South Vietnam should be settled by the exercise of a free choice by its people. 'Neither the exercise of such a choice nor application of the Geneva Agreements was possible at the moment.' The Paris talks should not fail. Wilson and Kosygin had agreed to do what they could for a settlement.

Stewart said he was encouraged that North Vietnam had made some statements about the type of government it would consider satisfactory in South Vietnam. That had to be covered in a later stage of the talks, 'but he was glad that North Viet-Nam believed that South Viet-Nam had a right to exist and to have a Government'. He agreed with the US that such a government should be chosen freely by the people. That was 'a wholly legitimate concept', said Gromyko. It had been envisaged in the Geneva agreements, which the US had, however, 'wholly undermined'. 'It was impossible to conceive of free elections being conducted in the presence in South Viet-Nam of an American army of half a million.' The conversation ended with more repetition but no agreement.[90]

The SD had asked Bruce to urge Stewart to take the line that if the US were to stop the bombing totally, the SU should cut back on its military supplies to the North and also those that went to the South.[91] The question was not raised. On his return Stewart said he had tried to make it clear to Gromyko that North Vietnam should make some response to the restriction of the bombing. He pointed out that 'failing that there might be a strong swing of public opinion in the United States that would feel that stopping the bombing was an unwise step'.[92] Gromyko was 'perfectly friendly', Stewart told Rusk, but his presentation of the North Vietnamese position was 'entirely orthodox and uncompromising'. Under pressure, he fell back on the thesis that it was up to the US as the aggressor to make the next moves. 'We brought home no bacon today. At the same time I am sure it is right to keep pegging away at the Russians both to keep them, as they would wish to be, in the picture and because I am sure that they cannot afford not to pass on all that I said to Hanoi and Xuan Thuy in Paris.'[93]

Why had the Russians wanted to talk about Vietnam if they had nothing new to say? They had waited till the US/North Vietnam meeting had been arranged, and then invited Stewart to Moscow in the hope of finding out more about the US position. The postponement of the visit, however, partly frustrated their objective: by the time it took place, it was clear that there was little 'give' in the American position. So the British ambassador in Moscow, Sir G. Harrison, argued.[94] The Russians were always part of Britain's diplomacy. They had perhaps become more so by Wilson's time, but not to much advantage. The year 1968 was to be the bloodiest year of the war. Over 1,000 American soldiers died each month, and the Vietnamese fatalities were eight times as high.[95]

Conclusion

The prime feature of Britain's diplomacy in the post-war period as in the Second World War itself was, of course, the 'special relationship' with the United States. In face of the other great superpower, Britain needed an American security guarantee, and throughout the period with which this book is concerned, and indeed beyond, it sought to avoid a clash with its essential ally. It also hoped, more ambitiously, to influence it. In particular it sought to discourage its adoption of policies that might generate a further war and so undermine the main objective of the policy itself. At the same time, it had to show some support. The policy was difficult to carry out, since its two objectives were not entirely compatible. Nor did the US consider the relationship quite so special as the British considered it.

Over time, moreover, Britain's power diminished. The Second World War, like the First, had imposed vast costs, and the further demands of participation in the Korean War made it hard to restore or revive British industry. Nor was the attempt to draw on colonial resources successful. By the late 1950s, Britain was anxious to rid itself of colonial burdens, though doing it in a more responsible way than other colonial powers. Decolonisation was something the US encouraged, but it was anxious that Britain should nevertheless remain active in the world, and, of course, support American priorities. For some time at least US administrations were, moreover, unwilling to act or seem to act unilaterally. The support of Western powers, in particular Britain, was necessary to justify its actions overseas to the domestic audience. Otherwise it might not be able to resist a recurrence of isolationism.

Personal quarrels—such as that between Eden and Dulles over Geneva—did not help. But after Suez Macmillan did his best to restore the relationship, enjoying some success with Eisenhower, and even more with Kennedy. As early as 1958 he rather optimistically told Britain's representatives in East Asia that 'Anglo-American cooperation had been put back on the footing of our old war-time relationship'.[1] In the following years the British were able to lead the US into a second Geneva conference and its chairman, Malcolm MacDonald, to play a major role in securing the agreement over Laos. But that was Britain's last diplomatic triumph in Southeast Asia. Its efforts over Vietnam—which the Laos agreement made even more a focus for American efforts—were unsuccessful.

Britain, moreover, had even less leverage than before. Its interest in Southeast Asia was diminishing. Malaya, in the early post-war years a dollar-earner, was now less rewarding, and, both as a means of terminating the Emergency, and a sign of the successful struggle against it, Malaya secured its independence in 1957. There was all the more pressure in Singapore for constitutional advance. That made it difficult to think that it could for long remain the major base for British forces in East Asia, and it was recognised that their tenure could not extend beyond another decade. In the meantime Malaysia might provide an answer, offering a means of constraining the leftward tendency of Singapore's politics and providing its nascent industries with a market. The bargain would be more acceptable in Malaya if the Borneo territories were also included. Malaysia was rather hastily pushed together during 1961–63. Too little account had been taken of Indonesia, however, and, led by Sukarno, it confronted the new Federation and the British and Commonwealth forces that came to its support. The scheme had not solved Britain's problem but intensified it.

Why had the British undertaken the scheme even though they thought they would not be able to retain the Singapore base for much longer? The Treasury wanted economy on defence in order to avoid a collapse of the pound, and the Left wanted to avoid cuts in welfare. The FO argued that the economies could not be effected until the end of Confrontation. It also argued that retaining the base supported the Anglo-American relationship. With no effective forces in the East, Britain's influence in the 'special relationship' would diminish. But while its forces were engaged with Indonesia, it could do little elsewhere. Earlier it had argued that it was fighting Communism in Malaya, while the US was fighting it on the mainland. Now, however, it was facing an Indonesian nationalism with which the US had some sympathy. The best Home could do was to obtain in February 1964—in the context of growing evidence of the new president's commitment to South Vietnam—LBJ's agreement to a rather general statement of mutual support. But, designed to limit US interference in the Malay world, that, of course, also diminished any influence Britain had on mainland policy.

Like leftists at the time, Logevall argues that Wilson could have had more influence if he had spoken out against Johnson's policies.[2] But, as Young says, he and Stewart 'were always convinced that such a course would have alienated them from Johnson completely, destroying any chance they might have had of moderating him'.[3] And LBJ hardly encouraged them.

'It is unbearably hard to fight a limited war,' wrote Lady Bird Johnson.[4] The president was fighting within narrow limits, imposed by international factors, but also by his unwillingness to risk the domestic impact of a wider war. He was 'said to have rejected the view of some of his advisers that in order to hold the support of the country he would have to engage in some outright chauvinistic rabble-rousing and provide the American people with a vivid foe. Such a mobilization of patriotic sentiments … could force him into unduly risky actions … which, in turn, could lead to a confrontation with Communist China or Russia. At the very least, a widening of the war might prevent the achievement of his domestic "Great Society" programs.'[5] LBJ, as Frank Ninkovich argues, was 'reluctant … to stir up patriotic emotions that could not be controlled'.[6]

'For Hanoi's leaders,' as George Ball recognised, 'control of the whole of Vietnam was a fanatical, almost religious, objective they had relentlessly pursued for twenty years; for America, the war was a marginal affair not worth a head-on clash with Peking or Moscow, a struggle to be waged with a limited commitment of manpower and weaponry. … The conflict was a limited war for limited objectives—a type of warfare for which a democracy is organically badly suited.' Could America, as a democratic state, 'fight a limited war that lasted more than a year or so and still keep it limited'?[7] 'Our American people,' Johnson told a press conference on 17 November 1967, 'when we get in a contest of any kind—whether it is in a war, an election, a football game, or whatever it is—want it decided and decided quickly: get in or get out … That is not the kind of war we are fighting in Vietnam.'[8]

In an article sympathetic to the president, written in September 1967, Louis Heren pointed to the limits on the war, 'dictated by the nuclear discipline. They are unpopular because they prolong the war and probably increase American casualties.' They had to be maintained against the pressure of Congress Committee chairmen and the chiefs of staff, supported by 'an impatient people'. Soundings were to be made of Hanoi. What if bombing stopped? And if talks began? And if no agreement were reached? A 'senior official put it to Heren that "[t]he result could be disastrous. After demonstrating that Hanoi was not prepared for peace except on its own terms, the demand here for total war could be irrepressible."'[9] Too often, indeed, it is forgotten that it was not only the left wing that criticised the president.

Clark Clifford exclaimed in November 1968 that for five years LBJ had received '[e]xcruciatingly unbearable awful advice' which had got the

US in so deeply without realising what its national interest was.[10] But he himself had been something of a hawk before he mutated into a dove. Searching for a consensus amidst all the advice he received, the president had to make the final decisions. No wonder he seemed arbitrary or secretive. No wonder advice from outside seemed an unwelcome complication in his decision-making.

'The Cold War turned into a cold peace because the destructive power of nuclear weaponry and delivery systems had evolved to a point that all-out war was rendered meaningless,' Frank Ninkovich writes. The key to avoiding it was 'a new politics in which the ability to maintain American credibility became an ersatz substitute for victory, while its loss became a token of defeat'.[11] Nguyen Cao Ky accepted that the US was wary of all-out war. But if it had to be a limited war, there was no need to send half a million men. 'Right from the start,' he argued, 'America should have adopted a long-term plan and a patient attitude and been prepared to accept a people's war that might have taken another ten years to win, without causing the divisiveness back home in the United States.' But '[t]he Americans believed that by bulldozing tactics they could win quickly, even though fighting a limited war'. The two, however, did not go together. 'The Americans also believed that they could win the people's war, the battle for the hearts of the people, while waging a military one. And they could not.'[12]

In a pamphlet published in August 1966 Eden advocated a new Geneva, with strong guarantees; a neutral belt; and a Locarno. Ten to 15 years would be allowed before the North and South had to decide for or against unification.[13] Well-meant, but not a programme Le Duan would accept. The FO itself had no answers on Vietnam that could be helpful. Cable and others thought that the 'war' was unwinnable, and that Britain should help to get the US out without loss of face. Maybe their well-argued proposals were after all too facile. In any case, beset by fiscal and economic problems, in which US help might be needed, the Labour government was cautious about raising the issue when the new PM first met the president. When the president began bombing the North he phoned LBJ and proposed to visit as Attlee had done when it was thought Truman might use the atomic bomb in the Korean War. The visit was unwelcome. LBJ—perhaps partly because he had reached his own decision with such doubt—was not an easy man to persuade. The personal relationship was never really restored.

It was in this context that Wilson turned increasingly to the Russians, whom he thought he knew. Over the Laos conference they had seemed to be helpful—and indeed Harriman had thought that the co-chairmen were the basis for a settlement—but Khrushchev lost interest. His successors revived the Russian interest in Vietnam, and Wilson believed that Britain could exercise some influence on them by pointing to Britain's influence with the US. In turn he could, he hoped, persuade them to influence the DRV, and so provide the US with a prospect for negotiating the end of the war. At the same time, that would demonstrate to left-wing critics at home that his government was trying to end the struggle, and persuade others that Britain was still playing a world role, even if it was not a world power. 'If the British can play a major, publicized role in terminating the war,' remarked General Wheeler, chairman of the Joint Chiefs of Staff in the US, 'it will further British desire to continue to be a leading power on the world stage.'[14]

The Russians were, however, unwilling or unable to do much to help. One reason was the attitude of the PRC. Abandoning the coexistence line that had prevailed at the time of the first Geneva conference, Mao's China had taken up the cause of the revolutionary struggle, and the Bloc, insofar as it had ever existed, disintegrated. But that did not make it easier for the SU to pursue a policy that differed completely from China's. The competition of the two powers for the leadership of world Communism was as conducive to extremism as their cooperation had been, if not more. The Russians could not be seen to be letting the North Vietnamese down while the Chinese were supporting them, and that they continued to do.[15] And not only were the Russians often unwilling to perform a mediating role: 'Hanoi also often took little notice when it did.'[16] They could not 'deliver' the DRV even as Wilson asserted he could 'deliver' the US. Despite the doubts of FO officials, he was active almost to the point of humiliation, but the end of the war was to come about through another route.

LBJ's policies did not work. Bombing did not have the effect his advisers suggested: it provoked the Vietnamese, intensifying Le Duan's dominance, and alienated opinion elsewhere. Introducing ground forces aroused domestic opposition, and its success, accompanied, like the bombing, by considerable losses, was not recognised as such. Then he drew back, hoping perhaps to avoid a Democrat defeat in the forthcoming presidential election. He realised, maybe too late, that more could have been done to build up an effective regime in the South. But that was perhaps not feasible even in the latter days of the Diem regime, let alone amid the expanded conflict that followed his overthrow. Maybe it was never feasible. Though Vietnam had known division in the past, the DRV could not only indulge in violence but could convincingly fly the banner of national unification while South Vietnam could not, even if the US had wanted it to. The determination of the DRV leaders was underestimated even by the British, who were so sure that nationalism was prevailing and would prevail in

Southeast Asia as elsewhere. 'Nationalism is as strong [in Southeast Asia] as elsewhere', Lord Avon [Eden] put it in 1967: 'too strong, if you like.'[17] This was not a proxy war, though influenced from outside: it was that bitterest of wars, a civil war.

When he left his post in Saigon in July 1966, Etherington-Smith had related, with the frankness the FO allowed its officers, his misgivings about Britain's policy in Vietnam. The PM had spoken in the Commons of political compromise. The idea was 'illusory': the issue was whether North Vietnam should get South Vietnam or not. Etherington-Smith believed that the threat to South Vietnam could still be defeated, and that the UK should do what it could to ensure that it was. The UK declared its support for the US, but its attitude was in fact one of 'hesitation, reticence and ambiguity', and its contribution on the ground most meagre. It used every excuse to explain its failure to do more: confrontation, financial difficulties, the role of co-chairman. It should step up its contribution in 'specific and limited ways'. As it was, friends and allies increasingly saw Britain's behaviour as 'negative, defeatist and hypocritical'.[18] The ambassador thought a satisfactory solution could be achieved if the West showed determination, Fyjis-Walker commented. But he foresaw a situation in which the Communists went underground, the US stopped bombing, and subversion was renewed. That was hardly a satisfactory solution. The FO's thinking—that the only real solution was a negotiated solution—was the right one.[19] It was a long way off even in 1968. And when the 'compromise' was made—without any Geneva or any role for Britain—the outcome was rather like the one Etherington-Smith prophesied.

Was Britain's way with LBJ—not all the way, but some—doomed to frustration? The influence it might have had was always limited. Many of the ideas developed in the FO were not even put to the Americans: it never seemed to be the right time, officials lamented. The politicians went further: they tried to reconcile misgivings and opposition at home with their overall reliance on the US. Did they exaggerate their potential influence? There is little doubt that they were still trying to play a world role, even as their power to do so diminished. Their efforts were unlikely to succeed, but it is understandable that they should have been made, and hard to conclude that they should not have been.

Notes

Introduction

1. Walsh to Foreign Secretary, 26 March 1942. FO 371/31751 [F4969/90/61], National Archives, Kew.
2. Jeffrey Pickering, *Britain's Withdrawal from East of Suez* (Houndsmills: Macmillan, 1998), p. 48.
3. Memorandum, 11.8.51. *British Documents on the End of Empire*, Series A, Vol. 4, Pt 2, London: TSO, 1992, Document 162, at p. 377.
4. Ibid., Doc 150, at p. 339.
5. MacLehose for SofS/Garvey, 29.3.65, Despatch 23. FO 371/185929 [FC 1022/8].
6. Graves/Morrison, 12.7.51. FO 371/93017 [FZ1022/94].
7. N. Tarling, *Britain, Southeast Asia and the Impact of the Korean War* (Singapore: NUS Press, 2005), p. 184.
8. DO (52) 2nd, 19.3.52. CAB 131/12, National Archives, Kew.
9. Tarling, pp. 191–2.
10. Quoted in Walter La Feber, 'The United States and Vietnam: The Enemies', in *The War That Never Ends*, ed. David L. Martin and John Ernst (Lexington: University Press of Kentucky, 2007), p. 47.
11. Cable/Addis, 2.3.64. FO 371/175066 [D1051/21].
12. Quoted in Ilya V. Gaiduk, *Confronting Vietnam: Soviet Policy towards the Indo-China Conflict* (Stanford University Press; Washington: Woodrow Wilson Center Press, 2003), p. 23.
13. Quoted in Weng Shao, *China, Britain and Businessmen* (Basingstoke: Macmillan, 1991), p. 145.
14. Joint Declaration, 28.6.54, in *Documents on China's Relations with South and South-East Asia (1949–1962)*, ed. G.V. Ambekar and V.D. Divedar (Bombay: Allied, 1964), pp. 7–8.
15. Tarling, pp. 306, 309, 315.
16. Ibid., p. 324.
17. Ibid., p. 334.
18. C (54) 207, 22.6.54. CAB 129/69.
19. CC (54) 43, 22.6.54, 2. CAB 128/27.
20. Hansard, 529, col. 433. Tel to HCs, 24.6.54, Y148. FO 371/112075 [DF1071/776].

21. Minute by Allen, 24.6.54. FO 371/111867 [D1074/155].
22. Makins/Eden, 3.8.54, 388. FO 371/112084 [DF1071/1012].
23. Meeting, 25.6.54. FRUS VI, p. 1083.
24. Hansard, 532, 8.11.54, col. 930.
25. Telegram, 27.6.54, 298S. FO 371/112075 [DF1071/792].
26. Memorandum, 26.6.54. FRUS VI, pp. 1091-2; XII, pp. 576–7.
27. Telegram, 27.6.54, 1300. FO 371/111867 [D1074/145].
28. Telegram, 26.6.54. P. Mendès-France, *Gouverner c'est choisir* (Paris: Gallimard, 1986), pp. 87–9. Telegram, 29.6.54, 375. FO 371/112075 [DF1071/785]. SofS/Embassy Paris, 28.6.54, cable 4852. FRUS XIII, pp. 1755-7; XVI, pp. 1257–9.
29. Telegram, 27.6.54, 1303. FO 371/112075 [DF1071/786].
30. Record, 27.6.54. FO 371/111869 [D1074/212].
31. Record, 29.6.54. DF1071/786.
32. Dulles/Embassy, 7.7.54, cable 77. FRUS XIII, p. 1792.
33. Allen/Jebb, 1.7.54. Ibid.
34. Telegram ex Makins, 30.6.54, 30S. FO 371/112090 [DF1073/41].
35. J.L. Gaddis, *We Now Know* (Oxford: Clarendon Press, 1997), p. 163.
36. Chen Jian, 'China and the First Indo-China War', *China Quarterly* 133 (1993): 109.
37. F. Joyaux, *La Chine et le règlement du premier conflit d'Indochine* (Paris: Sorbonne, 1979), pp. 262–3.
38. Quoted in Qiang Zhai, *China and the Vietnam Wars 1950–1975* (Chapel Hill, London: University of North Carolina Press, 2000), p. 60.
39. Telegram, 17.7.54, 952. FO 371/112079 [DF1071/884].
40. Telegram, 17.7.54, 956. FO 371/112078 [DF1071/880]. Diary, s.d. Avon Papers 20/17/231, Birmingham University Library.
41. Telegram, 17.7.54, 959. FO 371/112079 [DF1071/885].
42. Telegram, 19.7.54, 982. FO 371/112080 [DF1071/902].
43. Telegram, 19.7.54, 984. FO 371/112080 [DF1071/904].
44. Reply, 20.7.54. PREM 11/646, National Archives, Kew.
45. CC (54) 51st, 20.7.54, 1. CAB 128/27.
46. Telegram, 21.7.54, 1007. FO 371/112080 [DF1071/919].
47. Telegrams, 18.7.54, 966; 19.7, 969. FO 371/112079 [DF1071/889, 895].
48. Joyaux, pp. 282, 284.
49. Telegram 1007 as above.
50. See G. McT. Kahin and John W. Lewis, *The United States in Vietnam* (New York: Delta, 1967), pp. 372–3.
51. Telegram, 21.7.54, 1014. FO 371/112081 [DF1071/928].
52. CC (54) 52nd, 23.7.54, 4. CAB 128/27.
53. Eden/Lyttelton, 19.7.54. Avon Papers 20/17/146A.
54. Tarling, pp. 319–20.
55. Conversation, 19.8.54. FRUS XII, p. 735.
56. Damien Fenton, *To Cage the Dragon* (Singapore: NUS Press, 2012), pp. 234–5.
57. Memorandum, 14.12.68. FRUS 1964-68 VII Doc 255.

58. Eisenhower to 'President' Diem [thus Kahin's mistaken heading], 1.10.54, quoted in Kahin and Lewis, App 4, pp. 382–3.
59. R. Buzzanco, *Vietnam and the Transformation of American Life* (Malden, Mass.; Oxford: Blackwell, 1999), p. 53.
60. FRUS XII, p. 667.
61. Ibid., p. 730.
62. Graves/Tahourdin, 30.10.54. FO 371/112030 [DF1015/216].
63. Etherington-Smith/Tahourdin, 1.11.54. FO 371/112030 [DF1015/217].
64. Minute, 11.11.54. FO 371/112030 [DF1015/216].
65. Minute, 11.11.54. Ibid.
66. Minute, 15.11.54. FO 371/112030 [DF1015/221].
67. Brief, 15.12.54. FO 371/112100 [DF1075/18].
68. Memorandum, 15.12.54. FO 371/112100 [DF1075/22].
69. Conversation, 16.1.54. FO 371/112100 [DF1075/24].
70. Joy/Tahourdin, 8.1.55. FO 371/117176 [DF1072/9].
71. Minutes, 11, 12.1.55. Ibid.
72. Minute by Cable, 8.12.54. FO 371/112097 [DF1074/166].
73. Memorandum, 14.12.54. FO 371/112032 [DF1015/264].
74. Minute, 5.1.55. Ibid.
75. Minute, 11.1.55. FO 371/117115 [DF1018/15].
76. Minute, 17.1.55. FO 371/117176 [DF1072/10].
77. Minute, 18.1.55. Ibid.
78. Arthur Combs, 'The Path Not Taken: The British Alternative to U.S. Policy in Vietnam, 1954–1956', *Diplomatic History* 19, 1 (Winter 1995): 48.
79. Telegrams, 5.4.55, 223, 211. FO 371/117176 [DF1072/30].
80. Note, 16.4.55, in Telegram, 19.4.55, 222. FO 371/117176 [DF1072/46].
81. Minute, 26.4.55. FO 371/117176 [DF1072/47].
82. Telegram ex Baker, 7.6.55, 140. FO 371/117142 [DF1041/21].
83. Telegram, 7.7.55, 1569. FO 371/117143 [DF1041/77].
84. Millard/Graham, 9.7.55. Ibid.
85. SofS/Vietnam Embassy, 22.7.55, 4. FRUS I, p. 495.
86. Brief for Cabinet, 5.9.55. FO 371/117145 [DF1041/141].
87. Minute, 6.9.55. FO 371/117146 [DF1041/143].
88. Minute by Tomlinson, 20.2.56, quoted in Philip Hughes, 'Division and Discord: British Policy, Indochina, and the Origins of the Vietnam War, 1954–6', in *International Diplomacy and Colonial Retreat*, ed. Kent Fedorovich and Martin Thomas (London, Portland: Cass, 2001), p. 105.
89. Ilya Gaiduk, *Confronting Vietnam* (Stanford University Press; Washington: Woodrow Wilson Center Press, 2003), p. 82.
90. Minute, 14.6.56, quoted in Hughes, p. 106.
91. James Cable, *The Geneva Conference of 1954 in Indochina* (London: Macmillan, 1986), p. 140. The message is quoted by Eden in his *Towards Peace in Indo-China* (London: OUP/RIIA, 1966), pp. 53–5.
92. D.R. SarDesai, *Indian Foreign Policy in Cambodia, Laos and Vietnam, 1947–64* (Berkeley, Los Angeles: University of California Press, 1968), p. 103.

93. Hughes, p. 107.
94. Quoted in Robert K. Brigham, *Guerrilla Diplomacy: The NLF's Foreign Relations and the Viet Nam War* (Ithaca, London: Cornell University Press, 1999), p. 4.
95. Gaiduk, p. 84. Ang Cheng Guan, *The Vietnam War from the Other Side* (London: RoutledgeCurzon, 2002), pp. 16–7.
96. Lien-Hang T. Nguyen, *Hanoi's War* (Chapel Hill: University of North Carolina Press, 2012), p. 43.
97. Gaiduk, p. 110.
98. Ang, pp. 34–6. Nguyen Vu Tang, 'Coping with the United States: Hanoi's Search for an Effective Strategy', in *The Vietnam War*, ed. Peter Lowe (Basingstoke: Macmillan, 1998), p. 40.
99. William S. Turley, *The Second Indochina War* (Lanham: Rowman & Littlefield, 2009), p. 44.
100. Wallace J. Thies, *When Governments Collide* (Berkeley, Los Angeles: University of California Press, 1980), p. 242.
101. Pierre Asselin, *Hanoi's Road to the Vietnamese War, 1954–1965* (Berkeley, Los Angeles, London: University of California Press, 2013), p. 50.
102. Ibid., p. 89.
103. Keith W. Taylor, *A History of the Vietnamese* (Cambridge University Press, 2013), p. 574.
104. Gaiduk, p. 114.
105. Ibid., p. 114.
106. Chester Cooper, *The Lost Crusade* (London: McGibbon and Kee, 1971), p. 156.
107. Robert K. Brigham, *ARVN: Life and Death in the South Vietnamese Army* (Lawrence: University Press of Kansas, 2006), p. 4.
108. Nguyen Cao Ky, *How We Lost the Vietnam War* (New York: Cooper Square Press, 2000 [previously published in 1976]), p. 130.
109. Minute, 30.7.65. FO 371/180587 [DV 1075/168].
110. Michael Stewart, *Life and Labour* (London: Sidgwick and Jackson, 1980), p. 151.
111. Orrin Schwab, *A Clash of Cultures: Civil-Military Relations during the Vietnam War* (Westport, London: Praeger, 2006), p. 135.
112. Brigham, p. 121.
113. David L. DiLeo, *George Ball, Vietnam and the Rethinking of Containment* (Chapel Hill, London: University of North Carolina Press, 1991), p. 75.
114. Talking Paper prepared by Sullivan, 7.5.64. FRUS 1964-68, I, Doc 145.
115. Nguyen Cao Ky, p. 100.
116. Quoted in David Kaiser, *American Tragedy* (Cambridge: Belknap Press of Harvard University Press, 2000), p. 110.
117. Caccia/Home, 10.7.61, 132. FO 371/159712 [D 103145/13].
118. Memorandum, 21.6.61. FO 371 159715 [D 1053/2].
119. Minute, 1.11.61. FO 371/159722 [D 103113/9].
120. Quoted in D. Easter, *Britain and the Confrontation with Indonesia 1960–66* (London, New York: Tauris, 2004), p. 16.

121. Memorandum, Britain and Indo-China, 1.11.61. FO 371/159722 [D 103113/9].
122. Minute, 1.11.61. FO 371/159722 [D 103113/9].
123. P. Busch, *All the Way with JFK? Britain, the US, and the Vietnam War* (Oxford University Press, 2003), p. 54.
124. N. Tarling, *Britain and the Neutralisation of Laos* (Singapore: NUS Press, 2011), p. 438.
125. N. Tarling, *Britain and Sihanouk's Cambodia* (Singapore: NUS Press, 2014), pp. 58–9.
126. Heppel/Tomlinson, 23.5.56. FO 371/123419 [DF 1022/24].
127. Anderson/Warner, 8.5.61. FO 371/159722 [D 10133/3].
128. Quoted in V.B. Karnik, ed., *China Invades India* (Bombay: Allied, 1963), p. 221.
129. Visit of Mr Nehru, 4.11.61, South Vietnam, Brief for Prime Minister. FO 371/159715 [D 1053/9].
130. Talking Points. FO 371/159715 [D 1053/15].
131. Quoted in Busch, p. 73.
132. Quoted in Ibid., p. 89.
133. Home/Treasury, 25.2.63, quoted in Ian F.W. Beckett, 'Robert Thompson and the British Advisory Mission to South Vietnam, 1961–1965', *Small Wars and Insurgencies* 8, 3 (Winter 1997): 41–63, at p. 46.
134. Peter Lowe, *Contending with Nationalism and Communism* (Basingstoke: Palgrave Macmillan, 2009), pp. 140–1.
135. MacLehose for FSy/Garvey, 29.3.65, 23 FO 371/185929 [FC 1022/8].
136. Hohler/Warner, 1.8.62. FO 371/166706 [DV 1015/166].
137. Quoted in Charles G. Cogan, 'How Fuzzy Can One Be?', in *The Search for Peace in Vietnam 1964–1968*, ed. Lloyd C. Gardner and Ted Gittinger (College Station: Texas A&M University Press, 2004), p. 146; and in Pierre Journoud, *De Gaulle et le Vietnam, 1945–1969: La reconciliation* (Paris: Tallandier, 2011), pp. 117–8.
138. Warner/Hohler, 15.8.62. FO 371/166706 [DV 1015/166].
139. Joseph Buttinger, *Vietnam: A Dragon Embattled* (London: Pall Mall, 1967), p. 990.
140. Talking Points for Washington, 13.4.62. FO 371/166353 [D 1015/8].
141. Talking Points for Ottawa, 13.4.62. FO 371/166353 [D 1015/8].
142. Warner/Hohler, 24.5.62. FO 371/166353 [D 1015/13].
143. Record of a Discussion on South East Asia, 22.7.62. FO 371/166354 [D 1015/25].
144. Warner/Ormsby Gore, 26.7.62. Ibid.
145. Frederick Nolting, *From Trust to Tragedy* (New York: Praeger, 1988), pp. 132–3.
146. Quoted in Busch, p. 155.
147. Quoted in Ibid., p. 157.
148. Ibid., pp. 166–7.
149. Lyndon B. Johnson, *The Vantage Point* (London: Weidenfeld, 1972), p. 44.
150. Gaiduk, p. 183.

151. Arthur M. Schlesinger, *Robert Kennedy and His Times* (London: Deutsch, 1978), p. 725.
152. Quoted in Robert A. Caro, *The Years of Lyndon Johnson: The Passage of Power* (New York: Vintage, 2013), p. 402.
153. Ibid., p. 403.
154. Gareth Porter, *Perils of Dominance* (Berkeley, Los Angeles, London: University of California Press, 2005), pp. 183–4.
155. Qiang Zhai, p. 139. Randall B. Woods, *LBJ: Architect of American Ambition* (New York: Free Press, 2006), p. 504.
156. Woods, p. 505.
157. Quoted in John Lewis Gaddis, *George F. Kennan: An American Life* (New York: Penguin, 2011), p. 591.
158. Quoted in David Mayers, *George Kennan and the Dilemmas of American Foreign Policy* (New York, Oxford: Oxford University Press, 1988), p. 331.
159. Qiang Zhai, 'An Uneasy Relationship', in *International Perspectives on Vietnam*, ed. Lloyd C. Gardner and Ted Gittinger (College Station: Texas A&M University Press, 1999), p. 116.
160. Quoted in Nguyen Vu Tang, in Lowe, p. 46.
161. Ibid., pp. 46–7.
162. Asselin, pp. 135–6.
163. Quoted in Ibid., p. 166.
164. Nguyen, *Hanoi's War*, pp. 51–3, 59, 63, 74–5.
165. Gaiduk, p. 197.
166. Ilya V. Gaiduk, *The Soviet Union and the Vietnam War* (Chicago: Dee, 1996), p. 18.
167. Ibid., pp. 24, 27.

Chapter One

1. Telegram, 12.12.63. FRUS 1961-63, IV, Doc 365.
2. Thompson/Peck, 19.12.63. FO 371/170096 [DV 1015/144].
3. Trench/Cable, 27.12.63. FO 371/170096 [DV 1015/145].
4. Minute by Cable, 31.12.63. Ibid.
5. Forster/Wakefield, 8.1.64, and enclosure. FO 371/175493 [DV 103145/2]. Woods, p. 506.
6. Telegram ex Ormsby Gore, 3.2.64, 415. FO 371/175493 [DV 103145/8].
7. Notes for Possible Discussion between H.M. Ambassador, Washington, and President Johnson or Mr Rusk, 20.1.64. FO 371/175065 [D 1051/3].
8. Matthew Jones, *Conflict and Confrontation in South East Asia 1961–1965* (Cambridge University Press, 2002), pp. 250–1.
9. *Times*, 20.1.64.
10. Minute, 21.1.64. FO 371/175065 [D 1051/5].
11. Telegram, 21.1.64, 962. Ibid.; also FRUS 1964-8 XXVI, Doc 24.
12. The Western Position in South East Asia, 4.2.64. FO 371/175090 [D 1073/3]; also PM (W) (64) 30. FO 371/178904 [W2/62].

13. The British Position in South-East Asia in Its International Setting, 5.2.64. FO 371 175090 [D 1073/3].
14. Minute, 29.1.64. Ibid.
15. Minute, 3.2.64. Ibid.
16. Summary, n.d. FO 371/175090 [D 1073/12].
17. Minute by Peck, 11.2.64. Ibid.
18. Aide-memoire, 12.2.64. FO 371/175090 [D 1073/11].
19. Conversation, 12.2.64, White House, 3 p.m. FO 371/178904 [W2/80].
20. Extract, PM (W) (64) 2nd, 12.2.64. FO 371/175090 [D 1073/6].
21. Fn 5 to Doc 41, FRUS I.
22. *The Times*, 14.2.64. It also published the communiqué.
23. Minute, 20.2.64. FO 371/175090 [D 1073/13].
24. Telegram ex Dean, 11.2.64, 242. FO 371/175493 [DV 103145/11].
25. Minute, 12.2 64. Ibid.
26. Caccia/Greenhill, 17.2.64. Ibid.
27. Quoted in Porter, p. 185.
28. Telegram, 28.2.64, 3205. FO 371/175494 [DV 103145/22].
29. Telegrams, 28.2.64, 846, 848. Ibid.
30. Minute, 27.2.64. FO 371/175494 [DV 103145/26].
31. Minute, 29.2.64. FO 371/175494 [DV 103145/22].
32. Minute by Caccia, 29.2.64. Ibid.
33. CAB 128/38.
34. Message, 2.3.64. FO 371/175494 [DV 103145/22].
35. SD/London, 1.3.64, Telegram 5534. FRUS 1, Doc 64.
36. Cable/Etherington-Smith, 10.3.64. FO 371/175494 [DV 103145/35].
37. Telegram, 7.3.64, 222. FO 371/175494 [DV 103145/27].
38. Minute, 9.3.64. Ibid.
39. F. Logevall, *Choosing War* (Berkeley, Los Angeles, London: University of California Press, 1999), p. 151.
40. Quoted in Woods, p. 509.
41. Porter, p. 189.
42. Vietnam: Some Possible Solutions, n.d. [9.3.64] FO 371/175494 [DV 103145/33].
43. Addis/Cable, 25.3.64. Ibid.
44. Minute, 10.3.64. FO 371/175494 [DV 103145/27].
45. FO/Harlech, 11.3.64. FO 371/175494 [DV 103145/33].
46. Trench/Peck, 31.3.64. Ibid.
47. NSC Action Memo 288, quoted in David Kaiser, 'Discussions, Not Negotiations', in *Search for Peace*, ed. Lloyd C. Gardner and Ted Gittinger (College Station: Texas A&M University Press, 2004), p. 48.
48. Etherington-Smith/Cable, 25.3.64. FO 371/175495 [DV 103145/52].
49. Cable/Etherington-Smith, 13.4.64. FO 371/175495 [DV 103145/52].
50. Telegram, 18.4.64, 722. Ibid.
51. Trench/Cable, 22.4.64. FO 371/175495 [DV 103145/60].
52. Etherington-Smith/Cable, 22.4.64. FO 371/175496 [DV 103145/66].

53. Cable/Etherington-Smith, 1.5.64. Ibid.
54. Thompson/Peck, 22.4.64. FO 371/175496 [DV 103145/71].
55. Minute, 25.4.64. FO 371/175496 [DV 103145/70].
56. Minute, 16.4.64. FO 371/175506 [DV 1051/11].
57. Minute, 17.4.64. Ibid.
58. Minute, 7.5.64. FO 371/175506 [DV 1051/15].
59. Cable/Etherington-Smith, 9.6.64. FO 371/175496 [DV 103145/83].
60. Etherington-Smith/Cable, 18.6.64. FO 371/175068 [D 1051/65].
61. Murray/Cable, 20.5.64. FO 371/175068 [D 1051/62].
62. FRUS I, Doc 27.
63. Visit of the French Ambassador, Talking Points on South East Asia, 17.2.64. FO 371/175090 [D 1073/8].
64. DEA/Washington, 11.2.64, Savingram 37. FO 371/175091 [D 1074/1].
65. Cablegram, Austemba Paris/DEA, 13.2.64, 327. FO 371/175091 [D 1074/9].
66. Minute by J.B. Pedler in P.E. Ramsbotham/Cable, 24.3.64. FO 371/175091 [D 1074/5].
67. President/Bohlen, 23.4.64. FRUS I, Doc 96.
68. Telegram, 4.4.64, 248. FO 371/175091 [D 1074/8]. FRUS I, Doc 105, summarises the conversation less extensively.
69. Telegram 4.4.64, 252. FO 371/175091 [D 1074/7].
70. Dixon/Butler, 4.5.64, dispatch 59. FO 371/17509i [D 1074/11].
71. Peck/Dixon, 25.5.64. Ibid.
72. Addis/Butler, 12.5.64, dispatch 34. FO 371/175091 [D 1074/15].
73. Murray/Butler, 18.5.64. FO 371/175091 [D 1074/16].
74. Conversation, 8.6.64. FO 371/175091 [D 1074/19].
75. Telegram, 6.6.64, Secun 3. FRUS I, Doc 202. See also Journoud, *De Gaulle et le Vietnam*, p. 173.
76. Minute by Douglas Brown, SEAD, 8.6.64. FO 371/175091 [D 1074/20].
77. Telegram, 17.6.64, 111S. FO 371/175091 [D 1074/21A].
78. Telegram, 17.6.64, 112S. FO 371/175091 [D 1074/21].
79. Butler/Cable, 22.6.64. FO 371/175092 [D 1074/24].
80. Peck/Hohler, 23.6.64. FO 371/175092 [D 1074/23].
81. Minute, 29.6.64. Ibid.
82. Minute, 6.7.64. Ibid.
83. Telegram, 29.6.64, 671. FO 371/175092 [D 1074/25].
84. *The Johnson Press Conferences*, introd. Doris Kearns Goodwin (New York: Earl M. Coleman Enterprises, 1978), 2, 23.6.64. I, pp. 139, 148.
85. Minute, 29.6.64. FO 371/175092 [D 1074/25].
86. Telegram, 30.6.64, 8252. Ibid.
87. Dixon/Caccia, 30.6.64. FO 371/175092 [D 1074/30].
88. Burrows/Cable, 8.7.64. FO 371/175092 [D 1074/28].
89. P. Geyelin, *Lyndon B. Johnson and the World* (London, New York: Praeger/Pall Mall, 1966), p. 56.
90. Ramsbotham/Cable, 10.7.64. FO 371/175092 [D 1074/29].

91. Minute, 17.7.64. Ibid.
92. Minute, 20.7.64. Ibid.
93. Minute, 20.7.64. Ibid.
94. Telegram ex Dixon, 24.7.64, 537. FO 371/175092 [D 1074/32].
95. Mari Olsen, *Soviet-Vietnam Relations and the Role of China, 1949–64: Changing Alliances* (London, New York: Routledge, 2006), p. 132.
96. Memorandum, British Policy in Indo-China, 3.8.64. FO 371/175069 [D 1051/22].
97. Harlech/Caccia, 25.4.64. FO 371/175496 [DV 103145/67].
98. CC (64) 33rd, 25.6.64, 5. CAB 129/38.
99. Mac Bundy/President, 22.5.64. FRUS I, Doc 167.
100. Draft Memorandum for President, 25.5.64. Ibid., Doc 173.
101. SNIE, 25.6.64. Ibid., Doc 174.
102. Minute by Wakefield, 1.7.64. FO 371/175497 [DV 103145/93].
103. Quoted in Woods, p. 510.
104. Quoted in Mark K. Updegrove, *Indomitable Will: LBJ in the Presidency* (New York: Crown Publishers, 2012), p. 186.
105. Quoted in Porter, p. 192.
106. Blackwell/Cable, 25.2.64. FO 371/175495 [DV 103145/43].
107. Minute, 4.8.64. FO 371/175499 [DV 103145/131].
108. Thompson/Peck, 13.8.64. FO 371/175501 [DV 103145/178].
109. Minute, 17.8.64. Ibid.
110. Logewall, p. 202.
111. Ibid., p. 197. R.B. Frankum, *Like Rolling Thunder* (Lanham: Rowman & Littlefield, 2005), p. 13.
112. Lloyd C. Gardner, *Pay Any Price* (Chicago: Dee, 1995).
113. *Times*, 8.8.64. Joint Resolution, 10.8.64, in *Documents on American Foreign Policy 1964*, ed. Jules Davids (New York: Harper and Row, 1965), pp. 216–7.
114. Louis Heren, *No Hail, No Farewell* (London: Weidenfeld, 1970), p. 51.
115. *Times*, 8.8.64.
116. John Dumbrell, *President Lyndon Johnson and Soviet Communism* (Manchester, New York: Manchester University Press, 2004), p. 93.
117. Quoted in Woods, p. 517.
118. Johnson, *Vantage Point*, p. 119.
119. Gareth Porter, 'Coercive Diplomacy in Vietnam: The Tonkin Gulf Crisis Reconsidered', in *The American War in Vietnam*, ed. David Hunt and Jayne Werner (Ithaca: SEAP, 1993), pp. 10, 20; also editorial introduction, p. 4.
120. Asselin, *Hanoi's Road*, pp. 198, 200.
121. Douglas-Home is called Macmillan in FRUS I, Doc 282.
122. Telegram to Washington, 5.8.64, 9503. FO 371/175498 [DV 103145/110]; PREM 11/4760.
123. *Times*, 7.8.64.
124. Minute, 19.8.64. FO 371/175182 [DF 103145/18].
125. Forster/Cable, 2.10.64. FO 371/175502 [DV 103145/199].

Chapter Two

1. Trend/Burrows, 2.10.64. FO 371/175507 [DV 1051/37].
2. Sadi Dockrill, *Britain's Retreat from East of Suez* (Basingstoke: Macmillan, 2002), p. 51.
3. D.O. (O) (S) (64) 43; also O.P.P. (O) 64, 5, 21.10.64. CAB 148/10, National Archives, Kew. Extracts in *The Conservative Government and the End of Empire, 1957–1964, British Documents on the End of Empire*, Series A4, Part 1, HMSO, 2000, Doc 80.
4. DO (O) (64) 59, 22.9.64. CAB 148/7. Extracts in BDEE A4 Pt 1, and, as OPD (64) 10, 19.11.64, in BDEE A5 Pt I.
5. Memorandum, The Prospect in Viet-Nam and British Policy towards That Country, n.d. [?5 or 6.10.64]. FO 371/175507 [DV 1051/37].
6. Minute, 7.10.64. Ibid.
7. Burrows/Trend, 12.10.64. Ibid.
8. Minute, 13.10.64. Ibid.
9. Memorandum, The Future of Indo-China, Draft, n.d. Ibid.
10. Memorandum on Indo-China, 19.10.64. Ibid.
11. Minute by Peck, 20.10.64. Ibid.
12. Minute, 20.10.64. Ibid.
13. Background Note to Briefs Nos 7, 8, and 9, 21.10.64. FO 371/178907 [W2/162].
14. Record, 27.10.64. FO 371/175507 [DV 1051/40]; also PREM 13/692.
15. Cable/Etherington-Smith, 5.11.64. Ibid.
16. Etherington-Smith/Peck, 21.10.64. FO 371/175502 [DV 103145/202].
17. Minute, 28.10.64. Ibid.
18. Minute, 30.10.64. Ibid.
19. Minute, 10.11.64. FO 371/175095 [D 1077/1].
20. Minute, 10.11.64. Ibid.
21. Telegram, 14.11.64, 3751. FO 371/175095 [D 1077/2].
22. Telegram, 16.11.64, 13010. Ibid.
23. Telegram ex Harlech, 17.11.64, 3780. FO 371/175095 [D 1077/4].
24. Peck/M.N.F. Stewart, 18.11.64. Ibid.
25. Etherington-Smith/Peck, 5.11.64. FO 371/175503 [DV 103145/218].
26. Peck/Etherington-Smith, 12.11.64. Ibid.
27. Etherington-Smith/Peck, 18.11.64. FO 371/175503 [DV 103145/211].
28. Memorandum, 17.11.64. FO 371/175092 [D 1074/38].
29. Telegram, 12.11.64, 808. FO 371/175094 [D 1076/3].
30. Stewart/Peck, 9.11.64. FO 371/175503 [DV 103145/209].
31. Thies, pp. 56–7.
32. FRUS I, Doc 403, editorial note.
33. Telegram, SD/Saigon, 8.11.64, 1034. FRUS I, Doc 407.
34. *Courier-Mail* [Brisbane], 9.11.64.
35. Memorandum by Ehrlich, 18.11.64. FRUS I, Doc 416.
36. Telegram, Taylor/SD, 10.11.64, 1445. FRUS I, Doc 409.

37. Working Paper, 21.11.64. FRUS I, Doc 418.
38. Position Paper, 2.12.64. FRUS I, Doc 433.
39. Quoted in Gardner, *Pay Any Price*, pp. 157–8.
40. Porter, p. 208.
41. Telegram, 18.11.64, 3796. FO 371/175503 [DV 103145/209].
42. Minute, 19.11.64. FO 371/175092 [D 1074/38].
43. Minute, 19.11.64. FO 371/175503 [DV 103145/209].
44. Minute, 20.11.64. FO 371/175092 [DV 1074/38].
45. Anglo-U.S. Talks on South-East Asia. Western Co-operation on Indo-China, n.d. Ibid.
46. Peck/Stewart, 27.11.64. FO 371/175503 [DV 103145/215].
47. Anglo-American Talks on Indo-China Washington December 3–4, 1964. Points to be made orally, n.d. Ibid.
48. Peck/Stuart, 27.11.64. Ibid.
49. Memorandum by Peck, 24.11.64, and annex. FO 371/175095 [D 1077/6].
50. Telegram ex Harlech, 28.11.64, 3938. FO 371/175503 [DV 103145/215].
51. Telegram, 28.11.64, 3939. FO 371/175503 [DV 103145/213].
52. Memorandum, Washington Talks on Indo-China, SEAD, 1.12.64. FO 371/ 175095 [D 1077/6].
53. Visit to Washington by the Prime Minister and Foreign Secretary, Vietnam, sent to No. 10, 3.12.64. FO 371/175095 [D 1077/9]; also PREM 13/692.
54. Minute by Cable, 4.12.64. FO 371/175095 [D 1077/10].
55. Telegram, 3.12.64, 3986. FO 371/175503 [DV 103145/222].
56. Telegram, 3.12.64, 3987. FO 371/175503 [DV 103145/223].
57. Telegram Ball/London, 4.12.64, 3669. FRUS I, Doc 437.
58. Mac Bundy/President, 5.12.64. FRUS I, Doc 438.
59. Cable/Peck, 4.12.64. FO 371/175503 [DV 103145/223].
60. Suggested Line …, n.d. FO 371/175095 [D 1077A]; also PREM 13/692.
61. Memorandum, 4.12.64. FO 371/175095 [D 1077/10].
62. Introduction by S.R. Ashton and William Roger Louis to BDEE East of Suez, Pt 1, p. xxxiii.
63. Dockrill, p. 63.
64. Quoted in Derek McDougall, 'The Wilson Government and the British Defence Commitment in Malaysia-Singapore', *Journal of Southeast Asian Studies* 4, 2 (Sept. 1973): 231.
65. Pickering, p. 115.
66. Ibid., p. 149.
67. Memorandum of Conversation, 7.12.64. FRUS XII 1964-68, Doc 236.
68. Record of Prime Minister's Visit to Washington, 6-10.12.64. FO 371/184271 [W2/15].
69. Cf. Isabel Hull, *A Scrap of Paper* (Ithaca, London: Cornell University Press, 2014), p. 26.
70. Record of Conversation, 8.12.64. FO 371/175095 [D 1077/8].
71. Quoted in Jonathan Colman, *A 'Special Relationship'? Harold Wilson, Lyndon B. Johnson and Anglo-American Relations 'at the Summit', 1964–68* (Manchester, New York: Manchester University Press, 2004), p. 41.

72. Telegram, 11.12.64, 2142. FO 371/175095 [D 1077/12].
73. Minute, 1.1.65. FO 371/180539 [DV 103145/32].
74. Minute, 1.1.65. Ibid.
75. Minute for Prime Minister, PM/64/185, 29.12.64. FO 371/175503 [DV 103145/234]; also PREM 13/692.
76. Telegram, 29.12.64, 14242. FO 371/175503 [DV 103145/234].
77. Telegram, 31.12.64, 4229. Ibid.

Chapter Three

1. Telegram to NY, 6.1.65, 45. FO 371/184271 [W 2/1].
2. Telegram, 13.1.65, 80. FO 371/184271 [W 2/7].
3. CC (65), 5th, Item 2. CAB 128/39.
4. Minute, 1.2.65. FO 371/180539 [DV 103145/23].
5. Draft Brief for PM's Visit to Washington, 3.2.65. FO 371/180539 [DV 103145/24].
6. K.W. Taylor, *History of the Vietnamese*, p. 596.
7. Robert Topmiller, 'The Buddhist Anti-war Movement', in *The War That Never Ends*, ed. David L. Anderson and John Ernst (Lexington: University Press of Kentucky, 2007), pp. 147, 151–3.
8. George Kahin and John W. Lewis, *The United States in Vietnam* (n.p.: Delta Press, 1967), p. 168.
9. Telegram, 1.2.65, 93. FO 371/180539 [DV 103145/15].
10. Memorandum for President, 7.2.65. FRUS II, Doc 84.
11. Quoted in Paul Joseph, *Cracks in the Empire* (New York: Columbia University Press, 1987), p. 33.
12. Porter, p. 211.
13. Woods, p. 602.
14. *Times*, 9.2.65, 12.2.65.
15. Douglas Pike, *Vietnam and the Soviet Union* (Boulder, London: Westview, 1987), p. 78.
16. Heren, p. 74.
17. Thomson/Cooper, 10.2.65. FRUS II, Doc 102.
18. Crick/Burrows, 15.2.65. FO 371/180539 [DV 103145/29].
19. Ball/President, 13.2.65. FRUS II, Doc 113.
20. Memorandum to President, 16.2.65. Ibid., Doc 124.
21. R. McNamara, *In Retrospect, The Tragedy and Lessons of Vietnam* (New York: Times, 1995), pp. 173–4.
22. Herbert Schandler, *The Unmaking of a President* (Princeton University Press, 1977), p. 10.
23. Quoted in Robert A. Divine, 'Vietnam: An Episode in the Cold War', in *Vietnam: The Early Decisions*, ed. Lloyd C. Gardner and Ted Gittinger (Austin: University of Texas Press, 1997), p. 21.
24. Ralph Smith, *An International History of the Vietnam War*, Vol. 3 (Basingstoke: Macmillan, 1991), pp. 45–6, 48.

25. Woods, p. 603.
26. FO/Washington, 11.2.65, Despatch 39. FO 371/180594 [DV 1093/10].
27. Record of Conversation, 10.2.65. FO 371/180594 [DV 1093/25].
28. PR 65013, 10.65. FO 371/180594 [DV 1093/5].
29. Minute, 9.2.65.
30. Telegram, 2.2.65, 234. FO 371/184271 [W 2/7].
31. Minute by J.O. Wright, 11.2.65. PREM 13/692.
32. Harold Wilson, *The Labour Government 1964–1970, A Personal Record* (London: Weidenfeld and Joseph, 1971), pp. 79–80.
33. Memorandum of Telephone Conversation by Bundy, 10.2.65, 10.15 pm. FRUS II, Doc 103.
34. Record of a Telephone Conversation, 11.2.65, 3.15 am. PREM 13/692.
35. Seeking a Solution in Viet-Nam, 15.2.65. FO 371/180580 [DV 1075/17].
36. Geyelin, p. 222.
37. Memorandum, 15.2.65. Ibid.
38. Note on Ibid.
39. Conversation, 16.2.65. PREM 13/692.
40. Record of Conversation, 17.2.65, 10.30 am. PREM 13/692.
41. Minute, 17.2.65. FO 371/180580 [DV 1075/17].
42. Minute, 18.2.65. Ibid.
43. Telegrams, 16.2.65, 325, 326. FO 371/180580 [D 1075/1].
44. Telegrams, 17.2.65, 1211, 1212. FO 371/180580 [D 1075/1].
45. Telegram, 17.2.65, 384. FO 371/180580 [DV 1075/8]. US version, FRUS II, Doc 135. Rusk gave a press conference on 25 February. Richard P. Stebbins, ed., *Documents on American Foreign Relations 1965* (New York: Harper, 1966), pp. 131–4.
46. Telegram, 18.2.65, 1253. FO 371/180580 [DV 1075/15]. Speech quoted by Rusk in his press conference, 25.2.65, p. 134.
47. Draft, 18.2.65. FRUS II, Doc 136.
48. Telegram, 18.2.65, 401. FO 371/180580 [DV 1075/16].
49. Telegram, 19.2.65, 1299. FO 371/180580 [DV 1075/16].
50. Telegram, 19.2.65, 412. FO 371/180580 [DV 1075/15].
51. Telegram, 19.2.65, 533. FO 371/180580 [DV 1075/1].
52. Telegram, 20.2.65, 359. FO 371/180580 [DV 1075/10].
53. Telegram, 20.2.65, 360. Ibid.
54. Telegram, 20.2.65, 367. FO 371/180580 [DV 1075/11].
55. Telegram, 21.2.65, 429. Ibid.
56. Telegram, 22.2.65, 558. Ibid.
57. Telegram, 24.2.65, 447. FO 371/180581 [DV 1075/22].
58. Porter, p. 214.
59. Telegram, 27.2.65, 418. FO 371/180581 [DV 1075/38].
60. Telegram, 28.2.65, 426. Ibid.
61. Minute, 1.3.65. PREM 13/693.
62. Note on Ibid.
63. Telegram, 11.3.65, 517. FO 371/180583 [DV 1075/64].

64. Telegram, 2.3.65, 263. FO 371/180582 [DV 1075/49].
65. Telegrams, 15.3.65, 549, 551. FO 371/180583 [DV 1075/65].
66. Record of Conversation, 16.3.65. PREM 13/693.
67. *Times*, 20.3.65.
68. Ibid., 17.3.65.
69. Wilson, p. 85.
70. SEAD for Cabinet, 17.3.65. FO 371/180583 [DV 1075/74].
71. Minutes, 17.3.65. FO/18040 [DV 103145/59].
72. CC (65) 17th, 18.3.65, 2. CAB 128/39.
73. Etherington-Smith/Stewart, 3.3.65, Desp 22. FO 371/180594 [DV 1093/42].
74. Minute by Pestell, 9.3.65. Ibid.
75. Minute, 4.3.65. FO 371/180539 [DV 103145/37].
76. *Times*, 5.3.65.
77. MacGeorge Bundy/President, 6.3.65. FRUS II, Doc 183.
78. Hansard, cols 236-41.
79. *Times*, 9.3.65. *Australian*, 9.3.65.
80. Woods, p. 603.
81. *Times*, 12.3.65. Colman, p. 59.
82. Record of Conversation, 12.3.65. FO 371/180540 [DV 103145/47].
83. Memorandum, 15.3.65. Ibid.
84. Stewart/Caccia, 17.3.65. FO 371/180540 [DV 103145/69].
85. Peck/Stewart, 17.3.65. FO 371/180540 [DV 103145/48].
86. Stewart/Peck, 19.3.65. FO 371/180540 [DV 103145/50].
87. Brief No. 12, Secretary of State's Visit to Washington and New York, 23–24 March 1965 Viet-Nam, SEAD, 19.3.65. FO 371/180584 [DV 1075/104].
88. Telegram ex M.N.F. Stewart, 193.65, 691. FO 371/180583 [DV 1075/74].
89. Minute, 20.3.65. FO 371/180584 [DV 1075/104].
90. Minute, 18.3.65. FO 371/180540 [DV 103145/70].
91. Note on Ibid.
92. Press conferences, pp. 276, 280.
93. Etherington-Smith/Peck, 13.3.65. FO 371/180595 [DV 1093/55].
94. Peck/M.N.F. Stewart, 24.3.65. FO 371/180540 [DV 103145/58].
95. Telegram, 23.3.65, 713. FO 371/180540 [DV 103145/51]; also FO 371/184274 [W 2/94], Doc 1.
96. D. Hank Ellison, *Chemical Warfare during the Vietnam War: Riot Control Agents in Combat* (New York, London: Routledge, 2011), pp. 17, 19, 21, 24–5.
97. Record of Conversation, 23.3.65, 10.30am. FO 371/180540 [DV 103145/60]; also FO 371/184274 [W 2/94], Doc 6.
98. Telegram, 23.3.65, 731. FO 371/180540 [DV 103145/64].
99. Diary Entry by Bruce, 23.3.65. FRUS II, Doc 211.
100. *Times*, 26.3.65.
101. Stebbins, pp. 135–6.
102. Woods/SEAD, 29.3.65. FO 371/180595 [DV 1093/64].
103. Minute, 12.4.65. Ibid.
104. Telegram, 5.3.65, 560S. FO 371/180583 [DV 1075/62].

105. Telegram, 16.3.65, 187S. FO 371/180487 [DU 1072/1].
106. Telegram ex Garvey, 20.3.65, 357. FO 371/180487 [DU 1072/2].
107. Telegram, 22.3.65, 2293. FO 371/180583 [DV 1075/74].
108. P.E. Ramsbotham/Cable, 24.3.65. FO 371/180487 [DU 1072/6].
109. Telegram, 24.3.65, 149. FO 371/180583 [DV 1075/74].
110. Hohler/Peck, 25.3.65, FO 371/180854 [DV 1075/94].
111. Telegram, 23.3.65, 731. FO 371/180540 [DV 103145/64].
112. Telegram, 28.3.65, 774. FO 371/180208 [D 1052/1].
113. *Times*, 29.3.65.
114. Ibid., 30.3.65.
115. Minute, 1.4.65. FO 371/180584 [DV 1075/100].
116. Telegram, 1.4.65, 2634. FO 371/180583 [DV 1075/88].
117. Telegram, 1.4.64, 194. Ibid.
118. Telegram, 3.4.65, 684. FO 371/180487 [DU 1072/5].
119. Telegram, 7.4.65, 2834. Ibid.
120. Hohler/Peck, 9.4.65. FO 371/180487 [DU 1072/12].
121. Gardner, *Pay Any Price*, pp. 52–3.
122. Thomas J. Knock, 'George McGovern and Mr Johnson's War', in *The Search for Peace in Vietnam*, ed. Lloyd C. Gardner and Ted Gittinger (College Station: Texas A&M University Press, 2004), pp. 103, 106.
123. Gardner, *Pay Any Price*, pp. 191–2, 194, 197.
124. *Times*, 13.4.65.
125. Ibid., 12.4.65.
126. Speech, 7.4.65, in Kahin and Lewis, p. 424–5.
127. Quoted in Gardner, *Pay Any Price*, p. 196.
128. James Carter, *Inventing Vietnam* (Cambridge University Press, 2008), pp. 171, 173–4.
129. Logevall, *Choosing War*, pp. 371–2.
130. Statement, 8.4.65. PREM 13/694.
131. Kahin and Lewis, p. 425.
132. Telegram, 8.4.65, 2873. FO 371/180585 [DV 1075/111].
133. Telegram, 9.4.65, 735. Ibid.
134. Telegram, 9.4.65, 933. Ibid.
135. Stewart/Peck, 9.4.65. FO 371/150585 [DV 1075/120].
136. Telegram, 8.4.65, 155. FO 371/180584 [DV 1075/105].
137. *Times*, 15.4.65.
138. Smith, III, 88.
139. Thies, Appendix 1, pp. 421–2.
140. Luu Doan Huynh, 'The Perspective of a Vietnamese Witness', in Anderson and Ernst, p. 90. See also Ang, *Vietnam War*, pp. 86–9.
141. Kahin and Lewis, p. 210.
142. Quoted in Smith, III, p. 89. There was no ambiguity there.
143. Brigham, *Guerrilla Diplomacy*, p. 43.
144. Ibid., p. 40.
145. Quoted in Colman, p. 68.

146. *Times*, 23.4.65.
147. Brief in A.C. Maby/D.F. Murray, 9.4.65. FO 371/183729 [USC 1422/12].
148. OPD (65) 22nd, 13.4.65, 2. CAB 148/18, National Archives, Kew.
149. Minute, 13.4.65; also P.M.V. (U.S.) (65) 1. FO 371/180541 [DV 103145/93].
150. Colman, pp. 70–1.
151. Wilson, p. 95.
152. *Times*, 14.4.65.
153. N. Tarling, *Britain and Sihanouk's Cambodia* (Singapore: NUS Press, 2014), p. 233.
154. Minute by MacLehose, 26.4.65. FO 371/180488 [DU 1072/40].
155. Dumbrell, pp. 98–100.
156. Paul Gore-Booth, *With Great Truth and Respect* (London: Constable, 1974), p. 335.
157. Cable/Rumbold, 22.3.65. FO 371/180206 [D 1051/26].
158. Minute, 19.2.65. FO 371/180557 [DV 1051/55].
159. Minute, 23.2.65. Ibid.
160. Minutes by Peck, 24.2.65; Bridges, 1.3.65. Ibid.
161. Viet Nam and the Future, PC (65) 12, [3.65]. FO 371/180206 [D 1051/26.
162. Rumbold/Stewart, 5.4.65, Despatch 18. FO 371/180207 [D 1051/48].
163. Enclosure 1 in Ibid.; also in BDEE A5, Pt I, Doc 93.
164. Enclosure 2 in Rumbold's despatch; also in BDEE Doc 93.
165. Telegram ex Woods, 6.4.65, 158. FO 371/180208 [D 1052/17].
166. Telegram ex Woods, 12.4.65, 166. Ibid.
167. Qiang Zhai, *China and the Vietnam Wars*, p. 158.
168. Minute, 14.4.65. FO 371/180209 [D 1052/25].
169. Steering Brief, n.d. FO 371/180210 [D 1052/58].
170. Annexes to Steering Brief. Ibid.

Chapter Four

1. Telegram, 24.4.65, 1082. FO 371/180541 [DV 103145/102].
2. Memorandum, 21.4.65. FRUS II, Doc 267.
3. Press Conferences, 27.4.65, pp. 300–1.
4. Record of a Discussion, 2.5.65. PREM 13/694.
5. Conversation between Prime Minister and Ball, 10 Downing St, 5.5.65. FO 371/184274 [W 2/89].
6. Minute by Peck, Meeting between the Foreign Secretary and Mr George Ball, 10.5.65, 4pm, 11.5.65. FO 371/180586 [DV 1075/134].
7. Minute by Peck, 12.5.65. FO 371/180585 [DV 1075/132].
8. Peck/Dean, 13.5.65. FO 371/180586 [DV 1075/134].
9. Conversation at No. 10, 14.5.65. FO 371/184274 [W 2/93].
10. Conversation, 14.5.65. FO 371/184274 [W 2/92].
11. Memorandum, 10.5.65. FO 371/180586 [DV 1075/138].
12. Minute by Bridges, 18.5.65. Ibid.
13. Mac Bundy, 12.5.65. FRUS II, Doc 296.

14. Quoted in Dumbrell, p. 105.
15. Telegram ex Washington, 14.5.65, 1258. FO 371/180595 [DV 1093/80].
16. Telegram to Vienna for Foreign Secretary, 15.5.65, 248. Ibid.
17. Telegram ex Pilcher, 15.5.65, 155. Ibid.
18. Washington Telegram to Hanoi, 16.5.65, 16.5.65, 1272. Ibid.
19. Telegram 17.5.65, 287. Ibid.
20. Telegram 17.5.65, 219. Ibid.
21. Telegram, 18.5.65, 221. Ibid.
22. Ponsonby/Cable, 20.5.65. FO 371/180596 [DV 1093/88].
23. Telegram, 9.6.65. Ibid.
24. *Times*, 21.5.65.
25. Meeting, 16.5.65. FRUS II, Doc 304.
26. 552nd NSC, 11.6.65. FRUS II, Doc 347.
27. George Ball, *The Past Has Another Pattern* (New York: Norton, 1982), p. 404.
28. *Australian*, 13.5.65.
29. Report, 7.5.65. FO 371/180209 [D 1052/41].
30. FO/Etherington-Smith, 18.5.65, Despatch 48. FO 371/180209 [D 1052/41].
31. Cable/Etherington-Smith, 24.5.65. FO 371/180541 [DV 103145/118].
32. Stewart/Cable, 27.5.65. FO 371/180541 [DV 103145/126].
33. Memorandum, Effects of American Bombing of North Viet-Nam, 17.5.65. FO 371/180595 [DV 1093/81].
34. Thompson/Peck, 27.4.65. Ibid.
35. Etherington-Smith/Cable, 29.4.65. Ibid.
36. Minute, 2.5.65. Ibid.
37. Minute, 5.5.65. Ibid.
38. Stewart/Peck, 5.5.65. Ibid.
39. Cable/Stewart, 18.5.65. Ibid.
40. Etherington-Smith/Peck, 26.5.65. Ibid.
41. Minute, 2.6.65. Ibid.
42. Stebbins, pp. 163–4.
43. Trevelyan/Stewart, 19.5.65, despatch 28. FO 371/180534 [DV 103138/33].
44. Etherington-Smith/Cable, 16.6.65. FO 371/180586 [DV 1075/154].
45. *Times*, 2.4.65, 4.6.65. Telegram to Kabul, 14.6.65, 148. FO 371/180567 [DV 1062/36]. Belgrade Peace Appeal, 1.4.65. Stebbins, pp. 136–8.
46. *Australian*, 3.4.65.
47. Statement, 15.3.65. FO 371/180567 [DV 1062/36].
48. Telegram, 3.6.65, 5835. FRUS II, footnote to Doc 330.
49. McG. Bundy/President, 3.6.65. FRUS II, Doc 330.
50. Minute, 1.6.65. FO 371/180586 [DV 1075/152].
51. Minute, 3.6.65. Ibid.
52. Minute, 10.6.65. Ibid.
53. Telegram to Kabul, 14.6.65, 149. FO 371/180567/36].
54. Telegrams, 10.6.65, 4752, 4753. FO 371/150586 [DV 1075/152].
55. Minute by Peck, 19.6.65. Ibid.
56. *Times*, 9.6.65; also FRUS II, Doc 339.

57. *Times*, 10.6.65.
58. *Australian*, 10.6.65.
59. *Times*, 10.6.65.
60. Minute for Wright, 9.6.65. PREM 13/695.
61. Henderson/Reid, 9.6.65. Ibid.
62. Telegram, 10.6.65, 2043. FO 371/180642 [DV 2251/29].
63. Telegram, 10.6.65, 1420. Ibid.
64. Minute, 10.6.65. FO 371/180558 [DV 1051/148].
65. Memorandum, Viet-Nam Anglo-United States Relations, left with the PM on June 10. FO 371/180541 [DV 103145/137].
66. Wilson, p. 108.
67. Note for the Record, 15.6.65. PREM 13/690.
68. Telegram, 15.6.65, 4890. PREM 13/690.
69. Note by DJM, 15.6.65, midnight. PREM 13/690.
70. Philip Ziegler, *Wilson: The Authorised Life of Lord Wilson of Rievaulx* (London: Weidenfeld, 1993), p. 225.
71. R.H.S. Crossman, *The Diaries of a Cabinet Minister* (London: Hamilton and Cape, 1975), I, p. 253.
72. Telegram, 16.6.65, 1255. FO 371/180566 [DV 1062/7].
73. Telegram, 16.6.65, 1563. FO 371/180541 [DV 103145/136].
74. *Australian*, 19.6.65.
75. *Times*, 19.6.65.
76. Telegrams to New York, 17.6.65, 2178, 2179. FO 371/180586 [DV 1062/2].
77. *Times*, 21.6.65.
78. *Australian*, 21.6.65.
79. Draft by Ghana, Commonwealth Mission on Vietnam, Points for Establishing 'Guidelines' for the Mission, n.d. FO 371/180567 [DV 1062/40]; also PREM 13/690.
80. UK Revised Draft, n.d. PREM 13/690; also FO 371/180567 [DV 1062/40]. Memorandum by SEAD, Commentary on Draft Guide Lines, 23.6.65. Ibid.
81. Telegrams to Washington, 25.6.65, 5169, 5170. FO 371/180568 [DV 1062/42].
82. Telegram to Washington, 25.6.65, 5200. FO 371/180568 [DV 1062/42]. Final communiqué, 26.6.65, 12.05am, is in *Times*, 26.6.65.
83. Telegram, 25.6.65, 689. FO 371/180568 [DV 1062/61].
84. Telegram, 25.6.65, 1342. Ibid.
85. *Australian*, 19.6.65.
86. Telegram, 20.6.65, 800. FO 371/180566 [DV 1062/5].
87. *Times*, 22.6.65.
88. Telegram, 23.6.65, 1246. FO 371/180566 [DV 1062/20].
89. Telegram ex Duncan, 25.6.65, 346. FO 371/180568 [DV 1062/44].
90. *Réalités*, 25.6.65, pp. 3–4.
91. *New Zealand Herald*, 25.6.65. Roberto Rabel, *New Zealand and the Vietnam War* (Auckland: Auckland University Press, 2005), p. 129.
92. Hohler/Peck, 23.6.65. FO 371/180568 [DV 1062/53].

93. Note of a Conversation, 10 Downing St, 24.6.66, 10.15 pm. FO 371/180568 [DV 1062/41].
94. Nkrumah/Wilson, 23.6.65, T 235/65. PREM 13/690.
95. *Australian*, 22.6.65.
96. Telegram, 26.6.65, 820. FO 371/180568 [DV 1062/47].
97. *Times*, 26.6.65.
98. Note on Wilford's telegram of 25.6.65, 816. PREM 13/691.
99. Telegram, 26.6.65, 295. FO 371/180568 [DV 1062/57].
100. Minute, 25.6.65. FO 371/180569 [DV 103138/73].
101. Minute by Peck, 27.6.65. FO 371/180568 [DV 1062/57].
102. Telegram, 28.6.65, 299. FO 371/180568 [DV 1062/56].
103. Telegram, 30.6.65, 1311. FO 371/180596 [DV 1093/102].
104. Anatoly Dobrynin, *In Confidence* (New York: Times Books, 1995), p. 140.
105. Trevelyan/H.F.T. Smith, 1.7.65. FO 371/180596 [DV 1093/102].
106. Gaiduk, pp. 49–50, 53–4.
107. Memorandum, Bombing of North Vietnam, 5.7.65. FO 371/180596 [DV 1093/102].
108. Minute, 5.7.65. Ibid.
109. Minute, 6.7.65. Ibid.
110. Minute, 7.7.65. Ibid.
111. Smith/Brimelow, 8.7.65. Ibid.
112. Telegram, 9.7.65, 2262. Ibid.
113. Brimelow/Smith, 28.7.65. FO 371/180596 [DV/1093/108].
114. Brimelow/Smith, 27.8.65. FO 371/180596 [DV 1093/111].
115. John W. Young, 'The Wilson Government and the Davies Peace Mission to North Vietnam, July 1965', *Review of International Studies* 24, 4 (Oct. 1998): 547.
116. Telegram to Vientiane, 2.7.65, 716. FO 371/180570 [DV 1062/87].
117. Note for Mr Peck, 30.6.65. FO 371/180569 [DV 1062/84]. Note for the record, 30.6.65. PREM 13/691.
118. Minute, 30.6.65. FO 371/180570 [DV 1062/85].
119. Proposed Visit by Mr Harold Davies, M.P., to Hanoi, 1.7.65. FO 371/180569 [DV 1062/74].
120. Minute, 1.7.65, PM 65/103. Ibid.
121. *Australian*, 9.7.65.
122. Ibid., 10.7.65.
123. Crossman, *Diaries*, I, pp. 269–70.
124. Telegram, 3.7.65, 5380. Telegram ex Dean, 3.7.65, 1750. FO 371/180570 [DV 1062/87].
125. Telegram, 2.7.65, 716. FO 371/180570 [DV 1062/87].
126. Telegram, 8.7.65, 444. FO 371/180571 [DV 1062/109].
127. Telegram to Ponsonby, 10.7.65, 456. Telegram from Ponsonby, 12.7.65, 321. FO 371/180571 [DV 1062/111].
128. Minute, 14.7.65. FO 371/180571 [DV 1062/127].
129. *Australian*, 14.7.65.

130. Ibid., 17.7.65. Report in PREM 13/696.
131. *Times*, 13.7.65.
132. *Australian*, 21.7.65.
133. Young, p. 559.
134. Ibid., pp. 553, 555.
135. Simon Kear, 'The British Consulate-General in Hanoi, 1954–1973', *Diplomacy and Statecraft* 10, 1 (1999): 228.
136. FO/Etherington-Smith, 14.7.65, Despatch 69. FO 371/180571 [DV 1062/124].
137. Minute, 14.7.65. FO 371/180572 [DV 1062/136].
138. Minute, 30.6.65. FO 371/180570 [DV 1063/85].
139. Wright/Bridges, 8.7.65. FO 371/180571 [DV 1062/112].
140. Draft reply, 8.7.65. Ibid.
141. Telegram, 19.7.65, 470. FO 371/180572 [DV 1062/137].
142. Telegram, 21.7.65, 923. Ibid.
143. Qiang Zhai, p. 161.
144. Draft Wilson/Nkrumah, 3.9.65. FO 371/180572 [DV 1062/152].
145. PREM 13/1271.
146. Cable/Etherington-Smith, 30.6.65. FO 371/180559 [DV 1051/189].
147. Smith, III, pp. 154–5.
148. R.K. Brigham, *ARVN: Life and Death in the South Vietnamese Army* (Lawrence: University Press of Kansas, 2006), p. 88.
149. William Conrad Gibbons, *The U.S. Government and the Vietnam War* (Princeton University Press, 1995), IV, p. 52.
150. Quoted in Robert Buzzanco, 'Military Dissent and the Legacy of the Vietnam War', in Anderson and Ernst, p. 207.
151. Ball/President, 18.6.65. FRUS III, Doc 7.
152. Memorandum, 1.7.65. FRUS III, Doc 41.
153. Memorandum, 20.7.65. FRUS III, Doc 67.
154. Meeting, 21.7.65: Notes by Valenti. FRUS III, Doc 71. See also Porter, pp. 227–8.
155. Meeting, 22.7.65. FRUS III, Doc 78.
156. Meeting, 26.7.65. FRUS III, Doc 85.
157. Editorial note, FRUS III, Doc 97.
158. Cooper, p. 286.
159. Quoted in Gardner, *Pay Any Price*, p. 243.
160. DiLeo, pp. 129, 131.
161. Woods, p. 616.
162. Ibid., p. 750.
163. Joseph, pp. 96–7.
164. Press Conferences, pp. 348–52.
165. Minutes, 26.7.65. FO 371/180572 [DV 1062/147].
166. Memorandum, The Commonwealth Initiative on Vietnam, n.d. [?27.7.65]. Ibid.
167. Stewart/Bottomley, 27.7.65, FS/65/106. FO 371/180572 [DV 1062/147].

168. Bottomley/Stewart, 2.8.65. Ibid.
169. Telegram ex Jockling, 29.7.65, 146S, FO 371/180642 [DV 2251/39].
170. Telegram, 2.8.65, 6009. Ibid.
171. Telegram ex Dean, 2.8.65, 1993. Ibid.
172. Telegram ex Jockling, 3.8.65, 1783 FO 371/180642 [DV 2251/42].
173. Stewart/Commonwealth Secretary, 4.8.65, FS/65/113. FO 371/180572 [DV 1062/147].
174. Hughes/Foreign Secretary, 10.8.65. Ibid.
175. Telegram ex Caradon, 12.8.65, 1859. FO 371/180043 [DV 2251/48].
176. Greenhill/Caradon, 20.8.65. FO 371/1800642 [DV 2251/39].
177. Minute, 6.10.65. FO 371/180643 [DV 2251/67].
178. Minute, 7.10.65. Ibid.

Chapter Five

1. Mr Gordon Walker's Note on his talks in Washington 30 June 1965. FO 371/180542 [DV 103145/156].
2. Stewart/Peck, 6.7.65. FO 371/180542 [DV 103145/158].
3. Etherington-Smith/Peck, 22.7.65. FO 371/180542 [DV 103145/178].
4. Minute, 22.7.65. FO 371/180542 [DV 103145/174].
5. Telegram, 22.7.65, 1904. FO 371/180543 [DV 103145/183].
6. Minute, 26.7.65. Ibid.
7. Johnson/Wilson, recd 26.7.65. FO 371/180542 [DV 103145/180]; also BDEE A5, Pt 1, Doc 96].
8. Minute, 26.7.65. FO 371/180542 [DV 103145/181].
9. Minute for PM, 26.7.65. PM 65/12. PREM 13/697; also BDEE A5, Pt 1, Doc 96.
10. Minute, 30.7.65. FO 371/180542 [DV 103145/181].
11. Telegram, 30.7.65, 5966. Ibid.
12. Telegram, 30.7.65, 5967. Ibid.
13. Minute, 28.7.65. Ibid.
14. Minute, 28.7.65. FO 371/180543 [DV 103145/188]; also BDEE A5 Pt 1, Doc 97.
15. Telegram, 31.7.65, 1980. FO 371/180542 [DV 103145/181].
16. Wright/Palliser, 2.8.65. PREM 13/697. Telegram to Dean, 2.8.65, 6006. FO 371/180542 [DV 103145/181].
17. Telegram, 2.8.65, 1984. Ibid.
18. Telegram, 29.7.65, 1964. FO 371/180543 [DV 103145/184].
19. Etherington-Smith/Foreign Secretary, 14.6.65, Despatch 43. FO 371/180542 [DV 103145/139].
20. Peck/Etherington-Smith, 14.7.65. Ibid.
21. Minute by Cable, 12.7.65. FO 371/180587 [DV 1075/65].
22. Minute, 21.6 [for 7].65. Ibid.
23. Minute, 21.7.65. Ibid.

24. Minute, 23.7.65. Ibid.
25. Minute, 26.7.65. Ibid.
26. Memorandum, Viet-Nam and Escalation, 28.6.65. FO 371/180590 [DV 1091/33].
27. Likely Developments in the War in Vietnam during the Rest of 1965, sent by Murray to Etherington-Smith, 18.8.65. FO 371/180591 [DV 109/41].
28. Mansfield/Murray, 31.8.65. FO 371/180591 [DV 1091/54].
29. Etherington-Smith/Peck, 26.7.65. FO 371/180590 [DV 1091/44].
30. Cable/Etherington-Smith, 19.8.65. Ibid.
31. Vietnam and Escalation, 28.9.65. FO 371/180591 [DV 1091/60].
32. See Tarling, *Laos*, p. 412.
33. Minute, 28.9.65. FO 371/180591 [DV 1091/60].
34. Minute, 28.9.65. Ibid.
35. Note on Ibid.
36. The Possibility of a Negotiated Solution of the Conflict in Viet-Nam, SEAD, 26.8.65. FO 371/180588 [DV 1075/187].
37. Minute, 23.8.65. Ibid.
38. Minute by Peck, 24.8.65. Ibid.
39. Minute by Cable, 26.8.65. Ibid.
40. Addis/Peck, 25.8.65. FO 371/180544 [DV 103145/215].
41. Peck/Addis, 13.9.65. Ibid.
42. Minute, 6.9.65. FO 371/150588 [DV 1075/187].
43. Cable/Trench, 6.9.65. Ibid.
44. Comments in Brimelow/Cable, 16.9.65. Ibid.
45. Rumbold/Cable, 23.9.65. Ibid.
46. Ford/Cable, 23.9.65. Ibid.
47. Stewart/Peck, 2.9.65. FO 371/180544 [DV 103145/216].
48. Trench/Cable, 26.10.65. FO 371/180588 [DV 1075/187].
49. Trench/Cable, 26.10.65. FO 371/180589 [DV 1075/211].
50. Minute, 17.11.65. FO 371/180588 [DV 1075/187].
51. Minute, 18.11.65. FO 371/180545 [DV 103145/261].
52. Minute, 19.11.65. FO 371/186350[DV 1091/5].
53. Minute, 24.11.65. FO 371/180588 [DV 1075/187].
54. Minute, 14.12.65. Ibid.
55. The Possibility of a Negotiated Solution of the Conflict in Vietnam. PC (65) 54. FO 371/186350 [DV 1091/5].
56. Minute, 9.11.65. FO 371/180589 [DV 1075/211].
57. Trench/Cable, 15.12.65. FO 371/180596 [DV 1093/125].
58. Minute, 29.12.65. Ibid.
59. Conversation between Ball and Foreign Secretary, 8.9.65. FO 371/ 184275 [W 2/104].
60. Extract, Conversation, 26.11.65. FO 371/180546 [DV 103145/267].
61. Wilson, p. 187.
62. Telegram, 18.12.65, 3384. FO 371/184277 [W 2/135].
63. Record of Lunchtime Conversation, 17.12.65. FO 371/184277 [W 2/137].

64. Meeting, 17.12.65. FRUS III, Doc 231.
65. Mac Bundy/President, 27.11.65. FRUS III, Doc 208.
66. Gibbons, IV, pp. 113–4.
67. Quoted in Woods, p. 680.
68. Quoted in Ibid., p. 716.
69. Meeting, 18.12.65. FRUS III, Doc 235.
70. Gibbons, IV, pp. 123,126.
71. Ball, pp. 404–5.
72. Phone Conversation, 28.12.65. FRUS III, Doc 256.
73. Cooper, p. 293.
74. State/Rangoon, 28.12.65. 202. FRUS III, Doc 257.
75. Rusk at NSC, 5.1.66, quoted in Parker in Lowe, p. 214.
76. Telegram, 28.12.65, 3501. FO 371/180547 [DV 103145/297].
77. Johnson/Wilson, 29.12.65. FO 371/180547 [DV 103145/298].
78. Telegram, 29.12.65, 3518. Ibid.
79. Bridges/Reid, 30.12.65. Ibid.
80. Wilson/Johnson, 31.12.65. Ibid.
81. Quoted in Cooper, p. 294.
82. Stebbins, pp. 191–2; also in Kahin and Lewis, pp. 436–7.
83. Stebbins, p. 196.
84. Wilson, p. 192.
85. Notes of a Meeting, 1.1.66. PREM 13/1271.
86. Minute by Cable, 3.1.66. FO 371/186366 [DV 1072/14].
87. Telegrams 2,3.1.66, 11, 13.
88. *Times*, 5.1.66.
89. Telegram, 3.1.66, 2. FO 371/186366 [DV 1072/14].
90. Telegram, 6.1.66. FO 371/186366 [DV 1072/16].
91. Telegram, 2.1.66, 4. FO 371/186366 [DV 1072/5].
92. Telegram ex Ledwidge, 3.1.66, 10. FO 371/186366 [DV 1072/7].
93. Paris/SD, 31.12.65, 370. FRUS III, Doc 278.
94. Conversation, 10.1.66. PREM 13/1271.
95. Trench/Cable, 3.1.66. FO 371/186311 [DV 103145/3].
96. Minute, 17.12.65. FO 371/186350 [DV 1091/5].
97. Viet-Nam. The Present Situation, 20.12.65. Ibid.
98. Minute by Cable, 6.1.66. Ibid.
99. Etherington-Smith/Stewart, 15.12.65, Despatch 67. FO 371/180592 [DV 1091/81].
100. Minute, 6.1.66. FO 371/186350 [DV 1091/5].
101. Possible Initiative on Viet-Nam, 6.1.66. Ibid.
102. Minute, 14.1.66. Ibid.
103. Minute, 14.1.66. FO 371/186337 [DV 1072/67].
104. Telegram, 22.1.66, 270. FO 371/186337 [DV 1072/60].
105. Minute, 21.1.66. FO 371/186337 [DV 1072/70].
106. Minute, 7.1.66. FO 371/186307 [DV 103138/14].
107. Shepherd/Cable, 22.1.66. FO 371/186338 [DV 1072/85].

108. Etherington-Smith/Cable, 27.1.66. Ibid.
109. Johnson/Wilson, 24.1.66. T 48/66. FO 371/186311 [DV 103135/6]; also PREM 13/1272.
110. Minutes, 25.1.66. FO 371/186311 [DV 103145/11].
111. Minute, 25.1.66. Ibid.
112. PM/President, 26.1.66. FO 371/186311 [DV 103145/6].
113. FRUS IV, Doc 46.
114. Record of a Conversation over Lunch at State Department, 27.1.66. PREM 13/1272.
115. Minute of discussion, Vietnam and the Far East, 27.1.66. PREM 13/1272.
116. 25.1.66. FRUS IV, Doc 43.
117. Telegram, 27.1.66, 344. FO 371/186311 [DV 103145/12].
118. Telegram, 27.1.66, 173. FO 371/186337 [DV 1072/76].
119. Telegram, 29.1.66, 187. PREM 13/1272.
120. Telegram ex Clutton, 29.1.66, 47. FO 371/186311 [DV 103145/15].
121. Telegram, 29.1.66, 339. PREM 13/1272.
122. Telegram, 30.1.66, 193. Ibid.
123. Telegram, 30.1.66, 106. FO 371/186311 [DV 103145/15].
124. Telegram ex Clutton, 30.1.66, 51. Ibid.
125. Telegram ex Clutton, 2.2.66, 61. FO 371/186338 [DV 1072/92]; also PREM 13/1272.
126. Meeting, 28.1.66. FRUS IV, Doc 52.
127. Ibid., Doc 57. Broadcast in Stebbins, pp. 202–4.
128. Minute, 4.2.66. PREM 13/1272.
129. Telegram, 3.2.66, 1363. FO 186338 [DV 072/88].
130. Telegram, 3.2.66, 1386. Ibid.
131. Telegrams to Moscow, 3.2.66, 390; Hanoi, 3.2.66, 36; Warsaw, 3.2.66, 123. Ibid.
132. Telegram ex Harrison, 4.2.66, 332. FO 371/186338 [DV 1072/88].
133. Telegram, 5.2.66, 66. Ibid.
134. Minute, 4.2.66. PREM 13/1272.
135. Johnson/Wilson, 4.2.66, 434S. FO 371/186311 [DV 103145/24].
136. Harrison/Greenhill, 28.1.66. FO 371/186307 [DV 103138/21].
137. Dumbrell, p. 108.
138. Telegram, 7.2.66, 226. FO 371/186338 [DV DV 1072/98].
139. Telegram, 7.2.66, 261. FO 371/186307 [DV 103138/26].
140. Telegram, 7.2.66, 262. Ibid.
141. Minute, 7.2.66. FO 371/186329 [DV 1051/47].
142. Memorandum, Prime Minister's Visit to Moscow, Vietnam, 7.2.66. Ibid.
143. Minute, 7.2.66. FO 371/186329 [DV 1051/72].
144. Minute, 8.2.66. FO 371/186329 [DV 1051/47].
145. Minute, 10.2.66, PM/66/13, with Supporting Arguments. Ibid.
146. Wright/MacLehose, 14.2.66. Ibid.
147. MacLehose/Wright, 14.2.66. Ibid.
148. Telegram, 14.2.66, 1712. FO 371/186328 [DV 1051/33].
149. Telegram to Washington, 15.2.66, 1745. Ibid.

150. Telegram, 17.2.66, 364. Ibid.
151. Prime Minister's Visit to Moscow, Talk with North Vietnamese Representative, n.d. Ibid.
152. Telegram, 21.2.66, 407. PREM 13/1272.
153. Telegram, 21.2.66, 411. Ibid.
154. Telegram, 23.2.66, 446. FO 371/186329 [DV 1051/64]. Record of Conversation, 23.2.66. FO 371/186239 [DV 1051/90]; also PREM 13/1272.
155. Wilson, p. 214.
156. Record of Conversation, 22.2.66. PREM 13/1272.
157. Wilson, p. 213.
158. Record of Meeting, 23.2.66, extract. PREM 13/1272.
159. Wilson, p. 214.

Chapter Six

1. Cable/Wright, 13.10.65. FO 371/180207 [D 1051/61].
2. Wright/Cable, 4.11.65. Ibid.
3. Cable/Rumbold, 23.11.65. Ibid.
4. Rumbold/Cable, 7.12.65. FO 371/180207 [D 1051/68].
5. Warner/Cable, 22.12.65. FO 371/185929 [D 1091/2].
6. Etherington-Smith/Cable, 30.12.65. FO 371/185929 [D 1091/3].
7. Rumbold/Etherington-Smith, 6.1.66. Ibid.
8. Rumbold/Cable, 24.11.65. FO 371/180546 [DV 103145/273].
9. Cable/Rumbold, 10.12.65. Ibid.
10. Rumbold/Etherington-Smith, 21.12.65. FO 371/180547 [DV 103145/299].
11. Warner/Cable, 29.12.65. FO 371/185917 [D 103145/1].
12. Etherington-Smith/Rumbold, 14.1.66. FO 371/185917 [D 103145/8].
13. Rumbold/Etherington-Smith, 25.1.66. Ibid.
14. Etherington-Smith/Rumbold, 2.2.66. FO 371/186311 [DV 103145/28].
15. De la Mare/Rumbold, 2.2.66. FO 371/185917 [D 103145/8].
16. Adams/Cable, n.d, recd 31.1.66. FO 371/185929 [D 1091/6].
17. Cable/Adams, 11.2.66. Ibid.
18. Etherington-Smith/De la Mare, 10.3.66. Ibid.
19. Etherington-Smith/Stewart, 8.3.66, Despatch 9. FO 371/186350 [DV 1091/18].
20. Memorandum, The Prospects in Vietnam, 21.3.66. FO 371/186351 [DV 1091/24].
21. Minute, 21.3.66. Ibid.
22. Minute, 24.3.66. Ibid.
23. Minute, 24.3.66. Ibid.
24. Stewart/De la Mare, 8.3.66. FO 371/186312 [DV 103145/49].
25. Stewart/De la Mare, 3.3.66. FO 371/185917 [D 103145/11].
26. Minutes, 21.3.66. Ibid.
27. Addis/Foreign Secretary, 11.5.66, Despatch 14. FO 371/185917 [D 103145/16].

28. Minute, 2.6.66. Ibid.
29. Minute, 6.6.66. Ibid.
30. Minute, 15.6.66. Ibid.
31. Minute, 7.6.66. Ibid.
32. Etherington-Smith/Foreign Secretary, 26.5.66. FO 371/185917 [D 103145/17].
33. Minute, 21.6.66. Ibid.
34. Minute, 5.9.66. Ibid.
35. Minute, 13.10.66. FO 371/185917 [D 103145/22].
36. Minute, 17.3.67. Ibid.
37. Minute, 19.4.67. Ibid
38. Minute, 15.9.66. Ibid.
39. Minute, 19.1.66. FO 371/186238 [DV 1051/12].
40. PM's Minute for Foreign Secretary, 1.2.66, M7/66. PREM 13/1272.
41. Minute by Foreign Secretary, 7.2.66, PM 66/1. Ibid.
42. Wilson/Johnson, 9.2.66, T68/66. Ibid.
43. *New Zealand Herald*, 6.3.65.
44. John Young, 'Britain and "LBJ's War"', *Cold War History* 2, 3 (Apr. 2002): 68–9.
45. Ziegler, p. 248.
46. Telegrams ex Shepherd, 18.4.66, 33; ex Dean, 20.4.66, 1303. FO 371/186353 [DV 1093/2].
47. Stewart/De la Mare, 21.4.66. FO 371/186353 [DV 1093/7].
48. Telegram to Washington, 24.5.66, 5368. FO 371/186353 [DV 1093/11].
49. Telegram, 25.5.66, 5378. Ibid.
50. Wilson, p. 247.
51. Palliser/MacLehose, 2.6.66. FO 371/186353 [DV 1093/12].
52. PM's Telegram, 3.6.66, T209/66. FO Telegram, s.d., 5701. FO 371/186354 [DV 1093/58].
53. Conversation, 10.6.66. FRUS 1964–68, XXVII, Doc 72.
54. Palliser/MacLehose, 10.6.66. PREM 13/1274.
55. Telegram, 10.6.66, 5885. FO 371/186354 [DV 1093/58]; also T216/66 in PREM 13/1274.
56. PM Telegram to President, 10.6.66, T 215/66. Ibid.
57. FO Telegram to Washington, 14.6.66, 5960. FO 371/86353 [DV 1093/13]; also PREM 13/1274; and FRUS IV, Doc 156.
58. Telegram, 14.6.66, 5964. FO 371/186353 [DV 1093/13].
59. Press Conference, 18.6.66. Press Conferences, I, pp. 479–80.
60. *Times*, 20.6.66.
61. Telegram, 27.6.66, 129S. FO 371/186353 [DV 1093/22].
62. President's Meeting with NSC, 22.6.66. FRUS IV, Doc 161.
63. FO Telegram to Washington, 23.6.66, 6229. FO 371/186354 [DV 1093/58].
64. Telegram, 23.6.66, 6236. Ibid.; also PREM 13/1275.
65. Dean/Palliser, 22.6.66. FO 371/186354 [DV 1093/58].
66. FO Telegram to Washington, 26.6.66, 6311. Telegrams ex Dean, 27.6.66, 1912; 29.6.66, 1923. Ibid.

67. Telegram ex Etherington-Smith, 29.6.66, 542. FO 371/186353 [DV 1093/20].
68. Telegram, 25.6.66, 6298. FO 371/186354 [DV 1093/58]. CRO/Canberra, 25.6.66, 1787. PREM 13/1375.
69. Ibid. Wilson, pp. 247–8.
70. *Times*, 30.6.66.
71. Telegram, 1.7.66, 6493, T 236/66. PREM 13/1275. Tarling, *Sihanouk*, pp. 275–6.
72. Gibbons, IV, p. 371.
73. *Times*, 1.7.66.
74. *Times*, 8.7.66. *Australian*, 9.7.66.
75. Minute, 5.7.66. FO 371/186297 [DV 103110/33].
76. Telegram, 15.7.66, 410. FO 371/186339 [DV 1072/174].
77. Telegram, 13.7.66, 578. FO 371/186339 [DV 1072/175].
78. Minute by Palliser, 13.7.66. PREM 13/1276.
79. Wilson/Johnson, 15.7.66, T 246/66. Telegram, s.d., 6497. Ibid.
80. PMV (M) (2) (66) 1, PM's Visit to Moscow July 1966. Vietnam Brief by FO. Talking Points and Background Note, n.d. FO 371/186331 [DV 1051/201].
81. Discussion, 18.7.66, a.m. PREM 13/1276.
82. Gaiduk, pp. 62–3.
83. Record of Conversation, 18.7.66, lunch. PREM 13/1276.
84. Telegram, 19.7.66, 7035. Ibid.
85. *Times*, 20.7.66.
86. Memorandum, Chinese Military Intervention in Vietnam, [20.7.66]. FO 371/186298 [DV 103110/43].
87. Minute, 19.7.66. FO 371/186311 [DV 1051/229].
88. Minute, 21.7.66. Ibid.
89. Minute, 22.7.66. Ibid.
90. Minute, 27.7.66. Ibid.
91. Minute, 20.7.66. FO 371/186340 [DV 1072/186].
92. Minute, 20.7.76. Ibid.
93. Minute, 21.7.66. Ibid.
94. Minute, n.d. Ibid.
95. Palliser/MacLehose, 1.8.66. Ibid.
96. Memorandum, The Prime Minister's Visit to Washington, 18.7.66. FO 371/190525 [W 2/32].
97. PM (W) (66), 11, 21.7.66. FO 371/190526 [W 2/50].
98. Wilson, pp. 263–4.
99. Colman, p. 116.
100. Record of Meeting, White House, 29.7.66. FO 37/190528 [W 2/72].
101. Note of a Discussion, 29.7.66. Ibid.; also in FO 371/186340 [DV 1072/189].
102. Minute, 2.8.66. Ibid.
103. Telegram, 4.8.66, 7454. Ibid.; also PREM 13/1276.
104. Telegram, 4.8.66, 7455. FO 371/186340 [DV 1072/189].
105. Telegram, 10.8.66, 2238. Ibid.
106. Minute, 16.8.66. Ibid.

107. Minute by Murray, 1.8.66. FO 371/186340 [DV 1072/192].
108. Telegram, 2.9.66, 1640. FO 371/186340 [DV 1072/209].
109. Telegram, 6.9.66, 109. Ibid.
110. Telegram to Washington, 4.9.66, 8244. Ibid.
111. Fielding/Foreign Secretary, 9.5.66, Desp 10. DO 371/186240 [DU 103117/1].
112. *The Australian*, 26.8.66. See also Journoud, pp. 250–1.
113. *The Times*, 31.8.66.
114. Marianna P. Sullivan, *France's Vietnam Policy* (Westport: Greenwood, 1978), pp. 89–90. Stebbins, pp. 239–42.
115. Press conference, 8.9.66, II, p. 553.
116. Stewart/De la Mare, 9.9.66. FO 371/186340 [DV 1072/209].
117. Palliser/Forster, 5.9.66. FO 371/186340 [DV 1072/212].
118. Minute, 7.9.66. Ibid.
119. Minute, 7.9.66. Ibid.
120. Stewart/MacLehose, 12.9.66. FO 371/186313 [DV 103145/115].
121. Telegram, 15.9.66. FO 371/186340 [DV 1072/215].
122. Minute, 16.9.66. Ibid.
123. Minute, n.d. Ibid.
124. Pham, p. 117.
125. Speech in Stebbins, pp. 350–61.
126. Gibbons, IV, p. 402.
127. *Australian*, 26.9.66.
128. Telegram ex Dean, 29.9.66, 2650. FO 371/186341 [DV 1072/229].
129. Telegram ex NY, 8.10.66, 2154. FO 371/186341 [DV 1072/246].
130. Gaiduk, p. 89.
131. Lloyd C. Gardner, 'Fighting Vietnam; the Russian-American Conundrum', in *International Perspectives*, ed. Gardner and Gittinger, p. 40.

Chapter Seven

1. *Times*, 7.10.66. Foreign Secretary's Speech at Brighton, 6.10.66. FO 371/186341 [DV 1072/249].
2. Telegram ex Colvin, 10.10.66, 133. FO 371/186341 [DV 1072/248].
3. *Australian*, 12.10.66.
4. *Times*, 7.10.66.
5. Ibid., 10.11.66.
6. Ibid., 12.10.66.
7. Ibid., 18.10.66.
8. Ibid., 22.10.66.
9. Steering Brief and Brief No. 2 for Visit to US, 10.66. FO 371/190528 [W 2/64].
10. Telegram, 15.10.66, 2813. FO 371/186342 [DV 1072/266].
11. Telegram ex Dean, 15.10.66, 2806. FO 371/190528 [W 2/64].
12. Memorandum, 26.10.66. FRUS IV, Doc 284.

13. *New York Times*, quoted in Kahin and Lewis, p. 337n.
14. Cooper, p. 315.
15. E.g., *New Zealand Herald*, 26.10.66.
16. *Australian*, 27.10.66.
17. Minute, The Manila Conference, 27.10.66. FO 371/186343 [DV 1072/332].
18. Minute, 27.10.66. Ibid.
19. Note, 31.10.66. Ibid.
20. Telegram ex Dean, 17.10.66, 2835. FO 371/186344 [DV 1072/356].
21. Telegram to Moscow, 2.11.66, 2486. Ibid.
22. Notes for Discussion with Mr Harriman, Sections I and II, n.d. FO 371/186343 [DV 1072/337].
23. Record of Dinner Conversation, 6.11.66. FO 371/186344 [DV 1072/344].
24. Minute by Greenhill, 8.11.66. Ibid.
25. Minute, 8.11.66. Ibid.
26. Minute, 10.11.66. FO 371/186344 [DV 1072/347].
27. Minute, 14.11.66. FO 371/186344 [DV 1072/360].
28. Note on Ibid., n.d.
29. Meeting, 10.1.66. FRUS IV, Doc 300.
30. Telegram to Saigon, 13.11.66, 83786. Ibid., Doc 305.
31. Telegram, 14.11.66, 84238. Ibid., Doc 308.
32. James Hershberg, *Marigold: The Lost Chance for Peace in Vietnam* (Washington: Woodrow Wilson Center Press; Stanford University Press, 2012), pp. 111–5.
33. Ibid., pp. 207–8.
34. Telegram, 18.11.66, 876. FO 371/186344 [DV 1072/367].
35. *Australian*, 12.11.66.
36. *Times*, 16.11.66.
37. Note of the Foreign Secretary's Restricted Exchanges with Mr Gromyko, 'Document No. 1; Text of Unsigned Piece of Paper, 24.11.66', 'Document No. 2'. PREM 13/1917.
38. Record of a Meeting between the Foreign Secretary and the Chairman of the Council of Ministers, Kremlin, 25.11.66, 10.30am. PREM 13/1917.
39. Paragraph at the end of Document I. Ibid.
40. Minute by Greenhill, 28.11.66. FO 371/186345 [DV 1072/386]. Telegram, SD/London, 27.11.66, 91787. FRUS IV, Doc 317.
41. Record of Conversation, FO, 30.11.66. FO 371/186345 [DV 1072/406].
42. Telegram, 25.11.66, 312. FO 371/186345 [DV 1072/407].
43. Telegram, 29.11.66, 1303. Ibid.
44. Brown/Gromyko, 6.12.66. Ibid.
45. Minute, 13.12.66. FO 371/186308 [DV 103138/86].
46. Minute, 9.12.66. FO 371/186354 [DV 1093/69].
47. Memorandum for PM from Andrews, 30.12.66. PREM 13/1917.
48. Dean/Gore-Booth, 29.12.66. Ibid.
49. Telegram ex New York, 30.12.66, 3363. FO 371/186346 [DV 1072/430]. Thant/Goldberg, 30.12.66. Stebbins, p. 255.

50. Working Paper by Murray, n.d. [29 or 30.12.66]. FO 371/186347 [DV 1072/438].
51. Brown/Wilson, 30.12.66. PREM 13/1917. *The Times*, 31.12.66, reported that Washington was informed, not consulted.
52. Telegrams to Washington, 30.12.66, 11739. FO 371/186347 [DV 1072/437]. To Saigon, 30.12.66, 1708. FO 371/186347 [DV 1072/443]; also PREM 13/1917. To Hanoi, 30.12.66, 285. FO 371/186346 [DV 1072/430].
53. Telegram to Moscow, 31.12.66, 2939. Ibid.; also PREM 13/1917.
54. Press Conferences, II, p. 707.
55. FO statement, quoted in *Times*, 6.1.67.
56. Ibid., 3.1.67.
57. Ibid., 4.1.67.
58. Ibid., 6.1.67.
59. McNamara, p. 289.
60. Ang Cheng Guan, 'The Vietnam War from Both Sides: Revisiting "Marigold", "Sunflower", and "Pennsylvania"', *War and Society* 24, 2 (Nov. 2005): 101.
61. Telegram ex Warsaw, 19.12.66, 1513. FRUS IV, Doc 346.
62. Johnson, p. 252.
63. MacLehose/Palliser, 18.5.67. PREM 13/1912.
64. Hershberg, p. 496.
65. Thies, p. 343.
66. Minute for PM, 4.1.67. PREM 13/1917.
67. Hershberg, p. 246.
68. Letter to Dean, enclosed in PS/Palliser, 11.1.67. PREM 13/1917.
69. State/London, 10.1.67, 118905. Herring, *Secret Diplomacy*, pp. 333–5.
70. P. Gore-Booth, *With Great Truth and Respect* (London: Constable, 1974), p. 357.
71. Conversation, 11.1.67. PREM 13/1917.
72. Telegram, 12.1.67, 341. Ibid.
73. Rostow/President, 16.1.67, in FRUS V, editorial, Doc 15.
74. Conversation, 18.1.67. FCO 15/634 [52].
75. Wilson, p. 345.
76. Statement, 18.1.67. PREM 13/1917.
77. Minute, 18.1.67. FCO 15/621 [3].
78. Stewart/De la Mare, 30.1.67. FCO 15/633 [53].
79. Minute, 31.1.67. FCO 15/633 [54].
80. Minute by De la Mare, 1.2.67. FCO 15/633 [54].
81. Telegram, 31.1.67, 1001. FCO 15/634 [53].
82. *Times*, 4.1.67.
83. Interview, n.d., transmitted 28.1.67. PREM 13/1917. FRUS V, Doc 29. Stebbins, pp. 193–5. *Times*, 30.1.67.
84. Ang, *War and Society*, pp. 107, 109. FRUS V, Editorial Note, Doc 29.
85. Nguyen, p. 90.
86. Press Conferences, pp. 727–9.
87. *Australian*, 3.2.67.

88. Meeting, 4.2.67. PREM 13/1917.
89. Memorandum, The Kosygin Visit, A Study in Anglo-American Relations, February 1967. FCO 15/634 [60] [hereinafter: Study], pp. 4–5.
90. Ibid., pp. 1–2.
91. Conversation, 6.2.67, 3.30 pm. PREM 13/1917.
92. Record of a Meeting, 6.2.67, 4.30pm. FCO15/633 [21]; also PREM 13/1917.
93. Note by Murray for Secretary of State, 6.2.67. FCO 15/633 [3].
94. Record of a Conversation at Dinner, 6.2.67. PREM 13/1917.
95. Study, p. 7.
96. Rostow/President, 6.2.67, 8 pm. FRUS V, Doc 39.
97. Study, pp. 7–8.
98. Minute, 8.2.67. FCO 15/633 [59].
99. Minute, 7.2.67. FCO 15/633 [9].
100. Minute, 13.2.67. Ibid.
101. Minute, 8.2.67. FCO 15/634 [58].
102. Wilson/Johnson, 7.2.67, T 22/67. PREM 13/1917.
103. Johnson/Wilson, 6.2.67. Ibid.; also in Herring, *Secret Diplomacy*, pp. 436–8.
104. Minute by Palliser, 7.2.67. PREM 13/1917.
105. Study, p. 10, in margin.
106. Ang, *War and Society*, p. 112.
107. Chester Cooper, *The Lost Crusade* (London: McGibbon and Kee, 1971), p. 353.
108. Ibid., p. 368.
109. Johnson/Ho Chi Minh, 8.2.67. Stebbins, pp. 198–200; also in Johnson, App VIII. Telegram to Moscow, 7.2.67, 132608, sent 2.15am, with Note by Rusk. FRUS V, Doc 40.
110. Fn4 to Ibid.
111. Study, pp. 10–1.
112. Record of 4th Formal Meeting, 7.2.67, 4.30pm. PREM 13/1917; also FCO 15/633 [22].
113. Study, pp. 11–2.
114. Memorandum, Rostow/President, 7.2.67, 8pm. FRUS V, Doc 41.
115. Extracts in Herring, *Secret Diplomacy*, p. 442.
116. Study, pp. 12–3. Telegram ex Embassy, 9.2.67, 6399. FRUS V, Doc 46.
117. Note by Murray for Duty Clerk at No. 10. PREM 13/1917.
118. Telegram, 9.2.67, 6399. FRUS V, Doc 46.
119. Memorandum, 9 [?].2.67. FCO 15/633 [11]. Some of the dates in the Study are wrong.
120. Study, p. 13.
121. Meeting at Claridge's, 9.2.67. PREM 13/1917. Telegram ex Cooper, 9.2.67, 6411. FRUS V, Doc 49.
122. Phone Conversation, 9.2.67, 9.07 am. FRUS V, Doc 48.
123. Telegram, 9.2.67, 133907. Ibid., Doc 50.
124. Study, pp. 14–5.
125. Text of Message telephoned by Murray, 9.2.67. FCO 15/633 [61]. MacLehose/Palliser, 10.2.67. PREM 13/1918.

126. Study, p. 16. Record of Private Conversation, 10.2.67 PREM 13/1918.
127. Study, pp. 16–7.
128. Study, p. 17.
129. Telegram, Rostow/Trend, 10.2.67, CAP 67041. PREM 13/1918. Telegram ex Rostow, 10.2.67. FRUS V, Doc 51.
130. Memorandum, 10.2.67, 2.50pm. Ibid., Doc 54.
131. Cooper, pp. 360–1.
132. Study, p. 18.
133. Wilson/Kosygin, 10.2.67. PREM 13/1918.
134. Conversation at Soviet reception, 10.1.67. PREM 13/1918. Telegram ex Bruce and Cooper, 11.2.67, 1227. Herring, p. 456.
135. Telegram, drafted 10.2.67 evening, sent 11.2.67, T27/67. PREM 13/1918.
136. Study, pp. 18–9.
137. Wilson, p. 357.
138. Study, pp. 19–20.
139. Draft message, not sent. PREM 13/1918.
140. Study, p. 21.
141. Telegram ex Rusk for Bruce and Cooper, 10.2.67 [11.2.67 in London]. PREM 13/1918.
142. Record of a Meeting at 10 Downing Street, 11.2.67, 10.40pm, ending at 1.45am, 12.2.67. PREM 13/1918. Cooper's memorandum for the record, 11.2.67, is not much like this. FRUS V, Doc 63.
143. Telegram 12.2.67, T30/67. PREM 13/1918; also FRUS V, Doc 64.
144. Telegram, 12.2.67, T31/67. PREM 13/1918; also FRUS V, Doc 65.
145. Study, p. 23.
146. Telegram, 12.2.67, CAP 67043. PREM 13/1918; also IN FRUS V, Doc 66, and in Herring, pp. 462–4.
147. Telegram, 12.2.67, T33/67. PREM 13/1918; also FRUS V, Doc 67.
148. Cooper, p. 384.
149. Study, pp. 24–5.
150. Ibid., p. 25.
151. Telegram, Palliser/Rostow, 12.2.67. PREM 13/1918.
152. Telegram, Johnson/Wilson, 12.2.67, 2333Z CAP 67045. FRUS V, Doc 70; also as T34/67 in PREM 13/1918.
153. Study, p. 26.
154. Record of a Conversation at Claridge's, 13.2.67, 1am. PREM 13/1918.
155. Conversation with McNamara, 12.2.67, 10.13pm. FRUS V, Doc 71.
156. Wilson, p. 363.
157. Phone Conversation, 12.2.67, 11.17 pm. FRUS V, Doc 73. Johnson/Wilson, 11.2.67, CAP 67046. FRUS V, Doc 74; also PREM 13/1918.
158. Ang, *Other Side*, p. 114.
159. Study, pp. 28–9. Gore-Booth's diary of 13.2.67 pm, 16.2.67. FCO 15/633 [64].
160. Herring, p. 400. Hershberg, p. 570.
161. Gaiduk, p. 106.
162. Ibid.

163. Ho/Johnson, 15.2.67. Stebbins, pp. 200–2.
164. *Times*, 14.2.67.
165. Minute, 15.2.67. FCO 15/633 [17].
166. McNamara/Johnson, phone conversation, 13.2.67. FRUS V, Doc 77.
167. FRUS V, editorial, Doc 80. *Australian*, 16.2.67.
168. State/London, 14.2.67, 136999. Herring, p. 476.
169. Conversation, 24.2.67. PREM 13/1918. FRUS V, editorial, Doc 80.
170. Conversation, 24.3.67. PREM 13/1912.
171. Draft Message. PREM 13/2458; also FCO 15/633 [38].
172. Minute, 6.3.67. FCO 15/633 [40].
173. Draft. PREM 13/2458; also FCO 15/633 [34].
174. Minute, 14.3.67. Ibid.
175. Minute, 14.3.67. Ibid.
176. Minute for PM, 14.3.67, PM /67/31. FCO 15/633 [35].
177. PM/Foreign Secretary, 15.3.67, M24/67. FCO 15/633 [36].
178. Minute, n.d. Ibid.
179. Wilson/Johnson, 15.3.67, PM/67/32; also Telegram, 17.3.67, 2615. PREM 13/2458.
180. FO Telegram, 28.3.67, 2805. Ibid.
181. Minute, 23.3.67. PREM 13/1919.
182. Minute, 12.4.67. PREM 13/2458.
183. Note on Ibid.
184. George Brown, *In My Way* (London: Gollancz, 1971), p. 146.
185. Gore-Booth, p. 360.
186. Wilson, p. 365.
187. Brown, p. 146.
188. Ibid., pp. 145, 146.
189. Ang, *War and Society*, p. 111.
190. *Times*, 14.2.67.
191. Ibid., 15.2.67.
192. Crossman, II, p. 237.
193. Heren, pp. 155–6.
194. Gardner, in *Perspectives*, p. 44.

Chapter Eight

1. See Easter, pp. 191–2.
2. Memorandum, Vietnam and British Policy in East Asia, SC (67) 15, 24.2.67. FCO 49/9.
3. SC 94th, 8.3.67. Ibid.
4. De la Mare, British Policy in East Asia, 3.67. BDEE A5, Pt 1, Doc 101, pp. 349–53.
5. Gaiduk, pp. 117–8.
6. Ang, p. 115.
7. Record of a Meeting, Moscow, 24.5.67, 10.15 am, PREM 13/1919.

8. Telegram, 24.5.67, 875. FCO 15/621 [26].
9. Young is mistaken in thinking this was kept off the agenda. *Cold War History*, p. 76.
10. Conversation between PM and President, White House, 2.6.67, with brief reference to PM's Talk to Vice-President, 3.6.67. PREM 13/1919.
11. Visit of PM to Paris, June 1967, Vietnam, Talking Points, with Background. PMVG (67) 2 (a), 14.4.67. FCO 24/127.
12. Quoted in Woods, p. 802.
13. Gaiduk, pp. 128–30. Johnson, p. 247. Gardner, in *Perspectives*, pp. 49–50.
14. Stebbins, p. 242.
15. Quoted in David Schoenbrun, 'Hanoi's Terms for a Peace Conference', in *Australian*, 4.10.67.
16. Press Conference, 30.9.67. II, p. 842.
17. *Times*, 22.9.67.
18. Ibid., 27.9.67.
19. *Australian*, 28.9.67.
20. CC (67) 57th, 28.9.67, 2. CAB 128/42; also FCO 24/127.
21. Crossman, II, p. 498–9.
22. *Australian*, 7.9.67.
23. *Times*, 5.10.67.
24. Minute for Sir D. Allen, 1.11.67. FCO 15/619 [154]; also in BDEE A5, Pt 1, Doc 106.
25. Minute, 14.11.67, on Minute by Murray, s.d. FCO 15/618 [125].
26. Minute, 3.11.67. FCO 15/619 [155]; also BDEE A5 Pt 1, Doc 106.
27. De la Mare/Dean, 8.11.67. FCO 15/619 [156].
28. Minute, 13.11.67. FCO 15/618 [116].
29. Minute, 31.10.67. PREM 13/2459.
30. Minute, 31.10.67. Ibid.
31. Minute by Gore-Booth, 10.11.67. FCO 15/618 [115]; also BDEE A5 Pt 1, Doc 107.
32. Minute, 13.11.67. FCO 15/618 [116].
33. Minute by Murray, 14.11.67, and attached comments. FCO 15/618 [125].
34. Memorandum, 15.11.67, C (67) 180. CAB 129/134; also FCO 24/127 [102b]; FCO 15/618 [128], and, without the annex, BDEE A5 Pt 1, Doc 108.
35. Minute, 15.11.67. FCO 15/618 [126].
36. Minute, s.d. Ibid.
37. Minute for PM, 15.11.67. PREM 13/2459.
38. Brief for Cabinet of 16.11.67,15.11.67. FCO 24/127 [102a].
39. Pickering, p. 163.
40. Pham, p. 301.
41. Quoted in Joseph, p. 344n.
42. Ibid., p. 114.
43. Quoted in Pickering (2002), p. 157.
44. Ibid., p. 166.
45. Quoted in Ibid., p. 168.

46. Extract, PM's Talk with President Johnson in Melbournc, 22.12.67. PREM 13/2459.
47. Diaries, II, pp. 618–9.
48. Extract, FRUS V, editorial, DOC 451.
49. *Australian*, 2, 6.1.68.
50. Ibid., 4.1.68.
51. Extract, PM/Kosygin talks 22.1.68. PREM 13/2459.
52. Extract, PM/Brezhnev talks, 23.1.68. Ibid.
53. Moscow/FO, 23.1.68, retailing T33/68. Ibid.
54. Johnson/Wilson, 24.1.68, CAP 80370. FRUS VI, Doc 24; also Telegram to Moscow, 24.1.68, 255. PREM 13/2459.
55. Meeting, 24.1.68. *Documents on British Policy Overseas* [DBPO], Series III, Vol. 1 (1997), Doc 3, at pp. 18–20.
56. Passage for inclusion in Telegram to UK Mission, New York, amended by PM, n.d. PREM 13/2460.
57. Communiqué, 24.1.68, in *Times*, 25.1.68.
58. *Australian*, 1.2.68.
59. Ibid., 3.2.68.
60. Edward E. Moise, 'The Myths of the Tet Offensive', in *New Perspectives on the History and Historiography of Southeast Asia*, ed. M.A. Aung-Thwin and Kenneth R. Hall (London, New York: Routledge, 2011), p. 233.
61. R.K. Brigham, *Guerrilla Diplomacy: The NLF's Foreign Relations and the Vietnam War* (Ithaca, London: Cornell University Press, 1999), p. 73. See also Journoud, p. 280.
62. Nguyen, pp. 96, 98, 101.
63. Quoted in Luu Doan Huynh, 'The Perspective of a Vietnamese Witness', in *The War That Never Ends*, ed. David L. Anderson and John Ernst (Lexington: University Press of Kentucky, 2007), p. 91.
64. Brigham, *ARVN*, pp. 96–8.
65. Taylor, p. 604.
66. Quoted in Dumbrell, *Johnson and Soviet Communism*, p. 51.
67. Wilson, p. 497.
68. Record of Conversation, 8.2.68. PREM 13/2460.
69. Wilson, pp. 500–1.
70. Extract, Meeting, 9.2.68. PREM 13/2460.
71. Telegram to Moscow, 15.2.68. Ibid.
72. Palliser/Maitland, 15.2.68. Ibid.
73. *Times*, 14.2.68.
74. Press Conferences, II, p. 905.
75. Kosygin/PM, 29.2.68, 2436. Ibid.
76. Telegram, 11.3.68, 2436. Ibid.
77. Telegram ex Saigon, 2.4.68, 465. FCO 15/698 [8].
78. Johnson/Wilson, 30.6.68, T 85/68. PREM 13/2460.
79. Wilson/Johnson, 31.3.68, T 89/68. Ibid.
80. DBPO, III, 1, fn7, p. 35.
81. Telegram, 4.4.68, 3497. PREM 13/2461.

82. Minute for Allen, 8.4.68. FCO 15/621 [60].
83. DBPO, III, 1, p. 36.
84. Mitchell/Palliser, 15.5.68. PREM 13/2462.
85. Memorandum, 14.5.68. FCO 15/619 [140].
86. Memorandum, Vietnam Negotiations British Interests, 15.5.68. PREM 13/2461.
87. Minute, 17.5.68. Ibid.
88. Quoted in DBPO, III, 1, p. 36.
89. Our own correspondent, 22.5.68. *Times*, 23.5.68.
90. Record, 23.5.68, 10 am. PREM 13/2462.
91. Telegram, 18.5.68, 166803. FRUS VI, fn to Doc 246.
92. *Times*, 25.5.68.
93. SD Telegram to Paris, 24.5.68, 170294, Todel 220. FRUS VI, Doc 246.
94. Harrison/Hayman, 29.5.68. DBPO, III, 1, Doc 9.
95. Schwab, p. 72.

Conclusion

1. Record of Final Session of the Annual Conference of the Commissioner-General, South-East Asia, Eden Hall, 19.1.58. FO 371/135652 [D 1051/4].
2. Logevall, *Choosing War*, p. 401.
3. Young, *Cold War History*, p. 86.
4. Quoted in Woods, p. 751.
5. Guenter Lewy, *America in Vietnam* (New York: Oxford University Press, 1978), pp. 430–1.
6. Frank Ninkovich, *Morality and Power: A History of the Domino Theory* (Chicago, London: University of Chicago Press, 1994), p. 308.
7. Ball, pp. 376–7.
8. Press Conferences, II, p. 866.
9. *Times*, 18.9.67.
10. Notes of Meeting, Defense Department staff, 5.11.68. FRUS VII, Doc 95.
11. Frank Ninkovich, *The Global Republic* (University of Chicago Press, 2014), pp. 189–90.
12. Nguyen Cao Ky, p. 146.
13. Anthony Eden, Earl of Avon, *Towards Peace in Indo-China* (London: Oxford University Press/RIIA, 1966).
14. Wheeler/McNamara, 11.2.67. FRUS V, Doc 62.
15. Zhihua Shen and Danhui Li, *After Leaning to One Side: China and Its Allies in the Cold War* (Washington: Woodrow Wilson Center Press; Stanford University Press, 2011), pp. 225, 229, 234.
16. Dumbrell, p. 104.
17. Adlai Stevenson lecture, Illinois State University, reported in *Australian*, 30.3.67.
18. Etherington-Smith/Gore-Booth, 15.7.66. FO 371/186331 [DV 1051/208].
19. Minute, 3.8.66. Ibid.

Bibliography

Primary Sources

The National Archives, Kew

FO 371
FCO
PREM

Birmingham University Library
Avon Papers

British Documents on the End of Empire, ed. S.R. Ashton:

Series A Volume 4 *The Conservative Government and the End of Empire 1957–1964*, Parts 1 and 2. London: Stationery Office (2000).

Series A Volume 5 *East of Suez and the Commonwealth 1964–1971*, London; TSO, 2004.

Documents on British Policy Overseas, ed. G. Bennett and K.A. Hamilton, Series III, Vol. 1. London: The Stationery Office (1997).

Foreign Relations of the United States [FRUS] 1964–68, Vols I–VII, XXVII.

Documents on American Policy, ed. Jules Davids [1964], Richard P. Stebbins [1965–8]. New York: Harper & Row, 1965–69.

The Johnson Presidential Press Conferences, introd. Doris Kearns Goodwin.

Documents on China's Relations with South and Southeast Asia (1949–1962), ed. G.V. Ambekar and V.D. Divedar. Bombay: Allied, 1964.

Newspapers

The Times (London)
The Australian
The New Zealand Herald
Réalités (Phnom Penh)

Secondary Sources

Anderson, David L., ed. *The Columbia History of the Vietnam War*. New York: Columbia University Press, 2011.

Anderson, David L. and John Ernst, eds. *The War That Never Ends*. Lexington: University Press of Kentucky, 2007.

Ang Cheng Guan. *The Vietnam War from the Other Side*. London: RoutledgeCurzon, 2002.

———. 'The Vietnam War from Both Sides: Revisiting "Marigold", "Sunflower", and "Pennsylvania"', *War and Society* 24, 2 (Nov. 2005): 93–125.

———. *Southeast Asia and the Vietnam War*. London, New York: Routledge, 2010.

———. *Lee Kuan Yew's Strategic Thought*. London, New York: Routledge, 2013.

Asselin, Pierre. *Hanoi's Road to the Vietnam War*. Berkeley, Los Angeles, London: University of California Press, 2013.

Aung-Thwin, Michael Arthur and Kenneth R. Hall, eds. *New Perspectives on the History and Historiography of Southeast Asia*. London, New York: Routledge, 2011.

Axelrod, Alex. *The Real History of the Vietnam War*. New York: Sterling, 2013.

Ball, George. *The Past Has Another Pattern*. New York: Norton, 1982.

Ball, S.J. 'Selkirk in Singapore', *Twentieth-Century British History* 10, 2 (1999): 162–91.

Barnouin, Barbara and Yu Changgen. *Chinese Foreign Policy during the Cultural Revolution*. London: Kegan Paul, 1998.

Beckett, Ian F.W. 'Robert Thompson and the British Advisory Mission to South Vietnam, 1961–1965', *Small Wars and Emergencies* 8, 3 (1997): 41–63.

Bowles, Chester. *Promises to Keep*. New York: Harper & Row, 1971.

Bradley, Mark Philip and Marilyn B. Young, eds. *Making Sense of the Vietnam Wars: Local, National, and Transnational Perspectives*. Oxford University Press, 2008.

Brigham, Robert K. *Guerrilla Diplomacy*. Ithaca, London: Cornell University Press, 1999.

———. *ARVN: Life and Death in the South Vietnamese Army*. Lawrence: University Press of Kansas, 2006.

Brown, George. *In My Way*. London: Gollancz, 1971.

Busch, Peter. *All The Way with JFK? Britain, the US, and the Vietnam War*. Oxford University Press, 2003.

Buttinger, Joseph. *Vietnam: A Dragon Embattled*. London: Pall Mall Press, 1967.

Buzzanco, Robert. *Vietnam and the Transformation of American Life*. Malden, Oxford: Blackwell, 1999.

———. 'Military Dissent and the Legacy of the Vietnam War', in *The War That Never Ends*, ed. David L. Anderson and John Ernst. Lexington: University Press of Kentucky, 2007, pp. 191–218.

Cable, James. *The Geneva Conference of 1954 in Indochina*. London: Macmillan, 1986.

Caro, Robert A. *The Years of Lyndon Johnson: The Passage of Power*. New York: Vintage, 2013.

Carter, James M. *Inventing Vietnam: The United States and State Building, 1954–1968*. Cambridge University Press, 2008.

Chen Jian. 'China and the Vietnam Wars', in *The Vietnam War*, ed. Peter Lowe. Basingstoke: Macmillan, 1998, pp. 152–80.

Cole, Allan B. *Conflict in Indo-China and International Repercussion: A Documentary History*. Ithaca: Cornell University Press, 1956.

Colman, Jonathan. *A 'Special Relationship'? Harold Wilson, Lyndon B. Johnson, and Anglo-American Relations 'at the Summit'.* Manchester, New York: Manchester University Press, 2004.

Cooper, Chester. *The Lost Crusade.* London: McGibbon and Kee, 1971.

Crossman, R.H.S. *The Diaries of a Cabinet Minister.* London: Hamilton and Cape, Vol. I, 1975; Vol. 2, 1977.

DiLeo, David L. *George Ball, Vietnam, and the Rethinking of Containment.* Chapel Hill, London: University of North Carolina Press, 1991.

Divine, Robert A. 'Vietnam: An Episode in the Cold War', in *Vietnam: The Early Decisions,* ed. Lloyd C. Gardner and Ted Gittinger. Austin: University of Texas Press, 1997, pp. 11–23.

Dobrynin, Anatoly. *In Confidence.* New York: Times Books, 1995.

Dockrill, Saki. *Britain's Retreat from East of Suez.* Basingstoke: Macmillan, 2002.

Duiker, William J. *Ho Chi Minh.* Sydney: Allen & Unwin, 2000.

———. *U.S. Containment Policy and the Conflict in Indochina.* Stanford University Press, 2004.

Dumbrell, John. 'The Johnson Administration and the British Labour Government: Vietnam, the Pound and East of Suez', *Journal of American Studies,* 30, 2 (1996): 211–31.

———. *President Lyndon Johnson and Soviet Communism.* Manchester, New York: Manchester University Press, 2004.

Dumbrell, John and Sylvia Ellis. 'British Involvement in Vietnam Peace Initiatives, 1966–1967', *Diplomatic History* 27, 1 (Jan. 2003): 113–49.

Easter, David. *Britain and the Confrontation with Indonesia 1960–66.* London, New York: Tauris, 2004.

Eden, Anthony, Earl of Avon. *Towards Peace in Indo-China.* London: Oxford University Press and Chatham House, 1966.

Ellis, Sylvia. 'Lyndon Johnson, Harold Wilson and the Vietnam War: A Not So Special Relationship', in *Twentieth-Century Anglo-American Relations,* ed. Jonathan Hollowell. Basingstoke, New York: Palgrave, 2002, pp. 180–204.

Ellison, D. Hank. *Chemical Warfare during the Vietnam War: Riot Control Agents in Combat.* New York, London: Routledge, 2011.

Fedorowich, Kent and Martin Thomas, eds. *International Diplomacy and Colonial Retreat.* London, Portland: Cass, 2001.

Fenton, Damien. *To Cage the Red Dragon: SEATO and the Defence of Southeast Asia 1955–1965.* Singapore: NUS Press, 2012.

Frankum, Robert B. *Like Rolling Thunder: The Air War in Vietnam 1964–1975.* Lanham: Rowman & Littlefield, 2005.

Frey, Marc, Ronald W. Preussen and Tan Tai Yong, eds. *The Transformation of Southeast Asia: International Perspectives on Decolonisation.* Armonk, London: M.E. Sharpe, 2003.

Gaddis, John Lewis. *We Now Know.* Oxford: Clarendon Press, 1997.

———. *George F. Kennan: An American Life.* New York: Penguin, 2011.

Gaiduk, Ilya. *The Soviet Union and the Vietnam War.* Chicago: Dee, 1996.

———. 'Developing an Alliance: The Soviet Union and Vietnam, 1954–75', in *The Vietnam War*, ed. Peter Lowe. Basingstoke: Macmillan, 1998, pp. 133–51.

———. *Confronting Vietnam: Soviet Policy towards the Indo-China Conflict, 1954–1963*, Stanford University Press; Washington: Woodrow Wilson Center Press, 2003.

Gardner, Lloyd C. *Pay Any Price: Lyndon Johnson and the Wars for Vietnam.* Chicago: Dee, 1995.

———. 'Fighting Vietnam: The Russian-American Conundrum', in *International Perspectives on Vietnam*, ed. Lloyd C. Gardner and Ted Gittinger. College Station: Texas A&M University Press, 2000, pp. 23–57.

Gardner, Lloyd C. and Ted Gittinger, eds. *Vietnam: The Early Decisions*. Austin: University of Texas Press, 1997.

———, eds. *International Perspectives on Vietnam*. College Station: Texas A&M University Press, 2000.

———, eds. *The Search for Peace in Vietnam 1964–1968*. College Station: Texas A&M University Press, 2004.

Geyelin, Philip. *Lyndon B. Johnson and the World*. London: Pall Mall Press, 1966.

Gibbons, William Conrad. *The U.S. Government and the Vietnam War*, Vol. 4. Princeton University Press, 1995.

Gore-Booth, Paul. *With Great Truth and Respect*. London: Constable, 1974.

Gurtov, Melvin. *China and Southeast Asia: The Politics of Survival.* Baltimore, London: Johns Hopkins University Press, 1975.

Heren, Louis. *No Hail, No Farewell.* London: Weidenfeld, 1970.

Herring, George C. *The Secret Diplomacy of the Vietnam War: The Negotiating Volumes of the Pentagon Papers*. Austin: University of Texas Press, 1983.

Hershberg, James G. *Marigold: The Lost Chance for Peace in Vietnam*. Stanford University Press; Washington: Woodrow Wilson Center Press, 2012.

Hughes, Geraint. *Harold Wilson's Cold War: The Labour Government and East-West Politics, 1964–1970*. Woodbridge: Boydell/RHS, 2009.

Hughes, Philip. 'Division and Discord: British Policy, Indochina, and the Origins of the Vietnam War, 1954–56', in *International Diplomacy and Colonial Retreat*, ed. Kent Fedorowich and Martin Thomas. London, Portland: Cass, 2001, pp. 94–112.

Hull, Isabel. *A Scrap of Paper*. Ithaca, London: Cornell University Press, 2014.

Ives, Christopher K. *U.S. Special Forces and Counterinsurgency in Vietnam: Military Innovation and Institutional Failure, 1961–1963*. London, New York: Routledge, 2007.

Johnson, Lyndon B. *The Vantage Point*. London: Weidenfeld, 1972.

Jones, Matthew. *Conflict and Confrontation in South East Asia 1961–1965: Britain, the United States and the Creation of Malaysia*. Cambridge University Press, 2002.

Joseph, Paul. *Cracks in the Empire: State Politics in the Vietnam War*. New York: Columbia University Press, 1987.

Journoud, Pierre. *De Gaulle et le Vietnam, 1945–1969: La reconciliation*. Paris: Tallandier, 2011.

Joyaux, F. *La Chine et le règlement du premier conflit d'Indochine*. Paris: Sorbonne, 1979.

Kahin, George McT. and John W. Lewis. *The United States in Vietnam*. n.p.: Delta Press, 1967.

Kaiser, David. *American Tragedy*. Cambridge: Belknap Press of Harvard University Press, 2000.

———. 'Discussions, Not Negotiations', in *The Search for Peace in Vietnam 1964–1968*, ed. Lloyd C. Gardner and Ted Gittinger. College Station: Texas A&M University Press, 2004, pp. 45–58.

Karnik, V.B., ed. *China Invades India*. Bombay: Allied, 1963.

Kear, Simon. 'The British Consulate-General in Hanoi, 1954–73', *Diplomacy and Statecraft* 10, 1 (1999): 215–39.

Knock, Thomas J. 'George McGovern and Mr Johnson's War', in *The Search for Peace in Vietnam 1964–1968*, ed. Lloyd C. Gardner and Ted Gittinger. College Station: Texas A&M University Press, 2004, pp. 97–116.

La Feber, Walter. 'The United States and Vietnam: The Enemies', in *The War That Never Ends*, ed. David L. Anderson and John Ernst. Lexington: University Press of Kentucky, 2007, pp. 35–54.

Lawrence, Mark Atwood and Fredrik Logevall, eds. *The First Vietnam War: Colonial Conflict and Cold War Crisis*. Cambridge, London: Harvard University Press, 2007.

Lee, Edwin. *Singapore: The Unexpected Nation*. Singapore: ISEAS, 2008.

Li Mingjiang. *Mao's China and the Sino-Soviet Split*. London, New York: Routledge, 2012.

Logevall, Fredrik. 'De Gaulle, Neutralization, and American Involvement in Vietnam, 1963–1964', *Pacific Historical Review* 61 (1992): 69–102.

———. *Choosing War: The Lost Chance for Peace and the Escalation of War in Vietnam*. Berkeley, Los Angeles, London: University of California Press, 1999.

Lowe, Peter, ed. *The Vietnam War*. Basingstoke: Macmillan, 1998.

———. *Contending with Nationalism and Communism: British Policy towards Southeast Asia, 1945–65*. Basingstoke: Macmillan, 2009.

Luu Doan Huynh. 'The Perspective of a Vietnamese Witness', in *The War That Never Ends*, ed. David L. Anderson and John Ernst. Lexington: University Press of Kentucky, 2007, pp. 75–104.

Mayers, David. *George Kennan and the Dilemmas of US Foreign Policy*. New York, Oxford: Oxford University Press, 1988.

McNamara, Robert S. *In Retrospect: The Tragedy and Lessons of Vietnam*. New York: Times, 1995.

Mendès-France, P. *Gouverner c'est choisir*. Paris: Gallimard, 1986.

Moise, Edward E. 'Myths of the Tet Offensive', in *New Perspectives on the History and Historiography of Southeast Asia*, ed. Michael Arthur Aung-Thwin and Kenneth R. Hall. London, New York: Routledge, 2011, pp. 229–54.

Nguyen Cao Ky. *How We Lost the War in Vietnam*. New York: Cooper Square Books, 2000 (originally published 1976).

Nguyen Lien-Hang T. *Hanoi's War: An International History of the War for Peace in Vietnam*. Chapel Hill: University of North Carolina Press, 2012.

Nguyen Vu Tung. 'Coping with the United States: Hanoi's Search for an Effective Strategy', in *The Vietnam War*, ed. Peter Lowe. Basingstoke: Macmillan, 1998, pp. 30–61.

Ninkovich, Frank. *Morality and Power: A History of the Domino Theory in the Twentieth Century*. Chicago, London: University of Chicago Press, 1994.

———. *The Global Republic*. University of Chicago Press, 2014.

Nolting, Frederick. *From Trust to Tragedy*. New York: Praeger, 1988.

Olsen, Mari. *Soviet-Vietnam Relations and the Role of China, 1949–64: Changing Alliances*. London, New York: Routledge, 2006.

Parker, Alastair. 'International Aspects of the Vietnam War', in *The Vietnam War*, ed. Peter Lowe. Basingstoke: Macmillan, 1998, pp. 196–218.

Parker, Richard. *John Kenneth Galbraith: His Life, His Politics, His Economics*. New York: Farrar, Straus and Giroux, 2005.

Pham, P.L. *Ending 'East of Suez'*. Oxford University Press, 2010.

Pickering, Jeffrey. *Britain's Withdrawal from East of Suez*. Basingstoke: Macmillan, 1998.

———. 'Politics and "Black Tuesday": Shifting Power in the Cabinet and the Decision to Withdraw from East of Suez, November 1967–January 1968', *Twentieth Century British History* 13, 2 (2002): 144–70.

Pike, Douglas. *Vietnam and the Soviet Union*. Boulder, London: Westview, 1987.

Porter, Gareth. *Perils of Dominance: Imbalance of Power and the Road to War in Vietnam*. Berkeley, Los Angeles, London: University of California Press, 2005.

Preston, Andrew. *The War Council: McGeorge Bundy, the National Security Council, and Vietnam*. Cambridge: Harvard University Press, 2006.

Rabel, Roberto. *New Zealand and the Vietnam War Politics and Diplomacy*. Auckland: Auckland University Press, 2005.

Roberts, Priscilla, ed. *Behind the Bamboo Curtain: China, Vietnam and the World beyond Asia*. Stanford University Press; Washington: Woodrow Wilson Center Press, 2006.

Ruane, Kevin and James Ellison. 'Managing the Americans: Anthony Eden, Harold Macmillan and the Pursuit of "Power by Proxy" in the 1950s', in *The Foreign Office and British Diplomacy in the Twentieth Century*, ed. Gaynor Johnson. London, New York: Routledge, 2005, pp. 147–67.

Schaffer, Howard B. *Ellsworth Bunker Global Troubleshooter, Vietnam Hawk*. Chapel Hill, London: University of North Carolina Press, 2003.

Schandler, Herbert. *The Unmaking of a President*. Princeton University Press, 1977.

Schlesinger, A.M. *Robert Kennedy and His Times*. London: Deutsch, 1978.

Schulzinger, Robert D. *A Time for War: The United States and Vietnam, 1941–1975*. New York, Oxford: Oxford University Press, 1997.

Schwab, Orrin. *A Clash of Cultures: Civil-Military Relations during the Vietnam War*. Westport: Praeger, 2006.

Shen Zhihua and Danhui Li. *After Leaning to One Side: China and Its Allies in the Cold War*. Stanford University Press; Washington: Woodrow Wilson Center Press, 2011.

Smith, Ralph B. *An International History of the Vietnam War*, Vol. 3, *The Making of a Limited War*. Basingstoke: Macmillan, 1991.

Steininger, Rolf. '"The Americans Are in a Hopeless Position": Great Britain and the War in Vietnam, 1964–65', *Diplomacy and Statecraft* 8, 3 (1997): 237–85.

Stewart, Michael. *Life and Labour*. London: Sidgwick and Jackson, 1980.

Subritzky, John. *Confronting Sukarno: British, American, Australian and New Zealand Diplomacy in the Malaysian-Indonesian Confrontation, 1961–5*. Basingstoke: Macmillan; New York: St Martin's, 2000.

Sullivan, Marianna P. *France's Vietnam Policy: A Study in French-American Relations*. Westport: Greenwood, 1978.

Tarling, Nicholas. *Britain, Southeast Asia and the Impact of the Korean War*. Singapore: Singapore University Press, 2005.

———. *Britain and the Neutralisation of Laos*. Singapore: NUS Press, 2011.

———. *Britain and Sihanouk's Cambodia*. Singapore: NUS Press, 2014.

Taylor, Jay. *China and Southeast Asia: Peking's Relations with Revolutionary Movements*. New York, Washington, London: Praeger, 1976.

Taylor, K.W. *A History of the Vietnamese*. Cambridge University Press, 2013.

Thakur, Ramesh. *Peacekeeping in Vietnam: Canada, India, Poland and the International Commission*. Edmonton: University of Alberta Press, 1984.

Thies, Wallace J. *When Governments Collide: Coercion and Diplomacy in the Vietnam Conflict 1964–1968*. Berkeley, Los Angeles, London: University of California Press, 1980.

Topmiller, Robert. 'The Buddhist Antiwar Movement', in *The War That Never Ends*, ed. David L. Anderson and John Ernst. Lexington: University Press of Kentucky, 2007, pp. 143–66.

Turley, William. *The Second Indochina War: A Concise Political and Military History*, second edition. Lanham: Rowman & Littlefield, 2009.

Updegrove, Mark K. *Indomitable Will: LBJ in the Presidency*. New York: Crown Publishers, 2012.

Warner, Jayne and David Hunt, eds. *The American War in Vietnam*. Ithaca: Cornell University SEAP, 1993.

Wiest, Andrew and Michael J. Doidge, eds. *Triumph Revisited*. New York, London: Routledge, 2010.

Willbanks, James H. *The Tet Offensive: A Concise History*. New York: Columbia University Press, 2007.

Wilson, Harold. *The Labour Government 1964–1970*. London: Weidenfeld and Michael Joseph, 1971.

Woodruff, Mark W. *Unheralded Victory: Who Won the Vietnam War?* New York: HarperCollins, 1999.

Woods, Randall B., ed. *Vietnam and the American Political Tradition: The Politics of Dissent*. Cambridge University Press, 2003.

———. *LBJ Architect of American Ambition*. New York, London, Toronto, Sydney: Free Press, 2006.

Yang Kuisong. 'Mao and the Indochina Wars', in *Behind the Bamboo Curtain: China, Vietnam and the World beyond Asia*, ed. Priscilla Roberts. Stanford University Press; Washington: Woodrow Wilson Center Press, 2006, pp. 55–96.

Young, John W. 'The Wilson Government and the Davies Peace Mission to North Vietnam, July 1965', *Review of International Studies* 24, 4 (Oct. 1998): 545–62.

———. 'Britain and "LBJ's War", 1964–68', *Cold War History* 2, 3 (Apr. 2002): 63–92.

Zhai Qiang. *China and the Vietnam Wars 1950–1975*. Chapel Hill, London: University of North Carolina Press, 2000.

———. 'China's Response to French Peace Initiatives', in *The Search for Peace in Vietnam 1964–1968*, ed. Lloyd C. Gardner and Ted Gittinger. College Station: Texas A&M University Press, 2004, pp. 279–83.

Ziegler, Philip. *Wilson: The Authorised Life of Lord Wilson of Rievaulx*. London: Weidenfeld, 1993.

Index